Guiding Children's Learning of Mathematics

SIXTH EDITION

Guiding Children's Learning of Mathematics

Leonard M. Kennedy

California State University, Sacramento

Steve Tipps

Midwestern State University, Wichita Falls, Texas

Wadsworth Publishing Company

Belmont, California ● A Division of Wadsworth, Inc.

To Mary Kennedy and Rebecca Poplin

Education Editor: Suzanna Brabant
Editorial Assistant: Andrea Varni
Production: Stacey C. Sawyer, Sawyer & Williams
Print Buyer: Randy Hurst
Interior and Cover Designer: Adriane Bosworth
Copy Editor: Elizabeth Judd
Photo Researcher: Judy Mason
Illustrator: Pat Rogondino
Compositor: G & S Typesetters, Inc.
Cover Painting: Dina Herrmann, *Lunar Tide,* oil on canvas.

Printed in the United States of America

2 3 4 5 6 7 8 9 10—95 94 93 92 91

Library of Congress Cataloging in Publication Data
Kennedy, Leonard M.
  Guiding children's learning of mathematics / Leonard M. Kennedy, Steve Tipps.—6th ed.
      p.   cm.
  Includes bibliographical references and index.
  ISBN 0-534-14574-4
    1. Mathematics—Study and teaching (Elementary)   I. Tipps, Steve.
II. Title.
QA135.5.K43   1990
372.7—dc20
                                                                  90-46563
                                                                  CIP

PREFACE

This combination methods-and-resource book is written for preservice and inservice teachers who will teach mathematics in preschool through grade six. It presents a program based on the standards for curriculum and evaluation adopted by the National Council of Teachers of Mathematics, which establish goals for curriculum and evaluation for schools in the United States and Canada. The book presents materials and procedures that reflect the belief that mathematics *is* problem solving and that communications, reasoning, and connections are important aspects of a problem-solving program. The book is based on the learning theories of Piaget, Brownell, Skemp, Dienes, Bruner, and Gagne as well as successful classroom practices. In such a program and with teacher guidance, children first develop an understanding of underlying concepts and principles through many explorations, investigations, and teacher-led lessons with appropriate models of the mathematics they are learning. On achieving this understanding, children formulate generalizations that make learning more permanent and acquire the computational and other skills they need to use mathematics effectively now and in the future.

The material in this text will help you present mathematics concepts in ways that help children see the relevance of these concepts in a wide variety of situations. Each concept and skill is illustrated with one or more examples of how it can be presented to enhance children's learning. Numerous examples of how to use goals and objectives to plan lessons; organize a classroom; and present teacher-led, small-group, and individual activities are thoroughly explained. The place of cooperative-learning groups in mathematics is suggested and amply illustrated. Materials and procedures for presenting new topics and developing children's understanding of them are presented in Chapters 6 through 15.

This book reflects the latest beliefs about how children learn mathematics and how teachers should present it to them. The book presents a balanced program that incorporates both teacher-led and small-group activities. It retains the easy-to-read style, wide variety of problems, and clear illustrations of earlier editions.

■ CHANGES IN THIS EDITION _____

Every chapter in the text has been thoroughly revised to reflect contemporary thinking about how students learn mathematics and how teachers can present it so students will become confident and competent citizens of the twenty-first century.

1. Part One of the book deals with the nature of mathematics and how to organize instruction about it. Chapter 1 discusses the nature of mathematics instruction today. The importance of the standards for mathematics instruction adopted by the National Council of Teachers of Mathematics and the necessity of meeting the needs of all students are discussed.

2. Chapter 2 presents the role of learning theories and successful classroom practices. The reader is taken through the steps from standards to broad goals and objectives to specific objectives to see how they are used to plan effective lessons with a variety of materials.

3. Chapter 3 presents three modes of instruction: informal investigations, teacher-led lessons, cooperative-learning groups, and information about how to develop lessons in each mode. It contains a new section that illustrates commercial and teacher-made materials for the mathematics classroom. The role of calculators and computers is discussed in this chapter.

4. Chapter 4 discusses five areas of readiness and ways to assess children's standing with regard to each of them. An expanded discussion of evaluation and ways to record information about students is presented. This edition includes more information about Piaget-type interviews and teacher-developed diagnostic processes for primary and upper grades than earlier editions did, as well as forms for recording information.

5. Part Two discusses the four general NCTM standards. Chapter 5 discusses problem solving *as* mathematics. It includes a discussion of the problem-solving standard and ten problem-solving strategies. Each strategy is thoroughly examined, and examples of its applications are provided. There are one or more problems for each strategy for readers to solve.

6. Chapter 6 is a new chapter. It discusses the remaining three general standards to give examples of how mathematics can be presented so that children use a variety of ways to communicate mathematical ideas, develop reasoning skills, and make connections within the field of mathematics and between mathematics and other subjects as well as the real world.

7. Part Three discusses materials and procedures in such a way that you will see how mathematics can be presented to meet the standards. Chapter 7 contains a thoroughly revised presentation of materials and procedures for early childhood learning in mathematics.

8. Chapter 8 deals with the base-ten numeration system, estimation, number theory topics, and ways to introduce positive and negative integers.

9. Chapters 9 and 10 deal with whole number operations. Addition and subtraction are covered in Chapter 9 and multiplication and division in Chapter 10.

10. The chapter on geometry—Chapter 11—has been revised extensively and moved to follow whole number operations.

11. Common fractions are covered in Chapter 12 and decimal fractions and percent in Chapter 13. New activities and illustrations have been added to show how these topics can help students meet the standards that pertain to them.

12. Measurement is presented in Chapter 14. The format of the chapter has been changed to show how problem cards can be used for individual and small-group investigations about measurement.

13. Tools for data handling—tables, graphs, statistics, and probability—are the subject of Chapter 15. The chapter includes many new examples of activities dealing with each of the concepts.

14. Appendix A contains information about Logo commands. These commands were moved here in the belief that readers will be better served by having them all in one place rather than scattered through the book as in the fifth edition. Appendices B and C contain names, addresses, and phone numbers of software and mathematics learning aids suppliers, respectively.

The authors are indebted to the following reviewers, whose suggestions contributed to the improvement of this sixth edition.

Charles Allen
University of Pittsburgh

Gordon Eade
University of West Florida

Sue Brown
University of Houston, Clearlake

Helene Silverman
Lehman College

Edward J. Davis
University of Georgia

Also, thanks to Bennie Walker for her assistance with the bibliographies and to Kay Preston for the construction of teaching materials illustrated in the book.

We accept responsibility for any topics or materials that anyone feels are not adequately treated. We hope that readers will find much in this book that will help them present mathematics to children in such a way that all the standards for mathematics are met by their students.

CONTENTS

■ PART THREE: PROCEDURES AND MATERIALS   187

Chapter 10: Teaching Multiplication and Division of Whole Numbers   315

KEY FOR SYMBOLS IN ACTIVITIES

 Teacher-Led

 Group Activity

 Individual Activity

 Investigation

 Problem Solving

 Calculator Activity

 Game

ACTIVITIES

Chapter 5

Chapter 6

Chapter 9

Chapter 10

Chapter 11

Chapter 14

Chapter 15

Appendix A: Logo

PART One

FOUNDATIONS FOR TEACHING MATHEMATICS

CHAPTER 1

Mathematics Today for Elementary Schools

Every teacher faces the challenge of preparing children to learn in a rapidly changing world. Today's elementary school children will reach adulthood during the second decade of the twenty-first century. Changes in all facets of life are occurring so quickly that it is impossible to predict what life will be like in even a few years, let alone when children become adults. Therefore teachers must prepare children for a life of continuous learning in order for them to cope with unknown changes to come.

In this chapter you will read about

1. curriculum and evaluation standards for school mathematics adopted by the National Council of Teachers of Mathematics;

2. problems of equity and anxiety in mathematics and their effects on students' learning of mathematics;

3. guidelines for establishing a classroom atmosphere that promotes success in mathematics.

▧ A MATHEMATICS PROGRAM FOR TODAY

For teachers of mathematics in the elementary school, the challenge means helping children acquire a background of understanding and skill in mathematics that will allow them to face the future with confidence. The goal today is to develop problem solving, reasoning, and communications skills in mathematics; to connect the various facets of mathematics as a cohesive body of knowledge rather than treating them as unassociated facts and skills; and to connect mathematics and the real world.

Standards to achieve these goals have been formulated by the National Council of Teachers of Mathematics (NCTM). The NCTM is the professional organization of persons in the United States and Canada who are concerned with instruction of students from kindergarten through grade twelve. The members of this organization are classroom teachers at all levels, school administrators, mathematics coordinators and consultants, university professors of mathematics, teacher education professors, and other persons who are interested in school mathematics. The NCTM has national, regional, and local meetings and publishes the *Arithmetic Teacher,* a journal for elementary school teachers. For more than half a century, the National Council of Teachers of Mathematics has been an influential body in the field of school mathematics.

Curriculum and Evaluation Standards

In 1989 the NCTM presented its *Curriculum and Evaluation Standards for School Mathematics.* The publication contains a comprehensive statement of standards for mathematics for each of three grade ranges: kindergarten through grade four, grades five through eight, and grades nine through twelve. For three years a Commission on Standards for School Mathematics, appointed by the board of directors in 1986, worked to develop the standards. The commission had the mission of producing a set of standards for mathematics curricula in North American schools and of recommending ways to evaluate the quality of both the curriculum and student achievement. "The *Standards* is a document designed to establish a broad framework to guide reform in school mathematics in the [1990s]. In it a vision is given of what the mathematics curriculum should include in terms of content priority and emphasis."[1] The standards were endorsed by the NCTM and 15 other organizations concerned with mathematics education and supported by 25 other school and professional organizations.

We live in a society where information has attained unprecedented importance. Its importance and the speed with which it is transmitted and shared means that every person must be able to cope knowledgeably and skillfully with a vast amount of information each day. Today's society requires that education provide opportunities for all to become mathematically literate individuals capable of lifelong learning, and to be an informed electorate.[2] To meet these broad goals, the NCTM established five student goals related to mathematics:

- Learn to value mathematics
- Become confident in their ability to do mathematics
- Become mathematical problem solvers
- Learn to communicate mathematically
- Learn to reason mathematically[3]

The commission asserted that three premises for learning mathematics are embedded in the standards. The first is that ". . . 'knowing' mathematics is 'doing' mathematics." To learn mathematics effectively, students must be involved in an active learning process rather than in a receptive one built on the memorization of concepts and procedures. Second, the uses of mathematics have become broader. The quantification and logical analysis of data is done in fields such as linguistics, business, economics, biology, medicine, and sociology, as well as in science and engineering. Students must develop understandings and skills that enable them to deal with these broader applications. Third, tools of technology, particularly the calculator and computer, have changed ways in which data are stored, analyzed, transmitted, and used. Every student should have access to appropriate calculators at all times and to computers for individual and group work.[4]

Classroom instruction should grow out of genuine problems that are of interest and concern to students. As students deal with problems, they should engage in many small-group activities that include students-with-students and teacher-with-students discussions. There will also be expository lessons presented by the teacher and opportunities for students to practice basic skills and various mathematical processes.[5]

Standards That Apply to the Elementary School

Four standards that are broad in scope apply to all grades. Nine standards deal specifically with mathematics content for kindergarten through grade four and grades five through eight. The four broad standards encompass **problem solving**, **communication**, **reasoning**, and **mathematical connections**. At every grade level problem solving should be the central focus of mathematics instruction. There needs to be a wide variety of thought-provoking questions, speculations, investigations, and explorations so a teacher can promote a problem-solving approach to the learning of all mathematics content.[6] Mathematics should be considered to be a language that must be meaningful to students if they are to communicate mathematically and apply mathematics productively.[7] About mathematics as reasoning, the commission says, "A major goal of mathematics is to help children develop the belief that they have the power to do mathematics and that they have control over their own success or failure. This autonomy develops as children gain confidence in their ability to reason and to justify their thinking. It grows as children learn that mathematics is not simply memorizing rules and procedures but that mathematics makes sense, is logical, and is enjoyable."[8] The last of the four universal standards, called mathematical connections, helps children see how mathematical ideas are related. The ideas within and among the various strands of mathematics must be connected so that the subject is organized and makes logical sense to children. Connections must also be made between mathematics and other curriculum areas and topics outside of school.[9]

Beyond the common standards, nine standards for each of the levels pertain to various topical areas of mathematics. While overlapping between grades exists, the standards are directed toward the ages and capabilities of children at the two levels. The chart in Figure 1.1 lists these standards.

The NCTM standards provide an outline of the scope and content for elementary school mathematics. This book is devoted to further discussion of these standards and ways teachers can implement them in the classroom. The second section of the book deals with the four general standards. Ways to promote problem solving, reasoning, communication, and connections are presented. The remaining nine standards for each grade are discussed in the third section, where methods and procedures for presenting mathematics topics are discussed.

EXERCISE   Explain briefly why each of the universal standards is appropriate for all grades from kindergarten through high school.

Figure 1-1

NCTM standards for elementary mathematics

KINDERGARTEN–GRADE 4	GRADES 5–8
Estimation	Number and Number Relationships
Number Sense and Numeration	Number Systems and Number Theory
Concepts of Whole Number Operations	Computation and Estimation
Whole Number Computation	Patterns and Functions
Geometry and Spatial Sense	Algebra
Measurement	Statistics
Statistics and Probability	Probability
Fractions and Decimals	Geometry
Patterns and Relationships	Measurement

■ MATHEMATICS FOR ALL

A different challenge facing the teacher today is that of providing a mathematics program that assures success and achievement by all students. One major problem is that too many students fail to develop their full potential in mathematics; they lack prerequisites for many college and university degree programs or many occupations not requiring advanced education. In a technological world, this situation has many social and economic implications for both individuals and society as a whole. For the teacher of elementary school mathematics two crucial issues are equity in mathematics and children's attitudes toward the subject.

Equity in Mathematics

Equity in mathematics is an area of major concern. Equal opportunity for students of both genders and all minorities means that everyone has the chance to acquire the mathematical skills and knowledge that they will need to live in a technological world. Unfortunately, participation in mathematics by female students and many ethnic minority students has not been equal to that of Anglo males.

A 1972 survey by sociologist Lucy W. Sells showed that while 52 percent of the male students who entered the University of California at Berkeley had four years of high school mathematics, only 8 percent of the female students had the same background.[10] Sells also reported a 1978 survey of California high school students showing that 79 percent of students from Asian groups and 72 percent of the Anglo students were in a sequence of courses leading to calculus. Only 25 percent of the Hispanic students and 20 percent of the African-American students were in such a sequence. While 40 percent of all students taking mathematics were African-American, they comprised 79 percent of the students in remedial courses without access to even high school algebra and geometry. Only 5 percent of these students were enrolled in trigonometry, elementary functions, and calculus classes.[11]

The lack of adequate high school mathematics blocks access for many students to majors in science, medicine, and engineering. In addition, many fields that were once considered to be less dependent on advanced mathematics such as business, political science, psychology, and sociology have become increasingly quantitative in nature. The inability to enter college and university major programs is not the only limitation placed on the future by a lack of mathematics. A background in high school algebra and geometry alone may make a difference of 25 percent in scores for examinations required to enter many civil service positions and industrial jobs.[12] In a rapidly changing society, most individuals will change jobs three or four times as old jobs are eliminated and new ones, often requiring mathematical reasoning and skills, are created. Job advancement and promotions will go to workers comfortable with mathematics and willing to learn new skills that require mathematics.

Society as a whole seems to accept the myths that only a few people are "good" in mathematics and that mathematics is a male province. Although more males than females are in mathematics-oriented careers and females have lower scores on standardized mathematics tests, Elizabeth Fennema and Julia Sherman have found that such observations do not take into consideration the differences in students' mathematics background before being tested.[13] Enrollment differences cannot by themselves explain the differences in achievement, however.[14]

Many educators feel that during upper elementary grades students make the decisions about their future in mathematics. Girls perform as well as boys on tests during the elementary grades, but they begin to fall behind during the middle years on problem solving and applications. As children advance, teachers frequently interact more with males, pay more attention to their problems, give them more help and praise, and expect a higher level of achievement. Males are encouraged to become more independent as they work, while females are encouraged to become more dependent.[15] Hispanic and African-American students get consistently lower scores on mathematics achievement tests beginning in the primary years.[16] Observation in classrooms reveals that students experiencing difficulty get less content-related attention but receive many more discipline-related interactions.[17]

Erroneous beliefs about the superiority of one group of students over others in mathematics have led to differential treatment. Teachers who believe that females or minority children are less capable than white males treat them differently. Students who are treated with lowered expectations do not achieve as much as students for whom expectations are higher. The cycle of lower expectations and lower performance can be changed. Two programs have been developed to assist teachers in adjusting stereotypical beliefs about female or minority students: Teacher Expectations of Student Achievement (TESA)[18] and Multiplying Options and Subtracting Bias.[19] The success of these programs demonstrates that teacher expectations make a difference in how students perform in the classroom. Equity in mathematics is an issue that teachers must confront each day. Attitudes toward the students, expectations of learning by all students, and appropriate classroom teaching practices do make a difference.

EXERCISE   Do you recall any instances where mathematics teachers have treated students inequitably on the basis of gender or minority status? If so, describe the situation(s) and explain the consequences for the student or students.

Mathematics Anxiety and Attitudes

When people are asked to describe feelings about their own mathematics ability, they often respond with negative and self-deprecating statements. People typically remember bad or negative situations vividly.

I was never any good in mathematics. I just couldn't get the hang of it. I was too dumb even to ask a question when the teacher explained something.

I remember going to the board to work problems and crying because I was afraid that I would make a mistake.

One teacher made us stay in during recesses to copy the multiplication tables until we could get them all right on the test. I had to stay in for five weeks and never did get them all right.

I felt stupid the whole sixth grade in mathematics. The teacher said that mathematics was just something you got or didn't get. He said I was just one of those people who would never get it.

I did all right in elementary school, but algebra was impossible. What were those little X's and Y's? I was lost from the first day. Today I just stay away from numbers. I'm just not a mathematics person.

These statements are typical of those made by persons who dislike mathematics and have a high level of mathematics anxiety. **Mathematics anxiety** is a fear of mathematics or an intense, negative emotional reaction to the subject. Mathophobia is a serious problem for many people. When asked to recall good experiences in mathematics, many people struggle to find even one.

In his book *Innumeracy,* John Allen Paulos gives many examples of situations in which intelligent people resign themselves to a state of confusion and panic when dealing with relatively simple mathematical ideas. He attributes this failure at least in part to the lack of mathematical thinking required in school.[20]

Elementary schools by and large do manage to teach the basic algorithms of multiplication and division, addition and subtraction, as well as methods for handling fractions, decimals, and percentages. Unfortunately they don't do as effective a job of teaching when to add or subtract, when to multiply or divide, or how to convert from fractions to decimals or percentages. Seldom are arithmetic problems integrated into other school work—how much, how far, how old, how many. Older students fear word problems in part because they have not been asked to find solutions to such quantitative questions at the elementary level.[21]

Sheila Tobias has studied the phenomenon of mathematics anxiety for many years. She finds that students—many of them women—often have developed such negative attitudes in mathematics that they shut down rather than work with numbers. The problem is not with their ability; when they are able to let down their defenses, they are surprised and delighted that they can solve problems and think with numbers.[22]

Some researchers who have studied the problem contend that a majority of adults suffer from mathematics anxiety to some degree. Even though the problem does not manifest itself until after the elementary school years, evidence shows that it frequently gets started there.[23] Adults who suffer from mathematics anxiety report certain teacher practices and expectations that contributed to their anxieties:

- Lack of variety in teaching-learning processes
- Emphasis on memorization
- Emphasis on speed
- Emphasis on doing one's own work
- Authoritarian teaching

Lack of Variety in Teaching-Learning Processes

When the activity in an elementary mathematics class is analyzed, much of the time is spent in drill and practice. In many classes, more than 70 percent of the time is spent in independent practice, mostly with workbooks and paper-and-pencil tasks. This situation means that children often have received very little instruction in the mathematical concepts and processes that they are supposed to practice. When Thomas Good and Douglas Grouws[24] helped teachers change the teaching pattern to emphasize conceptual learning, use of concrete models, and discussion of ideas, not only was the amount of time spent in practice reduced to 30 percent, but the scores on tests improved greatly.

Lorelei Brush reported that students in grades six to twelve disliked mathematics and were bored with "repetitive assignments which require them to solve a series of very similar problems."[25] When thought-provoking problems were presented, the students enjoyed the challenge of thinking about "tough questions."

Emphasis on Memorization

If you had to memorize 100 three-letter combinations such as HJU, GPO, WTO, and PFA, you would be able to remember some of them for a short period of time. But you would soon forget both the letters and the tricks you used to remember them. Children who learn mathematics by rote memorization have the same problem. Rather than seeing mathematics as a structured body of knowledge, the mathematics they learn is a disconnected collection of isolated facts and tedious rules.

Most children can and should learn the basic facts for the four operations with whole numbers and an algorithm for each operation. When they are expected to learn these facts and processes by memorization alone without understanding what the facts mean or how the algorithms work, many children experience learning problems. Although they may be able to keep up by memorizing in the early grades, by the time students are in the fifth and sixth grades, they are overwhelmed by the number of facts and rules they have encountered. They become discouraged and develop progressively more negative attitudes toward themselves and toward mathematics. The emphasis on memorization in the classroom often crowds out other aspects of the curriculum such as problem solving and applications.

Emphasis on Speed

Memorization and speed often go hand in hand. Many teachers use drills, timed tests, and games that put a premium on speed. Some children can quickly recall the facts and are not negatively affected. However, many students work deliberately and need more time. When faced with a high-risk-of-failure situation, many students become very apprehensive and their work suffers. Some withdraw completely and can do little or no further work in mathematics.

Emphasis on Doing One's Own Work

Teachers commonly expect children to work alone in mathematics. "Do your own work" is a dictum in many elementary classrooms. Children may be forbidden to help others or to ask others for help. However, some teachers encourage "group work" because they know that there are social and academic benefits for children who work together, share ideas, and explain concepts to help one another understand mathematics.

In the last ten years, research evidence is clear that teachers' intuitions about group learning are well founded. The **cooperative-learning** movement has shown positive benefits for groups in many areas:

- Academic achievement
- Self-esteem and self-confidence as learners
- Intergroup relations, including cross-race and cross-culture friendships
- Social acceptance of mainstreamed children
- Ability to use social skills (when these are taught)[26]

Research evidence has consistently supported the benefits of small-group approaches. More information about cooperative learning is contained in Chapter 2.

Authoritarian Teaching

Lack of variety, emphasis on speed and memorization, and insistence on doing one's own work are often symptoms of authoritarian teaching. Persons who suffer from mathematics anxiety frequently remember teachers accepting only "one right way" of working problems. They recall how teachers gave them step-by-step procedures and a list of rules for doing computations. In authoritarian teaching, the teacher controls the classroom completely and discourages any variation from prescribed routines. Even when children do not understand, the authoritarian teacher holds to a rigid way of teaching, often with abstract words and symbols. Such practices lead to the belief that mathematics is inflexible and lacking in creativity and prevent students from seeing the usefulness and fun in mathematics.[27]

GUIDING CHILDREN'S LEARNING OF MATHEMATICS

Centering mathematics instruction on paper-and-pencil exercises, speed drills, and timed tests is uninspiring and repetitive and contributes to children's dislike of mathematics. Teachers who structure their classes to reduce stress, improve attitudes, and encourage students to continue with their study of mathematics will develop students who are well rounded in mathematics. The following practices reduce classroom tensions and enhance students' attitudes.

- The teacher provides a relaxed atmosphere for learning. Students should know that they will complete each assignment in a reasonable time if they stay on task.

- The teacher gives credit for processes and thinking as well as for answers. When students work individually and in groups to solve problems, they engage in processes for which credit should be given, even when a solution is not completed or is wrong.

- The teacher is sensitive to students' feelings. Humiliation, sarcasm, and ridicule are not used. Students' mistakes are usually the result of incomplete understanding of a concept or a procedure. Mistakes are used by the teacher as a basis for reteaching and clarifying concepts and processes.

- The teacher avoids the "open-your-book-and-work-problems-1-to-35" routine by introducing topics with meaningful materials and explanations such as are suggested in this book or in other resources. After children understand a concept, independent work with a text or workbook can be used as one way to practice.

- The teacher balances all aspects of mathematics. Computation is important, but there are many other equally important topics that are exciting and that provide variety in the classroom.

- The teacher does not use mathematics as punishment. Having students work 100 long division problems or write the multiplication table ten times does nothing to correct behavior problems and creates negative attitudes toward mathematics.

The style of teaching we advocate is democratic in nature. Both the teacher and the children have roles in the teaching-learning process. The teacher must have a repertoire of skills and procedures that encourages children to explore, investigate, expand, and consolidate mathematical meanings. In the activities and examples throughout the book, we suggest ways in which the teacher can present concepts so that children build their own understandings.

The democratic classroom works to overcome many of the problems that have led to poor mathematics attitudes and mathematics anxiety.

- Students are encouraged to understand how mathematics works by using various concrete materials to model operations and concepts. Understanding develops when concrete and pictorial models are linked to written symbols. Students begin by recording with pictures or written symbols what they see with materials. These written records serve as links to other symbolic materials, such as numerals, number words, and computational algorithms, which are used after the children understand concepts.

- Students are encouraged to work together in a variety of settings. They should discuss the materials they are using with others, both students and teacher. A teacher can guide interactions by asking probing and open-ended questions so that students find patterns, discover relationships, and draw conclusions. The teacher may also be silent and listen to what children say. Children's comments provide information that may be used in more formal teaching situations to clarify concepts.

- Students are encouraged to use the facts and processes in meaningful contexts. Applications of mathematics provide motivation for learning and connections to the real life of the students. Whenever possible, examples from the students' world and interests should be used to introduce concepts.

- Students are encouraged to be active participants in the process of creating mathematics. They should be asked to make up problems, extend situations in the lesson or with the materials, explain their reasoning, bring materials or situations from home or playground that illustrate mathematics concepts, draw pictures, build models, ask questions, and be fully engaged in the process of learning.

Teachers often feel pressures for students to perform at certain achievement levels. Teachers do have responsibility for student performance, but approaches based on test results and memorization of facts are likely to have a long-range negative impact on students. Evidence points to the fact that the teaching practices advocated in this book develop students who are capable of performing well on standardized achievement tests and in all other areas of performance.

We hope that instructors or students using this book are engaged in the same process we advocate for elementary school students. We envision a college or university classroom with a variety of manipulatives, much cooperative work and discussion, and opportunities for students to discover and rediscover important mathematics concepts and skills.

If you suffer from mathematics anxiety, now is the time to do something about it. Do not be afraid to admit it, you are not alone! Almost everyone has some incident to relate about feeling inadequate in mathematics. You *can* improve your attitude and you *can* improve your knowledge. You may wish to read some of the books and articles contained in this chapter's bibliography to help you get started.

The remaining chapters in this section of the book provide the background every teacher needs for teaching mathematics effectively. Chapter 2 provides information about foundations for effective instruction. Chapter 3 discusses ways to organize for teaching and materials for the classroom. Chapter 4 discusses procedures for assessing children's understanding of and skills with computational processes, problem-solving abilities, communication and reasoning skills, and inclinations toward mathematics.

EXERCISE   Prepare a chart with two headings: "Anxiety Prone" and "Reduced Anxiety." List characteristics of teachers and teaching practices that you believe are appropriate for each heading.

■ SUMMARY

A mathematics program for a rapidly changing world must equip children with the skills and knowledge they will need to cope with the future. The National Council of Teachers of Mathematics has established a set of standards to guide instruction and evaluation of the mathematics curriculum. There are four broad standards that apply to mathematics at all levels. These deal with mathematics as problem solving, reasoning, and communication, and with mathematical connections. There are nine topical standards for both kindergarten through grade four and grades five through nine. The standards give direction to textbook publishers, program developers, and classroom teachers.

Teachers need to be concerned with providing a program that encourages students of both genders and all minorities to attain mathematical competence. In the past, stereotypical thinking resulted in beliefs that female and minority males, except Asian males, were not as capable of learning mathematics as Anglo males. Such thinking resulted in differential treatment of students. Females and minorities received less positive reinforcement and encouragement. Research has shown that females and minority males are as capable of succeeding in mathematics as Anglo and Asian males. Teachers must avoid discriminatory attitudes and procedures for any students.

Anxieties cause many students to feel inadequate and ineffective with mathematics. Certain teaching practices tend to cause anxiety and should be avoided: lack of variety; emphasis on memorization, speed, and doing one's own work; and authoritarian teaching. Mathematics anxiety is lessened in a democratic classroom that provides concrete learning aids, encourages group work, puts mathematics in meaningful settings, and has students extend their thinking to situations where mathematics is used outside of the mathematics lesson.

Teachers-to-be should experience the types of learning activities advocated in this book. They should read, manipulate, reason, discuss, and make connections as they acquire the knowledge and skills they need to become effective teachers of elementary school mathematics. Those who have anxieties about mathematics should strive to overcome their apprehensions before they work with children.

■ STUDY QUESTIONS AND ACTIVITIES

1. The mathematics standards established by the National Council of Teachers of Mathematics are presented in this book. They are found at the front of each chapter beginning with Chapter 5, where standards for problem solving are listed. Read the standards at the beginning of each chapter. Are there any statements that you did not expect to find? If so, list them and tell why they were unexpected. Are there any standards you do not understand? If so, list them. Discuss statements you do not understand with classmates to see if you can clarify your understanding of them.

2. The standards cover a broad range of topics and ideas. Write a paragraph that describes mathematics classes, either elementary or secondary, that you experienced. To what extent did your classes meet the standards? Do you believe they met most of them, some of them, or only a few?

3. According to Kogelman and Warren, each of the following statements is a myth about mathematics that contributes to mathematics anxiety. Read all of the myths and put them in order from the most believable to the least believable. Compare your list with the list of two or three other students. Which of these myths are the most detrimental to people's attitudes toward mathematics?

   ■ Men are better in math than women.
   ■ Math requires logic, not intuition.
   ■ You must always know how you got your answer.
   ■ Math is not creative.
   ■ There is a best way to do a math problem.

- It's always important to get the answer exactly right.
- It's bad to count on your fingers.
- Mathematicians do problems quickly, in their heads.
- Math requires a good memory.
- Math is done by working intensely until the problem is solved.
- Some people have a "math mind" and some don't.
- There is a magic key to doing math.[28]

Martha L. Frank (see For Further Reading) had preservice elementary teachers answer the questions. Compare her results with yours.

4. Read Lorelei Brush's article in the December 1981 *Arithmetic Teacher* (see For Further Reading). Write a statement explaining how you can prevent your students from developing the four attitudes reported to Brush by students in her study.

TEACHER'S BOOKSHELF

Brush, Lorelei. 1980. *Encouraging Girls in Mathematics*. Cambridge, MA: Abt Books.

Cooney, Thomas J., ed. 1990 Yearbook. *Teaching and Learning Mathematics in the 1990s*. Reston, VA: National Council of Teachers of Mathematics.

Fox, Lynn H., Linda Brody, and Dianne Tobin, eds. 1980. *Women and the Mathematical Mystique*. Baltimore: Johns Hopkins University Press.

National Council of Teachers of Mathematics. 1989. *Curriculum and Evaluation Standards for School Mathematics*. Reston, VA: National Council of Teachers of Mathematics.

Trafton, Paul R., ed. 1989 Yearbook. *New Directions for Elementary School Mathematics*. Reston, VA: National Council of Teachers of Mathematics.

Tobias, Sheila. 1987. *Succeed with Math: Every Student's Guide to Conquering Math Anxiety*. New York: College Examination Board.

FOR FURTHER READING

Brush, Lorelei. 1981, December. Some thoughts for teachers on mathematics anxiety. *Arithmetic Teacher* 29(4), 37–39.

Some reasons for not liking mathematics reported by students are summarized. Brush discusses actions teachers can take to prevent mathematics anxiety.

Fennema, Elizabeth. 1981, November. Women and mathematics: Does research matter? *Journal for Research in Mathematics Education* 12(5), 380–385.

Fennema cites a number of myths about abilities and interests in mathematics. These myths have been damaging but are amenable to change. Causes that are due to social factors can be modified, and educators have a responsibility to know the truth about females' abilities and interests in mathematics.

————. 1980, March. Teachers and sex bias in mathematics. *Mathematics Teacher 73*(3), 169–173.

Research evidence supporting the belief that teachers treat females differently from male students is cited. Five practices that result in greater equity are discussed.

————. November, 1979. Women and girls in mathematics—Equity in mathematics education. *Educational Studies in Mathematics 10*(4), 389–401.

This article discusses beliefs about cognitive, affective, and educational variables in the mathematics education of females. The author concludes that there is nothing inherent that keeps females from learning mathematics. The article contains an extensive bibliography.

————, and Julia Sherman. 1977 Winter. Sex-related differences in mathematics achievement, spatial visualization, and affective factors. *Amercian Education Research Journal 14*(1), 51–71.

A comprehensive study of 589 female and 644 male, predominantly white, students in grades 9–12 revealed few sex-related cognitive differences but many attitudinal differences. The study strongly supports the contention that sex differences are the result of sociocultural rather than cognitive factors.

Fox, Lynn H. 1981, February. Mathematically able girls: A special challenge. *Arithmetic Teacher 28*(6), 22–23.

Recent research indicates that many able girls elect not to continue their study of mathematics beyond minimum courses. Fox discusses six practices that will encourage mathematically able girls to continue their studies.

Frank, Martha L. 1990, January. What myths about mathematics are held and conveyed by teachers? *Arithmetic Teacher 37*(5), 10–12.

An informal study using the myths from Kogelman and Warren reports how students respond to each myth (see Study Question 3 on pp. 15–16).

Hannifin, Michael J. 1981, May/June. Effects of teacher and student goal setting and evaluations on mathematics achievement and students' attitudes. *Journal of Educational Research 74*(5), 323–326.

The author cites a study showing that children who are given opportunities to participate in establishing goals in mathematics have a better sense of what they can accomplish than their teachers. Students given opportunities for self-regulation of instruction had greater confidence in their ability to manage portions of their instruction than those who did not.

Hill, Jan. 1980, February. The nonsexist classroom. *Instructor 84*(7), 78–80.

Discusses ways to lessen gender stereotypes about female and male roles in an elementary classroom. Includes a consciousness-raising attitude scale for teachers prepared by Barbara Samuel.

Hitch, Chris. 1990, May. How can I get others to implement the *Standards*? I'm just a teacher! *Arithmetic Teacher 37*(9), 2–4.

Hitch discusses strategies teachers can use to involve others in implementing the standards.

Hodges, Helene L. B. 1983, March. Learning styles: Rx for mathophobia. *Arithmetic Teacher 30*(7), 17–20.

Describes three mathophobic children, and discusses four aspects of learning styles teachers should consider to lessen mathematics anxiety in students.

Lazarus, Mitchell. 1974, January/February. Mathophobia: Some personal speculations. *National Elementary Principal 53*(2), 16–22.

Gives a good explanation of mathophobia and discusses some of its causes and its effects on ordinary adult life.

Sells, Lucy. 1978, February. Mathematics—A critical filter. *Science Teacher 45*(2), 28–29.

This was one of the first articles to call attention to the fact that females were blocked from taking many courses of advanced study by a lack of mathematics courses in high school.

Sherard, Wade E. 1981, November. Math anxiety in the classroom. *Clearing House 55*(3), 106–110.

The author cites some causes of anxiety and discusses eight practices to help reduce it.

Tobias, Sheila. 1978, September/October. Managing math anxiety: A new look at an old problem. *Children Today 7*(5), 7–9, 36.

Discusses mathematics anxiety and describes how clinical intervention can help students and adults overcome it.

———. 1980, September/October. Math anxiety: What can be done about it? *Today's Education 59*(3), 26GS–29GS.

Tobias states that elementary school teachers who feel uncomfortable about teaching mathematics owe it to their students to overcome their feelings of anxiety. She discusses some ways they can do this.

Tracy, Dyanne M., and Susan M. Davis. 1989, December. Females in mathematics: Erasing a gender-related math myth. *Arithmetic Teacher 37*(4), 8–11.

Presents a teaching unit including an interview form and reports on a famous female mathematician to increase awareness of the role of females in mathematics past and present.

■ NOTES

[1] National Council of Teachers of Mathematics. 1989. *Curriculum and Evaluation Standards for School Mathematics.* Reston, VA: 1989, v.

[2] NCTM, 3.

[3] NCTM, 5.

[4] NCTM, 7–8.

[5] NCTM, 9–10.

[6] NCTM, 23.

[7] NCTM, 26.

[8] NCTM, 29.

[9] NCTM, 32.

[10] Lucy W. Sells. 1978, February. Mathematics—A critical filter. *Science Teacher 45*(2), 28.

[11] Lucy W. Sells. 1980. The mathematics filter and the education of women and minorities, in Lynn H. Fox, Linda Brody, and Dianne Tobin, eds., *Women and the Mathematical Mystique.* Baltimore: Johns Hopkins University Press, 68.

[12] Sheila Tobias. 1978, September/October. Managing math anxiety: A new look at an old problem. *Children Today 7*(5), 8.

[13] Elizabeth Fennema and Julia Sherman. 1977, Winter. Sex-related differences in mathematics achievement, spatial visualization, and affective factors. *American Education Research Journal 14*(1), 31–71.

[14] Elizabeth Fennema. 1984. Girls, women, and mathematics, in Elizabeth Fennema and M. Jane Ayer, eds., *Women and Education: Equity or Equality.* Berkeley, CA: McCutchan Publishing Corp.

[15] Curtis McKnight, Joe Crosswhite, John Dossey, Edward Kifer, Jane Swafford, Kenneth Travers, and Thomas Cooney. *The Underachieving Curriculum: Assessing U.S. School Mathematics from an International Perspective.* Champaign, IL: Stipes Publishing Co.

[16] Elizabeth Fennema. 1980, March. Teachers and sex bias in mathematics. *Mathematics Teacher 73*(3), 169–171.

[17] Thomas L. Good and Jere Brophy. 1971. Analyzing classroom interaction: A more powerful alternative. *Educational Technology 11*(10), 36–41.

[18] Sam Kerman, Tom Kimball, and Mary Martin. 1980. *Teacher Expectations and Student Achievement.* Bloomington, IN: Phi Delta Kappa.

[19] E. Fennema, A. D. Becker, P. L. Wollent, and J. D. Pedro. 1981. *Multiplying Options and Subtracting Bias* (videotapes). Reston, VA: National Council of Teachers of Mathematics.

[20] John Allen Paulos. 1988. *Innumeracy.* New York: Hill and Wang.

[21] Paulos, p. 73.

[22] Sheila Tobias. 1981, January. Stress in the math classroom. *Learning 9*(6), 38.

[23] Mitchell Lazarus. 1974, January/February. Mathophobia: Some personal speculations. *National Elementary Principal 53*(2), 16–22; Sheila Tobias. 1978. *Overcoming Math Anxiety.* New York: W. W. Norton.

[24] Thomas Good and Douglas Grouws. 1979. The Missouri Mathematics Effectiveness Project: An experimental study in fourth grade classrooms. *Journal of Educational Psychology 71*(3), 75–81.

[25] Lorelei Brush, 1980. *Encouraging Girls in Mathematics.* Cambridge, MA: Abt Books, 49–50.

[26] Neil Davidson. 1989. Small-group cooperative learning in mathematics: A review of research. Research in small-group cooperative learning in mathematics. Edited by Neil Davidson and Roberta Dees. Reston, VA: *Journal for Research in Mathematics Education* monograph.

[27] Wade H. Sherard. 1981, November. Math anxiety in the classroom. *Clearing House 55*(3), 106.

[28] Stanley Kogelman and Joseph Warren. 1978. *Mind over Math.* New York: Dial Press, 30–43.

CHAPTER 2

Foundations for Planning Effective Instruction

Teachers need to know the subject they are to teach, but they also need to know about the teaching-learning process. Research in learning and effective teaching and successful classroom practices provide guidelines that help them to choose teaching strategies that work with children. This chapter reviews important research in teaching and learning mathematics as a foundation for planning effective instruction. Suggestions are made for using goals and objectives to plan instruction.

In this chapter you will read about

1. research on learning and its implications for elementary mathematics instruction;

2. research on teaching mathematics and instructional suggestions from it;

3. examples of classroom practice that reflect research on teaching and learning;

4. how goals are used for developing instructional objectives;

5. the role of instructional objectives in designing effective instruction.

21

■ FOUNDATIONS FOR INSTRUCTION

Take a step inside three classrooms to see how teachers interact with students and use materials. Lessons in a first-grade, a third-grade, and a fifth-grade class deal with subtraction of whole numbers, but the lessons are very different. The teachers' instructional purposes and expectations change at each level.

First Grade

Children are working with their "math boxes," which contain a collection of related objects, such as plastic airplanes and cars, toy bears, bottle caps, and rubber worms. Ms. Liu counts four bears out on her counting mat and asks how many bears the children see. She then removes one and asks again. She repeats the actions and adds a story. "Four bears were having a party. One had to go home." Next the children are asked to count a set of five bears onto a counting mat. After she verifies each child's work, she instructs each student to remove three bears. The children count the number of bears that remain on the mat. She asks if someone can tell a story about these bears.

After another example in which all the children are successful, she tells a short story—"Seven bears were playing ball; four went home"—for the children to model with the objects. She then asks the children to work in pairs to give each other stories or problems. She monitors the activities, pausing to listen to several stories and watch the action. After several minutes, she calls the students to attention and says, "You have been doing subtraction problems with your bears. Now I am going to write a subtraction statement with numbers." She writes $8 - 2$ on the board and reads it, "Eight minus two. Can anyone tell me what this '$-$' means?" Several students answer "went home," "move," "remove," or "left." She acknowledges all of these meanings and summarizes them, "Good. One meaning for the '$-$' sign is remove or take away." She asks the children to create a story to go with the subtraction statement and read the problem to each other. She tells them that they can use subtraction cards she has made or write their own problems for more practice.

Third Grade

Children are working on the decomposition algorithm for subtraction. They have already used base-ten blocks and beansticks for place-value lessons and subtraction. Today the teacher has the students bundle file cards in packs of 100 and 10. He presents a situation: "Mr. Cardwell had 362 greeting cards on Monday of Valentine week. By Friday, only 67 were in the rack. How many had been sold?" Students work in groups of three or four at their desks. One group is at the chalkboard. They place three packs of 100 cards, six packs of 10 cards, and two loose cards on the chalk tray. They do not have seven loose cards, so they take a bundle of 10 apart, making 12 loose cards. Then they put seven singles at the end of the chalk tray. Now they need six packs of 10, but they only have five. So they take a 100-pack apart to make ten packs of 10. Finally they get six packs of 10 and move them to the end of the chalk tray. They have two packs of 100, nine packs of 10, and five singles and determine that 295 cards were sold during the week.

Mr. Cardwell asks if anyone has a different answer or worked the problem a different way. One group wants to remove the six packs of 10 first. Mr. Cardwell works through the problem, taking directions from the class. Eventually the children decide the answer would be the same but that their way was more confusing than starting with the ones. Other problem situations are worked with the cards. Mr. Cardwell encourages children to make up problems for each other. Students find that some of their problems need regrouping, while others are worked without regrouping.

Fifth Grade

Ms. Calhoun wants to expand her children's mental arithmetic skills. She has determined that they are ready to learn to subtract a number like 43 from 69 without paper and pencil or a calculator. She says, "You can already estimate the answer to 69 minus 43. What would that be?" After some thought, students answer "70 minus 40 is 30." The lesson continues.

> T: Good. Now let's see if we can work out the exact answer in our heads by using mental arithmetic. One method is called *equal compensation*. Let me show some examples to see if you can figure out how compensation works. What do you notice that is the same or different about the examples? You have two minutes.

She reveals four problems on the overhead transparency.

$$
\begin{array}{cccc}
61 & 65 & 67 & 69 \\
-43 & -47 & -49 & -51 \\
\hline
18 & 18 & 18 & 18
\end{array}
$$

The students work in small groups to discuss the examples until Ms. Calhoun asks them to report what they have noticed about the problems. She records their answers without comment.

> C1: All the answers are 18.
>
> C2: All the problems are subtraction.
>
> C3: The numbers each get bigger as you go to the right.
>
> C4: The same number has been added to both the sum and the addend.
>
> C5: There is a pattern because first you added 4s, then 6s, then 8s.

After the comments are written, she asks if they can give other examples that work the same way. After a minute or two, several other examples have been written on the overhead.

$$
\begin{array}{r} 62 \\ -44 \\ \hline 18 \end{array} \qquad
\begin{array}{r} 68 \\ -50 \\ \hline 18 \end{array} \qquad
\begin{array}{r} 70 \\ -52 \\ \hline 18 \end{array} \qquad
\begin{array}{r} 180 \\ -162 \\ \hline 18 \end{array}
$$

Ms. Calhoun asks if any of the earlier comments apply to the new examples.

T: Which comments seem most important?

C1:   The pattern idea isn't really important because compensation works with adding any numbers.

C2:   As long as the numbers are the same for both the top and bottom.

C3:   I wonder if you could subtract the same number from the sum and addend.

The students try this out with new examples subtracting 1, 2, and 20.

$$
\begin{array}{r} 61 \\ -43 \\ \hline 18 \end{array} \qquad
\begin{array}{r} 60 \\ -42 \\ \hline 18 \end{array} \qquad
\begin{array}{r} 59 \\ -41 \\ \hline 18 \end{array} \qquad
\begin{array}{r} 41 \\ -23 \\ \hline 18 \end{array}
$$

C: Subtracting the same number from the sum and the addend also works. The answer is still 18.

T: My original problem was 69 minus 43. Let me show how I can do that in my head. What happens if I subtract 3 from 43?

C: It becomes 40.

T: If I subtract 3 from 40, what must I do with the 69?

C: Subtract 3 from it.

T: What is 66 minus 40?

C: It is 26.

T: How does compensation help you subtract mentally?

C1:   When you have a hard problem you can make it into an easier problem.

C2:   You can make an easier problem by adding (or subtracting) the same value to the top and bottom.

C3:   To the sum and the addend.

C4:   And then subtracting.

C5:   You need to get numbers that are easy to add in your head, too.

T: Now that you have the idea about how equal compensation works, let's try it with other examples. How would it work for 52 minus 38? For 67 minus 25? 43 minus 16?

The teachers who prepared these lessons followed guidelines for effective instruction: basing instruction on the knowledge and experience of the children, using concrete materials and visual aids, allowing children to work together, and encouraging involvement. They were aware of what researchers in learning and teaching of mathematics have said about how mathematics should be presented to children. They also knew about some of the materials and procedures used by successful teachers in classrooms like their own. Knowledge of research and classroom practice helped them develop good lessons for their children. The principles will help any teacher plan lessons that are effective.

EXERCISE   List three or four characteristics of the foregoing mathematics lessons that distinguish them from lessons you have observed recently or recall from your years in elementary school.

Research on Learning and Learning Mathematics

During the late nineteenth century, the mental discipline theory of learning had a great influence on mathematics teachers. According to this theory, the mind was like a muscle and benefited from exercise as muscles do. Mathematics was used to give the mind mental exercise; lengthy computations were regularly used to "train" the mind. Early in the present century, Edward Thorndike's stimulus-response theory supplanted the mental discipline theory. This theory was based on the belief that learning occurred when a bond or connection is established between a stimulus and an appropriate response. Mathematics lessons consisted primarily of presenting many number combinations so that children could establish strong bonds between combinations and their answers. Drill was heavily emphasized.

In the mid-twentieth century, a number of researchers and theoreticians challenged the simple stimulus-response description for human learning. William Brownell, Zoltan Dienes, Jean Piaget, Richard Skemp, Jerome Bruner, and Robert Gagne emphasized development of understanding as fundamental in learning mathematics. The meaning theory, introduced by Brownell in the 1930s, is based on the belief that children must understand what they are learning if learning is to be permanent. The theory supports the use of many objects to manipulate so that children can understand the meanings of new concepts and skills.[1]

Zoltan Dienes' work convinced him that various representations of a concept rather than a single representation are needed for children to fully understand the concept. "Multiple embodiment" of a concept occurs when beansticks, base-ten blocks, Unifix cubes, and packs of cards are used in a sequence of related lessons to represent the place-value system and various number values.[2]

Jean Piaget and Richard Skemp concluded that all individuals pass through stages as they mature intellectually. Piaget identified four stages through which he believed all individuals pass.

- Sensorimotor stage (ages 0–2), during which infants and children develop concepts primarily through interactions with the physical world.

- Preoperational stage (ages 2–7), during which children begin using language to express ideas but the ideas are still very dependent on perceptions.

- Concrete operations stage (ages 7–12), during which children develop many concepts using concrete objects to explore relationships and model abstract ideas. Language is a very important vehicle for expressing and remembering concepts.

- Formal operations stage (age 12 through adulthood), during which children begin to think abstractly, can hypothesize from abstract possibilities to the real world, and are not as dependent on concrete objects.

During early stages children do not have the mental maturity to grasp mathematical concepts presented by words and symbols alone. They need experiences with concrete objects to represent abstract ideas and the operations involving those ideas. During the elementary years, children in the concrete operational stage are developing mathematical concepts such as number, length, area, time, mass, and volume.

Piaget also emphasized that the process of learning is one of continual assimilation and accommodation. As students have new experiences, they actively try to make sense of the new ideas in relation to old experiences and old ideas. A general term for Piaget's theory of learning is *constructivism,* because of the belief that learners must construct their own meanings rather than being passive receivers of information.[3] A state of *disequilibrium* means that students are struggling as they try to make sense of the new and old ideas. Piaget sees this disequilibrium as being an essential part of the learning process. Children who are passive learners tend to accept information without working out the connections and meanings.

Skemp did not define stages in the same way that Piaget did but the similarities are evident.[4] Skemp separates learning into two stages. At the first level, manipulation of objects provides the learner with the basis for further learning and internalization of ideas. He advocates interaction of students with many physical objects during the early stages of concept learning. These early experiences form the basis for later learning at the abstract, or second level. Time for reflection and opportunity to act on knowledge assist students in organizing their thoughts and internalizing their learning. Skemp's ideas of a conceptual structure, or schema, that students develop for mathematics is also very similar to Piaget's constructivism. The underlying structure is crucial to using prior knowledge for future learning and applying knowledge in new situations.

Bruner also was interested in how children represented their understandings.[5] His three stages of representation are *enactive,* suggesting the role of physical objects in learning; *ikonic,* referring to pictorial and graphic representations; and *symbolic,* characterizing the ability to use words and symbols in learning. The parallels to Piaget's psychomotor stage, preoperational thought, concrete operational stage, and formal operational stage are easy to find. Bruner was also an advocate of discovery learning and encouraged the use of discovery learning in mathematics curricula.[6]

Robert Gagne[7] took a different approach in his research on learning. He believed that learning was improved when the subtasks needed to master a larger task were clearly identified and sequenced. The target task or goal might be to learn to subtract a pair of numbers of any size. The chart in Figure 9.2 shows one way to sequence the subtasks for meeting the target task of subtracting numbers of any size. According to Gagne, task analysis helps the teacher plan instruction by considering all the subtasks.

Cognitive theories of learning have made a significant contribution to knowledge about learning. The computer can be used as a metaphor for describing how learning takes place according to cognitive, or information processing, theories. Short-term memory stores new information that is received, but it has a limited capacity and a limited duration. Long-term memory is a complex web, or schema, of concepts, ideas, and relationships that represent important existing knowledge. For learning to occur, new ideas and experiences must be transferred from short-term memory into long-term memory. These ideas can then be retrieved and used repeatedly if they are stored with many meaningful connections.[8] Ellen Gagne describes implications of cognitive psychology for mathematics learning.

- Mathematics competence includes computational skill and conceptual understanding.

- If students are using an incorrect procedure or less-than-optimal procedure in computation, they may be helped with verbal instructions and corrective feedback.

- Failure to master prerequisite skills hampers students in computation.

- People organize information in different ways. What people understand about mathematics is very individual and shows up in the way that they approach problems.

- Estimation is an important competence because people learn to monitor their performance and judge what makes sense for them.[9]

Cognitive theories extend earlier research and theories that portrayed learning as a process of building meanings.

EXERCISE   Write a phrase or two that best identifies the learning theory of each of these individuals: Brownell, Dienes, Piaget, Skemp, Bruner, R. Gagne.

Research on Teaching and Mathematics Teaching

Research on teaching methods has not produced any single method or approach that is superior to all other approaches. Several instructional approaches and methods have been supported consistently in the research on mathematics teaching: cooperative learning, use of manipulatives, inquiry and induction, and direct instruction.

Cooperative Learning

In a general sense, students are cooperating in groups when they are working together to complete a geometry puzzle, measure the playground, or study for a test. However, cooperative learning has come to mean more than group work. The attribute that probably distinguishes general group work from cooperative learning the most is individual accountability. In cooperative learning all students in a group are accountable for developing group understanding and knowing what has been accomplished by the group. The group as a social unit makes a commitment to all the members. General and specific strategies for organizing learning with groups have been developed by many teachers and researchers.[10]

Cooperative learning is a good strategy for exploration and discovery of mathematical principles.[11] A mathematical challenge is presented for students to resolve. The situation might be a problem that has many possibilities; a set of materials with task cards; or a new process to figure out, such as the vignette on using compensation for mental subtraction. Sometimes students work in pairs, other times in groups of three or four. Some teachers assign roles for children in a group. The principal investigator is responsible for keeping the group working on the task, the recorder is responsible for notes of the group's ideas, and the materials manager is responsible for any materials needed for the investigation. Roles are rotated so that all the children have an opportunity to learn the jobs. Effective classroom management is an additional benefit of the cooperative learning technique.

Support for cooperative learning comes from the research of David Johnson and Roger Johnson, who have worked with teachers on cooperative learning since 1970.[12] They have described three types of classrooms: individualistic, competitive, and cooperative. In individualistic classrooms, the rule for achievement is "I'll get mine." In the competitive classroom, the achievement ethic is "I'll get mine by keeping you from getting yours." In the cooperative classroom, students learn that the whole group benefits when everyone learns, or "One for all, all for one." The Johnsons reported benefits for students in cooperative classrooms.

- Cooperation promotes higher achievement than do individualistic or competitive methods. Knowledge of basic facts and principles, reasoning, and sharing of problem-solving strategies were increased in group work.

- Students gain confidence in their individual abilities. Working together alleviates anxiety and promotes self-esteem with regard to mathematics.

- Students are influenced in their career choices and type of mathematics courses to take. More students see advanced mathematics as possible for them.[13]

The cooperative strategies used by the Johnsons emphasize explicit teaching and processing of group interaction skills. These skills may be developed in any mathematics activity in which group work and individual accountability are involved.

Some teachers use cross-age and peer tutoring as an effective means of improving instruction. In cross-age tutoring, students from one grade level work with students from another grade level. In peer tutoring, students from the same grade or class work together to learn content. Many of the strategies and processes developed by Robert Slavin resemble peer tutoring formalized into cooperative learning strategies.[14] He and faculty members at Johns Hopkins University have developed several specific techniques that they call Student Team Learning. Each of the techniques involves team members directly teaching and coaching each other for improved academic performance on a test or in a class tournament. Teams score points on how well all the members of the group do. The team goal may be set at an 80 percent mastery for all team members or be based on improvement from the previous test or tournament. There is competition between teams, but internally the members of a team function to improve all the members' learning. The Johns Hopkins techniques tend to be more structured than many other cooperative techniques, but they can be used with any content and at any grade level.

Different teachers use cooperative learning in various ways. Cooperative learning is not limited to any particular teaching style or process; it can be used in conjunction with many types of lessons. However, many teachers and observers also warn that cooperative learning requires careful planning and organization. Without adequate preparation, students may not gain all that they might.

Use of Manipulatives

Manipulative materials include a wide variety of teaching-learning aids that model and demonstrate mathematical concepts and processes. Manipulatives may be as simple as a piece of paper folded to show a fraction or as extensive as a kit of metric measures for length, volume, and mass. The research on manipulatives and student achievement has been consistent in support of these materials in all areas of mathematics.[15] Fennema found that a learning environment rich in manipulative models suited to the developmental level of the learner facilitates learning better than an environment that ignores the developmental level of the learner.[16] Marilyn Suydam and Jon Higgins concluded that lessons using manipulatives were much more likely to produce better mathematics achievement than lessons without manipulatives.[17] Even though these benefits have been found consistently, many teachers do not use manipulatives in their teaching. Patrick Scott found that fewer than half of the teachers in kindergarten through grade five used manipulatives as often as five times a year.[18]

Inquiry and Induction

Bruce Joyce and Marsha Weil report over 20 different instructional strategies that have been found effective.[19] These strategies include mnemonics (memory techniques), induction, concept attainment, synectics (creativity), and group investigation. Two strategies that many mathematics teachers use effectively are those of inquiry and induction. In inquiry, sometimes called guided discovery, students discover or invent concepts and principles with teacher assistance. The inductive method moves from specific examples to a general conclusion.

Learners work with materials or sets of unorganized data in both methods. An element of puzzlement or incongruity is often used to motivate the inquiry. After a time of work, students are asked to describe the patterns and relationships they have found. Observations become conjectures and hypotheses about what was found with the materials or data. The hypotheses are tested as the teacher probes and extends student thinking with new situations or examples. Generalizations, or statements of rules, come from the students rather than being stated by the teacher. Both techniques require that a teacher do much preplanning by gathering materials, structuring tasks, preparing questions, and creating extensions. Cooperative learning and manipulatives are often aspects of guided discovery and inductive-type lessons.

Direct Instruction

Direct teaching is the mode of learning experienced by many people. A teacher presents a lesson, usually oral, to a group of five, ten, thirty, or a thousand people. Students listen to the teacher; the teacher asks questions and gives tests to see how well students have learned the lesson. Learning in this manner tends to be very passive and memory based and makes low cognitive demands on learners.

Robert Gagne has challenged this type of direct instruction as ineffective. He believes eight events of instruction will bring about meaningful learning. These eight events require that the teacher actively engage the student in the learning from the beginning of instruction.

- Gain the learner's attention.

- Inform the learner of the learning objective.

- Recall prior experiences, information, or prerequisite skills.

- Present new content or skill.

- Provide learning guidance.

- Elicit performance.

- Provide feedback and assess performance.

- Apply content or skill in a new situation.[20]

The first three events prepare the learner for instruction. This is sometimes called creating a *learning set* or *expectancy* by relating the importance of the new knowledge to existing knowledge and making sure that the learner knows how this new information will be useful or helpful.

The next three events allow the teacher to structure the learning situation, or lesson, so that students work directly with the new information or skill while receiving corrective feedback about their performance. Both "showing" and "telling" are important in communicating the meaning and the process of the new content. After giving instructions, the teacher asks the learner to echo, or model, what has been taught. At first the modeling may be a simple repetition of the teacher's actions, but the teacher will also ask the students to demonstrate their understanding with different examples or situations. Guided practice is a very important step in the instructional cycle.

Independent practice comes after the teacher is sure that the learner is skilled enough to work independently. If the student is making many mistakes during guided practice, the teacher will reteach the lesson with other materials, new examples, or a different explanation before assigning independent practice. The goal of independent practice is to increase proficiency and expand the new skill with new situations. When the learner has had sufficient practice, evaluation is useful to pinpoint strengths and areas for further improvement. Finally, the new skill or information should be used in some manner. The new learning is put into a useful context. This step enhances retention by showing the utility of new learning.

EXERCISE   Look back at the vignettes at the beginning of the chapter. Find examples in the lessons that illustrate cooperative learning, use of manipulatives, inquiry and induction, and direct instruction.

A Comprehensive View of Instruction

Conclusions from research on effective learning and teaching are consistent. Students must be actively involved in their learning. They need opportunities to explore, discover, discuss, and apply mathematics in their world. They need a variety of materials that allow them to understand relationships rather than memorize steps. They should follow a sequence that moves from concrete materials to abstract symbols. The social climate, or how children feel in the classroom, makes a difference in how much mathematics and how well mathematics is learned.

Classroom teachers who have used meaningful approaches to help children learn mathematics support the research evidence by demonstrating their success. Mary Baratta-Lorton successfully used a variety of materials and procedures that became the basis of books for primary-grade teachers.[21] In Minnesota a program based on the theories of Piaget and using a wide variety of manipulatives has been successfully used in primary classrooms.[22] Marilyn Jacobson described how three sets of materials helped middle-grade children understand decimal fractions and their uses.[23] Susan Strand, a teacher in California, reported that her students acted out regrouping situations using base-ten blocks.[24] She wrote: "The skits are a high-interest vehicle for daily discussion of number, operations, place value, and problem solving. . . . Regularly using manipulatives in conjunction with student-centered activities gives pupils the opportunity to own mathematical concepts."

Research and classroom practice argue against teaching mathematics by lecture and recitation. Reliance on these methods has been responsible for the failure of many students to learn and like mathematics. Teachers have much freedom in determining the methods of instruction they will use. The evidence is clear on which practices will be the most successful for children.

Gagne's events of instruction provide a comprehensive way of thinking about instruction. The sequence allows teacher flexibility and creativity for accomplishing each step. Cooperative learning, use of manipulatives, and guided discovery may be incorporated into the broad guidelines. Classroom techniques such as learning centers, task cards, games, mathematics-based or interdisciplinary projects, and computer instruction also may deliver one or more of the events of instruction effectively. The comprehensive view of instruction presented in this text incorporates many different classroom strategies and instructional practices.

PLANNING A COMPREHENSIVE MATHEMATICS PROGRAM

Establishing Instructional Purposes

Purposes include the goals and objectives that teachers plan for learners to achieve. Both cognitive and attitudinal, or affective, goals should be part of the long-range planning for the classroom. Most state education agencies or local school districts have adopted goals and objectives for each grade level. These provide teachers with a scope and sequence of mathematics skills and concepts. The new National Council of Teachers of Mathematics standards provide goals that will be used when states and school districts update their curriculum statements. Textbooks and other teaching materials should be chosen because they match the goals and objectives of the school district. A scope and sequence chart in a textbook contains the concepts and skills that are presented during each of the elementary school years.

A scope and sequence chart in a textbook or curriculum guide gives teachers a sense of the mathematics experiences that children should have during the elementary school years. In the fall, each teacher should outline a plan for the year so that students will experience all the areas of the curriculum. This long-range plan should be seen as an overview rather than a rigid calendar. The needs and interests of the students mean that parts of the plan may shift during the year. Without a year-long plan, students may miss important topics. The plan should include a variety of topics to provide change in mathematics during the year. Students become bored by a constant agenda of number, numeration, and computation. Topics from geometry, measurement, probability and statistics, number theory, and graphing can be included throughout the year. Problem-solving projects and skills can also be included as the plan is developed. Figure 2.1 illustrates one teacher's yearly plan.

Figure 2-1
A planning guide containing a year-long plan for grade 4

SEPTEMBER	Geometry (Symmetry) and Patterns—1 week Applications of Addition and Subtraction—2 weeks Review of Common Fractions—1 week
OCTOBER	Introduction to Multiplication—2 weeks Basic Facts in Multiplication—1 week Applications with Addition, Subtraction, and Multiplication—1 week
NOVEMBER	Geometry (Tessellations) and Patterns—1 week Addition and Subtraction with Common Fractions—2 weeks Probability and Common Fractions—1 week
DECEMBER	Common Fractions into Decimal Fractions—1 week Applications with Fractions—2 weeks
JANUARY	Measurement: Length, Area, Volume—3 weeks Introduction to Division—1 week
FEBRUARY	Division and Multiplication Facts—1 week Division and Multiplication Algorithms with Calculator—2 weeks Applications with Division and Multiplication—1 week
MARCH	Probability—2 weeks Multiplication and Division of Fractions—2 weeks
APRIL	Statistics—2 weeks Coordinate Geometry—2 weeks
MAY	Measurement: Weight—1 week Problem-Solving Fair—2 weeks Applications—1 week

Instructional Goals and Objectives

Instructional goals provide the framework for a mathematics program. Objectives are specific statements that direct instruction of children.

Goals

Goals are broad statements of instructional purpose. The NCTM standards are goals because they are general guidelines. These kindergarten through fourth grade standards for data analysis and probability illustrate instructional goals.

Standard 11:   Statistics and Probability   In grades K–4, the mathematics curriculum should include experiences with data analysis and probability so that students can:

- collect, organize, and describe data;

- construct, read, and interpret displays of data;

- formulate and solve problems that involve collecting and analyzing data;

- explore concepts of chance.[25]

Goals into Process Objectives

Instructional objectives may be phrased in several ways to show different instructional purposes. Some objectives are called *process objectives* because they suggest the type of activity or experiences that should be provided. The instructional objectives from the *Mathematics Framework, Kindergarten–12* from Texas list process objectives for students at each grade level. The process objectives for probability and statistics specify which activities should be included at each grade level.

GRADE ONE: THE STUDENT SHALL BE PROVIDED OPPORTUNITIES TO:

A.   classify objects;

B.   order numbers.

GRADE TWO: THE STUDENT SHALL BE PROVIDED OPPORTUNITIES TO:

A.   collect and organize information;

B.   read bar graphs;

C.   make picture graphs.

GRADE THREE: THE STUDENT SHALL BE PROVIDED OPPORTUNITIES TO:

A. collect and organize information;

B. interpret and construct picture and bar graphs.

GRADE FOUR: THE STUDENT SHALL BE PROVIDED OPPORTUNITIES TO:

A. collect data and use to construct graphs;

B. interpret pictographs and use information to solve story problems;

C. list the possible outcomes in a given situation;

D. read and interpret line graphs.

GRADE FIVE: THE STUDENT SHALL BE PROVIDED OPPORTUNITIES TO:

A. collect data and use to construct graphs;

B. interpret and construct charts and graphs;

C. use counting arrangements;

D. predict possible outcomes from a sample.

GRADE SIX: THE STUDENT SHALL BE PROVIDED OPPORTUNITIES TO:

A. collect data and use to construct graphs;

B. interpret and construct charts and graphs;

C. construct sample spaces;

D. determine and interpret fractional probability;

E. find averages;

F. apply probability and statistics concepts to solve problems.[26]

Process Objectives into Performance Objectives

A teacher begins planning units, lessons, and activities with process objectives. As specific activities are developed, a different kind of instructional objective is used. Performance objectives, or behavioral objectives, specify the learning outcomes by stating what behaviors the teacher expects to observe in the learner. A complete performance objective includes the behavior, the situation, and the level of mastery. Sample objectives on statistics and probability demonstrate how performance objectives might be phrased.

- GRADE ONE: The student will be able to sort 20 wooden cubes painted in primary colors into three groups by color with 100 percent accuracy.

- GRADE ONE: The student will be able to make sets of 1 to 9 using Unifix cubes and arrange them in order from 1 to 9.

- GRADE FOUR: Given centimeter-squared paper, students will be able to collect data on a topic of their choice and construct a bar graph showing the results. Title and key should be included.

- GRADE SIX: Given a chart of the monthly rainfall in the county for the last ten years, students will average the rainfall for each month, create a bar graph showing the average monthly rainfall, and write a short paragraph describing the wettest and driest seasons.

Performance Objectives into Teaching Activities

Teachers write performance objectives while planning specific teaching activities. These teaching activities may take many forms as different teaching strategies are used. Few objectives are achieved in a single lesson. Most require that students encounter a skill or concept in a variety of ways with different materials over time: several days, weeks, or even years. So teachers need several lessons or activities on the same or related performance objectives. The following four examples show how teachers might plan activities for each of the performance objectives.

- GRADE ONE: The student will be able to sort 20 wooden cubes painted in primary colors into three groups by color with 100 percent accuracy.

Mr. Snell begins by putting a red flower on a red piece of paper, a blue glove on a blue piece of paper, and a yellow fire truck on a yellow piece of paper. He asks why the objects are where he put them. The students answer that the objects match the color of the paper they are on. He has several more objects that children place on the colored paper. He then gives each pair of students a box of 20 wooden blocks and three primary-colored pieces of construction paper. With no instructions, the students begin sorting the blocks by color. Students also record how many they have of each color by making a picture of their collection on squared paper. Mr. Snell extends the activity into counting and addition with questions: "Who has the most red cubes?" "The most blue cubes?" "The most yellow cubes?" "The most red cubes and yellow cubes?"

If students have difficulty with the lesson, the teacher might want to try a similar lesson the next day with fewer objects to classify. If this lesson is very easy for the students, additional objects with more than one color on them might be on hand for classifying. Classifying as a skill would be addressed many times during the year. Both directed lessons and learning-center activities will be planned with different materials and different classifying schemes.

MATERIALS	CLASSIFYING SCHEMES
Buttons	Color, size, number of holes, texture, shank or hole
Shoes	Size; tie, Velcro, or slip-on; brands; color
Cuisenaire rods	Length (color)
Attribute blocks	Color, shape, texture, thickness

■ GRADE ONE: The student will be able to make sets of 1 to 9 using Unifix cubes and arrange them in order from 1 to 9.

Ordering numbers can be taught using toy cars, plastic bears, or other counters in teacher-directed lessons. Ms. Randell has nine circles ordered in sequence from a small circle on the left to a large circle on the right on a large sheet of paper. She places one object in the smallest circle, two in the next largest circle, and asks who knows how many belong in the next circle. Children see that each circle has one more than the previous circle. Similar lessons might be repeated for several days if needed. The next week a learning center of Unifix cubes with the Unifix boats or ladder allows the student more experience with ordering sets. (See photograph of Unifix materials in Chapter 3.) During the lessons and while working with the Unifix materials, the students also label the sets with numerals. Ms. Randell is working toward a performance objective on ordering numerals without the sets, such as "Given a set of numeral cards, the students will be able to place the cards in numerical order from 1 to 9."

■ GRADE FOUR: Given centimeter-squared paper, students will be able to collect data on a topic of their choice and construct a bar graph showing the results. Title and key should be included.

Mr. Rodriguez asks the children to name their favorite sandwich and makes a simple chart labeled with types of sandwiches: "peanut butter," "peanut butter with jelly," "grilled cheese," "bologna," "bacon and tomato," "turkey," or "other." He then has them write their names on the chart in the column for the sandwich of their choice. On the overhead projector he shows a transparency with seven columns of squares. He labels each column with a type of sandwich and writes in the initials of a child in each square. He says that it is like voting because everyone has one box to fill. Then he colors in the boxes for one kind of sandwich with the same color. Finally he asks the group to name the graph. After several suggestions, the group decides that "Yum Yum Our Favorite Sandwiches" is the best title. He asks the students to suggest some other things they could make graphs about. They list kinds of pizza, kinds of ice cream, favorite sports teams, pets, favorite recording groups, hair styles, dream cars, and many others. Students move into their groups to choose a topic, collect data, and create a graph. This is the first lesson of the year on graphing. Each student later in the year will individually conduct his or her own survey and construct a graph.

■   GRADE SIX: Given a chart of the monthly rainfall in the county for the last ten years, students will average the rainfall for each month, create a bar graph showing the average monthly rainfall, and write a short paragraph describing the wettest and driest seasons.

The assignment is part of an interdisciplinary science/mathematics/social studies unit on weather and environment. Ms. Morris has created a task card in the learning center with the newspaper report of monthly rainfall for the last ten years. Although students might work on the activity as either an individual or group task, Ms. Morris has decided to have each student make her or his own graph without consulting with the group. Then she plans to have them compare their results and make one chart for the whole group. The activity relates not only to the process objective and goals on statistics, but also to goals pertaining to applications of mathematics, communication using mathematics, and connections between mathematics concepts and other subjects.

Instructional standards and goals provide the overall framework for a mathematics program. Within that framework performance objectives provide guidance for teachers making instructional decisions. They provide direction for daily lesson planning and a basis for judging children's learning. Chapter 3 presents information about ways to organize a class for instruction and how to plan daily lessons, as well as discussing concrete learning aids and calculators and computers.

EXERCISE   Distinguish between a goal and an objective in mathematics education. With which of these is the classroom instructor more directly concerned? Why?

■   SUMMARY

Effective instruction requires that teachers develop lessons that are more than lecture and recitation. Research into the ways children learn and research on the methods and strategies that enhance learning provide a basis for making instructional decisions. Use of many concrete manipulatives, active involvement of students in exploring and generalizing mathematical principles, organizing cooperative learning groups, and attention to developmental needs of different learners are practices that teachers should include in planning lessons and learning activities. Teachers who employ such techniques report with satisfaction how much the children understand and how excited they are about learning mathematics. Teachers also must refer to state or district goals and objectives in developing activities. Goals and objectives, such as those stated in the NCTM *Curriculum and Evaluation Standards for School Mathematics,* guide planning for a variety of learning activities in a well-balanced mathematics program.

■ STUDY QUESTIONS AND ACTIVITIES

1. Examine the goals of an elementary school mathematics textbook series to see how well they reflect the NCTM standards. How well will the series help students meet the standards? Are some standards neglected? Which standards receive the greatest attention?

2. Several learning theories, including some no longer believed to be creditable, are mentioned in this chapter. Which of the theories did the mathematics teachers who instructed you use as the basis for their teaching? Do you believe there are still persons who believe in the stimulus-response theory of learning teaching in schools? If so, how do they manifest this in their teaching? At what level of schooling— early elementary, intermediate grades, junior high, senior high, or college—do you believe the best mathematics teaching occurs? Why?

3. Berman and Friederwitzer (see the For Further Reading section) indicate that elementary school children can understand algebraic equations if the work is made concrete. Read the article. What materials are used and what are the algebraic equations children learn? How much problem solving is there in the activities? Do you believe the activities are worthwhile?

4. Read Skemp's article on instrumental and relational learning (see For Further Reading section). Distinguish between the two types of understanding. Based on your experiences with mathematics, which of these understandings have you developed? Give examples of either or both types of understanding you presently possess. Can you think of any situations in which instrumental understanding might be preferred over relational understanding?

■ TEACHER'S BOOKSHELF

Gagne, Robert. 1985. *The Conditions of Learning and Theory of Instruction.* New York: Holt, Rinehart & Winston.

Joyce, Bruce, and Marsha Weil. 1986. *Models of Teaching,* Third Edition. Englewood Cliffs, NJ: Prentice-Hall.

Piaget, Jean. 1952. *The Child's Conception of Number.* New York: Humanities Press.

■ FOR FURTHER READING

Adler, Irving. 1966, November. Mental growth and the art of teaching. *Arithmetic Teacher 13*(7), 576–584.

A discussion of a dozen facets of Piaget's theory of mental growth and thirteen implications of the theory for teaching mathematics.

Arithmetic Teacher. 1986, February. *33*(6).

This theme issue focuses on manipulative materials in mathematics learning; it contains many articles on how to use concrete materials.

Berman, Barbara, and Fredda Friederwitzer. 1989, April. Algebra can be elementary . . . when it's concrete. *Arithmetic Teacher 36*(8), 21–24.

This article provides the reader with a model to aid children as they progress from the concrete to the abstract in solving algebraic equations.

Brown, Sue D. 1980, January. A look at the past. *Arithmetic Teacher 27*(5), 34–37.

Teaching methods of the past century, as reflected in mathematics books, are briefly described. Excerpts from many books are presented.

Driscoll, Mark. 1986, May. Effective teaching. *Arithmetic Teacher 33*(9), 19, 48.

Recent research indicates the factors that contribute to effective mathematics teaching.

Duckworth, Eleanor. 1964, May. Piaget rediscovered. *Arithmetic Teacher 11*(7), 496–499.

A discussion of Piaget's theories on intellectual development, teaching, and teacher training.

Fennema, Elizabeth. 1973, May. Manipulatives in the classroom. *Arithmetic Teacher 20*(5), 350–352.

The author discusses seven reasons for using manipulatives, or learning aids, while teaching mathematics. She also cautions against the use of manipulatives in a random way.

Fielder, Dorothy R. 1989, April. Project hands-on math: making a difference in K–2 classrooms. *Arithmetic Teacher 36*(8), 14–16.

Fielder supports the power of manipulatives in early childhood mathematics. She emphasizes the need for available materials and appropriate staff development.

Gibb, E. Glenadine. 1982, March. Teaching effectively and efficiently. *Arithmetic Teacher 29*(7), 2.

Gibb discusses different interpretations of what efficiency and effectiveness in mathematics are. She concludes by saying that if changes in curriculum are to take place, the expected learning outcome and expected content cannot be overlooked.

Greenwood, Jay, and Robert Anderson. 1983, November. Some thoughts on teaching and learning mathematics. *Arithmetic Teacher 31*(3), 42–49.

Greenwood and Anderson discuss opinions about mathematics goals and methods, and they include suggestions for resolving conflicts.

Skemp, Richard R. 1978, November. Relational understanding and instrumental understanding. *Arithmetic Teacher 26*(3), 9–15.

Relational understanding indicates that the learner knows the relationships among parts—knows the schema—of a topic or concept, while instrumental understanding relies on rules only. The advantages of relational understanding outweigh those of instrumental understanding, according to Skemp, even though it is a harder type of understanding to develop.

Suydam, Marilyn N. 1986, February. Manipulative material and achievement. *Arithmetic Teacher 33*(6), 10, 32.

Suydam summarizes recent findings on the use of manipulative materials in elementary school mathematics.

◼ NOTES

[1] An interesting review of research in mathematics during the first half of the twentieth century is found in William A. Brownell. 1986, October. The revolution in arithmetic. *Arithmetic Teacher 34*(2), 38–42. This article is a reprint of the original that appeared in the first issue of the *Arithmetic Teacher* in February, 1954.

[2] Zoltan P. Dienes. 1960. *Building Up Mathematics.* London: Hutchison Education.

[3] Jean Piaget. 1952. *The Child's Conception of Number.* New York: Humanities Press; Barry J. Wadsworth. 1984. *Piaget's Theory of Cognitive and Affective Development,* Third Edition. New York: Longman, 1.

[4] Richard Skemp. Mathematics as an activity of our intelligence: A model for diagnosing and remediation of learning difficulties in mathematics, in Ian D. Beattie, ed., *1981 Research Monograph: Research Reports from the Seventh Annual National Conference on Diagnostic and Prescriptive Mathematics.* Bowling Green, OH: Research Council for Diagnostic and Prescriptive Mathematics, 2–4; Richard S. Skemp. 1971. *The Psychology of Learning Mathematics.* Hammondsworth, England: Penguin Books.

[5] Jerome Bruner. 1960. *The Process of Education.* Cambridge, MA: Harvard University Press.

[6] Diana Lambdin Kroll, Connections between psychological learning theories and elementary mathematics curriculum, in *1989 Yearbook: New Directions for Elementary School Mathematics.* Reston, VA: National Council of Teachers of Mathematics, 206.

[7] Robert Gagne. 1985. *The Conditions of Learning and Theory of Instruction.* New York: Holt, Rinehart & Winston.

[8] Ellen D. Gagne. 1983. *The Cognitive Psychology of School Learning.* Boston, MA: Little, Brown.

[9] Ellen D. Gagne, 229–230.

[10] Neil Davidson, ed. 1990. *Cooperative Learning in Mathematics.* Menlo Park, CA: Addison-Wesley.

[11] Marilyn Burns. The math solution, using groups of four, in Neil Davidson, ed. 1990. *Cooperative Learning in Mathematics.* Menlo Park, CA: Addison-Wesley, 89–97.

[12] D. W. Johnson, R. Johnson, and E. Holubec. 1986. *Circles of Learning.* Edina, MN: Interaction Book Company.

[13] David W. Johnson and Roger T. Johnson. Using cooperative learning in math, in Neil Davidson, ed. 1990. *Cooperative Learning in Mathematics.* Menlo Park, CA: Addison-Wesley, 103–125.

[14] Robert Slavin. Student team learning in mathematics, in Neil Davidson, ed. 1990. *Cooperative Learning in Mathematics.* Menlo Park, CA: Addison-Wesley, 89–97.

[15] Marilyn N. Suydam. 1984, January. Research report: Manipulative materials. *Arithmetic Teacher 31*(5), 27; Marie E. Canny. 1984, September. The relation-

ship of manipulative materials to achievement in three areas of fourth-grade mathematics: Computation, concept development, and problem solving. *Dissertation Abstracts International 44A,* 775–776.

[16] Elizabeth H. Fennema. 1972, December. Models and mathematics. *Arithmetic Teacher 19*(6), 635–649.

[17] Marilyn Suydam and Jon L. Higgins. 1977. *Activity-Based Learning in Elementary School Mathematics: Recommendations from Research.* Columbus, OH: ERIC/SMEAC.

[18] Patrick B. Scott. 1983, January. A survey of perceived use of mathematics materials by elementary teachers in a large urban school district. *School Science and Mathematics 83*(1), 61–68.

[19] Bruce Joyce and Marsha Weil. 1986. *Models of Teaching,* Third Edition. Englewood Cliffs, NJ: Prentice-Hall.

[20] Robert Gagne. 1985. *The Conditions of Learning and Theory of Instruction.* New York: Holt, Rinehart & Winston.

[21] Mary Baratta-Lorton. 1989. *Mathematics Their Way.* Menlo Park, CA: Addison-Wesley; 1988. *Workjobs.* Menlo Park, CA: Addison-Wesley; 1988. *Workjobs II.* Menlo Park, CA: Addison-Wesley.

[22] A. Dean Hendrickson. 1981. *Mathematics the Piaget Way.* St. Paul, MN: Minnesota Council on Quality Education.

[23] Marilyn H. Jacobson. 1984, February. Teaching rational numbers—intermediate grades. *Arithmetic Teacher 31*(6), 40–42.

[24] Susan Strand. 1990, January. Acting out numbers. *Arithmetic Teacher 37*(5), 6–9.

[25] National Council of Teachers of Mathematics. 1989. *Curriculum and Evaluation Standards for School Mathematics.* Reston, VA: The Council, 54.

[26] Texas Education Agency. *Mathematics Framework Kindergarten–Grade 12.* Austin, TX: The Agency, n.d., 13–18.

Organizing for Instruction

Individual teachers are seldom responsible for establishing instructional objectives, but they usually have great flexibility in the instructional methods they use to implement those objectives. They may choose from teacher-directed lessons, informal exploration with games and activities, learning centers or mathematics laboratories, cooperative learning groups, or individualized study plans.

In this chapter you will read about

1. three modes of instruction that provide a well-balanced instructional program;

2. the importance of informal experiences in introducing concepts;

3. steps in a teacher-directed lesson;

4. facilitating mathematics investigations with students;

5. arranging the classroom for instruction;

6. using learning centers and mathematics laboratories;

7. teaching mathematics for gifted and talented students;

8. adapting mathematics instruction for students with handicaps;

9. suggestions for working with parents;

10. a variety of manipulative materials for mathematics instruction;

11. the importance of calculators and computers as learning tools.

■ THREE INSTRUCTIONAL MODES

As teachers organize for instruction, they have various instructional goals in mind and may adopt different modes of instruction to meet their goals. Three different modes of instruction are suggested:

- ■ Informal introduction to concepts, procedures, and materials
- ■ Teacher-directed lessons
- ■ Mathematical investigations

Each of the instructional modes contributes to a comprehensive mathematics program for elementary students.

Informal Introduction

Teachers often introduce mathematical concepts and ideas to students in an informal manner. An informal approach is taken when children need experiences with an idea before it is introduced in a lesson. The teacher structures the environment with materials, allows the children to explore and manipulate the materials, watches children as they work, asks questions, probes for understanding, and makes decisions about the next activity needed to provide mathematical background.

Most of the mathematical experiences in preschool and kindergarten are informal. A sand or water table allows children to explore weight and volume. A block corner is excellent for developing concepts such as proximity and enclosure as well as length and area. Unit blocks, double blocks, half blocks, and quad blocks introduce children to early fractional ideas. Cooking provides informal measuring activities. Playing store provides opportunities for children to work with play money and exchange money for goods. Finger plays and rhymes often include counting up and counting down. Many pictures have mathematical concepts in them. The entire kindergarten day is full of informal experiences that contribute to children's mathematical background.

Older children also need informal introductions to concepts and procedures in mathematics. Games with spinners or cards are important for basic

Figure 3-1
Cuisenaire stairs
illustrating the idea
of adding one

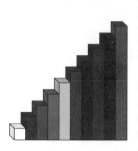

understanding of probability. The card game "Battle" is an introduction to inequalities; children turn over playing cards one at a time, with the highest card winning. Some teachers have students record their grades to demonstrate fractions (8/10) and percentage (80 percent) before teaching formal lessons. With skip counting (3, 6, 9, 12, . . .), children learn some multiplication facts. When informal introductions are a regular part of mathematics instruction, children come to direct instruction with the background for understanding new concepts.

Children should be introduced to manipulatives informally before the materials are used in a lesson. As children build and manipulate Cuisenaire rods (see page 73), they invent many designs that display number concepts. Cuisenaire stairs in Figure 3.1 show the idea of adding one. Children should have informal time with geoboards (see page 76) to explore concepts such as symmetry, similarity, congruence, and area.

Children who have a chance to work informally with mathematical concepts have time to build basic understandings. These basic understandings are a foundation for formal concepts and procedures to be introduced in more directed ways. The activities also develop children's pedagogical and affective readiness for later activities. Some teachers find that informal experiences are so powerful that children need very little direct instruction. Most of the manipulatives that are pictured later in this chapter should be introduced informally.

Teacher-Directed Lesson

In a teacher-directed lesson, a teacher works with a group of children on a skill or concept. A teacher should use observations and discussions during informal work to evaluate children's readiness for a formal presentation. The teacher should know the mathematics content and where each new skill fits in the curriculum scope and sequence. The teacher should have identified a performance objective that makes the expected level of performance clear. Then the teacher should prepare a well-developed lesson plan as the foundation for good teaching. Complete mastery of a skill or concept is not expected early in a sequence of lessons but as a culmination of many lessons and experiences over a period of time.

A lesson based on Gagne's events of instruction will include motivational introduction, presentation of the new content, guided practice, and independent practice. A lesson cycle developed by Madeline Hunter and Douglas Russell has been used extensively by many teachers. The lesson cycle suggests seven parts for an effective lesson.

- Setting the stage
- Statement of objective
- Instructional input

- Modeling
- Checking for understanding
- Guided practice
- Independent practice

The Hunter plan is called the *lesson cycle* because the steps are not linear, contrary to what the list implies. Instead the lesson is taught in small increments, with each new piece of information cycled through several steps before new information is added. Figure 3.2 demonstrates how the lesson cycle operates. Figure 3.3 is a lesson plan format for a teacher-directed lesson.

Figure 3-2
Lesson cycle

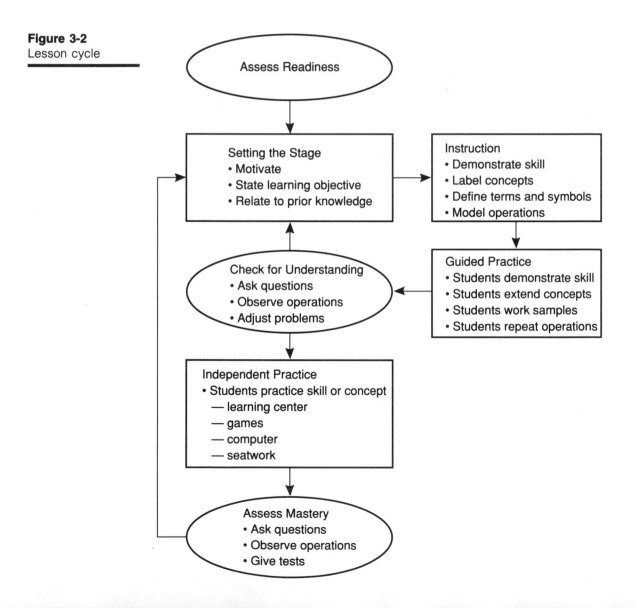

Figure 3-3 Blank lesson plan and sample lesson plan for a teacher-directed lesson

TEACHER _____ DATE _____

TOPIC _____

OBJECTIVE _____

_____

SETTING THE STAGE _____

_____

INSTRUCTIONAL INPUT AND MODELING _____

_____

GUIDED PRACTICE AND CHECK FOR UNDERSTANDING _____

_____

INDEPENDENT PRACTICE _____

MATERIALS NEEDED _____

(continued)

Figure 3-3 *(continued)*

TEACHER   K. Morris   DATE   March 3

TOPIC Linear Measurement - measuring in centimeters

OBJECTIVE

Students will be able to measure objects in centimeters using orange and white
Cuisenaire rods.

SETTING THE STAGE

Have groups of five children line up from the tallest to the shortest. Then have
them arrange a group of drinking straws of various length from longest to
shortest. Let three children walk off the length of the room in heel-to-
toe fashion and record the lengths (42 Ashley feet, 45 Shawna feet, 38 Au feet)

INSTRUCTIONAL INPUT AND MODELING

Ask children what the difficulty is with having three different children measure
the room with their own feet. (People's feet are different so the measurements are
different.)
Say "We need to have a consistent unit for measuring so that everyone will
understand what we mean. When measuring we use two different systems: the
customary and the metric. Today we are measuring objects using the metric
system."
Hold up a white Cuisenaire rod and say "This rod is one centimeter long."
Hold up an orange rod and ask how long it is. (10 centimeters.)
Say "Let me show you how to measure this pencil with the centimeter rods" and
line up the centimeter rods starting at one end of the pencil.
Ask "How long is it?" Children will answer by counting.
Write 16 cm (without period) to record the answer.
Ask "Is there an easier and quicker way to measure the pencil?" (Use orange rod.)
Model the measurement with the orange rod or rods and the white rods.
Repeat modeling if needed.

GUIDED PRACTICE AND CHECK FOR UNDERSTANDING

Say "You have four things at your table to measure. Work together to measure
the objects using the orange and white rod. Record your answers in your log."
Move among students to see how they are working and recording the answer.
Ask the groups to trade objects and measure again, then compare answers.
Ask if the groups agree on the length of objects.
Ask whether all the objects were measured exactly using the rods.
The answer should be "No." Say "Measurement is always an approximation."

INDEPENDENT PRACTICE

Have students cut paper strips the length of the orange and white rod.
Ask them to measure the length of ten objects at home.

MATERIALS NEEDED

White and orange Cuisenaire rods
Collection of objects for measuring

Setting the Stage

Hunter and Russell use the term *anticipatory set* for all the things a teacher does to prepare students for learning. Good teachers have many ways to focus students on a lesson and create excitement about learning. A mystery box or bag is a good attention grabber. The contents may be materials for the lesson, a pertinent book, or a puppet. Some teachers begin a lesson with a story or felt-board demonstration. Many teachers find that a puzzle on the overhead projector is good for gaining attention of the group. *Building Thinking Skills* ® and *Math Mind Benders* ® have many activities suitable for opening a mathematics lesson.[1] A puzzling event, a cartoon, or a newspaper headline may provide motivation. A good beginning helps the student shift from a previous activity such as reading or recess to the mathematics topic. Regardless of the method, helping children focus on the lesson is the first step in a good lesson.

Statement of Objective

When a teacher describes clearly for the students what the learning expectations are, the students know what is coming, what they are expected to do, and what they will be learning. A statement as simple as "Today you are going to learn to multiply by tens" may be sufficient. The teacher may wish to extend the statement of objective by relating the skill to previous or future knowledge: "Multiplying by tens is like skip counting by tens," or "Knowing how to multiply by tens makes multiplication and division with larger numbers much easier." The objective can be related to a previous experience. "Last week we had a jar of dimes here and guessed that there were 150 dimes in it. When we counted, there were actually 93 dimes. Multiplying the number of dimes by ten will give us the amount of money in the jar."

Instructional Input and Modeling

Having manipulatives and visual aids is critical during this part of the lesson because the teacher should both tell and show students what they are learning. Concrete and pictorial representations of the mathematical concept or procedure give children several opportunities to see what is happening. Showing and telling occur simultaneously. The teacher verbalizes each step or asks the students to verbalize the steps or process.

If the children are learning to measure with the centimeter ruler, a teacher might begin with Cuisenaire rods, which have metric sizes. First the teacher might demonstrate measuring the width of a mathematics book with white Cuisenaire rods. By lining up twenty-six white centimeter rods along the edge of the book and counting them, the teacher models the process of measurement. Then, the teacher may use two decimeter-long orange rods and six white rods, counting the orange rods by tens and the white rods by ones: 10, 20, 21, 22, 23, 24, 25, 26 centimeters. The orange rod takes the place of ten white rods. Finally, the centimeter ruler is used to verify that the measure is the same. The teacher places the end of the ruler at one edge of the book and looks at the mark on the ruler at the other edge of the book. This gives the same number as counting the cubes—26 centimeters.

Guided Practice and Checking for Understanding

While the instructional input is an important step, it often occurs in a cycle with guided instruction. Instead of doing all the instructional input in a lesson before asking children to respond, good teachers will ask for the students to model or repeat each of the steps.

Following the teacher's first demonstration for the measurement lesson, students would be asked to measure the length of the mathematics book or the top of their desk with white centimeter rods so that the teacher could see that they understood that step. After the demonstration with orange and white rods, children would be asked to measure using both orange and white rods. If they have difficulty, the teacher might ask them to measure one or two more objects to make sure that they were lining up the rods and counting accurately. When the teacher is satisfied that students are measuring accurately with the orange rods, students would demonstrate how to measure with the centimeter ruler. The teacher walks around the class, watching the children work, asking questions, giving individual help, and seeing that children are using the correct process for measuring.

The guided instruction helps the teacher decide whether to proceed or stay on that stage of the lesson for a longer time. The best reteaching is done at this stage of the lesson. When children have difficulties, the teacher gives more examples, explains the procedure again, uses different materials, or in some way provides more instructional input.

At the end of instruction, the teacher will close the lesson by emphasizing what has been learned. Many different methods can be used for closure. Some teachers write the main points on the chalkboard or on an overhead transparency. Other teachers ask the students to verbalize the main points or to demonstrate the procedures. Students may be challenged with a problem that is slightly different from any of the examples. Negative examples of the concept may be posed to delimit the concept or idea. The teacher may wish to relate the new learning to some other situation or example or to the beginning of the lesson. A teacher uses many different ways of wrapping up a lesson prior to assigning independent work.

Independent Practice

When students have demonstrated understanding during guided practice, they are ready for independent practice. The most infamous method for independent practice is to have children complete workbook pages or practice problems from a text. Practice pages have a role in independent practice; however, many other ways are available for students to gain speed and accuracy with mathematical ideas and procedures. For practice with measurement, problem cards like the ones in Chapter 14 can direct children's independent practice. Many games offer good practice; teachers adapt traditional games such as bingo, tic-tac-toe, baseball, and dominoes for mathematics concepts. Teachers also find that students are familiar with television quiz shows and family board games and adapt such games as Jeopardy®, Concentration®, and Trivial Pursuit® to mathematics. Computer software provides drill and practice; some software has record-keeping features and can be adjusted for level of difficulty. Teachers may also ask students to continue their lesson at home. Finding solid geometric shapes at home or examples of percentages in the newspaper are ways of tying the instruction to the real world. All of these strategies for independent practice extend students' understanding and encourage practice of the skills and concepts being studied.

Mathematical Investigations

Several teaching strategies are subsumed under the label of *mathematical investigations:* group investigation, induction, inquiry, and concept attainment. Each of these strategies, or models of instruction—described by Bruce Joyce and Marsha Weil[2]—requires careful planning and preparation before a lesson and materials are presented. The role of the teacher is less directive than in the Hunter lesson cycle. The teacher serves as a facilitator rather than as a lesson director. Investigative lessons are less rigid than teacher-directed lessons. Although some of the same elements exist in both types of lessons, they are less obvious in the investigation. Instructional input and modeling are usually less important, unless the teacher needs to give directions for working with materials or a procedure such as data collection.

Setting the Stage

The inquiry lesson often begins with a challenge or puzzling observation. In a lesson on probability for the sixth grade, the teacher may begin with a question about the likelihood that two children in the class have the same birthdate. The children generally say that it is unlikely because there are 30 children and 366 possible birthdates. However, in a survey of the room, they discover that two people do in fact have the same birthdate. Such an observation may begin a unit on complex probability. (See Chapter 15 for a discussion of this activity.)

In another investigation, students have been rolling a die to find out whether the die is fair. If it is fair, each of the numbers one through six has an equal probability of turning up. The teacher asks a leading question about the probability of each number occurring when rolling two dice. The students, based on their prior experience with one die, answer that all the numbers one through twelve have an equal probability of being rolled. This conjecture serves as the basis for further investigation.

Statement of Objective

In an inquiry or induction lesson, the objective is stated differently than for a directed lesson because the teacher wants the students to reason and come to a conclusion. Instead of telling the student what they are going to conclude, the objective is more of a challenge or query. "I wonder if the fact that our class has two birthdays on the same day was just a coincidence or if it would happen again in another group. I have the birthdays for all the students in school on the computer database. How could you find if two or more children in each homeroom have the same birthdate? See if you can figure out a strategy that will work to answer our question."

For rolling two dice, the teacher might draw a record form with spaces for one through twelve on it and ask groups of students to roll the dice 50 times to see if their conjecture is correct. "As you fill in the table, you will find out if the probabilities are equal or unequal. See if there is a pattern in your table. Compare your group's results with another group's results. Some of you might use the computer program for rolling dice." (See Activity 15.10 for more on this investigation.)

Investigating and Checking for Understanding

Instead of direct instructional input, the teacher works as a facilitator during a mathematical investigation. After the task is outlined or the challenge given, the teacher monitors the students' progress, asks questions, and probes for understanding. Either individually or in groups, the children are asked about their work. "Was the conjecture about birthdates true or false?" "How many classes had two people with the same birthdate?" "What would happen if you randomly choose 30 people; how many times would two people have the same birthdate?"

For the lesson on rolling dice, the teacher might ask other questions to help students focus on the results. "Were all the probabilities equal for numbers one through twelve?" "Was there a pattern to the number of times that a certain number came up?" "Was the pattern consistent from group to group?" The teacher asks many questions to draw out students' thinking. At the end of the investigation, children are asked to state their observations and draw conclusions.

Extensions

Closure of an investigation is often the beginning of another investigation to extend or apply the conclusion. For the birthdate investigation, students might write down the names of 30 people in their family or neighborhood and do another investigation. If everyone in the class entered names in a computer database, they could generate random lists of names to see the frequency of same birthdates in groups of 10, 20, 30, or 50 people. The investigation with two dice could be continued with a computer simulation or with probabilities for rolling three dice. Some students might want to investigate the use of probabilities in weather, building design, or genetic combinations. Investigations are especially good for applications of mathematics in the real world and connecting mathematics to other subjects. A source for 20 mathematical investigations is *Teaching with Student Math Notes*.[3] The first level of activities in each is rather simple, but numerous possibilities for deeper investigations develop with each topic.

Cooperative-Learning Groups

Cooperative-learning groups can be used for exploratory, teacher-directed, and investigative lessons. Having children work together toward the common goal of understanding mathematics has both social and academic benefits. Children of all abilities learn to work together and develop skills that make them more independent and confident in their work. The research reviewed in Chapter 2 shows that cooperative learning results in greater achievement, more positive attitudes toward learning, improved social skills, and high self-confidence.[4]

Structuring the cooperative situation is important so that children understand what is expected. When a teacher forms groups, the nature of the task needs to be explained. The expectations will vary with the mode of instruction. Expectations for behavior must also be established. Carol Meyer and Tom Sallee list three "Groups of Four Rules" for students:

1.   You are responsible for your own behavior.
2.   You must be willing to help anyone in your group who asks.
3.   You may not ask the teacher for help unless all four of you have the same question.[5]

The rules are established so that students learn to depend on one another. The teacher monitors the activities and lends assistance only when needed. Teachers also take time to debrief the groups so that they can share their discoveries and conclusions as well as how well they did on social skills such as listening, sharing, and helping. Teachers who use cooperative-learning groups are good resources for teachers who are just beginning. They are usually willing to explain their rules and routines.

EXERCISE   Name the three modes of instruction discussed in the preceding section. Identify a characteristic of each that distinguishes it from the other two.

Variety and Flexibility in Instruction

No single type of lesson or instruction provides the variety and flexibility needed for a comprehensive mathematics program. Using each of the three modes of instruction reduces the pressure and anxiety many students associate with mathematics and the monotony many children find in mathematics instruction. Charles Wolfgang and Carl Glickman have suggested the

Figure 3-4
Teacher Behavior
Continuum (adapted
from Wolfgang and
Glickman)

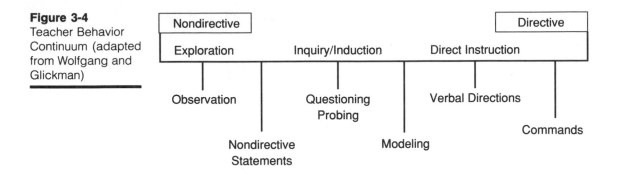

"Teacher Behavior Continuum" in Figure 3.4 as a way of looking at differing instructional approaches.[6] Informal introduction, teacher-directed lessons, and mathematics investigations represent the range of instructional practices on the "Teacher Behavior Continuum." Informal introduction is the most child-centered approach. The lesson cycle is the most teacher-directed. Mathematical investigation is in the center where authority and control are shared between teacher and students.

When only one instructional mode is used in a classroom, students miss important mathematical experiences. The informal approach may not focus students on needed skills and concepts. It leaves much learning to chance. The teacher-directed lesson is very strong at developing mathematical skills and processes; however, alone it may be too confining and limit independent thinking. Mathematical investigations are excellent for developing understandings and extending mathematics with applications. But investigations depend on some prior knowledge and skill. Only when all three modes of instruction are used do students get a well-rounded instructional program.

Some teachers use the textbook as their instructional guide. Certainly if the content matches the goals and objectives of the school, the textbook can be used. However, a textbook alone is not sufficient for a well-rounded program. Teaching that is too dependent on a textbook does not provide sufficient time or opportunity for students to build understandings. When a textbook is used, teachers must be careful to avoid the routine of opening the book, working an example, and giving the assignment. Many textbooks now have lesson plans designed around the lesson cycle with activities that incorporate manipulatives. Teachers should use these suggestions for a lesson or supplement them with ideas and materials of their own.

A variety of resources and ideas are available to help teachers keep mathematics exciting. The *Arithmetic Teacher* is one important source of teaching ideas. Many of the activities from the *Arithmetic Teacher* are collected in other publications from National Council of Teachers of Mathematics. *Student Math Notes*[7] is a collection of activities that are especially good for mathematical investigations. "SSMILES"[8] is a monthly feature in *School Science and Mathematics* that shows connections between mathematics and science. AIMS is another source of integrated science and mathematics activities.[9]

■ ORGANIZING THE CLASSROOM

Classroom Arrangement

The arrangement of a classroom is one way teachers can adapt different teaching styles. While the traditional classroom with five rows of six desks may work well for a teacher who works with the whole class, many teachers find that other arrangements are more flexible and encourage exploration and group work. One way to organize the room is with clusters of four to six desks. Students can work together to explore materials and make investigations. Other teachers find that a U-shaped arrangement of desks or slanted rows is best for them. Figure 3.5 shows several different classroom arrange-

Figure 3-5
Classroom arrangements: (a) traditional classroom; (b) classroom with table and rug for group work, games, or manipulatives; (c) classroom with tables for projects and learning centers; (d) mathematics laboratory

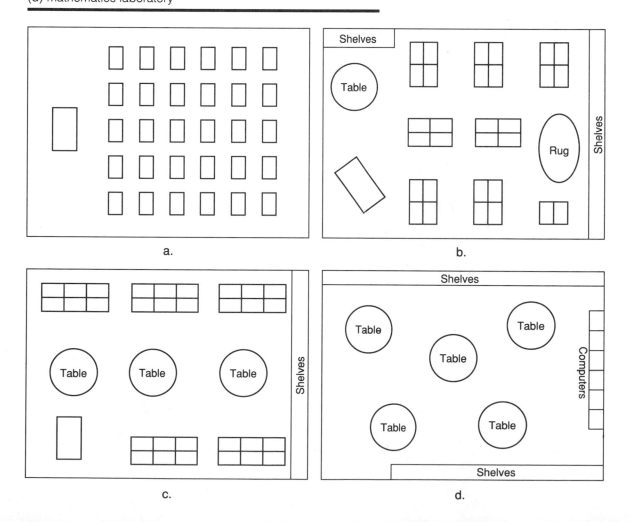

ments. Since classroom arrangement can help or hinder instruction, teachers should take time to organize the class to suit them and their students. Many teachers like to have a teaching area where they keep instructional materials: textbooks, manipulatives, overhead projector, squared paper, and pencils. Whether this is at a desk, at a table arranged for small-group work, or on a rolling cart with the overhead projector, it can save many steps as a teacher organizes for instruction.

Learning Centers

Teachers may arrange a learning center with mathematics materials on shelves or cabinets for easy access by students. In a mathematics center, students find measuring instruments, geoboards, commercial games, cards, dice, base-ten materials, Cuisenaire rods, Unifix cubes, or dozens of other commercial or teacher-made materials. Students can go to the shelf, get the materials they need, and work at their desk, at a table, or on the floor. If the classroom has a computer or computers, a computer learning center may be set up with activities and software. Some teachers establish several centers in their rooms: writing center, science center, library corner, and art area.

Learning centers are especially good for the informal introduction and investigation modes of instruction. Materials that apply to the topics to be studied or that are being studied are placed in the center. For instance, for several weeks before beginning a geometry unit, geoboards, tangrams, pentominoes, squared paper, and dot paper are in a learning center. Task cards (see Figure 3.6) or directions on paper may be available to direct students' work with challenging activities.

Figure 3-6
Task card for geoboard (courtesy of Gary Goldberg)

Students who are not used to working independently may not understand that the learning center activities are as important as those with their workbook and text. When learning centers are first introduced, students need help to establish purposes and ground rules. Procedures for recording learning center work are also needed. Some teachers ask students to record their work in a mathematics journal or to keep it in a folder. Sometimes special response sheets are provided. Either method gives a teacher some way to monitor the students' progress in a learning center.

Rotation of materials in a learning center is important. If a center always contains the same things, students can become bored. Interest can be maintained by replacing one or two old items with new things each week. When materials are brought out a second time, students find new interest with them. At times, a teacher may organize a learning center around a particular topic or skill. When the topic is subtraction, students practice, extend, and apply their knowledge of subtraction by completing eight to ten subtraction activities. A learning center of this kind may last two or three weeks. A theme—such as the circus or treasure hunt—adds interest to any center.

Teachers who have not worked with a learning center are sometimes concerned that their classroom will get out of hand. In a well-organized learning center students are too busy to be unruly. A good way to learn about learning centers is to visit a teacher who uses them. Teachers who have success with learning centers are usually eager to help others. They will share their guidelines and rules to get others started. Once a teacher has worked with learning centers, the rules can be adapted to suit his or her situation.

Mathematics Laboratory

In some schools, one teacher teaches all the mathematics for one or more grades. A mathematics specialist can turn an entire room into a mathematics center, or a mathematics laboratory. Instead of learning centers for all the subject areas, the mathematics laboratory may have centers for several different mathematics topics. In one area of the room, measuring materials are displayed; in another, the numeration materials and counters are available. A computer corner may include four or five microcomputers. Even in the mathematics laboratory, teachers employ informal activities, directed lessons, and investigations.

WORKING WITH EXCEPTIONAL CHILDREN

Individuals learn in unique ways based on their prior experiences, interests, and abilities. When teachers use different ways of teaching and organizing classrooms to encourage a variety of mathematical behaviors, most students make progress in mathematics. Even so, some students may have needs that require special attention. Gifted-talented students and children with learning handicaps are two groups who require special consideration.

Gifted-Talented Students

No single criterion identifies gifted students. At one time, scores on intelligence tests were used. However, H. Laurence Ridge and Joseph Renzulli believe that three clusters of traits should be used in identification of students at the upper end of the creativity-productivity scale:

- Above-average general ability
- Task commitment
- Creativity [10]

Scores on general intelligence tests are only one source of information. If they are used alone, students who immerse themselves in a particular area of interest (task commitment) and who show originality of thinking and diversity in approaches and inventive solutions to problems (creativity) may not be identified. Your awareness of each cluster of characteristics will help you identify gifted and talented students.

- Above-average general ability
  —Accelerated pace of learning; learning earlier and faster
  —Sees relationship, readily grasps big ideas
  —Higher levels of thinking; applications and analysis easily accomplished
  —Verbal fluency; large vocabulary, expresses self well orally and in writing
  —Extraordinary amount of information
  —Intuition; easily leaps from problem to solution
  —Tolerates ambiguity
  —Achievement and potential have close fit
  —Masters advanced concepts in field of interest
- Task commitment
  —Highly motivated
  —Self-directed
  —Accepts challenges, may be highly competitive
  —Extended attention to one area of interest
  —Reads avidly in area of interest

—Relates every topic to own area of interest

—Industrious and persevering

—High energy and enthusiasm

■ Creativity

—Curious

—Imaginative and perceptive

—Questions standard procedures

—Original approaches and solutions

—Flexible

—Risk taker and independent

Gifted students do not learn concepts and skills automatically; they should participate in a planned, systematic mathematics program. Work with concrete materials, pictorial representations, and symbols is as important for gifted as for other students. Not all gifted and talented students are equally interested in mathematics, so a teacher cannot expect the same level of accomplishment from each of them. However, all children are expected to learn basic concepts, skillfully compute with whole numbers and fractions, use common instruments of measure, and apply mathematics in both in-school and out-of-school situations.

At the same time, teachers should find ways for gifted students to be challenged mathematically. If confined to a one-dimensional curriculum, gifted children become bored and some even develop behavior problems. The stereotype of gifted children is that they are ideal students in every way. Gifted students are individuals with the full range of behaviors, including being messy, forgetful, or rebellious. Traits of gifted students such as questioning authority, extreme imagination, and absolute concentration on one topic dismay teachers. Some schools meet the needs of gifted students through special programs. The program may be conducted in regular classrooms by the regular teacher or in a separate room or location by special teachers.

Some programs for the gifted concentrate on vertical enrichment or acceleration, while others provide horizontal enrichment or elaboration of ideas. **Vertical enrichment** allows students to move to a more advanced topic or one that would usually appear at a higher grade level. Students in first grade might work with division, which is not usually introduced until third or fourth grade. Some programs attempt to provide acceleration by allowing students to work through textbooks at their own pace. This questionable practice deprives students of direct instruction, interaction with others, and adequate developmental work with concrete materials. When a program concentrates on symbolic manipulation, gifted students may be able to perform operations without grasping the meaning of a process. Their verbal fluency allows them to parrot answers without understanding. **Horizontal enrichment** encourages students to explore a topic by making connections to other fields and ideas. This practice encourages students to delve more deeply into topics they study. Third graders might compare the Hindu-Arabic numeration system with the binary, Mayan, or Egyptian system to broaden their understanding of how numeration systems work. Older students might extend investigations to include activities beyond those done by most students. The birth date problem mentioned earlier and elaborated on in Chapter 15 would intrigue some gifted students.

Ridge and Renzulli recommend a three-level program for gifted students.[11] Exploratory experiences introduce ideas and stimulate interests. Students then receive direct instruction on their topic to develop skills and concepts needed before moving on. Finally, students are engaged in individual or small-group study of a topic. These three levels parallel the three modes of instruction recommended earlier in the chapter.

Mathematical investigations are an excellent way to accommodate gifted students. After demonstrating understanding of a concept or skill, students work on other projects. They often devise their own games and activities when given the opportunity. Many teacher resource books discuss projects. The role of gifted students in cooperative groups is important because children learn much from each other. A cooperative group has students with high, middle, and low ability. One of the benefits of cooperative learning is the social skill that children learn from the different roles. The gifted student may be a leader in one group and a materials monitor or recorder in another; he or she should not dominate leadership positions.

The concentration of a gifted child on a single topic is often unsettling to the teacher charged with providing a balanced curriculum. One elementary student became fascinated by trains and wanted to work on nothing else for several weeks. The student's independent investigation of trains included the history of the railroad and its impact on American history, types of fuel used for locomotion and the advantages or disadvantages of each, a map of the United States and Canada showing mileage on major routes, speed of trains including the Japanese bullet train, and the setting up of a model train track. The student learned mathematics in many practical ways integrated with science, social studies, language arts, and art. The teacher who is concerned about the student's knowledge of topics covered can interview or test the student to make sure that skills and concepts are developed.

EXERCISE   Distinguish between vertical and horizontal enrichment. What are some advantages and disadvantages of each approach? Do you believe it is a question of selecting one mode over the other when a program for gifted children is planned? Explain.

Learning-Handicapped Children

Legislation enacted more than 30 years ago requires that all handicapped children have the opportunity for free public education in the "least restrictive environment." Children who in earlier days might have stayed at home or gone to special schools or institutions are now in local schools. These students may have diagnosed physical impairments or have learning or emotional disabilities. Teachers adapt teaching strategies, materials, and expectations to match the needs of the students.

Students who have been identified as having learning problems may also be inattentive or disruptive. Instead of recognizing these as symptoms of learning problems, teachers may reprimand children. Teachers should be alert to students who do not understand their work and use distracting behavior as a cover. Ways to diagnose student understandings and skills are discussed in Chapter 4. With information gained through assessment, a teacher can provide activities that meet the needs of these special students.

Teachers must also be aware of students who have auditory or visual problems. Prescription eyeglasses may help students with visual deficiencies. The teacher needs to notice if students are straining to see or hear during class and refer them to the school nurse or bring problems to the attention of parents or guardians. Concrete materials and large-print books are important for severely visually impaired learners. Functionally blind children may use braille, have their lessons recorded, or use the computer as a learning aid. A computer can be adapted so that students can overcome many sensory impairments.

Physical impairments may also affect children's ability to function in the classroom. Health problems such as asthma, diabetes, and nervous system disorders like cerebral palsy or muscular dystrophy may interfere with a student's ability to take part in class. The severity varies with each student, and modifications in the mathematics program will vary for individuals.

Some children in the classroom also may have emotional handicaps. These students may have a history of unsatisfactory interpersonal relations with teachers and students, inappropriate behavior or feelings in the classroom, changes in emotions including extreme depression or unhappiness, or a tendency to develop physical symptoms as a response to fears. J. F. Weaver and William C. Morse broaden the definition of emotional handicaps to include socially maladjusted children, or "socially-emotionally impaired" children, who make up a large part of the segment of children who have problems in schools.[12]

A teacher does not work alone when special plans for handicapped students are developed. PL 94-142 requires that an individualized educational plan (IEP) be developed for each child. The plan is prepared by a team composed of the child's parent(s), teacher, a person other than the teacher who is qualified to provide or supervise the program, and the child when appropriate. Other persons such as the school psychologist, educational diagnostician, special education teachers, or mathematics specialist may also provide input for the plan. The following generalizations should be considered when a plan for what is best for the student is developed.

- All handicapped children progress through Piaget's stages of mental development. The rate at which they progress and level of attainment vary according to the type and degree of handicap. Piagetian-type interviews and diagnostic tests (discussed in Chapter 4) are useful for determining the level of mental development and the mathematical skills and understandings of handicapped children.

- The sequence of subtasks for a topic must be considered when selecting content. Gaps in a child's knowledge and understanding are often more critical when handicaps are present because the handicaps make catching up and bridging gaps more difficult and time consuming.

- Appropriate learning objectives based on criterion-referenced diagnostic tests should be established for each child.

- The teaching-learning sequence—concrete manipulative, pictorial representation, and abstract-symbolic—should be followed with most handicapped students. These children are capable of learning concepts and solving problems, so rote learning and memorization are no more appropriate for them than for other children.

- Instructional modes for handicapped students may need to be adapted for them, but they still need informal, directed, and investigative experiences in mathematics.

- Conditions that prevent students from writing or manipulating learning materials require special learning aids and ways of responding to assignments. Specially adapted computer arrangements have touch or electronic panels that allow students to respond with a probe or muscle-activated light sensor. Physically impaired students may need to work with a fellow student or a teacher's aide.

- The teacher should call on specialists to assist in modification of instruction.

EXERCISE   In your judgment, should there be any limitations on the placement of handicapped children in regular classrooms for mathematics instruction? Explain.

■ WORKING WITH THE HOME

Teachers have another resource for helping children. Teachers can involve parents to help children learn mathematics. Teachers have a variety of ways in which to include parents or guardians in the program. Some write weekly or monthly newsletters that communicate the topics being studied and make suggestions for home activities. Some textbooks now include model newsletters in their teacher's manuals. Other teachers ask parents to volunteer in the classroom. Parent volunteers need tasks organized for them such as reading books or working with a mathematics game. Some teachers have created take-home versions of mathematics materials. Students check out the games, manipulatives, or investigations to use with parents at home. Homework can also be designed to include home projects. A geometry scavenger hunt and a survey of food favorites are good ways to involve parents and siblings. The involvement of parents or guardians may not be easy to achieve, but the extra effort teachers take to work with parents has many positive benefits for student learning.

TOOLS FOR LEARNING AND TEACHING

When the mathematics curriculum consisted entirely of number operations and mental calculations, no one required materials more elaborate than a chalkboard and a piece of chalk. Today's curriculum is much more complex and what we know about teaching and learning is more complete. The mathematics program advocated by National Council of Teachers of Mathematics, mathematics educators, and many individual teachers is founded on the knowledge that students learn better when many tools for learning mathematics are available.

The teaching-learning materials in this chapter are basic to the teaching and learning of mathematics in elementary school. The materials range from counting and place-value manipulatives to electronic calculators and computers. Materials for teaching mathematics should be included in a school's budget, just as paper and paste, reading supplies, and physical education equipment are. When money is a problem, as it often is in schools, teacher-made materials can substitute for many commercial items. There should be a sufficient quantity of both commercial and teacher-made materials for an entire class or for small-group work. Not every teacher in the school needs a classroom set of each of the materials. A mathematics closet in the school can be used to store materials until needed by teachers. Materials that are in constant demand may require multiple sets.

This book is based on the assumption that you have these materials to work with as you read about activities. Working with a geoboard is very different from seeing a picture and reading about it. Playing the "Banker's Game" with Chip Trading materials is not the same as seeing a picture of it. You should take time to work with these materials while you are learning about teaching mathematics.

Mathematics Manipulatives

Well-chosen, properly used manipulatives enhance understanding, generate interest, and promote problem solving and understanding of concepts. They may be used for introducing, reinforcing, reteaching, and extending concepts for small groups, entire classes, or individual students. Materials make even the most difficult mathematical concepts easier to understand. Manipulatives enable students to connect real objects and abstract mathematical concepts. Throughout the remainder of the book, references will be made to a variety of mathematic manipulatives. Many of the materials can be used with more than one mathematics topic.

Interlocking Counting Cubes

Plastic cubes that snap together are used to demonstrate numeration concepts and basic computation concepts. Unifix cubes may be purchased with a variety of supporting materials for counting and learning numbers (see photo 1).

Linking Materials

Linking materials come in a variety of colors and shapes (see photo 2). They are used for counting, pattern, and classification activities.

Photo 1
Unifix materials (courtesy of Didax Educational Resources, Peabody, MA)

Photo 2
Linking materials
(courtesy of
Cuisenaire
Company of
America, Inc.,
New Rochelle, NY)

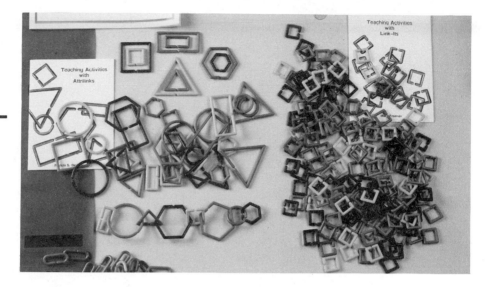

Attribute Blocks

Wooden or plastic attribute blocks, which are geometric shapes in various colors and sizes, are used for sorting, classifying, and problem solving (see photo 3). Some have different textures and thickness. Exploration of geometric concepts such as similarity and congruence is also possible with the shapes. Other attribute sets contain shapes that permit a variety of investi-

Photo 3
Attribute blocks
(courtesy of
Cuisenaire
Company of
America, Inc.,
New Rochelle, NY)

gations. These materials help children investigate patterns and relationships, fraction concepts, and similarity, congruence, and symmetry in geometry. (see photo 4).

Photo 4
Geometric attribute shapes (courtesy of Cuisenaire Company of America, Inc., New Rochelle, NY)

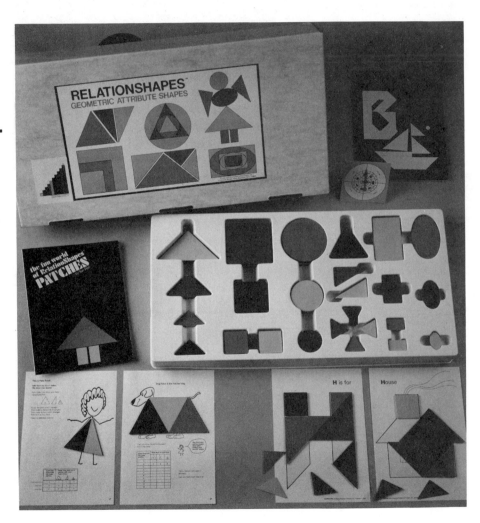

Math Box or Junk Box

Teacher-assembled collections of buttons, shells, plastic toys and animals, keys, and other safe objects provide many opportunities in mathematics (see photo 5). They can be used for sorting and classifying, patterning, seriation, counting, and for modeling situations in problem solving and number operations. Objects in a math box should contain both likenesses and differences.

Photo 5
Math boxes
(courtesy of Gary
Goldberg)

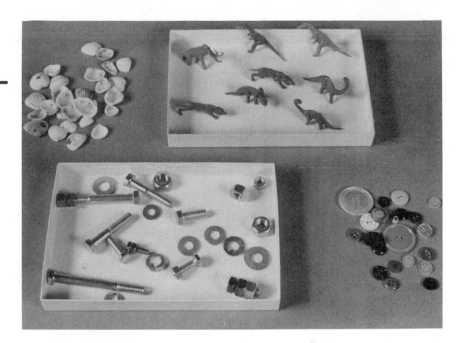

Measuring Instruments

Materials for measuring include devices for determining length, area, volume, weight or mass, and temperature (see photo 6). Foot rulers

Photo 6
Measuring devices
(courtesy of
Cuisenaire Com-
pany of America,
Inc., New Rochelle,
NY)

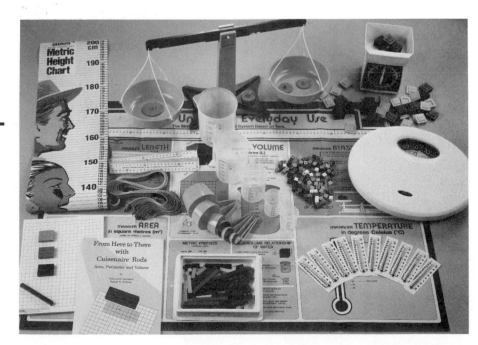

marked in inches and fractions, yardsticks, trundle wheels, tape measures in metric and customary units, and metric centimeter and meter rulers are essential for linear measurement. Jars and bottles can be combined with measuring spoons and standard-capacity measures in both the customary and metric systems. Volume is explored with centimeter cubes and inch cubes. Balances, spring scales, and household scales provide experiences with weight and mass. A large classroom thermometer or an indoor-outdoor thermometer is good for science and mathematics. Time is learned on both digital and analog time pieces in the classroom (see photo 7). Special devices are used for teaching children how to measure angles, as photo 8 shows.

Photo 7
Clocks (courtesy of Cuisenaire Company of America, Inc., New Rochelle, NY)

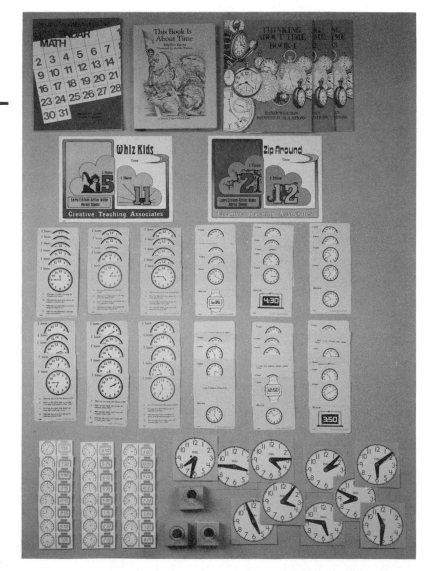

Photo 8
Measuring angles (courtesy of Creative Publications, Sunnyvale, CA)

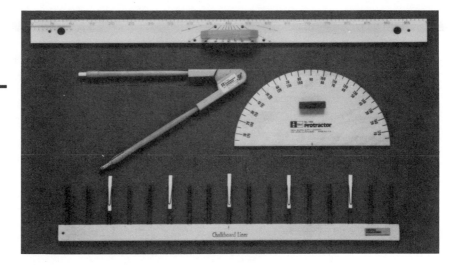

Play Money

Play coins of plastic or paper are available in classroom sets (see photo 9). Coin stamps and printed paper bills are available.

Photo 9
Play money (courtesy of Cuisenaire Company of America, Inc., New Rochelle, NY)

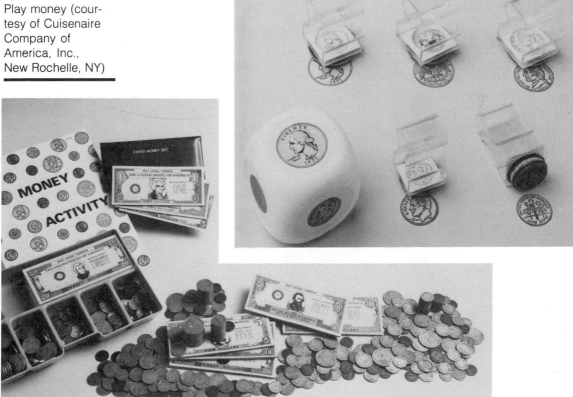

Base-Ten Materials

Several types of base-ten materials can be purchased commercially. Wooden or plastic models of units, tens, hundreds, and thousands are used to model place value and four basic operations. They are sometimes called *flu* materials (*f* for flat, *l* for long, and *u* for unit) (see photo 10). Other place-value models are: beansticks (see photo 11), bundled tongue depressors, and chips for trading. Cuisenaire rods can be used as decimal models when a rod is designated as the unit (see photo 12).

Chip Trading Materials

A kit contains four colors of chips, chipboards, chip tills, abacus board, dice, and numeral and operations cards (see photo 13). Manuals describe a variety of activities that develop students' understanding of place value, grouping and regrouping concepts, and problem-solving skills.

Photo 10
"Flu" materials
(courtesy of
Didax Educational
Resources,
Peabody, MA)

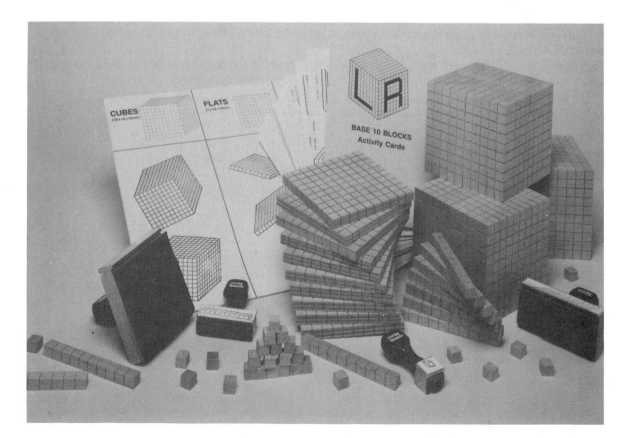

Photo 11
Beansticks
(courtesy of
Gary Goldberg)

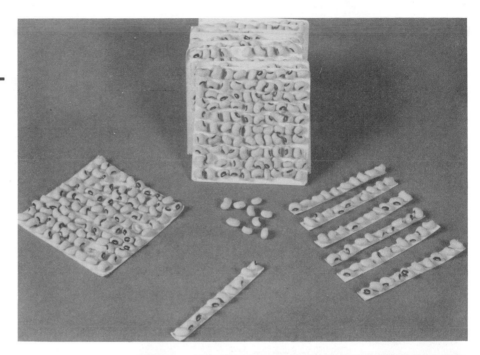

Photo 13   Chip trading materials
(right) (courtesy of Scott Resources,
Fort Collins, CO)

Photo 12   Cuisenaire rods (courtesy of
Cuisenaire Company of America, Inc.,
New Rochelle, NY)

Fraction Models

There are a variety of plastic, wooden, or rubber models of fractional pieces available (see photo 14). They come in many sizes and shapes. Cuisenaire rods may also be used as fraction models.

Tangrams

Tangrams are a set of seven plastic, wooden, or pasteboard pieces constructed from a square according to a specific pattern (see photo 15). These are used to develop concepts in geometry, measurement, and problem solving. They can be used to develop certain fraction concepts. Supertangrams are a more complex set of shapes.

Photo 14

Fraction materials (courtesy of Cuisenaire Company of America, Inc., New Rochelle, NY)

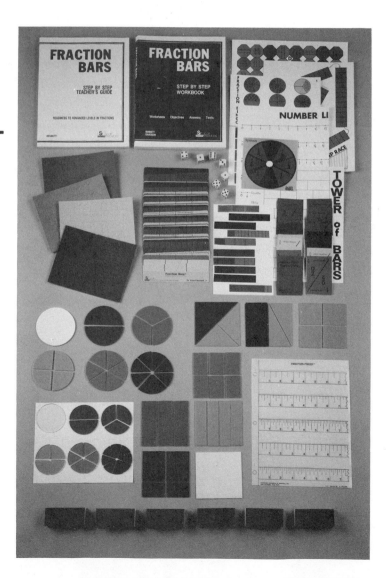

Photo 15
Tangrams (courtesy of Didax Educational Resources, Peabody, MA)

Photo 16
Geometric models (courtesy of Cuisenaire Company of America, Inc., New Rochelle, NY)

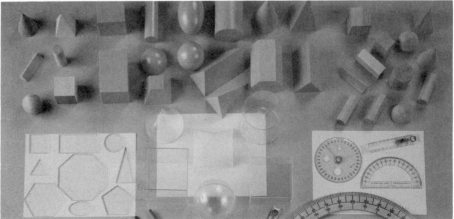

Geometric Models

Wooden or plastic models of basic plane and solid shapes can be purchased. Two-dimensional shapes include squares, circles, triangles, rectangles, parallelograms, and regular 5-, 6-, 8-, 10-, and 12-sided polygons. Three-dimensional models include spheres, cubes, cones, rectangular solids, pyramids, various prisms, and regular solids (see photo 16).

Geoboards

Geoboards are square boards made of plastic or wooden boards with pegs or nails in 5 × 5 to 11 × 11 arrays or circular arrangements (see photo 17). Geometric and measurement concepts are explored. Children use dot paper to record geoboard designs.

Probability Devices

Many simple probability devices are available (see photo 18). Spinners with different configurations, regular dice, or polyhedrons with colors, numbers, and letters on the faces are used to develop concepts of chance and probability.

Photo 17
Geoboard and dot paper (courtesy of Gary Goldberg)

Photo 18
Probability devices (courtesy of Creative Publications, Sunnyvale, CA)

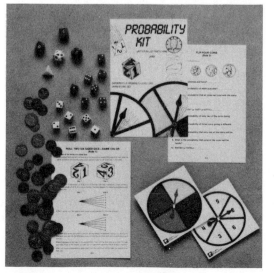

Overhead Projector Materials

Base-ten, common and decimal fraction, counting, money, and probability materials are available to use with an overhead projector (see photo 19).

Photo 19
Overhead projector materials (courtesy of Cuisenaire Company of America, Inc., New Rochelle, NY)

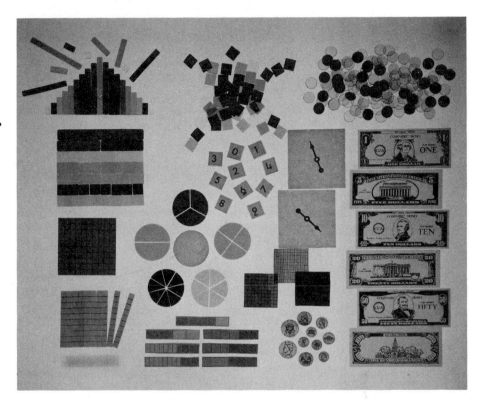

EXERCISE   Briefly describe the role of manipulative materials in mathematics.

Calculators

Since 1980, the National Council of Teachers of Mathematics has recommended that teachers at all levels take full advantage of the power of computers and calculators.[13] Full power means that students learn to use it as a learning and computing tool in the same way that they learn paper-and-pencil algorithms and mental computation processes. Once the meaning of an operation is understood and one or more algorithms for computing have been learned, children should also learn to use a calculator for computing the operation. The calculator frees children from routine, often tedious and time-consuming computation and gives them more time to consider problems and how to solve them. In addition to being a problem-solving tool, calculators have other uses in the classroom:

■ Developing understanding of numbers. With a calculator, children can count by ones, two, sixes, eights, or any other number. Most calculators have a simple way to repeatedly add or subtract. Pressing ①, then ⊕, ①, and ⊜ gives the answer 2. Repeatedly pressing ⊜ causes the calculator to add 1 each time. A child who counts up to 1,000 by ones or fives or tens has an experience with large and small numbers.

■ Gain insight into operations. While counting up, students also learn about addition and multiplication. If students repeatedly subtract a number, they learn about subtraction and division.

By subtracting 64 from 237, students find out the number of times 64 can be subtracted and whether there is a remainder. The problem 237 ÷ 64 on the calculator can be compared to the repeated subtraction. Sometimes solving a problem with a calculator helps students focus on how the algorithm works by reducing the emphasis on the computation per se. A multiple-digit multiplication problem can be worked with partial products.

362	CALCULATOR WORK
× 489	
18	9×2
540	9×60
2700	9×300
160	80×2
4800	80×60
24000	80×300
800	400×2
24000	400×60
120000	400×300
177018	Add all the products

■ Extend children's mathematical experiences. The calculator opens the door to many activities that would be very difficult and time consuming otherwise. For instance, children can study the pattern that develops as the following multiplications are completed.

$$
\begin{aligned}
1 \times 1 &= 1 \\
11 \times 11 &= 121 \\
111 \times 111 &= 12321 \\
1111 \times 1111 &= ?
\end{aligned}
$$

Once these are completed, the students should be able to predict the product of 11,111 multiplied by 11,111. Some calculators do not have enough places to show the answer and will show an overflow error. Others will convert the large number to scientific notation. Either of these events might begin another investigation into the largest number that can be displayed.

■ Rounding off and estimating. A person using a calculator should learn to estimate answers before calculating. If an answer does not reasonably fit the estimate, the problem should be recalculated. Estimated answers are frequently used in problem-solving situations, and rounding is often used in real life. The following example shows how these skills apply to a real problem.

SITUATION

The sales tax is 6.75 percent on a set of tires costing $163.25 on sale.

■ What was the total cost?

ESTIMATION OF ANSWER

■ First a student might want to estimate the tax of about 7 percent on $160: $.07 \times \$160$ is about $10, which means that the total bill will be about $163 + $10 or $173.

CALCULATOR SOLUTION

■ Now the calculator is used: $.0675 \times \$163.25 = \$11.019375$, which is rounded to the nearest penny or $11.02. This is added to the cost of the tires: $163.25 + $11.02 = $174.27.

Work with calculators does not replace the need for knowledge of basic facts and paper-and-pencil computation skills. Even though calculators will get correct answers, a child must understand the operation well enough to know which keys to press and why. A student should also develop a sense of when an estimation serves as well as an exact answer. Many simple mental computations are easier than keying a problem on a calculator. The few students who have problems with memorizing basic facts can use a calculator to help them learn the facts.

Studies of calculator use in elementary school indicate that they enhance learning of computational skills and problem-solving processes, or at least are not detrimental. Robert Reys and his associates report that many teachers who have used calculators say that the children can work more problems and cover more topics.[14] More than 80 percent of the teachers in Reys' study reported that students were more eager to work and had an enhanced confidence in their ability to solve problems. This finding suggests that calculators may be helpful in lessening mathematics anxiety, which is another justification for their use.

Calculators come in all sizes and shapes. For the classroom, however, certain features are important. The calculator should have at least an eight-digit display and a floating decimal. A memory function is useful for upper elementary grades because it permits an operation or number to be entered once and then used many times. Percent and square root calculations are also helpful for older children. The size and placement of the keys are other considerations. If the keys are too small or crowded, students can be frustrated because they touch the wrong numbers. Solar-powered calculators are inexpensive and have long lives.

A number of calculators are marketed for schools. One designed specifically for elementary schools is the Texas Instruments Math Explorer™ (see photo 20). In addition to having all the regular functions, this calculator has a unique feature: the ability to compute and give answers with common fractions. It also automatically converts common fractions to decimal fractions and vice versa and simplifies (reduces) common fractions. Calculators are now relatively inexpensive. A set of ten almost indestructible devices may cost less than $100. Ten Math Explorers™ cost around $250. When calculators are used for exploratory activities and investigations, not every child will need one. More will be needed when students use them as computational and problem-solving tools.

Photo 20
Math Explorer™
(courtesy of
Texas Instruments,
Dallas, TX)

Despite the availability of calculators and their widespread use among adults and evidence of their benefits to children, some educators and parents object to their use in elementary school. Teachers who choose to have calculators in their classrooms may need to persuade administrators and parents that the calculators will not replace development of mathematics skills. Regular use in a comprehensive program enhances mathematical skills and broadens mathematics concepts and problem-solving activities.

If there is no official policy about using calculators, a teacher should work with other teachers to establish one. The authors of this book recommend that once children learn to use a calculator, they should use it extensively in both routine and nonroutine problem-solving situations, including tests and homework. Some recently published standardized tests include calculator problems.

EXERCISE   Why do you believe the use of calculators in elementary school mathematics is not a universally accepted practice? What are your views on their use?

Photo 21
Computer system
(courtesy of Apple
Computer, Inc.,
Cupertino, CA)

Computers in Elementary School

Students should have access to computers and software that offer a full range of mathematics topics and styles of interactions (see photo 21). Com-

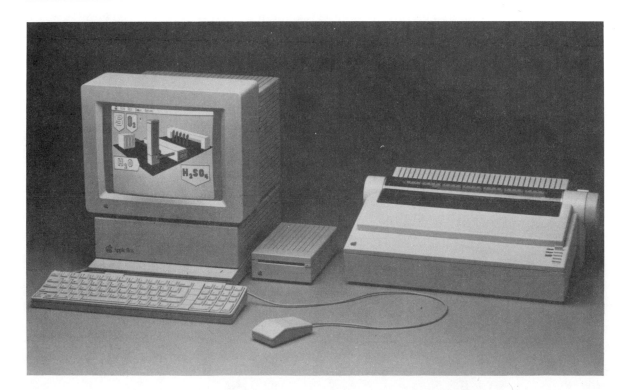

puters for schools can now be purchased for less than $1,000, and a full computer system with color monitor and printer is less than $2,000. These inexpensive computers are more powerful, faster, and have more memory than computers that controlled the entire space program 20 years ago. A wide selection of software allows children to use the computer in many ways: word processing, data management, writing and playing music, making posters and puzzles, and creating graphics and animation. The information age is *now* and students need many experiences with computers and their varied uses.

Learning with Computers

Learning with computers depends on the type of software being used. The generic name for educational software is *computer-assisted instruction,* or *CAI.* CAI comes in many forms. Some software provides drill and practice on content that has been learned previously. Teachers have to be careful that the prerequisite knowledge and skills have been learned before children use these programs. Tutorial software provides a complete lesson. A good tutorial follows Gagne's steps of effective teaching, including motivation, objectives, instructional input, guided practice, independent practice, and application. Some complete packages of lessons and sequenced tests also keep records and allow the teacher to monitor student progress. These comprehensive programs are called *computer-managed instruction* or *CMI.*

Other programs offer exploratory or investigative activities such as games and simulations. Some games are really drill-and-practice programs, while others have content or skill being learned while the student plays the game. In simulations, a situation is established in which learners must participate until they learn the rules or procedures to accomplish a task. In *Donald Duck's Playground,*[15] students help Donald work in a variety of stores to earn money. When enough money is earned, the playground is completed. Games and simulations require problem-solving skills because answers are not immediately apparent. Students work through a simulation several times before they become skilled with it.

Evaluating Software

Before any program is purchased, it should be evaluated thoroughly. Instructional objectives, technical aspects, and practical considerations should be taken into account. Instructional objectives refer to the learning that takes place in the program. The content and presentation must be accurate. A good drill-and-practice program can provide independent practice after a skill has been taught and the children have been checked for understanding. Simulations may provide motivation and extend ideas and problem-solving skills. By knowing what a program does, the teacher determines how to prepare students for using it and what follow-up activities to plan.

The technical aspects of software refer to how well the program makes use of a computer's capabilities. The most important media characteristic is the interactive quality. Is the learner meaningfully engaged in the learning process and does the computer react to the student in meaningful ways? If the student is only a button pusher and the software only responds "Good job," the interaction between the learner and computer is very stilted. The more natural and engaging the interaction between the learner and the computer, the better the program is. Other technical aspects are the use of color, music and speech, graphics, and animation. Color and sound should focus the learner on the content. If they are only there to impress, they may get in the way of the learning. Pictures and other graphics should be meaningful to children. Speed is also important; presentation of materials or responses should not be so fast that a child cannot keep up, yet the program should not be so slow that a child becomes restless. One or two seconds becomes a long time to wait.

Finally, consideration should be given to how the program can be used. Does the software add something unique to the instructional program not supplied by other classroom materials? Can the program be used for small-group and whole-group instruction, or is it limited to one child? Does the program come with good documentation that suggests preparation and follow-up activities? Is the cost reasonable for its utility?

All of these questions can only be answered by a thorough hands-on preview of software. Software reviews can help a teacher decide which software is worth reviewing. Every issue of the *Arithmetic Teacher* and *School Science and Mathematics* reviews software. *Teaching and Computers*[16] and *Classroom Computer Learning*[17] magazines review software in all curricular areas. Both computer magazines list recent teacher favorites and award-winning educational software dealing with mathematics. Software companies and suppliers are listed in Appendix B.

TEACHERS' FAVORITE SOFTWARE[18]

All-Time Favorite: Logo

K–2 Mathematics

Counting Critters (MECC)	Stickybear Numbers (Optimum Resources)
Math Rabbit (Learning Co.)	
Clock Works (MECC)	Measure Works (MECC)
Fish Scales (MECC)	Logo and LogoWriter (LCSI or Terrapin)
Patterns (MECC)	
The Pond (MECC)	Gertrude's Secrets/Puzzles (Learning Co.)
Math Blaster/Math Blaster Plus (Davidson)	Moptown Parade (Learning Co.)

2–4 Mathematics

Number Munchers (MECC)
Math Man (Scholastic)
Money Works (MECC)
Money (Gamco)
Logo (LCSI and Terrapin)
LogoWriter (LCSI)
Mastering Math Series (MECC)

Math Blaster/Math Blaster Plus
  (Davidson)
Fraction Munchers (MECC)
Money! Money! (Hartley)
Measure Works (MECC)
Bumble Games (Learning Co.)

4–6 Mathematics

Conquering Math Series (MECC)
Fraction Munchers (MECC)
Logo (LCSI and Terrapin)
Bake and Taste (MindPlay)
The Factory (Sunburst)
Teasers by Tobbs (Sunburst)
Math Blaster/Math Blaster Plus
  (Davidson)

Math Shop (Scholastic)
LogoWriter (LCSI)
Puzzle Tanks (Sunburst)
Math Blaster Mystery (Davidson)
How the West Was One (Sunburst)

AWARD-WINNING SOFTWARE[19]

Talking Math and Me

Grades K–2. This entertaining speech-based program introduces young children to shapes, numbers, patterns, and addition. For each concept, there are three sequential games involving such skills as identification, matching, comparing, and counting. (Davidson.)

Exploring Measurement, Time, and Money

Grades K–2. In this program, young children learn concepts of measurement, time, and money by manipulating colorful graphic figures on the screen. The four parts present activities to explore in unstructured and structured situations. (IBM.)

Elastic Lines: The Electronic Geoboard

Grades 2–8. *Elastic Lines* is a fun and challenging program that functions as a geoboard on which students construct and manipulate two-dimensional figures. It is a powerful tool that provides a flexible environment for illustrating and exploring geometric concepts such as area, perimeter, similarity, congruence, and symmetry. (Sunburst.)

Logo Plus

Grades K and up. *Logo Plus* does it all—graphics, simple word processing, animation, and music—including the ability to add text to graphics screens in a variety of styles, colors, and fonts; to design new turtle shapes, and create animation; and to edit a Logo design in detail. (Terrapin Software.)

Logo

Logo is a computer language designed to develop creativity and problem-solving skills with the computer. With only a few commands to the computer, children begin to explore numbers and geometry in interesting and often exciting ways. Logo is special because it allows complete control of the learning environment by the learner. As students learn to make shapes and perform other tasks, they create and name new commands for later use. In this way, they are actually building their own computer language as they learn. Appendix A includes an introductory experience with Logo and lists several additional programs that can be used to explore other mathematical topics. Logo is a classroom learning tool that is underutilized, but teachers and students who have experience with it understand its power. Logo is listed in the Teachers' Favorite Software List at all elementary grade levels.

EXERCISE   With your present understanding of and skill in using a computer, how do you believe you would use computers in your classroom? List four different uses of the computer in mathematics instruction. Which do you think have the most value for development of problem solving and reasoning skills?

■ SUMMARY

Teachers have considerable control over the type of instruction that goes on in their classes. A well-balanced instructional program includes informal exploratory activities, teacher-directed lessons, and mathematical investigations. Exploratory activities provide students with experiences and materials that build background for formal instruction. Teacher-directed lessons give students a structured experience for learning concepts and skills. Teachers use the lesson cycle to motivate, introduce and model concepts, provide guided practice and check for understanding, and assign independent practice. In mathematical investigations, the teacher presents a challenging problem to the students and acts as a facilitator while students work toward solutions. Cooperative-learning groups are appropriate with any of these modes of instruction. When a teacher plans a variety of instructional activities, students have many opportunities to learn and use mathematics.

Classroom arrangement is one way a teacher can structure learning activities. When desks or tables are arranged in clusters, the teacher encourages students to work together. Learning centers and mathematics laboratories are organized so that students have access to a variety of teaching-learning materials. Mathematics manipulatives are concrete learning aids that are very helpful as students learn new concepts. Manipulatives of many types and for nearly every mathematical topic can be purchased or made by a teacher.

Calculators and computers are important learning aids. The calculator enhances mathematical knowledge and attitudes. Students need to be proficient with their calculator; this includes the estimation of answers. Computers and computer software provide many possibilities for children to learn mathematics. Some programs are drill and practice, some teach an entire lesson, while some are exploratory or encourage investigations. All software needs to be previewed to make sure that it meets instructional objectives and has good technical qualities. Reviews and lists of award-winning software give teachers ideas about which software they might preview for purchase. Logo is a powerful computer language that allows exploration of many mathematics concepts and that is popular with many teachers and students.

STUDY QUESTIONS AND ACTIVITIES

1. Examine a teacher's manual from a recent elementary mathematics series. Compare the lesson cycle from Hunter with several lesson plans suggested in the manual. How closely do the textbook lessons resemble the lesson cycle? Does the textbook lesson emphasize manipulatives or paper-and-pencil activities?

2. Interview a teacher who uses learning centers or cooperative learning to discuss time management, types of activities, and evaluation techniques. Ask about the guidelines and rules used as well as the benefits and problems.

3. Interview a teacher who has special training and experience with gifted or handicapped students. What kind of mathematics program do these special students have? Does their mathematics program include all the topics and opportunities for exploration and investigation?

4. Preview three of the titles from the Teachers' Favorite Software list. If possible, have an elementary-age student work the programs with you and observe his or her reactions. What did the student like best? What characteristics do you think make each one a favorite? How would you rate each on the technical qualities, instructional characteristics, and usefulness in a classroom?

5. Get a mathematics materials catalog and make a wish list of $500 worth of equipment for your classroom. Rank the items on your list in order of priority and justify your list. At the end of the book, you may wish to look back and see if you would change your list.

■ TEACHER'S BOOKSHELF

Clements, Douglas. 1989. *Computers in Elementary Mathematics Education.* Englewood Cliffs, NJ: Prentice-Hall.

Collis, Betty. 1988. *Computers, Curriculum, and Whole Class Instruction.* Belmont, CA: Wadsworth.

Joyce, Bruce, and Marsha Weil. 1986. *Models of Teaching,* 3rd ed. Englewood Cliffs, NJ: Prentice-Hall.

Computer Magazines for Teachers

Classroom Computer Learning. Peter Li, Inc., 2451 E. River Rd., Dayton, OH 45439.

Computing Teacher. ISTE, 787 Agate St., Eugene, OR 97403.

Electronic Learning. Scholastic Inc., P.O. Box 644, Lyndhurst, NJ 07071-9985.

■ FOR FURTHER READING

Arithmetic Teacher. 1987, February *34*(6).

> *This theme issue on calculators features 15 articles on curricular questions and instructional activities and updates the 1976 theme issue on calculators.*

Barson, Alan, and Lois Barson. 1987, October. Calculator counting. *Arithmetic Teacher 35*(2), 27–32.

> *Ideas section features calculator activities and investigations.*

Bartalo, Donald B. 1983, January. Calculators and problem-solving instruction: They were made for each other. *Arithmetic Teacher 30*(5), 18–21.

> *A ten-day sequence of activities involving children with calculators and problem solving is reported along with seven teaching suggestions. The lessons were designed to focus children's attention on problem-solving skills.*

Binswanger, Richard. 1988, December. Discovering division with Logo. *Arithmetic Teacher 36*(4), 44–49.

> *Binswanger provides the reader with a search-and-discover format for Logo-based lessons on division. The exercises are relatively simple and provide active student involvement.*

Bright, George W. 1989, January. Logo and geometry. *Arithmetic Teacher 36*(5), 32–34.

> *Three programs written in LogoWriter teach geometry concepts.*

Danforth, Marion M. 1978, December. Aids for learning mathematics. *Arithmetic Teacher 26*(4), 26–27.

The aids Danforth describes are procedures for helping individuals overcome learning difficulties. Included are such things as giving specific objectives, having a child verbalize thought processes, using error-analysis cards, using analogies, giving directions several ways, using concrete materials, using cues to avoid errors, and removing frustration.

DeRidder, Charleen, and Donald J. Dessart. 1982, November. Using a directed lesson. *Arithmetic Teacher 30*(3), 16–17.

A five-step sequence for presenting a specific mathematics skill is described. Teachers' activities at each step are explained.

Duea, Joan, and Earl Ockenga. 1982, February. Classroom problem solving with calculators. *Arithmetic Teacher 29*(6), 50–51.

Examples of student-created problems and their uses in a classroom are presented. Calculators improve the quality and number of student-produced problems.

Easley, Jack, Harold A. Taylor, and Judy K. Taylor. 1990, March. Dialogue and conceptual splatter in mathematics classes. *Arithmetic Teacher 37*(7), 34–37.

"Splatter" refers to students' varied ideas about a mathematics topic and how they express them. The encouragement of splatter through dialogue is one way to help students clarify their thinking.

Fennell, Francis (Skip). 1984, November. Mainstreaming and the mathematics classroom. *Arithmetic Teacher 32*(3), 22–27.

Presents ways to assess children with special needs and to develop Individualized Education Plans (IEPs).

Forish-Ferguson, Laura. 1989, April. Two technological fables. *Arithmetic Teacher 36*(8), 50–51.

This article contains a rationale for the use of calculators and computers in the classroom. The author uses specific student experiences to support this posture.

Greer, John, and Bonnie Greer. 1988, September. Public domain software: A formula for better classroom computing. *Arithmetic Teacher 36*(1), 26–30.

A good resource for identifying available software and where to get it.

Hembree, Ray. 1986, September. Research gives calculators a green light. *Arithmetic Teacher 34*(1), 18–21.

Calculators have an important place in today's mathematics classes, according to research of the past ten years.

Higgins, Jon L. March, 1990. Calculators and common sense. *Arithmetic Teacher 37*(7), 4–5.

Higgins contends that the question of whether to use calculators in the classroom is a nonissue. The issue is how to use them. Using calculators to explore mathematics is one crucial use.

Johnson, Martin L. 1983, January. Identifying and teaching mathematically gifted elementary school children. *Arithmetic Teacher 30*(5), 25–26, 55.

Provides rationale and guidelines for mathematics programs with the gifted.

Lappan, Glenda, Elizabeth Phillips, and M. J. Winter. 1982, October. Powers and patterns: Problem solving with calculators. *Arithmetic Teacher 30*(2), 42–44.

A study of number patterns generated by working with the powers of numbers provides problem-solving experiences, practice with calculators, and application of calculator skills.

Larson, Carol Novillis. 1983, September. Organizing for mathematics instruction. *Arithmetic Teacher 33*(1), 16–19.

Both content and process are included in a model for mathematics instruction.

Lauritzen, Carol. 1985, December. Using every pupil response in mathematics instruction. *Arithmetic Teacher 33*(4), 46–47.

Get every child involved with answer cards.

Markuson, Carolyn, Joyce Tobias, and Tom Lough. 1983, September. Logo fever: The computer language every school is catching. *Arithmetic Teacher 31*(1), 48–51.

Describes advantages of Logo as a problem-solving language for elementary students.

Rees, Rebecca D. 1990, April. Station break: A mathematics game using cooperative learning. *Arithmetic Teacher 37*(8), 8–12.

Learning centers based on practical problems and equipped with the necessary aids for solving them are used. Problems center around buying fast food, sports equipment, and admissions to an amusement park, and preparing cookies.

Reys, Robert E. 1980, November. Calculators in the elementary classroom: How can we go wrong? *Arithmetic Teacher 28*(3), 38–40.

This author favors the use of calculators. He discusses ten ways we can go wrong if they are used improperly.

Sears, Carol J. 1986, January. Mathematics for the learning disabled child in the regular classroom. *Arithmetic Teacher 33*(5), 5–11.

Sears suggests a variety of planning strategies to engage children who have different kinds of disabilities.

Thornton, Carol A., and Sally C. Tucker. 1989, February. Lesson planning: The key to developing number sense. *Arithmetic Teacher 36*(6), 18–21.

Teachers can plan for number sense development from warm-ups to sponge activities to soak up empty seconds in the day.

Thornton, Carol A., and Barbara Wilmot. 1986, February. Special learners. *Arithmetic Teacher 33*(6), 38–41.

Describes how manipulatives are useful in all elementary mathematics topics for special learners; suggestions are equally useful for regular students.

Vacc, Nancy N. 1987, March. Individualizing mathematics drill and practice: Variations on a computer program. *Arithmetic Teacher 34*(7), 43–47.

A "core microcomputer program" and instructions for modifying the program to fit other needs within the mathematics program.

West, Tommie A. 1982, October. Using a textbook effectively. *Arithmetic Teacher 30*(2), 8–9.

Steps in planning lessons around a text are explained. Ways to structure lessons, problems to assign, overcoming a text's weaknesses, and ways of correcting homework are discussed.

Wiebe, James H. 1981, November. Using a calculator to develop mathematical understanding. *Arithmetic Teacher 29*(3), 36–38.

Understanding of counting, estimating, and computation can all be improved through calculator work. Examples of activities are given.

Williams, David E. 1984, September. Warm-ups—Keys to effective mathematics lessons. *Arithmetic Teacher 32*(1), 40–43.

Warm-up activities establish the "set" for a good lesson.

■ NOTES

[1] *Building Thinking Skills* ® is a five-book sequence and *Math Mind Benders* ® is a four-book series of thinking puzzles from Midwest Publications, P.O. Box 448, Pacific Grove, CA 93950-0448.

[2] Bruce Joyce and Marsha Weil. 1986. *Models of Teaching,* 3rd ed. Englewood Cliffs, NJ: Prentice-Hall. Joyce and Weil describe in detail how each of these teaching strategies may be implemented.

[3] Evan Maletsky, ed. 1987. *Teaching with Student Math Notes.* Reston, VA: National Council of Teachers of Mathematics.

[4] David W. Johnson and Roger T. Johnson. 1989. Cooperative learning in mathematics, in Paul R. Trafton and Albert P. Shulte, eds., 1989 Yearbook, *New Directions for Elementary School Mathematics.* Reston, VA: National Council of Teachers of Mathematics, 234–245.

[5] Carol Meyer and Tom Sallee. 1983. *Make It Simpler.* Menlo Park, CA: Addison-Wesley, 5.

[6] Charles Wolfgang and Carl Glickman. 1988. *Solving Behavior Problems,* 3rd ed. New York: Allyn and Bacon.

[7] National Council of Teachers of Mathematics. 1989. *Student Math Notes.* Reston, VA: National Council of Teachers of Mathematics.

[8] Donna Berlin, ed. "SSMILES" (monthly feature), *School Science and Mathematics,* School Science and Mathematics Association, Bowling Green, OH 45403-0256.

[9] *Project AIMS Update,* AIMS Education Foundation, P.O. Box 7766, Fresno, CA 93747.

[10] H. Laurence Ridge and Joseph S. Renzulli. 1981. Teaching mathematics to the talented and gifted, in Vincent J. Glennon, ed., *The Mathematics Education of Exceptional Children and Youth, an Interdisciplinary Approach.* Reston, VA: National Council of Teachers of Mathematics, 196–201.

[11] Ridge and Renzulli, 218–222.

[12] J. F. Weaver and William C. Morse. 1981. Teaching mathematics to socially and emotionally impaired pupils, in Vincent J. Glennon, ed., *The Mathematics Education of Exceptional Children and Youth, an Interdisciplinary Approach.* Reston, VA: National Council of Teachers of Mathematics, 96.

[13] National Council of Teachers of Mathematics. 1980. *An Agenda for Action: Recommendations for School Mathematics in the 1980s.* Reston, VA: National Council of Teachers of Mathematics, 1.

[14] Robert Reys and others. 1980. Hand calculators—What's happening in schools today? *Arithmetic Teacher 28*(6), 41.

[15] *Donald Duck's Playground,* Walt Disney Productions, Sierra On-Line, Coarsegold, CA 93614.

[16] *Teaching and Computers,* Scholastic Publications, P.O. Box 2040, Mahopac, NY 10541-9963.

[17] *Classroom Computer Learning,* Peter Li, Inc., 2451 E. River Rd., Dayton, OH 45439.

[18] From Teachers' favorite software, *Teaching and Computers 7*(4), (January/February, 1990), 20–28.

[19] From Teacher's Software 1989–1990. *Classroom Computer Learning,* Software Awards. *Classroom Computer Learning 10*(3) (November/December, 1989), 14–30.

Assessment in Elementary School Mathematics

The standards for school mathematics from the National Council of Teachers of Mathematics provide information about the nature of good mathematics programs and content. From these standards, state and district goals and objectives are formulated that give direction and information to teachers responsible for implementing mathematics programs in schools and classrooms. The goals and objectives also provide the basis for assessing students' progress in mathematics.

The success of a mathematics program depends on the extent to which it accomplishes its goals and objectives. A classroom assessment program must give a teacher information about each student's current status and progress toward goals. The assessment program must reflect the goals and objectives of the school. Standardized achievement tests are not enough to determine students' success in a comprehensive program such as the one outlined in the NCTM standards. Assessment of students' readiness for learning mathematics; their ability to solve problems, to reason and communicate mathematically, and to make connections between and among concepts and other curriculum areas; and their dispositions toward mathematics must also be made. Written work, observations and interview, and testing all have a role in the assessment program.

93

In this chapter you will read about

1. the purposes of assessment in mathematics;

2. five types of readiness applicable to mathematics;

3. five ways of assessing students' readiness, understandings, skills, and inclinations in mathematics;

4. ways to record information about students.

◼ AREAS OF READINESS

Readiness refers to a child's ability to learn new ideas. Robert B. Underhill named five areas or components of readiness that teachers need to consider as they plan and teach mathematics:

- Content Readiness
- Pedagogical Readiness
- Maturational Readiness
- Affective Readiness
- Contextual Readiness[1]

Content Readiness

Content readiness refers to the mathematical skills and knowledge that a student possesses. For example, a student who counts objects accurately, can demonstrate a "take-away" situation with cubes, knows all or most of the 100 basic subtraction facts, and understands place value for numbers between 9 and 99 has a high degree of content readiness for learning an algorithm to compute answers in examples like these:

$$\begin{array}{ccc} 34 & 47 & 50 \\ -\ 6 & -\ 9 & -\ 7 \end{array}$$

A variety of procedures can be used to assess content readiness. Interviews and observations of students at work reveal their ability to count accurately and to use cubes and other materials to demonstrate "take-away" subtraction situations. Small-group and whole-class discussions can be used to determine their understanding of place-value concepts. Students' oral and written responses to basic-fact combinations indicate their knowledge of basic facts.

Pedagogical Readiness

247
− 182

Work with a variety of materials—objects, pictures, representations of objects, and symbols—is advocated because children gain the experiences they need for understanding and using mathematics. Pedagogical readiness is concerned with a student's understanding of and skill with a particular learning aid. For example, a student is ready to use beansticks (see the photograph of beansticks in Chapter 3, p. 73) to learn the meaning of the problem in the margin if she or he can represent the number 247 with the sticks and can exchange a hundreds raft for 10 tens sticks to show the regrouping needed to complete the algorithm. Students must understand a learning aid before the aid is used to clarify a concept.

Children must also understand the meanings of pictures and other representations. Unless they understand that the picture of animals in a first-grade workbook portrays one set of puppies joining another set of puppies, they do not know that it represents addition; the picture does not serve its intended purpose. A drawing of a triangular prism is of no value to students who do not know how to interpret the two-dimensional drawing of a three-dimensional object. A teacher must be alert to the misinterpretations children make of pictures and drawings. Observing and listening to students as they work with learning aids, pictures, and drawings, and interviewing them are some of the ways a teacher can determine students' pedagogical readiness.

Maturational Readiness

Maturational readiness refers to students' levels of mental maturity. Jean Piaget's research led him to conclude that each person passes through four stages of mental maturity:

- The sensorimotor stage (zero to two years)
- The preoperational stage (two to seven years)
- The concrete operations stage (seven to twelve years)
- The formal operations stage (twelve years and beyond)

The sensorimotor stage occupies the years of life prior to verbal communication. It is during this stage that foundations for later mental growth and mathematical learning are developed. The preoperational stage sees the onset of a child's use of words and understanding that objects and symbols can be used to stand for other objects. A. Dean Hendrickson describes preoperational children:

> Children who are not yet concrete operational are most likely to make judgments about situations based on immediate appearances of things. . . .

Preoperational thinkers tend to center on single features rather than to coordinate features, often making decisions based on one attribute and then switching to a different attribute. . . .

[They] tend to focus on states and to ignore the transformations made in going from one state to another. In a similar fashion, the child's thinking is irreversible in that an opposite set of transformations needed to reverse a change, or a compensatory plan to undo something, cannot be conceptualized.

In forming classes, or part-whole relations, the preoperational or transitional child finds it difficult to see that one class can be a subclass of a larger one.[2]

During kindergarten and grade one, children come to understand a lasting correspondence between two equal sets when the elements in one or both sets are moved. Children learn that the number of objects in each set remains constant. Primary-grade teachers who know that a child may not yet be at this level of maturity refrain from premature introduction of operations, such as addition and subtraction, that depend on lasting correspondence.

Children are in the concrete operations stage during most of the elementary school years. During this period they begin to form mental images of objects and start to use the images for reasoning. They can mentally integrate the parts to form a whole and separate the whole into its parts. Children who can perform these mental operations have achieved what Piaget called *reversibility*. During this stage children become ready to deal with inverse operations, such as addition and subtraction, and to group and regroup numbers, such as is done when adding numbers like those in the margin example.

$$\begin{array}{r} 89 \\ + 78 \\ \hline \end{array}$$

The final stage of maturity, the formal-operations stage, begins after elementary school. Children gradually become able to think abstractly and are able to form hypotheses, analyze situations to consider all aspects of them, and draw conclusions and test them against reality.

Observations of children at work in groups or individually with manipulative materials, interviews, children's responses to questions and during class discussions, and Piaget-type tests are ways to determine a student's maturational readiness.

Affective Readiness

A student's disposition toward mathematics governs to a large extent the degree of success she or he has in learning and using mathematics. "*Disposition* refers not simply to attitudes but to a tendency to think and to act in positive ways. Students' mathematical dispositions are manifested in the way they approach tasks—whether with confidence, willingness to explore alternatives, perseverance, and interest—and in their tendency to reflect on their own thinking. The assessment of mathematical knowledge includes evaluations of these indicators and students' appreciation of the role and value of mathematics."[3] Observations of students at work reveal the enthusiasm and confidence with which they undertake mathematics tasks and the ways in which they apply mathematics in other school activities.

Contextual Readiness

Contextual readiness refers to the awareness of children about ways in which mathematics is used. Students with a high level of contextual readiness are aware of different real-world applications of mathematics and realize their importance. A teacher can assess students' contextual readiness by observing their uses of mathematics both during the times devoted to its study and when they engage in art, social studies, science, physical education, and other in-school activities.

EXERCISE Cite instances from your experiences as a student or as an observer of teachers in a classroom where you have seen teachers who are aware of areas of mathematics readiness other than content readiness.

■ ASSESSMENT PROCEDURES

Teachers need information about each student's status with regard to the five areas of readiness as they prepare activities for children. The nature of each area precludes reliance on written tests as the sole determiner of a child's readiness for a particular mathematics concept. A variety of processes for assessing readiness in each area should be used. A teacher should make systematic use of these procedures:

- Observation of children
- Interviews with children
- Evaluation of recorded work
- Conferences with parents or guardians
- Tests

The National Council of Teachers of Mathematics standards document emphasizes the importance of a broad assessment program. According to its authors,

> The advantage of using several kinds of assessments, some of which are embedded in instruction, is that students' evolving understanding can be continuously monitored. The disadvantage is that such a procedure is perceived as cumbersome. Records of students' progress should be more than a set of numerical grades or checklists; they can include brief notes or samples of stu-

dents' work. Such records are evidence of students' continued growth in understanding. Students should also maintain their own records. At all grades, students can keep portfolios of their work; in the higher grades, as they become more verbally fluent and reflective, they should be encouraged to keep a mathematics journal. These journals can contain goals, discoveries, thoughts, and observations, as well as descriptions of activities. Journals not only allow students to chart their progress in understanding but also act as a focus for discussion between student and teacher, thereby fostering communication about mathematics itself.[4]

Observation of Children

Observations of students during class discussions, cooperative-group activities, independent work periods, and tests reveal a variety of information about students' readiness for and growth in understanding of mathematics concepts. Observations need not be highly structured nor do they need to detract from a teacher's other activities. They can be done during class discussions and as children engage in seatwork and problem-solving activities. As students discuss a topic, note a child's contribution. Note whether the child tends to withdraw from the discussion. If so, is the withdrawal caused by a lack of understanding of the concept involved? Or, is it caused by a past experience during which the child was ridiculed for an incorrect answer? Note the quality of a child's contribution. Does the contribution signify insight into the concept? Does the student demonstrate that she or he is able to connect the new concept to one previously encountered? Observations as students use learning aids provide clues that indicate how well they understand the aids and their uses. Does a child use an aid mechanically in an imitative way that suggests a lack of understanding of its meaning? Or, does the child apply it to new situations with confidence? Can the child use several devices to portray a given concept?

Observations during test and study periods help determine children's work habits and abilities to use and apply mathematics. When children begin work promptly and apply themselves to a task, an observer would conclude that they understand what they are doing and feel confident in their ability to complete the task. On the other hand, children who begin work slowly or cannot focus on it show that they may not understand what they are trying to do or lack confidence in their ability. By circulating among children as they work, a teacher can note those who appear to be having difficulty and give them immediate assistance. Often a child can overcome a difficulty in a short time when given immediate help. When several children are observed to have a common problem, they can be organized into a small group for immediate help or a structured cooperative-learning activity.

A teacher should observe students as they use measuring tools, calculators, and computers to determine their skill in applying them in useful ways. Do children select and use an appropriate measuring instrument to determine the size of a piece of paper for an art project? Do children choose to use a calculator in situations where its use is appropriate, such as to determine the total points earned on a series of spelling tests? Do children spontaneously select and use a computer graphing program to organize and display data collected during a research project?

When students are working, they should be offered encouragement and praise. "That's the way" or "You're on the right track" is often the only acknowledgment needed by children who are uncertain about whether they are working correctly.

A plan can be devised to guide a teacher's systematic observation of a group of children. Five children who are to be observed are identified, and notes about their performance are made during a day's activities. This plan lets a teacher focus on a manageable portion of a class. Over a period of about two weeks, all children in a class can be observed. When there are children about whom there are particular concerns a teacher can observe them over a period of several days to note their work habits, perseverance, curiosity, and other attributes.

Interviews with Children

An interview can be planned or spontaneous. Neither type of interview need be highly formal or time consuming. Five situations illustrate the usefulness of spontaneous interviews.

- When a new student transfers to a classroom, the child can be asked to demonstrate what she or he understands about a given concept or operation with manipulative materials or an algorithm. Although the interview does not reveal all that a teacher needs to know about the student's mathematical background, it provides an idea of where to begin more intensive assessment and of where to begin instruction.

- If a teacher observes a student who has a unique or special method of approaching a problem or shortcutting a process, a brief talk can reveal the child's thought processes and allow the teacher to decide if the method is accurate.

- When a student is having difficulty with a concept or skill, the teacher can identify the basis of the problem and determine appropriate materials and activities to help the child overcome the problem.

- A child understands a process but is temporarily "blocked" and cannot continue. A teacher listens as the child talks through the problem and supports the child's attempts to clarify the next steps.

- A fourth-grade child is using a time-consuming procedure, such as counting fingers. A teacher talks to the child to help him or her select and use a more appropriate way of working, such as using a table of facts or a calculator to make the work more efficient.

A teacher who talks to a child for a few moments to give support, contact, or proximity approval often gains worthwhile information about the child and at the same time gives support to the student merely by tendering the attention.

Interviews should not be threatening to a child. A child being interviewed to determine thought processes during an operation, for example, can be told to "think aloud" as the work is completed. "Tell me what you do when you complete this subtraction algorithm." A child should not be interrupted during the explanation. Errors and possible reasons for misconceptions should be recorded and used later to reteach the student.

Interviews may be planned around reviewing the contents of a portfolio or journal. A young child's portfolio reveals growth in the student's understanding of concepts. When discussing the portfolio with a child, a teacher can call attention to the growth that has taken place. "Look at how much more you can do today than you could four weeks ago when you started this collection." The portfolio may also show where a student's understanding of a concept begins to break down. This information enables the teacher to plan strategies to overcome the problem. An older student's journal may contain examples of work products, but it also contains other information. Discussion can center around such things as the student's goals and expectations in mathematics, insights and discoveries, and descriptions of activities. A teacher who has good rapport with students learns much about students' attitudes, interests, and anxieties and about their confidence in using mathematics during discussion of a journal's contents.

More structured interviews may also be planned. Piaget developed interview techniques, or protocols, for concepts such as conservation of number, length, area, time, mass, and liquid volume.[5] The steps in an interview are the same for each concept.

- Step 1: Establish equivalence for two sets or objects.
- Step 2: Transform one of the sets or objects.
- Step 3: Ask whether the two sets or objects are still equivalent.
- Step 4: Probe for the child's reasoning.
- Step 5: Determine the level of reasoning on the task.

When interviewing for conservation, or constancy, of number, the teacher is finding out whether or not the child can keep the abstract concept of number fixed even while the objects are rearranged. An interview would be conducted in this manner.

PIAGET INTERVIEW ON CONSERVATION OF NUMBER

- *Step 1:* Establish equivalence for two sets or objects (see Figure 4.1).

  Teacher: I have some red checkers and black checkers. I want to find out if I have the same number of red checkers and black checkers.

The teacher puts seven red checkers in a row and seven black checkers in a row. The checkers should be lined up so that one-to-one correspondence between the rows is obvious.

Figure 4-1
Establish
equivalence

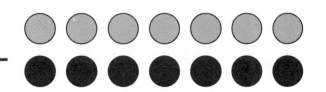

Teacher: Do I have the same number of red checkers and black checkers?

If the child does not recognize that the number of checkers is the same, the interview is over. If the child responds that there are the same number of red and black checkers, the interview continues.

- *Step 2:* Transform one of the sets or objects (see Figure 4.2).

The teacher then transforms, or changes, the way one of the rows of checkers looks. This may be done by pushing the checkers closer together, spreading them out, or clustering them as a group.

Figure 4-2
Transform, or distort,
one row

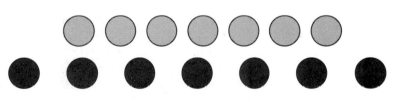

- *Step 3:* Ask whether the two sets or objects are still equivalent.

Teacher: Now are there more checkers here (pointing to the top row), more checkers here (pointing to the bottom row), or is the number of checkers the same?

The child will respond more red, more black, the same, or occasionally will become confused and not respond at all. In the latter case, the interview ends. However, if the student answers red, black, or same, the teacher follows up with a question on reasoning.

- *Step 4:* Probe for the child's reasoning.

Teacher: Can you tell me why you think that?

The student will then give a reason for her or his belief. The reasoning is the most important part of the interview because the teacher has a chance to understand how the child is thinking.

■   *Step 5:* Determine the level of reasoning on the task.

The reasons that children give for the number being the same are often related to not having removed any of the checkers. Some will count the two groups to confirm equivalence, while others will return the checkers to a one-to-one correspondence. If both the answer and the reasoning are accurate, the teacher may conclude that the student is a conserver of number.

If the child says that the number is not the same, the teacher also listens for the reasoning. Some children say the checkers are longer or they "stick out." Others say that the group that is closer together is more because they are "all together." Some can give no reason for their opinion. The reasons that children give for the number of checkers being different are often surprising to an adult who sees this task as easy. But the reasons are showing the intellectual development of the child.

All the other Piaget interviews are conducted in the same manner. For conservation of liquid volume, two identical glasses are filled with liquid to the same level to establish equivalence. Then the liquid in one glass is poured into a shallow dish or a tall thin bottle. The questions and probes for reasoning are adapted to the task. Conservation of mass is done with two balls of clay. After establishing that two balls have the same amount of clay, one is rolled into a hotdog shape or into a pancake.

The Piaget-type interview is not a time to teach; the child is revealing a level of understanding to the teacher. Telling students that the number is the same does not work because the students become confused; they "know" that the two groups are not equal. Instead of attempting to teach at the time of the interview, a teacher should note which children need additional experiences with sets or objects to be provided in many different ways. Activities of this type are found in Chapter 7.

Teachers may wish to develop their own set of structured interviews. Constance Kamii suggests an interview that reveals whether students have an understanding of place value.[6] She asks students to pick out 16 cubes and draw a picture of them on a paper. Then she has them write "16" on the paper. Next she asks the students to draw a circle around the number of cubes represented by the "16." Then she points to the "6" in the numeral and asks them to circle the number of cubes represented by the "6." Finally, she asks them to circle the number of cubes represented by the "1." The results of several students' work is shown in Figure 4.3. Most students can find the "16" and the "6" correctly, but for "1" they circle only one block instead of ten. Based on her interviews, Kamii concludes that most students do not develop a complete understanding of place value until about the fourth grade. However, most mathematics textbooks and curricula require that children work with regrouping in addition and subtraction earlier. This conflict alerts teachers to the need for careful concept development of place value and for concrete materials to model processes throughout the elementary grades.

Figure 4-3
Kamii interview:
students' work

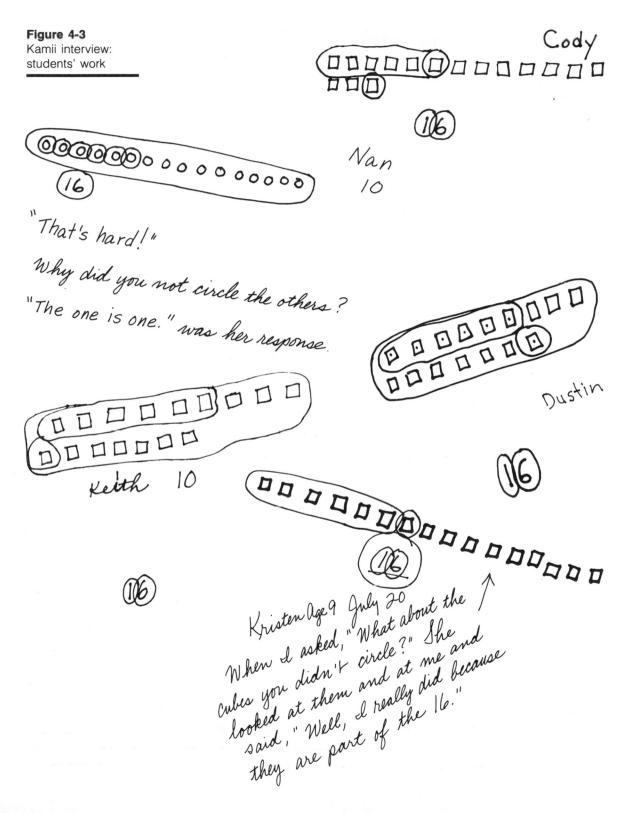

Cody

16

Nan
10

"That's hard!"

Why did you not circle the others?

"The one is one." was her response.

Dustin

16

Keith   10

16

16

Kristen Age 9   July 20
When I asked, "What about the ↑
cubes you didn't circle?" She
looked at them and at me and
said, "Well, I really did because
they are part of the 16."

Evaluation of Recorded Assignments

During the course of a year, children complete many recorded assignments. These assignments include the preparation of tables, charts, graphs, and diagrams, which may be made with paper and pencil or computer graphics; written work based on exercises in workbooks and textbooks; solutions to problems; and journals. A teacher's careful study of students' work products and journals yields much worthwhile information.

The tables, charts, graphs, and diagrams children prepare during mathematics and other school activities should be carefully studied to detect any errors in their construction or misrepresentations of the data. A study may reveal a more appropriate way to display the information than was selected; perhaps another type of graph or a table will show the information better than the graph chosen by the children.

Teachers who have students maintain journals in which records of problem-solving activities are kept have a ready source of information to discuss with a child. Other written information that pertains to problem solving should also be reviewed by a teacher. A teacher should examine more than answers to problems. He or she may ask students to turn in worksheets they used as a problem was solved. A student's or group's paper that shows a well-conceived series of steps leading to a solution indicates that the student or group is confident and capable in problem-solving situations. One that shows erasures, marked-out parts, or dead ends may indicate that the student or group does not know what to do or lacks confidence and is uncertain of a solution process.

An example of how examination of a daily paper can assist a child is provided in the following situation: A teacher introduced the decomposition algorithm for subtraction by having students use a place-value device to comprehend the regrouping process. Work with the device was allowed until students indicated understanding of the process. This was followed by work with an algorithm modeled by the teacher and some of the children. The teacher assigned a page from the textbook when he thought the children were ready for a written exercise. He examined the practice paper completed by each child. The following errors were committed on one paper:

$$
\begin{array}{ccc}
42 & 67 & 85 \\
-19 & -48 & -36 \\
\hline
37 & 21 & 51
\end{array}
$$

The teacher saw that the child subtracted the smaller number from the larger number regardless of where the numbers appeared in the algorithm. He knew immediately that the child had not understood the process. Rather than allow the student to do independent practice on an incorrect process until it became habituated, the teacher used a different device and additional modeling to reteach the regrouping process with the student. A practice page completed later showed that the child comprehended the decomposition algorithm process and could use it to deal with other subtraction examples.

Robert Ashlock has studied "patterned errors," such as the one cited in the preceding example. His book *Error Patterns in Computation* [7] provides insight into errors that children make as they add, subtract, multiply, and divide whole numbers, common fractions, and decimal fractions. For example, if the three problems below were on a practice page for subtraction, the teacher would find a systematic error.

ERROR PATTERNS IN COMPUTATION

779	297	632
− 204	− 103	− 400
505	104	200

What error do you find in these three problems?
What misunderstanding does the student have about subtraction?
What would you do to correct the misunderstanding?

After recognizing the systematic error, the teacher can provide instruction to correct it. Ashlock's book lists common error patterns and suggests corrective techniques. (It is included in the Teacher's Bookshelf at the end of this chapter.)

CONFERENCES WITH PARENTS OR GUARDIANS

Parents or guardians can provide information that is often unavailable from other sources. Many children enter kindergarten from a preschool where they had valuable experiences with pattern blocks, counting materials, and other number-oriented materials; where they made simple graphs and charts; and where they learned to recognize some written number symbols. Some children have opportunities to use computers for number and counting activities. Other children have meager experience with number and other mathematical ideas. Interviews with parents and guardians reveal information about children's early experiences with mathematics-oriented activities and help teachers organize and present activities that are appropriate for all children.

Parents of older children can provide information about their children's exposure to mathematics, uses of mathematics, attitudes toward the subject, and other significant information such as computer experience. A parent's personal anxiety about mathematics is sometimes revealed during an interview. Children may exhibit the anxieties of a parent. A parent may also talk about how important it is that the child excel in mathematics. Children react to pressures to succeed in different ways. One child may respond with enthusiasm and assurance, whereas another may succumb under the pressure. Children sometimes experience problems because of a conflict between ways mathematics is presented in the classroom and ways a parent believes it should be presented.

Problems that arise because of parental attitudes, expectations, and ways of doing mathematics should be discussed openly and frankly during conferences. At the same time, a teacher should enlist the help of parents in their child's mathematics learning. A student's portfolio or journal can also be explained and discussed during a conference as one means of informing parents about their child's progress and accomplishments.

EXERCISE Name at least one way to assess a child's level of performance in each of these tasks:

1. Compute the answer for 48 × 39 =
2. Use a balance scale to weigh a bunch of carrots.
3. Measure the area of the floor in a room at home.
4. Make a graph of data about television preferences of classmates.

 ## USING TESTS

Both commercial and teacher-made tests are used for assessing children's knowledge and skills in mathematics. Commercial tests are provided by companies that develop and publish achievement and diagnostic tests and by textbook publishers. Teacher-made tests are usually prepared by individual teachers to meet their specific needs.

Commercial Tests

Two types of commercially produced tests are commonly used in elementary schools—achievement and diagnostic. Achievement tests are designed to assess what children know about a subject or group of subjects. They are frequently used for statewide or districtwide testing programs, where they are given to all children or to those in selected grades according to a prescribed schedule. This allows the district to compare performance of students in the local schools against the performance of similar students nationwide.

For example, the *California Achievement Test*[8] includes tests for reading, language arts, mathematics, and other subjects. Each subtest is administered to a group of children. The test has eleven overlapping levels with six levels covering elementary grades. The *Metropolitan Achievement Test*[9] is another widely used broad-range achievement test. It also has six levels for elementary school.

Commercially produced achievement tests have standardized procedures for administering them, analyzing results, and determining each child's standing, which is usually reported in terms of a grade-level or percentile ranking for the test as a whole and for each of its subject subtests. Teachers use commercial tests as one source of information about a child's general level of achievement with the mathematics covered on the tests.

A textbook series usually contains a beginning-of-the-year inventory and end-of-unit and end-of-year mastery tests. These tests match the mathematics content of the series for which they are designed. They can be used to determine where to place a child when a series is used as the basis for a program.

Commercially produced diagnostic tests are also available. A diagnostic test is designed to provide information about strengths and weaknesses in specific areas of mathematics, such as the addition or subtraction of whole numbers. A commercial test will be useful as long as its items match those of a specific mathematics program.

The *Keymath Diagnostic Test,*[10] which is a diagnostic inventory of essential mathematics, consists of a large looseleaf book containing one test item per page. It covers a range of mathematics concepts and addition, subtraction, multiplication, and division algorithms arranged in an increasingly difficult order. The test is administered to one child at a time. The test administrator shows the student a page from the book, gives oral instructions, and receives the child's oral response. A written record of responses is made on a sheet provided with the test. The oral test is stopped when the student is no longer able to respond to the test items. In addition to taking the oral test, the student writes answers on a separate paper for each operation to demonstrate skill in paper-and-pencil computation. The test is an indicator of a child's level of understanding of the concepts and skills it contains.

Paper-and-pencil diagnostic tests indicate strengths and weaknesses in the topics and concepts they contain. The *Tests of Early Mathematics Ability*[11] is designed for children four to nine years of age and covers both formal mathematics concepts, such as number facts, calculation skills, and base-ten concepts, and informal concepts, such as counting, informal calculations, and comparisons of more and less. For 20 minutes, a teacher asks the questions and a single child responds orally or writes calculations in the test booklet. The *Stanford Diagnostic Achievement Test,*[12] an example of a group-administered test, has four different levels for four different grade ranges. A student receives a copy of a test booklet and records a written response for each test item.

Commercial achievement and diagnostic tests provide useful information, but they do not cover all aspects of a child's mathematics education. They must be considered as only one part of a comprehensive evaluation program, along with the other processes already discussed in this chapter.

Teacher-Made Tests

Teachers often find that commercial tests are inadequate for their diagnostic needs because the specific information they want about a child's skill or understanding cannot be obtained from them. Teacher-made tests can be designed to pinpoint particular areas of competence or weakness. Two teacher diagnostic processes are described: individual or small-group primary-level tests and an intermediate-grade test.

Primary-Level Diagnostic Test

When designing a diagnostic test for primary grades, a teacher has several choices of format: interview, observation, or paper-and-pencil. Regardless of the format, incorporating manipulative materials in the test will give better information because the teacher can see what the child is thinking as he or she manipulates them. The test can be given individually or to small groups of students. Giving a test to the entire group is difficult because a teacher cannot see what each student is doing.

Making a test involves three steps. First, choose the topic and the objectives. Second, decide the specific questions or tasks to include. Third, analyze the results. If a teacher wishes to assess children's understanding of numbers and numerals, the specific objective might be whether children can create and match sets from 6 to 10 using Unifix cubes. The testing objective might read: "Given a box of Unifix cubes and Unifix number indicators, the student will make towers for 6, 7, 8, 9, 10 and attach the correct number indicator to each tower." This objective includes the behavior being observed, the situation in which it is being observed, and the standard of acceptable performance. Children who have mastered the skill have the background to move into addition facts beyond 10 to 11–18. Children who cannot complete the task need additional informal and teacher-directed activities.

Children who are learning strategies for addition and subtraction should understand that the commutative law assists in learning facts. The teacher might write as a testing objective: "Given a picture of Unifix rod towers for sums 6–8, students will write all the combinations that have combinations of cubes totaling 6, 7, and 8." Figure 4.4 shows a page that might be used for such a test. Students who are successful with this should be ready to work on quick recall of the facts and work on facts with sums of 9 and higher.

A quick way to diagnose knowledge of subtraction facts is to show subtraction flash cards; a student keeps cards for facts that are known. These facts can be colored on an addition table; the uncolored facts show those that need work. The teacher should look at the addition table to see if there is a pattern of facts that need work and help the student with appropriate strategies.

Figure 4-4
Unifix rod towers
test

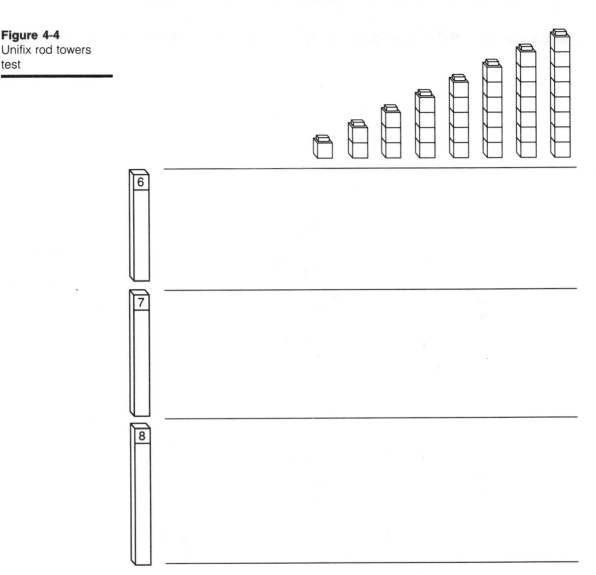

Intermediate-Grade Test

When a teacher wants to determine children's ability to use a paper-and-pencil algorithm for a particular topic, a diagnostic test can be constructed to discover which skills the child has or has not mastered. A sequence of steps for teaching children how to use an algorithm for subtraction is given in Figure 9.2 on page 269. The level of difficulty of the work increases from the bottom to the top of the chart. A teacher should know where each child is in relation to the stages when she or he plans activities that deal with subtraction. Figure 4.5 shows a test designed to pinpoint a child's standing in relation to stages 4 through 7 of the flowchart. There are fifteen items, with three problem examples for each of the levels 4, 5, and 7, and two sets of

Figure 4-5
Subtraction test:
Stages 4–7

Subtraction with Whole Numbers

Name _____

Date _____

A   36
    − 7
	B 43
	    − 21
		C 40
		    − 8

D   36
    − 19
	E 43
	    − 9
		F 50
		    − 27

G   70
    − 2
	H 45
	    − 22
		I 60
		    − 25

J   38
    − 19
	K 80
	    − 29
		L 78
		    − 42

M   90
    − 3
	N 86
	    − 18
		O 31
		    − 4

examples for level 6 because there are two different types of subtraction in it. The three problems at each level are sufficient to determine a child's ability to cope with it. It is assumed that a child who gets all three correct or misses only one item has developed computational skill at that level. On the other hand, a child who misses two or all three items may need additional instruction at that level. Note that the items are mixed on the page and not grouped by types. This forces a student to deal with each item separately rather than relying on patterns to complete the second and third items of a type after the first one is completed. A wide variety of basic facts are included in the test. Do not set a time limit for completing a diagnostic test; give each child all the time needed to complete it.

$$\begin{array}{r} 81 \\ -\ 26 \\ \hline \end{array}$$

An interview is better than a test to determine a child's understanding and comprehension of a subtraction algorithm. Give an example like the one in the margin, and ask the child to explain the work as it is completed. Review the suggestions for conducting an interview on pages 99–102.

One way to test a child's routine application of subtraction in a practical situation is to present a number sentence such as $256 - 149 = 107$ and ask the child to make up a story problem about the sentence. A paper containing a mixture of printed story problems requiring addition and subtraction, or a combination of other operations, can also be used to test a child's knowledge of how operations are used in routine problem situations.

The purpose of a diagnostic test is to determine a child's strengths and weaknesses in mathematics. Therefore it is necessary that a teacher carefully analyze responses for each test that a child completes. The analysis requires attention to more than the number of items missed. Note such things as the types of examples that were done correctly or incorrectly and any patterns of errors that may occur. In addition, it should be determined whether there are basic fact combinations that are missed regularly.

EXERCISE   Describe a circumstance that would lead a teacher to prepare a diagnostic test rather than using a commercially produced test.

RECORDING ASSESSMENT INFORMATION

Much information gathered through assessment activities is anecdotal. A numerical or letter ranking cannot be assigned to observational and interview information. Each teacher must devise a scheme for recording information about students.

One scheme is to maintain a cumulative anecdotal record for each child. A simple form (Figure 4.6) contains cells for recording a date and activity. Entries are made following a planned observation of a child, during

Figure 4-6
Form for recording anecdotal information about a single child

2/7 Sorted 20 blocks by color	2/12 Summarized the group's activities
2/9 Made picture of sorting activity on squared paper	
2/10 Compared sets and identified the one with most red blocks	
2/11 Was effective as materials manager	

Figure 4-7
Form for recording information about five children
during a planned observation (adapted from National
Council of Teachers of Mathematics, *Curriculum
and Evaluation Standards for School Mathematics*.
Reston, VA: 1989, p. 235)

	Student	Student	Student	Student	Student
Average numbers					
Constructs bar graph					
Interprets data					
Works cooperatively					
Helps others					

or following interviews, and following any other opportunity to note a child's activity, performance, or behavior.

A more detailed form might be used when there are specific skills or behaviors a teacher wants to assess. The form illustrated in Figure 4.7 can be used by a teacher who has selected a group of five students to observe on a specific day. Behaviors or skills are listed down the side and a student's name is written above each column. A check mark or anecdotal record is written in the appropriate box after the teacher has observed or otherwise noted a behavior or skill.

The records a teacher maintains for grading and reporting purposes will be determined by the nature of the grading system used in a school or district. There is no "best" scheme for recording scores, points, or letter grades for daily work, tests, and other work completed by children. Some teachers use standard grade books that contain spaces for letter or numerical grades. Some schools or districts provide forms that contain grade-level goals or objectives and cells in which checks or other marks are made when a goal or objective is accomplished. Some teachers determine what information they need and devise their own scheme for recording it.

EXERCISE   Some school systems use only narrative report forms, while others use only graded reports. What are advantages and disadvantages of each way of reporting students' progress in mathematics to parents and guardians?

■ SUMMARY

Teachers need current information about each child in order to plan effective lessons and activities. An assessment program that is aligned with the goals and objectives of a school's mathematics program provides this information. Each child's content, pedagogical, maturational, affective, and contextual readiness should be assessed. Content readiness refers to knowledge and understanding of mathematical concepts and skills. Pedagogical readiness refers to knowledge and understanding of materials—concrete, pictorial, and representational—that are used to teach mathematics. Maturational readiness is concerned with the mental maturity of children. The disposition of children toward mathematics is the concern of affective readiness. And the knowledge of the uses of mathematics that children possess is the subject of contextual readiness.

Five assessment procedures are discussed as ways to determine a student's position with regard to each of the areas of readiness: formal and informal observations, interviews, evaluation of recorded work, conferences with parents, and tests. Observations and interviews are particularly useful for obtaining information about content, pedagogical, affective, and contextual readiness. A careful study of students' assigned written work reveals areas of weakness that may need special attention. Conferences with parents or guardians may give information about affective and contextual readiness.

Both commercial and teacher-made tests are used in many assessment programs. Commercial achievement tests are provided by test-publishing companies and textbook publishers. There are commercially prepared tests that have been developed to help teachers diagnose children's strengths and weaknesses. Some teachers develop their own diagnostic tests in order to have tests that are more closely aligned with their programs' objectives than commercial tests. Piaget-type tests are used to determine children's levels of mental maturity. Anecdotal statements can be used to record information about students. Forms that list goals or objectives and on which check marks and anecdotal comments are placed provide a means for noting children's standing in specific areas of mathematics. Information that is needed for grading purposes should be kept in some orderly fashion.

STUDY QUESTIONS AND ACTIVITIES

1. Five areas of readiness are discussed in this chapter. Select five students to observe during at least three mathematics class periods. Use a form similar to the one in Figure 4.6 on which to write anecdotal records during your observations of these children. What is your assessment of each one's readiness for the work they are engaged in? Are there some areas where they appear to be better prepared than others? If so, identify them and explain why you believe this is true.
2. Conduct a Piaget-type interview with several kindergarten or first-grade children. Identify the subject of your interview and comment on each child's thinking. Based on your interviews, identify the type of work you believe each child should engage in over the next several weeks. *The Piaget Primer* (see footnote 5) will help you select a topic and give further help in structuring your interviews.
3. Examine a commercial diagnostic test and its manual. What specific mathematical skills and understandings does it diagnose? Critique the test in terms of the attention to facts and skills, comprehension and understanding, and applications of mathematics. Do you believe there is a good balance?
4. Look at the testing materials available with a comprehensive textbook series. Which specific mathematical skills and understandings are assessed? Compare a commercial test to the series' materials. How well do the two agree on content, vocabulary, and notation? What problems might arise for children when a test and a book do not use the same vocabulary and notation?
5. Use this chapter's suggestions for preparing a teacher-made diagnostic test. Select a topic from one of the charts at the beginning of Chapter 9 or 10 and a sequence of five subtasks from it, then write appropriate objectives and items and design your test. Administer the test to a group of children and analyze the results. What skills or subskills seem to be understood? How would this knowledge help you plan your teaching if you were teaching the children?
6. Ashlock's book (see the Teacher's Bookshelf section) and some articles listed in the For Further Reading section contain examples of error patterns found in students' work. Examine several of the error patterns. Give problems similar to the examples to several students. Do you find any of the error patterns in their work? How can a teacher use the results of such an examination to plan instruction?

■ TEACHER'S BOOKSHELF

Ashlock, Robert. 1990. *Error Patterns in Computation,* 5th ed. Columbus, OH: Charles E. Merrill.

■ FOR FURTHER READING

Arithmetic Teacher. 1979, November *27*(3).

> *This theme issue contains eight articles on assessment.*

Brumfield, Robert D., and Bobby D. Moore. 1985, November. Problems with the basic facts may not be the problem. *Arithmetic Teacher 33*(3), 17–18.

> *The authors describe types of error patterns students may make that prevent them from computing accurately with algorithms.*

Clark, H. Clifford. 1986, September. How to check elementary mathematics papers. *Arithmetic Teacher 34*(1), 37–38.

> *Clark recommends that teachers use evaluation of daily work for diagnostic purposes.*

Corbitt, Mary Kay. 1984, April. When students talk. . . . *Arithmetic Teacher 31*(8), 16–20.

> *Interviewing students gives the teacher an idea of mathematics from the students' point of view.*

Elliott, Portia. 1990, April. Reclaiming school mathematics. *Arithmetic Teacher 37*(8), 4–5.

> *Elliott stresses that students' performance on tests should not be the sole determiner of success in mathematics. Evaluation must be broad in conception and be made by a variety of means.*

Engelhardt, Jon M. 1982, May. Using computational errors in diagnostic teaching. *Arithmetic Teacher 29*(8), 16–19.

> *Engelhardt discusses four types of errors: mechanical, careless, conceptual, and procedural. Teachers must attend to each type of error and not concentrate on procedural errors, which they commonly do, according to the author.*

Fowler, Mary Anne. 1980, March. Diagnostic teaching for elementary school mathematics. *Arithmetic Teacher 27*(7), 34–37.

> *Diagnostic teaching requires three things: determination of types of errors, rationale for each type of error, and establishment of what needs to be learned in order to overcome each type of error. The article discusses how to do these things.*

Freeman, Donald J., et al. 1982, March. A closer look at standardized tests. *Arithmetic Teacher 29*(7), 50–54.

> *Four standardized tests are discussed. The authors found considerable variation in their content. A test should be selected carefully to provide the closest possible match between its content and a program's content.*

Hodges, Helene L. B. 1983, March. Learning styles: Rx for mathophobia. *Arithmetic Teacher 30*(7), 17–20.

Identification of different learning styles in children may help a teacher aid children in overcoming anxiety.

Norton, Mary Ann. 1983, May. Improve your evaluation techniques. *Arithmetic Teacher 30*(9), 6–7.

Norton suggests alternative ways a teacher can evaluate children's understanding of mathematics.

Peck, Donald M., Stanley M. Jencks, and Michael L. Connell. 1989, November. Improving instruction through brief interviews. *Arithmetic Teacher 37*(3), 15–17.

Comparing the results of a paper-and-pencil test and an interview shows that many children are misjudged based on test results alone.

Rudinsky, Allan N., Priscilla Drickamer, and Roberta Handy. 1981, April. Talking mathematics with children. *Arithmetic Teacher 28*(8), 14–16.

The article presents guidelines and strategies for conducting interviews.

Sadowski, Barbara R., and Delayne Houston McIlveen. 1984, January. Diagnosis and remediation of sentence-solving error patterns. *Arithmetic Teacher 31*(5), 42–45.

The article shows how analysis of students' papers reveals misunderstandings and suggests activities for remediation.

Shaw, Robert A., and Philip A. Pelosi. 1983, March. In search of computational errors. *Arithmetic Teacher 30*(7), 50–51.

Observations and student interviews reveal the nature of students' computational errors. Four situations are discussed.

Sowder, Larry, Judith Threadgill-Sowder, Margaret B. Moyer, and John C. Moyer. 1986, May. Diagnosing a student's understanding of operations. *Arithmetic Teacher 33*(9), 22–25.

These authors provide evaluation techniques for determining meanings of operations.

■ NOTES

[1] Robert B. Underhill. 1976. Classroom diagnosis, in John L. Higgins and James W. Heddens, eds., *Remedial Mathematics: Diagnostic and Prescriptive Approaches.* Columbus, OH: ERIC Center for Science, Mathematics, and Environmental Education, College of Education, Ohio State University, 33–35. Used by permission.

[2] A. Dean Hendrickson. 1981. *Mathematics the Piaget Way.* St. Paul, MN: Council for Quality Education, 2–3. Used by permission.

[3] National Council of Teachers of Mathematics. 1989. *Curriculum and Evaluation Standards for School Mathematics.* Reston, VA: National Council of Teachers of Mathematics, 233.

[4] NCTM, 197.

[5] Richard Copeland. 1984. *How Children Learn Mathematics.* New York: Macmillan; Ed Labinowicz. 1981. *The Piaget Primer,* 3rd ed. Menlo Park, CA: Addison-Wesley.

[6] Constance Kamii. 1986. *Children Reinvent Arithmetic.* New York: Teachers College Press.

[7] Robert Ashlock. 1990. *Error Patterns in Computation.* Columbus, OH: Charles E. Merrill.

[8] *California Achievement Test, Forms E and F.* 1985. Monterey, CA: CTB/McGraw-Hill.

[9] *Metropolitan Achievement Test.* 1987. San Antonio, TX: Psychological Corporation.

[10] *Keymath Diagnostic Test.* 1988, rev. version. Circle Pines, MN: American Guidance Service.

[11] *Tests of Early Mathematics Ability.* 1983. Austin, TX: PRO-ED.

[12] *Stanford Diagnostic Achievement Test.* 1976. San Antonio, TX: Psychological Corporation.

PART Two

FOUR GENERAL STANDARDS

Mathematics and Problem Solving

The task of preparing students for roles in society was once much simpler. In a slow-changing society, mathematics skills necessary for business, industry, and home were easily determined and taught. But over the years, occupational skills and the subject of mathematics as well as the requirements for learning it have expanded and become less definite. A fast-changing technological world offers few occupations for which mathematical requirements can be explicitly defined and developed during the school years. Today's students must understand a wide range of concepts and skills, be familiar with modern technological tools, and know and use a variety of problem-solving strategies. "Problem solving should be the central focus of the mathematics curriculum. As such, it is a primary goal of all mathematics instruction and an integral part of all mathematical study. Problem solving is not a distinct topic, but a process that should permeate the entire program and provide the context in which concepts and skills can be learned." [1]

In this chapter you will read about

1. the significance of mathematics *as* problem solving;
2. ten problem-solving strategies and ways to teach them;
3. examples of realistic problems children can solve in the classroom.

121

NCTM STANDARDS THAT PERTAIN TO PROBLEM SOLVING

Kindergarten Through Grade Four

Standard 1: Mathematics as Problem Solving In grades K–4, the study of mathematics should emphasize problem solving so that students can:

- use problem-solving approaches to investigate and understand mathematical content;
- formulate problems from everyday and mathematical situations;
- develop and apply strategies to solve a wide variety of problems;
- verify and interpret results with respect to the original problem;
- acquire confidence in using mathematics meaningfully.[2]

Grades Five Through Eight

Standard 1: Mathematics as Problem Solving In grades 5–8, the mathematics curriculum should include numerous and varied experiences with problem solving as a method of inquiry and application so that students can:

- use problem-solving approaches to investigate and understand mathematical content;
- formulate problems from situations within and outside mathematics;

- develop and apply a variety of strategies to solve problems, which emphasize multistep and nonroutine problems;
- verify and interpret results with respect to the original problem situation;
- generalize solutions and strategies to new problem situations;
- acquire confidence in using mathematics meaningfully.[3]

Standard 8: Patterns and Functions In grades 5–8, the mathematics curriculum should include explorations of patterns and functions so that students can:

- analyze functional relationships to explain how a change in one quantity results in a change in another;
- use patterns and functions to represent and solve problems.[4]

Standard 9: Algebra In grades 5–8, the mathematics curriculum should include explorations of algebraic concepts and processes so that students can:

- develop confidence in solving linear equations using concrete, informal, . . . methods.[5]

■ MATHEMATICS *AS* PROBLEM SOLVING

A new notion of what problem solving is has evolved in recent years. In the past, "problem solving" was a topic, like addition, geometry, or measurement. It was something that was taught to children, just as other topics were taught. And like other topics, problem solving was studied periodically, usually following a topic such as addition. Children worked with addition for a period of time, then were given word, or story, problems to solve using addition. About the only strategy children learned for solving problems was to use "cue" words. They learned that words like *altogether* and *total* usually indicated addition, and *difference* or *remainder* usually indicated subtraction. The relationship between problem solving in mathematics classes and elsewhere was vague or nonexistent.

In 1980 the National Council of Teachers of Mathematics shifted the focus from this narrow view to a much broader view in its *Agenda for Action: Recommendations for School Mathematics in the 1980s.* The NCTM placed problem solving at the top of the agenda. Other agencies soon followed this lead. In the mid-1980s, the California Department of Education said, "Instruction in mathematics must be planned to maximize each student's experience in solving challenging real-world and abstract problems."[6] In its most recent mathematics framework, the Texas Education Agency said, "The major focus of the mathematics program is to teach students to use mathematics to solve problems."[7] Problem solving became the most talked-about aspect of the mathematics curriculum.

The new view of problem solving led to changes in published materials and in the way problem solving is taught in many classrooms. The four-step problem-solving process developed by George Polya, of Stanford University, in his book *How to Solve It*[8] was simplified for children and was described and used in problem-solving activities in textbooks and other printed materials. The four steps are:

- Understanding the problem
- Devising a plan
- Carrying out the plan
- Looking back

Along with the Polya process a much wider variety of problem-solving strategies have been introduced. Today problem-solving activities with both routine and nonroutine problems frequently appear in textbooks. Activities are usually based on Polya's four steps and emphasize one or another of the problem-solving strategies so that children have frequent opportunities to learn and apply effective processes.

In the *Curriculum and Evaluation Standards for School Mathematics* the view of problem solving is broadened even further. Now problem solving is viewed *as* mathematics. It is through a problem-solving approach to all of the mathematics they learn that children acquire the understandings and skills they need in a technological society. Mathematics is not merely a collection of concepts and facts to be learned and then applied to the solution of problems, it *is* problem solving.

This view is explained by Thomas Schroeder and Frank Lester, Jr. They discuss three approaches to teaching problem solving: (1) teaching *about* problem solving, (2) teaching *for* problem solving, and (3) teaching *via* problem solving.[9] Teachers who use the first approach explain Polya's four-step problem-solving process and introduce strategies. Then they provide problems for children to solve. Children are taught to methodically apply the four-step process a step at a time and to be aware of where they are in the process. Problems may be solved independently or in small groups. Discussion of students' processes should follow completion of the problems. Teachers who use the second approach are continually aware of applications of the mathematics they are teaching. They use real-world situations to introduce children to new concepts and skills, and following development of the new work, in practice materials to emphasize applications. The Polya process and strategies are introduced and used. Connections between mathematics and the real world are made, but the emphasis is still on the mathematics that is being learned. With respect to the third approach, Schroeder and Lester explain that

> In teaching *via* problem solving, problems are valued not only as a purpose for learning mathematics but also as a primary means of doing so. The teaching of a mathematical topic begins with a problem situation that embodies key aspects of the topic, and mathematical techniques are developed as reasonable responses to reasonable problems. A goal of mathematics is to transform certain nonroutine problems into routine ones. The learning of mathematics in this way can be viewed as a movement from the concrete (a real-world problem that serves as an instance of the mathematical concept or technique) to the abstract (a symbolic representation of a class of problems and techniques for operating with these symbols).[10]

Further, Schroeder and Lester state that while the three approaches can be separated in theory, in practice they overlap. The first two approaches, if used more or less exclusively, narrow the focus of problem solving in the classroom. Therefore, they believe that the third approach is the most fruitful one. In the first two approaches the tendency is for the problem solver to move from the real-world situation to the mathematical world, where the problem is represented and solved mathematically, and then to return to the real world with its solution (Figure 5.1). In the third approach the problem solver moves from the real world to the mathematical world and back any number of times as a problem is solved. The arrows going upward in Figure 5.2 represent the process of abstraction and generalization, while the arrows going downward represent the process of returning to the real world to explain mathematical actions. The downward arrows might also suggest that the learner has returned to the real world for a model of the mathematical situation. Students in the early stages of learn-

Figure 5-1
A simplistic model of the process of solving mathematics problems (Thomas L. Schroeder and Frank K. Lester, Jr. 1989. Developing understanding in mathematics via problem solving. *New Directions for Elementary School Mathematics,* 1989 Yearbook, National Council of Teachers of Mathematics, 1989, 31–42.)

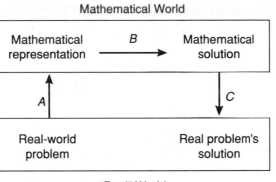

Figure 5-2
A model of the process of solving process problems (Thomas L. Schroeder and Frank K. Lester, Jr. 1989. Developing understanding in mathematics via problem solving. *New Directions for Elementary School Mathematics,* 1989 Yearbook, National Council of Teachers of Mathematics, 1989, 31–42.)

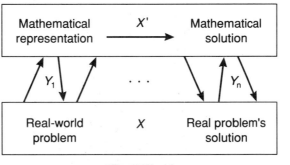

ing a new concept or skill will move between the two worlds frequently as they work. As the learner gains knowledge of concepts and skills, the processes become more routine and the actions are closer to those represented in Figure 5.1.[11]

The three vignettes at the beginning of Chapter 2 exemplify the learning of mathematics via problem solving. In the first classroom, children use toy bears to visualize and think about the meaning of subtraction. The third-grade class has a similar experience with more abstract, though just as meaningful, materials as they learn about regrouping with a subtraction algorithm. In each situation students move from the bears or cards (real world) to symbols (mathematical world) and back several times as they learn about subtraction. The fifth-grade class does not use concrete materials but does use a problem-solving approach to learn how to use compensation to subtract mentally. You will learn more about teaching mathematics as problem solving as you read about teaching specific topics in Part Three of this book.

■ PROBLEM-SOLVING STRATEGIES

When faced with a problem, a person must explore the situation and select appropriate materials and strategies to solve it. Teachers will make many of the selections and direct problem-solving processes until students learn concepts and strategies and develop computational skills. As children become more mature, they will select materials and strategies for themselves. Ten strategies are discussed in this chapter.

- Look for patterns.
- Use a model.
- Draw a picture or diagram.
- Act it out.
- Construct a table and/or graph.

- Guess and check.
- Account for all possibilities.
- Simplify or break into parts.
- Work backward.
- Break set or change point of view.

Look for Patterns

Patterns appear in many natural and person-made objects and situations. They are prominent in mathematics, so finding and using patterns has wide applicability in mathematical problem solving. Young children can find patterns in strings of beads, arrangements of blocks, and beats of a drum. Later, primary-grade children find and describe number patterns in sequences such as 0, 2, 4, 6, . . . ; 15, 20, 25, 30, . . . ; and 21, 18, 15, 12, ... Older students work with number patterns in more abstract and sophisticated ways.

Activity 5.1 is a teacher-led lesson in which kindergarten children investigate patterns in T-shirts. In Activity 5.2 older children use calculators to investigate number patterns and solve problems about them. A situation where more than one strategy may be used to solve a problem is illustrated in Activity 5.3. To solve it children might use wooden blocks (a model) to help find each pattern and then the pattern to solve the problem. Some of the activities in this chapter appear without solutions so that you may practice the strategies as you read. Answers and additional discussion of these problems are at the end of the chapter.

Number patterns similar to the ones in Activities 5.2 and 5.3 are used in a pair of computer programs called *The King's Rule* and *The Royal Rules*.[12] In both programs students figure out increasingly difficult number patterns to progress through a castle. In *The King's Rule* students generate and use working hypotheses by asking questions, trying new number combinations, and getting recaps of the data. With the discovery of each new pattern they advance toward the royal suite. *The Royal Rules* is an advanced version of the program in which students generate and test hypotheses and can create their own library of rules, save them, and challenge classmates to solve them.

ACTIVITY 5.1   T-Shirt Patterns

- Select a child who is wearing a T-shirt that has a simple design, such as one with alternate blue-and-white stripes. Have the child describe the shirt. Talk about the pattern.

- Select other children who have simple patterns on their shirts. Have each child describe the pattern on his or her shirt. Write words for patterns on the chalkboard, such as white, red, blue, white, red, blue, ...

- Tell each child to use crayons to draw a T-shirt and show its pattern.

- Show the children how letters can be used to represent a T-shirt's pattern. An alternating pattern can be represented as a-b-a-b-a-b- ··· and a three-color sequence as a-b-c-a-b-c-a-b-c- ··· . A narrow stripe that separates wider stripes is not counted as part of a pattern. A pattern of wide red, blue, and yellow stripes with narrow white stripes between colors is an a-b-c-a-b-c-a-b-c- ··· pattern.

- Write letter patterns such as a-b-c-d-a-b-c-d- ··· , a-b-a-c-a-b-a-c- ··· , and a-b-b-c-a-b-b-c- ··· on three-by-five cards, one pattern to a card. Give a card to each child. Each child is to use crayons to color the pattern for the letters on his or her card.

ACTIVITY 5.2   Arithmetic Patterns

- Write the first five even numbers on the chalkboard. Ask someone to write the next five numbers in the sequence after your numbers.

- Write the first five numbers of each of these sequences on the chalkboard and have a student write the next five for each sequence.

$$1, 3, 5, 7, 9, \ldots$$
$$3, 6, 9, 12, 15, \ldots$$
$$5, 10, 15, 20, 25, \ldots$$

- Ask, "What can you tell me about the first sequence?" "The second sequence?" "The third sequence?" Explain that a sequence that has a constant difference between each pair of numbers is called an *arithmetic (a rith MET ik) sequence*.

- Write the sequence 1, 2, 3, 4, 5, . . . on the chalkboard. Ask, "Is this an arithmetic sequence?" (Yes.) "How can you tell?" (The difference between each number is one.) "What is the hundredth number in this sequence?" (100.)

- Refer to the sequence of even numbers. Ask, "What is the hundredth number in this sequence?" Organize students into cooperative-learning groups and allow time for each group to answer the question. Let them use calculators if they wish. Discuss their solutions.

- Allow time for each of the groups to determine the hundredth number in one or more of the 1, 3, 5, . . . ; 3, 6, 9, . . . ; and 5, 10, 15, . . . sequences.

- Discuss the students' responses and procedures for determining each answer.

- Help the students express a general rule for determining any given number in an arithmetic sequence. (Do this only if their discussion suggests that they are ready to make such a generalization.)

ACTIVITY 5.3   Stacking Boxes

- Present this situation: A stock person in a grocery story made a display of boxes. The display was six boxes tall. Each layer formed a square. The single box on the top rested on four boxes. Each of these boxes rested on four boxes. This pattern was used to stack all of the boxes. How many boxes are in the display?

three cans, and each of the other cans rests on three.

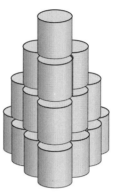

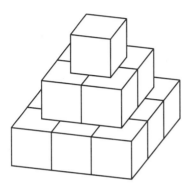

- Have students work in cooperative-learning groups to solve the problem. Suggest that they use wooden blocks to model the situation.

- Have students determine the number of cans in a six-high stack when the stack forms an equilateral triangle, the first can rests on

- Have each group explain its process for determining each of the answers.

- Have students determine the number of boxes in a square stack that is ten boxes high. Fifteen boxes high.

- Have students determine the number of cans in a triangular stack that is ten cans high. Fifteen cans high.

- Discuss the students' processes. Help them determine a general rule for each of the two types of stacks, if they are ready to do this.

Use a Model

Models abound in mathematics. Many of the learning aids illustrated in Chapter 3 are models that illustrate mathematical concepts and processes. Activities with the models offer many opportunities for children to deal with mathematics as problem solving. Models are also useful for solving many routine and nonroutine problems. Blocks that served as models of boxes aided in the solution to the problems in Activity 5.3, if students chose to use them. Other equally common materials can serve as models: disks for wheels, dried beans or blocks for people, and so on. Read Activity 5.4 to see some of the ways models are used to solve problems. Other sorts of problems are solved with models in Activities 5.5 and 5.6.

ACTIVITY 5.4   Some Birds

- Present this problem: Some birds flew overhead. One bird was behind two birds, one bird ahead of two birds, and one bird between two birds. How many birds flew overhead?

- Have children work in cooperative-learning groups to determine an answer. Suggest that if they use toy birds from their math kits they can make different arrangements of "birds" as they work.

- Have the groups demonstrate with models how they solved the problem.

- The arrangement shows that one bird is ahead of two birds, one bird is behind two birds, and one bird is between two birds.

- Here are similar problems to solve with models:
  —Five robots are walking in a parade. Bocko is 25 meters ahead of Rocko. Locko is 10 meters behind Bocko. Mocko is 5 meters behind Locko. Mocko is 15 meters behind Socko. In what order were the robots walking?

  —Six aliens stepped out of their spaceship. Alien 1 leaves first. Alien 3 is ahead of alien 6; alien 2 is behind alien 5; alien 4 is ahead of alien 5 and behind alien 6. In which order did the aliens leave their spaceship?

ACTIVITY 5.5   Rows and Rows

Present this problem: My sister was fooling around with her money the other night and left the coins in a pattern of four coins in each row. Each row had exactly one penny, one nickel, one dime, and one quarter; no row, either horizontal or vertical, had more than one coin of each kind. How were the coins arranged?[13]

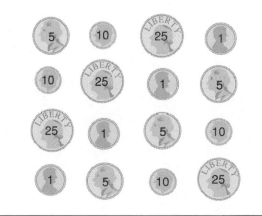

- Have children work in pairs with coin models to solve the problem.

- Discuss the students' solutions.

- Here are similar problems that can be solved with models:
  —My neighbor has a peculiar orchard. He has five apple trees, five peach trees, five pear trees, five apricot trees, and five plum trees. The trees are planted in a square of five rows of five trees each. Each row (in each direction) has exactly one tree of each variety and so do the center diagonals.[14]

  —Another neighbor had ten trees that she planted in five rows of four trees each. How did she do this?

  —How can you use six new lead pencils to form four congruent equilateral triangles?

ACTIVITY 5.6 Wheels

- Present this problem: I counted 7 cycle riders and 19 cycle wheels go past my house one morning. On how many cycles were the riders as they passed my house?[15]

- Ask, "Could all of the riders have been on bicycles?" (No.) "How do you know?" (There were 7 riders and 19 wheels. If they had all been on bicycles there would have been 14 wheels, assuming there were no tandem riders.) "What other types of cycles could there be?" (Unicycles, tricycles.)

- Have the students work in cooperative-learning groups to solve the problem.

- Have the students demonstrate and discuss their processes.

- Use disks on a magnetic board to demonstrate how a model can help solve the problem.

- Here are similar problems that can be solved with the same models:
  —Sara saw 10 cycle riders and 22 wheels pass her house. How many cycles did she see?
  —There were 10 vehicles on a ferryboat. Some were cars, some were motorcycles, and some were motorcycles with sidecars. If there were 18 wheels, what combinations of vehicles could there have been?

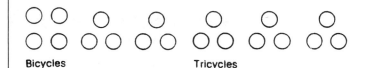

Bicycles   **Tricycles**

Draw a Picture or Diagram

Pictures and diagrams serve the same role as models; they help students visualize problems. A picture or diagram can show relationships among various parts of a problem and may suggest a process for solving it. They are especially helpful in solving complex, or multistep, problems. In the following examples, a variety of pictures and diagrams are illustrated. Simple line drawings are used in Activity 5.7. In Activity 5.8 tree diagrams are suggested, while in Activity 5.9 Venn diagrams are used.

ACTIVITY 5.7   Using Pictures

- Tell the students that a road sign appears at the city limits of the town of Adamsville.

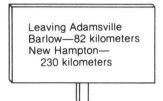

Leaving Adamsville
Barlow—82 kilometers
New Hampton—
    230 kilometers

- Ask, "How far will you travel before you reach the rest stop that is halfway between Barlow and New Hampton?"[16]

- Have students work in cooperative-learning groups to solve the problem. Suggest that they draw a picture to illustrate the situation.

- Here are other problems that can be solved with pictures:
  —Abdul lives 2-1/2 miles from school; Juan lives on the same street and 1-3/4 miles from school. How far apart do the two boys live from each other?

  —A baker rolled a piece of dough into a 15-inch by 18-inch rectangle. She cut the rectangle into three-inch by five-inch loaves. How many loaves did she make? If each loaf was laid end to end, how long would the row be?

  —An elevator stopped at the middle floor of a building. It then moved up three floors and stopped. It moved down five floors, then went up eight floors, where it stopped two floors below the top floor. How many floors does the building have?

230 kilometers
82 kilometers   *148 kilometers*

Adamsville   Barlow   New Hampton

- Discuss the students' pictures and solutions. The drawing shows that it is 148 kilometers from Barlow to New Hampton. Half that distance is 74 kilometers. Add 74 to 82 to determine the distance to go from Adamsville to be halfway between the two towns.

ACTIVITY 5.8   Tree Diagrams

- Introduce this situation: Eight schools had a softball tournament. Teams that won continued in the competition; those that lost were out. How many games were played before the winner was determined?

- Allow time for pairs of children to determine the answer. Have pairs of children who used different ways of solving the problem demonstrate and explain their procedures. Discuss how a tree diagram is useful to show how the tournament was conducted.   *(continued)*

Activity 5.8   *continued*

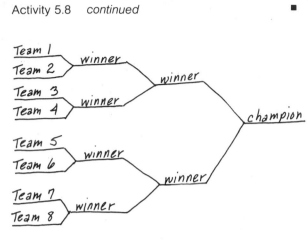

■ Here is another problem that can be solved with a tree diagram:

—In a tournament teams or individuals are often *seeded*. This means that they are listed in order from best to worst according to some standard, such as their records during a season. The best rated team or person is the no. 1 seed, the second rated is the no. 2 seed, and so on down to the worst team or person, which is no. 16 if there are that many teams or players. Sixteen tennis players competed in a tournament in which to lose meant to leave the tournament. How many matches were played? How many matches did the winner play?

ACTIVITY 5.9   Venn Diagrams

■ Present this problem: John and Joe owned four dogs jointly. John owned three himself. Altogether they had 12 dogs in a kennel. How many did each have?[17]

■ Allow time for pairs of students to determine the answer, using whatever process they wish.

■ Demonstrate and discuss how a Venn diagram can be used. Explain that "3" in the left circle indicates the dogs owned by John, "4" in both circles indicates the dogs the boys owned together, and "5" in the right circle represents the dogs owned by Joe. Point out that the sum of the numbers is 12, the number of dogs.

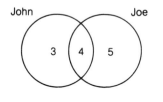

■ Here are other problems that can be solved with Venn diagrams:

—The 32 students in Ms. Markham's class were polled to see whether they liked pizza best or hamburgers best. Twenty children said they liked pizza, and 24 said they liked hamburgers. Obviously, some children could not choose just one and said they liked both pizza and hamburgers equally. How many children gave that answer?

—A math teacher conducted a survey of her classes. Forty-two students chewed gum in class; 55 talked incessantly; while 25 fell asleep during class. Four people both talked and fell asleep but didn't chew gum. Six students fell asleep and chewed gum but at least didn't talk. Forty students only talked. Ten students talked and chewed gum but didn't fall asleep. How many students were there in all? How many students talked and chewed gum and fell asleep (UGH)?[18]

Act It Out

The acting-out strategy is different from dramatization or simulation. Children who dramatize perform in a real-world or fantasy situation without solving a problem. In the primary grades children may dramatize a buying situation when they make "purchases" at a make-believe classroom store stocked with empty food and household product containers. Older children simulate a banking situation when they earn credits for accurate and on-time work, good behavior, courtesy, and so on, and "deposit" these credits in a classroom "bank." The credits are "withdrawn" to buy free time, school supplies, and other desired objects. Both situations give children opportunities to learn worthwhile consumer skills, but they solve no mathematical problems.

The acting-out strategy solves a problem, is often spontaneous, and is usually not very elaborate. Consider the situations in Activity 5.10. What props, if any, are needed for each one?

ACTIVITY 5.10   Acting It Out

- Present this situation: Cookies are sold singly and in packages containing three or six cookies. In what ways can a person buy one dozen cookies?

- Have two children role play the situation. When they have demonstrated one way to buy a dozen cookies, have another pair demonstrate a different way. Have other pairs of children role play until all combinations have been determined. (A written record will help children keep track of the combinations as they work.)

- Have children count the different ways of buying cookies.

- Here are other problems that can be solved by the act-it-out strategy:
  —Juanita shared a bag of 15 peanuts with friends. As the bag was passed around, each person took one. Juanita took the first and the last peanuts, and may have taken some in between. Including Juanita, how many children could have been in the group?

  —A woman bought a horse for $40. She then sold the horse for $50. Later, she bought the horse back for $60. She was offered $70 for the horse, which she accepted. How much money did she earn or lose on her transactions?

Record for cookie purchases

12 cookies	1	3	6
M & B	12	0	0
J & J	0	4	0
C & Z	0	0	2
L & H	3	3	0
M & M	6	0	1
T & D	6	2	0
B & T	9	1	0
K & M	3	1	1

Construct a Table and/or Graph

The handling of data is an important part of many occupations. An architect uses data about a new building's occupants to plan rooms, furnishings, and safety features; an insurance actuary uses data about births, deaths, ages, occupations, and places of residence to establish insurance rates; and a shipping agent uses data about production schedules, product destinations, weather, highway distances, and truck capacities to plan shipping schedules.

The data with which children deal is less complex than that in the examples above. Nevertheless, opportunities abound for children to deal with data in problems that are important to them. There are situations where a table is used to solve a problem. One such situation is shown in Activity 5.10, where a table was used to keep track of cookie combinations. Examples of other situations are in Activity 5.11. In some situations data are

---

ACTIVITY 5.11   Solving Problems with Tables

- Present this situation: Lana had 17 cents. What is the smallest number of coins she could have?

- Have children work in cooperative-learning groups to solve this problem.

- Have each group share its procedure with other students. They may suggest several

Pennies	Nickels	Dimes
17	0	0
12	1	0
7	2	0
2	3	0
7	0	1
2	1	1

combinations that they tried. If one or more groups made a table, have them show it. If none did, draw this table on the chalkboard and have the children help you fill it in.

- Point out that the combination of two pennies, one nickel, and one dime is the one with the fewest coins in it.

- Here are some other problems that can be solved by using tables:

—Kareem had 16 stools. There were 55 legs on all of the stools. There were more three-legged stools than four-legged stools. What is the smallest number of three-legged stools he could have?

—Beverley made papercraft flowers to sell at a school bazaar. Some flowers required three sheets of paper and others required four sheets of paper. When she was finished she found she had used 28 pieces of paper. What different combinations of birds could she have made?

more easily interpreted when they are represented by a graph. In Activity 5.12 primary-grade children make a graph of their favorite ice creams. Older students use a table and graph to solve a problem involving speed and distance in Activity 5.13.

ACTIVITY 5.12   Our Favorite Ice Creams

- Tell the children that you want to know each one's favorite ice cream. "When I call on you, you tell me your favorite ice cream; I will give you a paper rectangle that is the same color as your ice cream." Give a brown square for chocolate, a pink square for strawberry, and so on.

- After the squares are distributed, make a table that shows the poll's results.

Our Favorite Ice Cream						
Chocolate	Vanilla	Strawberry	Rocky Road	Almond Mocha	Banana	Miscellaneous
////	///////	///	////////	///	//	////

- After the table is completed, have the children paste their squares in columns by color on a large piece of butcher paper on which a baseline has been marked. Caution them against leaving gaps or having pieces overlap. Write the name of the ice cream represented by each color beneath the column.

Ask questions like: "Which ice cream is most popular?" "Which ice creams are equally popular?" "How many fewer children like chocolate ice cream than like rocky road ice cream?"

- Other subjects for primary-grade tables and graphs are: eye colors, shoe styles, numbers of brothers and sisters, pets.

Graph for ice cream table

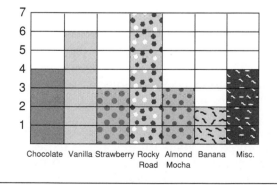

Chocolate Vanilla Strawberry Rocky Road Almond Mocha Banana Misc.

ACTIVITY 5.13   How Far?

- Present this situation: Amiko rode in a cyclethon to raise money for a charity. She bicycled at an average speed of six miles each hour. How far did she go if it took her eight hours to complete the cyclethon?

- Help the students make a table to show the distances she traveled during the eight-hour ride.

- Project a blank graph on a screen. Show the students how to indicate the hours Amiko rode across the bottom and the miles she rode up the left side. Mark the point where the first hour and six miles intersect to show the results of the first hour's ride. Ask, "Where will the mark for the second hour's ride go?" "The third hour's ride?" and so on.

Amiko's Ride								
Hours	1	2	3	4	5	6	7	8
Distance	6	12	18	24	30	36	42	48

- Use the graph to answer questions like these:
  —How far did Amiko ride in four hours?
  —How far did she ride in two and a half hours?
  —If she had ridden for nine hours, how far would she have cycled?

- Here are other problems that can be solved with this type of graph:
  —Milton made a braided key chain from thin strips of leather. If he braided one inch every two minutes, how many inches did he braid in fourteen minutes?
  —Carol practiced ballet for three-fourths of an hour each day. How many hours did she practice in one week?

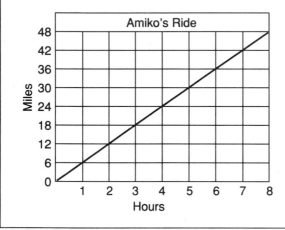

Guess and Check

This strategy is dependent on the problem solver using reason to make responsible guesses. A responsible guess is one that considers the critical parts of a problem; blind or wild guesses are not acceptable. Once a guess has been made it is checked against the demands of the problem. Sometimes the original guess solves the problems; many times it needs to be refined until the problem is solved. Each of the problems in Activity 5.14 can be solved with the guess-and-check strategy. Name another strategy that you would recommend be used along with guess-and-check for each problem.

ACTIVITY 5.14   Guess and Check

- Introduce this problem: How can you arrange the numbers 1, 2, 3, 4, 5, and 6 around this triangle so that the sum along each side is 9?

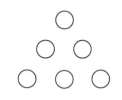

- Have children work in pairs using six pieces of paper, each marked with one of the numbers. Check triangles as students finish; challenge early finishers to see if they can find a second arrangement that also works.

- Have students share their arrangements and discuss their procedures.

- Challenge the children to make arrangements with the same six numbers that have the sums of 10, 11, and 12 along each side.

- Here are other problems that can be solved by the guess-and-check strategy.
  —Hiroko took a bag of coins when she went shopping. She spent 79 cents. What is the largest number of coins she could have used? What is the smallest number she could have used? What are three ways she could have used between ten and fifteen coins for her purchase?

  —A pair of numbers has a product of 144 and a quotient of 4. What are the two numbers?

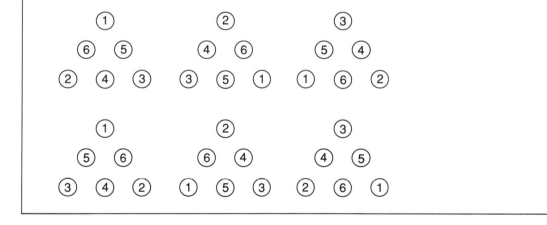

Account for All Possibilities

George Lenchner uses the expression "making an organized list" to identify this strategy. He says, "A useful problem solving strategy is organizing information into some type of list, a technique that may serve a variety of pur-

poses. When a problem requires you to generate a large amount of data, a
list may help you account for all possibilities and avoid repetitions."[19] Examples that can be solved with this strategy are in Activity 5.15.

ACTIVITY 5.15   Account for All Possibilities

Present this situation: A school has a "fish" pond
that contains four magnetized "fish." One fish has
a "2" on its bottom; the others have a "4," "6," or "8."
You pay 25 cents to catch four fish. Each time you
catch a fish you note its number and return it to the
pond. Prizes are awarded for the four highest
scores. What scores will win you a prize? What
other scores can you get?

Fish Pond

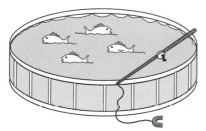

■ Have children work in cooperative-learning
groups to determine the answer. Tell them
to make models of the fish and work out a
scheme to keep track of all possible scores.

■ Have students explain how they solved the
problem and give their answers.

■ If no students used an organized list to account for all possibilities, prepare a list with
students' help.

■ Discuss the list to emphasize how it accounts for all possibilities.

■ Here are other problems for which this strategy is useful.
—An ice cream parlor has four flavors of ice
cream and six flavors of topping. Are there
enough combinations of ice cream and
topping so that 19 children can each have
a different sundae?

—Antonio needed 33 pounds of dog food. A
5-pound bag cost $2.49 and a 12-pound
bag cost $5.46. What combination of bags
will give him at least 33 pounds of dog
food for the best possible price?

Organized list

No #8 Fish	One #8 Fish	Two #8 Fish	Three #8 Fish	Four #8 Fish
2 + 2 + 2 + 2	2 + 2 + 2 + 8	2 + 2 + 8 + 8	2 + 8 + 8 + 8	8 + 8 + 8 + 8
2 + 2 + 2 + 4	2 + 2 + 4 + 8	2 + 4 + 8 + 8	4 + 8 + 8 + 8	
2 + 2 + 4 + 4	2 + 4 + 4 + 8	4 + 4 + 8 + 8	6 + 8 + 8 + 8	
2 + 4 + 4 + 4	4 + 4 + 4 + 8	4 + 6 + 8 + 8		
4 + 4 + 4 + 4	4 + 4 + 6 + 8	6 + 6 + 8 + 8		
4 + 4 + 4 + 6	4 + 6 + 6 + 8			
4 + 4 + 6 + 6	6 + 6 + 6 + 6			
4 + 6 + 6 + 6				
6 + 6 + 6 + 6				

Simplify or Break into Parts

Sometimes a problem seems overwhelming because of the size of the numbers or its complexity. When this is true, simplifying the problem may help solve it. One way to simplify a problem is to break it into parts, or to begin at a less complex level. The problem developed in Activity 5.16 involves eight people, but by simplifying it the solution becomes clear and can be determined by using a pattern. The activity has two additional problems that can be solved by breaking them into parts.

ACTIVITY 5.16   Simplifying Problems

- Present this situation: Eight girls rode on each of the rides at an amusement park. By day's end, each girl had taken one ride with each of the other girls. How many rides did the girls take that day?

- Discuss the situation with the students to make certain it is clear. Ask, "What does it mean when it says that each girl had taken a ride with each of the other girls?" "Would simplifying the problem help you understand the problem better?" "How can you simplify it?" "How many rides would be taken if two girls went to the park?" "Three girls?" "Four girls?"

- Make a record of the rides.

- Ask, "Is there a pattern in the way the numbers that show rides increase?" (The increase for each pair is one more than the increase for the preceding pair.) "How can we use that information to determine the number of amusement rides for eight people?" (We can extend the pattern to show rides for eight people.)

- If the discussion indicates that the children are ready to make a general rule for finding the number of rides for any number of people, help them do it.

2 girls	girl 1 with girl 2
3 girls	girl 1 with girl 2
	girl 1 with girl 3
	girl 2 with girl 3
4 girls	girl 1 with girl 2
	girl 1 with girl 3
	girl 1 with girl 4
	girl 2 with girl 3
	girl 2 with girl 4
	girl 3 with girl 4

5 girls	girl 1 with girl 2
	girl 1 with girl 3
	girl 1 with girl 4
	girl 1 with girl 5
	girl 2 with girl 3
	girl 2 with girl 4
	girl 2 with girl 5
	girl 3 with girl 4
	girl 3 with girl 5
	girl 4 with girl 5

- Demonstrate how a table can organize the data and help solve the problem.

No. of girls	2	3	4	5	6	7	8
No. of rides	1	3	6	10	?	?	?

(continued)

Activity 5.16   *continued*

■ Here are other problems that can be solved by breaking them into parts or simplifying them.
—Find the area of the plane figure.

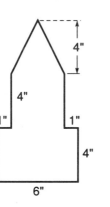

—Postal boxes in a post office are numbered from 1000 to 1200. How many of the box numbers contain the numeral "3"?

Work Backward

When only the conditions that exist at the end of a problem are known, it is necessary to work backward to find the beginning conditions and solve the problem. All through children's problem-solving experiences the need for carefully analyzing each problem should be emphasized. This emphasis pays off when children deal with problems that must be solved backward. It is critical that children determine the conditions that are known and those that they must determine by working backward. A puzzle is used to develop this strategy in Activity 5.17.

ACTIVITY 5.17   Working Backward

■ Present this situation: I found this puzzle in one of my books. It says,
"Pick a number, triple it, add three, double the result, subtract six, divide by three."
When I did it to a number, my answer was 12. What was my beginning number?

■ Discuss the problem. Ask questions: "What are you to find?" (The number that started the puzzle.) "What do you know?" (The answer and what was done to the number.) "What can we do to find the number?" Help the students see that by completing the steps backward and using inverse operations, they can undo what was done to the original number.

Activity 5.17   *continued*

■ Show how diagrams are useful for illustrat-
    ing this problem. The steps used to solve
    the problem are shown in the first diagram.
    The second diagram shows the steps for the
    original puzzle.

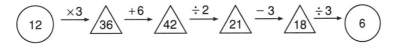

Solution

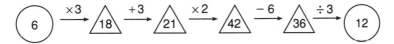

Original problem

■ Here are other problems that can be solved
    by working backward.
    —Chen took $20 to the grocery store. He
      bought a chicken for $2.09, celery for
      $0.79, milk for $1.02, and some bread. He
      received $14.42 change. How much did
      the bread cost?

    —A scout troop had six more 13-year-old
      members than 12-year-old members. At
      one meeting there were eight 13-year-old

    members present. They were one-half of
    the 13-year-olds. How many 12-year-old
    members were in the troop?

    —The sixth-grade class at Bayview School
      sold cupcakes at a carnival and collected
      $50. They sold single cupcakes for 25
      cents and packages of three for 50 cents.
      They collected $30 for the sale of single
      cupcakes. How many cupcakes did they
      sell?

Change Your Point of View

Changing your point of view is less of a strategy than it is a way of thinking.
What did you visualize as you began to solve the problem about ten trees
planted in five rows or the six pencils making four equilateral triangles in
Activity 5.5? How did you approach each of these problems? Did you think
about each one in a *conventional* way? If so, were you able to change your
mind-set so you could visualize each situation in a new way, or were you
stymied and unable to complete the problems? Activity 5.18 presents two
more problems about which you may need to change your point of view
before you can solve them.

It must be clear by now that there are few times when a problem is solved by
a single strategy. The ten strategies were separated for discussion, but in

---

ACTIVITY 5.18   Change Your Point of View?

■ Draw four lines to connect all of the dots. You may not lift your pencil from the paper once you begin your drawing.

    ● ● ●
    ● ● ●
    ● ● ●

■ Show how you can make a square that has an area of two units on dot paper. Make a

square with an area of five units on dot paper.

---

practice combinations of strategies are used to solve most problems. Teachers should keep the following points in mind as they present strategies to children.

■ Most of the strategies can be used to solve a variety of problems.

■ A problem may be solved in several ways. It is usually not necessary to employ a particular strategy for a given type of problem.

■ A child will not reach the same level of sophistication in using each strategy. Neither will all children reach the same level of sophistication in using a given strategy.

■ During the time students are learning to use strategies, processes of selecting and employing strategies are as important as correctly solving problems. Students should receive credit for choosing and using appropriate strategies, even when their solutions are not correct.

■ During their years in school, all students should learn each of the strategies and apply them to a variety of problems. By the time they complete the sixth grade, students should have skills to confidently tackle a variety of problems in and out of school.

EXERCISE   Indicate the problem-solving strategies with which you were most familiar at the time you read this chapter. Are any of the strategies in this chapter new to you? If so, which ones? Do you believe some strategies are more important than others? If so, which ones? Why?

CLASSROOM PROBLEMS

Alert teachers will be aware of the many opportunities that arise in the course of a school year for students to have realistic problem-solving experiences. The following are examples of common situations that can be used to give children experiences in applying processes and problem-solving strategies.

- A class needs sashes for a school program. Each sash has three stripes of different-colored material, and each stripe is four inches wide and forty-eight inches long. How many sashes are needed? How many yards of each color of material are needed? What is the cost of one yard of material? What will be the cost of all of the sashes?

- Two computers are in the classroom. What is the best way to schedule children's use of the computers so that everybody has an equal opportunity to use them with the least interruption of other activities?

- A class will sell pizzas at a Parent's Night program. How much will materials for one pizza cost? How many slices can be cut from one pizza? What is the fairest price to charge for one slice to make a reasonable profit? How many slices will need to be sold in order to buy a copy of *The King's Rule* computer program? How many pizzas will be needed?

- A science project dealing with the growth of plants under varying light conditions will be conducted. What measurements will need to be made? How frequently should the measurements be made? What types of records should be maintained? How should the results of the project be reported?

- A new surface is to be put down on the school's playground; all of the old markings for games will be covered. What game spaces should be laid out on the new surface? What is the best way to lay out the spaces to economize on space and provide for the least possible interference among players of different games? How much paint will be needed? How much will the paint and painting equipment cost?

- A class is investigating climatic changes in its region of the country. What is the average monthly rainfall for the past five years? How do these averages compare with the same averages for the past 100 years? Does it appear that the average for any given month has changed? Make the same comparisons for temperature. What, if any, climatic changes appear to have taken place over the past 100 years?

- A class is studying nutrition as part of a health unit. What number of calories is recommended for girls the age of those in the class? For boys? What distribution of calories by food groups is recommended? What is the average daily intake of calories of each child in the class? How are the calories for each child distributed among the food groups? By how much does each child's calorie intake vary from what is recommended?

■ SUMMARY

The importance of problem solving in a comprehensive mathematics program cannot be overstated. The view of the role of problem solving in the curriculum has evolved from one where mathematics was taught so that individuals could learn to solve problems to one where problem solving permeates the entire program. In its statement about standards for school mathematics, the National Council of Teachers of Mathematics maintains that problem solving *is* mathematics. According to this view, all children should learn mathematics through problem solving.

Textbooks and other published materials emphasize problem solving to a greater extent than ever before. In many classrooms, children learn George Polya's four-step problem-solving process and use it as they learn a variety of strategies. The four steps are: (1) understand the problem, (2) devise a plan, (3) carry out the plan, and (4) look back, or review the problem and its solution. Ten problem-solving strategies are discussed: (1) look for patterns, (2) use a model, (3) draw a picture or diagram, (4) act it out, (5) construct a table and/or graph, (6) guess and check, (7) account for all possibilities, (8) simplify or break into parts, (9) work backward, and (10) break set or change point of view. In practice it is seldom that a single strategy is used to solve a problem; usually a combination of strategies is used. During the time children are in elementary school they should have frequent opportunities to work with the ten strategies with a variety of problems. One primary goal of mathematics is to give each child skills and confidence to deal with problems both in and out of school.

Teachers should avail themselves of real problems in school or in the classroom that require students to use mathematics. Health, art, science, and fund-raising projects often contain problems that require a mathematical solution.

■ DISCUSSION AND ANSWERS TO PROBLEMS

Look for Patterns—Discussion

Number patterns for elementary school students should not be too complex. Arithmetic patterns (Activity 5.2) and addition patterns (Activity 5.3) are suitable for most students. Some multiplication patterns can also be used. You may be familiar with this one: "A person works for 1 cent the first day on the job, has the pay increased to 2 cents the second day, 4 cents the third day, 8 cents the fourth day, and so on. How much does the person earn on the twentieth day on the job?" (Use a calculator to solve this problem!)

ACTIVITY 5.2   Arithmetic Patterns

The hundredth number in the 1, 2, 3, 4, 5, . . . , sequence is 100.
The hundredth number in the 1, 3, 5, 7, 9, . . . , sequence is 199.
The hundredth number in the 3, 6, 9, 12, 15, . . . , sequence is 300.
The hundredth number in the 5, 10, 15, 20, 25, . . . , sequence is 500.

0	1	3	5	7	9	11	13	15	17	19		

$1 + (2 \times 0) = 1$
$1 + (2 \times 1) = 3$
$1 + (2 \times 2) = 5$
$1 + (2 \times 3) = 7$
$1 + (2 \times 4) = 9$

Children will probably use a calculator to determine the hundredth term in each sequence. This done, the problem will end for many children. For students who are ready to move on to determine a general rule for finding a given term in a sequence, a number line may be helpful. The number line shows that each number is two greater than the preceding number (except for 0 and 1). In the pattern beneath the line, 1 is shown as $1 + (0 \times 2) = 1$. The "2" represents the difference, or constant, between each term, while the "0" shows that 2 was not added to the one. Three is shown as $1 + (2 \times 1) = 3$ because it is one 2 greater than one; five is shown as $5 = 1 + (2 \times 2)$ because it is two 2s greater than one. The pattern continues with $7 = 1 + (2 \times 3)$, $9 = 1 + (2 \times 4)$, and so on. When you omit the starting number in a sequence, 1 in this case, the 99th number is the 100th term. Thus the hundredth term in the sequence of odd numbers must be $1 + (2 \times 99)$, or 199. The general rule for finding the 100th term is $1 + (c \times 99) = n$, where c is the constant and n is the number.

ACTIVITY 5.3   Stacking Boxes

These problems contain addition patterns, but the terms do not increase by a constant value as they do in an arithmetic pattern. A table to develop each pattern is a useful way to solve the problems. The table for the stack of boxes shows that the number in each layer is the square of its position in the stack. Therefore the general rule is $n = l^2$, where n is the number of boxes and l is the number of the layer.

Layer	1	2	3	4	5	6
Boxes	1	4	9	16	25	?

The table for the cans shows that beginning with 3, the number is the sum of consecutive

Layer	1	2	3	4	5	6
Cans	1	3	6	10	15	?

$1 = 1$
$1 + 2 = 3$
$1 + 2 + 3 = 6$
$1 + 2 + 3 + 4 = 10$
$1 + 2 + 3 + 4 + 5 = 15$

(continued)

Activity 5.3   *continued*

whole numbers. This is verified in the sentences beneath the table. In the second layer, there are two cans along each side; three is the sum of the first two consecutive whole numbers, 1 + 2. The next layer has three cans on a side; the number of cans is 1 + 2 + 3, or 6. This pattern leads to the general rule $n(n + 1) \div 2$, where *n* is the number of cans along one side of the stack.

The numbers in the first problem are called *square* numbers and those in the second problem are called *triangular* numbers.

Many students who understand how to use tables or calculators to solve number-pattern problems will not fully understand how a general rule is developed from a pattern. A teacher must use judgment in how sophisticated to make the work for children and not try to go too far with ones who are not mature enough to understand general rules.

Use a Model—Discussion

Any object can be a model for a problem-solving situation. Realistic materials are better for younger children, while more abstract representations can be used with older ones. Models are superior to drawings for some problems because they can be moved about to make new arrangements. Children frequently become discouraged when they see many erasures or marked-out trials. Models leave no "record" of mistakes, so children are less prone to give up. The materials used in Activities 5.4 through 5.6 are representative of the models children can use.

ACTIVITY 5.4   Some Birds

Toy birds from a math kit were used as models for the first problem. If birds are not in the kits, change the characters to bears, or dogs, or whatever else is available.

Toy robots, or other characters, can be arranged to solve the robot problem.

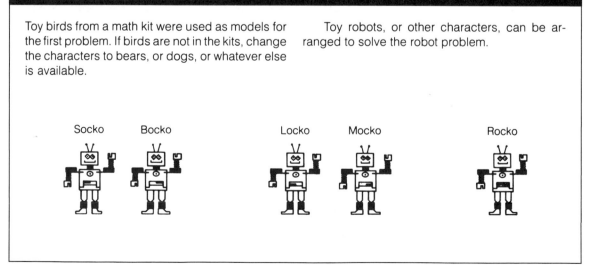

Socko   Bocko   Locko   Mocko   Rocko

Activity 5.4   *continued*

Alien "critters" can model the third situation.

ACTIVITY 5.5   Rows and Rows

Toy money, of course, is the natural model for the coin problem. Colored blocks or disks, one color for each type of tree, can model the tree problems. Give children unsharpened pencils or short dowels to model the final problem. Note that with the last two problems it may be necessary to change your point of view, or "break set," before you can solve each one.

Here is one arrangement for the 25 trees.*

Apple	Plum	Peach	Pear	Apricot
Apricot	Peach	Apple	Plum	Pear
Plum	Apricot	Pear	Peach	Apple
Pear	Apple	Plum	Apricot	Peach
Peach	Pear	Apricot	Apple	Plum

The ten trees are arranged in a star-shaped pattern, not in conventional rows.

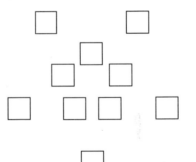

The six pencils form a pyramid (tetrahedron) to make four equilateral triangles.

*Adapted from Carol Meyer and Tom Sallee. 1983. *Make It Simpler: A Practical Guide to Problem Solving in Mathematics.* Menlo Park, CA: Addison-Wesley, 79. Copyright 1983. Used by permission of the publisher.

ACTIVITY 5.6   Wheels

Plastic disks are good models for "bicycles," "tri-cycles," and other vehicles for these problems. Here are solutions for the two problems.

First illustration of wheels

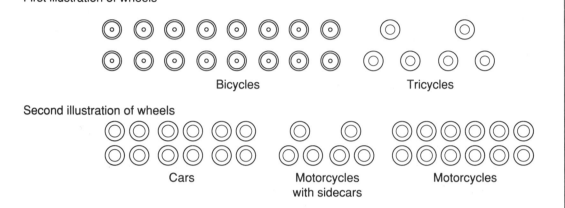

Bicycles   Tricycles

Second illustration of wheels

Cars   Motorcycles with sidecars   Motorcycles

Draw a Picture or Diagram— Discussion

The pictures used to solve the problems in Activity 5.7 illustrate the simplicity of this strategy. Elaborate pictures or drawings are not necessary. Tree and Venn diagrams are special kinds of diagrams that apply to a variety of situations. The ones shown in Activities 5.8 and 5.9 are typical of their uses.

ACTIVITY 5.7   Using Pictures

The road-sign situation is discussed in the original problem. A drawing of the school situation indicates that there are two solutions. The problem does not state that the two students live on the same side of the school. If they do, the first drawing illustrates the situation and shows that the houses are three-quarters of a mile apart. However, if the houses are on opposite sides of the school, as shown in the second drawing, they are four and one-quarter miles apart.

Activity 5.7   *continued*

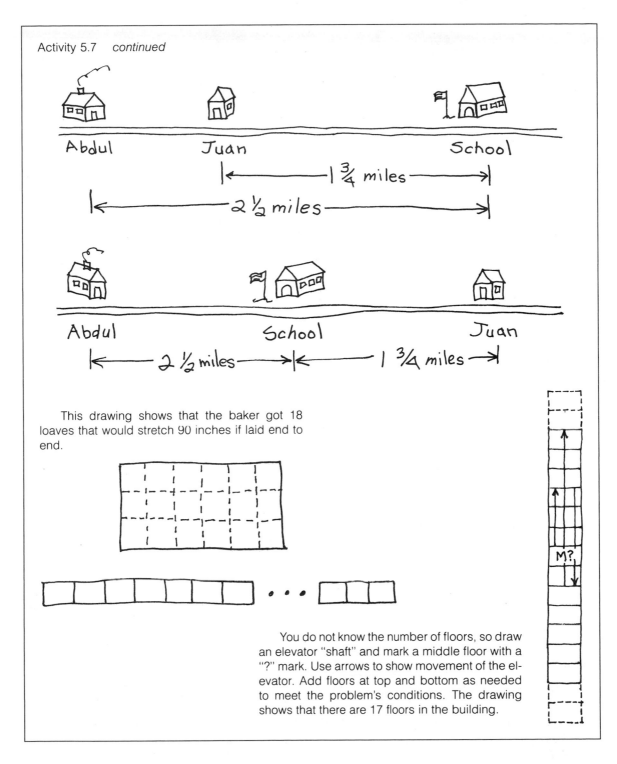

Abdul   Juan   School

|←———— 1 ¾ miles ————→|

|←———————— 2 ½ miles ————————→|

Abdul   School   Juan

|←——— 2 ½ miles ———→|←——— 1 ¾ miles —→|

This drawing shows that the baker got 18 loaves that would stretch 90 inches if laid end to end.

You do not know the number of floors, so draw an elevator "shaft" and mark a middle floor with a "?" mark. Use arrows to show movement of the elevator. Add floors at top and bottom as needed to meet the problem's conditions. The drawing shows that there are 17 floors in the building.

ACTIVITY 5.8 Tree Diagrams

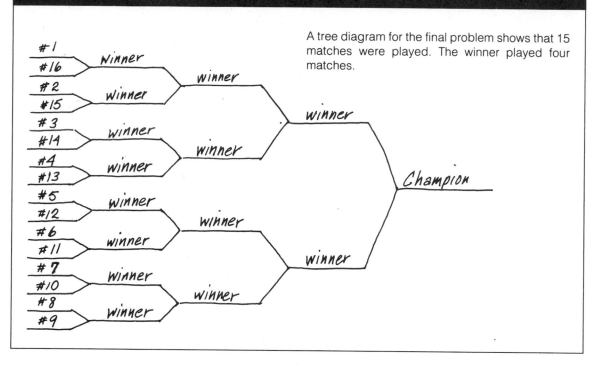

A tree diagram for the final problem shows that 15 matches were played. The winner played four matches.

ACTIVITY 5.9 Venn Diagrams

A two-circle diagram is used to solve the first classroom situation. The guess-and-check strategy can be used to determine the number of students who liked only pizza, only hamburgers, or who liked both.

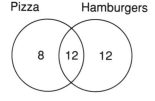

Use a three-circle diagram to solve the second classroom problem. First fill in the information you know for certain (underlined in the diagram).

Once this information is in place, use it to determine the unknown information. The known information accounts for 54 of the talkers (40 + 10 + 4 = 54). This tells you that there is only one student who talks, chews gum, and sleeps. Once you know this, you can determine the number of students who only sleep or only chew gum.

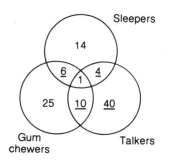

Act It Out—Discussion

Most students enjoy solving problems with this strategy; it involves action, which is not always a part of other strategies. Because no records are made at the time actions take place, children should be encouraged to make a drawing or diagram to illustrate results when the acting-it-out strategy is used, as in Activity 5.10.

ACTIVITY 5.10   Acting It Out

The drawings show that there is more than one solution to the problem of how many children could share peanuts with Juanita.

Juanita   Friend

1-3-5-7-9-11-13-15   2-4-6-8-10-12-14

Peanuts

Juanita	Friend 1	Friend 2	Friend 3	Friend 4	Friend 5	Friend 6
1	2	3	4	5	6	7
8	9	10	11	12	13	14
15						

Peanuts

Juanita	Friend 1	Friend 2	Friend 3	Friend 4	Friend 5	Friend 6	Friend 7
1	2	3	4	5	6	7	8
15							

Friend 8	Friend 9	Friend 10	Friend 11	Friend 12	Friend 13
9	10	11	12	13	14

Peanuts

The woman must have had $40 with which to make the original purchase. She made a profit of $10 from the first sale. Then she spent the original $40, her $10 profit, and another $10 to buy it back. The final sale returned $70. Her profit is the difference between her own $50 and the $70, or $20.

(continued)

Activity 5.10 *continued*

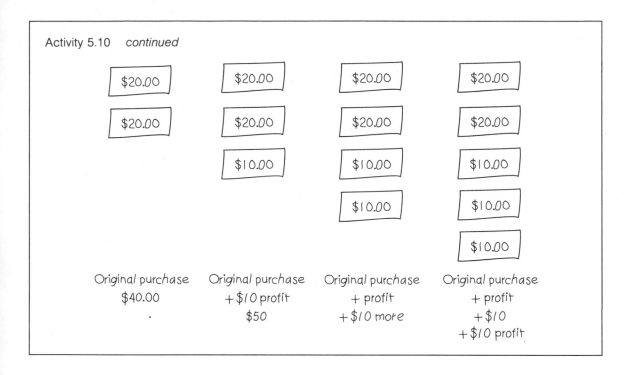

| Original purchase $40.00 | Original purchase + $10 profit $50 | Original purchase + profit + $10 more | Original purchase + profit + $10 + $10 profit |

Construct a Table and/or Graph—Discussion

The use of tables and graphs is a common problem-solving process. Tables are frequently used for problems that involve patterns, as illustrated in situations already discussed. Graphs are sometimes helpful to clarify data in tables. The tables and graphs in Activities 5.11 and 5.13 illustrate specific applications of this strategy that can be used by most children.

ACTIVITY 5.11 Solving Problems with Tables

The table shows the different combinations of three- and four-legged stools Kareem could make.

3-legged stools	0	1	2	3	4	5	6	7	8	9	10	11	12	13	14	15	16
Number of legs	64	63	62	61	60	59	58	57	56	55	54	53	52	51	50	49	48
4-legged stools	16	15	14	13	12	11	10	9	8	7	6	5	4	3	2	1	0

Activity 5.11   *continued*

Beverley could have made either seven flowers with four sheets of paper each or four of each kind of flower. She used the "account-for-all possibilities" strategy.

3-sheet flowers	0	1	2	2	3	4	5	5	6	6	6
Paper	28	27	30	26	29	28	27	31	22	26	30
4-sheet flowers	7	6	6	5	5	4	3	4	1	2	3

ACTIVITY 5.13   How Far?

Each of the situations is a simple rate-pair type of problem. The tables and graphs shown here are typical of ones children use until they can deal with these problems in more abstract ways. These types of problems involve proportions, which are discussed in Chapter 12.

Table for Milton's braided key chain

Inches	1	2	3	4	5	6	7	8	9
Minutes	2	4	6	8	10	12	14	?	?

Graph for Milton's braided key chain

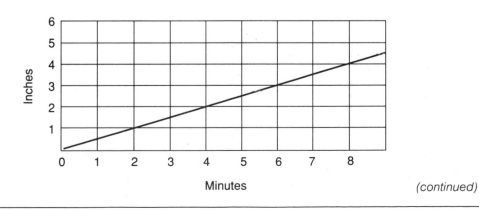

(continued)

Activity 5.13 *continued*

Table for ballet practice

Days	1	2	3	4	5	6	7	8
Hours	3/4	1 1/2	2 1/4	3	3 3/4	4 1/2	5 1/4	6

Graph for ballet practice

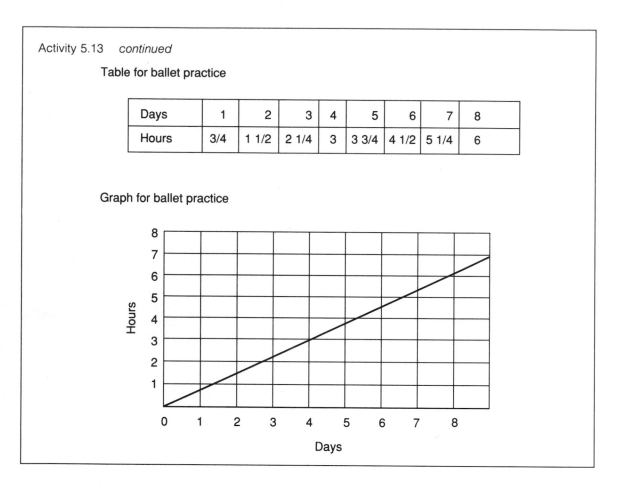

Guess and Check—Discussion

As indicated in the original discussion, wild guesses are not acceptable. Reasonable guesses are shown for the solution to each of the problems in Activity 5.14.

ACTIVITY 5.14   Guess and Check

Models in the form of squares of paper containing the numbers 1 through 6 were suggested as a way to solve the problems involving sums along the sides of the triangles. To avoid wild guesses, the problem solver should look at the conditions of a problem. The sum for the original problem is 9. Small numbers were used at the corner. As the size of the sum increases, larger numbers are needed at the corners. To determine arrangements for a sum of 10 or 11 the corner numbers

Activity 5.14   *continued*

should be larger than when the sum is 9, but not as large as when the sum is 12. The triangles show one solution for each of the sums 10, 11, and 12.

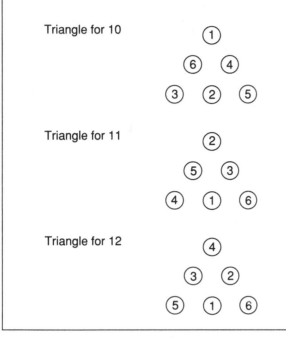

Triangle for 10

Triangle for 11

Triangle for 12

To guess the coins Hiroko used, a student needs to consider the value of each coin. A child with good knowledge of money will do less guessing than one whose knowledge is meager. The answer to the first question should be obvious; 79 pennies is the most Hiroko could spend. A guess for the fewest coins might begin with seven dimes, a nickel, and four pennies and then be refined to three quarters and four pennies. There are a number of ways Hiroko could have used between ten and fifteen coins. It is left to you to list some of them.

Naming factors for a number helps determine the two numbers in the final problem. List the factors of 144: 1, 2, 3, 4, 6, 8, 12, 18, 24, 36, 48, 72, 144. Once these have been listed check for combinations that have both a product of 144 and a quotient of 4. The product of 12 and 12 is 144, but the quotient is 1. Try 8 and 18; the product is okay, but the quotient is not. Try 6 and 24; the product is okay and the quotient is okay. Does any other pair work? Reasoning shows that the answer is "no." When the difference between the two factors increases, the size of the quotient also increases, so other pairs of factors will give quotients greater than four.

Account for All Possibilities— Discussion

This strategy works best when there are a limited number of possibilities. This strategy is another one with which a table is frequently used, as illustrated by the ice cream and dog food situations in Activity 5.15 and in the flower problem in Activity 5.11.

ACTIVITY 5.15   Account for All Possibilities

The ice cream situation is one that can be solved by multiplication. Until students are familiar with Cartesian—or cross-multiplication—situations, a table is a good way to account for all of the possibilities.

Topping	Ice Cream			
	Vanilla	Coffee	Banana	Walnut
Marshmallow	M-V	M-C	M-B	M-W
Cherry	Ch-V	Ch-C	Ch-B	Ch-W
Chocolate	Choc-V	Choc-C	Choc-B	Choc-W
Strawberry	S-V	S-C	S-B	S-W
Caramel	Car-V	Car-C	Car-B	Car-W
Raspberry	R-Y	R-C	R-B	R-W

There are four possible ways to buy at least 33 pounds of dog food, none of which gives 33 pounds exactly. The table clearly shows that buying three 12-pound bags is less expensive than buying seven 5-pound bags. It is less clear about the other situations. To be certain that buying three 12-pound bags is the overall best buy, find the cost per pound for each of the three situations: 37 pounds for $18.09 costs almost 49 cents a pound; 34 pounds for $16.26 costs slightly more than 48 cents a pound; 36 pounds for $16.38 costs 45.5 cents per pound.

Number of 5-lb bags	Cost($)	Number of 12-lb bags	Cost($)	Total weight(lb)	Total Cost($)
7	17.43	0	0	35	17.43
5	12.45	1	5.64	37	18.09
2	4.98	2	11.28	34	16.26
0	0	3	16.38	36	16.38

Simplify or Break into Parts—Discussion

This strategy works two ways. One is to use a simpler version of the problem and look for a pattern, which was done with the girls and rides in the amusement park. The other way is to break the problem into parts, which can be done with the other two problems in Activity 5.16.

ACTIVITY 5.16   Simplifying Problems

To find the area of the geometric figure, find the area of each of the parts, then add the numbers to find the area of the entire figure. Processes and formulas for finding area of plane figures are discussed in Chapter 14. The area of the triangle is 8 square inches, the area of the square is 16 square inches, and the area of the rectangle is 24 square inches; the total area is 48 square inches.

Break the mailbox problem into parts and solve it by steps. How many times does a "3" appear in the ones place in numbers between 1000 and 1200? (A "3" appears in the ones place 20 times.) How many times does a "3" appear in the tens place? (It appears in the tens place 20 times, but two of the numbers also contain three in the ones place and have already been counted.) Eighteen of the numbers have "3" in them.

Work Backward—Discussion

Puzzle situations like the one used to discuss the work-backward strategy are good to use for warm-ups and at moments in the day when a few minutes of waiting time occur. You can devise problems like the one used in Activity 5.17 for such occasions. The other three problems require careful study by children to be certain that they understand the information that is given and the information that must be determined.

ACTIVITY 5.17   Working Backward

The break-into-parts strategy can be used to solve the grocery store problem. First, determine the amount of change by subtracting $14.41 from $20.00. Then determine the cost of the groceries for which prices are given and subtract that amount for the cost of all of the groceries.

You must determine the total number of 13-year-old scouts to solve the second problem. Since eight 13-year-olds are half the total, there must be 16 of them in the troop. There are six more 13-year-olds than 12-year-olds, so there are ten 12-year-old scouts.

The students sold 120 single cupcakes to collect $30 because each one sold for 25 cents, or one-fourth of a dollar. They sold $20 worth of cupcakes at three for 50 cents, which is six for every dollar; they sold 20 times 6, or 120, at three for 50 cents. They sold 240 cupcakes.

Change Your Point of View— Discussion

The problems in Activity 5.18 may be more difficult for adults than for children. It is necessary to view these problems from different perspectives to solve them, and children are less set in the ways they view things and may be able to visualize each situation more imaginatively than many adults.

ACTIVITY 5.18 Change Your Point of View

You go beyond the bounds of the problem to solve the connect-the-dots problem.

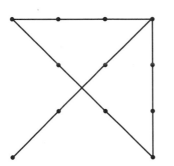

People who tend to view things on horizontal and vertical planes have difficulty with the area problem. The lines forming the squares are not horizontal and vertical.

Squares with 2 and 5 units of area

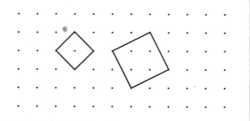

EXERCISE   Recall and list the ten problem-solving strategies.

■ STUDY QUESTIONS AND ACTIVITIES

1. Recall problem-solving experiences you had in elementary school. Was problem solving an integral part of mathematics instruction? If not, how was problem solving presented? What is your reaction to the problem-solving standard for kindergarten through grade four? For grades five through eight?

2. Look at the examples of problems used in this chapter. Using them as a model, create alternative problems of your own for five strategies. You may want to read Randall Charles's article (see the For Further Reading section) on "Writing Variations of a Problem." Then use other published sources to find alternative problems for five more strategies, noting the sources. Indicate a grade range for which you believe each alternative problem is suitable. Share your problems with fellow students to build a file of classroom problems.

3. List three school or classroom situations that could be used as the basis for genuine problem solving. How would you organize and present each situation so that children would gain the most problem-solving experience from it?

4. Some teachers post a "Problem of the Week," which is frequently a puzzle, on a bulletin board for children to solve. Talk to teachers who follow this practice to learn about the problems they use and their sources for finding them. Find out what kinds of puzzles they use, why they use them, and the responses of children to the practice. Do certain children work the problems while others do not? What characteristics, if any, differentiate those who solve puzzles from those who do not? What do teachers do with the puzzles that children complete? What are the strengths and potential problems of this practice?

▪ TEACHER'S BOOKSHELF

Buckeye, Donald A., William A. Ewbank, and John L. Ginther. 1989. *Cloudburst of Creative Mathematics Activities,* Vol. I and Vol. II. Pacific Grove, CA: Midwest Publications.

Dolan, Daniel T., and James Williamson. 1983. *Teaching Problem Solving Strategies.* Menlo Park, CA: Addison-Wesley.

Lenchner, George. 1983. *Creative Problem Solving in School Mathematics.* Boston: Houghton Mifflin.

Maletsky, Evan M., ed. 1987. *Teaching with Student Math Notes.* Reston, VA: National Council of Teachers of Mathematics.

Meyer, Carol, and Tom Sallee. 1983. *Make it Simpler: A Practical Guide to Problem Solving in Mathematics.* Menlo Park, CA: Addison-Wesley.

Morris, Janet. 1981. *How to Develop Problem Solving Using a Calculator.* Reston, VA: National Council of Teachers of Mathematics.

Overholt, James L., Jane B. Rincon, and Constance A. Ryan. 1983. *Math Problem Solving for Grades 4 Through 8.* Boston: Allyn and Bacon.

Stephens, Lillian S. 1983. *Developing Thinking Skills Through Real-Life Activities.* Boston: Allyn and Bacon.

▪ FOR FURTHER READING

Arithmetic Teacher. 1982, February *29*(6).

> *This issue contains ten articles about problem solving. There are both how-to and opinion articles.*

Barson, Alan. 1985, September. And the last one loses. *Arithmetic Teacher 33*(1), 35–37.

> *Suggests several strategy games that are won by the last move.*

Bartalo, Donald B. 1983, January. Calculators and problem-solving instruction: They were made for each other. *Arithmetic Teacher 30*(5), 18–21.

> *Describes a classroom experience for enhancing problem solving with a calculator.*

Brickman, Mary. 1986, September. Food for math. *Arithmetic Teacher 34*(1), 48–49.

A classroom grocery store provides many opportunities for problem solving.

Bush, William S., and Ann Fiala. 1986, December. Problem stories: A new twist on problem posing. *Arithmetic Teacher 34*(4), 6–9.

Nonroutine problem stories can provide motivation and unusual opportunities for creative thinking.

Campbell, Patricia F., and Honi J. Bamberger. 1990, May. The vision of problem solving in the *Standards. Arithmetic Teacher 37*(9), 14–17.

Problem solving as defined by the NCTM Standards *and examples at primary and intermediate levels are presented.*

Cemen, Pamala Byrd. 1989, October. Developing a problem-solving lesson. *Arithmetic Teacher 37*(2), 14–19.

Emphasizes questioning skills and outlines the development of Polya's four stages of problem solving.

Charles, Randall I. 1981, November. Get the most out of 'word problems'. *Arithmetic Teacher 29*(3), 39–40.

Most textbook word problems illustrate applications of mathematics topics. Charles describes ways to make the same problems contribute to developing mathematical concepts and improving problem-solving skills.

———. 1983, January. Evaluation and problem solving. *Arithmetic Teacher 30*(5), 6–7, 54.

Suggests ways to evaluate problem solving other than by looking for the right answer.

———. 1986, May. Writing variations of a problem. *Arithmetic Teacher 33*(9), 26–27.

Tips for extending problems by changing them or having students change them.

Daugherty, Barbara J., and Terry Crites. 1989, February. Applying number sense to problem solving. *Arithmetic Teacher 36*(6), 22–24.

Discusses how number sense can help students begin the process of solving problems and then help them judge the reasonableness of solutions. There are suggestions for developing children's number sense.

Greenes, Carole E., and Linda Schulman. 1982, October. Developing problem-solving ability with multiple-condition problems. *Arithmetic Teacher 30*(2), 18–21.

Polya's four-step problem-solving model is applied to problems having more than one condition. Guess-the-number problems are used as examples for discussing procedures for all grades.

Hosmer, Patricia C. 1984, December. Students can write their own problems. *Arithmetic Teacher 34*(4), 10–11.

Students can invent their own problems as a classroom challenge.

Huinker, DeAnn M. 1989, October. Multiplication and division word problems: Improving students' understanding. *Arithmetic Teacher 37*(2), 8–12.

This article has good ideas to help teachers become better enablers in the area of word problems.

Jones, Billie M. 1983, April. Put your children in the picture for better problem solving. *Arithmetic Teacher 30*(8), 30–33.

Problems based on information contained in the Guinness Book of World Records *and the mathematical and reading skills required to solve them are presented.*

Moses, Barbara. 1982, December. Individual differences in problem solving. *Arithmetic Teacher 30*(4), 10–14.

Children's varying levels of understanding and skills need to be considered during problem-solving activities. Examples of materials and procedures for developing understanding and skills are illustrated and discussed.

Pagni, David. 1989, January. A television programming challenge: A cooperative group activity that uses mathematics. *Arithmetic Teacher 36*(5), 7–8.

This is a good cross-curriculum problem-solving activity.

Rosenbaum, Linda, and others. 1989, March. Step into problem solving with cooperative learning. *Arithmetic Teacher 36*(7), 7.

The authors provide a good step-by-step plan for putting cooperative learning into operation. An especially good article for a beginning teacher.

Shaw, Jean. 1984, April. Newspapers add spark to mathematics activities. *Arithmetic Teacher 31*(8), 8–13.

Problems can be found on every page of the newspaper.

Walter, Marion. 1980, October. Frame geometry. *Arithmetic Teacher 28*(2), 16–18.

A picture-frame-making problem is posed. How many different frames can be made? Strategies for this and similar problems are considered.

Willcutt, Bob. 1982, September. 'Stamp collector's nightmare,' Phase two. *Arithmetic Teacher 31*(1), 21–25.

Many strategy problems develop from placement of different value "stamps" in a grid.

▮ NOTES

[1] National Council of Teachers of Mathematics, 1989. *Curriculum and Evaluation Standards for School Mathematics.* Reston, VA: National Council of Teachers of Mathematics, 23. Used by permission.

[2] NCTM, 75. Used by permission.

[3] NCTM, 98. Used by permission.

[4] NCTM, 102. Used by permission.

[5] NCTM, 23. Used by permission.

[6] California Department of Education, 1985. *Mathematics Framework for California Public Schools Kindergarten Through Grade 12.* Sacramento: California Department of Education, 13.

[7] Texas Education Agency. n.d. *Mathematics Framework Kindergarten–Grade 12.* Austin: Texas Education Agency, 4.

[8] George Polya. 1957. *How to Solve it.* Garden City, NY: Doubleday.

[9] Thomas L. Schroeder and Frank K. Lester, Jr. 1989. Developing understanding in mathematics via problem solving, in 1989 Yearbook, *New Directions for Elementary School Mathematics.* Reston, VA: National Council of Teachers of Mathematics, 31–42. Used by permission.

[10] Schroeder and Lester, 33. Used by permission.

[11] Schroeder and Lester, 36. Used by permission.

[12] Available from Sunburst Communications, 39 Washington Ave., Pleasantville, NY 10570-2898.

[13] Adapted from Carol Meyer and Tom Sallee. 1983. *Make It Simpler: A Practical Guide to Problem Solving in Mathematics.* Menlo Park, CA: Addison-Wesley, 79. Used by permission.

[14] Meyer and Sallee, 121. Used by permission.

[15] Adapted from Ohio State Department of Education. n.d. *Problem Solving—A Basic Mathematics Goal, Book 1, Becoming a Better Problem Solver.* Columbus: Ohio Department of Education, 16. Used by permission.

[16] Adapted from Carol Greenes and others. *Techniques of Problem Solving: Problem Card Decks.* Palo Alto, CA: Dale Seymour Publications, Card 48-C.

[17] Adapted from Maria Marolda. 1976. *Attribute Games and Activities.* Palo Alto, CA: Creative Publications, 141. Used by permission.

[18] Marolda, 141. Used by permission.

[19] George Lenchner. 1983. *Creative Problem Solving in School Mathematics.* Boston: Houghton Mifflin, 24.

Communication, Reasoning, and Connections

The attention given to a changing view of elementary school mathematics has caused many people to examine the way the subject is taught. Today the focus of mathematics instruction is on mathematics *as* problem solving. Because of this focus, students are exposed to an entirely different way of learning mathematics than in the past. Active student participation with concrete materials, group activities, and problem-solving situations is central to learning mathematics today. The topics of this chapter—communication, reasoning, and connections—are important parts of the current view of how children should learn mathematics.

In this chapter you will read about

1. The role of communication in students' learning of mathematics;

2. Ways to promote discussion and communication in mathematics;

3. The importance of reasoning in mathematics;

4. Activities that develop students' reasoning;

5. How connections among mathematics topics and between mathematics and the real world can be promoted.

165

NCTM STANDARDS THAT PERTAIN TO COMMUNICATION, REASONING, AND CONNECTIONS

Kindergarten Through Grade Four

Standard 2: Mathematics as Communication   In grades K–4, the study of mathematics should include numerous opportunities for communication so that students can:

- relate physical materials, pictures, and diagrams to mathematical ideas;
- reflect on and clarify their thinking about mathematical ideas and situations;
- relate their everyday language to mathematical language and symbols;
- realize that representing, discussing, reading, writing, and listening to mathematics are a vital part of learning and using mathematics.[1]

Standard 3: Mathematics as Reasoning   In grades K–4, the study of mathematics should emphasize reasoning so that students can:

- draw logical conclusions about mathematics;
- use models, known facts, properties, and relationships to explain their thinking;
- justify their answers and solution processes;
- use patterns and relationships to analyze mathematical situations;
- believe that mathematics makes sense.[2]

Standard 4: Mathematical Connections   In grades K–4, the study of mathematics should include opportunities to make connections so that students can:

- link conceptual and procedural knowledge;
- relate various representations of concepts and procedures to one another;
- recognize relationships among different topics in mathematics;
- use mathematics in other curricular areas;
- use mathematics in their daily lives.[3]

Grades Five Through Eight

Standard 2: Mathematics as Communication   In grades 5–8, the study of mathematics should include opportunities to communicate so that students can:

- model situations using oral, written, concrete, pictorial, graphical, and algebraic methods;
- reflect on and clarify their own thinking about mathematical ideas and situations;
- develop common understandings of mathematical ideas, including the role of definitions;
- use the skills of reading, listening, and viewing to interpret and evaluate mathematical ideas;
- discuss mathematical ideas and make conjectures and convincing arguments;
- appreciate the value of mathematical notation and its role in the development of mathematical ideas.[4]

Standard 3: Mathematics as Reasoning   In grades 5–8, reasoning shall permeate the mathematics curriculum so that students can:

- recognize and apply deductive and inductive reasoning;
- understand and apply reasoning processes, with special attention to spatial reasoning and reasoning with proportions and graphs;
- make and evaluate mathematical conjectures and arguments;
- validate their own thinking;
- appreciate the pervasive use and power of reasoning as a part of mathematics.[5]

Standard 4: Mathematical Connections   In grades 5–8, the mathematics curriculum should include the investigation of mathematical connections so that students can:

- see mathematics as an integrated whole;

- explore problems and describe results using graphical, numerical, physical, algebraic, and verbal mathematical models or representations;

- use a mathematical idea to further their understanding of other mathematical ideas;

- apply mathematical thinking and modeling to solve problems that arise in other disciplines, such as art, music, psychology, science, and business;

- value the role of mathematics in our culture and society.[6]

■ COMMUNICATION ABOUT MATHEMATICS

An important goal of mathematics instruction is to help children learn to communicate about mathematics. Today's technological society depends on computers and other devices that receive, manipulate, store, and transmit data and ideas. Individuals who lack an understanding of and ability to use these devices and who cannot communicate about them meaningfully with others will be unable to compete in the business, scientific, governmental, medical, and social communities of tomorrow. Even while they are growing up, children need to use and understand mathematical ideas in and out of school. Classroom practices that promote the children's skill in communicating—not just in mathematics but in all aspects of life—must be provided if today's children are to make positive contributions to society in the twenty-first century.

Mathematics as a Language

The view that mathematics is a language that children must learn is new. The National Council of Teachers of Mathematics includes mathematics as a language as a general standard for each of the three grade ranges for which standards were prepared. The authors say that

> Mathematics can be thought of as a language that must be meaningful if students are to communicate mathematically and apply mathematics productively. Communication plays an important role in helping children construct links between their informal, intuitive notions and the abstract language and symbolism of mathematics; it also plays a key role in helping children make important connections among physical, pictorial, graphic, symbolic, verbal, and mental representations of mathematical ideas. When children see that one representation, such as an equation, can describe many situations, they begin to understand the power of mathematics; when they realize that some ways of representing a problem are more helpful than others, they begin to understand the flexibility and usefulness of mathematics.[7]

Practices That Promote Communication

One feature of today's mathematics classroom that distinguishes it from classrooms of the past is the opportunity for children to communicate their thoughts about mathematics. No longer is the emphasis on doing one's own work and getting the "right" answer. There are few occupations today where an individual is solely responsible for developing an idea or making a product. Rather the importance of solving problems through shared investigations of concepts, discussions of ideas, and group responses is recognized in the workplace. Many teachers have grasped the importance of this process, and the practice is finding its way into the classroom. The three vignettes in Chapter 2 and many of the problems in Chapter 5 illustrate situations in which communication plays an active role as children learn new concepts. Each teacher in the vignettes presented a lesson in which discussion was central to the learning process. Many of the problems should be solved in cooperative-learning groups, where discussion is a key part of each activity.

Teacher-Led Activities

Teacher-led lessons should provide ample opportunities for students to engage in discussions about the work they are doing and to express opinions and ideas about the mathematics they are learning.

Robert Baratta-Lorton developed a set of lessons that he presented in *Mathematics . . . A Way of Thinking.*[8] Most of the lessons are presented to an entire class at a time. Grouping by ability—which can reinforce the impression that some students are less capable than others—is avoided. Rather Baratta-Lorton advocates that the questions a teacher asks be varied to account for different levels of understanding and comprehension and that variations in student responses be anticipated and accepted. A second advantage is that group instruction sets up an environment that challenges students' curiosity and feeds back information that tells them if their discoveries are valid. Baratta-Lorton says, "Students develop language skills and learn to communicate their ideas by working with others."[9] Discussion is a significant part of most of the lessons in the book. The following lessons from the book illustrate how a teacher can foster communication skills.[10] These two lessons deal with number facts.

Lesson 4-10

Number Facts with Tiles

Purpose: To provide experience in developing problems to match a given answer.

Materials: 1. If no overhead projector is available, square shapes
2. Tiles

    3. Individual blackboards
    4. Unlined paper

The following two lessons focus student attention specifically on the variety of number combinations or "number facts" in addition and subtraction that are associated with a given sum. The students learn that many different combinations of numbers will produce the same answer.

TEACHER: Take out eight tiles. Before, when you worked with tiles, I asked you to either add or subtract to get an answer. This time, I'll give you the answer and you can tell me what the problem might have been.

              The answer we will start with is "eight." What was the problem?

The teacher's question is meant to lead the class into a general discussion of what problems have an answer of eight. However, the class may need a more specific explanation of what is wanted.

TEACHER: If I divide my eight tiles into two equal groups, what problem did I start with?

STUDENT: Four and four.

TEACHER: That's one problem. Can you tell me another that might have eight as its answer?

The problems need not be limited to addition and subtraction. The students' imaginations should be the only limit.

When the teacher's question is understood, the students begin devising and recording their own problems. Once they feel they have exhausted the possibilities for eight, they may choose another number.

While constructing problems to go with their numbers, students may explore the answers to the following questions:

Are there more problems that can be made up for eight than for seven? How about six?
How many problems can you make up with zero as an answer? Do more or less problems have zero as an answer than eight? How do you know?
What is the highest number of problems you can make up for nine?
What would be the most if you only used addition? Subtraction?
What is the most unusual problem you can make up?
What is the longest problem you can make up? The shortest?

A student may decide that $0 + 8$ is different from $0 + 0 + 0 + 8$. This permits the student to generate an endless number of problems simply by adding zero. Whether $0 + 8$ is different from $0 + 0 + 0 + 8$ is a matter for the class to discuss and decide. Once discussed, the class resolves the issue by voting. Whatever the class decides will be the rule for resolving all similar questions. The rule thus created stays in effect until the class decides to change it.

Lesson 4-11

Number Facts with Tiles

Purpose: To provide experience in developing specific problems to match a given answer.

Materials: 1. Tiles
2. Individual blackboards
3. Unlined paper

TEACHER: Take out eight tiles. This time I want you to find problems that have the answer eight, but only use *two* groups of tiles.
 When you think of a problem, tell me and I'll write it down. Be sure to check the overhead to see if the problem you have made has already been recorded.

STUDENT: Three plus five.

STUDENT: One and seven.

STUDENT: Four and four.

STUDENT: Two plus six.

STUDENT: Five plus three.

STUDENT: Five plus three is already up there. It's the same as three plus five.

The teacher has an opinion about whether five plus three is the same as three plus five, but it isn't shared with the class. The students must resolve this issue to their own satisfaction through discussion then vote. If the students decide the two ways are the same, they will find this decision challenged when they reach coordinate graphing. If the class decides the ways are different, then how different are they? Shall the students now count problems such as the one shown with tiles [in Figure 6.1] as a different problem depending on one's physical location? A student sitting in front of the problem sees five plus three. A student facing the problem from the back sees three plus five. However the vote comes out, events in the future will cause them to rethink the issue. They must never be completely satisfied with their decision.

Figure 6-1
Whether you see
5 + 3 or 3 + 5
depends on how
you see the tiles.

Even the most valid rules or axioms of mathematics are only the product of our ancestors' ability to extend what seemed reasonable and to convince their fellows that what seemed reasonable to a few should be accepted as reasonable for all. Our students' understanding of the rules of mathematics is enhanced if they can decide for themselves what is reasonable and live with their collective decision.

Once the students have told the teacher as many ways as they can think of to get eight as an answer using two groups of tiles, they pick a new starting number, such as seven or nine, and continue as before. Whatever rules the class has chosen when finding ways to make eight are binding on each new number attempted.

The Baratta-Lorton lessons provide opportunities for students to represent numbers with tiles, to talk and listen, and to write and read mathematical, or symbolic, sentences for numbers. Students who engage in these activities are able to communicate mathematical ideas in many ways. An added benefit is that children will have little need to spend endless hours committing number facts to memory through drill-and-practice exercises; they remember facts because of their varied experiences with them.

Cooperative-Learning Groups

Cooperative-learning groups are an especially important way to promote discussion about mathematics. Neil Davidson states that cooperative-learning groups encourage communication by providing opportunities for students to exchange and explain ideas, to ask questions and clarify their thinking, and to help others understand ideas. The sharing of ideas helps every student achieve a measure of success in mathematics.[11] Davidson also points out that mathematics is ideal for helping students develop communication skills because most problems can be solved in a reasonable period of time, there are usually different ways a problem can be solved so discussion of the merits of different approaches is encouraged, and the field of mathematics is filled with topics that are of interest to students.[12]

Marilyn Burns is an advocate of cooperative-group learning. She believes children's learning is enhanced when teachers structure lessons according to the maturity of their students, children interact with physical objects before abstract mathematical ideas are introduced, and there is social interaction among the children and teacher.[13] In the following description of a third-grade lesson Burns describes a cooperative-learning activity.[14]

Dee Uyeda's third grade class had not had any formal instruction in fractions yet this school year. This was December, and Dee was interested in giving the students an opportunity to develop understanding of fractions and fractional equivalents. At the same time, she would give herself the opportunity to assess the students' present level of understanding.

The children were told that they would be working in groups for this activity. Dee settled the children into six groups, five groups of four and one group of five.

"I've cut many small circles that you'll use for this activity," Dee explained, introducing the children to the materials they would be using. The circles were cut from ditto paper and were about 2 inches in diameter. "You'll also have worksheets on which your group will record your work."

Before passing out any materials, Dee posed the following question to the class: "If I gave each group of 4 children 4 cookies to share equally, how much would each person get?" As Dee had predicted, this was obvious to them. But it gave her the chance to discuss sharing equally, an important concept for dealing with fractions.

Dee then told the children that they would have a similar problem to solve in their groups. "Your first task will be to figure out how to share 6 cookies equally among 4 people. You are to use the circles I've cut as the cookies, and actually share them. Use scissors, and paste each person's share on the worksheet." The worksheet had space for the group members' names at the top and was divided into four spaces in which they could paste their "cookie shares." A question was written beneath these four spaces at the bottom of the sheet: How much did each person get?

"When you have shared the cookies," Dee explained further, "you are to discuss together how to record at the bottom of the sheet to tell how much each person got."

Dee also told the children that when they had solved the problem with 6 cookies, they should come and get another worksheet and try the problem with 5 cookies, then 3 cookies, 2 cookies, and finally with 1 cookie.

The goal of this lesson was to provide the children with a problem-solving experience that required them to interact with fractional concepts. The "cookies" gave them the opportunity to learn from physical materials. This way, rather than focusing on the abstract symbolization of fractions, they could verify their thinking in the actual material they were using. Asking them to record how much each person got would give Dee the opportunity to learn what, if anything, the children knew about how to write fractions. She was curious how they would answer that question on their worksheets.

Dee asked that one person from each group come up for their materials. She gave each of them 6 circles and a worksheet. During the exploring time, all groups were able to work with ease. Dee worried a bit that perhaps this was too easy for them, but the children were involved and interested.

The class worked for about half an hour. In that time, each group of 4 did all the problems, with 6, 5, 3, 2, and 1 cookies, and several groups asked for more problems. For an extension to those groups who finished first, Dee gave them the problem of sharing 7 cookies among 4 people.

When Dee offered the 7-cookie problem to one group, a girl in the group commented that it was too easy to do. "Let us do 8 cookies," she said. But then she continued thinking aloud, "But that's even easier; it would be 2 cookies." And then the group started to think aloud together. "What about 9 cookies?" "Easy, two and a quarter." "Ten would be two and a half." Dee left them and they didn't even notice.

Dee gave one particularly interested and speedy group the problem of sharing 7 cookies again, but this time she said she was going to attend their party also, so they needed to divide the cookies equally among five people. They did not feel this was difficult. Though they were satisfied with their solution, it revealed that they were unable to deal with these fractional parts. They had pasted Dee's share on the back of the paper and had recorded: "Everyone gets 2 halves, 1 quarter, and one sliver."

The group of 5 students had difficulty that Dee was not immediately aware of. They began assuming that each person in their group needed a share, a decision that is commendable for its sense of fairness. But that meant they had to tackle the problem of sharing 6 cookies among 5 people as their first problem. This was difficult for them, and once Dee noticed their struggle, she suggested they include her and share 4 cookies among the 6 of them. They did fine with that, but it was all they had time for. Because of their different experience, the summarizing was not very valuable to them.

The lesson was a rich one for summarizing. First Dee discussed with the children how they organized themselves for working. The children reported the different ways they divided up the jobs of cutting, pasting, and writing, how they took turns, and how they helped each other. The children had worked cooperatively in a natural way. This occurred only because Dee had taken the time to develop the classroom atmosphere, working hard to develop the children's attention to the social skills needed for cooperation.

Dee began the discussion of fractions with 6 cookies. They had all reached the same conclusion—each person gets one and a half. Most groups wrote this in words; two groups had used symbols. "So," Dee concluded, "you all agree on each person's share. Here's how we write this." She wrote 1½ on the board, and all the children nodded that they were familiar with this. In this way, Dee was connecting the standard symbolism to the thinking they had already done.

With the 5-cookie situation, each read what they recorded to indicate each person's share. "A whole cookie and a quarter of a cookie." "One and a quarter." "Everyone gets one and a quarter." None of the groups used symbols for their recording, however.

Dee took this opportunity to introduce the symbolism. "Does anyone know how to write the fraction for one quarter?" she asked.

Brad volunteered, hesitantly, "Three over one?" This response did not surprise Dee. Children do not always think that the symbolism is supposed to make sense and often resort to guessing.

Dee said, "Let me explain to you why one half is written as a 1 over a 2." She then took a circle and cut it into two equal pieces. "The 2," she said, pointing to the denominator, "tells us that we cut the cookie into 2 pieces. The 1 on top tells how many pieces I have. If I have half a cookie, I have just 1 of the 2 pieces." Dee did not introduce the words "numerator" and "denominator." Instead, she kept the cookie as the reference for the children.

She continued with fourths. "Here's how you divided a cookie into four equal parts," she said, cutting a circle into quarters. "To write how much one piece is, I need to write a 4 on the bottom. Who can explain why?" Several children volunteered. "And what do I write on top?" Dee continued. In this way, she showed them the symbolism for one fourth. She used "one fourth" and "one quarter" interchangeably as she did this. In this teaching, Dee was again connecting their experience to the standard fractional number.

When Dee asked the groups to report how they shared 3 cookies among 4 people, most agreed that each person got a half and a quarter, and Dee wrote this on the board as 1/2 + 1/4. One group, however, reported that each person got three quarters. They had cut each of the 3 cookies into 4 pieces and each student had taken a piece from each cookie. This gave Dee the opportunity to introduce the symbolism for three fourths: 3/4.

"Though the answers are different," Dee asked them, "did each group divide up the cookies equally?" There was some initial disagreement before they were comfortable with 1/2 + 1/4 being the same amount as 3/4.

As Dee continued to discuss each problem, she wrote the fractions on the board to connect the children's findings to the symbolism. The most interesting variation came from one group's solution to sharing 2 cookies among 4 people. Most groups solved this problem by giving each person half a cookie. But this group cut each half into half and knew they had two quarters. Then they cut each quarter in half. Their final conclusion stated: "Each person gets four halves of a quarter." Complicated, for sure, but it was understood clearly by the group.

Dee feels strongly that the attention to the children's language is essential for them to develop concepts and that working in cooperative groups provides many opportunities for this to occur. She was pleased and surprised by the quality of the children's thinking during this experience. Not only did the children seem to learn, but she gained useful insights into their thinking. Dee planned to follow this with additional fractional work using other concrete models.

The Burns lesson provides opportunities for students to shift their thinking from objects to symbols, both written and oral, as they work with the models. First there is student-to-student discussion in the groups. This is followed by a teacher-led discussion where the interchange is sometimes teacher-student and sometimes student-student.

EXERCISES   Describe the teacher's role in each of the teaching situations about which you have just read. How could the Baratta-Lorton lessons be adapted to become cooperative-learning lessons? How could the Burns lesson be adapted to become a whole-class lesson?

What features characterize lessons that promote children-to-children and teacher-to-children communication about mathematics? Do you believe these characteristics are present in most elementary school mathematics lessons? Explain the reason for your response.

■ REASONING IN MATHEMATICS

In the conventional classroom of the past a textbook was the basis for most lessons. Students learned mathematics through a teacher's demonstration and explanation of a lesson's material and by independently completing an exercise from the book. There were usually no opportunities for students to develop reasoning skills through group investigations of meaningful situations. The NCTM's third general standard is "Mathematics as Reasoning." To reason a person must think, and to think a person must be challenged by an important and interesting problem or situation. A teacher controls children's thinking about mathematics. In the past children had limited opportunities to reason about mathematics. The teacher's explanation of a process was accepted without question and practiced until it became habitual. Today's classroom offers many opportunities for children to think about the concepts and processes they are learning. The three classrooms in Chapter 2, the problem-solving activities in Chapter 5, and the Baratta-Lorton lessons and Burns's description of a classroom all show ways teachers can help students use reasoning to develop their understanding of concepts and processes. Teachers in situations like those are open to children's ideas and suggestions and accepting of diverse points of view, have patience while children take time to understand processes and concepts and grope for answers, and view processes as more important than answers.

Throughout their years in elementary school, students' thinking about mathematics should be based on concrete materials and realistic situations. Primary-grade children learn mathematics by engaging in much informal thinking, conjecturing, and hypothesizing. Fifth- and sixth-grade children have the maturity to reason more abstractly, but are still dependent on concrete representations of the mathematics they learn. As you read Activities 6.1 to 6.4, think about how the teacher's comments and questions and the problems and materials promote learning and develop reasoning skills.

ACTIVITY 6.1   Straightening Up

- The kindergarten's classroom "store" is a mess. The teacher assigns a group of children to make some sort of order out of the mess simply by telling them to "straighten things up in the store" and leaving them to work.

- When the store has been straightened up, the teacher returns to the group and talks to them about their work.
  —Tell me why you put these boxes on this shelf.

  —Was there a special reason for putting these things together?

  —I wonder how having these things over here will help whoever is the next clerk?

  —You've had some time to think about what you have done to organize the store; are there any ways you would do it differently another time?

  —How is a real grocery store arranged?

- Similar experiences come from straightening up the classroom playhouse, the block corner, and shelves in the reading corner, and by working with commercial sorting materials and items from math boxes.

ACTIVITY 6.2   What Am I?

■ These are examples of puzzles that develop reasoning skills. The simplest ones can be used with kindergarten and primary-grade children; the most difficult ones are for mature upper-grade children.

—I am a number that is smaller than ten. I am greater than five and smaller than seven. What number am I? (6.)

—I have six faces. Each face is the same size. I have nothing but square corners. What am I? (A cube.)

—I have three or four sides. My angles are all the same size. My sides are not all the same length. What am I?[15] (A rectangle.)

—I am an even number. I am more than 20 and less than 30. I am not 25. The sum of my digits is eight. What number am I?[16] (26.)

—I am a metric unit of measure. You would use me to measure the width of your reading book but not the length of the hallway outside your classroom. What unit am I? (A centimeter.)

—I am a pair of numbers. My sum is 12 and my product is 35. What numbers am I? (5 and 7.)

—Name the next letter in this sequence: O, T, T, F, F, S, S, E, N, ... (These are the first letters of one, two, three, . . . nine, so the next letter is T.)

—I am a plane figure. My perimeter is 24 inches and my area is 27 square inches. What are the lengths of my sides? (Length is 9 and width is 3.)

—I am the smallest prime number that is not a factor of a number less than 40. What number am I? (23.)

—How is it possible to have $63 without having any one-dollar bills? (You could have $55.00 in fives and tens and four two-dollar bills.)

—Name the next number in this set of numbers: 3, 4, 6, 8, 12, 14, 18, 20, 24, ... (These are successors of prime numbers, so the next number is 30.)

Note that the last two might require the break-set, or change-your-point-of-view, strategy.

ACTIVITY 6.3   The Chinese Suan-Pan

■ Explain that a *suan-pan* is a counting and computing device still used in some parts of the world. Merchants use it to compute the cost of goods being sold and to figure the profits and losses for their businesses. (This and the Japanese *saroban,* a similar device, can be purchased at some novelty and souvenir shops.)

■ Organize the children for a cooperative-learning activity. Give each group a picture of this suan-pan and ask them to determine the number it represents. Have other illustrations of this or other counting devices for the groups to interpret.[17]

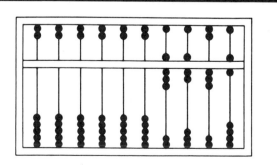

■ Have groups explain how the device(s) represent each number. Have them compare the suan-pan and other devices with place-value devices in their classroom.

ACTIVITY 6.4   Vacation Time

- Prepare copies of this temperature and precipitation chart.

- Give each student a copy of the chart.

- Have a child locate each city on a map. Have students tell what they know about the cities. Discuss such things as oceans, mountains, and other topographical information that is significant. Discuss the information contained in the chart.

- Organize cooperative-learning groups. Tell each group that they are to use the chart and map to plan a summer vacation and a winter vacation. Each vacation should be in a different city. Tell them that they will need to make conjectures about the weather to expect in each city in the winter and the summer. When a group has agreed on their choice of city for each vacation, they are to prepare a written report that explains the things they would do and the types of clothing they would take for each vacation. They should also explain how the map and chart helped them make their decisions.

TEMPERATURE AND PRECIPITATION CHART

City	Jan T	Jan P	Feb T	Feb P	Mar T	Mar P	Apr T	Apr P	May T	May P	Jun T	Jun P	Jul T	Jul P	Aug T	Aug P	Sep T	Sep P	Oct T	Oct P	Nov T	Nov P	Dec T	Dec P
Anchorage	13	0.8	18	0.9	24	0.7	35	0.7	46	0.6	54	1.1	58	2.0	56	2.1	48	2.5	35	1.7	22	1.1	14	1.1
Denver	30	0.5	34	0.7	38	1.2	47	1.8	57	2.5	67	1.6	73	1.9	71	1.5	63	1.2	52	1.0	39	0.8	33	0.6
Honolulu	73	3.8	73	2.7	74	3.5	76	1.6	78	1.2	79	0.5	80	0.5	81	0.6	81	0.6	80	1.9	77	3.2	74	3.4
Miami	67	2.1	68	2.1	72	1.9	75	3.1	79	6.5	81	9.2	83	6.0	83	7.0	82	8.1	78	7.1	73	2.7	69	1.9
San Francisco	49	4.7	52	3.2	53	2.6	55	1.5	58	0.3	61	0.1	62	L	63	0.1	64	0.2	61	1.1	55	2.4	49	3.6
Wash'ton DC	31	2.8	34	2.6	42	3.4	53	3.1	62	3.6	71	4.2	76	3.8	74	4.2	67	3.3	55	3.0	45	3.0	35	3.3

Through a broad range of activities students become skillful in drawing conclusions and making generalizations about numbers, in making inferences, and in using inductive and deductive reasoning to solve problems. They see that there is beauty in mathematics and that it makes sense. Gradually each student develops confidence about his or her ability to use mathematics to solve worthwhile problems.

EXERCISES   In your judgment, how does teaching mathematics as demonstrated in the examples of lessons and discussion of practices about which you have read to this point promote students' reasoning about mathematics?

Three of the four activities in the reasoning section of the chapter are cooperative learning activities. Why do you believe cooperative learning situations are good ones for involving children in reasoning about mathematics?

■ CONNECTIONS IN MATHEMATICS

This standard is crucial. To understand mathematics students must learn that mathematical ideas are related and make connections between the concrete, pictorial, diagrammatic, symbolic, and verbal forms of representing concepts and processes. Mathematics must have value to them as a way to solve problems, so they need to make connections between mathematics and the real world.

These connections are interrelated, and during instruction they are occurring continuously. A teacher does not say, "Today my goal is to relate the children's intuitive knowledge of numbers to the process of counting," or "This lesson will teach the children that mathematics has utility in the real world." The connections are made as children work with concrete materials and translate actions with them into pictures, diagrams, charts, graphs, and symbolic forms. The third-grade teacher in the Burns lesson helped students make connections between their "cookies" and written symbols for fractions. Students in that classroom were also making a connection between mathematics in the classroom and mathematics in the real world as they solved realistic problems with their "cookies."

A comprehensive mathematics program includes many topics that have only recently become a part of the elementary school curriculum. If these topics were taught today as topics were in the past, they would be presented isolated one from the other, with a textbook dictating their sequence during the year. Today topics are not isolated. The following activities illustrate how topics can be integrated. In Activity 6.5 a zoo serves as the setting in which measurement provides the context for doing addition. Geometry and measurement are integrated in Activities 6.6 and 6.7. Activity 6.7 can also integrate algebra with geometry and measurement for mature students.

ACTIVITY 6.5 At the Zoo

- Give each child the zoo map and a calculator.

- Have children justify their answers by pointing out routes on an overhead projector map of the zoo.[18]

Park City Zoo Plan

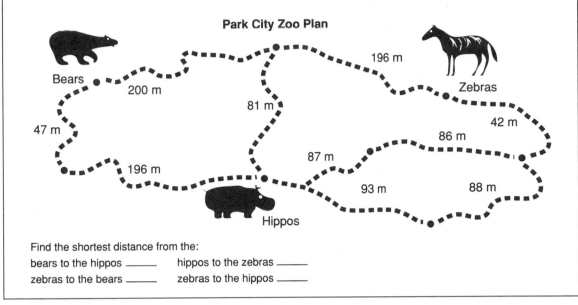

Find the shortest distance from the:

bears to the hippos _____   hippos to the zebras _____

zebras to the bears _____   zebras to the hippos _____

ACTIVITY 6.6 Perimeters

- Cut a 12-centimeter by 16-centimeter rectangle on a diagonal as shown. What geometric shapes can you make? Which ones have the same perimeter?

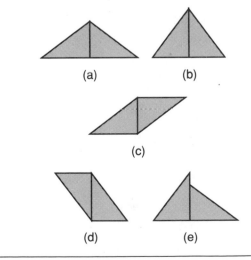

- Children can answer the question without numbers. They can see that figures (a) and (c) have the same perimeter and that figures (b) and (d) have the same perimeter. It may be more difficult for them to see that the quadrilateral (e) has the same perimeter as (a) and (c).

- Mature students may understand and use the Pythagorean theorem to determine the length of the long side of the triangle so they can determine the number of centimeters in the perimeter of each figure. This theorem states that the square of the length of the hypotenuse of a triangle is equal to the sum of the squares of the other two sides. In the example here the sum of the squares of the two sides is 400, so the length of the side of the triangle that is cut is 20 centimeters.[19]

ACTIVITY 6.7 Patterns

■ Organize the class into cooperative-learning groups. Give each group a representation of this pattern.

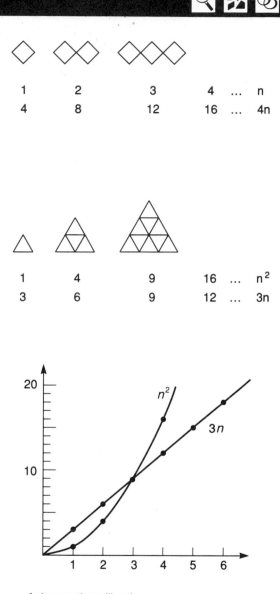

No. of squares	1	2	3	4	...	n
Perimeter	4	8	12	16	...	4n

■ Present these instructions: Describe the pattern. What are some questions you can ask about the pattern?

■ Have one group read one of its questions for other students' responses. Consider all questions.

■ Give each group a representation of this pattern.

No. of triangles	1	4	9	16	...	n^2
Perimeter	3	6	9	12	...	3n

■ Have students determine the pattern and write questions about it. Their questions might ask for the number of triangles in each successive figure, which deals with the concept of area, and for the perimeter of each successive figure.

■ Discuss the questions. Have students who answer the questions support the validity of their responses through demonstrations with a pictorial extension of the pattern, a verbal explanation of the number pattern, or other means.

■ Students' responses may indicate that they are ready to deal with an algebraic rule for finding the number of triangles in a triangle with n sides. Explain that the expression n^2 is used for this pattern. (The same pattern and rule are used in Activity 5.3, where the situation involves stacking cans.)

■ Mature students may be ready to compare the growth of the perimeter and the number of triangles to use a graph. Have students help as you make and explain a graph.

■ Ask questions like these.
—In which figures are the areas less than the perimeter? In which figure are both the area and perimeter the same? Why does the slope of the line for n^2 increase more rapidly than the slope for $3n$ after the point where area and perimeter are the same?[20]

Interdisciplinary and Real-World Connections

Connections between mathematics and other curriculum areas and the real world are numerous. The following examples illustrate ways a teacher can make connections between mathematics and other areas of the curriculum.

Mathematics and Science

- Weighing food and animals during a study of small animals
- Classifying animals as birds, mammals, insects, or reptiles and rocks as igneous, sedimentary, and metamorphic
- Taking and recording temperature, wind speed, and air pressure in a weather unit
- Measuring plants during a long-term growth experiment
- Establishing a scale and making a model of the solar system

Mathematics and Social Studies

- Making maps of a classroom and school grounds; using scaling and proportions to make a map of a neighborhood
- Setting up a classroom store; operating a school store
- Making a timeline of a day's events; a timeline of a historical period
- Classifying occupations by uniforms and nonuniforms; as research, service, manufacturing, military, farming
- Comparing the highest and lowest places on land; the highest place on land and the deepest place under water

Mathematics and Art

- Measuring crepe paper for a border around a mural; paper to cut for mounting a finger painting
- Making a scale drawing of a backdrop for a class play; measuring and preparing paper for the backdrop
- Measuring powder and water for tempera paint
- Reading and following directions for a Japanese origami creation

Mathematics and Health

- Measuring heights of children; recording them on a chart and graph
- Determining calorie intake; reading labels for nutrition information; learning about cholesterol levels during the health unit

Mathematics and Reading and Language Arts

- Looking for patterns in words; classifying words as rhyming and non-rhyming; looking for palindromic words
- Researching the origin of mathematical prefixes and suffixes
- Doing research and writing about famous mathematicians
- Doing research and writing about numbers and superstitions

Mathematics and Physical Education

- Counting the number of hops while jumping rope
- Measuring the length of a broad jump, vertical jump, softball throw
- Laying out a play area
- Timing races

Mathematics and Real-World Connections

Connections between mathematics and the real world can be made in many ways. Newspapers and magazines contain articles dealing with probability, economic trends, weather, and science. Bulletin boards on special topics can be prepared with articles and pictures from these publications. Individuals can be invited to the classroom to discuss ways in which they use mathematics in their occupations. Field trips to harbors, rail yards, and airports can provide information about some of the mathematical factors that govern the location of such facilities. A study of ecological problems, such as automobile and factory emissions or garbage disposal, offers many opportunities for students to connect mathematics to vital concerns of the day. An alert teacher has no problem in integrating mathematics, other curricular areas, and real-world problems on an almost daily basis.

EXERCISES Identify other examples of real-world and mathematics connections. Your list might contain additional examples for the areas discussed in this chapter or for areas entirely different from any mentioned here.

■ SUMMARY

The ability to communicate effectively is a necessity in a technological society. There is a language of mathematics that students must understand and use meaningfully. Communication plays a role in helping students connect their intuitive understanding of mathematical ideas with the processes and symbolism of mathematics. Teachers foster communication by providing teacher-led lessons, cooperative-learning situations, and explorations and investigations during which student-teacher and student-student discussions are encouraged. Children at all levels need opportunities to ask and answer questions, explain processes, make hypotheses and predictions, make charts and graphs, and to write statements about the mathematics they are learning.

An important goal of mathematics education is to develop students' confidence in doing and using mathematics. Confidence is high in students who know that they have the ability to think about mathematics in reasonable ways and can explain concepts and processes. Teachers influence the types of thinking students do about mathematics. The classroom atmosphere that promotes communication will also promote the development of thinking and reasoning skills. Children need many opportunities to make oral and written explanations of processes with manipulative materials, describe charts and graphs, make inferences and predictions from data, and draw conclusions and make generalizations about the mathematics they are learning.

Children need to make connections within the field of mathematics so that they see it as an integrated whole rather than a set of independent and unconnected ideas. Teachers do this when they help students connect such concepts and topics as common and decimal fractions to percent, multiplication to addition and division to subtraction, and measurement to geometry. Students also need to connect mathematics and other areas of the curriculum and mathematics and the real world. Opportunities to make connections arise almost daily; an alert teacher is aware of these opportunities and takes advantage of them.

■ STUDY QUESTIONS AND ACTIVITIES

1. Scan the activities in Part Three of this book for ones you believe are particularly good for fostering communication, reasoning, or connections. Locate at least two activities for each standard. Identify the activity, name the standard, and explain why you believe the activity is a good one for the standard you named.

2. Devise a method for keeping track of children's actions that indicate that they are using mathematics as communication and reasoning and are making connections within mathematics and between mathematics and the real world. Observe a group of children during a mathematics period and make a record of their actions in these three areas. What percent of the total time was spent in actions relating to these standards? Did it appear that the teacher was making a conscious effort to promote communication, reasoning, and connections? Do you think the teacher overlooked opportunities to promote one or another of

the standards? If so, what might she or he have done to take advantage of the opportunity?

3. A number of ways connections can be made between mathematics and other curricular areas are listed in this chapter. List at least two additional activities for each subject area to expand the list. Discuss your list with classmates to see the many different ways connections can be made.

■ TEACHER'S BOOKSHELF

Baratta-Lorton, Robert. 1977. *Mathematics . . . A Way of Thinking.* Menlo Park, CA: Addison-Wesley.

Labinowicz, Ed. 1980. *The Piaget Primer.* Menlo Park, CA: Addison-Wesley.

■ FOR FURTHER READING

Bowan, Thomas E., and David Kufakwami Mtetwa. 1990, January. Mathematics as reasoning. *Arithmetic Teacher 37*(5), 16–18.

Bowan and Mtetwa discuss mathematical reasoning and cite three educational benefits from an approach that fosters reasoning in the classroom.

Katterns, Bob, and Ken Carr. 1986, April. Talking with young children about mathematics. *Arithmetic Teacher 33*(8), 18–21.

The authors interviewed children about their understanding of multiplication. Some responses were written to indicate children's thinking. The authors conclude that learning needs to be grounded in a wide variety of concrete experiences and that children need ample opportunities to explain ideas and processes.

Silver, Edward A., and Margaret S. Smith. 1990, April. Teaching mathematics and thinking. *Arithmetic Teacher 37*(8), 34–37.

Research into thinking is reviewed, then classroom practices that promote thinking are described. There is an extensive bibliography on thinking.

Sgroi, Richard J. 1990, February. Communicating about spatial relationships. *Arithmetic Teacher 37*(6), 21–23.

Students work in groups of two or three. One student gives oral instructions to another; the receiver makes a copy of the pattern, model, or other object described by the giver. Clear instructions and careful listening are mandatory for good copies. Four activities are described.

Small, Marion S. 1990, January. Do you speak math? *Arithmetic Teacher 37*(5), 26–29.

Small believes teachers should abandon much of the paper-and-pencil activity commonly used in favor of more discussion of mathematical ideas. Students who solve problems mentally rather than with paper and pencil are forced to think about mathematics as opposed to using rote processes. Teachers also need to discuss mathematics with children and have children write about the mathematics they are learning.

Whitin, David J. 1989, February. Number sense and the importance of asking "why." *Arithmetic Teacher 36*(6), 26–29.

> *Teachers should encourage children to ask "why" as they work with processes and ponder operations. Allowing children to investigate the "why" of an operation or process strengthens their number sense, pushes them into thinking about mathematics, fosters a spirit of inquisitiveness, and encourages them to take risks in mathematics.*

Zaslavsky, Claudia. 1989, September. People who live in round houses. *Arithmetic Teacher 37*(1), 18–21.

> *Talks about making mathematics relevant through integration with social studies and other subjects.*

◼ NOTES

[1] National Council of Teachers of Mathematics. 1989. *Curriculum and Evaluation Standards for School Mathematics.* Reston, VA: National Council of Teachers of Mathematics, 26. Used by permission.

[2] NCTM, 29. Used by permission.

[3] NCTM, 32. Used by permission.

[4] NCTM, 78. Used by permission.

[5] NCTM, 81. Used by permission.

[6] NCTM, 84. Used by permission.

[7] NCTM, 26.

[8] Robert Baratta-Lorton. 1977. *Mathematics . . . A Way of Thinking.* Menlo Park, CA: Addison-Wesley.

[9] Baratta-Lorton, 286.

[10] These are lessons 4-10 and 4-11 from Baratta-Lorton, 33–34. Used by permission.

[11] Neil Davidson, ed. 1990. *Cooperative Learning in Mathematics.* Menlo Park, CA: Addison-Wesley, 4.

[12] Davidson, 4.

[13] Marilyn Burns. 1990. The math solution: Using groups of four, in Neil Davidson, ed., *Cooperative Learning in Mathematics.* Menlo Park, CA: Addison-Wesley, 23.

[14] This lesson is from Davidson, 41–45. Used by permission of Marilyn Burns.

[15] Adapted from National Council of Teachers of Mathematics. 1989. *Curriculum and Evaluation Standards for School Mathematics.* Reston, VA: National Council of Teachers of Mathematics, 30.

[16] NCTM, 30.

[17] For information about early devices, see Florian Cajori. 1928. *A History of Mathematical Notations,* Vol. I. La Salle, IL: Open Court, 30–40; and H. A. Freebury. 1961. *A History of Mathematics.* New York: Macmillan, 160.

[18] Adapted from National Council of Teachers of Mathematics. 1989. *Curriculum and Evaluation Standards for School Mathematics.* Reston, VA: National Council of Teachers of Mathematics, 34. Used by permission.

[19] Adapted from NCTM, 34. Used by permission.

[20] Adapted from NCTM, 85–86. Used by permission.

PART Three

PROCEDURES
AND MATERIALS

CHAPTER 7

Early Experiences in Mathematics

Mathematics learning does not begin on the first day of school. Development of mathematics concepts such as number, shape, size, and patterning starts with sensory experiences in the crib. Playing with toys, talking and singing, walking and exploring are important in providing the foundations for strong mathematical structures. Informal explorations with a wide variety of materials should continue through the early childhood years and into primary grades. Teacher-led lessons and mathematical investigations also play a part in early mathematics learning in preschool, kindergarten, and the early grades.

In this chapter you will read about

1. concrete experiences in the home and at school that build mathematics concepts;

2. children's work with discrete and continuous materials;

3. classification as a basic thinking skill based on recognition of similarities;

4. order and seriation activities for arranging objects based on differences;

5. children's work with patterns of many kinds;

6. activities to develop spatial understandings such as proximity, separation, order, and enclosure;

7. development of rote and rational counting;

8. five principles that govern counting;

9. activities to relate the number in a set with number words and symbols;

10. children's learning to write numerals;

11. special problems that some children have with counting and numerals;

12. the appropriate role of computers in early childhood mathematics.

NCTM STANDARDS THAT PERTAIN TO EARLY MATHEMATICS EXPERIENCES

Kindergarten Through Grade Four

Standard 6: Number Sense and Numeration
In grades K–4, the mathematics curriculum should include whole number concepts and skills so that students can:

- construct number meanings through real-world experiences and the use of physical materials;

- develop number sense;

- interpret the multiple uses of numbers encountered in the real world.[1]

Standard 9: Geometry and Spatial Sense   In grades K–4, the mathematics curriculum should include two- and three-dimensional geometry so that students can:

- develop spatial sense.[2]

Standard 13: Patterns and Relationships   In grades K–4, the mathematics curriculum should include the study of patterns and relationships so that students can:

- recognize, extend, and create a wide variety of patterns.[3]

   ## A GOOD START IN MATHEMATICS

Many skills are acquired incidentally through children's play at home. In the same way that language is learned spontaneously, mathematics skills are learned. Children use counting processes; fit shapes into forms; make symmetrical patterns; build block structures; crawl over, under, and around objects; and engage in other activities with a mathematics orientation. Not only are these experiences fun, they also help children acquire vocabularies and background on which later learning is based.

Informal, play-type experiences should continue in preschool and kindergarten classrooms. Children from ages four to seven are making a transition from being totally dependent on their perceptions to being able to think more abstractly with concrete objects as aids. A variety of commercial and teacher-made materials allow children to develop an understanding of many topics.

In a room stocked with ample materials, children confront mathematical ideas continually as they manipulate objects and talk about them. The learning is not likely to be segmented into distinct lessons or class times but grows from the experiences that the teacher has organized by careful selection and arrangement of materials. Teachers who recognize that children learn through play choose materials and ask questions to help children understand the meanings in the materials. The activities and suggestions found in this chapter will alert you to many opportunities.

■ EXPERIENCES WITH DISCRETE AND CONTINUOUS MATERIALS

Children need experiences with both discrete and continuous materials. **Discrete materials** are those that can be counted, such as cookies, children, cars, and dots on a piece of paper. Children may use unit blocks or cubes for counting and stacking. Other discrete materials include color links, pegboard pegs, toys, beads on a string, flannel board cutouts, and magnetic pieces.

Continuous materials are not counted but are measured in terms of length, area, height, weight, volume, capacity, or temperature. The numerical value of a child's height, a container of milk, and a package of rice is determined by comparing it to a unit of measure. When children build towers of blocks and compare the heights, they are talking about a continuous quality—height. When they count the number of blocks in the towers, the blocks are not just discrete objects but are also units of measure.

A water table or sand table is an important part of the primary classroom. As children pour water or sand from one container to another using funnels, tubing, plastic cups, and bowls of various sizes, they develop ideas about capacity, volume, weight, and mass. In classrooms where a water table or sand table is impractical, a small plastic tub or sink may be used. Rather than water or sand, rice, beans, or even plastic packing pellets may be substituted as continuous materials. Although individual grains of rice or beans can be counted, they are considered to be continuous materials when used this way.

DISCRETE MATERIALS

More cars	Fewer cars
More beads	Fewer beads
Most dolls	Fewest dolls

CONTINUOUS MATERIALS

More juice	Less juice
More clay	Less clay
Most soup	Least soup

While children work with discrete and continuous materials, they learn to compare quantities based on number or size. The ideas of *more* and *less* are explored in a general sense as objects are compared without counting or exact measurement. The teacher may make comments and ask questions to help children focus on the comparisons:

- "Juan has more blocks."
- "Who has fewer cars?"
- "Ina has more water in her cup."
- "Which cup holds less sand?"
- "Can you tell who has the most cards?"

When the teacher models the language and processes of comparison, children begin to use them. Math boxes are a good way to provide many different materials for children to explore. These boxes contain collections of materials that encourage children to explore a variety of mathematical ideas. They may contain "junk" assortments of colored toothpicks, plastic fishing worms, washers of various sizes, nails of different lengths, assorted keys, small plastic toys, plastic bread closers, buttons, or collections of other items. Early activities with math boxes lay foundations for later work with one-to-one matching, counting, addition, subtraction, common fractions, and other concepts. Mary Baratta-Lorton developed a series of activities based on math boxes.[4] Activity 7.1 describes some ways to utilize math boxes. (See photographs of math boxes in Chapter 3).

Teachers may also make games and activities that are more specific than math boxes. Activities in which children make one-to-one matchings refine their understanding of number concepts *as many as, more than,* and *fewer than.* The first activities should involve real objects or toys, as in Activities 7.2 and 7.3. Activities that are more pictorial can be constructed with tagboard to use on a magnetic or flannel board, as in Activity 7.4.

ACTIVITY 7.1   Math Box Exploration

- Give the children math boxes.
- Watch the children work with the contents. Some will "play" with materials—flying airplanes or setting the table with plates and cups. Some will begin to sort based on color; others will group by size, shape, or other common attributes. Some children will form lines or trains with their objects, with or without a pattern.

- Make a statement about the collection: "I see two blue cars." "I see four big dinosaurs." Watch how the children respond to this statement.
- The actions of the children tell the teacher about each child's understanding of sets and classification.

ACTIVITY 7.2   Nuts and Bolts

- Collect an assortment of nuts and bolts. You may want to have them all the same size or a variety of sizes.

- Make several groups of nuts and bolts and place them in containers such as butter tubs. The number of nuts and bolts you use may vary from three or four to ten or fifteen. Vary the number of nuts and bolts so some tubs have different amounts. Some have more bolts, some have more nuts, and others have the same number.

- Ask students to find out whether there are more nuts or bolts in each tub by matching them.

- Variations:
  —Punch holes in the lid for students to put the bolts through before fastening the nut.

—Label the lid with a numeral and punch that number of holes so that students are matching the same number of nuts and bolts.

—Paint numerals on the head of a large bolt and provide washers so that students can put the correct number of washers on before putting on the nut.

ACTIVITY 7.3   Matching Outlines

- Put outlines of common objects on a large sheet of heavy tagboard.
- Have a collection of common objects in a box.
- Have children match the real objects with their outlines.

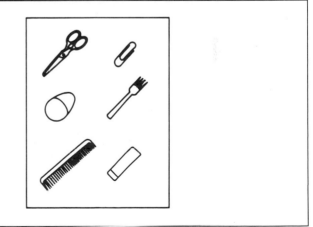

ACTIVITY 7.4   Matching Airplanes and Wings

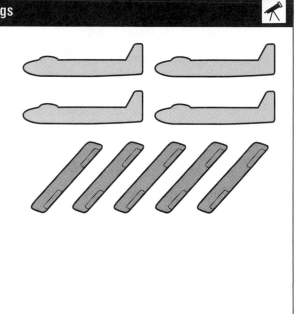

- Make a set of tagboard cards with wingless airplanes on them. Put different numbers of airplanes on the cards. Make the planes on some cards one color; mix colors on others. Make wings to match the colors of the planes. Put pieces of small magnets or pieces of flannel on the back of each piece.

- Have children match the wings to the airplanes.

- Have children tell whether there are *as many as, more than,* or *fewer than* when matchings are complete.

- Variations: Use canoes and paddles, toy cars and garages made of small boxes, cut-out dolls and pieces of clothing, cups and saucers, or other commonly matched objects.

EXERCISE   Create an activity similar to one of those in Activities 7.1 through 7.4 to provide young children with an exploratory experience with discrete or continuous materials.

■ BUILDING LEARNING SKILLS

Working and playing with a variety of discrete and continuous materials develops basic learning skills. Sorting and classification, seriation and order, and sequence and patterning are basic skills used in learning all subjects. They are necessary for problem solving and all higher-order thinking. Teachers develop activities with both discrete and continuous materials so that children in preschool and the primary grades have many chances to develop these skills.

Sorting and Classifying

Classification may be the first and most fundamental of all thinking skills. The world is a very chaotic place to persons without the ability to understand how people, events, or objects are similar. Children develop classification schemes to make sense of their world. The evidence of this **classifica-**

tion, or grouping by similarity, is seen when a child calls a dog "kitty" or refers to any man as "daddy." These humorous events belie a very powerful thinking tool that becomes more accurate with time and experience.

When working with a collection of objects, children, like adults, usually group the objects into meaningful subsets. They may use classification schemes such as color, shape, size, purpose, or materials. Classification should begin with real objects because they are much more complex and interesting than classification materials made especially for school use. Every classroom should be full of things to classify. The math boxes are convenient sources of materials. By observing children classifying a box of buttons, teachers gain insight into their thinking. If students only classify buttons by color, the teacher may intervene. Sometimes the teacher only asks, "Is there another way to classify the buttons?" Other times more leading questions or statements can be used.

- "I see two big buttons. Can you find any more big buttons?"
- "This button is very rough. This button is smooth."
- "Do all the buttons have four holes?"

These interventions come only after children have had time to explore and invent classification schemes for themselves. During early experiences, children may not be consistent in their classification plans. When confronted with a set of buttons, they may sort them into a group of big buttons, a group of shiny buttons, and a group of red buttons. Most children move toward a more consistent classification plan without prompting. However, if a child does not become consistent, the teacher may ask the child to name all the colors of buttons and suggest using only colors for classification.

Children themselves are another source for classification materials. They can arrange themselves into groups by gender, hair color, wearing apparel, number of brothers or sisters, or type of pets. Shoes are another classification material described in Activity 7.5. Classification schemes based on single attributes or characteristics are fairly simple for most children. A double classification plan is more complicated, as shown in Activity 7.6. Sets of attribute blocks (see the photograph in Chapter 3) designed for classification activities have several characteristics that can be used for simple or multiple classification: color, shape, size, thickness, texture. A sample exercise with attribute materials is shown in Activity 7.7.

Classification skills are also important in many subject areas. In science children classify objects by whether they sink or float and whether they are living or nonliving. In reading children hear and see that words have similarities in sounds and letters, such as rhyming words with the same ending letters. In social studies they find similarities in how people live in different climates. Artworks can be classified as realistic or fanciful and music as fast or slow, soft or loud. Opportunities for various exercises and materials in classification help children develop flexibility of thinking and learn concepts of many kinds.

ACTIVITY 7.5   Sorting Shoes

- Have all the children take one of their shoes off and put it onto a piece of butcher paper with a large circle drawn on it. Have the children stand around a table or sit on the floor around the butcher paper.

- Ask children to describe the shoes. Ask whether some shoes are alike and have them name several characteristics: tennis shoes, shoes with laces, new shoes, big shoes, brown shoes.

- Ask one child to make one group of shoes. Ask another to make another group. If they begin classification with two attributes at the same time—color and type—see if they can resolve this dilemma themselves by reaching an agreement to use only color or type. If they cannot, suggest that they group by color this time and type next time.

- Ask how many different ways they can find to sort the shoes.

- Variations
  —Use a collection of shoes for all ages from a used clothing store.

  —Have the children classify pictures of shoes cut from catalogs and advertisements.

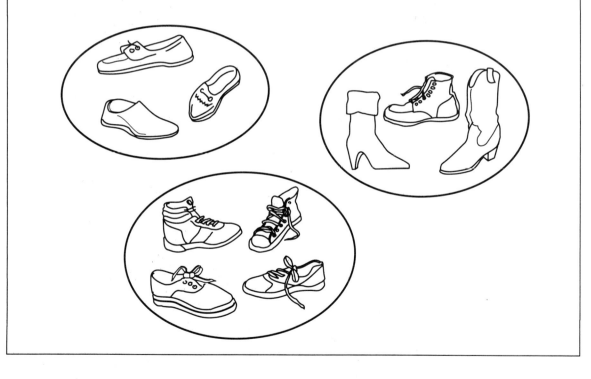

ACTIVITY 7.6   Double Classification

- Prepare a set of twenty-five cards using five shapes of five different colors: star, car, rabbit, balloon, and rocket in yellow, blue, orange, green, and red.

Activity 7.6   *continued*

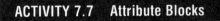

- Prepare a 5-by-5 space game board with room on the top and left for a key to the game. Across the top draw the outlines of the five shapes and down the sides put five colors.

- Have children draw one shape at a time from a bag or box and place it in the space at the intersection of the shape and color.

- Variations:
  —Play the game like bingo. Make a set of game boards. Have a child draw and call out the shape and color. Let the players mark the intersection with a black paper square.

  —Mark two blank dice with colors and shapes. Roll the dice to get the color and shape for the board.

ACTIVITY 7.7   Attribute Blocks

- Draw three separate areas on a piece of paper and put out ten or twelve assorted shapes.

- Place a yellow circle in one area. Place a red square in another area. Ask the children where to place a blue triangle. (In the third area.)

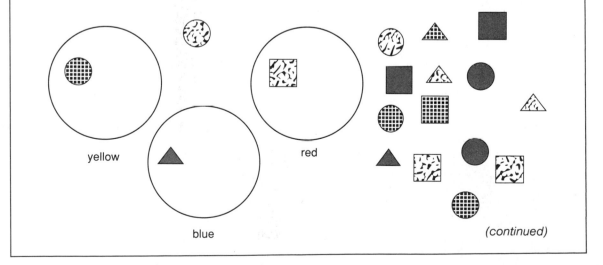

(continued)

Activity 7.7   *continued*

- Hold up a red circle and ask where it should go and why it belongs there. Children should see that it could go either with the red square or with the yellow circle. Tell them that you want them to guess what your rule for classification is and put the red circle with the red square. (The rule is classification by color.)

- Continue to hold up attribute pieces and ask the children to place them in the correct area. Probe why each piece belongs in a given area.

- Play the game again with different rules such

as shape, size, thickness, or texture, depending on the set of attributes.

- Draw two areas that overlap. Put several red and blue circles in one area and several yellow squares and triangles in the other area. Ask what the rule is for each classification area. Then ask if there is any piece that has both characteristics (circle and yellow). Put one yellow circle in the overlapping area. Ask them to find other yellow circles.

- Repeat double classification with other combination rules.

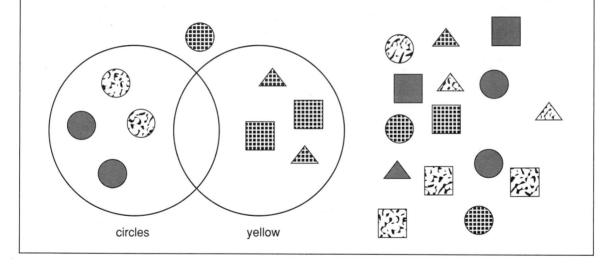

circles   yellow

Order and Seriation

Order and seriation apply to both discrete and continuous materials. Discrete materials are counted and their sets ordered by number. Continuous materials are measured and are *seriated,* or put in order, according to length, height, or weight. While classification is based on similarities, seriating is based on differences.

A variety of experiences help children see differences. Children can be lined up from shortest to tallest. Blue tiles may be ordered from lightest to darkest. Cuisenaire rods may be ordered from longest to shortest; Unifix cubes may be stacked so that each stack has one more cube on it. Children may be asked to vote for their favorite fruit snack, and a graph can be drawn to show the most favored, the next favored, down to the least favored. Many materials developed by Maria Montessori and used in Montessori schools, such as the pink tower and weight or length cylinders, were designed to develop order and seriation skills. Teachers may develop materials similar to the Montessori materials to provide seriation practice. Activity 7.8 describes a seriation activity for length using straws. Activity 7.9 shows how to use film canisters for a seriation-by-weight activity.

ACTIVITY 7.8   Drawing Straws

- Cut five or six drinking straws into two pieces so that you have ten or twelve different lengths. Line the straw pieces up on a piece of tagboard and make a playing board of them from the shortest to the longest.

- Put the straws into a bag or box and have students draw one straw piece at a time from the bag. As each piece is drawn, it is placed on the playing board until all the straw pieces are drawn out.

- Variations:
  - Play the same game without the playing board. Students decide where each piece goes without guidelines.
  - Make a board with only some of the sizes drawn on it. Have the children draw to find only the straws that are the right length to fit on the board.
  - Make a board on which the lines are marked at random.

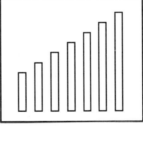

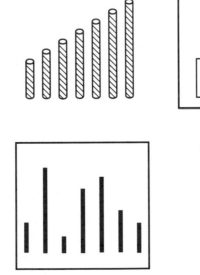

ACTIVITY 7.9   Sand Cans

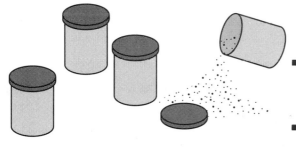

- Collect five to ten film canisters. Put different amounts of sand in each one. At first you may only have three cans with sand: very little sand, half-full, and nearly full.

- Ask the children to find the lightest can, the heaviest can, the middle-weight can.

- When the children are successful with three cans, add two more cans with other weights of sand in them. You can continue to add more cans until the children cannot discriminate accurately between the weights. Then they will begin to group them into three or four groups: heavy, light, middle.

- You may decide whether you wish to provide a self-checking system for the cans by numbering them or marking the bottom of the cans in colors keyed to an answer board.

- Variation: Use margarine tubs in place of canisters.

Sequences and Patterns

A *sequence* is a meaningful arrangement of objects or events and may be related to ordering. Cuisenaire rods arranged in stair steps from shortest to longest are a sequence based on a one-step difference between them. Events in the classroom may be ordered with a posted schedule so that the children know that the daily sequence of activities is group time, center time, snack time, story time, and outside time. The days of the weeks have their order shown on the calendar. Picture books are good sources for sequences. The story of "Three Billy Goats Gruff" can be told or acted out to emphasize its sequence of events. One sequence activity is a folder game (Activity 7.10) based on change rules using attribute materials or pattern blocks.

Patterns are based on sequences; a pattern is a sequence of objects, events, or ideas that repeats. The ability to recognize sequence and repetition is an important thinking skill used in all areas of the curriculum. Word and letter patterns are used by good readers; puns or other kinds of word play are based on some distortion of the usual pattern of words. Repetitions of colors and shapes in art and of sounds in music are fundamental in aesthetics. The field of science is based on finding regular and predictable occurrences in the natural world.

When young children work with patterns involving physical objects or drums and cymbal beats, they sharpen their perceptions and develop awareness of order, sequence, shapes, and aesthetics. A pattern center can be es-

ACTIVITY 7.10   Shape Changes

- Materials: Attribute materials or a set of objects with at least three attributes.

- Make a game board with six or seven squares with different lines between them.

- Tell the students what the different lines mean.

→ Change one attribute
⇒ Change two attributes

- Have children put a shape in the START box and follow the rules to the STOP box.

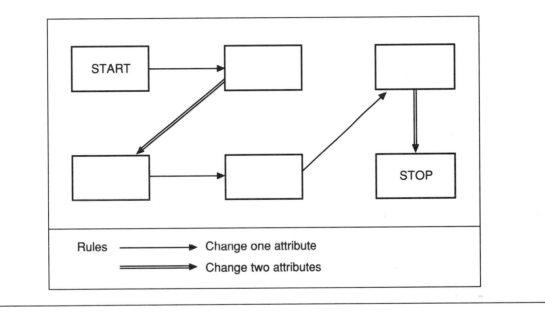

Rules ——————▶ Change one attribute
 ═════════▶ Change two attributes

tablished with such things as colored beads and cord, pegboards and golf tees, shapes cut from cardboard, pattern blocks, small colored tiles, and colored plastic disks. Children will make up many designs with these materials. Task cards for pegboards, beads, and patterns are available commercially (Figure 7.1), or teachers can make their own. Task cards direct children to replicate patterns and designs and should be used selectively so that they do not inhibit children's own creativity with the materials.

When working with patterns, some students may need assistance in recognizing where each sequence in a pattern begins and ends. Teacher-developed lessons alert students to patterns of sounds, shapes, or events. Activity 7.11 describes pattern activities with rhythm instruments that can be done throughout the entire year. Activity 7.12 shows how to get children to read and act out patterns.

Figure 7-1
Samples of pattern
cards

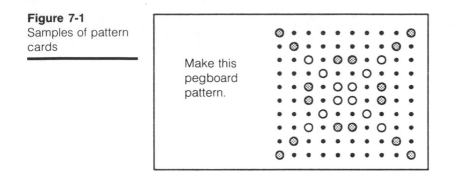

Make this
pegboard
pattern.

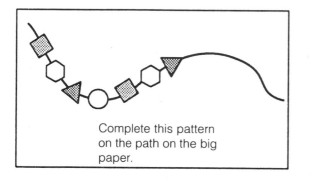

Complete this pattern
on the path on the big
paper.

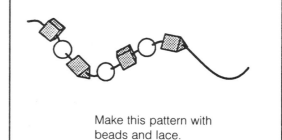

Make this pattern with
beads and lace.

ACTIVITY 7.11   Drums Across the Classroom

- Use a variety of percussion instruments: drum, cymbals, rhythm sticks, tambourine, and tone block.

- Have the children sit in a circle so they can see you. Begin beating the drum with a steady beat: thump, thump, thump. Have the children clap with you as you set the rhythm.

- When the students can keep the rhythm, stop them and ask them to listen to a new pattern. Instead of beating regularly, introduce pauses in the pattern.

  Thump, thump, thump, pause;
  thump, thump, thump, pause; . . .
  Thump, pause; thump, pause;
  thump, pause; . . .

Have students join you as soon as they understand the pattern. Nodding the head for the "pause" is a good way to maintain the rhythm.

- Ask for a volunteer to model another pattern of beats using another rhythm instrument.

- Variation: When students can keep a steady beat and follow the pattern, introduce various rhythms. Instead of thump, thump, pause, you may double the first beat for quick, quick, thump, pause. Let the children lead the rhythm patterns.

ACTIVITY 7.12   Acting Out Patterns

- Begin with a string of beads in a yellow-blue-yellow-blue pattern.

- Read the pattern "yellow, blue, yellow, blue, . . ." and have the children read it with you.

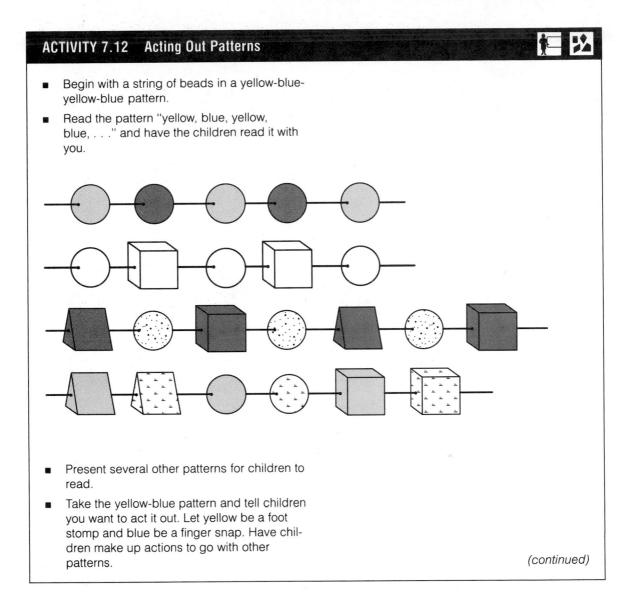

- Present several other patterns for children to read.

- Take the yellow-blue pattern and tell children you want to act it out. Let yellow be a foot stomp and blue be a finger snap. Have children make up actions to go with other patterns.

(continued)

Activity 7.12   continued

- Make a series of pattern strips on sentence strip cards. Have some show pictures indicating actions (stomp, snap, clap, blink, nod) and others show shapes that can be read or acted out.

- T-shirt patterns in Activity 5.1 can also be acted out.

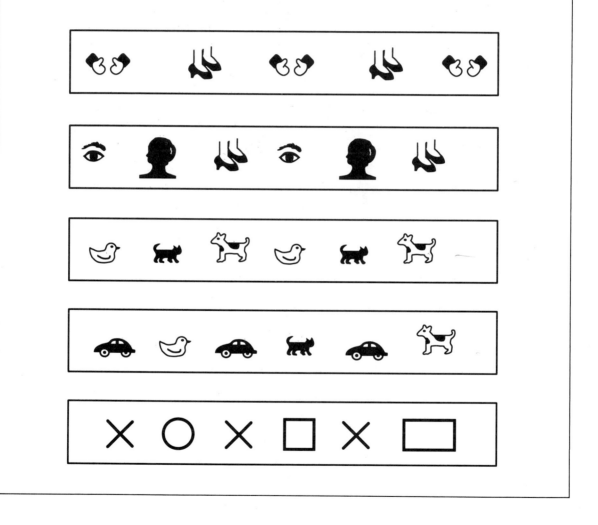

■ SPATIAL RELATIONSHIPS

A good understanding of spatial relationships is an important characteristic of an effective problem solver. Many problems deal with relationships between and among objects, places, and events. Packaging presents for mailing involves spatial visualization of how all the parts might fit inside the whole. Learning to throw a football or baseball accurately requires a well-developed spatial sense. Art projects and building designs are dependent on a sense of space, balance, and how different forms interrelate. Reading a map is another example of a spatial understanding that is fundamental to everyday living.

Spatial relationships of these kinds are a special kind of geometry called *topological geometry.* A topological view does not require that figures maintain a rigid or fixed shape as in Euclidean geometry. Rather, a shape may be altered so that it assumes a new configuration, much as it would if drawn on a sheet of rubber where it can be stretched in different directions. For example, a square may assume the shape of a rectangle or an oval or some other simple closed curve. An open figure such as the letter C can be reshaped to look like the letter S. As the configurations change, certain characteristics remain unchanged, even though the shape may take different forms.

Children's perspective on the world, including their understanding of space, is very **idiocentric,** or self-centered. According to Piaget young children do not view people and objects as being stable and unchanging but view them in the topological sense. To children in the sensorimotor and preoperational stages, people and objects change as the positions from which they are viewed change. Therefore, Piaget said that children's first concepts of the world are topological. Four topological relations—proximity, separation, order, and enclosure—are suitable for kindergarten and primary-grade children.

Proximity

Proximity refers to the location of objects in space and to how near one object is to another. Naturally, very young children are interested in things close to them because they can touch and manipulate them. Things that are out of their reach are usually of little interest, unless the child sees something that is eye-catching such as a shiny part of a swinging mobile. Objects that are out of sight do not exist in the mind of a child in the early sensorimotor stage.

Gradually children engage in activities that help them recognize that out-of-sight objects do exist and that clarify the location of objects in space. Early experiences with spatial relations and concepts such as *near, far, close to, under, above, below, up, down, beside, between, next to,* and so on come from children's everyday experiences and free play activities. In-class activities and teacher comments help to develop children's spatial understandings and give them practice in following directions.

- "Put the yellow block on top of the blue block."
- "Yusef is standing between Tara and Ramona."
- "The tower is going up. It is almost as tall as you are."
- "Pick up the book beside the globe."
- "Walk close to the wall during the fire drill."

As children become more proficient, two and three directions can be given at the same time.

Working with math boxes leads naturally to questions about location and proximity.

- "Which red car is nearest to the green car?"
- "Which bead is the farthest from the blue bead?"

A set of flannel board shapes or magnetized objects may also be placed so that teacher and students can talk about their locations.

- "Emily, please move the blue car close to the red truck."
- "Which car is closest to the red airplane? Farthest from it?"

Students may play a game modeled after "I Spy" as in Activity 7.13, or move through an obstacle course as in Activity 7.14, to practice spatial language and concepts.

ACTIVITY 7.13   I Spy

- Describe things in the room using the spatial terms.
  - "I see something yellow on top of the coat closet."
  - "I see something under the desk nearest the wall."
  - "I see someone far from Sean and close to Paulette."
  - "I see someone standing between Angelica and Jose."
- Variations:
  - Have the children place things around the room and have them lead the game.
  - Use pictures in an oversized picture book for the game.

ACTIVITY 7.14   Obstacle Course

- Make a classroom obstacle course by set-ting up the chairs, tables, trash cans, and bookshelves so that the children can move around them easily.

- Either verbally or with rebus cards, tell the students actions to take to complete the ob-stacle course.

- Variation: Play "Follow the Leader" with the teacher leading the children through a series of actions and announcing each one. The children should say exactly what has been said as they follow through a sequence of movements: "around the flagpole, on top of first base, under the monkey bar, beside the slide."

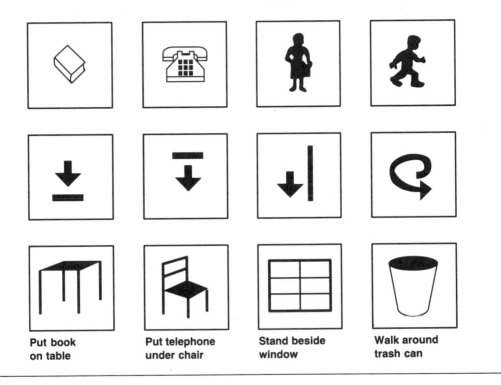

Put book on table   **Put telephone under chair**   **Stand beside window**   **Walk around trash can**

Separation

Until children achieve an understanding of *separation,* they cannot clearly visualize an object as having separate parts or a collection as being made up of separate objects. All the parts run together in the child's mind. Children's drawings, especially those of human figures, provide a good indication of their understanding of separation. Early drawings are usually an egg shape with odd lines for mouth, arms, and legs. Gradually children differentiate the body parts and add distinct head, torso, and limbs. Finally they draw details such as fingers, toes, and all the parts of the face and head in the proper places.

The process of recognizing parts and wholes takes several years. The teacher may find various opportunities to point out examples of separation.

- A fence separates the playground from the street.
- The red line is a boundary between two teams.
- The library separates picture books for the primary grades from books for the upper elementary children.
- Local rivers and streets serve as boundaries between neighborhoods or school attendance zones.
- The police officer's uniform has many special parts: badge, gun, whistle, cap, boots, belt, and so on.
- The cooperative group has four people with different jobs.

The classification activities already described also help children learn about parts and wholes. A set of toy animals can be divided into groups of dogs, cats, elephants, cows, horses, and monkeys. Recognizing sets and subsets is an important aspect of separation that leads to number concepts.

Order

A sequence of events has two orders: from beginning to end and from end to beginning. Developing a sense of reversibility or opposite direction is another thinking ability that children learn through working with materials. Children may be asked to make a pattern with beads that is the reverse of a given pattern. They may count up to ten, but counting down may be a little more difficult. Teachers in kindergarten or the primary grades may have a "Backward Day," in which the children do as many things backward as they can. They eat dessert first, wear their shirts backward, reverse the order of daily events, and find other ways to go in reverse.

An easy way to assess whether students can maintain a given order requires a tube and three beads or balls of different colors. As children watch, put the red ball in the tube, then the green, then the blue. Ask the children what order the balls will be in when they come out the other end of the tube. Some students will not be able to maintain the sense of order. They will need many more pattern and sequence activities before they are ready for reversibility.

Enclosure

Enclosure includes the position of one point between two others on a line, a point within a closed curve on a plane, and a point within a closed three-dimensional figure such as a cube. Enclosure on a line is important because children frequently encounter the idea of "between" in mathematics. Children's first work with enclosure should be at the concrete level. Activity 7.15 is for developing children's understanding of enclosure on a line. The block corner where children build corrals for horses and garages for cars and trucks is an excellent place for children to explore enclosure. Toys and pictures can also be used for the farm setting in Activity 7.16.

An activity for three-dimensional enclosure can be done by placing something inside a box or jar. Compare taking something out when the lid is off and when the lid is on. The children can look for other examples of enclosure in boxes, jars, and rooms inside and outside of the classroom.

ACTIVITY 7.15   Between Two Beads

- Put three different beads on a string.
- Have the children describe what they see. If they have worked with separation, they can mention that the center bead separates the other two.

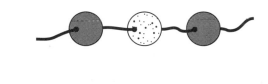

- Point out that the two outside beads enclose the bead in the middle. Ask how to get the middle bead off. The middle bead cannot be taken off without moving one of the two outside beads.
- Variations:
  —Have some children stand in line so that one is enclosed by others on either side.
  —Discuss how some chairs are enclosed by others in a row of chairs. How can people sit in the middle chair?

ACTIVITY 7.16   Fences

- Set up a scene with plastic fences, horses, cows, barns, and so on. Place some animals inside a closed fence and some outside of it.
- Ask questions.
  —"Who can tell which animals are inside the fence?"
  —"Is the brown horse inside or outside the fence?"

- —"Is the barn inside or outside the fence?"
- Point out that the things inside the fence are enclosed as long as the gate is closed. The animals outside cannot get inside.
- Variation: Use felt animals and a yarn loop on a flannel board.

EXERCISE   Activities dealing with classification, order and seriation, sequences and patterns, proximity, separation, and enclosure have been described. Do you believe most preschool, kindergarten, and first grade children have adequate opportunities to deal with each of these concepts? Explain the reason for your response.

■ COUNTING AND NUMBER RELATIONSHIPS

Understanding of mathematical concepts begins imperceptibly in infancy and grows so gradually that it is almost unnoticeable. Children under two years of age have acquired some idea of *more,* usually in connection with food, such as by taking the larger cookie or bigger glass of juice. Some counting behaviors are seen in two- and three-year-old children. Even though the counting may not be accurate, the children show that they are aware of the process.

Many children are taught to say the number words in sequence. Children can count to 10, 20, 50, or 100 using memorized verbal chains without regard to the meaning of the numbers. Such counting is called **rote** counting. Although this skill itself may not be valuable except as a performance piece for appropriately impressed relatives, it can be a foundation on which later understanding is built. A deliberate attempt to teach meaningful, or **rational,** counting occurs when an adult encourages children to connect number words to objects by counting tableware pieces or cars or fingers or toes. Children who play at game boards on which moves are determined by dice or spinners learn to count spots on the dice and read spinner numerals and move the designated number of spaces on the board.

Children who enter kindergarten and first grade with many informal number and counting experiences may need different experiences than those with a meager background. A teacher must take time early in the year to assess the level of understanding and skill. The Conservation of Number task described in Chapter 4 is very useful. Observing while children count a set of objects also gives insight into their understanding. Rachel Gelman and C. R. Gallistel have identified five principles of rational counting.[5]

1.   The abstraction principle states that any collection of real or imagined objects can be counted.

2.   The stable-order principle means that counting numbers are arranged in a sequence that does not change.

3.   The one-to-one principle involves ticking off the items in a set in such a way that one and only one number is used as each item is counted.

4. The order-irrelevance principle states that the order in which items are counted is irrelevant. The number stays the same regardless of the order.

5. The cardinal principle gives special significance to the last number named, because not only is it associated with the last item but it also represents the total number of items in the set. The number, which tells how many are in the set, is the cardinal number of the set.

Gelman and Gallistel also identify common errors observed in children's counting behavior.[6]

- A child may make a coordination error. This occurs when the count is not started until after the first item has been touched, which results in an undercount, or when the count continues after the final item has been touched, which results in an overcount.

- A child may make omit errors. This occurs when one or more items are skipped.

- A child may make a double-count error by counting one or more items more than once.

- The child may use idiosyncratic counting sequences such as "one, two, four, six, ten."

Understanding of number is built on a child's intuitive understanding of the number *one*. The only way to describe *one* is by holding one finger or one block or one of something else. When children have had many experiences with discrete materials and classification, they understand that the number two is *one-more-than-one*, three is *one-more-than-two* or *two-more-than-one*, and so on. A way to organize objects to emphasize counting order is shown in Activity 7.17.

ACTIVITY 7.17   Counting Cars

- Put a collection of plastic cars on the table so that there are one, two, three, and four cars of different colors. Ask the children to sort the cars by color.

- Have a piece of paper marked with squares large enough to hold the cars.

- Ask the children to line up the cars so that one car is in each square. Have them put the largest number on the top line and the smallest number on the bottom line.

- Ask the children to count the number of cars in each line. As they count each set ask if they can find other sets in the room with the same count.

- Make a chart of things found in twos, threes, and so on.   *(continued)*

Activity 7.17   *continued*

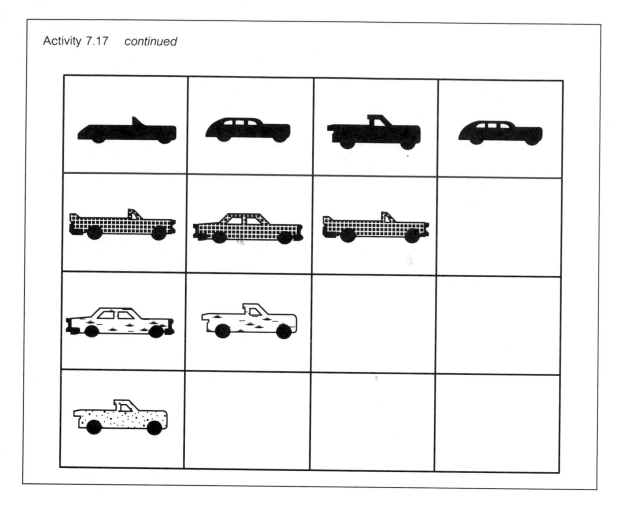

Sets for the rest of the numbers through nine should gradually be developed and studied with concrete materials. As counting is taught, stress numerical order. Also stress the cardinal number by emphasizing it each time you count a set: "One, two, three, four, *five*." After a child has counted, ask, "What is the last number you named? How many cars (shapes, books, dolls) are in the set?" A chart can be made that shows sets for all nine numbers. When the items are lined up accurately, the chart helps to demonstrate the one-more idea between counting numbers, as in Figure 7.2.

Zero requires special attention because children may not have encountered the number word for an empty set before starting to school. However, children have had experiences of "all gone," and those can be used to introduce zero. Story situations such as Activity 7.18 may be used.

Figure 7-2
Number sets

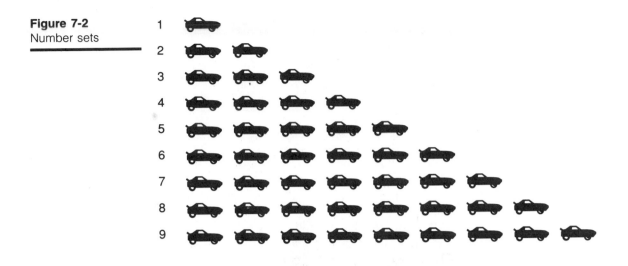

ACTIVITY 7.18   No More Flowers

- Put three felt flowers on a flannel board.

- Ask, "These flowers were growing in the garden. How many did I have?"

- Remove one of the flowers and ask, "I went to my garden on Saturday and picked one of the flowers. How many were left?"

- Remove two flowers and ask how many are left. Children will respond with "none," "not any," "they are all gone," and so on.

- Show several empty containers (boxes, bags, jars) and ask the children to describe their contents. Some will say they are empty. At this point introduce the word *zero* as the number that tells how many flowers were left and the number of things in each container.

Number rhymes, songs, and fingerplay activities familiarize children with number names and their sequence. The rhythm and rhyme of songs and poems stimulate children's enjoyment of language and support many concepts. "One Little Brown Bird" has the children counting in sequence.[7]

> One little brown bird, up and up he flew.
> Along came another and that made two.
>
> Two little brown birds, sitting in a tree.
> Along came another one and that made three.
>
> Three little brown birds, then up came one more.
> What's all the noise about? That made four.

"Five Little Monkeys" is a counting down favorite of many children. Each verse has one fewer monkeys jumping on the bed.

Five little monkeys jumping on the bed.
One fell off and bumped his head
Called the doctor and the doctor said
Bad little monkeys jumping on the bed.

Four little monkeys jumping on the bed.
. . .
. . .

One little monkey jumping on the bed
One fell off and bumped his head.
Called the doctor and the doctor said
No more monkeys jumping on the bed.

Books of fingerplays and poems for young children are available in most libraries. Many books for children have counting and number ideas. Some are listed in the Teacher's Bookshelf section at the end of the chapter.

Children need many experiences with rearranging and manipulating objects as they learn to count. Unifix materials provide students with many such experiences, as in Activity 7.19. Similar activities can be done with counting bears or flannel or magnetic materials, which are easy to arrange on an appropriate board. Activities 7.20 and 7.21 show two such activities. If children are having difficulty conserving number as shown by the Piaget conservation task in Chapter 4, take extra time and care with activities such as these.

ACTIVITY 7.19   Unifix Cube Towers

- Create a Unifix tower of seven cubes. Keep them all the same color.

- Ask the children to make other towers the same height as yours using two colors of cubes. They should make tower combinations of 1 + 6, 2 + 5, 3 + 4, 4 + 3, 5 + 2, and 6 + 1.

- Next ask for all the towers of three colors. Have children discuss all the combinations to see if they have found them all without duplication.

- Continue with four and five colors.

- Let the children compare all their towers with the original one. Ask how many were in your tower and how many are in each of the towers they made. If children do not see that they all are the same, note them for additional concrete work.

ACTIVITY 7.20   Seven Animals

- Materials: Pictures of animals such as penguins, rabbits, cats, and teddy bears on a flannel board or with magnetic tape for a magnetic board.
- Show two or three sets of seven animals. Put each set into a circle.

- Ask the question, "How are these sets different?" Discuss the differences the children see.
- Ask, "In what way are these sets the same?" (Each one has seven animals in it.)

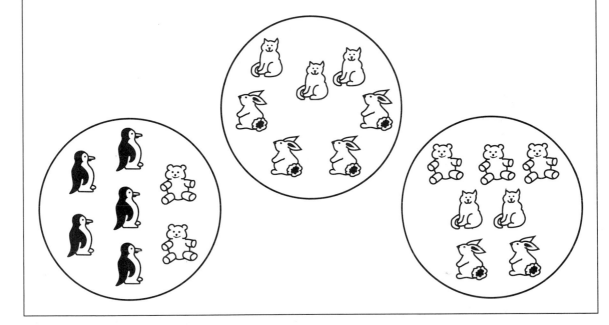

ACTIVITY 7.21   Arranging Seven

- Materials: Blue poker chips with magnetic tape on one side and a magnetic board.
- Show several arrangements of seven chips. Draw a loop around each one.

- Have the children make other arrangements of seven chips.
- Ask what is the same about all the sets.

EXERCISE   Identify three key features of lessons/activities dealing with the meaning of numbers that you believe are essential for establishing children's understanding of the meaning of the numbers one through ten.

■ NUMBER WORDS AND SYMBOLS

Children begin using numbers very early. The answer to "How old are you?" is two or three fingers. Then the answer changes to "Four" and four fingers are held up. By about six years of age, children will answer verbally without holding up fingers. This progression from concrete representation of a number idea to verbal abstraction is repeated many times as children learn to use the spoken word or the written word or symbol to stand for the idea of a number value. The written symbols **0, 1, 2, 3, 4, 5, 6, 7, 8, 9** are called **numerals.**

Children can make number books with one number on each page. On the page for "one," the child can draw or paste several single objects. On the "two" page, sets of two are drawn or pasted. At the end of several weeks, the child has a booklet to take home showing all the numbers and numerals. A number booklet is also a good home project for children to work on with parents or guardians.

Unifix Number Boats are designed so that a Unifix tower will fit exactly into the slot shown in Figure 7.3a. Unifix Number Indicators are less structured. Children may put the indicators on Unifix towers, as shown in Figure 7.3b. Peg number puzzles show the numeral and the correct number of peg holes. After children have worked all the pieces, they fit them together in the correct numerical order, as shown in Figure 7.3c. Activity 7.22 shows how you can make simple teacher-made puzzles for students to match numbers with numerals.

Most of the children's early work can be done without writing. Numeral cards are used instead of writing because the emphasis is on understanding the number value and recognition of the numerals. The manuscript form of writing numerals is used almost exclusively, although most people change to cursive form for writing words. When instruction in writing begins, most writing lessons begin with modeling the strokes and directions (see Figure 7.4). Some writing instruction systems have children trace over dotted or lightly drawn numerals while learning the shapes.

As children gain experience in writing numerals, most of them make numerals correctly and neatly during writing practice sessions. However, some are less careful at other times. A chart showing the correct way to write each numeral may be posted so that a child who is having difficulty can look to see how to form the letter.

Number words are usually taught in conjunction with the numerals. Many games and puzzles can be devised to relate the number of a set with

Figure 7-3
(a) Unifix cubes
and number boats;
(b) Unifix cubes and
number indicators;
(c) interlocking
number puzzles with
pegs.

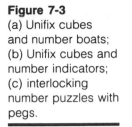
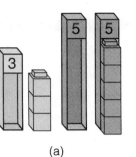

(a)

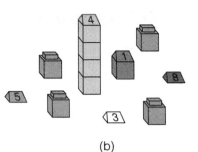

(b)

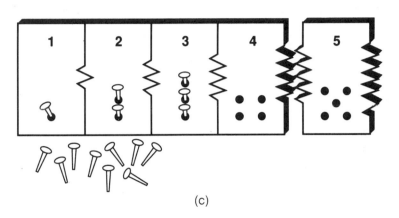

(c)

ACTIVITY 7.22   Plate Puzzles and Cup Puzzles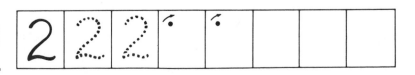

- Make a set of puzzles out of paper plates. Each plate should have a different cut so that only one number and the corresponding set will fit together.

- Put a number on a paper cup. Use golf tees to punch the correct number of holes in the top. Children fit the correct number of tees into the holes in the cup.

- Have children make their own cup and plate puzzles.

Figure 7-4
A sequence of steps
for teaching children
to write a numeral

2	2	´	´			

both the numeral and the number word. Children may match cards, numerals, and words in a pocket chart, as shown in Activity 7.23, or on a flannel or magnetic board. A concentration game with cards is described in Activity 7.24.

ACTIVITY 7.23   Matching Numeral and Set Cards

- Put set cards in a pocket chart. Give the children numeral cards to put in front of the sets.

- Variations:
  —Begin with nine and reverse the order of the sets.

—Mix up the order of the sets.

—Add a set of number words to match to the sets and numerals.

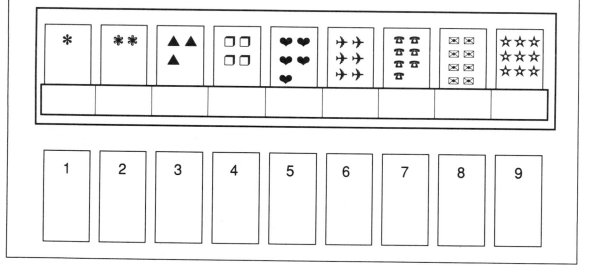

ACTIVITY 7.24   Concentration

- Take ten pairs of cards from a deck of playing cards, or make a set of cards having matching numeral cards and set cards.

- Have the children work in groups of two or three. Arrange the cards face down in a 4-by-5 array. A child should turn two cards over at a time. When a match of cards is made, the child keeps the two cards. If there is not a match, the cards are returned face down in their places and the next child turns over a pair.

- Variation: Introduce a set of number word cards into the game so that children have to remember three things to make a match.

A number line is a useful device for children of all ages because it puts the numbers in a spatial arrangement. Children in kindergarten and first grade can use a number line marked on the classroom floor as they learn to count and associate numbers with numerals. The points on the line should be about 14 inches apart, with the numerals printed on cards rather than on the floor to increase the number line's versatility. Activity 7.25 gives several different exercises with the number line to teach numerals and order.

ACTIVITY 7.25   Walking the Number Line

- Have a child stand at the left end of the number line. Begin working without numerals. As the child takes a step, have the children count "one." Continue counting with each step.

- Place the numerals on the number line beginning with "0" at the left-most mark. Have each child walk down the line beginning at "0," while others count the steps in unison.

- Variations:
  —Have the children begin at "9" and walk from there to "0." Count each step.

—When the children know the numerals' sequence, remove the cards and mix them up. Have the students rearrange them in order on the number line.

—Have the children close their eyes while you remove a card or two cards or exchange two cards. Have the children tell the names of the missing card or find the exchange and correct it.

Numbers are also used in the ordinal sense when the order of objects in a set or a series of events is important. *First, second, third,* and so on tell where the something belongs in relation to others in the sequence. Textbooks in primary grades usually instruct children in the use of ordinal words and middle and last. However, these exercises are more effective when children have real experiences. Ordinal concepts can be emphasized when children line up for recess or dismissal. The sequence of each day's events may be listed first, second, third on a wall chart. When the teacher points out ordinal ideas in context, most children will have little trouble with them in lessons.

SPECIAL PROBLEMS WITH COUNTING AND WRITING NUMBERS

Well-equipped settings for informal work and well-planned developmental lessons are essential for all children. Nevertheless, some children have problems learning to count or write numbers well. Some children need an extended amount of free play before directed lessons begin. The purpose of each activity and the connection between one activity and another should always be made clear to help children see relationships and to organize the concepts and skills they learn.

Children with handicaps may need special learning aids. Children with visual and certain physical handicaps, for example, need large-sized blocks. Structured rods cut from wood with a two-inch cross section can be substituted for much smaller Cuisenaire rods. Dowel rods rather than lengths of ribbon make it easier for some children to compare objects' lengths, while textured rather than drawn numerals make it easier for some to learn how numerals are formed.

Some children have difficulty with counting and make coordination, omit, or double-counting errors. One technique to help this is to draw a line down the center of the paper so that as children count they can move the object from the left side to the right. This activity diminishes the chance that the child will begin or end the count improperly, will fail to count one or more objects, or will double count some. Once accuracy is achieved, the child may be able to count in a row without moving the objects.

Counting on is a valuable skill that helps many children learn number values. Start with a set of five blue chips and have the children say "five." As you add red chips, have the children count *six, seven, eight,* . . . with you. One teacher began the counting on by having the children pop an open palm against their forehead as they say the starting number. This action pops the number into each child's head. Then as objects are added to the original set, each child holds up a finger for each number as it is counted on. To count down, the number is "popped" into the head and a finger is lowered for each number that is counted.

Reversal errors in writing numerals such as 6 and 9 or 5 and 2 are very common among children. If children are being successful with each number word and its set, teachers should not be overly worried about such writing reversals. If the problem persists into the second or third grade, the teacher might wish to check for learning impairments, such as visual handicaps, visual discrimination and spatial organization problems, and motor coordination weaknesses. Special materials for these children include large numerals cut from felt or sandpaper glued to cards and flat boxes with wet sand in which numerals can be drawn. As children use these materials, a kinesthetic reaction helps them remember each numeral's configuration. Writing numerals on the chalkboard and tracing them with chalk or a wet sponge are also helpful. Some children are helped by having someone trace a numeral on their back or on the back of their writing hand just before a numeral is traced or written.

EXERCISE   What things do you believe can be done to prevent the occurrence of many of the problems identified in the discussion of problems with counting and writing numerals?

◼ COMPUTER USE IN EARLY MATHEMATICS

Computers for young children offer many opportunities and also call for some precautions. The Southern Association for Children Under Six (SACUS) has issued five criteria for appropriate uses of the computer:

1. Integrate the computer into the environment so that children use it as a natural medium for learning.

2. Provide extensions of classroom computer activities in other learning centers in the classroom.

3. Use the computer as part of the total curriculum, relating its content to the context of other activities.

4. Select software that promotes children's active exploration of the environment.

5. Experiment with different uses of the computer so that the program avoids the tutorial design often associated with commercial learning tools.[8]

Good software for young children can be tied directly to other materials. *Moptown*[9] is an attribute and classification game. Before meeting the families of Bibbles and Gribbles, which have distinctive characteristics on the computer, students can create them with blocks.[10] *Stickybear Opposites* allows children to control the action while Stickybear demonstrates ideas such as up-down, inside-outside, and full-empty.[11] When used to expand ideas that have been experienced with materials, computer programs offer another transition from concrete to pictorial representation. Programs should not replace hands-on experiences and should extend the manipulative experiences in the classroom.

EXERCISE   What uses of computers in kindergarten/primary classrooms have you observed or are you aware of? Is it evident that computers were used according to guidelines given in the preceding section?

◼ SUMMARY

Mathematics begins for most children before they start school. Their early play experiences provide a basis for later learning. They should continue to have gamelike activities in preschool, kindergarten, and into the primary grades. These informal experiences build many thinking skills and understandings that are fundamental in mathematics and other subject areas. Children should have many experiences with both discrete (countable) and continuous (measurable) materials. Classification is a basic thinking skill based on recognition of similarities. When children sort objects by attributes, they are using classification skills. Order and seriation of objects are based on recognition of differences between them. Lining things up by length is a seriation skill. Children need experiences recognizing, making, and extending patterns. Patterns are repeated sequences.

Spatial relationships are an important area of exploration for young children. Children's first awareness of geometry is topological in nature as they explore the space in their world. They learn about location and proximity of objects in space and develop a large vocabulary of location words. Separation is the topological understanding of boundaries between objects and of the parts that make up the whole. Enclosure is the topological concept relating to being between or inside, while order relates to the fact that objects and events can be arranged in various ways. Concrete experiences and good language models are essential to building basic spatial understandings.

Counting is an early verbal skill, but children may need more time and experiences before the verbal chain of number words is more than a rote exercise. Working with many materials and relating them to the sequence of number words is vital. Five principles describe counting: the abstraction, stable-order, one-to-one, order-irrelevance, and cardinal principles. Children may miscount because they start or end the count improperly, skip or double count items, or use idiosyncratic counting sequences.

Carefully planned activities with manipulative materials enable children to understand the meaning of counting and the way numerals are used to record the number of items in a set. Games, songs, and books help children develop meaningful connections between the number in a set, the number word for a set, and the written symbol for a set. Writing the symbol, or numeral, need not be stressed because many activities can be conducted with number cards. When children do learn to write their numbers, kinesthetic experiences with sandpaper letters, tracing in the air or on the chalkboard, and accurate modeling of the numeral form are important teaching techniques.

The computer offers opportunities for young children to interact with classification, spatial relationships, counting, and other mathematics concepts. The computer should not replace experiences with manipulative materials, but it can supplement children's experiences to reinforce earlier learning and add variety to the mathematics program.

◼ STUDY QUESTIONS AND ACTIVITIES

1. Gather materials for three different math boxes or junk boxes. Use things that you have around the house or can purchase inexpensively

at the grocery store, hardware store, or department store. If you have the opportunity, watch while children work with the materials in the junk boxes. What language and mathematics skills do you see?

2. Find six different ways to show a pattern of three items: colors, shapes, numbers, motions, and so on. Make a pattern strip such as that shown in Activity 7.12. Extend the pattern to four items being repeated.

3. Read an article about Maria Montessori and write a short essay on her philosophy of education and the materials she developed for teaching children.

4. Proximity, separation, order, and enclosure are four ideas in topological geometry. List three sentences for each of them that demonstrate everyday uses of topological geometry.

5. Ask several young children to count aloud for you. Also ask them to count a set of pennies or other small objects for you. Record what each of them does. Did you find any differences in their rote and rational counting abilities? Did any of them demonstrate common counting errors (coordination, omission, double counting) that Gelman and Gallistel list? Use procedures suggested in this chapter to help them overcome their errors. Did the procedures work?

■ TEACHER'S BOOKSHELF

Baratta-Lorton, Mary. 1988. *Workjobs*. Menlo Park, CA: Addison-Wesley.

_____. 1989. *Mathematics Their Way*. Menlo Park, CA: Addison-Wesley.

_____. 1978a. *Workjobs II*. Menlo Park, CA: Addison-Wesley.

_____. 1978b. *Workjobs for Parents*. Menlo Park, CA: Addison-Wesley.

Baroody, Arthur J. 1987. *Children's Mathematical Thinking*. New York: Teachers College Press.

Barron, Linda. 1979. *Mathematics Experiences for the Early Childhood Years*. Columbus, OH: Merrill.

Burton, Grace. 1985. *Toward a Good Beginning*. Menlo Park, CA: Addison-Wesley.

Fulton, Oliver. 1987. *Mathways for Early Childhood*. New Rochelle, NY: Cuisenaire Co. of America.

Kamii, Constance, with Georgia DeClark. 1985. *Young Children Reinvent Arithmetic*. New York: Teachers College Press.

Payne, Joseph N., ed. 1975. *Mathematics Learning in Early Childhood*. Reston, VA: National Council of Teachers of Mathematics.

Schultz, Karen A., Ron P. Colarusso, and Virginia W. Strawderman. 1989. *Mathematics for Every Young Child.* Columbus, OH: Merrill.

Scott, Louise B., and Jesse J. Thompson. 1960. *Rhymes for Fingers and Flannelboards.* St. Louis, MO: Webster.

Stone, Janet. 1990. *Hands on Math: Manipulative Math for Young Children.* Glenview, IL: Scott, Foresman.

Selected Mathematic Concept and Counting Books for Young Children

Anno, Mitsumasa. 1977. *Anno's Counting Book.* New York: Crowell.

———. 1982. *Anno's Counting House.* New York: Crowell.

Bang, Molly. 1983. *Ten, Nine, Eight.* New York: Greenwillow.

Feelings, Muriel, and Tom Feelings. 1971. *Moja Means One: Swahili Counting Book.* New York: Dial Press.

Galdone, Paul. *The Three Billy Goats Gruff.* New York: Seabury Press, 1973.

Hoban, Tana. 1972. *Push Pull, Empty Full: A Book of Opposites.* New York: Macmillan.

———. 1973. *Over, Under, and Through, and Other Spatial Concepts.* New York: Macmillan.

———. 1974. *Circles, Triangles, and Squares.* New York: Macmillan.

———. 1976. *Big Ones, Little Ones.* New York: Greenwillow.

———. 1986. *Shapes, Shapes, Shapes.* New York: Greenwillow.

Maestro, Betsy, and Guilio Maestro. 1981. *Traffic: A Book of Opposites.* New York: Crown.

Oxenbury, Helen. 1968. *Numbers of Things.* New York: Watts.

Testa, Fulvio. 1982. *If You Take a Pencil.* New York: Dial Press.

———. 1983. *If You Look Around You.* New York: Dutton.

◼ FOR FURTHER READING

Arithmetic Teacher. 1982, December *30*(4).
   Focus issue with several articles on early childhood.

Arithmetic Teacher. 1988, February *35*(6).

Focus issue on early childhood with articles on Montessori, conservation, computers, children's literature, fractions, and problem solving with young children.

Carter, Beth W. 1985, September. Move over, Frank Lloyd Wright. *Arithmetic Teacher 33*(1), 8–11.

Blocks provide many opportunities for mathematics thinking.

Frank, Alan R. 1989, September. Counting skills—A foundation for early mathematics. *Arithmetic Teacher 37*(1), 14–17.

Counting on and skip counting are presented as foundations for later number skills.

Ginsburg, Herbert P. 1980, September. Children's surprising knowledge of arithmetic. *Arithmetic Teacher 28*(1), 42–44.

Research that shows young children exhibit surprising intellectual strengths, ranging from intuitions about more, *to counting procedures for mental addition, to invented strategies for school arithmetic.*

Hamrick, Kathy B. 1980, November. Are we introducing mathematical symbols too soon? *Arithmetic Teacher 28*(3), 14–15.

Hamrick believes many children are given mathematical symbols too soon. She believes children are ready for symbols only after they can discuss a topic meaningfully.

Heddens, James W. 1986, February. Bridging the gap between the concrete and the abstract. *Arithmetic Teacher 33*(6), 14–17.

Illustrates the use of pictures and tallies to develop numeration concepts.

Hiebert, James. 1989, March. The struggle to link written symbols with understanding: An update. *Arithmetic Teacher 36*(7), 38–44.

Ideas to help teachers connect written mathematical symbols, problem solving, and evaluation for their students.

Jensen, Rosalie, and Deborah C. Spector. 1986, April. Geometry links the two spheres. *Arithmetic Teacher 33*(8), 13–16.

Movement activities for young children encourage spatial understandings.

Maxim, George W. 1989, December. Developing preschool mathematical concepts. *Arithmetic Teacher 37*(4), 36–41.

Activities for understanding of number and numeral recognition.

Mueller, Delbert W. 1985, October. Building a scope and sequence for early childhood mathematics. *Arithmetic Teacher 33*(2), 8–11.

Both number and nonnumber activities are essential in early childhood mathematics.

Poggi, Jeanlee M. 1985, December. An invitation to topology. *Arithmetic Teacher 33*(4), 8–11.

Presents activities for exploration of topology.

Shaw, Jean. 1983, September. A-plus for counters. *Arithmetic Teacher 31*(1), 10–14.

Suggests many activities with counters to develop number and number system concepts.

Smith, Nancy J., and Karla Hawkins Wendelin. 1981, November. Using children's books to teach mathematics concepts. *Arithmetic Teacher 29*(3), 10–15.

Ten strands of mathematics concepts for kindergarten through grade three are identified, and children's books are listed for each one.

Swick, Kevin. 1989, February. Appropriate uses of computers with young children. *Educational Technology 23*, 6–10.

How computers might best be used with young children.

Suydam, Marilyn N. 1986, January. The process of counting. *Arithmetic Teacher 34*(5), 29.

Summarizes the latest findings about how children learn to count.

Tipps, Steve, and Lynne Mann. 1984, October. Computers: A new learning environment for children. *Dimensions 13*(1), 15–18.

Describes software for young children and ways to prepare children for the computer with concrete materials and activities.

Van de Walle, John A. 1978, March. Track cards. *Arithmetic Teacher 25*(6), 22–26.

Teacher-made track cards provide many kindergarten and primary-grade activities that enhance thinking, creativity, vocabulary, and understanding of topological and symmetry concepts. Includes ten different activities with directions for preparing track cards.

Van de Walle, John A., and Helen Holbrook. 1987, April. Patterns, thinking, and problem solving. *Arithmetic Teacher 34*(8), 6–12.

Problem-solving activities for the early grades.

Yvon, Bernard R., and Jane Dallinger Dopheide. 1984, January. Iggies come to kindergarten. *Arithmetic Teacher 31*(5), 36–38.

Many classification activities based on a created character, Iggie.

Yvon, Bernard R., and Eunice B. Spooner. 1982, January. Variations in kindergarten mathematics and what a teacher can do about it. *Arithmetic Teacher 29*(5), 46–52.

After surveying commercial kindergarten mathematics programs, the authors conclude that a single published program does not give children a well-rounded experience. They describe teacher-made materials for 16 activities to balance a kindergarten program.

 NOTES

[1] National Council of Teachers of Mathematics. 1989. *Curriculum and Evaluation Standards for School Mathematics.* Reston, VA: National Council of Teachers of Mathematics, 38. Used by permission.

[2] NCTM, 48. Used by permission.

[3] NCTM, 60. Used by permission.

[4] Mary Baratta-Lorton. 1989. *Mathematics Their Way.* Menlo Park, CA: Addison-Wesley. See the Teacher's Bookshelf section for other books by the same author.

[5] Rachel Gelman and C. R. Gallistel. 1978. *The Child's Understanding of Number* (Cambridge, MA: Harvard University Press), 131–135.

[6] Gelman and Gallistel, 106–108.

[7] *Sixty Songs for Little Children.* 1933. London: Oxford University Press. Used by permission.

[8] From Kevin Swick, quoted in *Appropriate Uses of Computers in Early Childhood Curriculum*. 1989. Southern Association for Children Under Six, Box 5403, Brady Station, Little Rock, AR 72215.

[9] The Learning Company, 6493 Kaiser Dr., Fremont, CA 94555.

[10] Steve Tipps and Lynne Mann. 1984. Computer: A new learning environment for young children. *Dimensions 13*(1) (October 1984), 15–18.

[11] Optimum Resource, Inc., 10 Station Place, Norfolk, CT, 06058.

Extending Understanding of Numbers and Numeration

If children are to work effectively with numbers and numerals using the Hindu-Arabic numeration system, they must understand the system thoroughly and not just have rote knowledge of it. Therefore the topics of this chapter—the base-ten numeration system; one-to-many, many-to-one, and many-to-many correspondences; odd and even numbers; prime and composite numbers; and integers—must be developed by teachers in ways that permit children to learn the fundamentals and the rationale behind them. Children's understanding of the concepts in this chapter is built on their earlier counting, matching, comparing, sorting, ordering, and other similar experiences.

In this chapter you will read about

1. the major characteristics of the base-ten numeration system;

2. how concrete materials, both proportional and non-proportional, are used to develop understanding of the base-ten system;

3. expanded notation forms for numbers that emphasize place value;

4. markers and other objects that demonstrate one-to-many, many-to-one, and many-to-many correspondences;

229

5. estimation and how to develop and encourage estimation skills;

6. the role of number theory topics in the elementary school curriculum;

7. activities for exploring odd and even numbers and prime and composite numbers;

8. ways to develop understanding of positive and negative integers using number lines and simple stories.

STANDARDS THAT PERTAIN TO NUMBERS AND NUMERATION

Kindergarten Through Grade Four

Standard 5: Estimation   In grades K–4, the curriculum should include estimation so that students can:

■ explore estimation strategies;[1]

Standard 6: Number Sense and Numeration
In grades K–4, the mathematics curriculum should include whole number concepts and skills so that students can:

■ construct number meanings through real-world experiences and the use of physical materials;

■ understand our numeration system by relating counting, grouping, and place-value concepts;

■ develop number sense;

■ interpret the multiple uses of numbers encountered in the real world.[2]

Grades Five Through Eight

Standard 5: Number and Number Relationships   In grades 5–8, the mathematics curriculum should include the continued development of number and number relationships so that students can:

■ develop number sense for whole numbers. . . .[3]

Standard 6: Number Systems and Number Theory   In grades 5–8, the mathematics curriculum should include the study of number systems and number theory so that students can:

■ develop and use order relations for whole numbers [and] integers . . .

■ develop and apply number theory concepts (e.g., primes, . . .) in real world and mathematical problem situations.[4]

■ THE BASE-TEN NUMERATION SYSTEM

The Hindu-Arabic, or base-ten, numeration system has its roots in the Middle East. Students need not be overwhelmed with details of its history, but some aspects are of interest. Early development took place in India, where numerals based on a place-value scheme were used as early as A.D. 600.[5] The forerunners of the numerals we use today made their appearance about A.D. 700. The origin of zero is uncertain. H. A. Freebury says zero appeared in the Devanagari numerals of the eighth century, while David E. Smith says they did not appear until the ninth century, where they were used in inscriptions at Gwalior in India.[6]

The Arabs' association with the system came more from their contribution to the transmission of information about it to other parts of the world rather than from any refinements they made to it. The Arabs translated into their language much of what was known about science and mathematics in Greece, India, and elsewhere. Some of these translations have been our only source of knowledge of Greek and Indian achievements. One translation, called *The Book of al-Khowarazmi on Hindu Number,* explained the use of Hindu numerals. From the author's name, al-Khowarazmi, came the modern word *algorithm,* which refers to the procedures we use to compute with numbers. This author also wrote a book called *Al jabr,* which is about reduction and cancellation. The name has been corrupted so that it is now *algebra,* which designates one of the important branches of mathematics.[7]

The Crusades, the increased trade among nations, and the Moorish conquest of North Africa and Spain spread the Hindu-Arabic numeration system to many parts of the Mediterranean world, including Europe. Roman numerals and the abacus were widespread in Europe before arrival of the Hindu-Arabic system, which gradually assumed a greater role in trade and commerce as people recognized its advantages over Roman numerals. For a time, the two systems coexisted, but eventually the *algorists* who computed with the new system won out over the *abacists,* and by the sixteenth century the Hindu-Arabic system was predominant.

The characteristics of the Hindu-Arabic system are summarized and explained in the following paragraphs.

1. There is a base number, which is ten. During their first counting experiences, people undoubtedly used their fingers to keep track of the count. After all fingers were used, it became necessary to use a supplemental means for keeping track of the count. It was natural that the grouping was based on ten, the number of fingers available.

2. There is a symbol for zero. It is the placeholder in a numeral like 302, where it indicates that there are no tens. It is also the number that indicates the size, or numerical value, of a set that has no objects in it.

3. There are as many symbols, including zero, as the number indicated by the base. The symbols for the Hindu-Arabic numeration system are 1, 2, 3, 4, 5, 6, 7, 8, 9, and 0.

4. The place-value scheme has a ones place on the right, a base position to the left of the ones place, a base times base (b^2) position next, a base times base times base (b^3) position next, and so on. Beginning at any place in the system, the next position to the left is ten times greater, and the position to the right is one-tenth as large. This char-

acteristic makes it possible to represent fractional numbers (decimals) as well as whole numbers with the system.

5. The system makes it possible to compute with paper and pencil and an algorithm for each operation. While paper-and-pencil computation is diminishing as calculators and computers take over many calculation chores, children should still learn an algorithm for each operation and ways in which they are used. (Algorithms are explored more deeply in later chapters.)

■ TEACHING THE BASE-TEN NUMERATION SYSTEM

Classrooms at every level should be well equipped with place-value materials. Concrete manipulative devices give children the means to represent numbers in ways that are more understandable than when only pictures and diagrams and verbal descriptions are used. A wide variety of both commercial and teacher-made materials should be available for children's use. Most materials that are used for developing children's understanding of place value in this chapter are illustrated in Chapter 3.

A progression of activities with place-value materials and concepts will occur over all of the years children are in elementary school. Initial activities with young children deal with counting and numbers under ten. When children begin learning about place value for numbers greater than ten, they should use proportional materials, such as Unifix cubes and tongue depressors (type one), followed by beansticks and base-ten and Cuisenaire (type two) materials. **Proportional materials** are those in which a ten-for-one exchange is made as regrouping is done. Beansticks are proportional because ten loose beans are exchanged for 1 tens stick as 10 ones are renamed as 1 ten. **Nonproportional materials** have a single object that represents a group of ten. An abacus is nonproportional because 10 ones beads are exchanged for a single bead that represents ten. Nonproportional materials should not be used during students' early activities. Their use should be delayed until children have the maturity to grasp the concept that one thing can stand for many, such as when one bead on a tens rod of an abacus stands for ten beads on the ones wire. An abacus is useful for helping older students represent large numbers and algorithms for addition, subtraction, and multiplication.

Introducing Place Value

Before a teacher begins activities that deal with place value, there are certain skills children must have. They must be able to do rational counting to at least nine and to read and write numerals for the numbers zero through nine. They should also be able to express numbers as addition combinations. For example, they should be able to express three as "3 + 0," "2 + 1," "1 + 2," and "0 + 3." This ability is not important for the combinations themselves but as a basis for understanding that a number like 12 can be represented as "1 ten + 2 ones" and as "10 + 2." When children are ready for numbers greater than nine, they can use any of the type-one place-value materials. The value of these materials over type-two materials is that children must combine ten loose pieces to make a tens piece rather than exchanging ten loose pieces for an already-made tens piece. Activity 8.1 is one way to begin.

Children will indicate through words and actions when their understanding of a concept is becoming internalized. Their descriptions of activities will become fluent and their actions with materials sure. When their actions with Unifix cubes and descriptions of what they are doing indicate that they understand the underlying concept of grouping by ten, a train/car mat can be introduced on which they can perform their actions (Activity 8.2). Activities 8.3 and 8.4 extend the new work to include numerals for identifying numbers greater than ten. Activity 8.3 is a counting activity in which children are introduced to the numerals 10–19. In Activity 8.4 they use beansticks to further their understanding of place value.

Frequent activities—both teacher-led and individual and small-group work spread over several months—are necessary for most children. Children who demonstrate skill and understanding while working under a teacher's direction are ready for individual and cooperative group work

---

ACTIVITY 8.1   Trains and Cars

- Give each child 19 same-colored Unifix cubes.

- Tell the children that they are to join 15 cars (single cubes) to make a train (a piece with 10 cubes). When the train has been made, have the children count the remaining cubes.

- Discuss the fact that they have one tens train and five ones cars.

- Have them make their own train and car combinations using anywhere from 11 to 19 cubes. Each time a train and loose cars are arranged, ask questions so that the children must think about the results of their work.
  —"Who has one train and three cars?"

  —"How many have a train and eight cars?"

  —"How many trains and cars do you have?"

ACTIVITY 8.2   Train/Car Mats

- Give each student 19 same-colored Unifix cubes and a mat.

- Each time the children assemble their train and some loose cubes, have them arrange them on the mat. Have them describe each arrangement as "1 train and _____ cars."

Trains	Cars

ACTIVITY 8.3   Place Value with Sticks and Chips

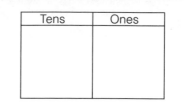

- Use counting chips and a magnetic board, tongue depressors, and a place-value mat. Put 15 chips on the board.

- Choose three children for the first activity: the first child to count the chips, the second to keep track of the count with sticks, and the third to record numerals on the chalkboard.

- As the first child counts the chips, the second one picks up a tongue depressor. At the same time, the third child records the count on the chalkboard.

- Have the children pause at nine and review what they have done so far.

- As the tenth chip is counted and the tenth stick is picked up, ask: "How many chips has Chen counted?" "How many sticks does Tricia have in her hand?" Give the child a rubber band to put around the ten sticks. Ask the child where the bundle should go on the place-value mat.

Tens	Ones

- Ask, "How many tens?" "How many ones?" "How can Abdul write '10' on the chalkboard?"

- Continue the count by representing "11" with a bundle and one stick and showing how "11" is written. Do the same with 12, 13, 14, and 15.

- Discuss the meaning of "11" as 10 and 1, "12" as 10 and 2, and so on.

- Repeat the exercise with other numbers of disks and different students playing the three roles.

ACTIVITY 8.4   Place Value and Beansticks

- Give each child 19 loose beans, a tens beanstick, and a place-value mat.

- Tell each child to count 13 loose beans and put them in the ones place on the mat; talk about the number of beans so the children will note that there are more than ten.

- Tell each child to separate the loose beans into a group of ten and a group of three, and to put the ten beans in the tens place and the three beans in the ones place on the mat.

- Have each child exchange the 10 loose beans for 1 tens stick; discuss the fact that there are 1 ten and 3 ones, or 13 beans.

- Write "1 ten and 3 ones," "10 + 3," and "13" on the chalkboard. Discuss the fact that they are all ways of writing the number 13.

- Repeat with other numbers up to 19.

with work sheets, problem cards, and games. Work sheets from children's workbooks can be used for individualized practice. Some work sheets contain pictures of common place-value devices; later only numerals and words are used. A teacher must be certain that a child has both content and pedagogical readiness before having him or her do workbook exercises.

Cards that contain problems, such as those in Figure 8.1, are particu-

Figure 8-1
Problem cards for activities with structured materials

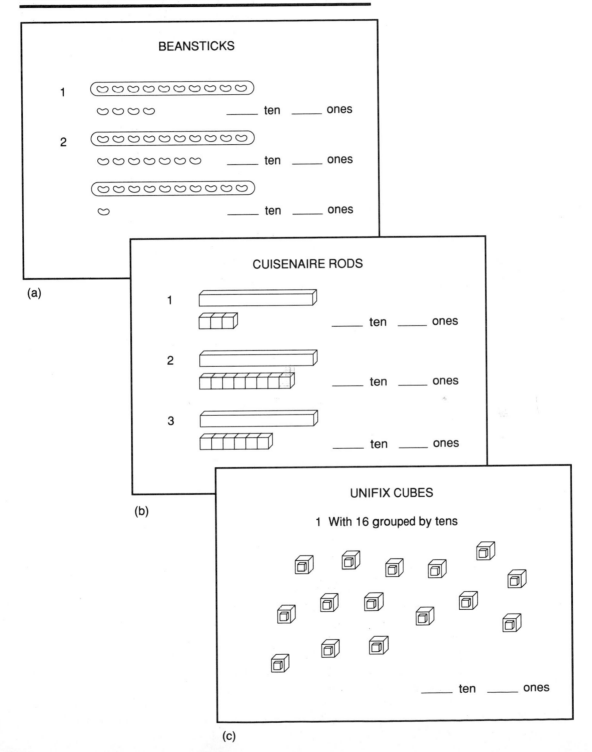

(a)

(b)

(c)

larly good because they can be drawn to match the concrete materials that children use during initial learning activities. These cards are only samples; a teacher can prepare several for each device. A duplicated answer sheet can be prepared for children's responses for each set of cards.

After children understand place value through 19, they should work with manipulative materials that show place value through 99. Activities like the ones in Activities 8.1 through 8.4 can be used for these numbers. Once understanding has been developed, a game offers opportunities for children to practice a particular skill in a grouping situation. In every grade a good game contributes to learning by giving children additional manipulative experiences with familiar materials. The changed setting in which the materials are used enlivens the practice session and heightens children's interest in maintaining their skills. An example of a place-value game for numbers between 9 and 100 is "Beans and Sticks" (Activity 8.5). Base-ten or Cuisenaire materials can be used in this game, too.

ACTIVITY 8.5   Beans and Sticks

- Materials: A set of 18 loose beans, 9 tens sticks, and a place-value mat for each player; one 0–9 spinner.

- Two to four students follow this order of play: Each player spins the spinner, with either the high or low spin determining the first player; the other players take turns clockwise.

- The first player spins the pointer and calls out the number on which it stops. The player counts that many beans and puts them on her or his mat. Each player has a first turn. The first player spins again, counts the beans, and puts them on the mat. If the count exceeds nine, the player exchanges ten loose beans for a tens stick and puts it on the mat in the tens place. Play continues until one player has a score in the nineties, or until an agreed-on number of turns have been played.

- Variation: For older students, include hundred rafts, more tens sticks, and two spinners. One spinner designates tens and the other ones. Play continues until a player's total exceeds 900.

Work with Larger Numbers

In later grades, students work with larger numbers. Their understanding of the meaning of numbers through 999 should be developed as they engage in activities similar to those used for learning about the numbers through 99. It is not necessary to continue counting objects, but place-value devices will remain useful in illustrating that 10 tens equal 1 hundred as 10 bundles of sticks are bundled together with a rubber band or 10 beansticks are exchanged for a hundreds raft. The flats and rods from a base-ten or Cuisenaire set show hundreds and tens, respectively, while small cubes represent ones.

As students work with a device, they also learn how the numeral for 10 tens, or 100, is written. They should note the relationship between the symbol "100" and the markers in a place-value set: single flat from a base-ten or Cuisenaire set or one raft from a set of beansticks. The numeral "200" stands for two flats or rafts, while "300" stands for three of either device.

Activity 8.6 provides an interesting setting in which children count a large number of pumpkin seeds to see how place value works with large numbers.

ACTIVITY 8.6 Pumpkin Seeds

- Have a pumpkin, some square sheets of dark-colored construction paper, and glue.

- Display the pumpkin for a few days to allow time for the students to guess the number of seeds it contains. Have each child record a guess and give it to you.

- Open the pumpkin and remove the seeds. Separate the seeds from the pulp and dry them.

- Have small groups of children each count a portion of the seeds. A useful scheme is to have some children in each group count sets of ten seeds; each time 100 seeds have been counted, another group glues the seeds in a 10-by-10 array on a piece of the paper. Groups of ten seeds fewer than 100 should be glued in rows of ten on strips of paper. Any set of fewer than ten seeds should be glued to small squares of paper.

- Arrange the cards with hundreds at the left side of a bulletin board. (If the count exceeds 1,000, arrange the thousand on the left, then the hundreds.) Cards with ten seeds and loose seeds go to the right of the hundreds. Write the number with expanded notation with words and numerals, and in compact form (see example below). This activity is a good class project for an outside-of-the-room bulletin board, such as one in a hallway or cafeteria.

- Check the guesses to see which student's guess was closest to the actual count. Discuss the fact that some guesses were close to being correct and (if there were some extremely large or small numbers guessed) that some were too far on either side to be reasonable.

7 hundreds + 6 tens + 5 ones

700 + 60 + 5

765

An abacus is a nonproportional place-value device that is practical for showing larger numbers. An abacus can be made from a wooden block and lengths of coat-hanger wire placed in holes and wooden beads. A four-rod abacus shows up to 9,999. A much larger abacus is shown in Figure 8.2, where the number 536,209,468,312 is displayed. When an abacus is first used children must learn that one bead on the tens wire represents 10 ones; one bead on the hundreds wire represents 10 tens, and so on. Under a teacher's guidance students will conclude that each rod represents a place-value position that has a value that is ten times greater than the rod to its immediate right, no matter where it is on the rod. As their understanding of place value increases, students will generalize that the Hindu-Arabic system has a place-value scheme based on ten and powers of ten. This same scheme is the basis for the metric system of measurement, which children discover as they learn about measurement.

Sources of data involving large numbers abound and should be used to provide real-world settings for such numbers. An almanac contains many tables on varied subjects that have large numbers. Activity 8.7 is based on a table listing the busiest U.S. airports. Only some of the airports are listed for the activity.

Space flights and the solar system also provide large numbers for students' work with larger numbers. These topics interest most students, and the numbers are large enough to extend place value into the millions and beyond.

A calculator is also an aid for learning about place value. As children work with an abacus and place-value chart, they can enter the numbers they deal with into a calculator. A calculator activity that deals with place value and operations, "Roll and Add" (Activity 9.28), provides practice with place-value concepts as children play a game. The "Wipeout" exercise in Activity 8.8 can be used to check children's understanding of place value in large numbers. Numbers into the millions can be supplied for older children.

Figure 8-2
Abacus representing the number 536,209,468,312

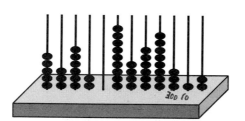

ACTIVITY 8.7 Busy Airports

- Display this table with data about U.S. airports on a large sheet of paper or an overhead projector.

Six Busiest U.S. Airports 1986			
Chicago O'Hare	54,770,673	Atlanta	45,191,480
Los Angeles	41,417,867	Dallas/Ft. Worth	39,945,326
Denver	34,685,944	Newark	29,433,048

- Have students work in cooperative-learning
  groups to complete questions and activities
  such as these:

Questions
  —Which airport had more than 50,000,000
  passengers in 1986?

  —Which number has an "8" in the ten thousands place?

  —Between which airports is the difference
  in the number of passengers approximately 10,000,000?

Activities
  —Write the name of the airport that has a
  "7" in the thousands place.

—Write the name of the airport that has a
  "5" in the millions place.

—Write the name of the airports that had
  approximately 40,000,000 passengers.

—Write the place-value position of each
  "9" that is in a number. Name the airport
  where each "9" appears.

—Use words to write the number of passengers for Los Angeles airport.

—Write the numbers for Dallas/Ft. Worth
  and Denver in this place-value chart.

—Show the number of passengers at
  Newark airport on a large abacus.

Billions Period			Millions Period			Thousands Period			Ones Period		

A game that alerts students to place value can be played with a spinner and paper and pencil, as in Activity 8.9. The object of the game is to write

---

ACTIVITY 8.8   Wipeout

- Children work singly or in pairs with a calculator.

- The object of the activity is to "wipe out" a number in a particular place-value position. For example, when shown the number 547, the child is to wipe out the 4 tens with one subtraction. In order to do this, the child must recognize that the "4" represents 4 tens, or 40: 40 is subtracted from 547, leaving 507.

- Present these numbers by writing them on the chalkboard or giving duplicated lists to each student or pair of students.

- Variation: Name a number such as 7,000 for children to display on their calculators. Call out values to add, such as "Add 4 tens," "Add 3 hundreds," "Add 8 ones." Have children compare the displays on their machines.

Wipe out tens	Wipe out hundreds	Wipe out thousands
798	2379	47,956
321	9999	71,233
475	7439	82,309

ACTIVITY 8.9   Spin to Win

- The entire class or small groups of students play.

- The teacher or a student serves as leader to call out numbers from a 0–9 spinner. (Spinners are available from school supply companies. See Appendix C.) Each student prepares playing spaces by marking lines on a piece of paper. The number of lines is determined by the size of number that will be made. There will be four lines for a four-place number:

_____   _____   _____   _____

- The leader turns the spinner four times to get four numbers to fill the spaces. Each time a

number is called it must be placed on one of the lines; once a number is placed, it cannot be moved to another line.

- If the object is to make the largest number, large numbers are put in large place-value positions and small numbers in the smaller positions; the reverse is done when the object is to make the smallest number.

- All students who have recorded the largest or smallest number must read it correctly to receive credit.

- Repeat as often as time and interest permit.

- Variations: The number of blanks can be increased to accommodate larger numbers.

the largest or smallest possible number with a given number of digits. Students need to develop strategies for placing numerals according to positions and size of numerals in order to win.

Computer software programs can be used to reinforce students' understanding of place value following group and individual work with manipulative materials. *Box™ Introduces Numbers*[8] includes counting skills, greater than and less than activities, and place value with tens and ones. Micro-Learningware[9] has *Place Value,* which is devoted entirely to activities dealing with the concept of place value and drill-and-practice exercises. *Bunny Hop*[10] is a program that not only helps develop a better understanding of numeration, but does it with an optional customized voice that talks to students. It is designed especially for special-needs students. One part of the *Understanding Math Series*[11] provides survey tests and prescriptive practice for meeting students' special needs in learning place-value concepts.

EXERCISE   A real-world situation that yields specific large numbers is given in Activity 8.7. Identify three other situations that can be used; identify at least one number associated with each situation.

▪ EXPRESSING NUMBERS WITH EXPANDED NOTATION

Students use both compact and expanded forms of numerals in elementary school mathematics. In the compact form—the one we normally use—the number 243 is written as "243." There are times, however, when one of the expanded forms is useful. For example, when children are learning about place value, the expanded forms "2 hundreds + 4 tens + 3 ones" and "200 + 40 + 3" emphasize place value in the base-ten system. Also, the simplest expanded forms help primary-grade children develop their understanding of the algorithms for addition and subtraction of small whole numbers. Intermediate-grade children need to understand expanded notation, eventually in its exponential form, because it serves as a foundation for the study of extremely large and small numbers and their expression in scientific notation.

The simplest form of expanded notation is the expression of a number using a combination of numerals and words, as when the number 17 is expressed as "1 ten and 7 ones." As children count objects and use place-value materials, they should repeatedly express numbers as so many tens and so many ones, and write numerals in both standard and expanded forms. After using the form "4 tens and 5 ones" to express the number 45, students move to the shorter "40 + 5" form. A game based on the television game "Concentration" provides practice in recognizing and naming expanded forms of numbers; see Activity 8.10.

ACTIVITY 8.10   Expanded Notation Concentration   ♟

Materials: Eight to twelve pairs of cards like these:

10 + 2	12
40 + 3	43
60 + 7	67

- Two to four children play the game.

- The cards are placed face down in an orderly arrangement with the same number of cards in each row and column. The first player turns two cards face up. If the cards match the player says, "ten plus two equals twelve." Each time a matched pair is drawn, the player gets another turn. If the cards do not match, the cards are returned to their places face down and play passes to the next player. Play continues until all cards have been matched. The player with the most matches is the winner.

As students mature they will use expanded forms for larger numbers, such as 53,489. As they use an abacus and place-value chart to represent such a number, older children should learn to express it in the following ways:

- With words: fifty-three thousand, four hundred eighty-nine

- With numerals
  and words: 5 ten thousands, 3 thousands, 4 hundreds, 8 tens,
                         9 ones
                       53 thousands, 4 hundreds, 8 tens, 9 ones

- With numerals: $50,000 + 3,000 + 400 + 80 + 9$
                       or
                       $$\begin{array}{r} 50,000 \\ 3,000 \\ 400 \\ 80 \\ 9 \\ \hline 53,489 \end{array}$$

After children can multiply by ten and powers of ten, they can express numbers in two other forms:

$$(5 \times 10,000) + (3 \times 1000) + (4 \times 100) + (8 \times 10) + 9$$

$$[5 \times (10 \times 10 \times 10 \times 10)] + [3 \times (10 \times 10 \times 10)] + [4 \times (10 \times 10)] + [8 \times 10] + [9 \times 1]$$

Older children can extend their knowledge of place value by expressing numbers with exponential notation. In exponential notation, 53,489 is expressed this way:

$$(5 \times 10^4) + (3 \times 10^3) + (4 \times 10^2) + (8 \times 10^1) + (9 \times 10^0)$$

■ REGROUPING

$$\begin{array}{r} 46 \\ -\ 19 \end{array} \qquad \begin{array}{r} ^3\cancel{4}^16 \\ -\ 19 \end{array}$$

Regrouping is a process used to express a number in a form that is convenient for computation. For example, when the algorithm in the margin is computed with paper and pencil using the decomposition algorithm, the process involves regrouping 46 as 3 tens and 16 ones so that 9 can be subtracted. The regrouping is shown in the algorithm by marking out the "4," writing a "3" in its place, and showing 16 ones. Children who are unfamiliar with regrouping are not pedagogically ready for learning addition and subtraction with larger whole numbers. Children need regrouping activities as they work with place-value materials. As children make exchanges of materials, such as when they exchange ten loose beans for a tens stick, they should also work in reverse to undo the exchanges; a tens stick will be exchanged for ten loose beans. The first variation of the "Banker's Game" (Activity 8.11) provides opportunities for children to regroup tens as they trade

---

ACTIVITY 8.11   Banker's Game

- Materials: 1 red, 15 each green, blue, and yellow chips, 1 chipboard for the banker, 1 chip till for each player, 1 die.

- Players: 3–5 (one serves as banker).

- A player is selected to start the game; play rotates clockwise.

- Rules: The banker sets up a till as shown.

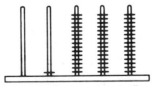

red green blue yellow

Chips are traded this way:

3 yellow = 1 blue
3 blue = 1 green
3 green = 1 red

The first player roles the die and asks the banker for the number of chips indicated on it. If five dots show, the player gets five chips. Three of the yellow chips are exchanged for one blue chip; all of the chips are put on the player's chip till. Next players take their turns in order. The first player to get a red chip is winner.

R	G	B	Y

- Variation: (1) Each player begins with one red chip. Players trade down until one player has cleared her or his till. (2) Change the rate of exchange. A ten-to-one rate gives practice in the base-ten system.

- Lima beans spray painted yellow, blue, green, and red are an inexpensive substitute for chip-trading materials. Chip tills can be outlined on pieces of construction paper or tagboard.

down. The "Beans and Sticks Game" (Activity 8.5) can be changed so that students begin with 9 tens sticks and trade down; the first one to have only loose beans in the ones place is winner.

An abacus is useful for showing regrouping with numbers larger than 999. The abacus in Figure 8.3 illustrates how the numbers 23,498 can be regrouped to subtract 9,129. In (a) the original number is represented. In (b) regrouping from tens to ones and ten thousands to thousands has been done.

Figure 8-3
Abacus representing 23,498—in (a) as 20,000 + 3000 + 400 + 90 + 8; in (b) as 10,000 + 13,000 + 400 + 80 + 18

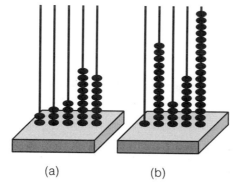

(a)   (b)

■ ONE-TO-MANY, MANY-TO-ONE, AND MANY-TO-MANY CORRESPONDENCES

Counting is a process of making a one-to-one correspondence between a collection of objects and the natural numbers 1, 2, 3, ... It is important that children understand one-to-one correspondence as the basis for counting. It is equally important that they understand one-to-many, many-to-one, and many-to-many correspondences.

One-to-many correspondences have useful applications. Examples are place value (1 ten is equal to 10 ones), money (1 nickel is equivalent to 5 pennies), linear measure (1 foot is equal to 12 inches, 1 meter is equal to 100 centimeters), and travel time/distance (1 hour for each 55 miles). Many-to-one correspondences are represented by the reverse of each of the above examples—that is, 10 ones equal 1 ten—as well as others (12 eggs for each carton, 24 hours equal 1 day).

Many problems are solved by using these and many-to-many correspondences. Consider this example: A truck driver averages 55 miles per hour. How far will the driver go in 8 hours?" The ratio between time and speed is 1 to 55. A proportion can be used to solve the problem: $1/55 = 8/n$. The ratio 8/440 has the same value as 1/55, and is a many-to-many correspondence. Further activities with ratio and proportion are in Chapters 12 and 13.

Commercial and teacher-made materials will help children understand these correspondences. The *Chip Trading Activities Kit*—which is illustrated in Chapter 3—offers a variety of activities. Activity 8.11 explains one.

EXERCISE   Have you dealt with numbers in expanded forms before reading about them in this chapter? If so, describe your experiences with them.

■ SKIP COUNTING

Skip counting is the process of counting by twos, fives, tens, or any other numbers. Teachers frequently have children do rote skip counting, with no reference to objects or other useful applications. Other than learning to recite numbers in some sequence, there is little benefit in this for children. Skip counting has uses that should be explored by children, as in Activities 8.12 through 8.14. Tally marks, coins, and organized collections of objects can be counted by skip counting. Children's first experiences with skip counting can be built on their understanding of patterns. A hundreds board reveals patterns that aid children as they learn skip counting. A calculator is also useful for helping children learn to skip count.

ACTIVITY 8.12   Skip Counting

- Show children a pattern consisting of colored beads on a string.

- Discuss the alternating patterns of shapes and/or colors. Count by ones.

- Ask, "Does anyone know another way to count the beads?" If counting by twos is not mentioned, explain how it is done.

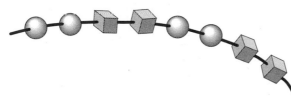

- Count other pairs, such as pennies grouped by twos, pairs of desks placed side by side, and pairs of children in a line.

- Do the same with patterns of five and ten. Groups of five and ten pennies work well. Later, nickels and dimes can be exchanged for the pennies. Have children note that the total is the same, whether it is groups of five pennies or nickels that are counted, because it is the value of the coins—not the quantity—that is determined.

ACTIVITY 8.13   Patterns

- Show a hundreds chart either on a large sheet of paper or with an overhead projector.

- Examine rows across to observe how counting by twos includes every other space, counting by fives includes every fifth space, and counting by tens every tenth space. Note that the tens sequence is in the right-hand column.

- Look at each column. The numbers in the ones places remain the same, while numbers in the tens place increase by one. Have children read in unison a sequence such as 12, 22, 32, ...

- A diagonal from the top left to the bottom right increases by eleven, while the one from top right to bottom left increases by nine. Have students study and discuss these patterns.

First hundreds chart

1	2	3	4	5	6	7	8	9	10
11	12	13	14	15	16	17	18	19	20
21	22	23	24	25	26	27	28	29	30
31	32	33	34	35	36	37	38	39	40
41	42	43	44	45	46	47	48	49	50
51	52	53	54	55	56	57	58	59	60
61	62	63	64	65	66	67	68	69	70
71	72	73	74	75	76	77	78	79	80
81	82	83	84	85	86	87	88	89	90
91	92	93	94	95	96	97	98	99	100

ACTIVITY 8.14   Calculator Counting

- Students work singly or in pairs with a calculator.

- Tell the children that they are to figure out how to make the calculator count by ones. When children have done this, have them count by twos, fives, tens, or any other number.

- Give challenges: (1) "Can anyone count by fives to 500 in a minute?" Have one child time the other with the second hand on a classroom clock or another timepiece. (2) Give problem cards with tasks like these on them:[12]

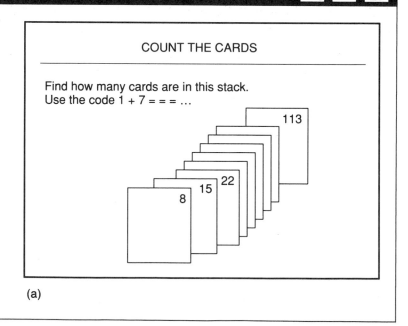

COUNT THE CARDS

Find how many cards are in this stack.
Use the code 1 + 7 = = = ...

113

22

15

8

(a)

Activity 8.14   *continued*

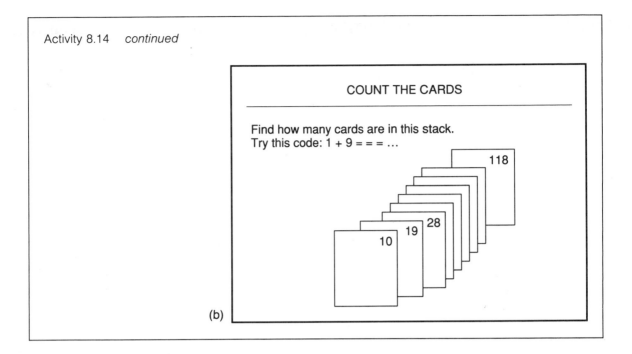

COUNT THE CARDS

Find how many cards are in this stack.
Try this code: 1 + 9 = = = ...

118

28

19

10

(b)

ESTIMATION

Estimation skills have wide application in mathematics. Children need to be able to make reasonable estimates when giving answers to problems and when computing. Skill in estimating answers has gained importance as its value in judging the reasonableness of answers to problems has become fully recognized. One way to judge the reasonableness of an answer is to make an estimate before the computation or other work is done. Procedures for making estimates of computed answers are discussed in chapters dealing with the operations of addition, subtraction, multiplication, and division with both whole and fractional numbers. One way to estimate an answer for an operation such as addition is to add rounded numbers. Children must have content readiness—that is, they must know how to round numbers—in order to use this process. To estimate the answer for the addition in the margin, a person must know how to round each number to the nearer hundred. A number line such as the one in Figure 8.4 helps children see that 290 is nearer 300 than 200. When 290 is located on the line and the steps are counted between 290 and 200 and between 290 and 300, the reason for rounding 290 to 300 becomes clear. After all four numbers have been rounded, the answer can be estimated by adding the rounded numbers.

$$\begin{array}{r} 290 \\ 320 \\ 380 \\ + \ 430 \end{array}$$

Figure 8-4
Number line used to help children round off numbers to the nearest hundred

0   10   260 270 280 290 300 310 320 330 340 350 360 370 380 390 400 410 420 430 440 450 460

Children should learn that to round numbers to the nearer ten, numbers ending in one, two, three, or four are rounded down, and that numbers ending in five, six, seven, eight, and nine are rounded up. A number line that shows tens makes it clear that numbers less than five are nearer the tens place number to the left of them and that numbers greater than five are nearer the tens to the right of them (Figure 8.5). The number line shows that a number ending in five is midway between the two tens numbers; children should be told that it is conventional to round these numbers to the next higher ten. Older students should learn to round larger whole numbers and decimal fractions. The rules for rounding tens and hundreds apply to rounding larger numbers. Procedures for rounding decimals are discussed in Chapter 13.

Once children understand how to round numbers, they should have activities that provide practice and then apply the process to estimating answers that are to be computed. Figure 8.6 illustrates a problem card that can be used to provide practice with rounding numbers. The problem cards in Figure 8.7 provide practice in estimating computed answers. Finally, a card in Figure 8.8 shows examples for which an estimated answer is sufficient for answering the problem.

EXERCISE   Create a problem card that gives children an experience with estimating computed answers (see Figure 8.7) or in using estimated answers to solve problems (see Figure 8.8).

Figure 8-5
Number line used to help children round off numbers to the nearest ten

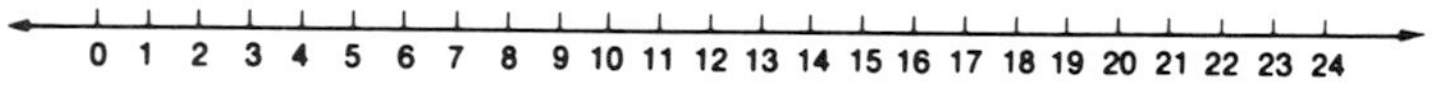

Figure 8-6
Problem card used to practice rounding numbers

ROUNDING NUMBERS

Round each of these numbers to the nearer ten:
    3291   4648   13,689

Round each of the numbers to the nearer hundred.

Round each of the numbers to the nearer thousand.

Figure 8-7
Problem cards used to practice estimating computed answers

ESTIMATING SUMS AND DIFFERENCES

Estimate each sum or difference.

23	18	67	63	48	64
+ 49	+ 21	+ 42	− 21	− 19	− 18

Check your estimates with those of a classmate.

(a)

ESTIMATING PRODUCTS AND QUOTIENTS

Estimate each product or quotient.

19	73	978	438 ÷ 11 = ☐
× 3	× 21	× 48	698 ÷ 35 = ☐

Check your estimates with those of a classmate.

(b)

ESTIMATING ANSWERS

Give an estimated answer for each of these word problems.

- What is the cost of a 69-cent can of fruit and a 59-cent quart of milk?

- How many passengers can 28 buses that each carry 54 passengers take to a parade?

- A stadium seats 54,298 people. If an equal number of people are seated in each of 18 sections, how many people are in each section?

Check your estimates with those of a classmate.

(c)

Figure 8-8
Examples of estimated numbers

NO EXACT ANSWER REQUIRED!

Use estimation to solve these problems.

- Sally wants to buy a baseball glove for $12.95 and a baseball for $3.25. She has $18.00. Does she have enough money to buy the glove and ball?

- A jet plane can carry enough fuel for a five-hour flight made at top speed. If it flies at a top speed of 890 miles, can it make a 5,000-mile trip without refueling?

ELEMENTARY NUMBER THEORY

According to Tobias Dantzig,[13] number theory was developed before the theory of arithmetic. Long before efficient ways to use algorithms were worked out, people began to study the relationships among numbers. Number lore, the study of prime and composite numbers, and other aspects of number theory have a long history. Certain areas of number theory have a prominent place in today's elementary school mathematics curriculum. Organized approaches to the study of odd and even numbers and prime and composite numbers are used to help children learn about these numbers. There are several reasons for this:

- The study of prime and composite numbers gives students skills and information they can use when they work with the common fraction form of representing fractional numbers. Children who know about prime and composite numbers can use them to factor composite numbers and to find *greatest common factors* (*GCF*) and the *least common multiple* (*LCM*) of two or more numbers. Later they can use the knowledge to find common denominators and to simplify, or reduce to *lowest terms*, common fractions.

- Many students find that work with number theory is challenging and interesting. Some find that work with prime and composite numbers leads to many intriguing areas of investigation.

- During the study of the various aspects of number theory, many opportunities arise to work with basic facts for the four operations, to practice computational skills, and to further develop mathematics vocabulary. For example, the process of factoring numbers involves factors, or divisors, and multiples of numbers.

Odd and Even Numbers

Investigations that deal with whole numbers to give children an understanding of odd and even numbers can begin in grades one and two. In Activity 8.15 children use plastic disks to determine why some numbers are odd and others are even. Small cubes and other objects can be used.

As students mature they can use number lines and hundreds charts for further investigations with odd and even numbers. They can locate an odd or even number greater than 20 on a number line and then count by twos forward or backward for ten counts, or to some designated number.

A hundreds chart like the one in Activity 8.13 can be used for similar counting experiences. These observations are among the ones children will make as they use a hundreds chart:

- Beginning at 2, every other number is an even number; beginning at 1, every other number is odd.

- The column on the left side of the chart contains all odd numbers ending in 1. Each alternate column ends in 3, 5, 7, and 9.

ACTIVITY 8.15   Even and Odd

- Have children work in pairs, using disks.

- Tell them to arrange eight disks in two rows, with the same number in each row. Count the number in each row.

- Repeat with 10, 2, 6, 14, 30, 18, or any other even numbers of disks.

- Have children choose other numbers of disks to make two equivalent rows.

- Have children arrange seven disks in two rows. The longer row should contain one extra disk.

- Repeat with 5, 11, 15, 21, 23, and other odd numbers. Emphasize that the longer row should contain only one more bead than the shorter row.

- Have the children recall some of the groupings that contained two equivalent rows (2, 6, 10, 14, 18, 30) and those that made nonequivalent rows (5, 11, 15, 21, 23).

- Ask, "Does anyone know the name for numbers that make two rows that are the same?" "Does anyone know the name for numbers that make two rows that are not the same?" Discuss the difference between even and odd numbers.

■ The second column from the left contains all even numbers that end in 2. Each alternate column across the chart contains even numbers ending in 2, 4, 6, 8, and 0.

■ The even numbers are all multiples of 2.

Intermediate-grade children can study odd and even numbers at a more abstract level. These generalizations can arise from their investigations:

■ Since every even number is a multiple of 2, an even number can be expressed as $2n$.

■ Since every successor of an even number is one greater and is odd, an odd number can be expressed as $2n + 1$.

■ Zero is an even number.

Prime and Composite Numbers

Intermediate-grade children can investigate the nature of prime and composite numbers in cooperative-learning groups, as in Activity 8.16. Activities with disks or cubes allow students to investigate different array patterns and factors of numbers. Directions for activities can be duplicated for distribution to each group.

ACTIVITY 8.16   Prime and Composite Numbers

■ Organize children in cooperative-learning groups. Give each group a paper containing the following information:

■ All of the possible arrays into which sets of six disks can be arranged are shown here:

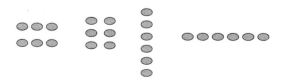

■ Arrange sets of 4, 8, 9, 10, 12, and 15 disks into all of their possible arrays. Make a record of each array for each number on the chart (see top left chart on next page).

■ Make arrays for sets of 2, 3, 5, 7, 11, 13, and 17 disks and record the results. (Arrays for 7 disks are shown.)

■ Determine the array for one disk and record it.

■ Examine your chart, then write a statement that tells how many arrays there are for one disk; for 4, 6, 8, 9, 10, 12, and 15 disks; and for 2, 3, 5, 7, 11, 13, and 17 disks. Statements similar to the ones shown at the right are acceptable:

Activity 8.16   *continued*

—Some whole numbers—2, 3, 5, 7, 11, 13, 17—have only two arrays. These form a straight line rather than a rectangular pattern. The numerical description of each array contains the numeral 1 and the number that tells how many disks are in the array.

—Some whole numbers—4, 6, 8, 9, 10, 12, 15—have more than two arrays. They can be arranged in one or more rectangular patterns as well as in straight lines. In addition to the numeral 1 and the number that tells how many disks there are, other numerals are used in numerical descriptions of these arrays.

—There is only one array for the number 1.

Whole Number	Arrays	Number of Different Arrays
6	2 by 3, 3 by 2, 6 by 1, 1 by 6	4

Whole Number	Arrays	Number of Different Arrays
1	1 by 1	1
2	1 by 2, 2 by 1	2
3	1 by 3, 3 by 1	2
4	2 by 2, 1 by 4, 4 by1	3
5	1 by 5, 5 by 1	2
6	2 by 3, 3 by 2, 6 by 1, 1 by 6	4
7	1 by 7, 7 by 1	2
8	2 by 4, 4 by2, 8 by 1, 1 by 8	4
9	3 by 3, 9 by 1, 1 by 9	3
10	2 by 5, 5 by 2, 10 by 1, 1 by 10	4

The generalizations open the way to discussions about prime and composite numbers. A large classroom chart like the one in Activity 8.16 with arrays for each of the numbers from 1 to 30 can be prepared to focus attention on the numbers. Students should be able to give a suitable definition of prime and composite numbers: "A prime number has only two different factors: 1 and the number itself." "A composite number has three or more different whole number factors." The special characteristics of the number 1 make it neither prime nor composite. It has only one factor—itself—and it is one factor of every other number.

Work with prime and composite numbers extends understanding of factors, divisors, and multiples. Students have already encountered these terms in their study of multiplication and division. Now they should see that *factor* and *divisor* mean the same thing and can be used interchangeably. When two whole numbers are multiplied, they yield a product; they can be

---

ACTIVITY 8.17   Sieve of Eratosthenes

- Begin with a hundreds chart, like the one in Activity 8.13.

- Ask students to give definitions of prime and composite numbers. Ask, "Why is zero neither prime nor composite?" Put a ring around "1" on the chart.

- Have a student identify the smallest prime number. Ask, "What are the multiples of two?" Mark these out as students identify them.

- Ask, "What is the next prime number?" "Are any multiples of three already marked out?" (Yes.) "Which ones?" (The ones that are multiples of two, or the even-numbered multiples of three.) Mark out the odd-numbered multiples of three.

- Ask, "Why are four and all of its multiples marked out?" (They are multiples of two.)

- Ask, "What is the next prime number?" Mark out the multiples of five that remain.

- Ask, "What is the smallest multiple of seven that remains?" (49.) "Why are no smaller multiples of seven unmarked?" (The smaller multiples are also multiples of other smaller prime numbers.) Mark out 49 and the remaining multiples of seven.

- Eleven is the next prime number. Ask, "What multiples of 11 are on the chart?" "Why are none of these multiples unmarked?"

- Have students examine the chart to identify the prime numbers under 100. List these numbers.

called either factors or divisors of their products. (An exception to this statement is that zero can be a factor but not a divisor.) The product of two numbers can also be said to be the multiple of the two numbers. Thus 5 and 7 are factors or divisors of 35; 35 is a multiple of 5 and 7.

Another investigation into prime and composite numbers for intermediate-grade children is done with the *sieve of Eratosthenes*. Eratosthenes was a Greek astronomer-geographer who lived in the third century B.C. He devised a scheme for separating any set of consecutive whole numbers larger than 1 into prime and composite numbers. Naturally, his scheme did not use base-ten numbers, as does the one in Activity 8.17.

A teacher-directed activity with the sieve of Eratosthenes yields additional prime and composite numbers. Once the sieve with numbers from 1 to 100 has been completed, interested students can complete one for numbers between 101 and 200, 101 and 300, or within any other limits to find the multiples of increasingly larger prime numbers: 11, 13, 17, 19, 23. Some students might be interested in searching for *twin primes*. Twin primes are ones that have only one composite number between them. Small twin primes are 3 and 5, 5 and 7, 11 and 13. Students can be challenged to find the largest twin primes less than 300, or less than some other number.

There are problem-solving activities that involve prime and composite numbers. Students in grades five and six can use calculators as they solve the three problems in Activities 8.18 through 8.20, respectively.

ACTIVITY 8.18   Prime and Composite Numbers

- Put numbers such as these on three-by-five inch cards:

421	221	161	151	247
539	457	803	587	937

- Challenge students to determine which of the numbers are prime and which are composite. Have them separate the cards into two piles according to type.

ACTIVITY 8.19   Goldbach's Conjecture

- Goldbach was a Russian mathematician who made a conjecture in 1742 that every even composite number greater than two can be written as the sum of a pair of prime numbers: 4 = 2 + 2, 6 = 3 + 3, 8 = 5 + 3, 10 = 7 + 3, or 5 + 5. Point out that a mathematical conjecture is an educated guess for which there is not sufficient evidence to prove its truth. This conjecture has never been proved true or false for all composite numbers.

- Challenge students to test the conjecture with composite numbers less than 100, or 200, or any other number.

ACTIVITY 8.20   Prime and Composite Numbers

- Prepare a large chart and post it in the room. (Make the chart in two or three sections.) Or, duplicate the chart for groups of students.

Number	Factors	Sum of Factors
1	1	1
2	1, 2	3
3	1, 3	4
4	1, 2, 4	7
5	1, 5	6
6	1, 2, 3, 6	12
7	1, 7	8
8	1, 2, 4, 8	15
9	1, 3, 9	13
10	1, 2, 5, 10	18
11	1, 11	12
12	1, 2, 3, 4, 6, 12	28
13	1, 13	14
14	1, 2, 7, 14	24
.		
.		
.		
30	1, 2, 3, 5, 6, 10, 15, 30	72

- Organize students into cooperative-learning groups. Give each group a paper that contains these questions:
  - —Which numbers have two and only two factors? What kind of numbers are these?
  - —Which numbers have three and only three factors? What will be the next number that has exactly three factors?
  - —Which numbers have four and only four factors? The numbers 8 and 27 have exactly four factors. How do they differ from the other numbers that have exactly four factors? Can you predict the next number of this kind? What number with exactly four factors follows next after 46?
  - —Which numbers have five and only five factors? Can you describe these numbers? What is the next number that has exactly five factors?
  - —Can you write a mathematical rule that tells how to determine the sum of factors when a number is prime? Can you write a rule for finding the sum when a number has exactly three factors?
- Discuss with the students the results of their work.

EXERCISE   At what grade level do you believe work with prime/composite numbers should begin? Explain the reason(s) for your answer.

■ INTEGERS

The numbers considered so far are used for counting discrete quantities or determining measures of magnitude such as length and volume. There are situations in which these numbers alone are not suitable. For example, there are situations in which a part of a unit or group is considered; fractional numbers, represented by common fractions, decimal fractions, and percent, are used to deal with these situations. (These numbers are considered in Chapters 12 and 13.) There are also situations in which measures such as temperature, distance, and altitude, and balances of money accounts require numbers that deal not only with magnitude but also direction. The numbers that do this are real numbers. Integers are the part of the set of real numbers that are studied by elementary school children.

Even though children have limited encounters with situations that require the use of integers, most have had some experience with them. When primary-grade children learn to use a thermometer, they will note that it contains numbers that register temperatures below zero. Older students learn about altitudes above and below sea level, experience or read about gains and losses in football, and see contestants "go in the hole" in the "Jeopardy" television game.

The study of integers in the elementary school is largely informal, with children having opportunities through stories and games to learn some basic concepts about them. There are many story lines that can be used to introduce integers. David Page used cricket jumps on a number line and Louis Cohen used postman stories as settings for introducing them.[14] The subject of a story may be real or fanciful, as long as the sequence of ideas can be readily understood. They should involve students in small-group or whole-class discussions to clarify concepts. The cricket jump theme can be used to introduce the concept and notation for integers (see Activity 8.21). Following the introductory activity are two games—in Activities 8.22 and 8.23—that reinforce understanding of integers.

ACTIVITY 8.21   Cricket Jumps

- Use a number line made on calculator-machine tape that extends both to the left and to the right of zero and a cardboard "cricket" on the end of a stick.

- Call the students' attention to the number line and point out numbers to the right of zero (positive integers) and numbers to the left of zero (negative integers). The children should note that each number to the right of zero has a "+" sign in front of it, and each number to the left of zero has a "−" sign in front of it. Tell them that these numbers are positive and negative integers.

- Use the cricket to review moves on the positive side of the line. Have the cricket jump from 0 to 7 in one-unit hops. Ask, "Where did the cricket start?" "Where did it stop?" "How many jumps did it make?" Write a "7" on the chalkboard. Start at 8 and make the cricket

jump to 3 in one-unit hops. Ask similar questions to clarify jumps to the left. Write "5" on the chalkboard.

- Have the cricket jump from zero to −5 with one-unit hops. Ask, "Where did the cricket start?" "Where did it stop?" "How many hops did it make?" Students should say that there were five hops to the left. Write "5" on the chalkboard; put a "−" sign in front of it. Help the children to understand that the "−5" indicates both the direction and the number of hops.

- Return to the "5" you wrote for the jumps from +8 to +3. Ask, "What should I do to make this five show that there were five jumps to the left?" (Put a "−" sign in front of it.) Ask, "Do both minus fives mean the same thing?" (Yes, each one indicates five hops to the left.)   *(continued)*

```
 •   •   •   •   •   •   •   •   •   •   •   •   •   •   •   •   •   •   •   •   •   •   •
─11─10 ─9  ─8  ─7  ─6  ─5  ─4  ─3  ─2  ─1   0  +1  +2  +3  +4  +5  +6  +7  +8  +9 +10 +11
```

Activity 8.21   *continued*

- Show the cricket taking one-unit hops from −8 to zero. Discuss the number that indicates the number of hops. (+8.) Tell the children that a "+" sign is placed in front of a number to indicate a positive integer, or a move to the right.

- Use other cricket hops to strengthen children's understanding of positive and negative integers and the symbols that represent them.

- Before they are finished with the activity, students should know that positive and negative integers have two roles: (1) they identify numbers in sequence to the right and to the left of zero, and (2) they indicate the direction and magnitude of moves along the number line.

ACTIVITY 8.22   Cricket Jump Game

- Materials: A number line on calculator-machine tape extending from −12 to +12; small construction-paper crickets for markers; and a pair of dice, one marked −1, −2, −3, −4, −5, and −6, and the other marked +1, +2, +3, +4, +5, and +6.

- Two to four students play, rotating turns in a clockwise direction.

- Rules: The first player tosses the dice and reads the number on each one. From "0," the player moves a cricket in the positive direction as many jumps as indicated by the plus die, and then in the negative direction by the number of jumps indicated by the minus die. Each player takes a turn in the same way. Play continues until a player is off the board or until the allotted time has passed. The player farthest from zero in either direction is winner if no player's cricket leaves the board.

ACTIVITY 8.23   Checks and Bills

- Materials: Play money in $1, $5, $10, and $20 denominations and a deck of cards with statements such as: "You receive a rebate of $2.00 from Wrangler jeans." "You receive $5.00 for doing yard work." "You pay $5.00 for an afternoon at Waterworld." "You buy a baseball for $6.00."

- Two to four players take turns in clockwise order. One player also serves as banker.

- Each player begins with five bills for $1, one for $5, two for $10, and one for $20. A bank containing $100 is set up. Cards are shuffled and put face down. The first player draws the top card and tells whether it is a positive card (money is received) or negative card (money is paid) and how much will be gained or lost. For example, "I have a negative card that will cost me $4.00." Players receive money from the bank for positive cards and give money to the bank for negative cards. Play rotates until one player is out of money or until the allotted time has elapsed. The winner is the player with the most money.

A vector, or directed segment, is a line segment with an arrow at one end to indicate direction on a number line. Each vector represents an integer, or directed number. An activity with number lines and vectors like Activity 8.24 enhances students' understanding of integers.

When whole numbers are ordered in sequence on a number line, it is easy to develop the concepts of *equal to, greater than,* and *less than.* The number to the right of a number is greater than the number and any other number to its left; a number to the left of a number is less than the number and any other number to its right. The same properties hold for numbers in the set of integers. When integers are ordered on a number line, their comparative properties can be determined by their locations. Zero and all positive numbers are greater than all negative numbers. To compare any two negative numbers, children should recognize that they are treated like whole numbers.

ACTIVITY 8.24   Vectors

- Show a horizontal number line. Draw an arrow that begins at zero and ends at +4. Tell the students that this vector is a "+4" vector. Ask, "Why is it named that way?" "If this vector represented cricket jumps, would the cricket move to the left or right?" "If it represented a money situation, would you give or receive money?"

- Show other vectors on the line. Ask similar questions about vectors, such as **b**, **c**, and **d**.

- Show a vertical number line. Mark vectors, such as **e**, **f**, **g**, **h**, and **i**. Ask questions about these vectors.

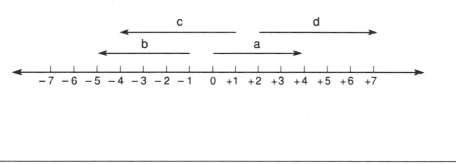

EXERCISE   What do you believe should be the role of work with integers in elementary school mathematics?

■ SUMMARY

Children must have a well-developed understanding of numbers and the Hindu-Arabic, or base-ten, numeration system if they are to be mathematically literate. Place-value materials, such as bundled tongue depressors, which are type-one proportional materials, and base-ten and Cuisenaire kit materials and beansticks, which are type-two proportional materials, are useful for clarifying the meaning of the base-ten system. An abacus is a non-proportional place-value device that is particularly good for clarifying the meaning of large numbers. Numerals can be written in both compact and expanded forms. Expanded forms are used to help children understand place value and algorithms for such operations as addition and subtraction. Regrouping is a process in which exchanges are made between adjacent place-value positions in a number during computation with the operations. Children need to understand regrouping thoroughly before they deal with algorithms. Beansticks and other place-value materials can be used in directed lessons and group activities to teach the process.

Children must understand one-to-many, many-to-one, and many-to-many correspondences, for which numerous applications are found in mathematics and real-world problem situations. Skip counting is a useful counting process that is applied to many situations. It should be learned by children in practical situations, such as counting money, vote tallies, and other grouped items. Estimation is frequently used in problem solving to determine the reasonableness of answers. One way to estimate is to round numbers and compute with the estimated numbers. Number lines are useful for helping children learn to round numbers.

Number theory topics contribute to children's understanding of numbers. Primary-grade children learn about odd and even numbers, while intermediate-grade students learn about prime and composite numbers. Children should be introduced to integers through stories and activities that are meaningful to them. Games involving cricket jumps on a number line and gaining and losing money provide settings for students to enhance their understanding of integers.

■ STUDY QUESTIONS AND ACTIVITIES

1. Three general standards are discussed in Chapter 6. In order for teachers to accomplish them, they must be aware of them and how activities in all areas of mathematics help achieve them. Select one of the three standards for either K–4 or 5–8, then write statements that explain how topics in this chapter and activities with them can help develop the subpoints for that standard.

2. You should be familiar with a variety of materials for teaching the meaning of place-value: beansticks, bundled tongue depressors, Unifix cubes, base-ten sticks, Cuisenaire rods, place-value chips, and the abacus. Show the meaning of each of the following numbers with the materials you have: (a) 136, (b) 95, (c) 308, (d) 4082. Make drawings to represent each number with three of the materials. Identify each of the materials as proportional or nonproportional.

3. Different forms of expanded notation are described in this chapter. Some forms are suitable for introducing place value to young children: "1 ten and 4 ones." A form using exponential notation is introduced to older students. Express each of the following numbers in four different expanded forms: (a) 654, (b) 47,825, (c) 200,409. Begin with the first form, then use two intermediate forms, and end with the exponential form.

4. Read "The Plight and Might of Number Seven," "Don't Be Blue, Number Two," or "Number Three Comes to See" (see the For Further Reading section) and list some student activities suggested by Shmuel Avital. How might you use these activities in your class for extension and enrichment of the topics in this chapter?

5. Prime numbers can be approached in several ways. Burton and Knifong (see the For Further Reading section) discuss six methods. List the approaches and discuss their strengths and weaknesses. Which method appeals the most to you? Why? Show that you understand the file card and toothpick activity discussed by the authors by picturing cards for these numbers: 2, 3, 4, 6, 7, 9.

6. Goldbach's conjecture holds that every even number can be expressed as the sum of two prime numbers. Hamann's conjecture suggests that every even number from 2 to 250 can be expressed as the *difference* between two prime numbers. Read more about Hamann's conjecture by reading Frame's article (see the For Further Reading section). Test Hamann's conjecture with at least 20 numbers between 2 and 250 to demonstrate that it is reasonable.

7. Makurat and West and Haar (see the For Further Reading section) discuss activities dealing with large numbers. What other types of materials of the sorts discussed in these two articles can be used to illustrate large numbers? How would you have children use the materials you identify?

▮ TEACHER'S BOOKSHELF

Freebury, H. A. 1961. *A History of Mathematics.* New York: Macmillan.

▓ FOR FURTHER READING

Avital, Shmuel. 1978, February. The might and plight of number seven. *Arithmetic Teacher 25*(5), 22–24.

The number 7 comes alive to visit the author and tells about its special characteristics. Many interesting possibilities for children's investigations of the number 7 arise in the article.

———. 1986, September. Don't be blue, number two. *Arithmetic Teacher 34*(1), 42–45.

Activities that illustrate interesting characteristics of the number 2 are presented.

Avital, Shmuel, and Uri Grinblat. 1983, March. Number three comes to see. *Arithmetic Teacher 30*(7), 46–49.

Activities in this article focus on the number 3.

Bickerton-Ross, Linda. 1988, December. A practical experience in problem solving: A "10 000" display. *Arithmetic Teacher 36*(4), 14–15.

Children brought in large numbers of objects (666 by each one) to make a display of 10,000. Each child wrote a story about her or his objects. Eventually they assembled all of the objects into a display of 10,000 objects.

Burton, Grace M., and J. Dan Knifong. 1980, February. Definitions for prime numbers. *Arithmetic Teacher 27*(6), 44–47.

Materials and procedures for teaching children about prime numbers are discussed. Other activities dealing with prime numbers are suggested.

Frame, Maxine R. 1976, January. Hamann's conjecture. *Arithmetic Teacher 23*(1), 34–35.

"Hamann's conjecture" was made by a seventh-grade boy when he discovered that every even number from 2 through 250 can be expressed as the difference between two prime numbers. (Later, when he did research on the subject, he found that his conjecture was not the first expression of the idea.)

Hopkins, Martha H. 1987, March. Number facts—or fantasy? *Arithmetic Teacher 34*(7), 38–42.

Hopkins provides us with a brief history of specific numbers and some beliefs associated with them.

Makurat, Phillip A. 1977, December. A look at a million. *Arithmetic Teacher 25*(3), 23.

A computer printout of a million dollar signs is relatively easy to get—much easier than a million bottle caps. With such a printout, children can figure how long it would take to make a million dots. Other activities are suggested.

West, Mike, and Ken Haar. 1978, September. It's neat being surrounded by peanuts. *Arithmetic Teacher 26*(1), 22.

Mike, a ten-year-old student, bought a 100-pound bag of peanuts and held a contest; fellow students guessed the number of peanuts. Mike and some of his friends counted the peanuts, grouping them by tens and powers of tens; there were 16,870. Guesses ranged from as low as 800 to well over a billion, prompting Ken, the teacher, to observe that even some high school students who made estimates lacked good number sense.

◼ NOTES

[1] National Council of Teachers of Mathematics. 1989. *Curriculum and Evaluation Standards for School Mathematics.* Reston, VA: National Council of Teachers of Mathematics, 36. Used by permission.

[2] NCTM, 38. Used by permission.

[3] NCTM, 87. Used by permission.

[4] NCTM, 91. Used by permission.

[5] H. A. Freebury. *A History of Mathematics.* 1961. New York: Macmillan, 72.

[6] David Eugene Smith. 1953. *History of Mathematics.* Boston: Ginn, 69.

[7] Freebury, 76–77.

[8] SVE, 1345 Diversey Parkway, Chicago, IL 60614-1299.

[9] Micro-Learningware, Rt. 1, Box 162, Amboy, MN, 56010-9762.

[10] Hartley Courseware, Inc., Box 419, Dimondale, MI 48821.

[11] Mindscape, Inc., 3444 Dundee Rd., Northbrook, IL 60062.

[12] Adapted from Project Impact. 1982. *Problem Solving Using the Calculator: Book I.* Cedar Falls, IA: Price Laboratory School, University of Northern Iowa, 3.

[13] Tobias Dantzig. 1954. *Number: The Language of Science,* 4th ed. New York: Doubleday, 38.

[14] See David A. Page. 1964. *Number Lines, Functions, and Fundamental Topics.* New York: Macmillan, Chapter 6, for a discussion of cricket jumps; and Louis Cohen. 1965. A rationale in working with signed numbers. *Arithmetic Teacher* 12(7) (November 1965), 563–567, for postman stories.

CHAPTER 9

Teaching Addition and Subtraction of Whole Numbers

Four basic arithmetic operations are learned by children in the elementary school: addition, subtraction, multiplication, and division. In former years, much of the curriculum was centered on these operations with whole numbers and common and decimal fractions. After students studied an operation for a period of time they were given a few story problems pertaining to the operation and then moved on to another operation. Today, operations are only one part of the curriculum and are learned through a problem-solving approach. This chapter discusses ways to help boys and girls learn about addition and subtraction with whole numbers. The next chapter discusses multiplication and division.

In this chapter you will read about

1. the NCTM standards that apply to developing students' understanding of and skills in adding and subtracting with whole numbers;

2. three ways of computing;

3. four different real-world situations associated with subtraction;

4. the importance of real-world situations in developing understanding of addition and subtraction;

5. activities for developing readiness for addition and subtraction;

6. ways to introduce addition and subtraction facts and number sentences for them;

7. strategies for helping students learn basic addition and subtraction facts;

8. place-value devices that represent addition and subtraction of two- and three-digit numbers with and without regrouping;

9. strategies students can learn for estimation and mental computation with addition and subtraction;

10. two algorithms for computing subtraction;

11. computer and calculator activities dealing with addition and subtraction.

NCTM STANDARDS THAT PERTAIN TO ADDITION AND SUBTRACTION OF WHOLE NUMBERS

Kindergarten Through Grade Four

Standard 5: Estimation   In grades K–4, the curriculum should include estimation so that students can:

- explore estimation strategies;
- recognize when estimation is appropriate;
- determine the reasonableness of results;
- apply estimation in working with . . . computation and problem solving.[1]

Standard 7: Concepts of Whole Number Operations In grades K–4, the mathematics curriculum should include concepts of addition [and] subtraction . . . of whole numbers so that students can:

- develop meaning for the operations by modeling and discussing a rich variety of problem situations;
- relate the mathematical language and symbolism of operations to problem situations and informal language;
- recognize that a wide variety of problem structures can be represented by a single process;
- develop operation sense.[2]

Standard 8: Whole Number Computation   In grades K–4, the mathematics curriculum should develop whole number computation so that students can:

- model, explain, and develop reasonable proficiency with basic facts and algorithms;
- use a variety of mental computation and estimation techniques;
- use calculators in appropriate computational situations;
- select and use computation techniques appropriate to specific problems and determine if the results are reasonable.[3]

Grades Five Through Eight

Standard 6: Number Systems and Number Theory
In grades 5–8, the mathematics curriculum should include the study of number systems and number theory so that students can:

- understand how basic arithmetic operations are related to one another.[4]

Standard 7: Computation and Estimation   In grades 5–8, the mathematics curriculum should develop the concepts underlying computation and estimation in various contexts so that students can:

- compute with whole numbers . . . ;

- develop, analyze, and explain procedures for computation and techniques for estimation;

- select and use an appropriate method for computing from among mental arithmetic, paper-and-pencil, calculator, and computer methods;

- use computation [and] estimation . . . to solve problems;

- use estimation to check the reasonableness of results.[5]

Standard 9: Algebra   In grades 5–8, the mathematics curriculum should include explorations of algebraic concepts so that students can:

- understand the concept of . . . equation.[6]

The charts in Figures 9.1 and 9.2 suggest sequences for teaching addition and subtraction. The sequences indicate in a general way the subtasks that most children learn in addition and subtraction; however, neither one should be followed without variation because children vary in the rate and manner in which they learn operations and an algorithm for each one. An **algorithm** is a step-by-step process for computing numbers with paper and pencil.

Figure 9-1
A series of steps
for learning to add
whole numbers

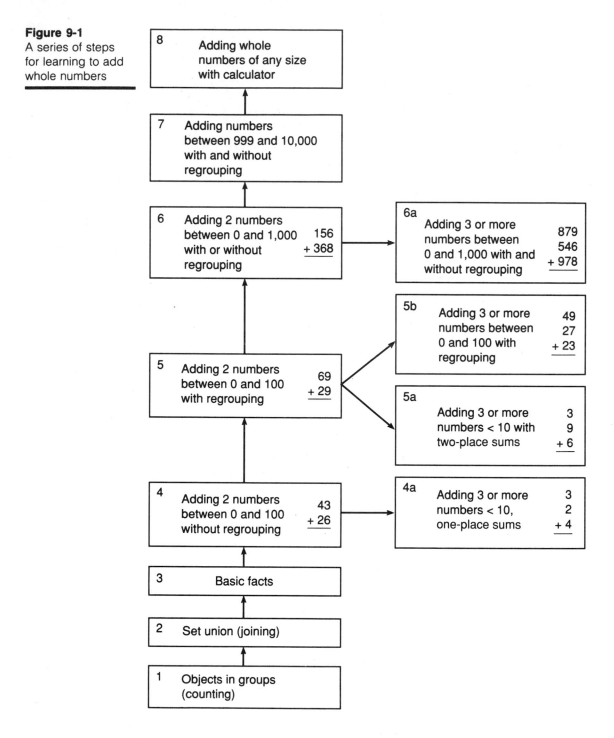

Figure 9-2
A sequence for
learning to subtract
whole numbers

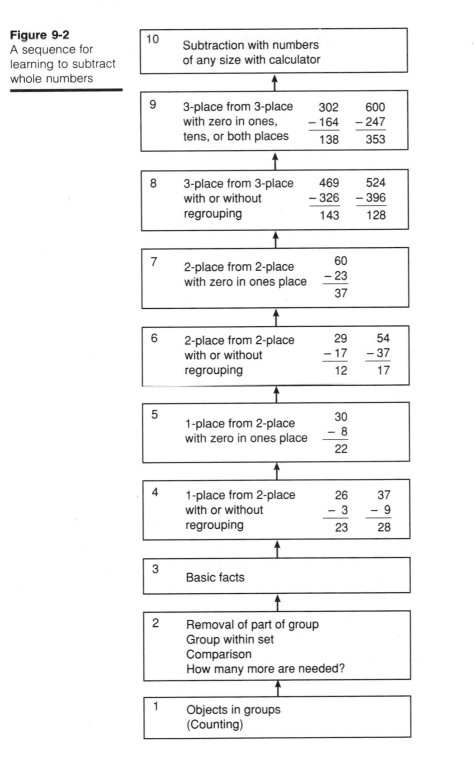

10	Subtraction with numbers of any size with calculator

9	3-place from 3-place with zero in ones, tens, or both places	302 − 164 138	600 − 247 353

| 8 | 3-place from 3-place with or without regrouping | 469
− 326
143 | 524
− 396
128 |

| 7 | 2-place from 2-place with zero in ones place | 60
− 23
37 |

| 6 | 2-place from 2-place with or without regrouping | 29
− 17
12 | 54
− 37
17 |

| 5 | 1-place from 2-place with zero in ones place | 30
− 8
22 |

| 4 | 1-place from 2-place with or without regrouping | 26
− 3
23 | 37
− 9
28 |

| 3 | Basic facts |

| 2 | Removal of part of group
Group within set
Comparison
How many more are needed? |

| 1 | Objects in groups (Counting) |

■ THE NCTM STANDARDS

Activities that lay the foundation for work with addition and subtraction begin in kindergarten or first grade. Once begun, work with the operations continues throughout the elementary school years. The National Council of Teachers of Mathematics standards recommend that children's early work with addition and subtraction of whole numbers provide opportunities for a variety of manipulative materials with which children learn the meanings of the operations and their algorithms. As children learn about addition and subtraction they should be encouraged to explain and discuss the operations and ways of computing with them. Over time, they should learn and use strategies for estimating sums and remainders and use a variety of processes for computing numbers. The work children do with addition and subtraction should always be linked with real-world situations so that they recognize how to use these tools for solving problems.

■ THREE TYPES OF COMPUTATION PROCESSES

Students should learn three ways to perform computation: paper-and-pencil, calculator, and mental. In the past, paper-and-pencil algorithms have been emphasized almost to the exclusion of calculator and mental processes. Today calculators and computers have almost universally replaced paper-and-pencil processes in science, industry, business, and the marketplace. A calculator is the instrument of choice for many people when balancing a checkbook, determining the better buy in a supermarket, and for other calculations that were formerly done with paper and pencil.

A well-conceived elementary school mathematics program will place the proper emphasis on each of the three calculation processes. In the program students learn the meaning of paper-and-pencil algorithms to determine sums, differences, products, and quotients. There are several reasons why students need to learn one or more algorithms for each of the four operations.

1. Skill in computation helps students understand concepts involved with the operations and more advanced skills. For example, students who have a good understanding of the concept of addition will quickly grasp that subtraction is the inverse of addition; it is the operation that undoes what is done by addition. Likewise, a good knowledge of addition helps students understand the repeated addition interpretation of multiplication. Knowledge of paper-and-pencil processes helps students learn proper ways of computing with a calculator.

2. Skill in computation helps students understand operations and their applications. Many people do not realize that counting can be used to solve almost every problem involving discrete objects. If a student wants to determine the total number of objects in two or more collections, he or she can count each object to determine the total. If the collections are of unequal size, it is easier to add to determine the total; if they are of equal size, it is easier to multiply. Rather than counting each object, a student with good understanding of operations will generally use the least difficult and the fastest method to determine a total.

3. Skill in computation helps students explore topics, generalize from data, and recognize mathematics principles. A common activity for helping students understand prime and composite numbers is to complete a sieve of Eratosthenes (see Activity 8.17). Students with a good understanding of multiplication and the meaning of factors will gain much from an investigation of prime and composite numbers using the sieve. They will be able to name all factors of a number, to recognize differences between prime and composite numbers, and to make generalizations about the numbers. Students lacking a good understanding will gain little from an investigation using the sieve.

4. Skill in computation has social utility. There are times when paper-and-pencil computation is more suitable than using a calculator. A quick bit of paper-and-pencil computation might be used to determine a person's share of the cost of an evening's entertainment. Many times a situation does not require an exact answer; an estimate is sufficient. Skill in estimating is dependent on a good understanding of an operation.[7]

Students need to learn to do mental arithmetic. Mental arithmetic is used to find exact answers, such as when a student mentally adds the numbers 42 and 30 to get 72, and to determine estimated answers, such as when a student estimates that the product of 5 and 48 is about 250. Mental computations may be done to find sums or differences, or as part of another operation. When a student mentally adds 42 and 30 to get 72, it is done to determine a final sum. When a student mentally adds 28 and 6 to get 34, which is done as part of the process used to find the product in the example in the margin, it is done as part of another operation. Both types of mental computation must be developed over time if students are to become proficient in their uses.

$$\begin{array}{r} 49 \\ \times\ 7 \\ \hline 343 \end{array}$$

Students should learn underlying concepts and a paper-and-pencil algorithm for each operation. Once these tasks are accomplished, calculators can be used for much of the computation formerly done with paper and pencil. Calculators can also be used to investigate number concepts and to solve problems. Students who use calculators regularly and with understanding do not have diminished understandings of computation. On the contrary, they usually have deepened understandings of computation and other areas of mathematics because a calculator frees the time formerly used to add and subtract large numbers using paper and pencil and gives more time for problem solving and other activities.

■ ADDITION AND SUBTRACTION SITUATIONS

There is only one type of real-world situation that gives rise to addition: the joining of two or more groups of objects. Subtraction, however, arises from several kinds of situations. Students should have experiences with these types:

- *Take-Away*—Subtraction is used to find the remainder when part of a set is removed. "Jamal had 394 baseball cards. He sold 154 of them at a card show. How many cards did he have after the show?" This is the type of situation most frequently encountered by children.

- *Comparison*—Subtraction is used to compare the sizes of two sets. "There were two circus performances. One was attended by 8,958 people and the other by 9,348 people. How many more people attended the second performance?"

- *Completion*—Subtraction is used to determine the size of a set that is put with a second set to make a third set. "Mr. Lopez finished filling the pages of a 1,200-stamp book. How many additional stamps did he put in if there were 949 stamps when he started?"

- *Part/Whole*—Subtraction is used to find the size of a group within a group. "Sally has 78 snapdragons. Thirty of them are white. How many have other colors?"

■ DEVELOPING READINESS FOR ADDITION AND SUBTRACTION

Children's early understandings of addition and subtraction concepts and procedures develop from informal experiences. As they play they have opportunities to share things, count objects, compare heights and distances, and engage in other background-building activities. Children whose experiences are meager have little background on which to build knowledge of mathematical concepts and skills. Young children in school need opportunities to participate in meaningful playlike activities to build background for understanding mathematics. As students become ready, new settings and materials should be introduced to broaden their knowledge.

Activities that develop students' intuitive understanding of addition and subtraction should be an integral part of their work as they learn to count to ten and beyond. You can ask questions to stimulate students' thinking about addition and subtraction situations as they learn to count with concrete materials:

- "You have put six clothespins on that card. I'll put two more on it. How many pins do you think are on the card now? Count to see if there are eight."

- "There are nine acorns in your basket. When I take three from the basket, how many will be left? Count to see if there are six in the basket."

- "You have six red golf tees and four blue golf tees in the pegboard. Are there more red tees or more blue tees? How do you know? How many more red tees are there?"

Students can use a walk-on number line for readiness activities. When the sequence of numbers from zero through nine has been learned, students can play "train" on a walk-on line (Figure 9.3). Each numeral card is a "station."

- "Begin at station zero and walk to station three. Now, take four more steps. On what station are you standing?"

- "Begin at station eight and walk four steps toward station zero. On what station are you standing?"

Figure 9-3
Students play "train" on a walk-on number line.

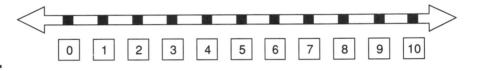

■ INTRODUCING ADDITION AND SUBTRACTION

Initial Addition Activities

All children are not ready to begin work with addition and subtraction at the same time. Those who are ready should not be delayed because of less mature classmates. You can use a concrete situation to introduce addition to students who are ready for the new work, as in Activity 9.1.

Provide many activities of these types, which teach the meaning of addition by joining sets of objects. Use the experiences as opportunities to de-

---

ACTIVITY 9.1   Introducing Addition

- Begin with familiar objects, such as a set of two dolls and a set of three dolls.

- Have students identify the number of dolls in each set.

- Put the sets together and have students determine the total number.

- Repeat with other numbers of familiar objects, such as toy cars, books, blocks, and paper plates.

velop students' oral descriptions of addition and understanding of the terminology applied to the operation. "A set of two dolls joined with a set of three dolls makes a set of five dolls." "Two dolls and three dolls make five dolls." "Two plus three is five." "Two and three equal five."

After students have had a variety of concrete experiences and can orally describe addition situations, introduce the addition sentence. Materials that can be moved around on a magnetic or flannel board and at students' desks are appropriate at this stage of learning, as suggested in Activity 9.2. As children use realistic objects and markers, they build up mental images of addition situations and number sentences. A child with a good store of mental images will have little difficulty in writing mathematical sentences when confronted by similar but not identical situations at a later time.

ACTIVITY 9.2   The Addition Sentence

- Put a set of three shapes and a set of four shapes on a flannel or magnetic board.

- Have a student count and put a felt or magnetic "3" beneath the first set. Have a second student do the same with the set of four shapes.

- Put a felt or magnetic "+" sign between the "3" and the "4" and discuss its meaning. Put

an "=" sign after the "4" and discuss its meaning. Complete the sentence by putting a "7" after the equal sign.

- Have students read the sentence in unison, "Three plus four equals seven."

- Repeat with other combinations having sums less than nine.

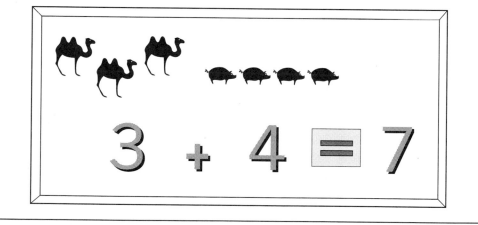

Initial Subtraction Activities

Subtraction activities generally follow activities dealing with addition. All addition combinations need not be introduced before work with subtraction is begun. Once a teacher is certain that children have a good grasp of the meaning of addition and can model and describe simple addition situations, the children can begin work with subtraction. Activity 9.3 suggests some ways of getting started.

Students need not use subtraction sentences during their initial activities. Neither is it necessary that they learn any terms, such as *sum, addend,* and *missing addend.* It is better first to establish an understanding of the take-away situation. Once students recognize this meaning of subtraction and can distinguish it from addition, the sentence can be introduced—as in Activity 9.4.

ACTIVITY 9.3   Introducing Subtraction

- Begin with six objects, such as books. "I am going to give two of these books to Nita. How many books will I keep?"

- Have students count the original set to confirm that there are six books. Many students will just "know" that you kept four books. Even so, either a single child or the group in unison should count them.

- Repeat with other collections and different combinations.

ACTIVITY 9.4   The Subtraction Sentence

- Put a set of seven shapes on a magnetic or flannel board. Put a magnetic or felt "7" beneath the shapes.

- Say, "I am going to take four of the shapes off the board."

- Take four shapes off the board and have a student tell how many are left.

- Complete the subtraction sentence by putting a magnetic or felt "−" sign, "4," "=" sign, and "3" after the "7." Relate the parts of the sentence with the just-completed actions to the shapes. Help the students see that "7" represents the original set; the "−" sign indicates that some shapes were removed; "4" indicates how many were taken away; and the "=" sign shows that "3" is equal to "7 − 4."

- Repeat with additional sets containing nine or fewer objects.

Activities for Reinforcing the Meaning of Addition and Subtraction

Activities with a variety of concrete materials will reinforce students' understanding of addition and subtraction. Children who are given activities like the ones that follow will need fewer practice exercises at a later time because they have a greater understanding of the operations and because they learn many of the basic facts as they manipulate objects. (See Activities 9.5 through 9.9.)

Later, students can use chalkboard or paper number lines. Figure 9.4 shows how the sentence $3 + 4 = 7$ can be represented. A number line is

---

ACTIVITY 9.5   Adding with Beads

- Give a pair of children a nine-by-twelve card with beads strung across the face.

- Tell them to separate the beads into two groups and write the addition sentence that describes the arrangement of beads.

- Have the students separate the beads in other ways and write the addition sentence for each arrangement.[8]

- A student can use the cards to arrange groups and write sentences for part/whole subtraction sentences.

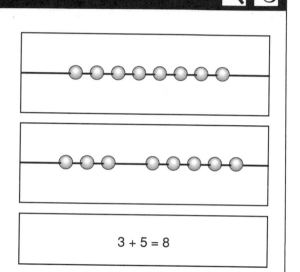

$3 + 5 = 8$

ACTIVITY 9.6   Adding with Beans

- Give a pair of students a group of six, seven, eight, or nine lima beans that have been painted on one side and a sheet of colored construction paper.

- Tell the students to drop all of the beans onto the sheet of paper at one time. The students count the beans with plain sides up and write the number as the first addend; count the beans with the painted side up and write a "+" sign and the number of the second addend; then they write the sum after an "=" sign.

- Tell the students to complete the activity five times.

- Ask, "Is each sentence different?" If there are matching sentences, have the students identify them.

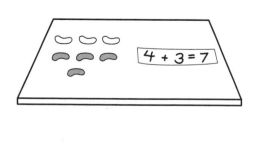

Figure 9-4
Number line show-
ing how to illus-
trate the sentence
$3 + 4 = 7$

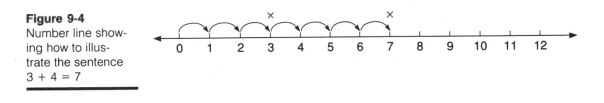

ACTIVITY 9.7   Subtracting with Blocks

- Give a pair of students an aluminum pie tin and several small blocks.

- One child chooses a number, say six, and puts that many blocks into the tin. The child removes a few of the blocks, puts the tin upside down over them, and puts the remaining blocks on top of the tin.

- The other child writes two number sentences for the action. If two blocks are covered, the sentences are $6 - 2 = 4$ and $6 - 4 = 2$.

- Repeat with different combinations of six blocks and with more or fewer than six blocks.[9]

ACTIVITY 9.8   Dropping Beads

- Enclose seven small beads in your hand. Open the hand so a group of children can count the beads. Close your hand.

- Drop a bead onto a table or the floor. Ask, "How many beads are in my hand now?" Drop another bead. Ask, "How many beads are in my hand now?" "How many beads did I drop?" Have students confirm both num-

bers by counting the beads in your hand and on the table or floor.

- Have a student write the subtraction sentence $7 - 2 = 5$ on the chalkboard; discuss its meaning.

- Repeat with other combinations for seven beads and other quantities of beads.[10]

ACTIVITY 9.9   Using a Number Line

- Put a walk-on number line on the floor. (See Figure 9.3.)

- Write "6" on the chalkboard. Tell a student to begin at "0" and take six steps. Write "3" after "6" with a space between. Tell the student to take three more steps. Have another

student complete the addition sentence by writing "+," "=," and "9" in the proper places.

- Repeat with other combinations having sums less than ten.

useful for showing that subtraction and addition are inverse operations. First write the sentence 6 + 3 = 9 on the chalkboard and represent it on a number line, as in Figure 9.5(a). Then represent the related subtraction sentence on a number line, as in Figure 9.5(b). Write the subtraction sentence 9 − 3 = 6 on the chalkboard. During discussion of the two sentences, stress that moves for addition are made to the right and moves for subtraction are made to the left on the number line. Activities 9.10 and 9.11 provide helpful practice.

Figure 9-5
Number lines illustrating the inverse relationship between addition and subtraction. (a) The addition sentence 6 + 3 = 9. (b) The subtraction sentence 9 − 3 = 6.

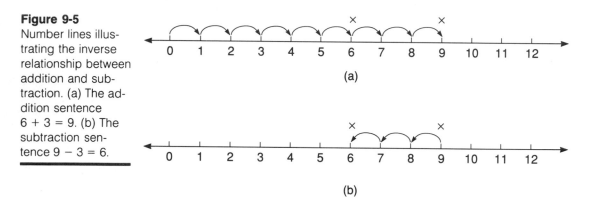

(a)

(b)

ACTIVITY 9.10   Cuisenaire Trains

- Give a pair of children some Cuisenaire rods. Tell them that letters will be used to represent the rods: "w" for white, "r" for red, "g" for green, . . . "o" for orange.

- Show how letters in sentences can represent trains: w + w = r, y + y = o

- Tell the children to select a rod such as dark green (dg) and make all of the trains with two rods that are the length of that rod.

- Tell the children to write a sentence for each train first using letters:

  w + y = dg, r + p = dg, g + g = dg,
    p + r = dg, y + w = dg
  then using numbers:
  5 + 1 = 6, 4 + 2 = 6, 3 + 3 = 6,
    2 + 4 = 6, 1 + 5 = 6
  Children may also write 0 + 6 = 6 and
    6 + 0 = 6 when they use numbers.

- Have students repeat with other rods.

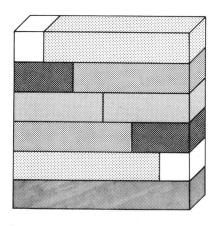

ACTIVITY 9.11   Addition and Subtraction

■ Have each child take two dozen Unifix cubes of four different colors. Tell them to sort and join all cubes of the same color.

■ Give directions and ask questions:
—Have each child hold up the cubes that form the longest link. "Who has the most reds?" "Blues?" "Yellows?" and so on.

—Have each child hold up the color that forms the shortest link. (It may be one cube.) "Who has the fewest reds?" "Blues?" "Yellows?" and so on.

—"How many more in your longest link than in your shortest link?" Allow time for students to respond.

—"Can you find two shorter links that together make one as long as your longest link?" [11]

Activities with real-world situations that involve the completion and part/whole situations for subtraction should be developed and used so that students will also become familiar with them. Here are some examples.

■ "Clarissa is saving inner seals from the lids of her favorite yogurt dessert for a free kite. She must have nine seals for the kite she wants. She has six seals. How many more seals does she need?"

■ "Bill watched eight airplanes fly overhead. Before they disappeared from sight, he saw that four of the planes were red. How many of the planes were not red?"

Introducing the Vertical Notation Form

The mathematical sentence, rather than the vertical notation form, is most often used when children are introduced to addition and subtraction. There are at least two reasons for this:

■ A sentence can be considered a shorthand form of a longer word sentence; hence its meaning is more easily recognized.

■ A sentence gives students a means of writing a notation for real-world situations that involve addition and subtraction.

Students also need to learn the vertical form because it is used in algorithms. You will lessen confusion for students if you are consistent in the ways you convert addition and subtraction sentences to vertical forms. For example, when you convert the sentence $4 + 6 = 10$ to vertical form, write

$$\begin{array}{r} 4 \\ +6 \\ \hline 10 \end{array}$$

For the sentence 6 + 4 = 10, write

$$
\begin{array}{r}
6 \\
+4 \\
\hline
10
\end{array}
$$

A magnetic or flannel board can be used to introduce vertical notation, as in Activity 9.12.

Once students are familiar with the addition form introduce the vertical form for subtraction.

Students also need manipulative activities that deal with addition and subtraction combinations with sums greater than ten. Activities like the ones already discussed can be used with larger sets. During all early work with combinations, each addend should not exceed ten; subtraction combinations should be inverses of the addition combinations with which students work.

EXERCISE   Write a subtraction question for each of the following situations. Label each situation with the type of subtraction it illustrates.
1. Mr. Ramirez had 16 boys in his class of 25 students.
2. Joan weighed 34 kg and Yusef weighed 81 kg.

ACTIVITY 9.12   Addition Sentence to Vertical Form

■ Arrange two sets of shapes horizontally on a felt or magnetic board. Use felt or magnetic symbols beneath the shapes to show the addition sentence.

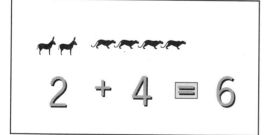

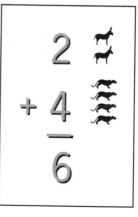

■ Turn the board so the shapes are vertical. Put felt or magnetic symbols alongside the shapes to show the vertical form.

■ Discuss the way the two forms are alike. (They both show addition.) Discuss the way they are different.

■ Repeat with other sets of shapes.

3. Mrs. Bennett bought two dozen oranges and served 14 of them to the girls after hockey practice.
4. Mr. Hoang had 18 mathematics books for 27 students.
5. Diego had 34 cents. The whistle cost 63 cents.

REINFORCING THE LEARNING OF BASIC FACTS

A **basic addition fact** is an ordered pair of whole number addends, each smaller than ten, and their sum. Altogether there are 100 addition facts that include all of the possible combinations using numbers less than ten and their sums. Every addition fact has a subtraction that is its inverse, so there are 100 subtraction facts. Ultimately each child who is capable of doing so should learn each fact for rapid recall. Otherwise the child will be handicapped when working with an algorithm for each operation and, later, when computing multiplication and division.

Students should learn strategies that increase the speed and accuracy with which they respond to the basic facts. Students who are denied opportunities to learn the strategies use inefficient and less effective ones, which very often do not lead to quick, sure responses. You must take time to present strategies to students and give them opportunities to practice them. The following strategies have been found to be effective.

One strategy for addition is counting on. It is particularly effective when one addend is four or less. A student who uses this strategy begins with the larger addend, and counts on from it the number of times indicated by the other addend. To find the answer for 8 plus 4, the student begins with eight and counts on four more: "8, 9, 10, 11, 12."

Another effective strategy is to use facts in "family" groups. Addition and subtraction facts can be grouped by families in two ways:

- All sentences for a given sum are grouped together: $3 + 0 = 3$, $2 + 1 = 3$, $1 + 2 = 3$, $0 + 3 = 3$, and $3 - 0 = 3$, $3 - 1 = 2$, $3 - 2 = 1$, $3 - 3 = 0$.

This scheme works best when the addends are relatively small and there are just a few combinations in each family.

- Or, the four combinations involving a given pair of addends and their sum are grouped together: $6 + 2 = 8$, $2 + 6 = 8$, $8 - 2 = 6$, and $8 - 6 = 2$.

Textbook work pages and games are good sources of practice exercises using families.

Most students readily learn the answers for doubles, or facts with two like addends, such as 8 + 8 = 16. There is a strategy to learn the near doubles, which include combinations like 8 + 9 and 7 + 8. Two other strategies are one for adding numbers to nine and one using ten. Activities 9.13 through 9.15 present these strategies.

ACTIVITY 9.13   Near Doubles

- Have each child make a set of double cards.

- Hold up a near-double card, such as one with the combination 5 + 6. Say, "Hold up the double card that will help us with this addition." Some children will hold up 5 + 5, while others might hold up 6 + 6. The first card suggests a "double plus 1" combination, while the second one suggests a

"double minus 1" combination. Either strategy is useful, and students should be encouraged to consider them both.

- Repeat with other combinations of numbers.

- Reinforce with work sheets containing examples like this: "Ring the doubles you would use to solve the combination above each truck."

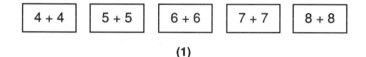

(1)

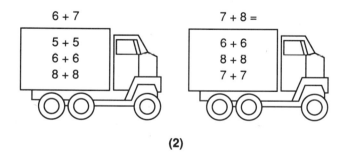

(2)

ACTIVITY 9.14   Adding One Less Than Ten

- Present a combination that contains ten as an addend orally: 4 + 10. Have a student name the sum.

- Present a combination that contains nine as an addend orally: 4 + 9. Have a student name the sum.

- Write both sentences on the chalkboard: 4 + 10 = 14   4 + 9 = 13.

- Say, "Four plus ten equals 14, so four plus nine equals 13."

- Use other combinations, such as 10 + 6, 9 + 6 and 8 + 10, 8 + 9.[12]

ACTIVITY 9.15   Add to Ten

- Write an addition sentence on the chalk-board, such as 7 + 6 = □.

- Model the sentence with shapes on a flannel or magnetic board.

- Ask, "What do you add to seven to make ten?" Rearrange the display to group three of the six shapes with the seven shapes.

- Ask, "Ten and three more make how much?" Combine the remaining three shapes with the ten shapes. Say, "Seven and three make ten and three more make 13. Seven and six make 13."

- Repeat with other combinations with sums of 11 or more.

■ COMMITTING BASIC FACTS TO MEMORY

Memorization of facts should begin when students demonstrate that they are capable of showing physical embodiments and orally describing the meaning of the facts to be committed to memory. Once a group of children demonstrates these skills, you should provide organized activities for memorizing facts. The following principles should guide the activities:

- The amount of practice is unlikely to be the same for all students at the same time. Some students require a limited number of practice sessions, while others need many activities to commit facts to memory. Change groupings frequently to accommodate the different rates of learning.

- Present a limited number of new facts in each practice session. Review already-learned facts often.

- Practice sessions should be brief and occur often. Five minutes a day are sufficient for most practice activities. Once underway, practice activities should occur almost daily until students are proficient in naming the facts. Periodic review sessions should occur to maintain skills.

- A variety of materials and procedures should be used. Students become bored with activities that are repetitious.

- Give frequent praise. "Just think, Juanita, you know all of the facts with six as an addend. You couldn't give answers for them last week."

During practice sessions, encourage rapid recall. If a child hesitates with a flash card or oral combination, do not give an explanation or allow time for finger counting or tally marks. Instead, show or name the answer. Then show the flash card, or repeat the combination orally, and have the child give the answer immediately. Have students maintain a record of progress. Some teachers have students simply separate their cards into stacks of known combinations and unknown combinations. Others have students record combinations as they are memorized. Others have students write brief entries in their journals: "Today I learned facts with 9 as an addend." Such entries are an excellent way for young students to communicate their thoughts about the mathematics they are learning.[13]

Practice materials come from many sources. Flash cards presented by a teacher or student are commonly used. Oral combinations dictated by a teacher or presented on tape can be used with older students who need reinforcement and practice. Cards and oral presentations should be given at a steady rate that encourages immediate responses. Practice pages from workbooks and texts are available to most teachers. A weakness of these materials is that the rate at which a student responds cannot be controlled, and some students are prone to revert to finger counting or tally marks when given a page of facts to complete. These materials have a place in the program, but should not be used to the exclusion of other materials.

Many computer programs emphasize learning strategies and practice of basic facts for addition and subtraction. In *Stickybear Math*[14] students help the Stickybear character move through a series of adventures by completing addition and subtraction combinations in the first of the 20 levels into which the program is arranged. Subsequent levels provide practice with addition and subtraction of larger numbers. Both horizontal and vertical notations are used. With *Math Rabbit*[15] students practice addition and subtraction facts by engaging in games involving a rabbit. *Math Blaster™* and *Math Blaster™ Plus*[16] provide pure drill and practice in an arcade-game format that emphasizes speed. Graphics, sound, and avoidance of negative feedback contribute to the popularity of these two software programs. Students may choose problems from addition, subtraction, multiplication, or division, and a problem editor allows individualizing practice problems for a student or group. Appendix B contains names, addresses, and phone numbers of companies from which you can get catalogs listing programs to review and evaluate.

Calculators can also be used for practicing basic facts. In Activity 9.16, students begin working with simple combinations, but the activity can also be extended to three or more addends. Activity 9.17 not only provides practice, but also points out an advantage of knowing the facts.

ACTIVITY 9.16   House Numbers

- Duplicate a simple picture of a house on ½-inch-square paper. Make a door, windows, and a chimney that each cover two squares. Write a digit 1–9 in each square inside the house.

				3				
	7	3	4	9	9			
	2	4	8	4	8	4	2	
1	2	3	4	5	6	7	8	9
3	3	8	2	7	7	2	6	8
5	7	6	2	4	8	3	4	5

- Have students work in pairs. One child names the sum in the door, each window, and chimney. The second student keys the numbers in a calculator to find their sum.

- Extensions:
  —Prepare cards that contain sentences like these: The sum of the numbers in the chimney and door is _____. The sum of the numbers in the chimney and left window is _____. The difference between the sum in both windows and the sum in the chimney is _____.

  —Find the sum of the numbers in the roof. Find the sum of the row of squares above the windows and door. Find the sum of the numbers outside the door and windows.

  —Find the sum of all the house numbers.[17]

ACTIVITY 9.17   Brain Versus Button

- Use this activity after children are reasonably proficient with basic facts for addition and subtraction.

- Divide the class into pairs. Each pair of students has two sets of 15 identical fact cards and a calculator. One child is the "Brain" who will determine each answer mentally and write answers on paper. The other is the "Button" who must key in all of the facts into a calculator, then write the answers.

- Ask the children who they believe will complete the 15 combinations first.

- Start the race and time how long it takes the "Brain" and how long it takes the "Button." Timing can be done with a sweep second hand; write times beginning with six seconds—6, 8, 10, . . .—on the chalkboard. Each child writes the last recorded time on his or her paper. Have the children exchange roles to complete a second set of 15 cards.

- You may want to account for accuracy by adding a second to a player's time for each incorrect answer.

- Variations:
  —Use subtraction rather than addition combinations.

  —Present older children with examples that have three or four single-digit addends.

Preprogrammed devices, games, and puzzles provide other sources of activities. Examples of preprogrammed devices are *Drillmaster* and *Skillmaster*.[18] Each device provides practice with basic facts for addition, subtraction, multiplication, and division. *Drillmaster* records elapsed time and correct or incorrect items for each group of 25 facts. *Skillmaster* can also be adjusted to set time limits for responses.

Addition bingo is an example of a large group game (see Activity 9.18). Each player has a different card, which contains 24 sums for basic facts and a free space. Bingo cards for each of the operations are available commercially or may be made by a teacher. To solve a "What's My Rule" puzzle, as in Activity 9.19, students must listen and think carefully to determine the rule that applies during each round.

ACTIVITY 9.18   Addition Bingo

- Materials: Game board and markers for each player, sheet with 100 addition facts or a set of addition flash cards.

- Give each child one game board and about 20 markers.

0	6	18	9	15
4	3	11	8	7
5	7	Free	17	16
6	15	13	2	4
10	1	12	14	6

- One at a time, read a combination from the fact sheet or show one of the flash cards. If the sum of the combination is on a game board, a child puts a marker on it. Only one number is covered at a time, even though some numbers appear more than once on each game board.

- The winner is the first child who has five markers in a row, column, or diagonal. A game of "blackout" requires that all 25 squares be covered. Variation: Write combinations for basic facts, such as 6 + 2, 9 + 4, and 8 + 7, in squares. Hold up answer cards or call out sums; players cover a combination that matches the sum.

ACTIVITY 9.19   What's My Rule?

- Tell the students that you are going to pretend to be an "operations" machine. This special machine is able to perform operations on numbers. When a number is given, the machine gives an answer. If the students are learning addition facts, make it an "add" machine. (It could be a "subtract," "multiply," or "divide" machine.)

  The students are to listen to each number that is given to the machine and to your (the machine's) response and determine the "rule" that the machine uses on each number.

- Begin with a simple rule. An "add-2" rule is a good first rule.

- Tell the children to give you a number from zero to nine. When a number is given, for example four, you think "4 + 2 = 6" and say "six." If eight is given you say "ten." You never state the rule.

- Students who grasp the rule for a round are not to say what it is, but are to raise a hand. When you see raised hands, invite those students to join you as you give the next response. If the answers are correct, you will know that they have determined the rule; they can continue answering with you or replace you as the machine's responder. If a child's answer is incorrect, have the child listen again and rethink the rule.

■ TEACHING SOME PROPERTIES OF ADDITION AND SUBTRACTION

The commutative and associative properties and the identity element for addition need not be stressed in highly formal ways in the primary grades. However, their meanings and applications will be developed over time through activities with the concrete materials children use to learn about addition. Students in grades four through six should be able to explain the properties and demonstrate them with concrete and symbolic representations and many will even name them.

The Commutative Property

The procedures in Activity 9.20 are effective ones for helping children understand the commutative property of addition.

ACTIVITY 9.20   Commutative Property

- Have each child put a few lima beans on each half of a paper plate and write the addition sentence for those beans.

- Have each child turn the plate halfway around without disturbing the beans and write the number sentence for the new configuration.

- Discuss each sentence and point out that the sums are the same, even though the sentences are reversed.

- Variations:
  —Have the children make Cuisenaire rod trains.
  —Have the children use a number line.

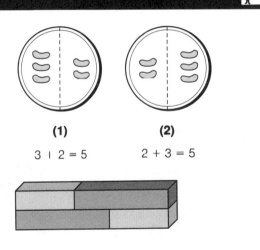

(1)　　　　**(2)**

3 | 2 = 5　　　2 + 3 = 5

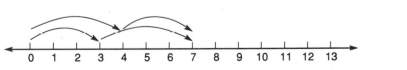

The Associative Property

The associative property of addition is used when there are three or more addends. Addition can be done with only two addends at a time (it is a binary operation); when there are three addends it is necessary to select two of the addends to add first, then add the third number to the sum of the first two.

Addition with three addends is frequently introduced before all 100 of the facts have been studied. No specific number of facts is a prerequisite, but the students must previously have worked with all of the basic facts they will use when they first work with three addends. The sum of any pair of addends should be less than ten. As with other new topics, this one should be introduced through exercises with manipulative materials, such as those suggested in Activity 9.21.

As students mature, they should be introduced to useful applications of the commutative and associative properties. Students who study examples such as these will realize that it is easier and faster to complete some computation mentally than with paper and pencil. In the first example, the 397 and 3 can be added, then 246 can be added to 400. In the second example,

$$246 + 397 + 3 = \square$$
$$496 + 385 + 4 = \square$$
$$20 + 392 + 680 = \square$$
$$16 + 23 + 7 + 4 = \square$$

both the commutative and associative properties are used so that 385 can be added to 500 after the 496 and 4 are added. How are the properties used in the last two examples? In these examples, the pairs of numbers with sums that are tens or hundreds are compatible numbers.

ACTIVITY 9.21   Beans and Cups

- Give each pair of children a small handful of lima beans and three small paper cups. Have them align the cups horizontally and put two beans in the left-hand cup, three beans in the middle cup, and three beans in the right-hand cup.

- Have them remove the beans from the first two cups and combine them. Ask, "How many beans are there altogether?" Have them remove the beans from the third cup and combine them with the rest. Ask, "How many beans?"

- Repeat the activity, beginning with the two cups on the right.

- Discuss the fact that the sum is the same, regardless of the order in which they have been combined.

- Repeat with other numbers of beans.

The Identity Element for Addition

Children who understand the meaning of zero will have little difficulty learning its role in addition. As they deal with concrete materials to learn about addition, they will realize that when zero is an addend, there will be no materials representing that number. Paper plates, like those in Activity 9.20, can be used to illustrate this. Have students put some beans on one side of a plate and no beans on the other side. Have each one write the sentence for the beans on his or her plate. If there are five beans on one side, the sentence will be $0 + 5 = 5$ or $5 + 0 = 5$. Eventually students will see that if zero is one addend, the sum will always be the other addend. Zero is the identity element for addition.

During work with subtraction, students should have opportunities to make clear the role of zero in that operation. Activities should lead them to generalize that when zero is subtracted from a number, the answer is always the other number. And when a number is subtracted from itself, the answer is always zero.

EXERCISE   Describe how the commutative and associative laws and the identity property help children learn the basic addition facts.

TEACHING ADDITION WITH LARGER WHOLE NUMBERS

Children who have a good understanding of whole numbers and place value and who have learned basic facts are ready to start adding tens and hundreds. This work receives much emphasis in grade two, but is not complete until the late intermediate grades. A first lesson should begin with a common problem situation and proportional place-value materials, such as beansticks (see Activity 9.22).

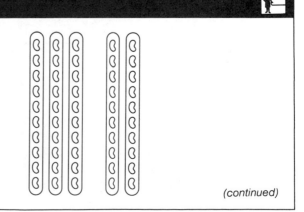

ACTIVITY 9.22   Adding Tens

- Give each student nine of the tens sticks.
- Tell the story, "Yesterday Chu had 30 baseball cards. He got 20 more today. How many cards does he have now?"
- Have students show 30 with three tens sticks to represent the 30 cards; have them represent the 20 cards with two tens sticks.
- Ask, "How many cards are there altogether?"
- Write the addition sentence $30 + 20 = 50$ on the chalkboard.

(continued)

Activity 9.22   *continued*

- Write the problem in vertical (algorithm) form:

$$\begin{array}{r} 30 \\ +20 \\ \hline \end{array}$$

- Discuss the fact that 30 means 3 tens and represents 30 cards and 20 means 2 tens and represents 20 cards. Ask, "What is three tens and two tens?"

- Put the answer in the algorithm. Have students read the algorithm in unison as you point to the parts: "30 plus 20 equals 50."

- Repeat with similar situations and numbers.

- Variations: The same activity can be done with Cuisenaire or base-ten rods or Unifix cubes.

In subsequent lessons, students can complete work sheets that contain pictures of a place-value model. Instead of using beansticks (concrete mode), they use pictures (pictorial mode). Figure 9.6 illustrates a problem that uses base-ten rods. Children write a number sentence and the sum for the picture. A worksheet can contain six or eight problems.

Addition of multiples of ten will not present any special problems to most students. This should be followed by two-place addition with numbers other than zero in the ones place. Most textbooks present this with examples that do not require regrouping (sometimes referred to as "carrying"). Some authorities believe students should learn this type of addition with examples that require regrouping. They believe that when students add a pair of numbers not requiring regrouping, such as 23 and 46, using the conventional algorithm form (see margin) they will begin the addition in either the tens or the ones place first. Students who learn regrouping from the beginning will immediately see the reason for starting addition in the ones column. Addition in Activity 9.23 requires regrouping. Teachers who believe that work should start with no regrouping can alter the examples described here to eliminate the need for regrouping.

$$\begin{array}{r} 23 \\ +46 \\ \hline \end{array}$$

Figure 9-6
Base ten rods illustrating the addition
40 + 30 = 70.

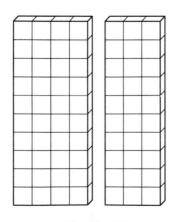

40 + 30 = 70

ACTIVITY 9.23   Using Beansticks to Add

- Tell a story. "Jemetta had 26 marbles. Her grandmother gave her 17 more. How many marbles does she now have?"

- Have the students determine the addition sentence for the problem:

$$26 + 17 = \square$$

- Have each student show the two numbers with beansticks.

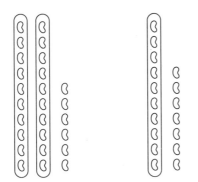

- Tell each child to combine the loose beans and determine how many there are. Ask, "Are there more than nine loose beans?" (Yes.) "What do you do when there are more than nine loose beans?" (Exchange ten of them for a tens stick.) Have each child do this.

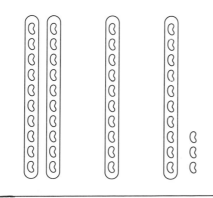

- Ask, "How many loose beans are there now?" (Three.)

- Have each child combine the tens sticks. Ask, "How many tens sticks do you have?" (Four.) "How many tens and how many ones do you have?" (Four tens and three ones.)

- Write the sum, 43, in the sentence.

- Repeat with similar stories and numbers.

Note that an algorithm was not included in this activity. Students were manipulating concrete materials and recording the results; they need ample time to clarify the process before an algorithm is introduced. When an algorithm is introduced, the connection between it and the concrete materials should be made. Using the problem in Activity 8.20 as an example, students will use this algorithm:

$$
\begin{array}{r}
\overset{\prime}{2}6 \\
+17 \\
\hline
43
\end{array}
$$

Help them associate the addition of the 6 and the 7 with the combining of the loose beans. The "3" in the ones place is associated with the remaining loose beans. Relate the 1 that is regrouped in the algorithm to the exchange of the ten loose beans for one tens stick; and the addition of the 1, the 2, and the 1 should be associated with combining the tens sticks. The "4" is associated with the four tens sticks. Only when a teacher makes conscious efforts to help students make connections between actions with concrete materials and actions with symbols will most children understand relationships between concrete and symbolic materials.

Beansticks and Cuisenaire and base-ten materials are also useful for representing addition with hundreds. The progression of steps for adding

$$
\begin{array}{r}
358 \\
+267
\end{array}
$$

are shown with beansticks in Figure 9.7. In (a) two sets of beansticks are shown to illustrate the original addends. In (b) 15 single beans are exchanged for one tens stick, with five loose beans remaining. In (c) 12 tens sticks are exchanged for a hundreds raft, with two sticks remaining, and the hundreds rafts are combined. Steps in the algorithm should be associated with the beanstick actions.

$$
\begin{array}{ccc}
358 & \overset{\prime}{3}58 & \overset{\prime\prime}{3}58 \\
+267 & +267 & +267 \\
\hline
 & 5 & 625 \\
\text{(a)} & \text{(b)} & \text{(c)}
\end{array}
$$

Once students understand regrouping through hundreds, they should recognize that addition with larger numbers proceeds in the same manner as with tens and hundreds. It is not recommended that time be devoted to making students proficient in using a paper-and-pencil algorithm to compute with larger numbers. Rather they should use a calculator to compute answers.

EXERCISE   Why should children use proportional rather than nonproportional base-ten materials in their early work with multiple-digit addition and subtraction?

Figure 9-7
Beansticks illus-
trate addition of
358 + 267 = 623.

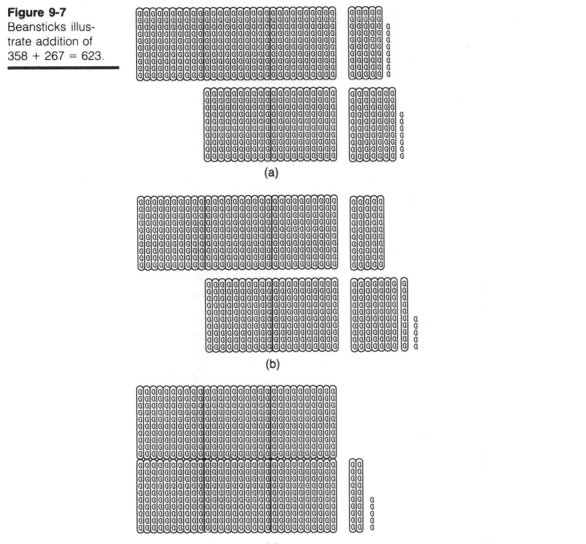

(a)

(b)

(c)

■ ESTIMATING SUMS AND MENTAL ADDITION

Skills for estimating answers and for doing mental computations should be developed over time once students are capable of adding tens and hundreds.

Estimating Sums

Estimation is used to determine the reasonableness of answers and in situations where exact answers are not needed. Three processes for estimating sums are described here: rounded numbers, front-end addition, and compatible numbers.

Rounded Numbers

Students need to know how to round numbers before they can use the rounding process to estimate sums. Procedures for teaching students to round numbers are presented in Chapter 8. A first lesson in estimating sums should be presented in two parts. Students estimate only the sums during the first part of a lesson that might include 20 examples like these:

$$
\begin{array}{ccccc}
49 & 36 & 22 & 84 & 31 \\
23 & 54 & 28 & 31 & 56 \\
+33 & +28 & +37 & +45 & +52 \\
\end{array}
$$

During the second part of the lesson three or four pairs of students should use a calculator to compute the exact sums for the examples. Once all of the sums have been computed, have the students compare their estimates and the exact sums. If there are major discrepancies, discuss each one to clear away possible misunderstandings.

Front-End Addition

Front-end addition is based on the idea that numbers in high place-value positions are more significant to an answer than are numbers in the low positions. Intermediate-grade students can learn to make an estimate with front-end addition with an example like this:

$$
\begin{array}{r}
125 \\
345 \\
226 \\
45 \\
+152 \\
\end{array}
$$

Add the numbers in the hundreds place—700. Add the tens—170. Add the 170 and 700 hundreds—870. Add a little more for the ones. An estimate of about 900 is adequate for this example.

To estimate a sum for these four numbers

$$
\begin{array}{r}
5266 \\
8942 \\
372 \\
+1217 \\
\end{array}
$$

add the numbers in the thousands place—14,000. Add the numbers in the hundreds place—1,600. Add 1,600 and 14,000—15,600. With larger numbers, the tens and ones are disregarded.

Compatible Numbers

Numbers that "fit" together because they are easy to deal with mentally are called *compatible numbers*. Intermediate-grade students should have exercises that familiarize them with compatible numbers. You can help children recognize compatible pairs by having them examine sets of numbers such as these:

$$45, 72, 25 \qquad 278, 935, 756 \qquad 6732, 3279, 8472$$

In the first set, students find the pair that fits together to make approximately 100. In the second set, what pair fits to make about 1,000? In the third set, what pair fits to make about 10,000? When students demonstrate that they are able to select compatible pairs, they can use the strategy to estimate sums. In the example in the margin, the first and third, the second and fifth, and the fourth and sixth pairs of numbers each fit to give a sum of about 100. Since there are three pairs of numbers, the sum is estimated to be about 300.[19]

```
  55
  78
  42
  11
  23
+ 86
```

Frequent, short practice exercises for each of the three estimation processes should be made available from time to time. Also, stress using estimation in problem-solving situations so students recognize that exact answers are not always necessary and see its value in determining whether answers are reasonable.

EXERCISE   What are three estimation strategies for addition? Write a sample problem to illustrate each of the strategies.

Mental Computation

```
    86
  × 49
   774
   344
  4214
```

Estimations are usually made by using mental computation processes. Mental computation is sometimes used to determine exact sums. Mental addition is also a part of much of the multiplication children do. For example, when the product of 49 and 86 is determined with the algorithm in the margin, it is necessary to add both 72 and 5 and 32 and 2 mentally. (Study the algorithm to see where these additions are made.)

Addition done during multiplication usually involves the addition of a one-place number to a two-place number. In the example in the margin, you record "4" and regroup the 5 tens. The 5 is added to 72 after the product of 9 and 8 is determined. As the multiplication of 40 times 86 is completed, you add 2 to 32.

Even though students do much mental computation when they compute with paper and pencil, the term *mental computation,* or *mental arithmetic,* is commonly meant to be computation without paper and pencil or any mechanical device. Students should learn ways to compute answers in their heads.

Students should learn to mentally add when there are three or more addends. When they add 8 + 9 + 7 + 8, they might begin with 8 + 9, then add 7 to 17 and then add 8 to 24 to get the sum 32. Or, they might see that 9 + 7 is 16, that 8 + 8 is 16, and that 16 + 16 is 32. Third- and fourth-grade students should have introductory and practice activities designed specifically to enhance their understanding of this addition. Some are suggested in Activity 9.24.

After students understand what is involved with this addition, they need practice so they can do it mentally. Here are examples of both written and oral exercises:

- Prepare a worksheet that has about 20 sets of addition sentences written according to a pattern:

$$5 + 3 = \square, 15 + 3 = \square, 25 + 3 = \square, \ldots, 95 + 3 = \square$$
$$7 + 8 = \square, 17 + 8 = \square, 27 + 8 = \square, \ldots, 97 + 8 = \square$$

- Prepare a worksheet that has about 30 sentences written in a random order:

$$14 + 9 = \square, 35 + 7 = \square, 64 + 8 = \square$$

- Dictate sentences to which students give oral responses: "Add six to 45." "Add four to the product of six and seven."

There are other mental addition processes intermediate-grade children can learn. All are suitable for adding a pair of two-place numbers.

ACTIVITY 9.24   Adding Two-Place and One-Place Numbers

- Display a hundreds chart.

1	2	3	4	5	6	7	8	9	10
11	12	13	14	15	16	17	18	19	20
21	22	23	24	25	26	27	28	29	30
31	32	33	34	35	36	37	38	39	40
41	42	43	44	45	46	47	48	49	50
51	52	53	54	55	56	57	58	59	60
61	62	63	64	65	66	67	68	69	70
71	72	73	74	75	76	77	78	79	80
81	82	83	84	85	86	87	88	89	90
91	92	93	94	95	96	97	98	99	100

- Use a sentence like 45 + 7 = $\square$. Call students' attention to 45 on the chart, then have them count on 7. Ask, "Where did we stop?" (52.)

- Ask, "If we begin at 55 and count on 7, where will we stop?" "What is 65 + 7?" "75 + 7?" "85 + 7?"

- Repeat with other numbers.

- Do a similar activity using a 0–100 number line.

47
+28

- One process reverses the usual order of adding numbers. For the example in the margin, students add the tens numbers first, then add the sum of the ones numbers to the first sum: $40 + 20 = 60$, $15 + 60 = 75$.

- In a second process the first addend is added to the number in the ones place of the second addend, and that sum is added to the remaining tens: $47 + 8 = 55, 55 + 20 = 75$.

- A third process uses compensation. Three is added to 47 to make 50. Three is subtracted from 28 to make 25. Finally, 25 and 50 are added to make 75.[20]

■ INTRODUCING SUBTRACTION WITH LARGER NUMBERS

Introductory work for subtraction with larger whole numbers should parallel introductory work for addition. That is, first work should be with realistic situations and adequate time for students to explore the operation's meaning. "A rope 70 feet long is being cut into shorter 10-foot ropes. If 40 feet of the rope have been cut from it, how many feet remain to be cut?" Allow time for students to use pictures, Unifix cubes, or place-value materials to determine the answer, then have them share their procedures. Place-value models should be brought into the discussion, either by a student or by you. Cuisenaire rods are illustrated here, but any of the models can be used. In Figure 9.8(a) the 70 feet of rope is represented by seven tens rods. The removal of 40 feet of rope is indicated by the removal of four of the rods. The answer, 30 feet of rope, is represented by the three tens rods that remain (b).

Figure 9-8
Cuisenaire rods illustrate the subtraction $70 - 40 = 30$. In (a) 7 rods represent 70. After 4 rods (40) are removed, 3 rods (30) remain.

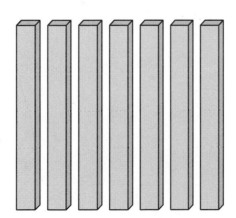
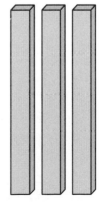

(a)   (b)

Other similar situations should be modeled with place-value devices until the meaning of the subtraction is clear.

TWO SUBTRACTION ALGORITHMS

Two algorithms for subtraction are discussed.[21] They are the decomposition algorithm, which is the inverse of the commonly used addition algorithm, and the equal-additions algorithm. The decomposition algorithm is taught most frequently, although the equal-additions algorithm has many advocates.

The Decomposition Algorithm

The decomposition method of subtracting is generally favored because it can easily be modeled with familiar place-value devices. The relationship between addition and subtraction is emphasized by this method, because the steps in subtraction are the exact reverse of those for addition with regrouping.

An understanding of place value is a prerequisite of the decomposition method of subtraction. An understanding of expanded notation is also useful. For example, students should know that the number 36 can be expressed as "36," "3 tens and 6 ones," "30 + 6," and "20 + 16." Activity 9.25 will introduce students to subtraction using decomposition.

After the regrouping process is clear, introduce the decomposition algorithm. Again it is important to relate each step in the algorithm to each step in the place-value model. These are the steps for the subtraction situation in Activity 9.25.

$$
\begin{array}{c}
82 \\
-53 \\
\hline
\end{array}
\qquad
\begin{array}{c}
{}^{7}\!\!\!\not{8}\,'2 \\
-5\ 3 \\
\hline
9
\end{array}
\qquad
\begin{array}{c}
{}^{7}\!\!\!\not{8}\,'2 \\
-5\ 3 \\
\hline
2\ 9
\end{array}
$$

First the original problem is shown. Next the regrouping of one ten as ten ones is shown by the marked-out 8, the small 7, and the 12 ones. The work is then completed with subtraction of 3 from 12 and of 5 from 7. The line through the 8, the small 7, and the 1 beside the 2 are memory aids that help children keep track of each step as they compute. Students can be encouraged to discontinue using these aids whenever dropping them will not interfere with their ability to compute accurately.

Once students understand the decomposition process with tens, they should deal with hundreds. Examples like the ones in the margin can be presented along with place-value devices so that students can see the neces-

$$
\begin{array}{c}
453 \\
-137 \\
\hline
\end{array}
$$

$$
\begin{array}{c}
948 \\
-362 \\
\hline
\end{array}
$$

$$
\begin{array}{c}
573 \\
-385 \\
\hline
\end{array}
$$

ACTIVITY 9.25 Decomposition

- Present this situation: "There were 82 boxes of apples at a fruit stand when it opened. During the day 53 boxes were sold. How many boxes were left at the end of the day?"

- Have a student write the mathematical sentence

$$82 - 53 = \square$$

- Have pairs of students represent the situation with base-ten materials.

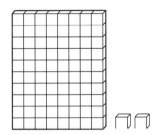

- Discuss the fact that there are not enough small cubes to take away three of them. Ask, "What can we do to get enough small cubes?" (Exchange a tens rod for ten cubes.) Have students do this.

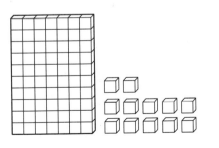

- Have students remove three of the cubes. Ask, "How many cubes are left?"

- Ask, "How many tens rods should be removed?" Have students remove five of the tens rods.

- Ask, "How many tens rods are left?" "How many boxes of apples were left at the end of the day?"

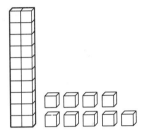

- Repeat with other similar situations.
- Variations: Students use beansticks, Cuisenaire rods, Unifix cubes.

---

sity of regrouping from either the tens or hundreds place or from both places. The base-ten rods in Figure 9.9 illustrate one way to model subtraction for the third example.

Students sometimes have difficulty using the decomposition process with subtraction that has a zero in the minuend, such as in the example in

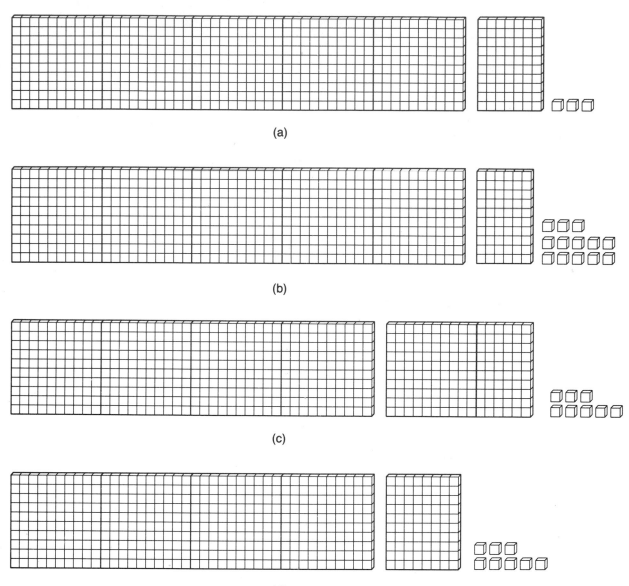

(a)

(b)

(c)

(d)

Figure 9.9
Base-ten blocks illustrate the subtraction of
573 − 385. In (a) there are 5 flats, 7 rods,
and 3 cubes. In (b) 1 rod is exchanged for
10 cubes. In (c) 5 cubes are removed. and
1 flat is exchanged for 10 rods. In (d) 8 rods
are removed. Finally, in (e), 3 flats are removed, leaving 1 flat, 8 rods, and 8 cubes.

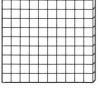

(e)

$$\begin{array}{r} 306 \\ -148 \\ \hline \end{array}$$

$$\begin{array}{r} 29 \\ \cancel{30}\,{}^1 6 \\ -14\ \ 8 \\ \hline \end{array}$$

the margin. A common error is that students will regroup from the hundreds place to the ones place, leaving the tens place intact. Then they are confused because there is still a zero in the tens place. One way you can avert the confusion is to have students consider the number as 30 tens and 6 ones. Now when they regroup they rename 30 as 29 tens and 10 ones. The algorithm is changed as in the second example in the margin. Subtraction is completed by subtracting 8 from 16, 4 from 9, and 1 from 2.

The Equal-Additions Method

The equal-additions method of subtraction is based on the mathematical concept that there are an infinite number of equivalent subtraction combinations for a given remainder. Two equivalent combinations are $68 - 14$ and $70 - 16$, which both equal 54. Students who possess the mathematical maturity to understand this concept can learn to use the equal-additions algorithm.

A first step is to make certain that students understand the concept behind the procedure. Activity 9.26 will help develop this understanding.

In addition to understanding that the difference remains the same if a given number is added to both the minuend and the subtrahend, an understanding of place value is also essential before the equal-additions method of subtraction is introduced. Once an adequate background has been established, introduce the equal-additions algorithm. One procedure follows. Write a subtraction example on the chalkboard:

$$\begin{array}{r} 652 \\ -216 \\ \hline \end{array}$$

ACTIVITY 9.26   Equal Additions

- Put a sentence like $16 - 8 = 8$ on the chalkboard. Put the sentence $26 - 18 = 8$ beneath the first sentence.

- Ask, "What is the same about these two sentences?" (The answer, 8.) "What is different about them?" (The numbers in the minuend and subtrahend.)

- Discuss the fact that each number in the second sentence is ten larger than the corresponding number in the first sentence.

- Repeat with other examples, but omit a number from the second sentence: $35 - 12 = 23$, $45 - \square = 23$; $69 - 25 = 44$, $\square - 35 = 44$. Have students supply the correct number for each pair of sentences.

- Point out that when an equal amount is added to each number in a subtraction sentence the difference remains the same.

Students see that it is not possible to subtract 6 ones from 2 ones. It is possible to subtract in the ones place when 10 ones are added to the 2 ones in the minuend to make 12 ones. Subtract 6 ones from 12 ones, and record "6" (a).

$$
\begin{array}{r}
65\,{}^{/}2 \\
-21\ 6 \\
\hline
6
\end{array}
\qquad
\begin{array}{r}
6\ 5\,{}^{/}2 \\
-2\,{}^{2}1\ 6 \\
\hline
3\ 6
\end{array}
\qquad
\begin{array}{r}
6\ 5\ {}^{/}2 \\
-2\,{}^{2}1\ 6 \\
\hline
4\ 3\ 6
\end{array}
$$

(a)   (b)   (c)

Because 10 was added to the minuend, 10 is added to the subtrahend in the form of 1 ten. When this is done there are 2 tens to be subtracted from 5 tens; a "3" is recorded (b). Finally 2 hundreds are subtracted from 6 hundreds and "4" is recorded (c).

An advantage of equal-additions over decomposition is that once a student learns to use it efficiently, computation can be done quite rapidly. This can be demonstrated by considering an example with thousands. A mature user of the algorithm thinks: $16 - 7 = 9, 4 - 4 = 0, 12 - 9 = 3, 3 - 2 = 1$

$$
\begin{array}{r}
3\,{}^{/}2\ 4\ {}^{/}6 \\
-\,{}^{2}1\ 9\ {}^{4}3\ 7 \\
\hline
1\ 3\ 0\ 9
\end{array}
$$

When a number in a place-value position in the minuend is smaller than the number in the same place-value position in the subtrahend, increase it by 10, and complete the subtraction for that position. Each time this is done, increase the number in the place-value position to its immediate left in the subtrahend by 1. The process becomes automatic when it is well understood and sufficiently practiced. This process presents no particular difficulties when there are zeros in the minuend.

Children should not practice paper-and-pencil algorithms with numbers greater than 1,000. They should use a calculator for computing answers when numbers are large.

ESTIMATING DIFFERENCES AND MENTAL SUBTRACTION

There are never more than two numbers involved in subtraction. For that reason, rounding off is the most used estimation process. Numbers of any size can be rounded to an appropriate place-value position to make an estimate.

Two mental arithmetic processes for subtracting are discussed. The first process reverses one of the mental arithmetic processes for addition: Sub-

$\begin{array}{r} 69 \\ -45 \\ \hline \end{array}$ tract the tens number of the subtrahend from the minuend. To compute the answer mentally for the example in the margin, subtract the tens number in the subtrahend from the minuend: $69 - 40 = 29$. Then subtract the ones number of the subtrahend from the remainder: $29 - 5 = 24$.

The second process uses compensation. Change the subtrahend so it is a multiple of ten; add the same amount to the minuend: Add 5 to both 45 and 69 to make them 50 and 74. Then subtract the new numbers: $74 - 50 = 24$. (This process is explained in greater detail in the fifth-grade classroom vignette in Chapter 2.)

Mental computation with both addition and subtraction can become a part of daily warm-up and free-moment activities. At the beginning of a class period, write four addition or subtraction examples on the chalkboard. Have students write the mentally computed answers on a slip of paper. On signal, have students give a unison response for each problem. There are usually times during a day when there are unfilled moments, such as when waiting for a lunch period. Take advantage of these times to present oral problems involving addition of a two- and a one-place number or subtraction of two two-place numbers and call on individuals to respond.

EXERCISE   Describe the steps you would use solving $93 - 65$ using the strategies of left-to-right subtraction and compensation.

■ USING COMPUTERS AND CALCULATORS

Computers and calculators can be used to improve students' understanding of operations, application of addition and subtraction in real-life situations, and explorations of interesting mathematical ideas. Do not use computer activities as a substitute for concrete materials and interaction between you and students; do use programs with individual children who have demonstrated understanding and know many facts. Programs are more interesting to students who feel successful with them. A chart or record page in a journal that shows improvements and completion of lessons helps students follow their progress. Many addition and subtraction practice programs are available for elementary mathematics. Complete software packages that offer developmental and practice activities are part of some textbook series.

Three programs previously mentioned in this chapter for basic fact practice also contain more advanced exercises. *Stickybear Math* progresses through 20 levels to four-digit operations with regrouping. *Math Blaster*™ and *Math Blaster*™ *Plus* offer a full range of practice exercises. MECC[22] offers a variety of software programs for developing young children's skills with addition and subtraction. *Early Addition* and *Space Subtraction* are for grades one and two, *Circus Math*™ is for grade two, and *Addition Logician*™ and *Subtraction Puzzles* are for grade three. In *Mathman*[23] students help a construction worker complete a building by providing correct responses to addition and subtraction problems of varying levels of difficulty. A computational practice program that challenges students is *Quations*,[24] played on a grid similar to a Scrabble ™ board. Students fill in the blanks using numbers and all of the operations. Much strategy is needed to place numbers in the squares and maximize scores. Random House[25] has *Math Master* (grades one and two), *Building Your Math Skills* (three and four), and *Expanding Your Math Skills* (five and six).

Older students can also write their own drill programs. A prototype Logo program that randomly generates addition problems and is easy to modify for each of the other operations is discussed in Appendix A.

Activities 9.27 through 9.30 make use of calculators as children practice with a puzzle and three games.

ACTIVITY 9.27   What Is the Number?

- Give children this puzzle: Find the two-digit number that, when added to its reverse, is closest to 50 (23 and 32).

- Suggest that students use the guess-and-check strategy to solve the puzzle. Students will soon notice that some numbers are in-appropriate; 45 and 54 or 12 and 21 do not work. They will find that other numbers are appropriate; in this case 23 and 32.

- Have students find pairs of numbers closest to 100; 150; 200; and so on.

ACTIVITY 9.28   Roll and Add

- Materials: Calculators, die.

- Two to four children play. Each child marks three lines with places for four numbers in each line.

  ____ ____ ____ ____

  ____ ____ ____ ____

  + ____ ____ ____ ____
  (_____).

- Roll the die 12 times. As each number is rolled, each student writes it in one of the blank spaces. The objective is to create the largest possible sum. Once a number has been placed, it cannot be moved to another blank.

- Use calculators to determine each player's sum.

- Variations:
  a. Play with a spinner that contains the numerals 0–9 or card deck with face cards removed and the joker as zero.

  b. Play the game with the objective of creating the smallest possible sum.

  c. Use just two four-digit numbers. Students play for the largest or the smallest possible difference.

ACTIVITY 9.29   Bull's-Eye

- Create a pack of 20 cards with numerals on each card. A first set may contain numerals for numbers between 1 and 100; a second set between 100 and 1,000; a third set between 1,000 and 10,000. Use numerals according to students' abilities. Make a bull's-eye target for recording winners. For numbers between 10 and 100 a good range is center: 0–10, first ring: 11–30, second ring: 31–60, third ring: 61–100.

- Three or four children play the game. Each child draws three or four cards and estimates the sum of the numbers, which is written down.

- Each student uses a calculator to find the sum.

- Use a calculator to determine the difference between each sum and each estimate. The difference between the two numbers becomes a score.

- Play four rounds and find the sum of the four scores. The player with the lowest total difference between estimates and sums is the winner. Put colored markers on the target to show scores. Markers nearest the bull's-eye indicate players with the best estimates.

- Variation: Estimations can be done for subtraction involving the two numbers.

ACTIVITY 9.30   NIM

- Choose a target number, say 50.

- The first player enters a one-digit number into the calculator.

- The second player adds a second one-digit number to the first.

- Players alternate adding one-digit numbers until one player reaches exactly 50 and is winner.

- Encourage students to work out a strategy for winning. Suggest that they try strategies with smaller target numbers before working toward a large target number.

- Variation: Start at a number, such as 30, and subtract one-digit numbers smaller than five to reach zero.

■ SUMMARY

Addition and subtraction are usually introduced in the first grade, and once each is introduced, they are usually studied simultaneously. The real-life situation that gives rise to addition is the joining of two or more sets. There are four situations that give rise to subtraction: take-away, part-whole completion, and comparison of two sets.

Children develop a readiness for addition and subtraction as they learn to count using concrete materials. Working in the concrete-manipulative mode with real objects and markers gives children opportunities to join, separate, and compare the sizes of sets of objects; this is the basis for understanding the meaning of addition and subtraction and the use of abstract processes dealing with the operations.

Once students know the meaning of addition and subtraction, they need to use strategies for learning the facts and to engage in activities that will help them remember each fact. There are 100 basic addition facts, which are all of the possible combinations of pairs of addends smaller than ten and their sums. Each addition fact has a corresponding subtraction fact. Strategies that use families of facts, doubles and near doubles, and adding one less than ten should be used. Computer programs, calculators, and pre-programmed devices and games as well as practice pages from workbooks provide a variety of practice experiences. Children's understanding of the commutative and associative properties and the identity element should be developed.

When students have a good understanding of place value for numbers through 99 and of the meaning of addition and subtraction, they are ready for addition and subtraction with addends up to 99. Later, addition and subtraction are extended to the hundreds, and finally, through the use of calculators, to numbers of any size. Addition that requires regrouping should be developed with beansticks, Cuisenaire and base-ten materials, and other place-value devices. It is recommended that the time formerly devoted to paper-and-pencil calculations with large numbers be devoted to helping students learn to compute such numbers with calculators and work with other mathematics topics. Estimation and mental arithmetic skills should be developed. Rounding off, front-end addition, and use of compatible numbers are estimation skills for addition that children can learn. Mental arithmetic skills need to be developed because they are useful in performing operations on larger numbers and because there are times when mental computation is preferable to either paper and pencil or a calculator. Students can learn to add a one-place number to a two-place number and mental processes for adding numbers less than 100.

The decomposition method of subtracting is most commonly taught, although the equal-additions process has advocates. The decomposition process is generally favored because it is easily modeled with any place-value device. The equal-additions process is easy and rapid to use by persons who learn to do it. Rounding off is the most commonly used method of estimating subtraction answers. Mental processes for subtraction include subtracting the tens in the subtrahend from the minuend, then subtracting the ones number from the remainder; and using a compensation procedure to turn the subtrahend into a number with zero in the ones place.

There are computer programs that can be used to provide practice with basic facts and addition and subtraction with larger numbers. Some programs provide practice in game and puzzle situations. When students are prepared, they often enjoy success with the drill programs. Software should be seen as a supplement rather than a substitute for thorough instruction emphasizing understanding of operations. A calculator can be used to provide practice with the operations and to further develop problem-solving skills involving addition and subtraction.

▰ STUDY QUESTIONS AND ACTIVITIES

1. According to the NCTM standards, "In grades K–4, the study of mathematics should include opportunities to make connections so that students can relate various representations of concepts or procedures to one another." [26] Name some concepts or procedures that you believe should be connected as children learn about addition and subtraction. Describe teaching materials and procedures that you think will help students connect the mathematics concepts and/or procedures you named.

2. Real-world examples of the completion and part/whole procedures for subtraction are given on page 272. Read the two situations. Write an activity similar to the ones found on page 275 for each situation to show how you might introduce each one to first- or second-grade children. Use story situations that are different from the ones in the text. Some teachers instruct children to interpret the minus sign as "take away." What do you think of this practice? What difficulties might arise from its exclusive use?

3. Palindromic numbers are numbers that read the same forward and backward, such as 131 and 2,484,842. Palindromes can be generated by adding a number and its reverse. 13 + 31 generates the palindrome 44. Sometimes more than one addition is needed to generate a palindrome. In situations where this is true, reverse the digits in the sum and add that number to the sum. How many additions are required to generate a palindromic number with 596? With 69? Write a lesson in which you introduce palindromic numbers to fifth- or sixth-grade children. Include the calculator as a tool for this lesson. (See Nichol's article in the For Further Reading section.)

4. Estimate the sums of the following examples. Make a mental note of the process you use to arrive at your estimates.

	a.	b.	c.
	369	3789	711
	923	472	826
	128	2091	138
	554	8357	624
	721	1826	437
	+218	+6649	+448

Was your strategy rounding off, front-end estimation, or using compatible numbers? Did you use the same strategy for each problem? Ask several friends to estimate the sums, and ask them how they did it. They may not know the name of their strategy but will be able to describe their method. Ask several fifth- or sixth-grade students to estimate each sum and describe the method. Can you draw any conclusions from this activity about estimation strategies?

5. Use place-value devices, such as Unifix cubes, beansticks, and base-ten materials, to practice the following examples until you are proficient at demonstrating the process with each device. Which operation did you find more difficult to represent with the devices? Why was it more difficult for you?

a.	23	b.	68	c.	203	d.	685	e.	536
	$+41$		$+26$		$+428$		-204		-249

6. Rheins and Sherrill (see the For Further Reading section) each compared the performance of children who learned decomposition subtraction with another group who learned equal-additions in studies conducted more than 20 years apart. What were the results and what conclusions did they draw from their investigations? What implications do you draw from their reports of the children's performances?

7. Obtain a practice page of 100 addition or subtraction facts and take a one-minute timed test. (This is not an uncommon practice in many fifth- and sixth-grade classrooms.) How many did you complete? How many of the completed ones were correct? How did you feel at the end of the test? Discuss your memories of timed tests with your classmates. What are the possible harmful aspects of this practice? What ways can you think of to overcome the pressure and anxiety many students feel from such tests?

■ TEACHER'S BOOKSHELF

Kamii, Constance, with Linda Leslie Joseph. 1989. *Young Children Continue to Reinvent Arithmetic.* New York: Teachers College Press.
National Council of Teachers of Mathematics. 1978 Yearbook. *Developing Computational Skills.* Reston, VA: The Council.

■ FOR FURTHER READING

Balka, Don S. 1988, November. Digit delight: Problem-solving activities using 0 through 9. *Arithmetic Teacher 36*(3), 42–45.

A variety of puzzles using tiles with the numerals 0–9 are described. The puzzles deal with addition and subtraction and range from quite simple to challenging.

Baroody, Arthur. 1984, November. Children's difficulties in subtraction: Some causes and cures. *Arithmetic Teacher 32*(3), 14–19.

Counting strategies provide the basis for understanding subtraction facts.

_____. 1989, October. Manipulatives don't come with guarantees. *Arithmetic Teacher 37*(2), 4–5.

The author stresses that use of manipulative materials does not assure that children will learn with understanding. He states that when improperly used, manipulatives may do more harm than good. Teachers need to determine whether all materials—manipulative, pictorial, and oral or written symbolic—are familiar and make sense to children.

Beattie, Ian D. 1986, February. Modeling operations and algorithms. *Arithmetic Teacher 33*(6), 23–28.

Describes rationale and materials needed to demonstrate addition and subtraction algorithms.

Campbell, Melvin D. 1989, April. Basic facts drill: Card games. *Arithmetic Teacher 36*(8), 41–43.

Card games provide opportunities for students at all levels of skill and understanding to learn basic facts through competitions that are challenging and interesting. Games for all four operations are described.

Campbell, Patricia F. 1981, January. What do children see in mathematics textbook pictures? *Arithmetic Teacher 28*(5), 12–16.

The author interviewed first-grade children to get their interpretations of pictures portraying addition and subtraction situations. She found four levels of interpretation, ranging from no understanding to full understanding. She concludes that teachers need to know each child's level of understanding.

Evered, Lisa. 1989, December. How does a computer subtract? *Arithmetic Teacher 37*(4), 55–57.

The author describes a subtraction enrichment activity that uses a set of cards. One side of each card contains a one-digit number and the opposite side contains the number that when added to the first gives a sum of 9. The cards provide an experience that helps students understand how a computer subtracts.

Feinberg, Miriam M. 1990, April. Using patterns to practice basic facts. *Arithmetic Teacher 37*(8), 38–41.

Patterns in numbers provide strategies for helping children learn the basic addition and subtraction facts. Five different strategies are discussed.

Fuson, Karen. 1988, January. Subtracting by counting up with one-handed finger patterns. *Arithmetic Teacher 35*(5), 29–31.

The author describes a process for helping children learn to subtract. Children learn to count up as they determine the difference between two numbers. The process was helpful to all first-grade children.

Hutcheson, James W., and Carol E. Hutcheson. 1978, January. Homemade device for quick recall of basic facts. *Arithmetic Teacher 25*(4), 54–55.

An overhead transparency with a grid of random digits and paper shields that reveal rows and columns of digits offers opportunities for several skill-development activities— for example, recall of basic facts (addition and multiplication), comparing numbers, mental arithmetic, and reading three- and four-place numbers.

Kamii, Constance, and Linda Joseph. 1988, February. Teaching place value and double-column addition. *Arithmetic Teacher 35*(6), 48–52.

Kamii was a research fellow under Jean Piaget. The process of helping children learn double-column addition described in this article is based on her belief that children's own natural thinking should be fostered and that they should be encouraged to exchange points of view as they learn.

King, Julia A. 1981, September. Missing addends: A case of reading comprehension. *Arithmetic Teacher 30*(1), 44–45.

Children are frequently confused by simple missing-addend sentences. The author contends that it is a reading problem, not a mathematics problem. A game "Are You Kidding" is recommended as one way to help children who have this problem.

Logan, Henrietta I. 1978, September. Renaming with a money model. *Arithmetic Teacher 26*(1), 23–24.

Children who have difficulty grasping the meaning of subtraction with regrouping may be aided by using dollars, dimes, and pennies as models for place value. First, different ways of representing a given amount of money are practiced; then the money is used as a model for the subtraction algorithm.

Nichol, Margaret. 1978, December. Addition through palindromes. *Arithmetic Teacher 26*(4), 20–21.

There are both words and numbers that are palindromes. Of particular interest are suggestions for using palindromes to provide addition practice. Also of interest is the fact that it takes 24 steps to change 89 to a palindrome.

Reys, Barbara J., and Robert E. Reys. 1990, March. Estimation: Direction from the *Standards*. *Arithmetic Teacher 37*(7), 22–25.

Estimation is used in both measurement and computation situations. Sample activities in both areas are discussed.

Rheins, Gladys B., and Joel J. Rheins. 1955, October. A comparison of two methods of compound subtraction. *Arithmetic Teacher 2*(3), 63–59.

Reports the results of a study comparing groups of children taught by two subtraction methods, the decomposition and equal-additions. The conclusion is that the decomposition method is a better way to introduce compound subtraction.

Sherrill, James M. 1979, September. Subtraction: Decomposition versus equal addends. *Arithmetic Teacher 27*(1), 16–17.

Sherrill compared two groups of third-grade children to determine whether the group that learned the decomposition method or the one that learned the equal-additions method of subtraction performed better at the close of the instructional period. He confirmed the results of others who have compared children's performance on the two methods: Children who learned the decomposition method worked with greater accuracy and understanding.

Shoecraft, Paul. 1989, April. 'Equals' means 'Is the same as'. *Arithmetic Teacher 36*(8), 36–40.

Devices such as teeter-totters, pan balances, and mathematical balances can be used to develop the concepts of "equals." Illustrated examples offer suggestions for dealing with equalities and inequalities and operations.

Sowder, Judith T. 1990, March. Mental computation and number sense. *Arithmetic Teacher 37*(7), 18–20.

Mental computation depends on a good sense of the meaning of numbers. Skills in mental computation should be developed along with the meanings of the various operations. Sowder identifies six characteristics of "mental algorithms."

Starkey, Mary Ann. 1989, October. Calculating first graders. *Arithmetic Teacher* *37*(2), 6–7.

> *First-grade children learn to use the calculator to enhance their understanding of numbers and addition and subtraction. The use of calculators enables students to apply what they are learning to everyday situations.*

Thompson, Charles S., and William P. Dunlop. 1977, December. Basic facts: Do your children understand or do they memorize? *Arithmetic Teacher* *25*(3), 14–16.

> *Discusses two simple procedures for diagnosing and analyzing children's knowledge of basic facts, level of understanding, and rate of learning facts. Both require materials easily and inexpensively made by a teacher.*

Thompson, Charles S., and John Van de Walle. 1980, September. Paper dot plates give numbers meaning. *Arithmetic Teacher* *28*(1), 3–7.

> *Paper plates containing round dots serve to introduce counting, matching, addition and subtraction sentences, and other concepts.*

———. 1981, January. Transition boards: Moving from materials to symbolism in subtraction. *Arithmetic Teacher* *28*(5), 4–7, 9.

> *Transition boards provide a nonproportional model for playing trading games, such as the "Banker's Game" explained in Chapter 8. The authors show how to use a board to help children learn the decomposition method of subtraction.*

———. 1984. Modeling subtraction situations. *Arithmetic Teacher* *32*(2), 8–12.

> *Children need to be introduced to different situations that call for different understandings of subtraction.*

Thornton, Carol A., and Paula J. Smith. 1988, April. Action research: Strategies for learning subtraction facts. *Arithmetic Teacher* *35*(8), 8–12.

> *A variety of strategies to help children learn subtraction, including counting on, were used in a program planned to improve children's understanding of and responses to basic subtraction facts. The study supports the use of strategies to help children.*

■ NOTES

[1] National Council of Teachers of Mathematics, 1989. *Curriculum and Evaluation Standards for School Mathematics*. Reston, VA: National Council of Teachers of Mathematics, 36.

[2] NCTM, 41. Used by permission.

[3] NCTM, 44. Used by permission.

[4] NCTM, 91. Used by permission.

[5] NCTM, 94. Used by permission.

[6] NCTM, 102. Used by permission.

[7] This discussion was adapted from Katherine B. Hamrick and William D. McKillip. 1978. How computational skills contribute to the meaningful learning of arithmetic, in 1978 Yearbook *Developing Computational Skills*. Reston, VA: National Council of Teachers of Mathematics, 1–12.

[8] Adapted from Mary Baratta-Lorton. 1988. *Workjobs*. Menlo Park, CA: Addison-Wesley, 200–201.

[9] Adapted from Baratta-Lorton, 198–199.

[10] Adapted from Larry Leutzinger. 1981. *Strategies for Learning the Basic Facts.* Cedar Falls: Iowa Council of Teachers of Mathematics, 14.

[11] Adapted from A. Dean Hendrickson. 1980. *Mathematics the Piaget Way.* St. Paul: Minnesota Council on Quality Education, 9.

[12] Adapted from Leutzinger, 29.

[13] For a more extensive discussion of principles governing practice, see Edward J. Davis. 1978. Teaching the basic facts, in 1978 Yearbook *Developing Computational Skills.* Reston, VA: National Council of Teachers of Mathematics, 52–58.

[14] Optimum Resource, Inc., 10 Station Place, Norfolk, CT, 06058.

[15] The Learning Company, 6493 Kaiser Drive, Fremont, CA 94555.

[16] Davidson & Associates, Inc., 3135 Kashiwa St., Torrance, CA 90505.

[17] Adapted from Gary Bitter and Jerald Mikesell. 1980. *Activities Handbook for Teaching with the Handheld Calculator.* Boston: Allyn and Bacon, 68–69.

[18] Both devices are available from Educational Insights, 19560 S. Rancho Way, Dominguez Hills, CA 90220.

[19] For more information about compatible numbers, see Barbara Reys. 1986. Teaching computational estimation: Concepts and strategies, in 1986 Yearbook *Estimation and Mental Computation.* Reston, VA: National Council of Teachers of Mathematics, 41.

[20] For more information about both estimation and mental computation see Paul R. Trafton. 1978. Estimation and mental arithmetic: Important components of computation, in 1978 Yearbook *Developing Computational Skills.* Reston, VA: National Council of Teachers of Mathematics, 196–213.

[21] There are more than two algorithms. For a discussion of two others see Hitoshi Ikeda and Masui Ando. 1974, December. A new algorithm for subtraction? *Arithmetic Teacher 21*(8), 716–719; and Paul R. Neureiter. 1966, April. The 'ultimate' form of the subtraction algorithm. *Arithmetic Teacher 12*(4), 277–281.

[22] MECC, 3490 Lexington Avenue North, St. Paul, MN 55126.

[23] Scholastic, Inc., P.O. Box 7501, Jefferson City, MO 65102.

[24] *Quation* is also from Scholastic, Inc.

[25] Random House Media, Dept. 517, 400 Hahn Road, Westminster, MD 21157.

[26] National Council of Teachers, 1989. *Curriculum and Evaluation Standards for School Mathematics.* Reston, VA: National Council of Teachers of Mathematics, 32.

Teaching Multiplication and Division of Whole Numbers

Multiplication and division have many everyday uses. They may both be seen in the process of sorting a large number of items into equal-sized groups for the purpose of counting or for distributing the items. Multiplication and division algorithms for whole numbers are more complex than algorithms for addition and subtraction. Therefore, they are more difficult for students to learn. Work with these operations follows activities that acquaint children with the meanings of whole numbers and ways to represent them with symbols, and activities dealing with addition and subtraction.

In this chapter you will read about

1. the NCTM standards that apply to developing students' understanding and skills in multiplying and dividing with whole numbers;

2. three ways to interpret multiplication and models of each way to use with students;

3. two real-world division situations and ways to model them;

4. strategies for reinforcing basic multiplication and division facts;

5. the properties of multiplication students should learn;

6. ways to introduce a multiplication algorithm with manipulative materials;

7. using place-value materials to help children understand multiplication with regrouping;

8. estimation and mental arithmetic processes for multiplication;

9. use of multiplication and division patterns to aid in estimating quotients;

10. models and a question-and-answer sequence for developing understanding of a division algorithm;

11. ways to treat remainders in division to reflect different situations;

12. calculator and computer activities for multiplication and division.

NCTM STANDARDS THAT PERTAIN TO MULTIPLICATION AND DIVISION OF WHOLE NUMBERS

Kindergarten Through Grade Four

Standard 5: Estimation   In grades K–4, the curriculum should include estimation so that students can:

- explore estimation strategies;
- recognize when estimation is appropriate;
- determine the reasonableness of results;
- apply estimation in working with . . . computation and problem solving.[1]

Standard 7: Concepts of Whole Number Operations   In grades K–4, the mathematics curriculum should include concepts of . . . , multiplication, and division of whole numbers so that students can:

- develop meaning for the operations by modeling and discussing a rich variety of problem situations;

- relate the mathematical language and symbolism of operations to problem situations and informal language;
- recognize that a wide variety of problem structures can be represented by a single operation;
- develop operation sense.[2]

Standard 8: Whole Number Computation   In grades K–4, the mathematics curriculum should develop whole number computation so that students can:

- model, explain, and develop reasonable proficiency with basic facts and algorithms;
- use a variety of mental computation and estimation techniques;

- use calculators in appropriate computational situations;

- select and use computation techniques appropriate to specific problems and determine whether the results are reasonable.[3]

Standard 13: Patterns and Relationships   In grades K–4, the mathematics curriculum should include the study of patterns and relationships so that students can:

- explore the use of variables and open sentences to express relationships.[4]

Grades Five Through Eight

Standard 6: Number Systems and Number Theory   In grades 5–8, the mathematics curriculum should include the study of number systems and number theory so that students can:

- understand how basic arithmetic operations are related to one another.[5]

Standard 7: Computation and Estimation   In grades 5–8, the mathematics curriculum should develop the concepts underlying computation and estimation in various contexts so children can:

- compute with whole numbers;

- develop, analyze, and explain procedures for computation and techniques for estimation;

- select and use an appropriate method for computing from among mental arithmetic, paper-and-pencil, calculator, and computer methods;

- use computation [and] estimation . . . to solve problems.[6]

▨ THE NCTM STANDARDS ———————————————————

The NCTM standards for curriculum and evaluation in mathematics that apply to multiplication and division are similar to the ones for addition and subtraction. The standards indicate that just as children learn to model, explain, and use addition and subtraction, they need to learn to model, explain, and use multiplication and division. Skills are developed through a curriculum that employs many manipulative, pictorial, and diagrammatic materials, and that encourages students to work in groups and with their teacher to discuss and reflect on the work they are doing. Connections between addition and multiplication and between subtraction and division should be emphasized. Problem situations involving multiplication and division should be an integral part of the curriculum so that students will learn of the operations' varied applications.

Children's first work with multiplication and division begins informally in kindergarten and the primary grades as they learn to skip count, share things, and make recurring patterns with Unifix cubes and other pattern materials. Formal multiplication lessons may begin late in the second grade, although the majority of students' early work occurs in the third grade. Division is usually formally introduced in grade three. Work continues through the elementary grades as children develop understanding of the operations and algorithms for them. Multiplication and division with numbers greater than 1,000 should primarily deal with estimation or be done with a calculator. This frees students in the upper grades from time-consuming drill-and-practice exercises with multidigit factors and divisors. A sequence for presenting multiplication to children is shown in Figure 10.1; one for division is in Figure 10.2. As with addition and subtraction, the sequences are offered as guides rather than prescriptions for presenting the operations and algorithms to students.

■ INTRODUCING MULTIPLICATION

One definition of *multiplication* states that it is the operation on numbers that assigns a single number called the **product** to an ordered pair of numbers called **factors.** *Division* is defined as the operation used to find a missing factor when one factor and a product are known. These are abstract definitions that are useful at a mature level of understanding but are not suitable for school-age children. They need opportunities to see what multiplication is in terms of real situations and with materials they can manipulate and use to demonstrate multiplication applications. Three interpretations of multiplication are commonly presented in elementary schools: repeated addition, arrays, and Cartesian products.

Repeated Addition

Children's early free-play and teacher-directed activities lay foundations on which an understanding of multiplication can be developed. For example, children who make Unifix-cube trains with alternating pairs of two colors see a pattern for two. If children are led to count the cubes by twos, they are in fact using a counting-on strategy to determine a product. Similar visual patterns are useful for developing skip counting by other numbers, such as four, five, and ten.

For children who have had skip-counting experiences with Unifix trains, groups of buttons, small plastic animals, and similar materials, the repeated-addition interpretation of multiplication is an extension of an already-known idea. By using familiar situations to introduce multiplication, a teacher helps students use what they know to make connections between counting and multiplying and between adding and multiplying. When confronted with four sets of two objects, children can use skip counting (2, 4, 6, 8) to determine that there are eight objects. Children should then see that repeated addition—$2 + 2 + 2 + 2 = 8$—and multiplication—$4 \times 2 = 8$—are two ways to represent the same situation.

Figure 10-1
A sequence of steps for learning to multiply whole numbers

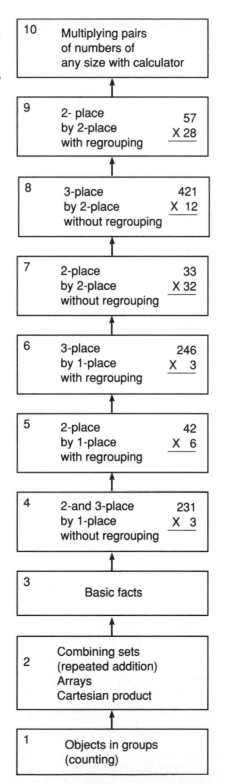

10 Multiplying pairs
of numbers of
any size with calculator

9 2- place   57
by 2-place   X 28
with regrouping

8 3-place   421
by 2-place   X 12
without regrouping

7 2-place   33
by 2-place   X 32
without regrouping

6 3-place   246
by 1-place   X 3
with regrouping

5 2-place   42
by 1-place   X 6
with regrouping

4 2-and 3-place   231
by 1-place   X 3
without regrouping

3 Basic facts

2 Combining sets
(repeated addition)
Arrays
Cartesian product

1 Objects in groups
(counting)

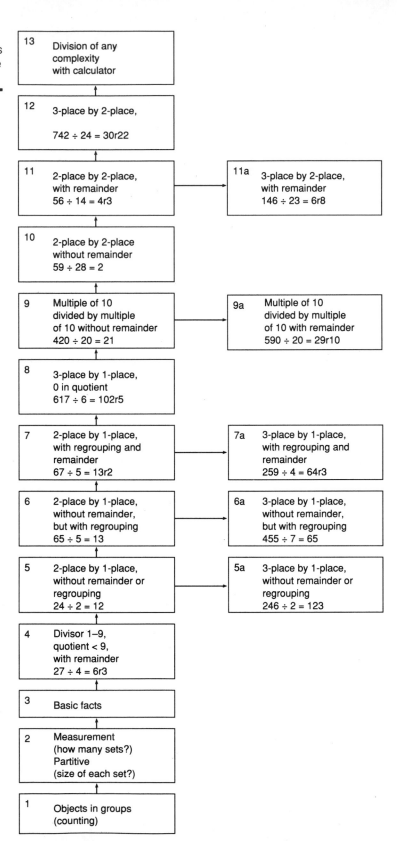

Figure 10-2
A sequence of steps for learning to divide whole numbers

13 Division of any complexity with calculator

12 3-place by 2-place,

742 ÷ 24 = 30r22

11 2-place by 2-place, with remainder
56 ÷ 14 = 4r3

11a 3-place by 2-place, with remainder
146 ÷ 23 = 6r8

10 2-place by 2-place without remainder
59 ÷ 28 = 2

9 Multiple of 10 divided by multiple of 10 without remainder
420 ÷ 20 = 21

9a Multiple of 10 divided by multiple of 10 with remainder
590 ÷ 20 = 29r10

8 3-place by 1-place, 0 in quotient
617 ÷ 6 = 102r5

7 2-place by 1-place, with regrouping and remainder
67 ÷ 5 = 13r2

7a 3-place by 1-place, with regrouping and remainder
259 ÷ 4 = 64r3

6 2-place by 1-place, without remainder, but with regrouping
65 ÷ 5 = 13

6a 3-place by 1-place, without remainder, but with regrouping
455 ÷ 7 = 65

5 2-place by 1-place, without remainder or regrouping
24 ÷ 2 = 12

5a 3-place by 1-place, without remainder or regrouping
246 ÷ 2 = 123

4 Divisor 1–9, quotient < 9, with remainder
27 ÷ 4 = 6r3

3 Basic facts

2 Measurement (how many sets?) Partitive (size of each set?)

1 Objects in groups (counting)

The introduction of the formal terms *factor* and *product* should be deferred until students can visualize, demonstrate with concrete materials, and orally explain the new operation. Activities with familiar objects and situations like those in Activity 10.1 can be used to develop understanding of repeated addition.

Spread students' experiences with concrete materials over a period of several days to give them opportunities for further group and individual activities with materials from their mathematics boxes, Unifix cubes, domino cards, and sets of markers on flannel or magnetic boards (see Figures 10.3 through 10.6).

Figure 10-3
Buttons from a mathematics box show four sets of three objects.

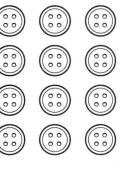

Figure 10-4
Unifix cubes linked to show $2 \times 3 = 6$

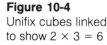

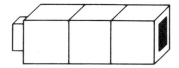

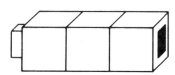

ACTIVITY 10.1   Buying Gum

- Organize students in groups for a cooperative-learning activity.

- Begin with a story: "Sadie buys gum in packages that each have seven sticks. When she buys four packages, how many sticks does she get?"

- Allow time for each group to use coffee stirrer sticks, or any other materials, or to use more abstract procedures to determine the answer. Move among the groups to observe their work and encourage promising approaches.

- Have groups demonstrate and explain what they did. If any group used a mathematical procedure, such as repeated addition or perhaps even multiplication, have the process explained.

- Give other similar situations for the groups to model with their materials.

Figure 10-5
Domino cards used to give children experience with counting by fours. These can be made by sticking adhesive labels to pieces of tagboard or colored poster board.

Figure 10-6
Markers used to illustrate the multiplication sentence $3 \times 7 = 21$

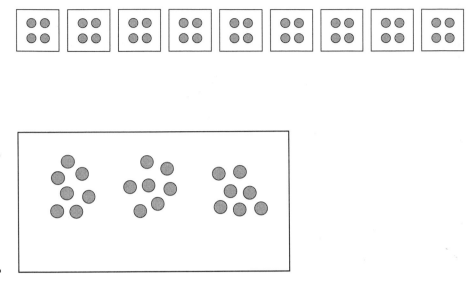

Once children have the background necessary to understand the terms and symbols for multiplication, use activities from earlier lessons to introduce both the terms and symbols. For the situation portrayed on the flannel board, write the addition sentence $7 + 7 + 7 = 21$ on the chalkboard. Have the students read it in unison. Then discuss the fact that there are three groups, each with seven markers. Write the multiplication sentence—$3 \times 7 = 21$—beneath the addition sentence. Ask the children how these two sentences are related. Most of them recognize that the "3" in the sentence identifies the number of sets, just as the three addends do. The "7" indicates the size of each set, and the "21" tells the total number of objects. Introduce the terms by saying that the "3" and "7" are *factors,* while the "21" is the *product.* The terms *multiplier,* for the first factor, and *multiplicand,* for the second factor, can be introduced in late third grade or in fourth grade.

Arrays

An array is an arrangement of items in a number of equal-sized rows. Cans on the shelves of a supermarket are a good example. There are four rows of cans with eight cans in each row in Figure 10.7. This is a 4-by-8 array; the "4" indicates the number of rows and the "8" the number of cans in each row.

Other examples include boxes on shelves in a shoe store, games on racks in a video rental shop, boxes of film in a camera shop, and rows of musicians in a marching band. Use an activity like Activity 10.2 to introduce arrays.

Figure 10-7
A 4-by-8 array of
cans on a grocery
shelf

ACTIVITY 10.2   Multiplication Arrays

- Group students in pairs. Give each pair a set of chips, lima beans, or similar markers.

- Demonstrate how to make a 2-by-4 array and a 4-by-2 array. Point out that the 2-by-4 array has two rows with four markers in each row, and that the 4-by-2 array has four rows with two markers in each row.

- Have students name the arrays as "two rows of four" and "four rows of two."

- Have each pair of students form other arrays: 2-by-7, 3-by-5, 6-by-3, and so on. Move among the students to observe their work and to hear students describe their arrays.

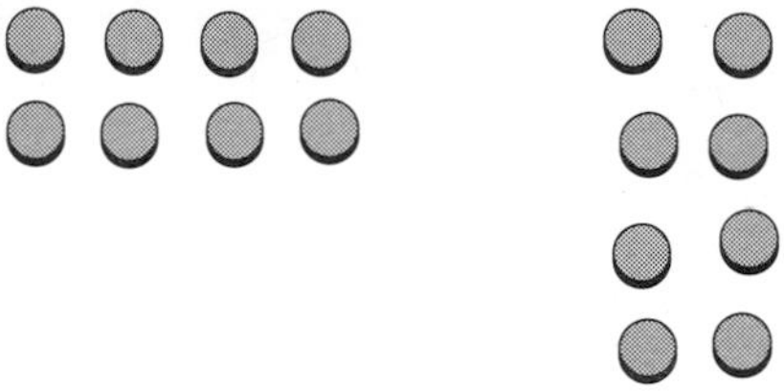

In addition to this activity, you can have students work with materials like these:

- *Adhesive-label arrays*—Patterns made with colored adhesive labels or bright stickers attached to colored cardboard make a simple learning aid showing arrays. Students can work in pairs, with one of the pair showing and the other naming the arrays. A 7-by-7 arrangement has 49 labels and can show 13 different arrays: 1-by-7, 2-by-7, 3-by-7, 4-by-7, 5-by-7, 6-by-7, 7-by-7, 7-by-1, 7-by-2, 7-by-3, 7-by-4, 7-by-5, and 7-by-6. The student showing a card covers and uncovers rows with a plain piece of paper to reveal different arrays. Figure 10.8 shows a 7-by-7 array (a), a 7-by-1 array (b), and a 1-by-7 array (c). A card with 36 labels will show 11 arrays; one with 64 labels will show 15 arrays; and one with 81 labels will show 17 arrays.

- *Squared paper*—Give students pieces of centimeter- or quarter-inch-squared paper. Have them roll dice to determine numbers for arrays to illustrate with crayons and to write multiplication sentences (see Figure 10.9).

Figure 10-8
(a) Card showing a 7-by-7 array. (b) The card is covered to show a 7-by-1 array. (c) The card is covered to show a 1-by-7 array.

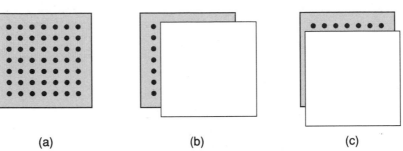

(a)   (b)   (c)

Figure 10-9
Samples of arrays drawn on squared paper

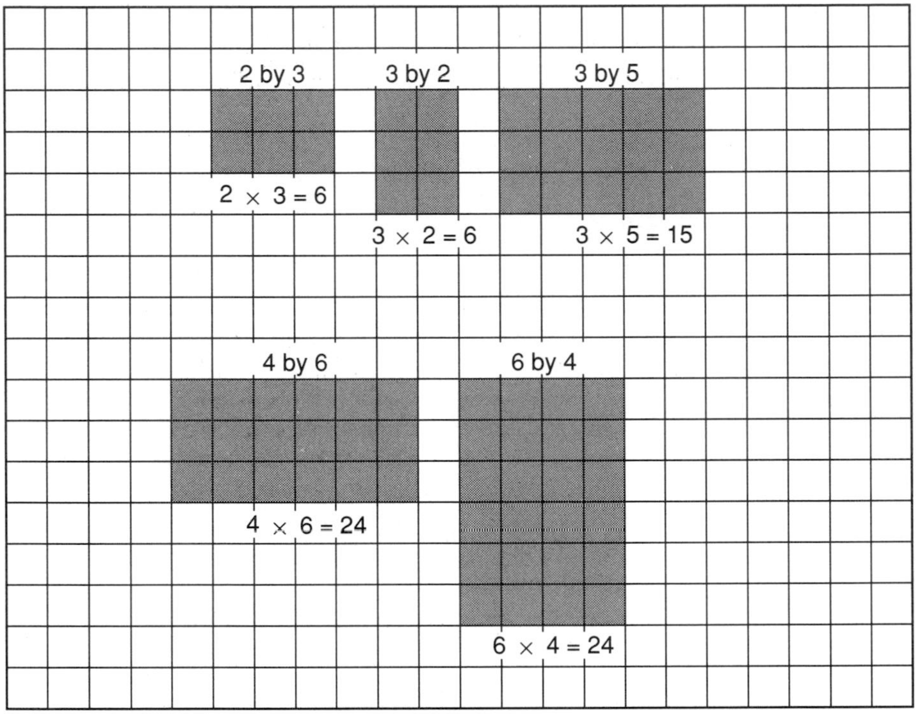

2 by 3   3 by 2   3 by 5

2 × 3 = 6
         3 × 2 = 6   3 × 5 = 15

4 by 6   6 by 4

4 × 6 = 24

6 × 4 = 24

Nearly every classroom has array patterns, such as panes of window glass, rows of ceiling or floor tiles, and sets of lights. You can also create arrays by arranging books on shelves and papers on bulletin boards. Have students search their room to detect objects arranged in arrays. You can challenge them to identify other arrays in the school building, on the playground, and in the neighborhood. An assignment for a language arts lesson might be to have students write a paragraph describing the arrays and their locations.

Cartesian Products

A **Cartesian,** or **cross, product** is used to determine how many combinations there are when each element in one group is matched with each element in a second group. A sandwich shop provides a setting for illustrating a Cartesian product situation. The shop has six different types of bread or rolls and eight different types of fillings. How many different types of sandwiches can be made when each type of bread is spread with each type of filling? There are 48 possible combinations when bread and fillings are considered. When additional foods such as sliced tomatoes, shredded lettuce, avocados, and alfalfa sprouts are used as a third ingredient, the situation becomes more complicated. How many combinations are possible when these four items are also available in addition to the filling? The idea of Cartesian product can be introduced informally by having students form all the combinations for three pairs of socks and four pairs of shoes or the combinations of ice cream servings when there are four flavors and either cups or cones. Children can use cutouts of shoes and socks or ice cream and cups/cones at a flannel board to show the combinations. A cooperative-learning activity can be used to formally introduce the concept; see Activity 10.3.

Activities dealing with the Cartesian-product concept can be designed around other situations. Help students decide on a procedure for dealing with each of these situations.

- How many different girl-boy partnerships can be formed from a given set of boys and a given set of girls?

- How many outfits can be arranged using a given number of shirts and trousers or skirts and blouses?

- How many different frosted cakes can be prepared from a given number of cake mixes and a given number of frostings?

ACTIVITY 10.3 Making Bicycles

- Organize the class for a cooperative-learning activity.

- Present this situation: Each group is to pretend that they are a team of designers in a bicycle manufacturing plant. Management has decided that the plant will produce red, silver, gold, and black bicycle frames. Each team is to decide on six colors for trim on the frames and then plan a scheme for determining how many different combinations of colors there will be if they use only one trim color on each frame and there are four frame and six trim colors.

- Provide each team with pieces of red, silver, gold, and black paper for frames and other colors of paper from which they can choose trim colors.

- When all teams are finished, have the children show their choices of colors and explain how they determined the numbers of combinations.

- Teams that finish the first task before others can determine the number of combinations when there are five frames and three trim colors; four frame and five trim colors.

The Cartesian-product interpretation is useful for explaining the roles of one and zero in multiplication. When one of the sets in a Cartesian-product situation contains only one element, there can be only as many combinations as there are elements in the other set. In the bicycle factory, if there are only gold bicycle frames there can be only as many combinations as there are trim colors. A situation like this explains why the product of one times a number is always the other number. It is obvious that if there are only frames and no trim colors it is not possible to produce bicycles trimmed with a color. This situation helps explain why zero times any number is always zero.

EXERCISE   Write stories for the multiplication sentence 3 × 5 = 15 that illustrate repeated subtraction, arrays, and Cartesian products.

◾ INTRODUCING DIVISION

Multiplication is the operation by which two factors yield a product. In division a product and one factor are known; the other factor is to be determined. Two types of situations lead to division. The serving of eggs illustrates each of the situations. "How many servings of scrambled eggs can be served from eight eggs if two eggs are used in each serving?" The eight eggs are measured out in servings of two eggs each. This is a **measurement** situation. In it, the size of the original set is known and the size of each serving, or group, is known. The problem is to determine the number of groups. "How many eggs are in a serving when eight eggs are served equally among four people?" The eight eggs are parceled out among the four people so that each person gets two eggs. This is a **partitive** situation. In it, the size of the original set and the number of subsets are known; the problem is to determine the size of each serving, or subset.

Introducing Measurement Situations

Either of the two situations mentioned can be used when division is introduced. Measurement situations are preferred by many mathematics specialists and teachers because they can be connected directly with repeated subtraction. Students can see that division modeled by repeatedly removing equal-sized groups is the opposite of multiplication modeled by repeatedly adding equal-sized groups. After studying how primary-grade children learn division, Marilyn Zweng concluded that understanding is enhanced when containers are used so that children can actually have places to put the objects when sets are separated.[7] To complete Activity 10.4, children put beans in paper cups as they investigate measurement situations. Marbles are used in Activity 10.5.

ACTIVITY 10.4   Dividing Beans Among Cups

- Give each child 15 to 20 lima beans and 9 small paper cups.

- Have each child count eight beans and hold them in one hand.

- Direct the children to put the eight beans into cups, two at a time until all of the beans have been distributed.

- Ask, "How many cups have two beans in them?" (4.)

- "Take 18 beans and distribute them three at a time into the cups. How many cups have three beans?"

- Repeat with other quantities and groupings of beans. Discuss each situation as it is completed to help children realize that each time they separate a set of beans into groups of a known size, they determine the number of cups (subsets) into which the beans are put.

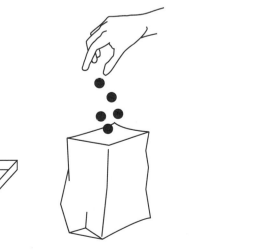

ACTIVITY 10.5   Putting Marbles into Bags

- Use marbles and small bags.

- Tell a story: "Susie has 15 marbles. She is going to put them into bags so that there are five marbles in each bag. How many bags will she need?"

- Show 15 marbles in an open box. Ask a student to come to the box and put five marbles into one bag. Have the student repeat the action until the 15 marbles are in bags.

- Have the student show that he or she has three bags and that there are five marbles in each bag.

- Repeat with other quantities of marbles and different groupings.

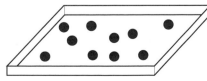

Use a situation similar to ones already used to introduce the division sentence. If the situation is the separation of 16 pencils into groups of two, the sentence is $16 \div 2 = 8$. After the sentence has been written on the chalkboard discuss its parts. Help the students see that "16" stands for the original group of pencils, "2" for the size of each equal-sized group of pencils, and "8" for the number of groups. The sentence is read: "Sixteen divided by two equals eight."

Introducing Partitive Situations

Most children have shared things with friends. Partitive division can be introduced through the familiar experience of sharing cookies, as in Activity 10.6.

After students understand partitive situations, help them relate the numbers in a sentence to the situation with which it is associated. For a situation with 24 cookies and the sentence $24 \div 3 = 8$, the "24" represents the original set of cookies, the "3" the number of groups into which they are divided, and the "8" the number of cookies in each group.

Eventually children should learn the terms associated with division. The number that is divided is the **dividend,** the number by which it is divided is the **divisor,** and the answer is the **quotient.** The meaning of the dividend in a sentence never changes; it always tells the size of the original group. But the roles of divisor and quotient are interchanged, depending on the situation. In a measurement situation, the divisor tells the size of each group, while the quotient tells the number of groups. In a partitive situation the divisor tells the number of groups, while the quotient tells the size of each group.

EXERCISE   Read the following multiplication situation. From it write division situations

---

ACTIVITY 10.6   Sharing Cookies

- Present this situation: Paul has 17 cookies. Three friends and he will share them as a snack after school. How many cookies will each one get?

- Use 17 disks cut from cardboard to represent cookies.

- Discuss with the children how to determine the answer. One way is to distribute the cookies one at a time to four children.

- "After we have shared 16 of the cookies there is one left over. What can be done with it?" (The children may suggest that one cookie can be saved for Paul's dinner or be cut into four equal-sized parts.)

- Repeat with other numbers of cookies and groupings of children.

that illustrate measurement (repeated subtraction) and partitive (sharing) division.

Graciella had four bags of apples. Each bag had five apples in it. How many apples did she have?

REINFORCING LEARNING OF THE FACTS

As children work with manipulative materials and use skip counting and repeated addition and subtraction to learn the meaning of multiplication and division, they will learn many of the 100 basic multiplication and 90 division facts. For example, many students see that multiplying by two is the same as doubling a number. Multiplication by five is not difficult for children who have had meaningful experiences with manipulatives and skip counting. When activities dealing with one and zero are understood, multiplication by these numbers presents no difficulties to most children.

Strategies for Multiplication

When children's work with manipulative materials indicates a good understanding of the meanings of multiplication, they should be given activities and materials that will help them learn the basic facts.

Many students develop strategies of their own for remembering multiplication and division facts. These children should be encouraged as long as their strategies lead to accurate results and reasonable speed. You can help all children to remember the facts by presenting activities like the following ones. In Activity 10.7 the multiplication table is used to help children realize that there are relatively few difficult combinations. Activities 10.8 and 10.9 focus on combinations that involve nine as a factor, which are difficult for many children to remember. The activities help children think about such combinations and aid their memory of them.[8]

Once children understand how to determine products when nine is a factor, they should have practice sheets that contain examples and questions similar to the ones in Activities 10.8 and 10.9. These worksheets should be followed by practice with other worksheets, fact cards, oral expressions, and other means of presenting basic facts containing nine as one factor.

Students can also use known facts to determine products for unknown facts. For example, a student who knows that $4 \times 8 = 32$ can use that knowledge to determine that $8 \times 8 = 64$. The thinking is: "If $4 \times 8 = 32$, then 8×8 will be twice as much because eight is twice as much as four. So, $8 \times 8 = 64$." Children who experience difficulty with the thinking involved in this process can be helped by using an array. Activity 10.10 involves a similar activity with a 4-by-8 array.

ACTIVITY 10.7   The Multiplication Table

- Begin with a blank multiplication table, either on an overhead transparency or a large sheet of paper.

- Point out that the numbers along the top and down the left side are factors; a product will

X	0	1	2	3	4	5	6	7	8	9
0										
1										
2										
3										
4										
5										
6										
7										
8										
0										

X	0	1	2	3	4	5	6	7	8	9
0	0	0	0	0	0	0	0	0	0	0
1	0	1	2	3	4	5	6	7	8	9
2	0	2	4	6	8	10	12	14	16	18
3	0	3	6	9	12	15				
4	0	4	8	12	16	20				
5	0	5	10	15	20	25	30	35	40	45
6	0	6	12			30				
7	0	7	14			35				
8	0	8	16			40				
0	0	9	18			45				

be placed in the cell beneath a top factor and to the right of a left-hand factor.

- Begin at the first row of cells. Say, "If we multiply each number in the top row by the number in the left-hand row, what are the products?" (They are all zero.) Ask, "Where else will there be products that are zero?" (Down the first column of cells.) Discuss why this is so. Ask, "How many multiplication facts have zero as a factor?" (19.)

- Ask similar questions about the second row and second column of cells, where one is a factor for each pair of numbers. There are seventeen more facts that have one as a factor. Point out to the children that by knowing the role of zero and one in multiplication they know more than one-third of the basic facts.

- Turn to the third row and third column of cells, where two is a factor. Remind students about skip counting by twos. Add the 15 products for these combinations to the table. Combinations with zero, one, and two account for more than half of the basic facts.

- Combinations with five as one factor offer little difficulty to most children because of skip counting by fives. Add these to the table. These contribute another 13 facts.

- The remaining combinations for cells in the upper left-hand part of the table are probably already known by most students. These are 3×3, 3×4, 4×3, and 4×4.

- Point out that among the 32 facts on which most students need to concentrate there are four doubles, leaving only 28 that may be troublesome.

ACTIVITY 10.8   Nines Are Easy

■ Begin with a discussion of multiplication by ten:

—"What are six tens?" (60.) "Will six nines be more or less?" (Less.) Point out that the answer for six nines will be in the fifties.

—"What are four tens?" (40.) "Will four nines be more or less?" (Less.) Point out that the answer for four nines will be in the thirties.

—Repeat with other tens and nines until students recognize the pattern.

■ Write these combinations on the chalkboard:

$$9 \times 6 = 54 \qquad 7 \times 9 = 63$$
$$9 \times 3 = 27 \qquad 8 \times 9 = 72$$
$$9 \times 4 = 36 \qquad 5 \times 9 = 45$$

Say, "Look at the number in each tens place. How does it compare with the number being multiplied by nine?" (It is one less.)

■ Show these combinations:

$$4 \times 9 = 36 \qquad 6 \times 9 = 54$$
$$7 \times 9 = 63 \qquad 9 \times 8 = 72$$
$$9 \times 9 = 81 \qquad 2 \times 9 = 18$$

Ask, "How can you describe the number in the tens place for each of these combinations?" (It is one less than the number being multiplied by nine.)

ACTIVITY 10.9   Products with Nine as One Factor

■ Show cards containing numerals such as 4, 8, 3. Ask, "What do we add to each of these numbers to make nine?" (5, 1, 6.)

■ Write some facts with nine on the chalkboard.

$$9 \times 4 = 36 \qquad 8 \times 9 = 72$$
$$9 \times 7 = 63 \qquad 6 \times 9 = 54$$
$$9 \times 5 = 45 \qquad 2 \times 9 = 18$$

Ask, "If we add the digits in each product, what is the sum?" (9.) Tell the students that in the nines facts, the sum of the digits is always nine.

■ Show some partially completed facts:

$$9 \times 3 = 2\_\_ \qquad 7 \times 9 = 6\_\_$$
$$9 \times 5 = 4\_\_ \qquad 8 \times 9 = 7\_\_$$

Point out that since $10 \times 3 = 30$, the answer to 9×3 will be in the twenties. Ask, "What is added to two to give nine?" (7.) So, $9 \times 3 = 27$.

■ Repeat with the other combinations.

ACTIVITY 10.10   Using an Array

- Have the children separate a 4-by-8 array into two 4-by-4 arrays.

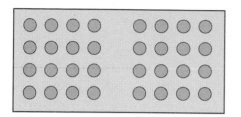

eight is twice four times four; when I double 16, I get 32, so 4 x 8 = 32."

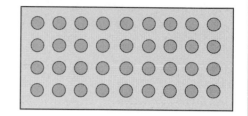

- Encourage the children to think: "Four times eight is twice as much as four times four; four times four equals 16, so four times

- Use other arrays, such as 8-by-7, 6-by-9, and 4-by-9.

Strategies for Division

Students who have learned to think of division as the process of using a product and a known factor to determine a missing factor can use multiplication facts to learn division facts. At first, activities should focus on a product and its factors. These activities should be followed by ones that have a factor and a product. (See Activities 10.11 and 10.12.) Worksheets and teacher-prepared audiocassette tapes can be used to provide practice with product-and-known-factor combinations.

A completed multiplication table like the one in Activity 10.7 can be used for learning division facts. To determine the quotient for 64 ÷ 8 = □, locate "64" in the column beneath "8" in the top row, then move to the left to the number in the left-hand column—"8." Once the process is understood, students can work in groups of two to four at a chart. One student can identify a product and one factor; the others can name the missing factor. Using the table this way is consistent with the way it is used for multiplication and reinforces students' understanding that multiplication and division are inverse operations.

Practice Materials

Flash cards that emphasize the relationship between multiplication and division can be used to provide some of the practice children need to commit the facts to memory. The cards in Figure 10.10 are particularly useful. The card in (a) is used this way: For multiplication, hold the card with thumb

---

ACTIVITY 10.11   Missing Factors

- Ask, "What numbers do we multiply to get 24?" Consider the combinations 4 × 6 and 3 × 8. (1 × 24 and 2 × 12 are not basic facts.) Ask, "What numbers do we multiply to get 36?" Consider 4 × 9 and 6 × 6. (1 × 36, 2 × 18, and 3 × 12 are not basic facts.)

- Repeat with other numbers that have at least two factors that are less than ten.

ACTIVITY 10.12   One Missing Factor

- Write the numbers 56 and 8 on the chalkboard. Ask, "What is the other factor when we have 56 and eight?" (7.)

- Write the numbers 48 and 8 on the chalkboard. Ask, "What is the other factor when we have 48 and eight?" (6.)

- Repeat with other products and one factor.

- Write these sentences on the chalkboard:

36 = 4 × □	36 ÷ 4 = □
49 = 7 × □	49 ÷ 7 = □
63 = 7 × □	63 ÷ 7 = □

- Call on individuals to read the completed sentences for each pair.

---

and forefinger covering "63." A student reads the sentence, "Seven times nine equals 63." For division, hold the card with thumb and forefinger covering a factor. The student says, "Sixty-three divided by seven equals nine." Or, "Sixty-three divided by nine equals seven." Each student can prepare cards for those combinations that he or she needs to practice.

The card in Figure 10.10(b) contains all of the facts involving eight as a factor. Children work in small groups with a single card. The side showing in the left-hand picture is for multiplication practice and the other side is for division practice. One student serves as leader, who provides input, while the others give responses. The leader places a pencil or fingertip in a notch, say at "9." The responding student will say, "Nine times eight equals

Figure 10-10

Two types of flash cards for practicing multiplication and division facts

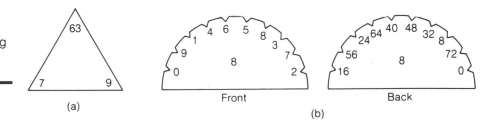

(a)   Front   Back   (b)

72." Or, "Eight times nine equals 72." Each time the pencil or fingertip is moved, a new combination is used. The leader can check each response by looking at a notch's number on the reverse side of the card. To practice division, show the other side so responders see quotients and the given factor. They respond by saying, "Sixteen divided by eight is two" or whatever the combination is. Procedures that apply to practice with addition and subtraction facts apply here. Instruct a leader not to allow time for responders to count or use other immature processes to determine a factor or quotient. Have the leader give the response and then reshow the combination to a child who is uncertain about an answer.

A well-equipped classroom will contain other practice materials. Textbooks contain pages of practice exercises dealing with basic facts, which can be used after students are familiar with the facts and have begun activities to commit them to memory. Computer programs such as *Number Operations*,[9] *Stickybear Math 2*,[10] and *Math Skills—Elementary Level*[11] contain practice exercises for multiplication and division facts. The calculator activity "Brain Versus Button," described in Activity 9.17, can be adapted for multiplication and division. Instead of responding to orally or visually presented facts for addition or subtraction, players respond to multiplication or division facts. Cassette tapes with orally presented facts can be prepared by a teacher. A set of 20 to 25 facts is sufficient for one practice exercise. Different rates of presentation can be recorded on separate tapes. An already-numbered answer sheet for each set of facts provides a means for students to record written responses. An answer key for each set allows a student to check his or her own work.

Calculators provide a good way for students to reinforce their understanding of connections among addition, subtraction, multiplication, and division. A student can use one to experience multiplication as repeated addition and division as repeated subtraction. To perform repeated addition, one factor is used as an addend; it is repeatedly added as many times as indicated by the other factor. For $9 \times 7 = \square$, seven is entered as an addend and the "=" key is pressed nine times to get the product. For repeated subtraction, the dividend (product) is entered. The divisor (known factor) is subtracted until zero or a number that is smaller than the divisor is reached. For $54 \div 9 = \square$, enter 54, then subtract nine until zero is reached. When children alternate the two operations with the same set of factors and product, they have achieved another way of seeing that multiplication and division are inverse operations. At the same time, the activities provide valuable practice with basic facts.

TEACHING PROPERTIES OF MULTIPLICATION

Before students can fully understand multiplication and the common algorithm for performing it, they need to understand some properties of multiplication. Activities that involve concrete, pictorial, and abstract experiences provide understanding of the commutative, associative, and distributive properties, as well as of the roles of zero and one.

The Commutative Property

Activities with arrays—as in Activity 10.13—provide ready illustrations of the **commutative** property, which allows two or more factors to be arranged in any order without affecting the product.

A number line is also useful for illustrating the commutative nature of multiplication. The number line in Figure 10.11 illustrates the sentences $5 \times 3 = 15$ and $3 \times 5 = 15$.

It is important that a teacher be consistent when using a model or illustration to represent a mathematical concept. When the repeated-addition interpretation of multiplication is explained, the first factor indicates the number of sets and the second factor indicates the size of each set. To illustrate the word problem "How many apples are used when eight apples are put in each of six boxes?", there are six sets of markers, each containing eight objects. The sentence $6 \times 8 = 48$ represents this situation. If there are

---

ACTIVITY 10.13   Commutative Property of Multiplication

- Show an array of markers on a flannel or magnetic board.

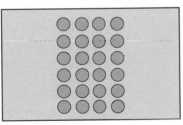

- Have a student write the sentence for the array on the chalkboard.

$$6 \times 4 = 24$$

- Rotate the board a quarter turn.

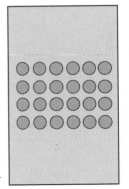

- Have the student write the sentence for the array as it now appears.

$$4 \times 6 = 24$$

- Repeat with other arrays. Discuss the fact that the order of the factors in each pair of sentences has no effect on the product.

Figure 10-11
Number line used to show that 5 × 3 = 3 × 5

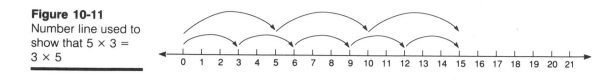

6
×8

198
× 8

eight boxes with six apples each, there are eight sets with six markers each and the sentence is 8 × 6 = 48. The multiplication is shown with vertical notation (see margin). As students mature, provide opportunities for them to see that because of the commutative property they do not need to adhere to this way of writing the sentence for a problem. Rather than writing the sentence for the problem "How many apples are needed when eight apples are to be put in each of 198 boxes?" as 198 × 8 = □, they can write it as 8 × 198, and use the algorithm in the margin to determine the answer.

The Associative Property

The **associative** property frees students to deal with pairs of factors in any order they choose when there are three or more factors. Students encounter situations involving three factors when they find the volume of solid figures. Activities with blocks—as in Activity 10.14—will help students understand the significance of this property of multiplication. The situation involving three ingredients for making sandwiches, discussed earlier in this chapter, is another one that involves three factors and can be used to illustrate this property.

This type of multiplication is also discussed in the section about finding the volume of solid figures in Chapter 14. (You should recognize that the commutative property is used along with the associative property in situations involving volume.)

Older students should deal with sentences such as these so they can see how the associative and commutative properties can be used to make it possible to compute answers mentally:

$$4 \times 9 \times 25 = \square \qquad 36 \times 2 \times 50 = \square$$

In the first example, think 4 times 25 is 100, 9 times 100 is 900. What thinking can be used in the second example to determine its product mentally?

The Distributive Property

The **distributive** property makes it possible to break down the more difficult multiplication facts into easier combinations. One strategy for learning multiplication facts is to use doubling of the product for the fact $4 \times 8 = 32$ to determine that the product of 8 times 8 is 64. The combination 8 times 8 is used in Activity 10.15 to show how the distributive property might be introduced.

The distributive property is also used when two two-place or larger numbers are multiplied with the conventional algorithm.

ACTIVITY 10.14   The Associative Property for Multiplication

- Have students work in pairs with at least 30 wooden or plastic cubes.

- Have students use 24 cubes to make a solid figure that has two layers, with the same number of cubes in each layer. (Figures with these dimensions can be made: $2 \times 2 \times 6$, $2 \times 3 \times 4$, or $2 \times 1 \times 12$.)

- Have each pair of students study their solid from different perspectives to determine the ways they can write sentences to represent the multiplication for it. Students who made a $2 \times 3 \times 4$ solid should write and explain these sentences:

$3 \times 4 \times 2 = 24$ $4 \times 3 \times 2 = 24$
$3 \times 2 \times 4 = 24$ $4 \times 2 \times 3 = 24$
$2 \times 4 \times 3 = 24$ $2 \times 3 \times 4 = 24$

- Discuss the sentences for the other solids. (If only one or two of the three solids are made by the children, demonstrate how to make the unmade one(s) before writing and discussing its sentences.)

- Repeat with other numbers of cubes and solids such as 36 and 54.

ACTIVITY 10.15   The Distributive Property

- Write a sentence like $8 \times 8 = 64$ on the chalkboard.

- Ask, "What are some ways we can use addition combinations to rename eight? $(1 + 7, 2 + 6, 3 + 5,$ and so on.)

- Rewrite the multiplication sentence, using one of the combinations for eight.

$$8 \times (4 + 4) = 64$$

- Rewrite the sentence once again.

$$(8 \times 4) + (8 \times 4) = 64$$

- Have students verify that the answer— 64—is still correct because $8 \times 4 = 32$, and $32 + 32 = 64$.

- Repeat using other combinations for eight in the rewritten sentences.

- Repeat with other multiplication combinations, such as $6 \times 9 = \square$ and $7 \times 6 = \square$.

The Identity Element

An **identity element** is a number that, when operated on by another number, results in an answer that is the same as the second number. Activities dealing with zero as the identity element for addition were discussed in the previous chapter. *One* is the identity element for multiplication. Activities with manipulative materials and the Cartesian product interpretation should make the role of one in multiplication clear to children.

One also plays an important role in division. Children need activities and discussions that help them generalize that whenever a number is divided by one, the quotient is the same as the dividend. They should also see that when a number is divided by itself, the answer is one, with zero divided by zero excepted.

The Role of Zero in Multiplication and Division

Zero has a special role in multiplication and division. In multiplication, the product is always zero when one of the factors is zero. Cartesian product situations, as already discussed, are particularly good ones for demonstrating the role of zero in multiplication. In division, zero has a special role. When the dividend is zero, the quotient is also zero. This is illustrated by the example $0 \div 9 = 0$. This is the inverse of the multiplication sentence $0 \times 9 = 0$. Zero is never used as a divisor, however, so there is no division sentence that is the inverse of the multiplication sentence $9 \times 0 = 0$. There are only 90 division facts, because the sentences $0 \times 0 = 0$, $1 \times 0 = 0$, $2 \times 0 = 0, \ldots, 9 \times 0 = 0$ have no inverses.

EXERCISE   How long should children engage in developmental activities with multiplication and division before being expected to know all the multiplication and division facts? What teaching materials and strategies might be used instead of timed tests?

■ INTRODUCING A MULTIPLICATION ALGORITHM

The conventional algorithm uses the distributive property, which makes it possible to do multiplication in a series of steps that yield partial products. Once all partial products are determined they are added to yield a complete product.

Students must have a good knowledge of the basic facts and of place value in the base-ten system before the multiplication algorithm is introduced. When children have the prerequisite knowledge, activities using familiar situations and appropriate place-value materials should be used. A lesson using books is described in Activity 10.16. Introductory lessons can be followed by cooperative-learning activities during which children use familiar place-value devices to portray multiplication sentences, as in Activity 10.17.

ACTIVITY 10.16   Introducing a Multiplication Algorithm

- Tell this story: "Carletta arranged some books in a bookcase. She found that 12 books fit on each of the three shelves. How many books did she put in the bookcase?"

- Display three sets, each with 12 books.

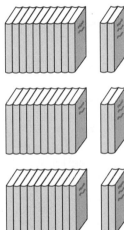

- Have students consider the situation and discuss ways to determine the answer. (Count the books, add 12 + 12 + 12, multiply 3 times 12.)

- Write the multiplication sentence: 3 × 12 = □.

- Write the algorithm:

$$\begin{array}{r} 12 \\ \times\ 3 \\ \hline \end{array}$$

- Separate the books so that each set shows ten books and two books.

- Ask, "How many books are there in these three parts of the sets?" (as you hold up the three groups of two books).

- Show the multiplication of three times two in the algorithm:

$$\begin{array}{r} 12 \\ \times\ 3 \\ \hline 6 \end{array}$$

- Ask, "How many books are there in these three parts of the sets? (as you point to the three groups of ten books).

- Show the multiplication of three times ten in the algorithm and add the partial products:

$$\begin{array}{r} 12 \\ \times\ 3 \\ \hline 6 \\ 30 \\ \hline 36 \end{array}$$

- Repeat with other collections of objects, such as boxed and loose pencils, empty milk cartons, and bundles of tongue depressors or popsicle sticks.

ACTIVITY 10.17 Using the Multiplication Algorithm 🔍 ⊘

- Organize the class into cooperative-learning groups.

- Give each group Cuisenaire or base-ten rods, an abacus, or beanstick materials, and three multiplication sentences, such as $6 \times 11 = \square$, $3 \times 13 = \square$, and $4 \times 22 = \square$.

- Each group should determine how to arrange its materials to represent one of the sentences, then make the arrangement. Once an arrangement is correctly made, have the group write an algorithm and show the answer with it.

- Have the groups show their arrangements of the place-value materials and explain the algorithm for each sentence to their classmates.

Figure 10.12 shows each sentence represented with a place-value device. The use of a variety of place-value materials rather than of a single model is recommended because a model that is meaningful to one child may not have the same meaning for another child. Under a teacher's careful guidance, most children will have each step in the algorithm clarified by one or several of the models.

Another way to show the algorithm is with expanded notation. This way may make the procedure clearer to some students.

$$
\begin{array}{r}
10 + 1 \\
\times \quad\quad 6 \\
\hline
60 + 6 = 66
\end{array}
$$

Figure 10-12
Place-value materials represent three multiplication algorithms: (a) Unifix cubes, (b) abacus, and (c) base-ten rods

After multiplication with numbers like the ones above, examples that have numbers larger than 100 and require no regrouping can be introduced. No particular difficulties are involved in this type of multiplication by children who have a good knowledge of the base-ten numeration system

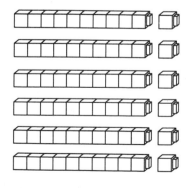

(a)

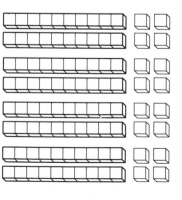

(b)

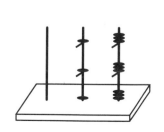

(c)

and multiplication with two-place numbers. They can use an abacus or other structured materials to demonstrate the process for examples like these:

$$
\begin{array}{r} 123 \\ \times\ 3 \\ \hline \end{array}
\qquad
\begin{array}{r} 241 \\ \times\ 2 \\ \hline \end{array}
\qquad
\begin{array}{r} 342 \\ \times\ 2 \\ \hline \end{array}
$$

■ MULTIPLICATION WITH REGROUPING

$$
\begin{array}{r} 27 \\ \times\ 2 \\ \hline 14 \\ 40 \\ \hline 54 \end{array}
$$

$$
\begin{array}{r} 27 \\ \times\ 2 \\ \hline 54 \end{array}
$$

As in all cases when new steps in a process are presented, meaningful materials should be used when children are introduced to multiplication with regrouping. Students should use these materials as they explore and discuss the meanings of the steps involved in regrouping. Arrays and base-ten materials are used in Activities 10.18 and 10.19.

During early work on multiplication with regrouping it may be helpful to show both partial products in full and then add them to determine the final product, as shown in the first example in the margin. Later, students should combine the two partial products into one, as shown in the second example.

ACTIVITY 10.18   Regrouping in Multiplication

- Organize students for a cooperative-learning experience.

- Write a sentence and algorithm on the chalkboard.

$$
7 \times 14 = \square
\qquad
\begin{array}{r} 14 \\ \times\ 7 \\ \hline \end{array}
$$

- Allow time for each group to use 1-centimeter or quarter-inch-squared paper to make a

- 7-by-14 array and figure out how to use it to determine the product for the sentence and algorithm.

- Repeat with examples such as 3×26, 6×12, and 4×24.

- Each group should arrive at a jointly prepared explanation of how the array illustrates the steps in each algorithm.

ACTIVITY 10.19   Regrouping with Base-Ten Materials

- Give base-ten materials to each group of two or three students.

- Write an algorithm on the chalkboard.

$$\begin{array}{r} 24 \\ \times\ 3 \\ \hline \end{array}$$

- Have each group show the numbers on their materials.

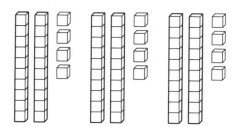

- Discuss the first step in regrouping. (Combine the ones cubes.) Ask, "How many cubes are there after they are combined?" (12.) "What must be done with the 12 cubes?" (They must be regrouped as 10 + 2.)

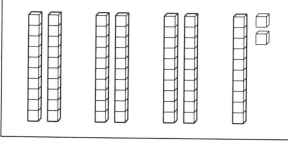

- Ask, "What do we do now?" (Combine the tens rods.) "How many rods are there when they are combined?" (7.) "What is the product of 3 times 24?" (72.)

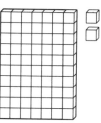

- Relate each step with the base-ten materials to each step in the algorithm.

$$\begin{array}{r} 24 \\ \times\ 3 \\ \hline \end{array} \qquad \begin{array}{r} \overset{1}{2}4 \\ \times\ 3 \\ \hline 2 \end{array} \qquad \begin{array}{r} \overset{1}{2}4 \\ \times\ 3 \\ \hline 72 \end{array}$$

- Repeat with examples like 4 × 13 = ☐ and 5 × 12 = ☐.

■ MULTIPLICATION WITH NUMBERS LARGER THAN TEN

$$\begin{array}{r} 53 \\ \times\ 36 \\ \hline 318 \\ 159 \\ \hline 1908 \end{array}$$

The commonly used algorithm for multiplying two numbers larger than ten is shown in the margin. Students build on their knowledge of expanded notation and multiplication of a two-place number by a one-place number to develop understanding of this algorithm. Start with an algorithm such as in (a):

```
        14          14          14
       ×12         × 12        × 12
                     8          28
                    20         140
                    40         168
                   100
                   168

       (a)         (b)         (c)
```

To multiply these numbers, students should think of the multiplier as $10 + 2$ and the multiplicand as $10 + 4$. When the multiplication has been completed, there will be four partial products, as shown in (b). By seeing each of the partial products separately, children are more likely to recognize that there are four separate pairs of numbers to multiply. Later the process is shortened so that only two partial products are written (c).

When partial products are indicated in the algorithm in the most mature form, the "0" is not written in the ones place of the second partial product. The "14" is written with the "4" in the tens place of the second partial product to show that it represents 14 tens. Children should realize that the zero is omitted only as a time-saving technique. Development of the algorithm in a sequence of steps enable them to understand why the numbers are written as they are in the final form.

```
   14
 × 12
   28
   14
  168
```

Regrouping

Multiplication that requires regrouping is taught after children understand how to multiply two two-place numbers with no regrouping. During early work with regrouping, students can write each partial product, as in the example in (a). In (b) the partial products from multiplying 8 times 36 are combined to give the first partial product—288. The partial products from multiplying by 40 are added as they are written, giving the second partial product—1,440. The mental addition required for this kind of multiplication should be learned through activities that develop students' skills with addition of a one-place number to a two-place number. Ways to do this are discussed in Chapter 9.

```
        36          36
      × 48        × 48
        48         288
       240        1440
       240        1728
      1200
      1728

       (a)         (b)
```

Large amounts of time should not be devoted to multiplication involving three-place and larger numbers. Once children understand the multiplication algorithm and how it works, a calculator should be used for computation with larger numbers.

▪ ESTIMATION AND MENTAL COMPUTATION

Rounded numbers are an efficient way to estimate products for two- and three-place numbers. To estimate the product of two two-place numbers, round each one to the nearer ten and multiply the rounded numbers, as in (a). Round two three-place numbers to the nearer hundred and multiply the rounded numbers, as in (b).

$$
\begin{array}{rr}
67 & 70 \\
\times\ 32 & \times\ 30 \\
\hline
& 2{,}100
\end{array}
\qquad
\begin{array}{rr}
483 & 500 \\
\times\ \ 731 & \times\ \ 700 \\
\hline
& 350{,}000
\end{array}
$$

         (a)   (b)

Front-end addition to estimate sums is described in Chapter 9. A front-end process works equally well to estimate products. The usual order for completing the algorithm in the margin is to multiply four times the number in the ones place, the tens place, and the hundreds place. A front-end estimate of the product begins in the largest place-value position rather than the smallest. The process is to think, "Four times 300 is 1,200." In this example, front-end estimation using just the largest place-value position gives the same result as rounding 348 to the nearer hundred and multiplying by four. The front-end estimate can be improved by adding the result of multiplying four times 40 to 1,200, giving an estimate of 1,360. This estimate is slightly less than the actual product.[12]

$$
\begin{array}{r}
348 \\
\times\ \ 4 \\
\hline
\end{array}
$$

The front-end multiplication process can also be used to mentally compute exact answers. To multiply 4×34 mentally, think: "Four times 30 is 120, four times four equals 16, 120 plus 16 is 136." A teacher can encourage students to multiply mentally by showing them how to use front-end multiplication with examples like these:

$$
\begin{array}{ccccc}
27 & 42 & 94 & 87 & 62 \\
\times\ 8 & \times\ 7 & \times\ 6 & \times\ 3 & \times\ 5 \\
\hline
\end{array}
$$

▪ CALCULATOR ACTIVITIES

Calculator activities that involve multiplication can be used to enhance students' problem-solving skills. The machine simplifies work so students can concentrate on the problem-solving aspects of each situation rather than toiling over time-consuming computation. Activities 10.20 and 10.21 introduce students to two interesting investigations.

ACTIVITY 10.20   Multiplying 27

- Have students work in pairs.
- Give them these written instructions:

  1. List the products for the combinations at the right.

  2. Study the sequence of numbers in the hundreds and ones places in the products as you go down the list. Write sentences that explain what you discover.

  3. Study the sequence in the tens place as you go down the list. Write a sentence that describes this sequence.

  4. Select any product, say 486 (18 × 27). Rearrange the digits by putting the "6" ahead of the "48." Is 648 divisible by 27? Put the "4" after the "86." Is 864 divisible by 27?

  5. Rearrange two other products in the same way. Is each different arrangement divisible by 27?

  6. What sequence of steps can you use on the calculator when you use 27 as a factor with several numbers so that you do not need to key in 27 each time you multiply?

  3 × 27
  6 × 27
  9 × 27
  12 × 27
  15 × 27
  18 × 27
  21 × 27
  24 × 27
  27 × 27
  30 × 27

ACTIVITY 10.21   Multiplying by 101

- Have students work in pairs.
- Give them these written instructions:

  1. Select a number greater than 10 and less than 100. Multiply the number by 101. Write the product.

  2. Select five other numbers and multiply each of them by 101. Write their products.

  3. Write a sentence that describes the digits in each of the products.

  4. Can you figure out why the digits are repeated in each of the numbers you chose? *Hint:* 101 can be renamed as 100 + 1.

  5. By what number will you multiply a factor that is between 100 and 1000 to get repeating digits in the product?[13]

■ INTRODUCING A DIVISION ALGORITHM

$$\begin{array}{r} 46 \\ 3\overline{)138} \\ \underline{12} \\ 18 \\ \underline{18} \end{array}$$

The standard division algorithm for the sentence $138 \div 3 = 46$ is shown in the margin. Before students can perform it with complete understanding, they must know and understand certain basic concepts and skills. These include (1) knowledge of both partitive and measurement division situations, (2) knowledge of multiplication and division facts, (3) ability to subtract, and (4) ability to multiply and divide by ten and its powers and multiples.

Situations teachers can use to promote understanding of the division algorithm abound. The activities and discussions that follow demonstrate a progression of lessons teachers can use over a period of time to help students understand how to divide with the standard algorithm. An activity such as Activity 10.22 can be used to introduce division by numbers smaller than ten.

"Think-back" flash cards will help develop children's skills in determining quotients. The card for 79 divided by 8 is shown in Figure 10.13. The front of the card (a) shows the division algorithm without the quotient, and

---

ACTIVITY 10.22   A Division Algorithm

- Present this situation: "Twenty-eight marbles will be shared equally by six children. How many marbles will each child get?"

- Have students suggest objects from their mathematics boxes to represent the 28 marbles. (They might even suggest marbles, if they know they are available.)

- Ask, "How can we use our materials to find out how many marbles each child will get?" (We can distribute them until each child has the same number.) Have one student distribute the objects to six classmates; there will be four objects left over.

- Show the algorithm for this situation:

$$6\overline{)28}$$

- Help the students develop a strategy for determining quotients without using concrete aids. One strategy is to relate division to multiplication. For this example, use these facts:

$6 \times 1 = 6, 6 \times 2 = 12, 6 \times 3 = 18,$
$6 \times 4 = 24, 6 \times 5 = 30$

- Ask, "Will each child get at least one marble?" "At least two marbles?" "At least three marbles?" "At least four marbles?" "At least five marbles?" Students will see that the answer is four marbles because there are not enough for each one to get five.

- Complete the algorithm:

$$\begin{array}{r} 4 \\ 6\overline{)28} \\ \underline{24} \\ 4 \end{array}$$

- Ask, "What does the '4' in the quotient mean?" (The number of marbles each child will get.) "What does the '4' at the bottom mean?" (The marbles that are left after each child gets a fair share.)

Figure 10-13
Example of a think-back flashcard.
(a) Front shows the division algorithm.
(b) Back shows the associated basic fact.

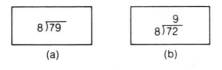

(a)

(b)

the back (b) shows the basic fact associated with the division. A student is shown the card and then thinks back to the related division fact and says, "Seventy-two divided by eight equals nine." (Avoid the expression "eight goes into 72 nine times.") When a student cannot think back to the correct basic fact, reverse the card so he or she can read it. Then show the front of the card again and have the student repeat the statement of the basic fact. Frequent group and individual work with these cards will help make children skillful in naming quotients.

Children's next work is usually with division that yields a quotient greater than ten without regrouping. In Activity 10.23, 48 ÷ 4 = 12 is the example. The dialogue used here suggests the types of questions a teacher should ask to help students develop their understanding of the process.

ACTIVITY 10.23   Division with No Regrouping

■ Present a situation: "John has 48 stamps that he is going to mount for a display at school. He plans to mount four stamps on a card. How many cards will he use?"

■ Write the algorithm for this situation:

$$4\overline{)48}$$

■ Use a dialogue similar to this to help students understand the algorithm:

T: "What does the 48 stand for?"

S: "The number of stamps John has."

T: "What does the 4 stand for?"

S: "The number of stamps for each card."

T: "Does John need at least ten cards?"

S: "Yes."

T: "How do you know?"

S: "Ten cards will hold 40 stamps; John has more than 40 stamps."

T: "Will he need at least 20 cards?"

S: "No, 20 cards will hold 80 stamps; he doesn't have that many."

T: "After John puts four stamps on each of ten cards, how many stamps will be left to be mounted?"

S: "Eight."

T: "How many cards will he need for the eight stamps?"

S: "Two."

T: "How many cards does he need for the 48 stamps?"

S: "Twelve."

■ During the discussion, relate each step in the algorithm with the question it answers.

```
 4)48
   40 | 10 × 4
    8
    8 | 2 × 4
```

■ Repeat with similar examples.

At this stage each partial quotient is shown with the divisor alongside the product rather than at the top of the algorithm. This makes its meaning clearer to students than when it is written at the top in the conventional manner. The change to writing quotients at the top will occur later.

■ DIVISION WITH REGROUPING

Regrouping is required in a two-place number when the number in the tens place is not a multiple of the divisor.

Using Concrete-Manipulative Models

Concrete-manipulative place-value materials can be used to illustrate the need for regrouping, as in Activity 10.24.

An Algorithm Form

$$3\overline{)45} \\ \underline{30} \mid 10 \times 3$$

(a)

$$\begin{array}{r} 1 \\ 3\overline{)45} \\ \underline{30} \end{array}$$

(b)

$$4\overline{)56} \\ \underline{40} \mid 10 \times 4 \\ 16$$

(a)

$$4\overline{)56} \\ \underline{40} \mid 10 \times 4 \\ 16 \\ \underline{16} \mid 4 \times 4$$

(b)

The algorithm form used for division with no regrouping is recommended for children's first work with regrouping. This form is beneficial because:

1. Each part of the quotient is shown in its complete form. In the example in the margin (a), the ten is shown as a "10" at the right, rather than as a "1" in the tens place above the dividend.

2. Multiplication is shown in a familiar form, 10×3, rather than in the abbreviated form shown in the margin (b).

3. The product of ten and three is shown as "30" beneath the dividend rather than as "3" in the tens place.

This form of the algorithm helps students see the meaning of the steps performed, because the different parts of the algorithm can be directly related to actions with beansticks or other manipulative materials.

A sufficient number of examples with dialogues such as the following will help students understand the algorithm.

T: "Will there be as many as ten fours in 56?"

S: "Yes, because ten times four is 40; 40 is less than 56."

T: "Will there be as many as 20 fours in 56?"

S: "No, because 20 times four is 80; 80 is more than 56."

T: "Let us show [in (a) in the margin] that ten times four equals 40 and then subtract 40 from 56 to see how much is left to be divided. What is 56 minus 40?"

ACTIVITY 10.24   Division with Regrouping

- Present a situation: "Gloria had 45 walnuts to put into three bags. How many walnuts will she put in each bag?"

- Have students suggest place-value models to represent the walnuts. (Beansticks, Cuisenaire or base-ten materials, bundled and loose tongue depressors, and an abacus might be mentioned.)

- Have pairs of students select the materials or device they will use. (Beansticks illustrate the process here.)

- Say, "Show 45 with your place-value materials."

- "Can you divide the four tens evenly by three?" (No.)

- Show the students how to separate three of the tens into three separate groups. "How many tens are left over?" (One.)

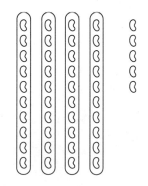

- "What can you do with the ten that is left over so you can divide it into three groups that are the same size?" (Exchange it for ten ones and put them with the five ones.)

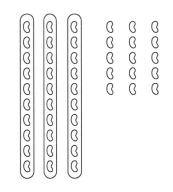

- "How many will be in each group when we divide 15 into three groups?" (Five.)

- "How many walnuts in each bag?" (15.)

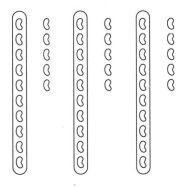

- Repeat with these divisions: 56 ÷ 4, 52 ÷ 2, 78 ÷ 6.

s: "Sixteen."

t: "What is 16 divided by four?"

s: "Four."

t: "We can show that in the algorithm too [in margin example (b)]. Now what is the answer to 56 divided by four?"

s: "Fourteen."

■ DIVISION WITH TWO-PLACE DIVISORS

Prerequisites to learning to divide by two-place divisors are a good understanding of division by one-place divisors and the ability to multiply by ten and its powers and multiples.

Two-Place Divisors and One-Place Quotients

Students' first work with two-place divisors is usually done with divisors that are multiples of ten. Previously understood patterns can be used to help develop skill in performing this division. Students should study patterns such as these so they can make generalizations about multiplying and dividing by ten and its multiples and 100 and its multiples.

$$1 \times 10 = 10 \qquad 10 \div 10 = 1$$
$$2 \times 10 = 20 \qquad 20 \div 10 = 2$$
$$3 \times 10 = 30 \qquad 30 \div 10 = 3$$
$$\cdot \qquad\qquad \cdot$$
$$\cdot \qquad\qquad \cdot$$
$$\cdot \qquad\qquad \cdot$$
$$9 \times 10 = 90 \qquad 90 \div 10 = 9$$

$$1 \times 100 = 100 \qquad 100 \div 100 = 1$$
$$2 \times 100 = 200 \qquad 200 \div 100 = 2$$
$$3 \times 100 = 300 \qquad 300 \div 100 = 3$$
$$\cdot \qquad\qquad \cdot$$
$$\cdot \qquad\qquad \cdot$$
$$\cdot \qquad\qquad \cdot$$
$$9 \times 100 = 900 \qquad 900 \div 100 = 9$$

Work with patterns like these will help students reach these generalizations:

_____ones × tens = _____tens   _____ones × hundreds = _____hundreds

_____tens ÷ tens = _____ones   _____hundreds ÷ hundreds = _____ones

So, for $270 \div 30 = \square$, the 27 tens are divided by 3 tens to determine that nine is the quotient.

A multiplication pattern is useful for determining answers for divisions, such as these, that have remainders:

$$1 \times 30 = 30 \qquad 2 \times 30 = 60 \qquad 3 \times 30 = 90$$
$$4 \times 30 = 120 \qquad 5 \times 30 = 150$$

$$30\overline{)123} \qquad 30\overline{)98} \qquad 30\overline{)72} \qquad 30\overline{)131}$$

The multiplication pattern shows that the quotient for the first example will be 4; it will be 3 for the second example; it will be 2 for the third example; and it will be 4 for the final example.

Because not all divisors are multiples of ten, strategies for estimating quotients for nonmultiples must be learned. A useful strategy is to round the divisor to the nearer ten and use multiples of the number:

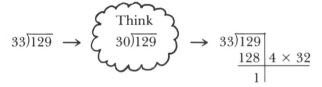

This process does not always yield the correct quotient.

$$33\overline{)129} \quad \rightarrow \quad \left(\text{Think} \atop 30\overline{)129}\right) \quad \rightarrow \quad 33\overline{)129} \atop \underline{132} \; | \; 4 \times 33$$

In this instance four times 33 yields a product that is larger than the dividend. Students must learn to adjust the quotient to correct the too-large figure by using a smaller number, in this case three.

Quotients with Two Digits

Real-world situations that students can easily visualize help them understand division involving larger numbers. By now students should be able to work without place-value models of the situations, but continued use of dialogues will enable most students to visualize the meaning of an algorithm. If students have a good understanding of the meaning of division, know how to multiply by tens and powers of ten, and know how to use the algorithm with smaller numbers, the first work they do with two-place divisors need not be restricted to examples that have one-place quotients. In the example in Activity 10.25, the quotient is larger than ten, but because of the setting in which it is considered and the dialogue, it is not overwhelming to students.

ACTIVITY 10.25 Bagging Oranges

- Present a problem situation: "A farmer has 288 oranges to bag for market. If she puts them into 24 bags, how many oranges will be in each bag?"

- Write a division sentence and algorithm for the situation:

$$288 \div 24 = \square \qquad 24\overline{)288}$$

- Use a dialogue similar to this to help students solve the problem and learn the algorithm.

  T: "What does the 288 stand for?"

  S: "The total number of oranges."

  T: "What does the 24 stand for?"

  S: "The number of bags into which oranges will be put."

  T: "Will there be at least ten oranges in each bag?"

  S: "Yes, because 24 times ten equals 240 and there are more than 240 oranges."

  T: "Will there be as many as 20 oranges in each bag?"

  S: "No, because 24 times 20 is 480 and there are not that many oranges."

- Show the result of putting ten oranges in each bag in the algorithm:

$$\begin{array}{r|l} 24\overline{)288} \\ 240 & 24 \times 10 \end{array}$$

  - Continue the dialogue:

  T: "After ten oranges have been put in each bag, how many are left to be bagged?"

  S: "48." (Help students determine this response, if necessary.)

- Show the algorithm with the remainder:

$$\begin{array}{r|l} 24\overline{)288} \\ 240 & 24 \times 10 \\ \hline 48 \end{array}$$

- Continue the dialogue:

  T: "Are there enough oranges to put one more in each bag?"

  S: "Yes, because that would only use 24 of the remaining oranges."

  T: "Can we put two more in each bag?"

  S: "Yes, because 24 × 2 equals 48; there are that many oranges."

  T: "The 48 oranges have been put in the 24 bags. I'll show that in the algorithm."

$$\begin{array}{r|l} 24\overline{)288} \\ 240 & 24 \times 10 \\ \hline 48 \\ 48 & 24 \times 2 \end{array}$$

  T: "When we add the ten and the two, we find that the farmer put 12 oranges in each of the 24 bags. So, 288 divided by 24 equals 12."

- Relate each numeral in the algorithm to the problem situation so that students will understand each one's meaning. Ask questions like, "What does the 240 in the algorithm mean?" (It represents the number of oranges that have been bagged after ten have been put in each bag.) What does the 48 stand for? (It stands for the number of oranges left to be bagged after 240 have been put in bags.)

- Repeat with similar problems until the algorithm is clear to students.

Estimating Quotients

Skills in determining quotients must be continually refined as numbers increase in size. The dialogue in Activity 10.26 suggests one way to help students estimate the size of quotients. Students who learn to make accurate estimates do not find it difficult to determine where to place the first quotient figure in an algorithm.

ACTIVITY 10.26   Estimating Quotients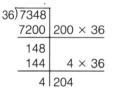

- Begin with an algorithm:

$$36\overline{)7348}$$

- Ask questions similar to these:

  T: "Are there at least ten thirty-sixes in 7,348?"

  S: "Yes. Ten times 36 is 360; that is less than 7,348."

  T: "Are there as many as 100 thirty-sixes in 7,348?"

  S: "Yes; 100 times 36 is 3,600; that is less than 7,348?"

  T: "Are there as many as 1,000 thirty-sixes in 7,348?"

  S: "No, 1,000 times 36 is 36,000; that is more than 7,348."

  T: "We know that the answer will be more than 100 but less than 1,000. Will there be 200 thirty-sixes in 7,348?"

  S: "Yes, 200 times 36 is 7,200, which is less than 7,348."

  T: "Will there be 300 thirty-sixes in 7,348?"

  S: "No, 300 times 36 is 10,800, which is too many."

- Show this step in the algorithm:

$$
\begin{array}{r|l}
36\overline{)7348} & \\
7200 & 200 \times 36 \\
\hline
148 &
\end{array}
$$

- Continue the dialogue:

  T: "After we multiply 36 by 200 and subtract, we have a remainder of 148. How many thirty-sixes are there in 148?"

  S: "There are four."

- Complete the algorithm:

$$
\begin{array}{r|l}
36\overline{)7348} & \\
7200 & 200 \times 36 \\
\hline
148 & \\
144 & 4 \times 36 \\
\hline
4 & 204
\end{array}
$$

- Review the meaning of each term in the algorithm, including the undivided remainder.
- Repeat with similar examples.

Shortened Forms

Older students will refine the division process so that the algorithm is used in more mature ways. In these refined forms the notation that is written is lessened. For example, the estimation process just described will help students determine where to put the first quotient figure in the algorithm for examples like these:

$$39\overline{)4869} \qquad 86\overline{)6243} \qquad 73\overline{)7421} \qquad 26\overline{)2438}$$

When estimation is used to determine whether the first quotient figure goes in the hundreds or the tens place, students know the approximate size of a quotient before they use the algorithm. In the first example, 100 times 39 is less than 4,869, so the first quotient figure goes in the hundreds place. In the second example, 100 times 86 is greater than 6,243, so the first quotient figure goes in the tens place. Where does the first quotient figure go in each of the other examples?

Once students can readily determine where to place the first quotient figure, they can begin to shorten steps in the algorithm. For the first example above, they can round the divisor to 40 to estimate that the first quotient figure is more than 100 but less than 200; so "100" is placed above the dividend and the product of 100 and 39 is placed beneath the dividend [see (a) below]. The number of thirty-nines in 960 is written as 20 above the dividend, and the product is written beneath the dividend, as in (b). The 780 is subtracted from 969. Finally, the number of thirty-nines in 189 is determined and written above the dividend. The product of four and 39 is subtracted from 189 and the remainder, 33, is written in the algorithm (c).

```
                                                          4
                                   20                    20
           100                    100                   100
       39)4869                 39)4869               39)4869
          3900                   3900                  3900
           969                    969                   969
                                  780                   780
                                  189                   189
                                                        156
                                                         33

          (a)                     (b)                   (c)
```

Children should learn how to reduce the written work still more, until finally they write the standard algorithm, as seen in (d).

```
          248r10
      32)7946
         64
         154
         128
         266
         256
          10

          (d)
```

There are students who understand the meaning of division and can determine when to use it in problem situations but who still have difficulty computing with an algorithm. These students should not be burdened with many time-consuming paper-and-pencil exercises in an effort to improve their computing skills; it is better to allow them to use a calculator to perform computation. It is recommended that no students spend time using an algorithm to compute with three- and four-place divisors. All students should use a calculator to do division that involves such numbers.

EXERCISE Describe how understanding multiplication problems such as 20 × 30, 500 × 40, 17 × 100, and 90 × 70 helps children when calculating and estimating answers for longer division and multiplication problems.

HANDLING REMAINDERS IN DIVISION

When the divisor is not a whole number factor of the dividend, a remainder occurs. From the first examples in division, students will work with problems that have remainders. In story and real-life situations remainders have different meanings, depending on the nature of the situation in which the division takes place. Children need to develop number sense about division and handle remainders according to situations, not by rule. The following situations illustrate four different ways to treat remainders.

- "There are 32 children in our class. If we play a game that requires three equal-sized teams, how many players will be on each team?" A paper-and-pencil-computed answer is 10r2. A calculator-computed answer is 10.666666. Either way, the quotient for this partitive situation is ten, with something left over. Since each team must have the same number of players, the answer is ten.

- "Sixty-eight apples are to be put in boxes. If each box holds eight apples, how many full boxes will there be?" This measurement situation is similar to the preceding partitive situation. The paper-and-pencil answer is 8r4, while a calculator answer is 8.5. There are enough apples to fill eight boxes, and there will be four apples, or one-half of a box, left over. In this and the preceding situation, the remainder is disregarded.

- "Jamelda baked 26 cookies, which she shared equally with three friends. How many did each one get?" The paper-and-pencil answer to this partitive situation is 6r2. There are four groups of six cookies, with two left over. The two cookies can be cut in two, so the remainder can be written as ½. A calculator already shows 6.5, which can be expressed as 6½. The acceptable answer is 6½.

- "It costs 79 cents for three note pads. What is the price of one pad?" The paper-and-pencil answer is 26r1, while a calculator answer is 26.333333. In this partitive situation the whole number quotient is 26, with something left over. Children should understand that a store is not likely to sell one pad for 26 cents, because then the price would be three pads for 78 cents. For this example, the answer needs to be changed to 27 cents when the price of one item is determined.

- "A group of 53 children will ride to camp in minivans. If each van can carry six children and their gear, how many vans will be used?" The answers to this measurement situation are 8r5 or 8.833333. The remainder shows that there are children without transportation after eight vans have been filled with six children each. One more van will be used to accommodate the five remaining children. Altogether, nine vans are used.

■ SUMMARY

There are three interpretations of multiplication with which children become acquainted. Each one can be demonstrated with story situations and manipulative materials to make them meaningful. These interpretations are repeated addition, the array, and Cartesian product. Repeated addition is used most often to introduce multiplication because it can be related to the already-understood addition operation. Arrays are an orderly arrangement of objects in rows and are easily represented by objects such as disks and dot patterns. Cartesian products result from situations in which all of the ordered pairs that result from matching each element in one set with each element in another set are determined.

Two types of situations give rise to division: measurement and partitive situations. Children should be introduced to both types through meaningful real-life problems and manipulative-material activities. Strategies for teaching basic facts and helping children learn them include use of the multiplication table, which can be used to show that there are relatively few facts that are difficult to remember, the special characteristic of nine as a factor, and relating divisors to multiplication with practice materials. There are many practice materials for learning basic facts, including flash cards, cassette tapes, and calculator and computer activities.

The basic properties of multiplication—commutativity, associativity, distribution of multiplication over addition, and the roles of one and zero—can be presented through activities with markers, arrays, multiplication tables, number lines, blocks, and other materials.

Care must be taken when children are taught to use algorithms for multiplication and division so the algorithms' meanings and applications will be clear. Materials to use include place-value devices, markers for magnetic or flannel boards, arrays, and structured materials. Real-life story problems play an important role in making applications of algorithms. Estimation by rounding and a front-end process are used to determine approximate answers for multiplication. The front-end process can be used to compute some multiplication answers mentally. Students should use calculators to compute answers for both multiplication and division with large numbers. Division situations frequently result in answers with remainders other than zero. Students should learn to handle remainders according to the nature of the situation, rather than by rule alone.

STUDY QUESTIONS AND ACTIVITIES

1. NCTM Standard 8 (Whole Number Computation) for Grades K–4 states that students should ". . . develop reasonable proficiency with basic facts. . . ." Write a statement in which you give your interpretation of what is "reasonable proficiency with basic facts" for multiplication and division.

2. NCTM Standard 2 (Mathematics as Communication) for Grades 5–8 states that students should have opportunities to model situations using oral, written, concrete, and pictorial means of communication. Write the number and title of activities in this chapter that promote each of the different means of communication cited in this standard. Identify the means of communication promoted by each activity.

3. Activity 10.14 discusses the associative property for multiplication. Multiplication sentences for three different solids containing 24 cubes are used in the activity. All possible ways of writing sentences for a $2 \times 3 \times 4$ arrangement of blocks are shown. Write all of the possible ways of writing multiplication sentences for the $2 \times 6 \times 2$ and the $1 \times 12 \times 2$ arrangements of blocks.

4. Dialogues are used in this chapter to illustrate how a teacher can help students develop an understanding of the conventional division algorithm. Write a word problem for each of these sentences: $216 \div 12 = 18$ and $645 \div 15 = 43$. Have one problem represent a measurement situation and one represent a partitive situation. Identify the type of situation that fits each problem. Write a dialogue similar to the one in Activity 10.23 for your measurement situation and a dialogue similar to the one in Activity 10.24 for your partitive situation. Include the step-by-step process for completing the algorithm for each situation.

5. Four ways of handling remainders in five different types of situations are explained in this chapter. Write a word problem for each type of situation. Identify each word problem as a measurement or partitive

situation. Explain how the remainder should be handled for each of your problems.

6. Frank Broadbent describes the lattice method of multiplying and dividing in an *Arithmetic Teacher* article (see the For Further Reading section). Read the article and use the algorithms to compute the answer for each of these sentences: $246 \times 195 = \square$ and $1176 \div 42 = \square$. Evaluate each algorithm in terms of its clarity and ease of use. Under what circumstances might you use one or both of these algorithms with children?

■ FOR FURTHER READING

Ando, Masue, and Hitoshi Ikeda. 1971, October. Learning multiplication facts—More than drill. *Arithmetic Teacher 18*(6), 359–364.

Presents activities that develop understanding of the basic multiplication facts, ways of organizing the facts in tables, and procedures for memorizing them.

Ashlock, Robert. 1977, April. Model switching: A consideration in the teaching of subtraction and division of whole numbers. *School Science and Mathematics 57*(4), 327–335.

Models are used to help children understand operations and their algorithms. Chips or blocks may be used to represent partitive and measurement division situations. Ashlock cautions teachers to use models consistently so that children do not become confused by discrepancies between how a model is used and the problem situation it represents.

Bolduc, Elroy J., Jr. 1980, November. The monsters of multiplication. *Arithmetic Teacher 28*(3), 24–26.

Ways to help children master the basic multiplication facts are discussed. Finger multiplication and the times table are suggested as worthwhile activities.

Broadbent, Frank W. 1987, January. Lattice multiplication and division. *Arithmetic Teacher 34*(5), 28–31.

The lattice algorithm was used in Europe in the early 1400s. A modern version of the algorithm for both multiplication and division is explained in this article. The author suggests that the lattice algorithm might substitute for the standard algorithms during instruction about multiplication and division.

Bruni, James V., and Helene J. Silverman. 1976, October. The multiplication facts: Once more, with understanding. *Arithmetic Teacher 23*(6), 402–409.

Several activities and games using arrays provide the means for developing understanding and memorization of the basic multiplication facts.

Cacha, Frances B. 1978, November. Exploring the multiplication table and beyond. *Arithmetic Teacher 26*(3), 46–48.

Careful study of the multiplication table reveals the properties of multiplication, information about odd and even factors, patterns on diagonals, and digit sums, all of which help children understand and master the facts.

Falco, Thomas. 1983, October. Multiplication clue: Game activity for the classroom. *Arithmetic Teacher 31*(2), 36–37.

Through dialogue and chalkboard examples, the author explains a game that requires students to analyze the teacher's responses to determine factors of numbers. The game helps students reinforce learning of the multiplication facts.

Huinker, DeAnn M. 1989, October. Multiplication and division word problems: Improving students' understanding. *Arithmetic Teacher 27*(2), 8–12.

Four examples of multiplication and division word problems and how they were presented to children are discussed. The activities are illustrated. The result of the process described was that students developed a solid understanding of the concepts involved in each story problem.

Jensen, Robert J. 1987, October. Teaching mathematics with technology: Division in the early grades. *Arithmetic Teacher 35*(2), 50–52.

A Logo computer program, included in the article, introduces early primary-grade children to the concept of division. Both partitive and measurement situations are illustrated by the program.

———. 1987, November. Teaching mathematics with technology: Multiples. *Arithmetic Teacher 35*(3), 52–53.

Computer and calculator activities that focus on multiples are described.

———. 1988, January. Teaching mathematics with technology: Introducing factors with a tiling simulation. *Arithmetic Teacher 35*(5), 36–38.

A Logo computer program, which is included in the article, is used so that students can perform in a simulated situation in which they are floor tilers seeking tiles of the appropriate sizes for different rooms. It is only when tiles with appropriate sizes are selected that the computer illustrates how a properly tiled room will look.

Killion, Kurt, and Leslie P. Steffe. 1989, September. Research into practice: Children's multiplication. *Arithmetic Teacher 37*(1), 34–36.

The authors discuss how two children thought about equal-sized groups of objects and the impact of their thinking on their readiness to understand multiplication facts and algorithms. Among the conclusions is the advice that teachers need to understand children's ways of thinking about numbers and number situations before they begin instruction about new topics.

Meyer, Ruth A., and James E. Riley. 1986, April. Multiplication games. *Arithmetic Teacher 33*(8), 22–25.

Five multiplication games with different levels of difficulty are illustrated and described. Each one deals with multiplication facts.

Remington, Jim. 1989, November. Introducing multiplication. *Arithmetic Teacher 37*(3), 12–14, 60.

This third-grade teacher introduces multiplication with paper plates and markers. The process from introduction to drill-and-practice activities is described.

Robold, Alice I. 1983, April. Grid arrays for multiplication. *Arithmetic Teacher 30*(8), 14–17.

Arrays are commonly used to introduce multiplication. Ways to use them with larger numbers are described in this article.

Rubenstein, Rheta. 1987, May. Estimation and mental calculation: Compatible numbers. *Arithmetic Teacher 34*(9), 24–25.

Procedures that will help students learn to estimate and mentally compute products and quotients using compatible numbers are presented. Ways to use an overhead projector and processes for testing students' skills are included.

Schoen, Harold L. 1987, February. Estimation and mental computation: Front-end estimation. *Arithmetic Teacher 34*(6), 28–29.

> *Front-end estimation is the focus of this article. Processes for operations other than multiplication and division are included.*

Smith, C. Winston, Jr. 1974, December. Tiger-bite cards and blank arrays. *Arithmetic Teacher 21*(8), 679–682.

> *Arrays with "bites" taken from them serve as a basis for students' searches for missing factors when totals (products) and number of rows (given factors) are known. The cards lead to a useful way of investigating the meaning of the division algorithm.*

Stuart, Maureen, and Barbara Bestgen. 1982, January. Productive pieces: Exploring multiplication on the overhead. *Arithmetic Teacher 29*(5), 22–23.

> *An overhead projector, a transparent grid, and colored transparent rectangles that fit the grid serve to develop students' understanding of multiplication. The materials make a nice tie-in between semiconcrete materials and the abstract multiplication table.*

Sundar, Viji K. 1990, March. Thou shalt not divide by zero. *Arithmetic Teacher 37*(7), 50–51.

> *Sundar discusses four examples of activities designed to help students understand why zero is not used as a divisor.*

Trafton, Paul R., and Judy Zawojewski. 1989, April. Estimation and mental computation: Rounding wisely. *Arithmetic Teacher 24*(8), 36–37.

> *The article suggests ways to help students learn to round numbers sensibly to fit a situation. Ideas for teaching rounding, how to adjust estimates, and decision making are presented. The authors cite a situation where an estimator might be penalized for using flexible estimation processes on a published test.*

◼ NOTES

[1] National Council of Teachers of Mathematics. 1989. *Curriculum and Evaluation Standards for School Mathematics.* Reston, VA: National Council of Teachers of Mathematics, 36. Used by permission.

[2] NCTM, 41. Used by permission.

[3] NCTM, 44. Used by permission.

[4] NCTM, 60. Used by permission.

[5] NCTM, 91. Used by permission.

[6] NCTM, 94. Used by permission.

[7] Marilyn J. Zweng. 1964, December. Division problems and the concept of rate. *Arithmetic Teacher 11*(8), 547–556.

[8] These two activities are adapted from Larry Leutzinger. 1981. *Strategies for Learning the Basic Facts.* Cedar Falls: Iowa Council of Teachers of Mathematics, 45, 50.

[9] Dorsett Educational Systems, P.O. Box 1226, Norman, OK 73070.

[10] Optimum Resources, Inc., 10 Station Place, Norwalk, CT 06058.

[11] Queue, Inc., 562 Boston Ave., Bridgeport, CT 06610.

[12] For further information about front-end multiplication, see Barbara S. Reys. 1986. Teaching computational estimation: Concepts and strategies, in 1986 Yearbook *Estimation and Mental Computation*. Reston, VA: National Council of Teachers of Mathematics, 38.

[13] This activity is adapted from Janet Morris. 1981. *How to Develop Problem Solving Using a Calculator*. Reston, VA: National Council of Teachers of Mathematics, 14.

CHAPTER 11

Informal Geometry

Geometry has long been part of the elementary school curriculum. For many years students have recognized and named common plane and space figures, measured angles, and learned some definitions. Geometry plays a more central role in elementary school mathematics today. The writers who prepared the National Council of Teachers of Mathematics standard on geometry and spatial sense said: "Geometry helps us represent and describe in an orderly manner the world in which we live. Children are naturally interested in geometry and find it intriguing and motivating; their spatial capabilities frequently exceed their numerical skills, and tapping these strengths can foster an interest in mathematics and improve number understandings and skills."[1] Experiences in geometry develop problem-solving and reasoning skills and support many other topics in mathematics.

In this chapter you will read about

1. why geometry plays an important part in elementary curriculum;

2. developmental stages in children's understanding of geometry;

3. plane shapes and activities that teach children about them;

4. activities for learning about points, lines, rays, and line segments;

5. solid figures and materials for learning about them;

6. motion geometry and how materials enhance understanding of transformations of shape;

7. activities for teaching about symmetry, congruence, and similarity;

8. coordinate geometry materials;

9. computer games and tools for learning about geometry.

NCTM STANDARDS THAT PERTAIN TO GEOMETRY

Kindergarten Through Grade Four

Standard 9: Geometry and Spatial Sense   In grades K–4, the mathematics curriculum should include two- and three-dimensional geometry so that students can:

- describe, model, draw, and classify shapes;
- investigate and predict the results of combining, subdividing, and changing shapes;
- develop spatial sense;
- relate geometric ideas to number and measurement ideas;
- recognize and appreciate geometry in their world.[2]

Grades Five Through Eight

Standard 12: Geometry   In grades 5–8, the mathematics curriculum should include the study of the geometry of one, two, and three dimensions in a variety of situations so that students can:

- identify, describe, compare, and classify geometric figures;
- visualize and represent geometric figures with special attention to developing spatial sense;
- represent and solve problems using geometric models;
- understand and apply geometric properties and relationships;
- develop an appreciation of geometry as a means of describing the physical world.[3]

 ## RATIONALE FOR GEOMETRY

Knowledge of geometry enhances children's understanding of their world. Kindergarten and primary-grade children who develop good spatial abilities through activities like those discussed in Chapter 7 dealing with proximity, separation, order, and enclosure can comprehend their surroundings better than children whose spatial abilities are less developed. Children's misunderstandings of pictures and diagrams used in textbooks to portray important mathematical concepts are usually the result of their poor spatial abilities. Intermediate-grade children learn to appreciate both practical and aesthetic reasons for geometric forms. Art and design, space exploration, clothing and automobile design, and home planning and architecture are topics of interest to students that draw on and develop their geometric abilities.

Reasoning and communication are inherent in a study of elementary geometry. Activities and materials require that children describe geometric forms and generalize about them, search for patterns, organize data, and draw conclusions. Geometry connects mathematics to the real world. It provides a change of pace and gives variety to the mathematics program. Children get away from numbers and operations when they work with geometry materials. Materials for teaching geometry are easy to adapt for informal activities and lend themselves to investigations that students can pursue independently or cooperatively.

Many topics and skills in elementary schools depend on children's spatial sense. Fractions, measurement, estimation, positive and negative integers on a number line, map reading, and various concepts in science and social studies have a spatial quality. Manipulation of objects in space also provides background for understanding algebra, trigonometry, calculus, and many topics in higher mathematics that require spatial thinking. Many of the world's great scientists, mathematicians, and inventors—including Einstein—report that they "saw" how things worked before they were able to explain or prove their discoveries.

■ DESIGN FOR LEARNING GEOMETRY

Piaget believed that children's first understanding of geometry is based on the world around them. The child is at the center of that world and views everything in relation to his or her location or perspective. In Chapter 7, a number of activities in topological geometry that help children develop this early sense of space were described. Euclidean geometry deals with geometric shapes that have fixed characteristics and that do not change. By ages four and five, students can recognize plane Euclidean shapes such as squares and circles in their environment.

A husband and wife team of Dutch mathematicians spent many years investigating and describing how children develop their understanding of Euclidean forms. Dina van Hiele-Geldof and Pierre Marie von Hiele described a number of stages in children's geometric understanding.[4] They concluded that individuals pass through five stages of development similar to the stages of Piaget.

■ *Stage 0*—Visualization—recognizing and naming the figures

- ▪ *Stage 1*—Analysis—describing the attributes
- ▪ *Stage 2*—Informal deduction—classifying and generalizing by attributes
- ▪ *Stage 3*—Deduction—developing proofs using axioms and definitions
- ▪ *Stage 4*—Rigor—working in various geometrical systems

Elementary teachers should be familiar with the first three stages, which occur during the elementary school years, so that they can design appropriate geometry learning activities. The first stage occurs in children's early years, during kindergarten, and in the primary grades. Children learn to recognize and label common plane figures such as circles, squares, triangles, and rectangles. They also recognize simple solids such as cubes, spheres, pyramids, and cones. They may learn the correct terminology or they may call cubes and spheres by more familiar names, "boxes" and "balls."

During the second stage students become more proficient at describing the attributes of the shapes and solids. They use a mixture of precise terminology and their own linguistic inventions. A triangle has three sides and three points or corners. A sphere is a "ball" and is round all over, but a cone is round and flat on one end and "pointy" or has a "round point" on the other. A square has "straight" corners. Teachers should accept the children's language until the right times to suggest "sphere" and "square" or "90 degree" angle come. Children eventually learn the general characteristics and can specify the number of sides and angles in plane figures and the number of sides, or **faces,** and points, or **vertices,** in solid figures.

The third stage occurs when children are in the upper elementary grades. In this stage they are capable of classifying shapes according to their characteristics. They recognize that all four-sided figures are quadrilaterals, and that quadrilaterals come in irregular and regular forms. They can talk about whether a square is a rectangle or a rectangle is a square and why. They may be interested in the reasons why certain shapes fit together to make a design while other shapes do not. The questions and problems encountered in elementary school provide background for the later more formal, deductive study of geometry, including proofs.

The activities teachers plan for children's study of geometry should be developed with these stages of development in mind. **Informal** means that students are not expected to use deductive proofs. The program should be informal so that children can establish a foundation on which to build in future years.

■ PLANE FIGURES

Plane figures include circles and ellipses and polygons, which are **closed figures** composed of line segments. Circles and ellipses are two regular curved figures. Irregular curved figures take many fanciful shapes. The common polygons are triangles, rectangles, pentagons, hexagons, and octagons. All regular polygons have congruent sides and angles. Each shape has a unique name. Drawings in Figure 11.1 illustrate several regular and irregular plane figures.

Plane figures are commonly introduced in preschool and kindergarten. Children learn to identify and classify circles by their shape and use the name *circle*. This term designates round objects of any size. They learn that *square* and *rectangle* are labels used to identify.four-sided figures. At first children may label only equilateral triangles as *triangle*. They are familiar with equilateral triangles because they are normally the only type of triangle found in kindergarten and early-grade materials. Isosceles, square, and obtuse triangles do not look the same and may not be "triangles" to some children. These children are not yet dealing with characteristics.

Children find many shapes in their environment. The shapes of traffic signs are important because of their meanings, and young children should learn to recognize them (see Figure 11.2). A classroom often has squares, rectangles, circles, and triangles that children can locate and identify. From time to time a teacher may prearrange new and different representations of

Figure 11-1
Regular polygons
(a) and irregular
polygons (b)

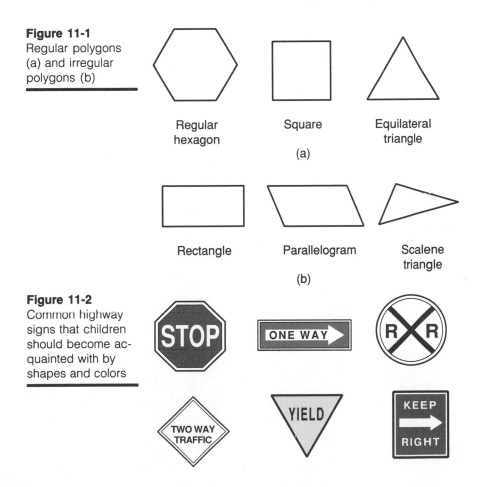

Regular
hexagon

Square

Equilateral
triangle

(a)

Rectangle

Parallelogram

Scalene
triangle

(b)

Figure 11-2
Common highway
signs that children
should become acquainted with by
shapes and colors

shapes for children to pick out. Pictures of shapes from magazines and sponges cut in geometric shapes and tempera paint provide other experiences with shapes. Activities with these and other materials give children chances to learn the names and become aware of the shape's characteristics.

Shape Templates

Experiences with a variety of models help children think about and visualize geometric figures. A set of shape templates is a simple way for children

ACTIVITY 11.1   Feeling and Finding Shapes

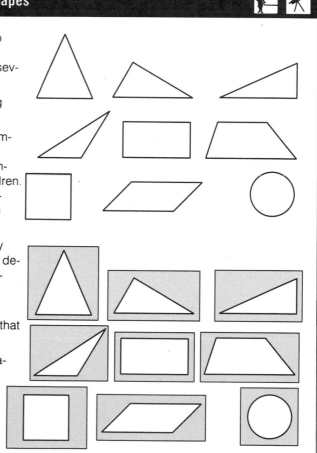

- Give the templates and cut-out shapes to children and have them rub their fingers around the hole and along the edges of several shapes.

- Let them put their shapes into the posting holes.

- Blindfold a child and give him or her a template. Have the child feel the outlines of shapes until the one that matches the template is identified. Repeat with other children. Some children are frightened when blindfolded; ask them to close their eyes while they feel the shapes.

- After the activity, ask them to tell how they knew which shape would fit. Accept their descriptions of the shapes. Have them compare their shape to a circle.

- Variations:
   —Have children find shapes in the room that are like the posting holes.

   —Have children look for pictures in magazines that show the same shapes and make a picture book of shapes.

to learn about many shapes. The templates shown in Activity 11.1 can be bought commercially or can be cut from plywood, masonite, cardboard, or even meat trays. The templates—sometimes called *posting holes*—and the cut-out forms can be used in a number of ways, including informal exploration in a learning center.

Geoboards

A geoboard has pegs arranged in an orderly fashion on a piece of wood or plastic. Geoboards may have a square grid arrangement of 9, 16, 25, 36, or more pegs or a circular arrangement (Figure 11.3). Rubber bands are put around the pegs to form shapes and designs. Large boards with an 11-by-11 array of pegs are large enough for several plane figures at the same time. Dot paper with the same arrangement as a geoboard is often used so children can copy their geoboard figures.

Geoboards can be used for many investigations from kindergarten through sixth grade. In the primary grades, children gain an intuitive understanding of plane figures, points, and line segments. Older children use them to study different types of triangles, quadrilaterals, and other figures and to learn about regular and irregular figures, concave and convex fig-

Figure 11-3
Examples of commonly used geoboards

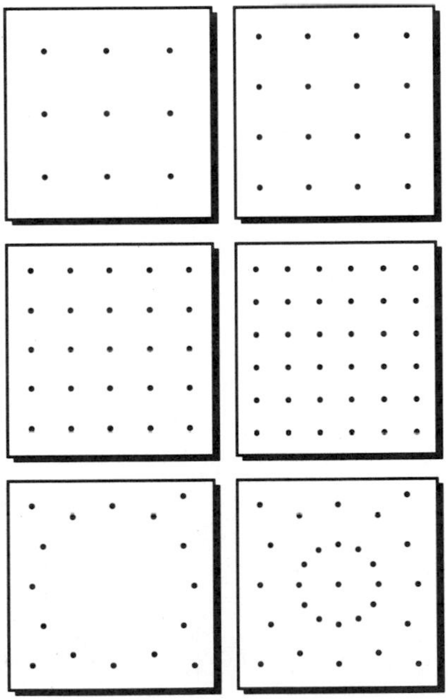

ures, congruence, similarity, and symmetry. Activity 11.2 has a lesson on triangles for third through sixth graders. Children will create many different types of triangles during this activity.

Activity 11.2 provides the basis for introducing two classification schemes for triangles. Triangles classified by their sides are **equilateral, isosceles,** or **scalene.** Equilateral triangles have three equal, or congruent, sides; isosceles triangles have two congruent sides, and scalene triangles have no congruent sides. Triangles are also classified by their angles. **Right** triangles have a 90 degree angle. All of the angles in **acute** triangles are less than 90 degrees; **obtuse** triangles have one angle larger than 90 degrees. (See Figure 11.4.)

ACTIVITY 11.2   Triangle Types

- Have the children work in pairs or triples.

- Tell them to use rubber bands to make as many triangles as they can on their board and to record them on dot paper.

- After each group has copied 15 to 20 different triangles, have them cut them out so that one shape is on each piece of paper.

- Ask them to sort the triangles into different groups and to name the different attributes they used to categorize the triangles, such

as "all three sides the same," "two sides same, one side different," "big angle and two little angles," or "all different sides."

- Challenge them to categorize them in several different ways and compare their categories with another group's.

- Have them label their category types and make a poster or display of the different groups of triangles.

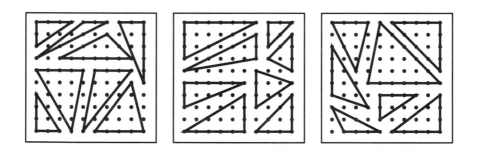

Figure 11-4
Right triangle (a), acute triangle (b), and obtuse triangle (c)

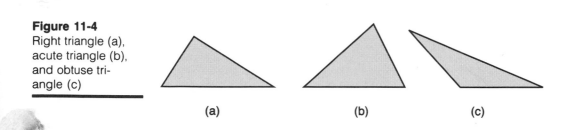

(a)   (b)   (c)

Similar geoboard investigation can also be done with four-sided figures, or quadrilaterals. After trying out all the various configurations and classifying them students have the background for naming quadrilaterals. Activity 11.3 helps students describe the characteristics of five quadrilaterals.

By the end of the sixth grade children should be familiar with the common plane figures. They should also be able to explain how each closed figure separates a plane into three distinct sets of points: the set that is the polygon itself, the set within the polygon, and the set outside the polygon. They should know about area and perimeter, which are discussed in Chapter 14.

Diagonals are explored in Activity 11.4. A chart is used to help children see a developing pattern as they work.

ACTIVITY 11.3   Quadrilaterals with Class

- Organize children in cooperative-learning groups.

- Have them make many four-sided figures on a geoboard. They should copy each figure on paper.

- Show an overhead transparency with five quadrilaterals on it. Ask students to compare their groupings to these five shapes. After they have compared their groups to these classifications, name each figure: square, rectangle, parallelogram, trapezoid, trapezium.

- Ask the children to fill in the chart to identify their figures by types of angles and sides.

FIGURE	ANGLES	SIDES
Square		
Rectangle		
Parallelogram		
Trapezoid		
Trapezium		

ACTIVITY 11.4   Diagonally Speaking

- Organize the children into cooperative-learning groups.

- Have the children make a triangle, quadrilateral, and pentagon on a geoboard; have them show the diagonals in each figure.

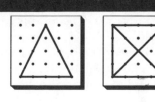

(continued)

Activity 11.4 *continued*

- Have the children count the diagonals and place the number for each on a chart. Ask the children to continue making other polygons with increasing numbers of sides and their diagonals and entering their numbers on the chart.

FIGURE	ANGLES	DIAGONALS
Triangle	3	0
Quadrilateral	4	2
Pentagon	5	5
Hexagon	6	9
Heptagon	?	?
Octagon	?	?

- Have the children examine the table for a pattern.
- When children think they have found a pattern, have them predict the number of diagonals for the next shape. Then check their hypothesis.
- Challenge the children to develop a formula for finding the number of diagonals in an *n*-sided figure.
- Extension: String art is a good way to explore diagonals.[5]

EXERCISE   Describe the geometric characteristics of the following shapes.

quadrilateral   rectangle
polygon   closed figure
square   parallelogram

Arrange the list of terms from the most general to the most specific.

■ POINTS, LINES, RAYS, AND LINE SEGMENTS

The abstract nature of geometric points and lines makes them difficult for children to understand. The definition of a **point** is an object without any dimension. A **line** is a set of points that extends infinitely. For children who are still using concrete models in thinking, infinity and something that has no dimensions are difficult to conceptualize. Piaget recommended that study of these concepts be postponed until children are eight or nine years old. Activity 11.5 uses real materials to represent points and lines and is recommended for an early experience with lines, segments, and rays; later children will be able to think about the concepts in abstract ways.

Lines may also be curved. In Activity 11.6 children explore simple closed curves. Activity 11.7 is an investigation of lines, points, and regions. Children can look for a pattern in the designs.

ACTIVITY 11.5   Segments and Rays

- Take the children to a play field. Stretch a skein of yarn or ball of twine across the field as far as it will go.

- Have the children hold onto the string and keep it taut. Tell the children that the string is part of a line that keeps going forever, even after the string comes to an end. Discuss what things the line would pass through as it moved beyond each end of the string.

- Each child who is touching the string is a point on the line. Tell the children that the space between each pair of them is a line segment, or part of the line. Name line segments by calling the names of children. "Line segment Latasha-Jason." The named children hold on to the string and the children between them let go. This shows how long each line segment is. Let children take turns calling pairs of names to identify line segments.

- Have children notice the children who are standing on either side of them. Return to the classroom and draw a picture of a line on the chalkboard. Put an arrow at each end to indicate that the line keeps going in both directions. See if the children can order their names on the line as they were outside.

- Ask the children to describe the difference between the experience outdoors and the chalkboard line and the ideas represented by the chalkboard line. (The arrows show that the line goes on without end. The points where children's names appear show that a line segment has definite ends. The names identify specific segments.)

- Draw a picture of a ray. Ask the children to tell what they see and what they think a ray is. (A ray includes an endpoint and all points extending in one direction from that point.)

- Introduce the way to write line $\overleftrightarrow{AB}$. Ask if the children can figure out how to write the notation for a segment ($\overline{AB}$) and a ray ($\overrightarrow{AB}$).

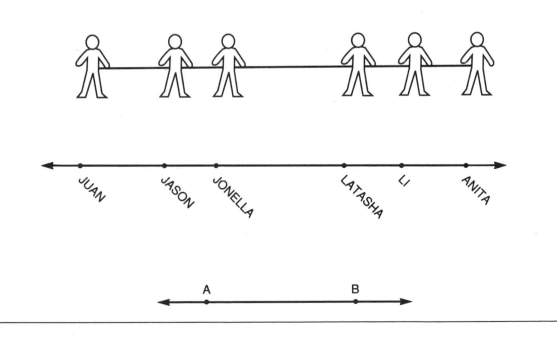

ACTIVITY 11.6   Simple Closed Curves

- Give each child a 50-centimeter length of yarn.

- Show a picture of several shapes and have the children make them with their yarn.

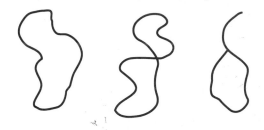

- Tell the students that the first figure is a simple closed curve. Ask them to make

other simple closed curves. The other two are not simple closed curves. Challenge the children to make other shapes that are not simple closed curves.

- Ask the children why the other two are not simple closed curves. (One crosses over itself and the other does not begin and end at the same place.)

- Ask for a definition of a simple closed curve. (A continuous line that begins and ends at the same point and does not cross over itself.)

- Extension: Create art designs with simple closed curves and curves that are not simple.

ACTIVITY 11.7   Doodle Geometry[6]

- Display a number of odd shapes with an overhead projector.

- Ask the children to count the points, the enclosed regions, and the line segments or simple closed curves in each figure. Make a table to organize the results.

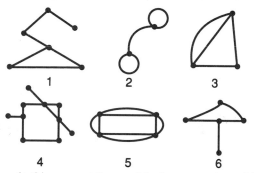

	POINTS	REGIONS	LINES
DOODLE 1	6	1	6
DOODLE 2	2	2	3
DOODLE 3	3	2	4
DOODLE 4	10	2	?
DOODLE 5	?	?	?
DOODLE 6	?	?	?

- After three or four examples, have the children count the points and the enclosed regions. Ask if they can predict the number of lines in the doodle. Suggest that they look at the three or four examples for a pattern. After their guess, have them count to see if the prediction was accurate. You may need to

do this several times while they come up with a plan for predicting the number of lines. (The number of lines is one less than the total of the points and regions.)

- Have the children draw doodles of their own to see if the relationship holds true for all their doodles. You may need to help them place the points at the end of any line segment and at all intersections.

- Variation: Leave the number of points or regions out of the chart and challenge students to fill in the correct number.

■ SPACE FIGURES

Children have many experiences inside and outside the home with objects that have three dimensions. Classroom activities should build on those experiences by using familiar three-dimensional models. A classroom grocery store is full of boxes with many shapes and sizes. Oatmeal boxes are cylinders; most cereal boxes are rectangular prisms. Common ice cream cones represent another geometric shape. Pyramids are less common, but are used for specialty boxes.

A block center or sets of desk blocks provide many opportunities for children to make three-dimensional designs. Children can also build three-dimensional collages from pasteboard boxes and tubes. Some may represent trucks or boats, while others will be quite fanciful. Glue and tempera paints are the only materials needed. Carpentry is another way in which children learn to put three-dimensional forms together. Children have a natural inclination to make patterns and structures that have balance and symmetry. A comment about the way a design balances will call their attention to this concept.

Children can take a geometry walk around school grounds to identify plane and solid figures. Specific tasks can be varied with the age of the children. Young children may simply be asked to find examples of familiar shapes and forms. Older children can discuss whether a shape is natural or human-made and whether it has utilitarian or aesthetic value. A grab bag of objects can be matched with models of the space figures or with line drawings of one face of the object. Magazines can be used for a scrapbook of pictures showing solid figures.

Many children cannot visualize a solid figure drawn in two dimensions. Many experiences of relating real objects to their flattened representation are important. Plastic and tagboard models allow children to explore how space figures are constructed. In Activity 11.8 children cut boxes to see flattened forms.

Another way to increase awareness of space figures is to have children sketch three-dimensional models. Display a model of a cube or tetrahedron for children to draw. Have them draw just the surfaces, corners, and edges that are visible. As they become more proficient have them show hidden edges with broken lines. Clear plastic models are good because hidden edges can be seen. To extend the activity have four or five children sit around a table with a solid figure on it. Each of them sketches the object. Take up the sketches and redistribute them to different students, who try to figure out where the original sketcher was sitting.

Clear plastic models are ideal for older children's analysis of spheres, cylinders, cones, prisms, and pyramids. Three solid figures associated with the circle are spheres, cylinders, and cones (Figure 11.5). A plastic model of each figure can be placed on an overhead projector to show that a circle can be projected from at least one placement. The sphere is a circle in every way as it is placed on the projector. Both the cylinder and the cone project a circle from both ends. They should also be projected from the side to show

---

ACTIVITY 11.8   This Side Up

- Collect a variety of food containers, such as cereal and round oatmeal boxes.

- Give one to each child, who counts the surfaces, corners, and edges.

- Ask each child to cut along edges of the box in such a way as to keep the parts together but let it be flattened. When the box is cut have the child flatten it and trace its edges.

- Color each congruent face the same color. Label the plane figures found in the tracing.

- Give the children a set of outlines of figures and ask them to predict which ones can be folded into boxes.

Cereal Box   Oatmeal Box

Figure 11-5

Representation of a sphere (a), cylinder (b), and cone (c)

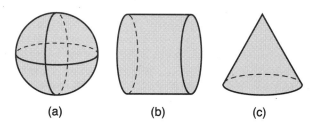

(a)   (b)   (c)

rectangular and triangular images. William Carroll suggests how students can learn to visualize parts of solid figures by slicing through figures made of modeling clay.[7]

Prisms should also be studied. A right prism has two parallel bases and sides, or faces, that are rectangles. All the sides are perpendicular to the bases. A rectangular prism has rectangular faces (Figure 11.6). A triangular prism has bases that are triangles (Figure 11.6).

Pyramids have only one base and triangular faces that meet at a point at the top, or apex. Pyramids studied in elementary school generally have regular polygons as bases, although pyramids can contain polygons that are irregular. Both prisms and pyramids are named according to the polygon at the base. In Figure 11.7, the base is a pentagon; the pyramid is a pentagonal pyramid. Polygons with any number of sides can form the bases of these figures.

Space figures with polygons for faces are called **polyhedrons.** *Poly* and *hedron* are ancient Greek words that mean "many" and "face," respectively. A special set of polyhedrons are the five Platonic solids (Figure 11.8). These solids have surfaces composed of four or more congruent regular polygons. A regular tetrahedron has four triangular faces. A cube or regular hexa-

Figure 11-6
Identification of the parts of (a) a rectangular prism and (b) a triangular prism

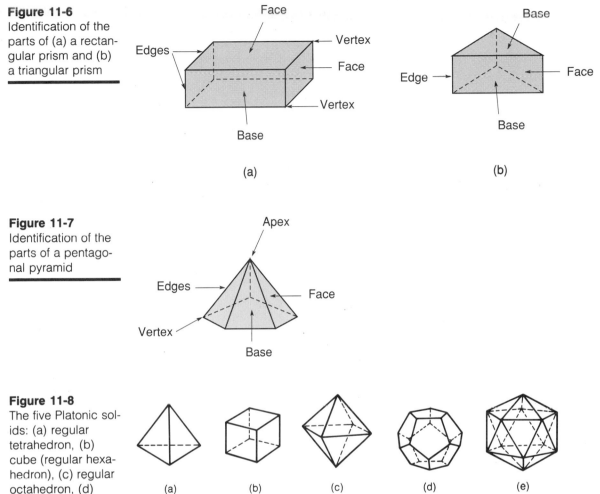

(a)

(b)

Figure 11-7
Identification of the parts of a pentagonal pyramid

Figure 11-8
The five Platonic solids: (a) regular tetrahedron, (b) cube (regular hexahedron), (c) regular octahedron, (d) regular dodecahedron, and (e) regular icosahedron

(a)   (b)   (c)   (d)   (e)

hedron has six square faces. A regular octahedron has eight triangular faces, while a regular dodecahedron and regular icosahedron have 12 pentagons and 20 triangles as faces, respectively. Older students should be able to identify the Platonic solids and their characteristics.

Children can construct their own solids using clay or playdough. Plastic straws can be threaded and joined with yarn or joined with special connectors or pipe cleaners to make models. Predrawn models can also be used so that children can cut and fold their own set of shapes.

During play and investigative activities children learn the terminology for solids—*face, edge, vertex, apex,* and *base*—and relate it to plane figures: corner, edge, square, triangle, and circle. Children should not be hurried to learn the specialized names and definitions. As children become ready for more precise terms to describe space figures, the terms can be introduced.

A net is a special shape which can be folded to form a box or cube. Activity 11.9 uses two-dimensional pentominoes as background for folding nets in Activity 11.10. Pentominoes are a geometric manipulative made of five squares joined together at their edges.

EXERCISE   On a cardboard box, label all the faces, edges, and vertices.

ACTIVITY 11.9   *Pentomino Patterns*

Materials: Overhead projector, set of plastic tiles or tagboard squares about 3 centimeters by 3 centimeters.

- Organize children into cooperative-learning groups of three or four.

- Place one square on the overhead projector and ask the children how many different shapes can be formed from a single square. (Only one because it has the same shape whichever way it is turned.)

- Place two squares on the overhead projector. Put the two squares together so that two sides are joined and ask how many shapes can be formed. (Still only one regardless of their position.)

- Place three squares on the overhead. Line them up to form a rectangle. Ask the children if there is another way to arrange the squares so that the sides join along edges. (One other shape is possible.)

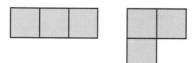

- Put four squares on the overhead and ask the children how many unique arrangements can be made with them. Give each group of children 20–30 squares. Have groups make different arrangements and draw them on paper.

- Tell the groups to make unique arrangements with five squares. Remind them that the sides must join fully, and "unique" means that the shape cannot be duplicated by turning it over or rotating it.

- Ask groups to name the various shapes; check to see if all groups agree. The twelve different shapes made from five squares are called *pentominoes*.

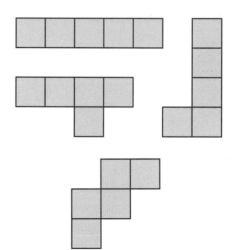

- Extension: Some students may be challenged to find the unique shapes with six or seven squares. Have them predict the number of shapes based on the pattern of one, two, three, four, and five squares.

ACTIVITY 11.10   Nets of Cubes

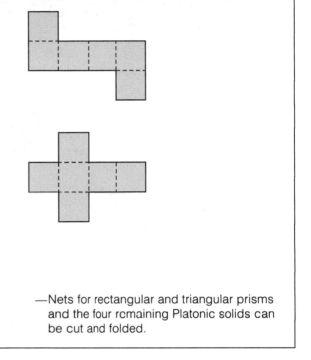

- Give cooperative-learning groups copies of the pentomino shapes. Tell the children to visualize which ones can be folded to make boxes without lids, and mark each of the pentominoes that they believe will fold.

- Have the children cut and fold the shapes to see which ones form boxes. Does each folded shape have a mark on it?

- Show the children a net with six squares and ask if it can be folded to make a closed cube. Give them a duplicated copy to cut and fold. Show a second net and ask if it can be folded to form a closed cube. Have them cut and fold a copy of it.

- Challenge the students to find five more six-square nets for a closed cube. Markers and tape are good for coloring and taping the cubes.

- Extensions:
  —Children can make mobiles of the decorated cubes.

—Nets for rectangular and triangular prisms and the four remaining Platonic solids can be cut and folded.

■ MOTION OR TRANSFORMATIONAL GEOMETRY

Motion or transformational geometry is the study of how shapes can be moved or transformed in space. Three basic motions are applied to geometric figures. **Translations** are sliding motions, **rotations** are turning motions, and **reflections** are flipping motions. *Slide, turn,* and *flip* are the terms generally used in elementary school. Figure 11.9 shows the three movements. When original triangle *ABC* is moved in space to a new location, it is transformed into triangle *A'B'C'*. The diamond shape *MNOP* can be transformed into diamond *M'N'O'P'* by a rotation movement. The parallelogram *ABCD* is flipped to the other side of a line to become parallelogram *A'B'C'D'*. The motions can also be combined.

Spatial visualization is an important outcome of working with motion geometry. Pattern blocks and tangrams are two useful materials for teaching motion geometry. Both materials can be used for informal exploration,

Figure 11-9
Transformational geometry is based on three motions that change shapes: (a) slide, or translation; (b) turn, or rotation; (c) flip, or reflection

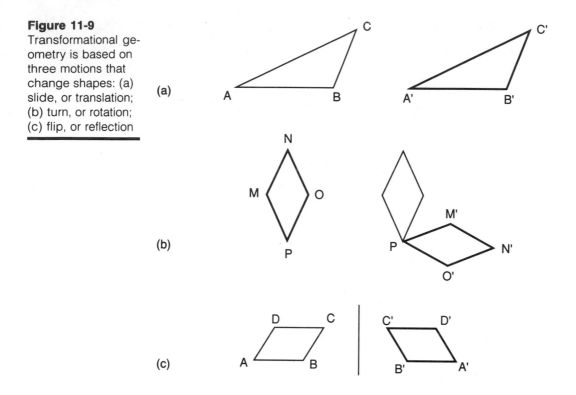

teacher-directed lessons, and group and individual investigations. Published tangram and pattern-block activity books are excellent for learning centers.

Pattern Blocks

Pattern blocks are colored wooden or plastic blocks that fit together to form designs or patterns. The patterns children can make with the blocks are limitless. Commercial sets are illustrated in Chapter 3. Pattern blocks encourage free exploration of motion geometry. In creating various designs and patterns children move the pieces, rotate them, and flip them over to fit. Many times a child's pattern will be symmetrical. If an unbreakable plastic mirror is placed on a line of symmetry, the image in the mirror will be an exact duplicate of the pattern behind it. Task cards or laminated sheets give children challenging design ideas.

Tiling activities are another way to use pattern blocks to show slide, flip, and turn motions. Tiling patterns, or **tessellations,** involve completely covering a surface with shapes. Students are challenged to determine which shapes fit together to tessellate a surface. Students find that certain shapes tessellate by themselves, while others work only in combination. Squares and regular hexagons cover a surface alone. Pentagons and octagons leave gaps that must be filled in with another shape (Figure 11.10). Ceramic bathroom

Figure 11-10
Tessellations:
(a) hexagons;
(b) squares;
(c) combinations of
shapes

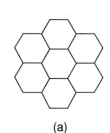

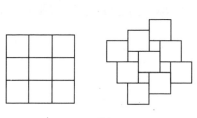

(a)   (b)

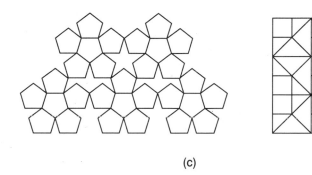

(c)

tiles of various shapes may be purchased for tiling activities. After working out a design with blocks, children can copy it on dot paper. The art of Escher is a good way to extend the study of motion geometry and tessellations. Children can study his artwork to see how shapes interconnect and fill a surface in an intricate puzzle-like drawing.[8]

EXERCISE   Take a pencil or some other small object. Transform the object by sliding, by turning, and by flipping. Try various combinations of the transformations.

Tangrams

A tangram is a seven-piece puzzle (see the photograph in Chapter 3). The seven pieces can be put together to form a square, but they can be put together to form many other shapes. Recognizable shapes, such as boats and birds, as well as fanciful designs can be made. Children's first work with tan-

Figure 11-11
Tangram pieces
and designs

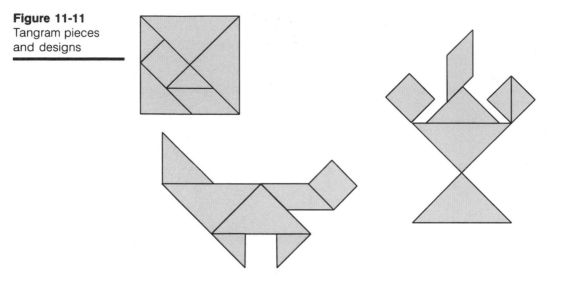

grams is often with designs from commercial sources (Figure 11.11). Children can be challenged to create and copy their own designs to add to the collection of commercial designs. As children work with tangrams, the pieces are moved, turned, and flipped to form a design.

SYMMETRY

Symmetry is often easier to show than to describe. Children report that symmetrical things are "the same on both sides." Understanding all the facets of symmetry requires many experiences with geometric manipulatives. Explorations and investigations help children develop an appreciation of geometry in art and find examples in many natural and human-made objects.

A line that separates a picture, design, or object into identical halves is a **line of symmetry.** Some objects have only one line of symmetry, while others have two or more. Children themselves are used to create symmetry in Activity 11.11. The art project described in Activity 11.12 is an interesting way to make symmetrical designs. Many of the blob designs look like butterflies with matching wings.

An object has **rotational symmetry** if its appearance is unchanged after it is turned part way around its axis. Block letters can be used to investigate both line and rotational symmetry (Figure 11.12). Consider all the letters and note that certain ones are symmetrical along a vertical axis; A and M are examples. Others are symmetrical along a horizontal axis, like D and E, and still others—such as I and O—have both horizontal and vertical lines of symmetry. Some letters also have rotational symmetry. When they are turned 90° or 180°, the same letter results; H, I, and O are examples.

ACTIVITY 11.11   Mirror Partners

- Have children choose partners. Have one pair come to the front of the room.

- Give the demonstrators instructions. "Raise your hands above your head." "Bend at the knees." "Turn around and put your backs together." "Put your hands straight in front of you." "Bend your knees as if you were sitting down."

- Give the same or similar instructions for all of the children to follow.

- After a little practice, ask one partner to be the leader and without talking make motions for the other to follow. Then have the other student be the leader.

- Have the children talk about the experience. "Both moved together." "They always did the same thing." "It was in slow motion." "It was like looking in a mirror."

ACTIVITY 11.12   Blob Art

- Give each child a piece of art paper and access to several pots of colored paint.

- Have the children fold their papers in half.

- On one side of the paper, have children put dabs of different colors of paint. Fold the other half of the paper over on the painted side and smooth it out.

- Open the picture to see the design. After they are dry, make a bulletin board of the pictures. Some children may want to decorate the pictures more by adding the same lines to both sides.

- Have an unbreakable mirror available for children to place on the fold. Discuss the fact that the mirror image is the same as the design hidden behind the mirror. Tell the children that the line along the fold is a line of symmetry. It divides the design into two like halves.

- Variation: Use a string to dip in the paint. Curl the string around on one side of the paper. Fold the clean half over the string and hold it down gently while pulling the string out the bottom of the fold.

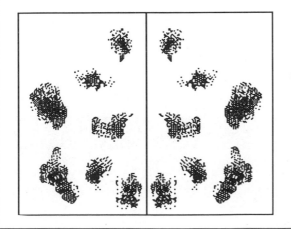

Figure 11-12
Block letters for
symmetry activity

A B C D E F G H I J K L M N

O P Q R S T U V W X Y Z

A paper-folding activity gives experiences with both line and point symmetry in Activity 11.13, while shape templates and boxes and lids provide a different type of investigation in Activity 11.14.

Children can find many examples of symmetry in everyday life. Many company logos are symmetrical. Students can make a scrapbook of company logos, classify them as being symmetrical or nonsymmetrical, and draw the appropriate lines of symmetry.[9] Most computer draw-and-paint programs have a feature called *mirrors* that allows children to make lines of symmetry (Figure 11.13).

ACTIVITY 11.13   Lines of Symmetry

- Give pairs of children paper cutouts of a square, rectangle, equilateral triangle, isosceles triangle, regular pentagon, and other polygons.

- Have them determine the different ways each figure can be folded so that one half exactly covers the other half.

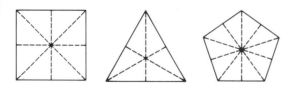

- Have the children record the number of lines of symmetry for each shape on a table.

SHAPE	SIDES	LINES OF SYMMETRY
Square	4	4
Triangle		
Pentagon		

- Challenge the children to determine if there is any relationship between the number of sides and the number of lines of symmetry in a regular polygon. Does this relationship exist for a rectangle and an isosceles triangle? What about other polygons? Are there any figures that have no lines of symmetry? What can be said about their shapes?

ACTIVITY 11.14   Fit to Be Rotated

- Use a template from Activity 11.1. Have the children determine different ways the shape can fit in its hole. A square can fit four different ways, while the parallelogram fits two ways.

- Have the children make a table of the number of ways that each shape can be placed in its posting hole.

Activity 11.14   *continued*

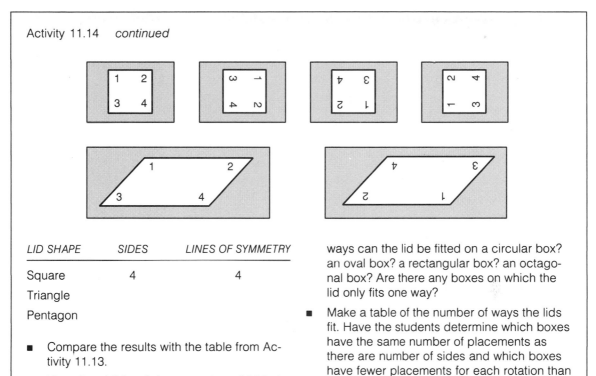

LID SHAPE	SIDES	LINES OF SYMMETRY
Square	4	4
Triangle		
Pentagon		

- Compare the results with the table from Activity 11.13.

- Have the children bring a number of lidded boxes to continue the investigation. The more odd-shaped boxes there are the more interesting the investigation will be.

- Ask the children to see how many ways each lid fits its box. The lid of a square box can be placed on it four different ways. How many ways can the lid be fitted on a circular box? an oval box? a rectangular box? an octagonal box? Are there any boxes on which the lid only fits one way?

- Make a table of the number of ways the lids fit. Have the students determine which boxes have the same number of placements as there are number of sides and which boxes have fewer placements for each rotation than there are number of sides.

- Compare the table with the results of the paper folding and posting-hole investigations.

- What conclusions can be drawn from these investigations?

Figure 11-13
Symmetrical design
from computer

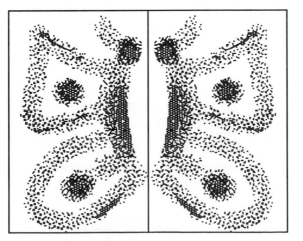

■ CONGRUENCE AND SIMILARITY

Two line segments are **congruent** when all points on one segment coincide exactly with all points on the other segment. Two plane figures or two space figures are congruent when all points of one figure coincide exactly with all points on the other figure. Congruent shapes cover each other exactly. This is the concept on which standardized measurement is based with its units for linear, area, and volume measure.

Two figures are **similar** when they have the same shape and all of their corresponding parts are proportional. All noncongruent squares, equilateral triangles, circles, and regular polygons are similar. Rectangles, pentagons, or hexagons need not be similar because they may have very different proportions. A scale drawing of a room is similar to the room because all of the dimensions are proportional to each other.

Children's work with tangrams and pattern blocks build intuitions about congruent and similar shapes. Sorting activities with attribute blocks from a kit include finding shapes that are congruent and shapes that are similar. For example, the large circles are congruent to one another and the small circles are congruent to one another, and all the large circles are similar to the small circles.

Geoboards are used in Activities 11.15 and 11.16 to help children find examples of congruent and similar figures.

ACTIVITY 11.15 Congruent Shapes and Tiling

- Have children work in pairs with a geoboard, rubber bands, and dot paper.

- Show a right triangle on an overhead geoboard. Instruct the children to make one exactly like yours. Tell them that the triangles are congruent because they have the same size and shape. Ask them to make another congruent triangle in a different position on the geoboard.

- Have the children draw their congruent triangles on dot paper.

- Tell the children to place triangles on the geoboard in such a way that all the space is filled up with congruent triangles. This is called *tiling*.

- Have them make a drawing of their geoboard to show how triangles fit together and cover the surface. Color the design.

- Repeat the same activity with geoboards and dot paper with isosceles triangles or rectangles. Ask the children to find ways to make a pattern with all congruent shapes. Make tile designs and color them.

Activity 11.5   *continued*

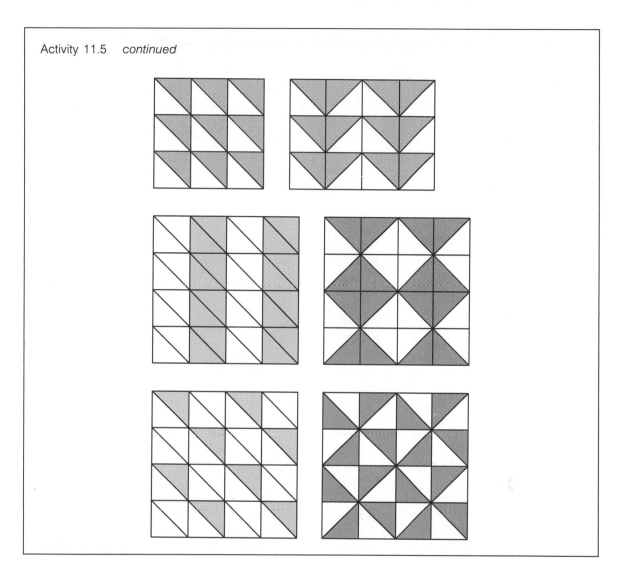

ACTIVITY 11.16   Similar Shapes

- Display a triangle on the overhead geo-board. Have the children make one like it.

- Challenge them to make one that has sides that are half as long.

- Discuss the differences between the two tri-angles. Make sure that the children see that each side on the smaller one is half as long.

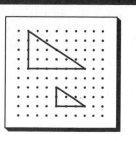

(continued)

Activity 11.16 *continued*

- Ask the children to make a triangle which is one and a half times as long on each side. Compare the triangle with the other two.

- Point out that all of the sides are proportional. The two figures have the same shape, but the sizes are different. These are called *similar figures*.

- Repeat with other figures: squares, rectangles, parallelograms, and so on.

- Extension: See if tiling patterns can be made of similar squares, similar triangles, similar rectangles, and similar hexagons.

EXERCISE   Draw two lines that are congruent. Draw two quadrilaterals that are congruent. Draw three similar triangles.

■ COORDINATE GEOMETRY

Rene Descartes (1596–1650) is credited with the development of coordinate geometry. Elementary school children can be introduced to the coordinate plane through activities that are both practical and fun. A prerequisite skill is that children be familiar with number lines. The coordinate plane can be introduced to children who have no knowledge of negative numbers, although knowledge of the numbers is necessary to work with the complete coordinate grid.

Activity 11.17 is designed to develop children's understanding of points on the coordinate plane. It begins with the whole number line as the basis for constructing the coordinate system.

A geoboard can also be used to develop the concept of the coordinate plane (Activity 11.18). Children who have worked with geoboards already know that its pegs form a grid, so naming the pegs with coordinate numbers is easily done. This activity is good for developing the guess-and-check problem-solving strategy.

■ COMPUTER ACTIVITIES FOR INFORMAL GEOMETRY

Many hands-on activities for geometry have been the basis for computer games and explorations. *Bumble Games*[10] is a series of games in which the Bumble character is hidden on a coordinate grid. In the first game, Bumble is hidden only on a horizontal number line; different levels of the game introduce the two axes and negative numbers. The *Factory*[11] uses square objects which are punched, striped, and rotated. Students must duplicate a piece by visualizing what was done to it and the order in which the actions occurred. The *Superfactory* is a more complex version of the same game.

ACTIVITY 11.17   Coordinating Points

- Make a horizontal drawing of a whole number line on the chalkboard or overhead projector with points 0–19. Review the way counting is done on a number line.

- Draw a vertical line from the zero point on the horizontal line and number it so that 0 is at the same place on both lines. Demonstrate how counting is done on the vertical line.

- Tell the children that the horizontal line is the first axis and the vertical line is the second axis. Each point on the grid is named by a set of ordered numbers; the first number is the horizontal number and the second is the vertical number.

- Give the children a list of ordered pairs that draws a picture when all the pairs are connected.

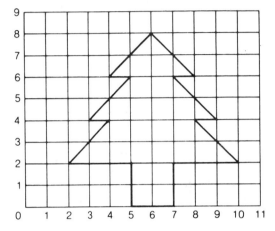

- Ask the children to draw pictures on the grid and make up a puzzle to share with the class.

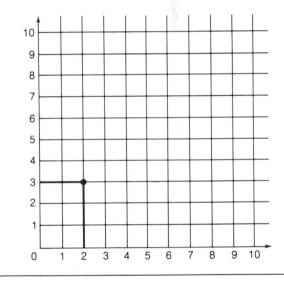

ACTIVITY 11.18   Geoboard Coordinate Grid

- Give each pair of children two geoboards and washers painted two colors.

- Have one student secretly put five washers in a row on pegs vertically, horizontally, or diagonally.

- The other student guesses where the washers are by calling out two numbers for the horizontal and vertical axes. The guesser keeps track of guesses on his or her board. Correct guesses are marked with one color of washer and incorrect with another color.

Draw-and-paint programs have features that can be used in exploring geometry. First students can use the shape tools to create congruent and similar shapes: squares, rectangles, circles, and ellipses. Irregular shapes and closed curves can also be made with shape tools. Many of the programs allow students to make grids with which they can print their own grid paper or grid designs for tessellations or nets to cut and fold into space figures after students have worked out the arrangements. Children enjoy working on the computer because the computer can be much more accurate in drawing.

Logo is another way of exploring geometry with the computer. As children move the turtle around on the screen, they make shapes and draw pictures. In the process they learn about sides and angles in a unique way because the lengths and angles allow them to control the turtle. Activities described in Appendix A only suggest some of the many ways Logo can be used to further geometric understanding.

■ SUMMARY

Geometry is an essential part of the comprehensive mathematics curriculum. Not only do children learn many useful concepts and skills of geometry, but geometry provides a foundation for many other topics in elementary and higher mathematics. Students' first experiences in geometry are topological, according to Piaget. Children learn about the space they live in and concepts such as location and proximity, enclosure, order, and separation. These ideas, described in Chapter 7, come before children are able to deal with fixed shapes in space.

Geometrical understanding has been described in five stages by Dina van Hiele-Geldof and Pierre Marie von Hiele. The first three stages provide guidance for the elementary teacher in designing appropriate experiences. Children learn to recognize and label shapes before they are able to pick out and describe the attributes of each shape. In the upper elementary grades, students should begin to use the attributes to generalize about the shapes and to understand the relationships between plane and solid figures.

Many geometric materials are available for teachers and students. Geoboards, pattern blocks, pentominoes, tangrams, shape templates, and models of solid figures provide opportunities for informal explorations, teacher directed lessons, and investigations. Students will learn the names and characteristics of plane and solid figures, geometric properties such as symmetry, congruence, and similarity, and applications such as tessellations and aesthetic uses. Problem-solving skills can also be developed with geometry materials. Computer games and drawing tools are yet another way students can expand their understanding of geometry.

■ STUDY QUESTIONS AND ACTIVITIES

1. Many activities in geometry are excellent for explorations and investigations. Select a geometry topic such as tessellations or coordinate geometry and design three task cards suitable for children's work on the topic. The articles in the For Further Reading section offer helpful ideas.

2. Glenda Lappan and Mary Jean Winter in the 1987 NCTM Yearbook have an article on improving children's spatial visualization skill. Use their article as a basis for designing a spatial visualization unit for fourth, fifth, or sixth graders.

3. Take some time to learn about Logo. Beginning Logo commands are given in Appendix A. Try making squares, triangles of several types, hexagons, octagons, and circles. What geometric ideas did you discover or rediscover for yourself? Read Bill Craig's article (see the For Further Reading section) for some ideas about students' work with Logo.

4. Use paper squares or plastic tiles to work out the pentomino shapes mentioned in Activity 11.9. Did you find them all? Which took the most time to discover? What names would you apply to the different shapes? Which of the shapes have line or rotational symmetry?

5. Complete Activity 11.7 on Doodle Geometry. After you have filled in the chart with examples, draw several of your own doodles to make sure the pattern works. Which NCTM standards are included in the activity?

6. Draw a tessellating pattern with equilateral triangles or triangles and hexagons. Color them three or four ways to see what different designs you can make from one basic pattern. Continue your study of tiling and tessellations by looking at quilt patterns. What shapes do you find most often in quilts?

7. The article by Barbara Renshaw (see the For Further Reading section) suggests using company trademarks for a symmetry lesson. Make a collection of pictures that illustrate symmetrical figures for a classroom bulletin board. Include examples of folding and rotational symmetry. Create the bulletin board so that students will interact with it in some way rather than just look at it.

8. Most of the graphics for this book were done with a computer draw or paint program. If you do not know how to use a graphics program, ask someone to show you how. Go through the chapter and see how many of the figures you can draw. Try drawing a tessellation using a graphics program.

▓ TEACHER'S BOOKSHELF

Engelhardt, Jon. 1987. *Geometry in Our World* (slides). Reston, VA: National Council of Teachers of Mathematics.

Lindquist, Mary Montgomery, and Albert Shulte, eds. 1987 Yearbook. *Learning and Teaching Geometry, K–12*. Reston, VA: National Council of Teachers of Mathematics.

Silvey, Linda, and James A. Smart, eds. 1982 Yearbook. *Mathematics for the Middle Grades (5–9)*. Reston, VA: National Council of Teachers of Mathematics.

Olsen, Alton T. 1975. *Mathematics Through Paper Folding*. Reston, VA: National Council of Teachers of Mathematics.

Wenninger, Magnus J. 1966. *Polyhedron Models for the Classroom*. Reston, VA: National Council of Teachers of Mathematics.

▓ FOR FURTHER READING

Arithmetic Teacher. 1990, February. *37*(6).

   Focus issue on spatial sense, spatial visualization, and geometry.

Arithmetic Teacher. 1979, February. *36*(6).

   Focus issue on geometry. Activities and materials for all grade levels are included.

Battista, Michael T. 1982, January. Distortions: An activity for practice and exploration. *Arithmetic Teacher 29*(5), 34–36.

   Morris the cat serves as the basis for a study of the plane coordinate system. He is first drawn on a normal grid. Then a variety of grids that distort the cat's appearance focus attention on different grid forms and the transformations that occur on them.

Bright, George W., and John G. Harvey. 1988, April. Learning and fun with geometry games. *Arithmetic Teacher 35*(8), 22–26.

   Card games help students visualize geometric shapes and properties.

Butzow, John W. 1986, January. Y is for yacht race: A game of angles. *Arithmetic Teacher 33*(5), 44–48.

   Materials and activities for upper-elementary students to explore angles by plotting the path of a sailboat.

Cangelosi, James S. 1985, November. A "fair" way to discover circles. *Arithmetic Teacher 33*(3), 11–13.

   Attributes of circles and polygons are explored.

Carroll, William M. 1988, March. Cross-sections of clay solids. *Arithmetic Teacher 35*(7), 6–11.

   By constructing geometric solids from clay and cutting cross-sections, children learn to visualize "inside" the shapes.

Craig, Bill. 1986, May. Polygons, stars, circles, and Logo. *Arithmetic Teacher 33*(9), 6–11.

Explores simple shapes with Logo and the mathematical ideas that can be learned from them.

Huekerott, Pamela Beth. 1988, January. Origami: Paper folding—The algorithmic way. *Arithmetic Teacher 35*(5), 4–8.

Origami in a learning center allows children to learn about shapes and angles while creating art works.

Holcomb, Jean. 1980, April. Using geoboards in the primary grades. *Arithmetic Teacher 27*(8), 22–25.

Kindergarten and first-grade children use geoboards to make designs and patterns, explore three- and four-sided figures, practice making letters, and learn about open and closed figures.

Horak, Virginia M., and Willis J. Horak. 1983, March. Using geometry tiles as a manipulative for developing basic concepts. *Arithmetic Teacher 30*(7), 8–15.

Geometry tiles are squares cut from heavy cardboard or flexible floor tiles. Directions for making tiles and activities for using them are explained.

Juraschek, William. 1990, April. Get in touch with shape. *Arithmetic Teacher 37*(8), 14–16.

Paper bags that contain two- and three-dimensional shapes are used to help children develop understanding of geometric shapes through the sense of touch.

Kaiser, Barbara. 1988, December. Explorations with tessellating polygons. *Arithmetic Teacher 36*(4), 19–24.

A student-posed question about why most floor tiles are square prompted an investigation. Tessellation activities with two-dimensional shapes, letters of the alphabet, and Escher-type drawings are illustrated and described.

Larke, Patricia J. 1988, September. Geometric extravaganza: Spicing up geometry. *Arithmetic Teacher 36*(1), 12–16.

A fair gives students the opportunity to display their geometry projects. The article offers suggestions for planning and carrying out a fair for students at all levels.

Nelson, Glenn, and Larry P. Leutzinger. 1979, November. Let's take a geometry walk. *Arithmetic Teacher 27*(3), 2–4.

A geometry walk helps children learn the relevance of geometry to their lives. Suggestions of things to view and questions to ask during a walk are presented.

Onslow, Barry. 1990, May. Pentominoes revisited. *Arithmetic Teacher 37*(9), 5–9.

Problem solving with pentominoes is discussed. Activities with tessellations, rectangles, squares, similar figures, area, and perimeter are included.

Renshaw, Barbara. 1986, September. Symmetry the trademark way. *Arithmetic Teacher 34*(1), 2–12.

Finds examples of symmetry in many commercial trademarks.

Sawada, Daiyo. 1985, December. Symmetry and tessellations from rotation transformations on transparencies. *Arithmetic Teacher 33*(4), 12–13.

Tessellation is a process of organizing tiles systematically to form patterns. This article provides an excursion into tessellations.

Smith, Robert F. 1986, April. Coordinate geometry for third graders. *Arithmetic Teacher 33*(8), 6–11.

Presents many activities that develop coordinate geometry with geoboards, dot paper, and maps.

Terc, Michael. 1985, October. Coordinate geometry—Art and mathematics. *Arithmetic Teacher 23*(2), 22–24.

Changing the scale on a drawing is easy with coordinate geometry.

Thiessen, Diane, and Margaret Matthias. 1989, December. Selected children's books for geometry. *Arithmetic Teacher 37*(4), 47–54.

Geometry concepts are found in many children's books. Activities and ideas for integrating children's books in mathematics.

Thornton, Carol A. 1979, October. Geometry: Perceptual-motor help for many handicapped learners. *Arithmetic Teacher 27*(2), 24–26.

The author believes that the benefits of geometry activities for handicapped learners are too great to be ignored. She indicates some activities for enriching children's perceptual awareness.

Van de Walle, John, and Charles S. Thompson. 1980, November. Concepts, art and fun from simple tiling patterns. *Arithmetic Teacher 28*(3), 4–8.

Tessellations are made with two different rectangles, a triangle, and a parallelogram. Basic patterns and the educational benefits are described.

_____. 1981, February. A triangle treasury. *Arithmetic Teacher 28*(6), 6–11.

Experiences with triangles in comparing likenesses and differences, studying and measuring angles, making quadrilaterals from triangles, measuring perimeters, working with symmetry, generating solids, and making tessellations.

Woodward, Ernest, and Patsy G. Bruckner. 1987, October. Reflections and symmetry—A second-grade miniunit. *Arithmetic Teacher 35*(2), 8–11.

Work with Mira (a plastic mirror) allows second graders to discover lines of symmetry.

Zurstadt, Betty K. 1984, January. Tessellations and the art of M. C. Escher. *Arithmetic Teacher 31*(5), 54–55.

Geometry and art are combined in tessellation projects.

■ NOTES

[1] National Council of Teachers of Mathematics. 1989. *Curriculum and Evaluation Standards for School Mathematics.* Reston, VA: National Council of Teachers of Mathematics, 48. Used by permission.

[2] NCTM, 48. Used by permission.

[3] NCTM, 112. Used by permission.

[4] Mary L. Crowley, 1987 Yearbook. *Learning and Teaching Geometry K–12.* Reston, VA: National Council of Teachers of Mathematics, 1–15.

[5] Pohl, Victoria. 1986. *How to Enrich Geometry Using String Designs.* Reston, VA: National Council of Teachers of Mathematics.

[6] Adapted from workshop by Margaret Kenney, Boston College, Chestnut Hill, MA, April 1988.

[7] William M. Carroll. 1988, March. Cross-sections of clay solids. *Arithmetic Teacher* *35*(7), 6–11.

[8] M. C. Escher and J. L. Locher. 1971. *The World of M. C. Escher.* New York: Harry N. Abrams, Inc.

[9] Barbara Renshaw. 1986, September. Symmetry the trademark way. *Arithmetic Teacher 34*(1), 6–12.

[10] The Learning Company, 6493 Kaiser Drive, Fremont, CA 94555.

[11] Sunburst Communications, 39 Washington Ave., Pleasantville, NY 10570-2898.

CHAPTER 12

Fractional Numbers: Common Fractions

Children's study of fractional numbers begins as early as kindergarten and continues through elementary school. The fractional numbers studied during the elementary school years are a part of the set of rational numbers that can be expressed in the form a/b, when a is any whole number and b is any nonzero whole number. Symbolically, fractional numbers can be expressed in one of three ways: as common fractions (½ and ⅔), decimal fractions (0.5 and 0.6666 . . .), and percent (50% and 66⅔%). Also, any fractional number can be expressed by an infinite number of numerals: ½ = ¼ = ⅜ = ⅛ = ⁵⁄₁₀ = ... As with other numbers, it is essential that early work allows students to intuitively develop a reasoned understanding of fractional numbers. In all grades, many concrete representations of fractional numbers help children develop a clear understanding of these numbers, their uses, and ways operations with them are performed. Common fractions are discussed in this chapter; decimal fractions and percent are treated in Chapter 13.

In this chapter you will read about

1. how the NCTM standards apply to developing children's understanding and use of common fractions;

2. four uses of common fractions from everyday life studied in elementary school;

3. the importance of understanding common fractions through concrete materials for representing parts of regions and sets;

4. a sequence of activities emphasizing equivalent fractions and comparison of unlike fractions;

5. strategies for naming or renaming equivalent fractions, including prime factorization;

6. concrete materials for modeling addition, subtraction, multiplication, and division with common fractions and developing understanding of these operations;

7. development of ideas behind cancellation and invert-and-multiply processes;

8. the role of calculators in work with common fractions;

9. activities emphasizing ratio and proportion.

NCTM STANDARDS THAT PERTAIN TO COMMON FRACTIONS

Kindergarten Through Grade Four

Standard 12: Fractions and Decimals   In grades K–4, the mathematics curriculum should include fractions . . . so that students can:

- develop concepts of fractions, mixed numbers, . . . ;

- develop number sense for fractions . . . ;

- use models to relate fractions to decimals and to find equivalent fractions;

- use models to explore operations on fractions . . . ;

- apply fractions . . . to problem situations.[1]

Grades Five Through Eight

Standard 6: Number Systems and Number Theory The mathematics curriculum should include the study of number systems and number theory so that students can:

- develop and use order relations for . . . , fractions, . . . ;

- develop and apply number theory concepts (for example, primes, factors, and multiples) in real-world and mathematical situations.[2]

Standard 7: Computation and Estimation   In grades 5–8, the mathematics curriculum should develop the concepts underlying computation and estimation in various contexts so that students can:

- compute with . . . , fractions, . . . ;

- develop, analyze, and explain procedures for computation . . . ;

- select and use an appropriate method for computing from among mental arithmetic, paper-and-pencil, calculator, and computer methods;

- use computation, estimation, and proportions to solve problems.[3]

■ THE NCTM STANDARDS

The National Council of Teachers of Mathematics provides this focus for instruction about common and decimal fractions in grades K–4:

> Fractions and decimals represent a significant extension of children's knowledge about numbers. When children possess a sound understanding of fraction and decimal concepts, they can use this knowledge to describe real-world phenomena and apply it to problems involving measurement, probability, and statistics. An understanding of fractions and decimals broadens students' awareness of the usefulness and power of numbers and extends their knowledge of the number system. It is critical in grades K–4 to develop concepts and relationships that will serve as a foundation for more advanced concepts and skills.
>
> The K–4 instruction should help students understand fractions and decimals, explore their relationship, and build initial concepts about order and equivalence. Because evidence suggests that children construct these ideas slowly, it is crucial that teachers use physical materials, diagrams, and real-world situations in conjunction with ongoing efforts to relate their learning experiences to oral language and symbols. This K–4 emphasis on basic ideas will reduce the amount of time currently spent in the upper grades in correcting students' misconceptions and procedural difficulties.[4]

The same spirit prevails for instruction in grades five and six. A continued development and extension of concepts through manipulative activities and discussion is necessary in order that students understand operations with common fractions and have a good foundation for later work with integers and other advanced number concepts.

■ MEANINGS OF COMMON FRACTIONS

Common fractions are numerals used to represent fractional numbers and ratios. There are a number of situations that give rise to common fractions; students need opportunities to deal with these situations during their years in elementary school.

Unit Subdivided into Equal-Sized Parts

Common fractions frequently arise from situations involving measurement. When it is necessary to subdivide a basic unit of measure, such as an inch, to make a more precise measurement than the whole unit allows, the inch is subdivided into equal-sized parts. Common fractions can be used to express the meaning of each subunit. When an inch is subdivided into two equal-sized parts, each part is one-half of an inch. Objects, such as a cake, are frequently cut into parts. When a cake is cut into four equal-sized parts, each part is one-fourth of the entire cake; the common fraction ¼ represents the size of each piece. The parts of a common fraction indicate the nature of the situation from which the numeral arises. In the numeral ½, the "2" indicates the number of equal-sized parts into which the whole, or unit, has been subdivided. This part of the fraction is the **denominator.** The "1" indicates the number of parts being considered at a particular time and is the **numerator.**

Set Subdivided into Equal-Sized Groups

When a set of objects is subdivided into groups of equal size the situation is clearly related to division. In a situation where a set of 12 objects is subdivided into two equal-sized groups, the mathematical sentence $12 \div 2 = 6$ represents what has taken place. The "6" represents ½ of the original set of 12. The sentence $½ \times 12 = 6$ describes the same situation. Students will often engage in activities that involve parts of sets of objects. To find ⅙ of 18, for instance, children must think of 18 objects that are subdivided into six groups of equal size. The size of each group relates to the size of the original set in such a way that each is ⅙ of the entire set. In this kind of situation the denominator indicates the number of equal-sized groups into which the set is subdivided, and the numerator indicates the number of groups being considered.

Expressions of Ratios

The relationship between a pair of numbers is often expressed as a ratio. Examples of common situations that give rise to ratios are:

- A relationship between objects in two groups is shown. In a classroom there are six books for each child. The ratio of children to books is one to six. This may be expressed by $1:6$, or by the common fraction ⅙.

- A relationship between a subset of objects and the set of which it is a part is shown. In a set of ten books there are three blue-covered books. The ratio of blue-covered books to all of the books is $3:10$, or ³⁄₁₀.

- A relationship between the sizes of two objects is shown. A ten-foot jump rope is compared with a 30-foot jump rope. The ratio between the two ropes is $10:30$, or ¹⁰⁄₃₀.

- A relationship between objects and their cost is shown. The price of two apples is 25 cents. The ratio between the apples and their cost is 2 : 25, or $\frac{2}{25}$.

Indicated Division

Sentences such as $3 \div 4 = \square$ and $17 \div 3 = \square$ indicate that division is to be performed. Cutting a piece of cloth that is three yards long into four equal-sized pieces illustrates a situation that leads to the first sentence. Another way to indicate this division is to use the common fraction $\frac{3}{4}$, which in this instance is the answer when the division is completed. A situation that illustrates the second sentence is the equal sharing of 17 cookies by three children. Division for the second sentence can be expressed as $\frac{17}{3}$, which can be renamed as the mixed numeral $5\frac{2}{3}$, the fair-share part of the 17 cookies for each child.

■ INTRODUCING COMMON FRACTIONS

Children in kindergarten and first grade are usually introduced to common fractions through activities with materials that show whole objects cut into two, three, and four parts and sets of up to perhaps ten objects separated into halves, thirds, and fourths. In grades two and three objects and sets are divided into smaller parts and the fractions that indicate their parts are introduced. Some aspects of simplifying fractions and adding and subtracting with them are introduced late in the primary years. Common denominators, least common multiple, and the more complex operations are introduced and developed in grades four through six and in grades beyond elementary school.

Using Regions

Geometric regions—such as squares, rectangles, circles, and triangles—cut from plain paper can be used to help young children understand the concept of common fractions. Children can match opposite corners of these figures and fold the paper to show halves, fourths, and eighths. It is difficult for young children to show thirds by folding blank paper, so lines should be marked to show where folds are made. Activity 12.1 suggests a way to introduce young children to the concept of one-half.

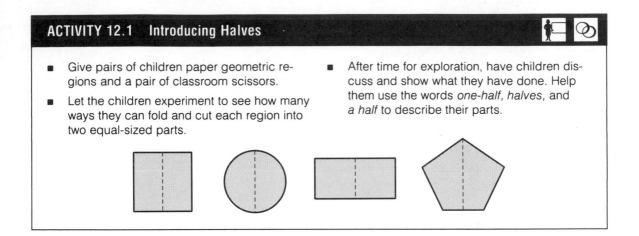

ACTIVITY 12.1 Introducing Halves

- Give pairs of children paper geometric regions and a pair of classroom scissors.

- Let the children experiment to see how many ways they can fold and cut each region into two equal-sized parts.

- After time for exploration, have children discuss and show what they have done. Help them use the words *one-half, halves,* and *a half* to describe their parts.

In subsequent lessons, children can fold and cut appropriate regions into fourths and eighths until the meaning of the subdivisions become clear (Figure 12.1). A piece of paper folded to show thirds can be folded by matching corners to show sixths (Figure 12.2). During this early work, do not use numerals for the fractions or the terms *numerator* and *denominator*. Numerals and terms should be delayed until the concepts are clearly understood.

Workbooks for grade one contain a limited number of pages that have pictures of objects marked to show fractions. You can prepare pictures of apples, pizzas, pies, and so on cut from magazines to show the fractions children are studying. Both types of materials provide worthwhile practice exercises.

Once the meanings of the shapes and their parts are clear, introduce the common fraction numerals. Relate the numerals to the shapes with which children have already worked. At first use only one part from each region to show the related unit fraction. A **unit fraction** is one in which the numerator is "1." Still do not use *numerator* and *denominator*. Do help children understand that the bottom part of the fraction indicates the number of parts into which a region has been cut, and the top part tells the part that is being considered at the moment.

Figure 12-1
Geometric regions to show fourths and eighths

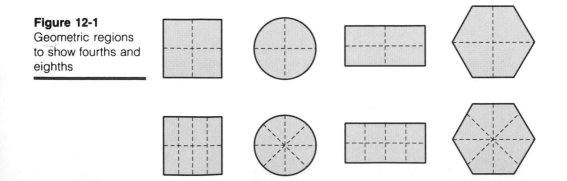

Figure 12-2
Squares (a) marked
to show where to
fold to make thirds
and (b) folded to
show sixths

(a)

(b)

Real-life situations provide opportunities for introducing numerators greater than one. "Tracy had pizza last night. Six people were expected, so the pizza was cut into six parts. Only five people ate a piece of the pizza. How much was eaten?" This and similar stories can be illustrated with pictures from magazines marked and cut to show fractional parts. Students need opportunities to deal with fractions greater than one, such as 5/4 and 9/5. Examples of such fractions can be shown with pictures of pizzas, pies, and similar objects. A whole pizza and one-fourth more show 5/4, while one pie and four-fifths of another one show 9/5. Fractions with numerators greater than the denominator have historically been called **improper fractions.** It is more meaningful to children to call them fractions that are greater, or larger, than one.

Using Sets of Objects

The concept of a fractional part of a set can be introduced only after children have a good grasp of whole numbers and are skillful in counting the number of objects in a set. Finding fractional parts of regions is often easier for children than recognizing fractional parts of a set, so work with regions should precede work with sets. Then the new work can be associated with regions. Activity 12.2 shows one way to relate understanding of parts of a set to fractional regions.

ACTIVITY 12.2   Berry Pies

- Cut several circles from construction paper or tagboard and mark them into halves, thirds, fourths, and sixths. These are the pies. Have children cut shapes to represent raspberries, cherries, strawberries, and blueberries. Have them make sets of 24 of each of the berries.

- Explain that the pies have been cut into equal-sized parts and that the children are to make certain that each person will receive an equal number of berries in each piece of pie.

- Have each child take a set of 12 berries and place them on a pie so that an equal number are in each region.

- Describe what is happening as each child completes a pie. "The pie has six parts. There are 12 berries. Two berries are in each piece of pie. One-sixth of 12 berries is two."

- Have children separate sets of 6, 18, and 24 berries on the 6-piece pie.

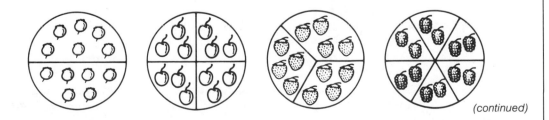

(continued)

Activity 12.2   *continued*

- Have children describe what they are doing and the results of dividing the sets into equal parts.

- Repeat with pies cut into three, four, or eight pieces and sets of berries that can be equally divided among them.

- Variation: After the idea is well established, ask children what they would do if a pie had 4 parts and 22 berries, 3 parts and 4 berries, and so on.

The children should soon be able to divide sets into equal groups without having the fractional regions as a cue. Eight objects can be arranged in two equal-sized groups, then four equal-sized groups. Other sets can be divided into two, three, four, or five equal-sized groups until the children understand. They may notice that some sets cannot be divided into equal-sized parts with a whole number answer for each subset. This realization sets the stage for operations with fractional numbers, discussed later in this chapter.

EXERCISE   Describe several common objects or situations to use during an introductory lesson for a part-of-a-whole and a part-of-a-set situation other than the ones used in the text.

■ COMPARING FRACTIONAL NUMBERS

As children study whole numbers, they learn to compare them so that they can tell when one number is greater than, less than, or equal to another. They use sets, number lines, and other means of comparing numbers until the idea is clear. They learn that one number is greater than another if it is to the right of the other on the number line. At the same time, they learn that every whole number has an immediate predecessor and an immediate successor. It is always possible to determine the predecessor of a whole number greater than zero by subtracting one from it. The successor of a number is determined by adding one to it. As children study fractional numbers, they learn that these numbers can be ordered by size, even though there is no constant value between fractional numbers as there is between each pair of whole numbers.

It is possible to compare a pair of fractions by changing one or both of them so they have common denominators. To compare $\frac{5}{8}$ and $\frac{11}{16}$, $\frac{5}{8}$ can be changed to $\frac{10}{16}$. When fractions have a common denominator, the one with the larger numerator is larger.

It should be clear that such an abstract way of comparing fractional numbers is unsuitable for young children. Initial experiences should come through investigations with models of various kinds. Later, more abstract procedures can be used as children's understanding of fractional numbers matures.

Using Congruent Geometric Shapes

Activity 12.3 uses materials that are appropriate in grades two and three to compare common fractions.

Congruent shapes are also useful for investigations in which children compare nonunit fractions. Pieces of paper folded and colored like those in Figure 12.3 help them see that $\frac{3}{4} > \frac{2}{3} > \frac{1}{2}$. As long as the shapes from which pieces are cut are congruent, children can see and order any fractional numbers that can be conveniently folded, cut, and colored to show parts.

ACTIVITY 12.3   Congruent Shapes

- Have the children work in pairs. Give each pair of children paper cut in circles, squares, and other shapes easily folded to show halves, fourths, and eighths.

- Have the children fold one piece to show halves, another piece of the same shape to show fourths, and a third piece to show eighths; each piece is cut into two, four, or eight parts. One piece of each size should be colored with a crayon. One unit piece should be left uncut and uncolored.

- Have the children place a half piece on top of a whole piece, a fourth piece on top of the half piece, and an eighth piece on top of the fourth piece. As the pieces are put in place, talk about which pieces are larger and which are smaller. As the pieces are discussed, order the numerals from larger to smaller and smaller to larger: $1 > \frac{1}{2} > \frac{1}{4} > \frac{1}{8}$ and $\frac{1}{8} < \frac{1}{4} < \frac{1}{2} < 1$.

- Shapes cut and colored to show thirds, sixths, ninths, and twelfths, as well as halves, fifths, and tenths, can be used to compare those fractions.

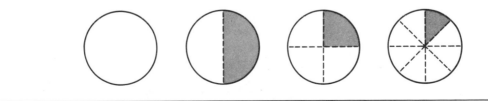

Figure 12-3
Geometric regions used to compare the size of $\frac{1}{2}$, $\frac{2}{3}$, and $\frac{3}{4}$

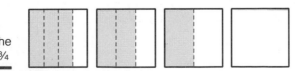

Using Fraction Strips

Fraction strips are useful for comparing common fractions, as in Activity 12.4. A set can be cut from colored cardboard and magnets attached to the backs for manipulation on a magnetic board. Sets for children's desktop investigations can be cut from colored construction paper.

ACTIVITY 12.4   Fraction Strips

- Organize the class for a cooperative-learning experience.

- Give each group a set of construction-paper fraction strips and a set of duplicated questions, such as these:

  —How many ½ strips are as long as the 1 strip? How many ⅓ strips are as long as the 1 strip? Which is longer, a ½ strip or a ⅓ strip?

  —What is the shortest fraction strip in this set? Which strips are longer than this strip?

  —Use the fraction strips to put these common fractions in order beginning with the largest and ending with the smallest: ⅛, ½, ⅓, ⅙, ¼.

  —Which is longer, two ½ strips or two ⅓ strips?

  —Which is longer, two ⅙ strips, or one ¼ strip?

  —Which is shorter, two ½ strips or two ⅛ strips?

  —Use the strips to put these common fractions in order, beginning with the smallest and ending with the largest: ⅔, ³⁄₆, ³⁄₈, ¾.

- Have the children explain their work as they discuss the questions.

- Variation: Have students make a fraction-strip book to compare common fractions. Cut a unit piece from construction paper; this will be the last page of the book. Twelve inches by two inches is a good size because twelve is easily divided into parts. Next, make quarter, two-quarter, and three-quarter pieces from another color of construction paper. Fold the two-quarter and the three-

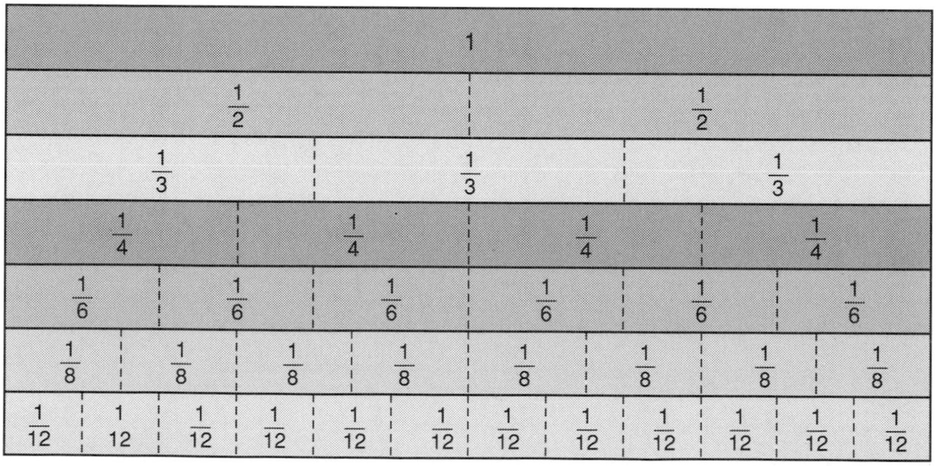

Activity 12.4   *continued*

quarter pieces to show their fractional parts. Make a one-third and a two-third piece from another color, and fold the two-third piece. Align the pieces along the left edge with the

shortest piece on top and the unit piece at the back. Staple along the left edge. The children can label each fraction and later add other pages to show sixths and eighths.

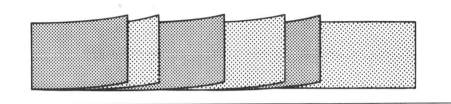

Using a Set of Number Lines

A set of number lines marked to show fractions is a more abstract way to show and compare fractions than are regions and fraction strips. Children who have a good understanding of common fractions can use number lines to compare fractions, as in Activity 12.5. Number lines are good for older students' review of ordering and comparing fractions.

ACTIVITY 12.5   Number-Line Chart

- Display a chart showing number lines with only whole numbers named. (Points for fractional numbers are lightly marked to make them easy to locate during the activity.)

- Direct students' attention to the top line and point out the unit segment.

- Go to the next line and mark the point midway between the "0" and "1" on the upper line. Have children identify and label the marks that show ½ and 2⁄2 points on the line.

- Go to the third line and mark points on it; have the children identify and label these points: ¼, 2⁄4, ¾, 4⁄4, 5⁄4.

- Continue until the bottom line that shows thirty-seconds has been marked and labeled.

- Raise and discuss questions such as these:

—How many of the ½ segments match the length of the unit segment?

—What is the shortest segment on the chart?

—How many of the ¹⁄16 segments are equivalent to a ⅛ segment?

—Which is longer, a ¹⁄16 segment or a ¼ segment?

—Which is shorter, two ⅛ segments or two ¼ segments?

—What number of eighths segments are equivalent to a ½ segment? to a fourth segment? to a whole segment?

—What is the order of these segments from longest to shortest?

$$\frac{1}{4} \quad \frac{3}{8} \quad \frac{19}{32} \quad \frac{1}{2} \quad \frac{3}{4} \quad \frac{30}{32} \quad \frac{3}{16} \; \textit{(cont'd)}$$

Activity 12.5   *continued*

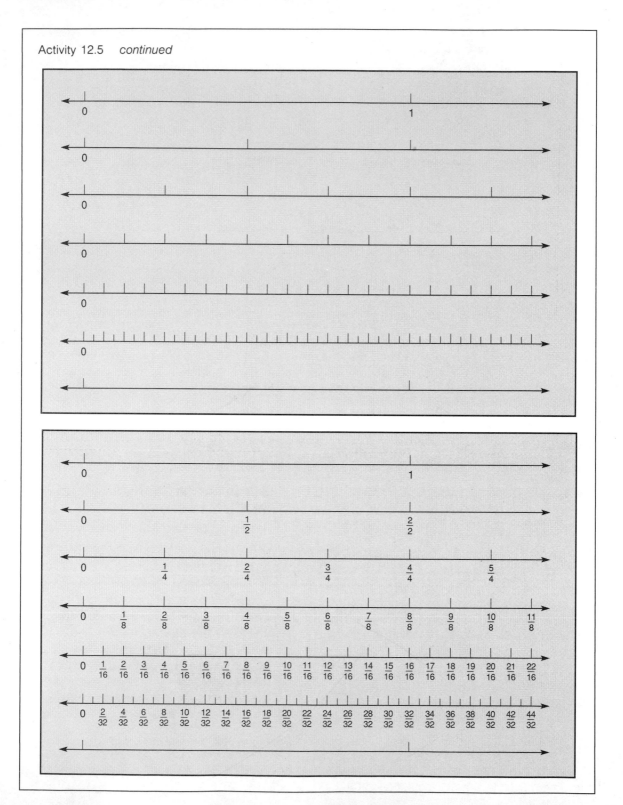

The concepts that a fractional number has no immediate predecessor or successor and that there are an infinite number of fractional numbers between any pair of fractions can be developed intuitively with a number-line chart. It is possible to explain these concepts mathematically, but the process is too abstract for most elementary school children. Questions like these can be used:

- "If we follow this pattern [the one used in Activity 12.5] of making points on number lines, what will be the name of the first point on the blank number line at the bottom of the chart?" (It will be $\frac{1}{64}$.)

- "I have run out of space on the chart for more number lines. Does that mean that there are no fractional numbers between $\frac{1}{32}$ and 0?" (No.)

- "Will the sequence ever end? Why not?" (It is always possible to indicate a point between two points on the line.)

Students in the fifth and sixth grades can use the number-line chart to learn how to determine fractional numbers that are midway between any pair of fractional numbers. They can eventually use an averaging process to find a number midway between a pair of fractional numbers, as in Activity 12.6.

Using Abstract Procedures

Students who understand the meaning of common fractions and who have a mature understanding of the procedures for comparing numbers that have already been discussed are ready to learn a multiplication process to compare fractions. The procedure works this way: To compare the fractions $\frac{2}{3}$ and $\frac{3}{5}$ multiply the numerator of the first fraction by the denomi-

---

ACTIVITY 12.6   Midpoints

- Have students locate the points $\frac{2}{4}$ and $\frac{3}{4}$ on the fourths line.

- Have them locate the point midway between them. "What is the simplest name we can give this point?" If students say "five-eighths" ask how they know. If the answer is not known, call attention to the point located at the same position on the eighths line.

- Use questions like these to focus attention on the averaging process:

  —"What will $\frac{2}{4}$ and $\frac{3}{4}$ be if we express them as eighths?"

  —"What is the sum of $\frac{4}{8}$ and $\frac{6}{8}$?"

  —"Can you figure what we can do to $\frac{10}{8}$ to determine the fraction midway between $\frac{4}{8}$ and $\frac{6}{8}$?" Help children see that $\frac{10}{8}$ is divided by two.

- Repeat with other pairs of fractions until the children recognize that by adding a pair of fractional numbers and dividing their sum by two, they can find a number that lies midway between that pair of numbers.

nator of the second and the denominator of the first fraction by the the numerator of the second—$2 \times 5 = 10$ and $3 \times 3 = 9$. When the product of the first numerator and second denominator is greater than the product of the first denominator and second numerator, the first fraction is greater than the second one. When the product is smaller, the second fraction is greater than the first one; when the products are the same, the fractions are equivalent. In this instance, $\frac{2}{3}$ is greater than $\frac{3}{5}$ because 2 times 5 is greater than 3 times 3.

FRACTIONAL NUMBERS GREATER THAN ONE

Fractional numbers that are greater than one require special attention. As children work with a number line, where such numbers are regularly displayed, they will see them represented to the right of "1" and see that such numbers can be expressed as either a common fraction or as a whole number and common fraction. Common fractions with numerators larger than denominators are called improper fractions. Calling them **fractions greater than one** is more meaningful to children, though.

After these fractions are understood, children should learn a procedure for changing a fraction greater than one to a **mixed numeral.** In the past, these have been called **mixed numbers,** but in the interest of distinguishing between number and numeral, it is more accurate to call them mixed numerals. The procedure to change an improper fraction to a mixed numeral is to divide the numerator of the fraction by the denominator. This yields a whole number or a whole number and a remainder. The remainder and the denominator of the fraction form the fraction part of the mixed numeral. The fraction $\frac{21}{9}$ is changed to $2\frac{1}{3}$ by dividing 21 by 9, and writing the fraction $\frac{3}{9}$, or $\frac{1}{3}$, after 2. It is not always the case that the fraction part of the mixed numeral is one that can be simplified.

Fractions greater than one can be changed to mixed numerals with the Math Explorer™ calculator. A key, [Ab/c], is used. To enter a fraction, say $\frac{15}{7}$, press [1], [5], [/], and [7]. To change $\frac{15}{7}$ to a mixed numeral enter the fraction and press [Ab/c]. The answer is displayed as 2 u $\frac{1}{7}$. The "2 u" indicates 2 units and the "$\frac{1}{7}$" indicates $\frac{1}{7}$ of another unit. A mixed numeral can be put into the calculator by entering the whole number, pressing [Unit], and the fraction. The display for $2\frac{1}{2}$ appears as 2 u $\frac{1}{2}$.

SYSTEMATIC PROCEDURES FOR NAMING EQUIVALENT FRACTIONS

Before students can understand all aspects of adding and subtracting fractional numbers and become proficient in performing the operations using common fractions, they must learn to express common fractions so that they have the same denominators. The process for doing this, commonly referred to as changing to a common denominator, must be developed carefully so that students will understand both the necessity for doing it and how to do it meaningfully. Children should learn that when they rename one fractional number to get an equivalent common fraction, the value of each number remains the same. Students who have had many experiences with the various learning aids illustrated in this chapter will have little difficulty with numbers such as $\frac{1}{2}$, $\frac{1}{4}$, $\frac{1}{8}$, $\frac{1}{3}$, and $\frac{1}{6}$. They will "just know" that $\frac{2}{4}$ and $\frac{4}{8}$ are other names for $\frac{1}{2}$ and that $\frac{2}{6}$ is another name for $\frac{1}{3}$. However, they need to learn systematic procedures for dealing with less familiar numbers.

Using Multiples

In some cases the denominator of one fraction is a multiple of the denominator of another fraction. When this is so, as with $\frac{2}{5}$ and $\frac{3}{20}$, the larger of the two denominators is a common denominator. The following thought process can be used:

- "Twenty is a multiple of five. By what number do we multiply five to get 20?" (4.)
- "To rename $\frac{2}{5}$ with a denominator of 20, multiply both the numerator, 2, and the denominator, 5, by 4. Two-fifths is equal to $\frac{8}{20}$."

When neither of the denominators is a common denominator, a different procedure must be used. The easiest procedure if denominators are small—for example, $\frac{1}{2}$ and $\frac{1}{5}$ or $\frac{1}{4}$ and $\frac{1}{6}$—is to use successive multiples. For $\frac{1}{2}$ and $\frac{1}{5}$, multiples of 2 and 5 are used (see Activity 12.7).

ACTIVITY 12.7 Least Common Multiple

- Write a "2" on the chalkboard. Ask, "What are the first several multiples of two?" Write the multiples after the "2."
- Write a "5" beneath the "2." Ask, "What are the first several multiples of five?" Write these on the chalkboard.

2	4	6	8	10	12	14	16	18	20
5	10	15	20	25	30	35	40	45	50

- Ask, "What numbers are on both lists?" Ring these numbers.

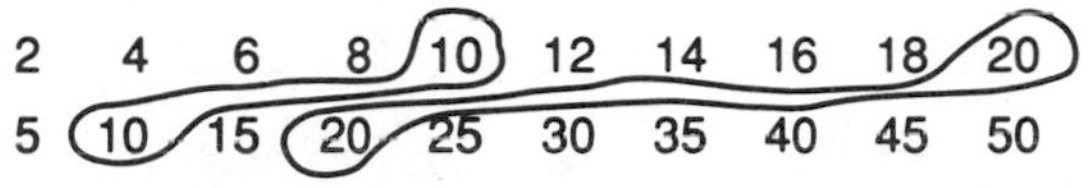

- Discuss the common numbers. Point out that each one is a common denominator for the two fractions, and that 10 is the least com-

(continued)

Activity 12.7   *continued*

mon denominator because it is the smallest of all common denominators.

- Repeat with other pairs of numbers.
- Show how the process works with three numbers.

4	8	12	16	20	24	28	32	40	44
5	10	15	20	25	30	35	40	45	50
8	16	24	32	40	48	56	64	64	88

Using Equivalent Classes

Another procedure for finding common denominators is to make a list of the first several numbers in the equivalence class for each fraction. To add ⅙ and ⅜, the following numerals would be listed:

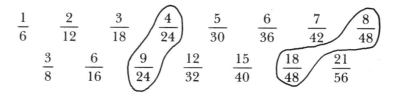

$$\frac{1}{6} \quad \frac{2}{12} \quad \frac{3}{18} \quad \frac{4}{24} \quad \frac{5}{30} \quad \frac{6}{36} \quad \frac{7}{42} \quad \frac{8}{48}$$

$$\frac{3}{8} \quad \frac{6}{16} \quad \frac{9}{24} \quad \frac{12}{32} \quad \frac{15}{40} \quad \frac{18}{48} \quad \frac{21}{56}$$

When students examine the two lists they find that there are some fractional numbers that have the same denominators. These should be ringed or identified by being written on the chalkboard: ⅙ = ⁴⁄₂₄ = ⁸⁄₄₈ and ⅜ = ⁹⁄₂₄ = ¹⁸⁄₄₈. Both of the pairs of numbers, ⁴⁄₂₄ and ⁹⁄₂₄ and ⁸⁄₄₈ and ¹⁸⁄₄₈ can be used to add ⅙ and ⅜.

$$
\begin{array}{ccc}
\dfrac{1}{6} & \dfrac{4}{24} & \dfrac{8}{48} \\[2mm]
+\ \dfrac{3}{8} & +\ \dfrac{9}{24} & +\ \dfrac{18}{48} \\[2mm]
& \dfrac{13}{24} & \dfrac{26}{48}
\end{array}
$$

Using Prime Factorizations

The process of determining common denominators for a pair of unlike fractions can be made systematic by using a factorization process. Students who learn to factor composite numbers can use a factorization process to determine the least common multiple, or least common denominator, when they add or subtract unlike fractions.

A composite number is factored completely when it is represented by a product expression that consists of two or more prime numbers. When the number 18 is factored completely, it is expressed as $2 \times 3 \times 3$; 36 is expressed as $2 \times 2 \times 3 \times 3$. Two ways of factoring numbers are described.

The first way is to determine factors by examination. It is useful when numbers are small, and particularly when there are only two prime factors. Numbers like 4, 6, 9, 14, and 15 are useful ones to introduce the concept to children. Children name the factors for each number and determine whether there are only prime numbers, or whether there is a composite number in a pair of factors. The above numbers all have two prime factors. When a number like 12 is used, there will be more than one way to factor it; either 2×6 or 3×4 can start the factorization. Either way there is a number that is composite, so further factoring is needed. The prime factorization of 12 is $2 \times 2 \times 3$.

Factor trees give a systematic way to factor numbers that are reasonably small but are the product of more than two prime numbers. Factor trees are created by expressing numbers in terms of successively smaller factors until all factors are prime numbers. The process is demonstrated in Activity 12.8, where different factor trees for 24 are made.

ACTIVITY 12.8   Factor Trees

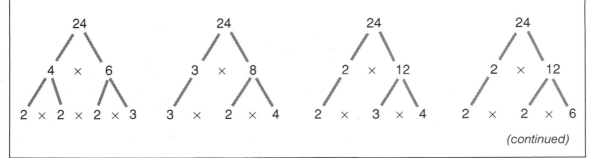

- Begin by writing three 24s on the chalkboard. Ask, "What are two numbers that when multiplied have a product of 24?"

(There are three pairs of numbers.) Write each pair beneath one of the 24s. Connect them to 24 with lines.

- Ask for factors of each of the factors of 24. Write them beneath their number. When a number is already prime, repeat it in the tree.

There are two ways to factor 12. Show one way in the original tree and make a second tree to show the other way.

(continued)

Activity 12.8   *continued*

- Complete the factor trees that still have composite numbers. (The factor tree on the left was complete after the second step.)

- Have students examine the bottom row of each factor tree. Discuss the way they are the same and how they might be different. (They will all have the same numbers; the numbers may be written in a different order in some of the rows.) The fact that every composite number has only one set of prime factors is called the **fundamental theorem of arithmetic**.

- Repeat with numbers such as 16, 18, 28, 30, 36, and 40.

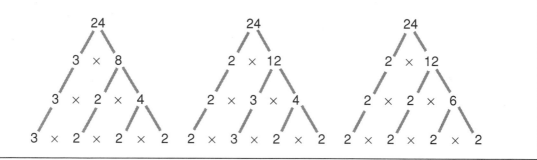

A prime number may appear more than once in a composite number's factorization, as 24, whose factorization is $2 \times 2 \times 2 \times 3$, or 18, whose factorization is $2 \times 3 \times 3$. Students who are familiar with exponential notation can express these factorizations with exponents. The expression $2 \times 2 \times 2 \times 3$ becomes $2^3 \times 3$ and $2 \times 3 \times 3$ becomes 2×3^2.

Once students understand that numbers can be expressed as the product of two or more prime numbers, they can use the knowledge to find least common multiples for two or more common fractions. For the pair of common fractions ⅙ and ⅛ the first step is to find the prime factorization of each denominator: 2×3 for 6 and $2 \times 2 \times 2$ for 8. A common multiple can be determined by finding the product of the two prime factorizations, but 48 is not the least common multiple. Since 2 is a factor of both 6 and 8 it needs to be used only as many times as it appears in the factorization with the most 2's. It appears three times in the factorization for 8, so three 2's are used with 3 from the factorization of 6 to yield the least common multiple: 24. The Venn diagram in Figure 12.4 illustrates why 2 is used as a factor only three times.

When the process is applied to addition, this sequence of steps is one way to proceed. First, determine the prime factorization of each denominator:

Figure 12-4
The Venn diagram illustrates why the least common multiple of 6 and 8 is 24.

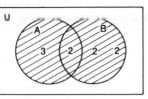

$$\frac{4}{15} = \frac{4}{3 \times 5}$$

$$\frac{5}{12} = \frac{5}{2 \times 2 \times 3}$$

Next, form the union of the sets of factors used in the prime factorization of the denominators: $2 \times 2 \times 3 \times 5$. This becomes the denominator that is used in renaming the fractional numbers:

$$\frac{4}{15} = \frac{4 \times 2 \times 2}{2 \times 2 \times 3 \times 5}$$

$$\frac{5}{12} = \frac{5 \times 5}{2 \times 2 \times 3 \times 5}$$

The number by which each numerator is multiplied is found by noting the factors by which the original denominator is multiplied to yield the new denominator: for $\frac{4}{15}$ the factors 2×2 are used, so the numerator is multiplied by 4; for $\frac{5}{12}$ the factor 5 is used, so the numerator is multiplied by 5.

$$\frac{4}{15} \rightarrow \frac{4}{3 \times 5} \rightarrow \frac{4 \times 2 \times 2}{2 \times 2 \times 3 \times 5} \rightarrow \frac{16}{60}$$

$$+ \frac{5}{12} \rightarrow + \frac{5}{2 \times 2 \times 3} \rightarrow + \frac{5 \times 5}{2 \times 2 \times 3 \times 5} \rightarrow + \frac{25}{60}$$

$$\frac{41}{60}$$

RENAMING COMMON FRACTIONS IN SIMPLEST FORM

A fractional number is expressed as a common fraction in its simplest form when the numbers represented by the numerator and the denominator have no common factor, or are **relatively prime.** There are times when the original answers to problems involving fractional numbers should be simplified. "There is $\frac{5}{8}$ of a cake left in the refrigerator. What part of the cake is left when Carlos takes a piece that is $\frac{1}{8}$ of the cake?" The answer $\frac{4}{8}$ is changed to $\frac{1}{2}$. Four ways to simplify fractions are discussed.

Using Number Lines

Number lines are particularly good for helping children learn about expressing common fractions in simplest form. (You may recognize the process of renaming a fraction in simplest form as "reducing a fraction to lowest terms.") During early work with number lines, children used them to compare common fractions and learned that a fraction like ½ can be renamed as ²⁄₄, ³⁄₆, ⁴⁄₈, and so on. At that time, they changed fractions to higher terms. Now they use the lines to do the reverse; they will simplify fractions, or express them in lower terms. Activity 12.9 suggests possible exercises.

Examining Numerator and Denominator

One commonly used procedure to simplify a fraction is to examine the numerator and denominator for the largest common divisor. Once a common divisor is determined, both numerator and denominator can be divided by it. Children who know the role of one in division will understand how one is used to simplify the fraction ⁹⁄₂₁:

$$\frac{9}{21} \rightarrow \frac{9}{21} \div 1 = \frac{9}{21} \div \frac{3}{3} = \frac{9 \div 3}{21 \div 3} = \frac{3}{7}$$

This procedure is satisfactory as long as the numbers are reasonably small and the greatest common divisor can be readily determined, as in ⁶⁄₁₂ or ⁹⁄₁₅. It will be less useful when the numerators and denominators are larger numbers.

Using Prime Factorizations

With larger numbers in the numerator and denominator, a better procedure is to find and use the prime factorization for each number. An example, ²⁴⁄₃₆, is treated in Activity 12.10 in the same way that students should proceed.

Simplifying with the Math Explorer™ Calculator

The Math Explorer™ calculator has a process for simplifying common fractions. When a student believes a fraction can be simplified, he or she presses ⌐Simp⌐. If the fraction is in simplest form, the display shows "SIMP". If the fraction can be simplified, the display shows the expression "N/D → n/d". The fraction is simplified by either entering a number that is a common factor of both numerator and denominator and pressing ⌐=⌐ or just by pressing ⌐=⌐. If the common factor is the greatest common factor, the simplest form of the fraction is displayed. If the common factor is not the greatest common factor, "ND → nd" appears to show that the number can be further simplified. Other common factors are entered until the simplest form is expressed on the display. If simplification is done solely by the calculator, press ⌐Simp⌐ and ⌐=⌐ alternately until the simplest form is displayed. These are the steps to simplify ¹⁸⁄₂₄:

STUDENT   Enter ¹⁸⁄₂₄ ; press ⌐Simp⌐, ⌐6⌐, and ⌐–⌐; ⅔ is displayed.

MACHINE   Enter ¹⁸⁄₂₄; press ⌐Simp⌐ and ⌐=⌐ alternately until ⅔ is displayed. (The machine uses 2, then 3, as common factors to get ⅔.)

EXERCISE   Activities for developing understanding of common fractions and for comparing fractions, learning about fractions greater than one, and simplifying

---

ACTIVITY 12.9   Simplifying Fractions

- Use a set of number lines like the completed one in Activity 12.5.

- Direct students' attention to ¹⁶⁄₃₂ at the bottom. "What fractions on other lines name the same point as ¹⁶⁄₃₂?" (⁸⁄₁₆, ⁴⁄₈, ²⁄₄, ½.) "Which of these has the smallest denominator?" (½.) "Is there a simpler way to name this point?" (No.)

- Discuss the fact that each of the fractions ¹⁶⁄₃₂, ⁸⁄₁₆, ⁴⁄₈, and ²⁄₄ is expressed in simplest form as ½.

- Repeat with other points on this chart, and on charts that show thirds, sixths, ninths, and twelfths, and fifths and tenths.

ACTIVITY 12.10   Prime Factorization

- Write the fraction ²⁴⁄₃₆ on the chalkboard. Ask, "What is the prime factorization of 24?" (2 × 2 × 2 × 3.) "What is the prime factorization of 36?" (2 × 2 × 3 × 3.)

$$\frac{24}{36} = \frac{2 \times 2 \times 2 \times 3}{2 \times 2 \times 3 \times 3}$$

- Ask, "What factors are common to both numbers?" (Two 2s and a 3.)

- Draw a Venn diagram to help students visualize the common factors.

$$\frac{24}{36} = \frac{24 \div 12}{36 \div 12} = \frac{2}{3}$$

- Have students determine the product of the common factors. (12.)

- Divide both terms of the fraction by 12.

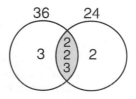

fractions progress from the concrete to the abstract. Review the discussions of activities beginning with introduction of fractions on page 401, and then list the steps from concrete to abstract for each one.

■ PRACTICING FRACTION SKILLS

Children's workbooks and textbooks contain pages that deal with each of the concepts included in the previous sections. These should be used whenever they are appropriate for a particular student or group of students.

Many computer programs for exploring common fraction concepts have been developed. Programs should be used only after children have developed understanding through activities with concrete materials. In *Fraction Munchers*,[5] students search for various types of fractional numbers to help "Munchers" avoid "Troggles." *Box™ Introduces Fractions*[6] provides work with identifying fractions, writing fractions, and comparing fractions. A pizza parlor provides a setting for learning about fractions in *Pizza Fractions*.[7] Students first learn to cut pizzas into fractional parts and identify the parts. At the highest level students fill orders by finding fractional parts of pizzas cut into various numbers of pieces. Two programs from Queue[8] provide background and instruction about the meanings of fractions. *The Meaning of Fractions* is a comprehensive introduction to fractions in which students write fractions from descriptions and demonstrate fractions by creating pictures, manipulating objects, or selecting representations. In *Fraction Concepts, Inc.,* students work in a factory to control machines on an assembly line containing fractions. Topics include the basic definition of a fraction, types of fractions, and simple equivalent fractions. There are other programs that cover a range of mathematics topics, including sections dealing with fractions. Consult catalogs from companies listed in Appendix B for these programs and more complete descriptions of programs mentioned here.

■ OPERATIONS WITH FRACTIONAL NUMBERS EXPRESSED AS COMMON FRACTIONS

By the time children are ready to perform the operations of addition, subtraction, multiplication, and division with fractional numbers, they have already developed skill in performing these operations with whole numbers. Armed with this knowledge, teachers frequently introduce operations with fractional numbers by using a series of rules: "If two fractions have the same denominator, the sum can be found by adding the numerators and placing the sum over the denominator." "If two fractions have unlike denominators, they must be changed to their least common denominator before they can be added." Rules for renaming fractional numbers with a common denominator are then posted so children can proceed with the addition. However, teaching these operations by rule alone means that many children will have little understanding of what they are doing and why they are doing it. Another weakness of teaching by rules is that students have little or no way to associate an operation with the real-world situations that give rise to it. Thus, they do not learn how to apply what they learn to problem-solving situations.

Procedures that help children visualize operations with fractional numbers are extensions of those used with whole numbers. Children's early counting experiences give them an intuitive understanding of addition and subtraction as they join and separate collections of objects. As children engage in more formal activities to learn to add and subtract whole numbers, they learn the meaning of the operations in terms of joining and separating sets. Objects, markers, number lines, and other devices are used so that children can discover the meanings of the operations. Children should learn to add and subtract fractional numbers in the same ways. Familiar physical models help extend children's understanding of addition and subtraction to fractional numbers.

■ ADDITION WITH COMMON FRACTIONS

There are several levels of complexity in situations that involve addition of common fractions. Addition with like denominators is easiest. Within that type of addition there are answers that do not need to be simplified, answers that do, and answers with sums greater than one. Addition with unlike denominators is more complex because a common denominator must be determined. Answers are of the same types as before. The most complex type of addition is with mixed numerals. All answers for this type are greater than one. Work with addition is spread over several years to account for the different levels of difficulty and children's maturity to cope with them.

$$\frac{1}{4} + \frac{1}{4} = \frac{2}{4}$$

$$\frac{1}{3} + \frac{1}{3} = \frac{2}{3}$$

$$\frac{1}{2} + \frac{1}{2} = \frac{2}{2}$$

$$\frac{1}{4} + \frac{2}{4} = \frac{3}{4}$$

Addition with Like Denominators

The setting within which children work should be stocked with familiar concrete materials: geometric regions left whole and cut into fractional parts, fraction-strip sets, fraction booklets, and number-line charts. Present a problem, such as the one in Activity 12.11.

After students have determined the answers for several problem situations, display the addition sentence for each one (if not already done for each one by students) and call attention to them: "What have we done in each sentence to determine the sum?" (See margin.)

Guide the children to see that the sum is determined by adding the numerators of the fractional numbers. It may be helpful to students to see the sentences rewritten as:

$$\frac{1 + 1}{4} = \frac{2}{4}, \qquad \frac{1 + 1}{3} = \frac{2}{3}, \qquad \frac{1 + 1}{2} = \frac{2}{2}, \qquad \text{and} \qquad \frac{1 + 2}{4} = \frac{3}{4}$$

This emphasizes the fact that the numerators are added. If children have difficulty understanding the process, the examples can be further simplified:

$$\begin{array}{llll} \quad 1 \text{ fourth} & \quad 1 \text{ third} & \quad 1 \text{ half} & \quad 1 \text{ fourth} \\ \underline{+ 1 \text{ fourth}} & \underline{+ 1 \text{ third}} & \underline{+ 1 \text{ half}} & \underline{+ 2 \text{ fourths}} \end{array}$$

Problems with answers greater than one can also be examined through activities with concrete materials, as in Activity 12.12.

ACTIVITY 12.11   Adding Common Fractions

"Last night Jim worked on his math assignment for ¼ hour before dinner and for ¼ hour after dinner. What part of an hour did he use for the math lesson?"

■ Let students work in pairs with concrete materials of their choice, if necessary, to determine the answer.

■ Discuss each pair's way of determining the answer. These are possibilities:
  —"We used fourths of circles to represent each of the two quarter hours. We put them together to make two-fourths, or one-half hour."

—"We used two pieces that show fourths in our fraction-strip set. They showed us that two-fourths is the same as one-half."

—"We used the number-line chart. When we showed two jumps that are each one-quarter unit long, we stopped at two-fourths, which is the same as one-half."
—Some children may say, "We just know that one-fourth and one-fourth equal one-half." Some of these children may have even used the addition sentence ¼ + ¼ = 2/4 (or ½) to determine the sentence. If so, have them write the sentence on the chalkboard and discuss it.

■ Present other, similar problem situations to be solved in the same ways.

Adding When Denominators are Different

Children's background for this new addition must include an understanding of the following things:

- The meaning of addition of whole numbers
- The basic facts for addition
- Common fractions and concrete models to represent them
- Addition of fractions with like denominators
- How to rename fractions so they have common denominators

The addition sentence ½ + ¼ = ☐ is used in Activity 12.13. One of the denominators is the common denominator in this sentence. In the sentence ½ + ⅓ = ☐ neither denominator is the common denominator. This sentence is the example in Activity 12.14.

ACTIVITY 12.12   Answers Greater Than One

"Josie is making a bandana and will use ⅔ of a yard of yellow material and ⅔ of a yard of green material. How much material will she use for the bandana?"

- Have students work in pairs to determine the answer, using self-selected concrete aids. Fraction strips and number lines are particularly useful because their properties parallel the linear measure used for determining the amount of material needed for the bandana.

- Have a student write the completed addition sentence on the chalkboard.

$$\frac{2}{3} + \frac{2}{3} = \frac{4}{3}$$

- Discuss the answer and have students demonstrate with their materials that ⁴⁄₃ is the same as 1⅓. Show this in the sentence.

$$\frac{2}{3} + \frac{2}{3} = \frac{4}{3} = 1\frac{1}{3}$$

Repeat with other situations having sums greater than one.

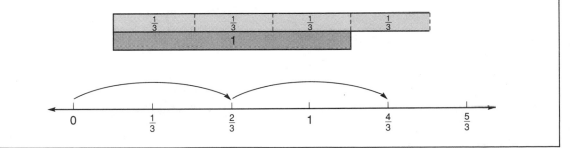

ACTIVITY 12.13   Adding with Unlike Denominators

"While making some clothes for her sister, Mae used ½ yard of material for the skirt and ¼ yard for the blouse. What part of a yard did she use for the outfit?"

- Let students work in pairs with concrete materials to determine the answer.

- Have students explain their procedures and demonstrate their materials. Fraction strips are used below.

- Have a student write the addition sentence on the chalkboard.

$$\frac{1}{2} + \frac{1}{4} = \square$$

- Point out that the denominators are not the same. Discuss what must be done to complete the addition with the algorithm. Some children will "just know" that ½ can be changed to ¾. Show this in the sentence.

$$\frac{2}{4} + \frac{1}{4} = \frac{3}{4}$$

- Verify this with the fraction strips by exchanging the half-strip for two of the fourth strips.

- Repeat with similar situations.

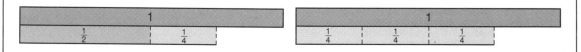

ACTIVITY 12.14   More Adding with Unlike Denominators

"Bubba ran halfway around the track for one wind sprint and a third of the way around for a second wind sprint. How far did he run for both sprints?"

- Write the sentence for this situation on the chalkboard.

$$\frac{1}{2} + \frac{1}{3} = \square$$

- Point out that neither denominator is a common denominator. (See next page).

- Use a number-line chart to help children determine a common denominator. Ask questions such as:
  —"Which lines have another name for one-half on them?" (The fourths, the sixths, the eighths, the sixteenths, the thirty-seconds.)

  —"Which lines have another name for one-third on them?" (Only the sixths.)

—"Which line should we use to find a common denominator for our sentence?" (The sixths.)

—"How many sixths is one-half?" (Three-sixths.) "One-third?" (Two-sixths.)

- Rewrite the sentence to change the fractions.

$$\frac{3}{6} + \frac{2}{6} = \square$$

- Complete the sentence.

$$\frac{3}{6} + \frac{2}{6} = \frac{5}{6}$$

- Verify this with the number line.

- Repeat with similar situations.

Ultimately students who understand least common multiples, or lowest common denominators, and processes for renaming fractions as equivalent fractions will use mature processes for completing algorithms with fractional numbers. As children learn these processes, they should also learn to use them when adding and subtracting fractions with unlike denominators. (Subtraction processes are discussed in the next section.)

Adding with Mixed Numerals

Historically the expression *adding with mixed numbers* has described addition algorithms in which both whole and fractional numbers are involved. An example of this addition is:

$$2\tfrac{1}{3}$$
$$+\ 3\tfrac{5}{6}$$

As explained earlier, in order to maintain a proper distinction between number and numeral, the expression **addition with mixed numerals** is a better description of addition of this kind (Activity 12.15).

Activity 12.14   *continued*

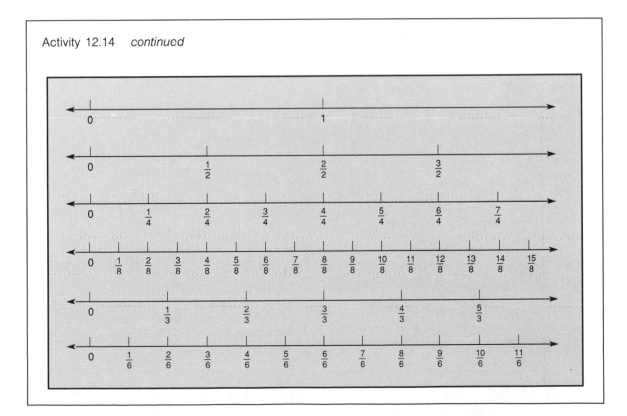

Adding with Math Explorer ™ Calculator

The Math Explorer™ calculator handles the addition of fractions in a straightforward manner. To add fractions, such as ⅔ and ⅓, enter the first fraction, press ⊞, enter the second fraction, press ⊟. The machine adds fractions and displays the answer with the least common denominator for the two numbers. If the answer can be simplified the machine displays "N/D → n/d". One of the two processes for simplifying a fraction can be used to change the answer. To add 4¼ and 3⅔, enter 4¼, press ⊞, enter 3⅔, press the ⊟. The display shows the answer as 7 u ¹¹⁄₁₂, or 7¹¹⁄₁₂.

Developing Number Sense About Addition with Fractions

Estimation processes are used to determine the reasonableness of responses in addition, subtraction, multiplication, and division with whole numbers. Because of the nature of common fractions, estimation processes are less useful for determining whether an answer is reasonable when computation is done with these numbers. However, students can develop a sense about

---

ACTIVITY 12.15   Addition with Mixed Numerals

"Jacques had 1½ pieces of brown posterboard and 1¼ pieces of green posterboard. How much posterboard was there when the pieces were put together?"

- Have students work in pairs to represent the situation with concrete aids. Pieces of geometric regions are used here, but other models can be used.

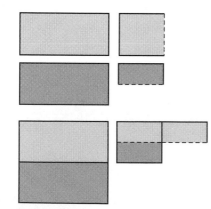

- Have students use their aids to determine the answer.

$$1 \tfrac{1}{2}$$
$$+ \; 1 \tfrac{1}{4}$$

$$1 \tfrac{1}{2} \; \longrightarrow \; 1 \tfrac{2}{4}$$
$$+ \; 1 \tfrac{1}{4} \; \longrightarrow \; + \; 1 \tfrac{1}{4}$$
$$\overline{\qquad 2 \tfrac{3}{4}}$$

- Write the algorithm on the chalkboard. Discuss how it relates to the original situation. Discuss the fact that the ½ must be changed to ²⁄₄ to add the fractions. Complete the addition and relate the completed algorithm to the concrete aids.

- Repeat with other mixed numerals.

fractions that can be used to determine an answer's reasonableness. Addition questions like these help students develop skill in determining the reasonableness of their sums:

- "When you add ⅓ and ¼, how do you know that the answer is less than one?" (Both fractions are less than ½, the sum of ½ and ½ is one, so the sum of ⅓ and ¼ will be less than one.)

- "When you add ½ and ¾, how do you know that the answer is more than one?" (Both fractions are equal to or greater than ½, so their sum will be greater than one.)

■ SUBTRACTION WITH COMMON FRACTIONS

Subtraction with fractional numbers arises from the same types of situations that use subtraction with whole numbers. Students should have numerous experiences with each type of situation by studying problems like the ones that follow. Both group-learning and teacher-directed activities, similar to the ones described for addition, can be developed and used for subtraction.

- *Take-Away*—"If there is ⅚ of a pizza in a pan, and Billy eats a piece that is ⅓ of the original pizza, how much pizza is left?" This situation is represented with pizza cutouts in Figure 12.5.

- *Comparison*—"Ted and Bev live on the same side of their school. It is ¾ of a mile from Ted's house to school and ⅞ of a mile from Bev's house to school. How much further from the school is Bev's house than Ted's house?" This situation is represented with a number line in Figure 12.6.

Figure 12-5
In (a) there is ⅚ of a pizza. In (b) a piece that is ⅓ of the pizza has been removed.

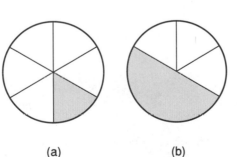

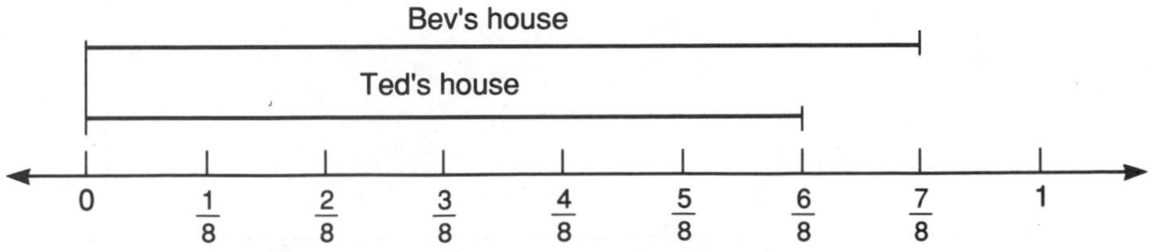

(a)   (b)

Figure 12-6
Number line used to compare distances from school to children's houses

Figure 12-7
Diagram showing amount of track to be laid to complete slot car layout

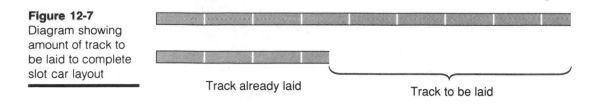

Track already laid   Track to be laid

Figure 12-8 (below)
A circle represents a pound. Thirteen-sixteenths is gray; $^{7}/_{16}$ of that represents sulfur and the rest a different chemical.

- *Completion*—"Judy is working on a new track layout for her slot car. She will have a total of 8½ yards of track in the new layout. If she has put down 3½ yards of track, how many more yards does she have left to put down?" This is represented by a diagram in Figure 12.7.

- *Part/Whole*—"Jametta has a mixture of two chemicals that weighs $^{13}/_{16}$ of a pound. She has $^{7}/_{16}$ of a pound of sulfur in the mixture. How much of the mixture is made up of the other chemical?" This situation is illustrated with the circular regions in Figure 12.8.

Children learn to add and subtract fractional numbers simultaneously. As with addition, the first subtraction work should have like denominators. The first and last examples have situations where this is so. Work with unlike denominators should follow the early work; the second example is of this type. Finally, they should deal with subtraction with mixed numerals; the slot car situation is of this type.

Subtraction with mixed numerals is bothersome for some children, especially when the common fraction part of the minuend is smaller than the common fraction part of the subtrahend. A child may rename the subtrahend as in the margin, where the process for regrouping with whole numbers is transferred to the new work. To avoid this error, instruction for this type of subtraction should begin with a situation such as in Activity 12.16.

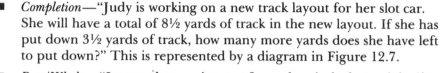

$$6\tfrac{1}{4} \qquad 5^{11}\!/_{4}$$
$$-\,3\tfrac{3}{4} \qquad -\,3\tfrac{3}{4}$$

ACTIVITY 12.16   Cake Sale

"Roberto was in charge of the cake sale at his school's bazaar. At 8:00 there were 3½ cakes on the table. By 8:15 he had sold 1¾ of these cakes. How many cakes were left at 8:15?"

- Show models of the 3½ cakes and the algorithm. (See next page.)
- Discuss the situation to determine what must be done before one and one-half cakes can be removed. Cut one cake into fourths and

combine it with the half cake, which is also cut into fourths. Show this change in the algorithm.

- Remove one and three-fourths of the model, leaving one and three-fourths; complete the algorithm.
- Relate each step in the model with each step in the algorithm.
- Repeat with similar situations and models.

Subtracting with the Math Explorer™ Calculator

The Math Explorer™ calculator handles subtraction as easily as it does addition. Enter the minuend, press ⊟, enter the subtrahend, press ⊜, and the answer appears on the display. To subtract 6¼ minus 3½ enter 6¼, press ⊟, enter 3½, and press ⊜. The answer is displayed as 2 u ¾, or 2¾.

Developing Number Sense About Subtraction with Fractions

Questions like these will help students learn to consider and judge the reasonableness of their answers when they subtract with common fractions:

- "When you subtract ½ from ¾, how do you know that the answer is less than one?" (Both fractions are less than one, so their difference will be less than one.)

- "When you subtract 1¾ from 1⅔, how do you know that the answer is less than one?" (The difference between the whole numbers is zero, and the fraction in the minuend is less than the fraction in the subtrahend.)

- "When you subtract 2¼ from 4⅔, how do you know that the answer is greater than one?" (The difference between the whole numbers is two; when the difference between the whole numbers is two or more, the answer is greater than one.)

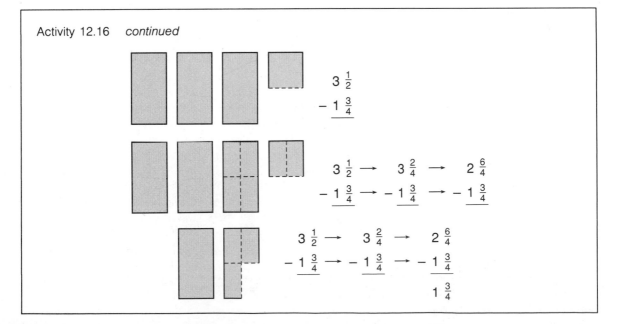

Activity 12.16   *continued*

■ MULTIPLICATION WITH COMMON FRACTIONS

The operations of multiplication and division are deceptively easy for teachers to teach and children to learn, but their meanings are elusive. Children can be taught rules for performing these two operations, and as long as they remember the rules, they can multiply or divide pairs of fractional numbers with ease. However, if children learn to perform these operations by rules alone, they probably will understand very little of the meanings behind them. Teachers who adopt the philosophy of this book will use realistic situations and learning aids, not simply rules, as they explore with students the meanings of these operations.

There are three situations involving multiplication with fractional numbers: multiplication of a fraction by a whole number, multiplication of a whole number by a fraction, and multiplication of a fraction by a fraction.

ACTIVITY 12.17   Multiplying a Fraction by a Whole Number

"Sarah practices ballet for three-quarters of an hour each day. How many hours does she practice in a week?"

■ Organize the class into cooperative-learning groups. Give the groups time to determine the answer with materials of their choice. Learning aids might be used to make these models of the situation:

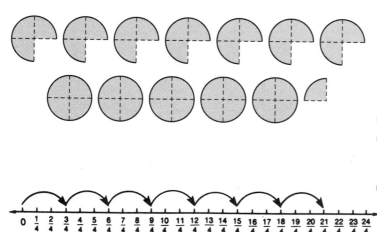

■ Have each group describe its model and how it represents the situation.

■ Write the multiplication sentence for this situation. (This is a repeated-addition situation, so the whole number is the first factor.)

$$7 \times \frac{3}{4} = \square$$

■ Demonstrate that by multiplying 7 times 3, the answer $2\frac{1}{4}$ is determined.

$$7 \times \frac{3}{4} = \frac{21}{4}$$

■ Change $2\frac{1}{4}$ to $5\frac{1}{4}$.

■ Compare the mixed numeral with the results of the children's work with the models.

■ Have the groups model and write multiplication sentences for other problem situations.

Multiplication of Fractional Numbers by Whole Numbers

Multiplication of fractional numbers by whole numbers is usually used for beginning work, because the examples are easily related to the repeated-addition process with which children are familiar. Activity 12.17 demonstrates this process.

Multiplication of a Whole Number by a Fractional Number

$$\frac{2 \times 18}{3} = \frac{36}{3} = 12$$

or

$$\frac{18}{3} \times 2 = 6 \times 2 = 12$$

Many practical situations give rise to the need for multiplying a whole number by a fractional number. When one cube of butter weighs one-fourth of a pound, the weight can be expressed as ¼ of 16 ounces, or 4 ounces. One-third of a foot is the same as ⅓ of 12 inches, or 4 inches; one-half of a dollar is ½ of 100 pennies, or 50 cents. Frequent encounters with these and similar applications enhance children's appreciation of the need for knowing how to perform such multiplication. Activity 12.18 presents a teacher-led lesson dealing with this type of multiplication. Eventually, students should learn that multiplication of a whole number by a common fraction can be completed by either of these procedures:

ACTIVITY 12.18   Multiplying a Whole Number by a Fractional Number

- Display a 6-by-3 array of disks on a magnetic board. Have the students recall the multiplication sentence for this array: $6 \times 3 = 18$.

- Say, "I want to set one-third of this array off to one side. How many disks should I move?"

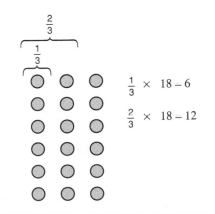

$$\frac{1}{3} \times 18 = 6$$

$$\frac{2}{3} \times 18 = 12$$

- Discuss the fact that to determine one-third of the set it is necessary to consider the disks as being in three equal-sized sub-groups. One of the groups is one-third of the entire array, so ⅓ of 18 is 6. Write the multiplication sentence ⅓ × 18 = 6 on the chalkboard.

- Ask, "How many disks will I set aside if I move two-thirds of the array?" Show this with the array and with a multiplication sentence: ⅔ × 18 = 12.

- Repeat with other sets that can be separated into equal-sized sets without remainders.

Multiplication of Fractional Numbers by Fractional Numbers

A paper-folding activity is a good activity for introducing multiplication of one fractional number by another; see Activity 12.19.

When students complete this activity, they should be ready to understand that to multiply two common fractions, the numerator of one fraction is multiplied by the numerator of the other fraction, the denominator of one fraction is multiplied by the denominator of the other, and the two products form another fraction. Thus the product for the sentence $\frac{3}{4} \times \frac{7}{8} = \square$ is determined by multiplying 3 times 7 to name the numerator and 4 times 8 to name the denominator.

Students also need opportunities to use this multiplication with examples from real-world situations.

- "Ben had $\frac{7}{8}$ of a piece of art foil. He used $\frac{1}{4}$ of the foil for an art project. What part of a sheet of foil did he use for his project?"

- A recipe uses $\frac{3}{4}$ of a cup of molasses. If only one-half of a recipe is prepared, how much molasses is used?"

ACTIVITY 12.19   Paper Folding

- Have students work in pairs. Give each pair of children several sheets of square paper. Some sheets should be marked to show fold lines for thirds.

- Instruct each group to fold one piece of paper in half.

- Ask, "What part of the whole square is one of the folded sides?" ($\frac{1}{2}$.)

- Instruct the students to fold the paper in half again.

- Ask, "Now what part of the whole square is one of the folded squares?" ($\frac{1}{4}$.) "What part of a half is one of the folded squares?" ($\frac{1}{2}$.) "The folding shows that one-half of one-half is one-fourth."

- Show the multiplication sentence for this situation.

$$\frac{1}{2} \times \frac{1}{2} = \frac{1}{4}$$

- Have students fold paper to represent these sentences. After the folding is done, have students show and discuss the results.

$\frac{1}{2} \times \frac{1}{4} = \square$ $\frac{1}{2} \times \frac{1}{3} = \square$ $\frac{1}{2} \times \frac{1}{6} = \square$

■ "Louie had ⅝ of a pound of ground beef. If he used one-third of the ground beef for a hamburger, what part of a pound did he use?"

Multiplication Involving Mixed Numerals

An example of multiplication involving mixed numerals is $2\frac{1}{2} \times 1\frac{1}{2} = \square$. A sentence of this sort usually arises from a situation involving measurement. A recipe illustrates one use in Activity 12.20.

Cancellation

Cancellation is a process for simplifying the common fractions used in multiplication before the work is done rather than simplifying the product after it is done. (Cancellation also can be used for certain division situations.)

ACTIVITY 12.20   Multiplying with Mixed Numerals

"A cookie recipe calls for 1½ cups of flour. If you want to make 2½ times as many cookies as one recipe makes, how many cups of flour will you use?"

■ Have the children work in cooperative-learning groups to work this problem. When they are finished, discuss their processes and answers.

■ Summarize the discussion by showing measuring cups to illustrate the situation.

■ Write the multiplication for this situation on the chalkboard.

$$2\frac{1}{2} \times 1\frac{1}{2} = \square$$

■ Change each mixed numeral to a fraction greater than one.

$$\frac{5}{2} \times \frac{3}{2} = \square$$

■ Complete the multiplication.

$$\frac{5}{2} \times \frac{3}{2} = \frac{15}{4} = 3\frac{3}{4}$$

■ Give the groups other examples from the same recipe.
—"The recipe calls for 1¼ tablespoons of baking soda. How much soda is needed for 1½ times the recipe?"
—"The recipe calls for ¾ teaspoon of salt. How much salt is needed for 3¼ times the recipe?"

(a) $\dfrac{2}{3} \times \dfrac{9}{10} = \square$

(b) $\dfrac{2 \times 9}{3 \times 10} = \square$

(c) $\dfrac{2 \times (3 \times 3)}{3 \times (2 \times 5)} = \square$

(d) $\dfrac{2 \times 3 \times 3}{2 \times 3 \times 5} = \square$

(e) $\dfrac{2}{2} \times \dfrac{3}{3} \times \dfrac{3}{5} = \square$

(f) $1 \times 1 \times \dfrac{3}{5} = \square$

The rationale for the process is given in the examples in the margin. The original multiplication is shown in (a). Rewrite the sentence as in (b). Next, factor the composite numbers, as in (c). Application of the commutative property permits rewriting the sentence as in (d). In (e) the sentence is rewritten to emphasize fractions that are names for one. Finally, in (f) two of the fractions are written as ones and multiplication is completed. Mature students with a good understanding of the role of one in multiplication and renaming of numbers will have little difficulty understanding this rationale.

In practice, the steps are omitted; multiplication sentences are inspected and cancellation is completed in one step through a mental arithmetic process. How do you use cancellation to simplify these sentences? What are the products of the sentences?

$$\dfrac{4}{5} \times \dfrac{3}{4} = \square \qquad \dfrac{3}{4} \times \dfrac{8}{9} = \square \qquad \dfrac{6}{8} \times \dfrac{2}{3} = \square \qquad \dfrac{5}{12} \times \dfrac{3}{4} = \square$$

Multiplying with the Math Explorer ™ Calculator

The product for the first multiplication sentence in the previous section is found by entering the fraction ⅘, pressing $\boxed{\times}$, entering the fraction ¾, and pressing $\boxed{=}$. The display shows the product, ¹²⁄₂₀, and "ND → nd" to indicate that the product is not in simplest form. To multiply the mixed numerals 2½ and 3¼: Enter 2½, press $\boxed{\times}$, enter 3¼, and press $\boxed{=}$. The display shows 8 u ¼, or 8¼.

Developing Number Sense About Multiplication of Fractions

After students have had ample experiences with models and they understand the algorithm, questions like the following will help them develop number sense and general rules about multiplication with common fractions:

■ "When you multiply ⅓ times 12, how do you know that the product will be less than 12?" (When you find a fractional part of a group, the part will be less than the group. Or, when one factor is a fraction less than one and the other is a whole number, the product will be less than the whole number.)

■ "When you multiply 12 times ⅓, how do you know that the product will be less than 12?" (The second rule above applies.)

■ "When you multiply ⅓ times ¼, how do you know that the product will be less than one?" (When you multiply two fractions less than one, their product is less than one.)

■ DIVISION WITH COMMON FRACTIONS

Division with fractions is not usually introduced before the fifth grade and sometimes not until the sixth grade. Some teachers present the rule, "Invert the divisor and multiply the fractions," as the only explanation for dividing with fractions. Students who know how to multiply fractions have no difficulty dividing with fractions when given this rule once they know what "invert" means. However, students may know how to apply the rule but have absolutely no knowledge about how the procedure works or when to use such division.

Situations That Illustrate Division with Common Fractions

Students should build on their understanding of both partitive and measurement situations to understand division with fractional numbers. As before, early experiences should include work with concrete models to aid in visualizing problem situations and the role of division in their solution. The role of early activities is not to teach students to use an algorithm but rather to understand division situations. The introductory lesson in Activity 12.21 uses a whole number situation to relate multiplication with common fractions to division with whole numbers.

A similar series of activities should be used to introduce partitive situations. Examples like these are appropriate:

■ "There is ¾ of a pie in a refrigerator. If it is cut into three equal-sized pieces, what part of the whole pie is each piece?"

■ "A half gallon of milk is divided into six equal-sized portions. What part of a gallon is each portion?"

Division Algorithms

Two algorithms are used for dividing with common fractions. Most commonly taught in the elementary school is the invert-and-multiply algorithm, which is based on the idea that dividing one number by another is the same as multiplying the number by the reciprocal of the divisor. Dividing 6 by 3 is the same as multiplying 6 by ⅓; 4 ÷ ½ is the same as 4 × 2. The algorithm is shown for each of these two division situations:

$$6 \div 3 = 6 \times \frac{1}{3} = 2$$

$$4 \div \frac{1}{2} = 4 \times \frac{2}{1} = 4 \times 2 = 8$$

ACTIVITY 12.21   Dividing a Fraction by a Whole Number

- Put 15 markers on a magnetic board. "If we put these markers into groups that each have three markers, how many groups will there be?" Review the idea that this measurement situation can be solved by repeated subtraction.

- Show a three-foot length of butcher paper and present this situation: "I have a piece of paper that is 3 feet long. If I cut it into pieces that are each ½ foot long, how many pieces will I have?"

- Help the students see that this situation is similar to the whole number situation. They know the size of the original object, 3 feet; they know the size of each part, ½ foot; they are to determine the number of pieces. Once the paper has been cut, the ½-foot pieces can be removed one at a time, just as sets containing three markers are removed.

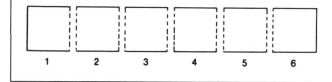

- Show a model of a sheet cake and present this situation: "I have ¾ of a cake. When I cut it into pieces that are each ¼ of the cake, how many pieces will there be?"

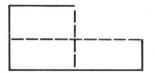

- This is also a measurement situation. The cake can be cut into quarter-size pieces and these can be removed one at a time. There are three pieces.

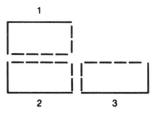

- Repeat with other situations that yield whole number answers.

The other algorithm requires that both fractions have the same denominator. Division is done by dividing the numerator of the dividend by the numerator of the divisor. Since the denominators are equal, their quotient will be 1, which has no effect on the quotient of the numerators. To divide ½ by ¼, rename ½ as ¾ and then divide 2 by 1. This set of steps shows this algorithm.

$$\frac{1}{2} \div \frac{1}{4} = \frac{2}{4} \div \frac{1}{4} = \frac{2 \div 1}{4 \div 4} = \frac{2}{1} = 2$$

Because the invert-and-multiply process is the most widely used algorithm, it is the only one for which lessons are described in this book. Teachers should avoid presenting this algorithm without developing adequate understanding of how and why it works.

Reciprocals

Before students are introduced to the invert-and-multiply process, they should have an understanding of reciprocals. They can be introduced to this concept through Activity 12.22.

ACTIVITY 12.22   Finding Reciprocals

■ Show a set of multiplication sentences:

$$\frac{3}{4} \times \square = \frac{12}{12}$$

$$\frac{6}{7} \times \square = \frac{42}{42}$$

$$\frac{2}{3} \times \square = \frac{6}{6}$$

■ Ask these questions:
—"By what number do we multiply ¾ to obtain the product ¹²⁄₁₂?" (⁴⁄₃.)

—"By what number do we multiply ⁶⁄₇ to obtain the product ⁴²⁄₄₂?" (⁷⁄₆.)

—"By what number do we multiply ⅔ to obtain the product ⁶⁄₆?" (³⁄₂.)

■ After the missing factor for each sentence has been identified, ask these questions:

—"What do you notice about each product in these sentences?" (They are all names for 1.)

—"What do you notice about the missing factors in each example?" (Each one is the reverse of the first factor in the sentence.)

■ Write these sentences on the chalkboard and ask students to name their products.

$$\frac{4}{15} \times \frac{15}{4} = \square$$

$$\frac{9}{7} \times \frac{7}{9} = \square$$

$$3 \times \frac{1}{3} = \square$$

■ After students know how to determine a reciprocal, help them compose a definition of it. For example, "The reciprocal of a number is the number by which the original number is multiplied to yield a product of one."

Invert and Multiply

When students can both describe measurement and partitive situations that involve fractional numbers and understand reciprocals, they are ready to comprehend the invert-and-multiply algorithm for dividing with common fractions. The algorithms in Activity 12.23 are based on the problems in Activity 12.21.

ACTIVITY 12.23   Using Reciprocals

- Begin with the sentence for the butcher paper situation.

$$3 \div \frac{1}{2} = 6$$

- Ask questions like these:
  —"What is the reciprocal of ½?" (²⁄₁, or 2.)
  —"What happens when we multiply 3 by the reciprocal of ½?" (The product is 6.)

- Show the sentence for the cake situation.

$$\frac{3}{4} \div \frac{1}{4} = 3$$

- Ask these questions:
  —"What is the reciprocal of ¼?" (⁴⁄₁, or 4.)
  —"What happens when we multiply ¾ by ⁴⁄₁ and simplify the answer?" (The product is 3.)

- Repeat with other examples that have been solved with models.

- Help students see that answers to these division situations are obtained by inverting (turning over) the divisor and then multiplying the two fractions. Show the sequence of steps with examples like these:

$$3 \div \frac{1}{3} = 3 \times \frac{3}{1} = 3 \times 3 = 9$$

$$\frac{5}{4} \div \frac{1}{4} = \frac{5}{4} \times \frac{4}{1} = \frac{5}{4} \times 4 = \frac{20}{4} = 5$$

$$\frac{2}{3} \div 6 = \frac{2}{3} \times \frac{1}{6} = \frac{2}{18} = \frac{1}{9}$$

$$6\frac{1}{2} \div 2\frac{1}{6} = \frac{13}{2} \div \frac{13}{6} = \frac{13}{2} \times \frac{6}{13} = \frac{78}{26} = 3$$

Division with the Math Explorer™ Calculator

The Math Explorer™ calculator can divide with common fractions in the same direct way it computes answers for other operations with fractions. To divide ⁶⁄₈ by ¼, enter ⁶⁄₈, press ÷, enter ¼, and press =. The answer is displayed as ²⁴⁄₈, which can be simplified mentally or by using the calculator. The final example in Activity 12.23 is divided this way: enter 6½, press ÷, enter 2⅙, press =. The answer appears as ⁷⁸⁄₂₆, which when simplified is 3.

Developing Number Sense About Division with Common Fractions

Questions like the following will help students develop number sense about division with common fractions:

- "When you divide 12 by ⅓, how do you know that the quotient will be greater than the dividend?" (When the divisor is smaller than the dividend, the quotient is greater than the dividend.)

- "When you divide ½ by 4, how do you know that the answer will be less than ½?" (When the divisor is greater than the dividend, the quotient will be less than the dividend.)

- "When you divide ½ by ¼, how do you know that the answer will be greater than one?" (When the divisor is smaller than the dividend, the quotient is greater than the dividend.)

- "When you divide ½ by ¾, how do you know that the answer will be less than one?" (When the divisor is greater than the dividend, the quotient will be less than the dividend.)

■ SIMPLIFYING ANSWERS

It was common practice in the past to have students record every fraction answer in its simplest form. Students' answers were often considered wrong if they could be but were not simplified, even when all other aspects of the work were correct. In keeping with the philosophy that students should understand what they are doing, it is better that they learn to consider each situation before deciding whether or not to simplify an answer. Consider these two examples: "Two pieces of wire are 3¼ inches long and 4¼ inches long. What is the total length of the two pieces?" If the answer is changed to 7½, there is no way to tell that each piece of wire was measured to the nearest quarter inch. Leaving the answer as 7¾ makes this clear and is the correct way to record the answer. "There were 29¼ yards of cloth. How much is left when 2¾ yards are cut from it?" This answer, 26¾, may be changed to 26½ because the precision of measurement is not significant in this example. Discussions that help students make decisions about how to treat fractions should replace the practice of having them simplify every answer.

Practicing Operations with Common Fractions

Middle-grade textbooks contain pages of practice exercises for addition, subtraction, multiplication, and division with common fractions. Students who need practice can use selected pages from these exercises to complete with paper and pencil or the Math Explorer™ calculator. Computer programs that provide practice with the four operations are also available. *Fraction Fuel-Up*[9] uses the fueling of space ships and making trips into space as a setting for addition and subtraction with fractional numbers. MECC[10] has *Conquering Fractions (+, −)* and *Conquering Fractions (×, ÷),* which provide timed practice on the four operations. Check with companies listed in Appendix B for information about their programs dealing with operations with common fractions.

EXERCISE   Children can use the Math Explorer ™ calculator to add, subtract, multiply, and divide with common fractions. Which of the concepts and computational processes for these four operations do you believe are crucial for children to master? Are any of the paper-and-pencil procedures for the operations made obsolete by the calculator?

RATIOS

One of the uses of fractions discussed at the beginning of this chapter is that of indicating ratio. When common fractions are used to indicate ratios, they are interpreted differently than when they represent parts of a whole or group. For example, the numerator of a ratio expression may tell the number of objects in one set, while the denominator tells the number of objects in an entirely different set. Ratios cannot be added, subtracted, multiplied, or divided. Consequently, care must be used when common fractions are introduced as ways of indicating ratios so that the concept is clear to children.

Rate Pairs and Tables

The introduction of ratios need not be delayed until children have mastered all the other uses of common fractions. A good way to make the introduction is through work with rate pairs. Activity 12.24 shows one way that this can be done.

ACTIVITY 12.24   Rate Pairs

- Introduce this situation: "Bubble gum costs 25 cents for three pieces."

- Have a student show a quarter and three objects that represent gum.

- Ask, "How much will six pieces of gum cost?" Have a student demonstrate this with six objects and two quarters.

- Through continued questions and representations students will see that for every three pieces of gum there is one quarter, or 25 cents.

- Make a table to show the ratios between gum and money.

Pieces of gum	3	6	9			
Cost of gum	25¢	50¢	75¢			

- Repeat with other situations and materials, such as: three pencils for 19 cents, five mini-boxes of raisins for 59 cents, three cans of cat food for 78 cents.

Proportions

Proportional relationships involving common fractions are frequently used in problem solving. Consider this situation:

- ■ "Carla and Carmen share responsibility for managing a gift shop. Carla is at the shop four days a week and Carmen is there three days. When Carla has been at the shop for 20 days, how many days has Carmen been there?"

The ratio for this situation is 4 to 3, or 4:3. A proportion can be used to solve the problem. Students must determine the number n that is used as a factor with 4 to give a product of 20:

$$\frac{4}{3} = \frac{20}{n}$$

Once the number is determined, it and 3 can be used as factors to determine the problem's answer. This is the same process that is used to rename a fraction in higher terms.

The missing term in any proportion can be solved by cross multiplication. To find the value of n in the expression above, multiply 3 times 20 and then divide by 4. When 20 is multiplied by 3 the product is 60; $60 \div 4 = 15$, so $4/3 = 20/15$. Naturally, more than one example needs to be used to make cross multiplication clear to children.

The use of proportions in problem solving is discussed further in the next chapter, in which their use in solving percent problems is considered.

EXERCISE   Name three additional examples of rate-pair situations. Money is involved in Activity 12.24. Include money in only one of your situations. Give three other examples of proportion situations.

■ SUMMARY

Common fractions have several meanings, depending on the situation in which they are used. Children learn that common fractions are used to express parts of a unit or set of objects that has been subdivided into equal-sized parts or groups, to express ratios, and to indicate division. Students need experiences with concrete and semiconcrete models that represent all of the meanings. Geometric regions, fraction strips, markers, and number lines are used during initial activities designed to make the common fraction representation of fractional numbers meaningful. These same materials, along with programs for computers and certain abstract procedures, help students learn to compare fractional numbers, to rename them as common fractions in simplest form, and to rename two or more fractional numbers so they are expressed as common fractions having the same denominator. Factorization of numbers is an abstract process that can be used to simplify common fractions and to find lowest common denominators. The Math Explorer™ calculator can be used to simplify fractions and to change improper fractions to mixed numerals.

Operations with fractional numbers expressed as common fractions require the same careful development that is made for operations with whole numbers. Even though children are older when operations with fractional numbers are developed, it is still necessary that the processes be developed through carefully sequenced activities with appropriate learning aids rather than by rules alone. Real-life problems can illustrate situations that give rise to addition, subtraction, multiplication, and division with fractional numbers. Geometric regions, fraction strips, markers, and number lines should accompany the real-life problems to give further meaning to the operations. References to similarities that exist between the operations with whole numbers and those with fractional numbers should be stressed whenever it is appropriate. There is a procedure for developing children's understanding of how cancellation is done when multiplying fractional numbers. Each of the four operations can be done on the Math Explorer™ calculator. Use of the device and computer programs and textbooks should follow development of each operation with real-life situations and concrete learning aids.

The use of common fractions to express ratios and solve problems involving proportions should be introduced through simple examples that involve patterns and tables. The cross-multiplication process for solving ratio problems can be explained in terms that are understood by mature elementary school children.

STUDY QUESTIONS AND ACTIVITIES

1. Read the NCTM standards at the beginning of this chapter. Think back to your own experiences with common fractions in elementary and junior high school. How well do you believe the instruction you received would meet the standards? Which, if any, of the standards would not have been met at all in the classrooms you recall? Envision a classroom in which the teacher invokes teaching procedures based on the philosophy of this chapter. How does the classroom you envision compare with classrooms of your experience?

2. Read the articles by Zalman Usiskin or by Usiskin and Max Bell (see the For Further Reading section) and summarize arguments for common fractions in the elementary school mathematics curriculum. Compare the ideas in the article you chose with Joseph Payne's article

on curriculum issues. How do you feel about the need for common fractions? State your position and tell how this position agrees or differs from the articles mentioned.

3. Ways in which the Math Explorer ™ calculator can simplify common fractions, change improper fractions to mixed numerals, and perform operations with fractional numbers are explained in this chapter. Practice each of the processes and operations until you are able to do them easily. Write a statement in which you explain your position on children's use of this calculator for work with common fractions. How do you envision that this calculator will change the way common fractions are taught and learned in the elementary school in the future, if indeed you believe it will? If you believe it will not or should not effect any changes, state your reasons.

4. Word problems are used frequently in this chapter to present situations leading to operations with common fractions. Develop your own skill in creating word problems for real-life situations by writing a problem for each of these sentences. Also draw a sketch of objects or use real objects to model how each operation would be done.

   a. $\frac{3}{4} + \frac{3}{4} = \frac{6}{4}$
   b. $1\frac{1}{2} + 3\frac{1}{4} = 4\frac{3}{4}$
   c. $\frac{7}{8} - \frac{3}{8} = \frac{4}{8}$
   d. $3 - 1\frac{1}{2} = 1\frac{1}{2}$
   e. $\frac{2}{3} \times 18 = 12$
   f. $2 \times \frac{3}{8} = \frac{6}{8}$
   g. $4 \div \frac{1}{2} = 8$
   h. $\frac{1}{2} \div 3 = \frac{1}{6}$

5. One way to assess fifth- or sixth-grade students' understanding of fraction sentences is by having them make up word sentences and use concrete materials or pictures to demonstrate a process for solving each problem. Use number sentences from Study Question 4 as you interview several children. Have each child make up a word problem and then demonstrate its solution with concrete materials or drawings. If you find a child who cannot successfully model his or her own stories, you can do the modeling and have the student explain what you are doing. Children who cannot create situations that correspond to the sentences show a lack of understanding of common fractions and their uses. As a teacher, you would need to consider reteaching common fraction concepts with concrete materials and familiar problem situations to develop children's understanding of the processes.

6. If you are familiar with Logo, you can use a computer to try the procedures developed by Steve Tipps (see the For Further Reading section) that allow students to play with common fractions. Both region and number-line formats are provided. If you are working with children, see how they respond to the procedures.

■ FOR FURTHER READING

Beedle, Ruby B. 1985, October. Dot method of renaming fractions. *Arithmetic Teacher 33*(2), 44–45.

Demonstrates transitional method for renaming fractions.

Bezuk, Nadine S. 1988, February. Fractions in the early childhood mathematics curriculum. *Arithmetic Teacher 35*(6), 56–60.

The article discusses components of instruction about common fractions in the early childhood years. The author stresses the importance of correct language and use of manipulative materials. She believes that once a variety of materials have been introduced, children should be given the option of choosing the ones they will use.

Chiosi, Lou. 1984, April. Fractions revisited. *Arithmetic Teacher 31*(8), 46–47.

Diagrams provide multiple ways of showing fractions.

Nelson, Rebecca S., and Donald R. Witaker. 1983, April. Another use for geo-boards. *Arithmetic Teacher 30*(8), 34–37.

Geo-islands provide many fractional activities.

Payne, Joseph N. 1984, February. Curricular issues: Teaching rational numbers. *Arithmetic Teacher 31*(6), 40–42.

Raises several questions about the teaching of fractions and decimals and makes recommendations about instruction.

Quintero, Ana Helvia. 1987, May. Helping children understand ratios. *Arithmetic Teacher 34*(9), 17–21.

The author discusses the levels of difficulty children experience with ratios and a sequence of activities aimed at developing the concept.

Rees, Jocelyn Marie. 1987, December. Two-sided pies: Help for improper fractions and mixed numbers. *Arithmetic Teacher 35*(4), 28–32.

A two-sided pie consists of one opaque circle and one transparent circle cut from colored report covers. Opaque circles are cut for fourths, thirds, and other fractions. Only one transparent circle is needed for each investigation. A variety of activities dealing with improper and mixed fractions are presented.

Silvia, Evelyn M. 1983, February. A look at division with fractions. *Arithmetic Teacher 30*(5), 38–41.

A graphic display of division with fractions increases understanding of the operation.

Steiner, Evelyn E. 1987, May. Division of fractions: Developing conceptual sense with dollars and cents. *Arithmetic Teacher 34*(9), 36–42.

The author describes an eight-level presentation of division with common fractions using money as the means of conceptualizing the process. The levels are presented sequentially over a period of time, with time devoted to each level determined by students' progress. Some levels can be consolidated for rapidly progressing students.

Swart, William L. 1981, October. Fractions vs. decimals—The wrong issue. *Arithmetic Teacher 29*(2), 17–18.

Swart argues that greater emphasis needs to be placed on concepts of fractions and less on computation with them. He uses an interesting problem to present his case.

Sweetland, Robert D. 1984, September. Understanding multiplication of fractions. *Arithmetic Teacher 32*(1), 48–52.

Sweetland explains activities with Cuisenaire rods that promote understanding of fractions and the multiplication algorithm.

Tipps, Steve. 1986, October. Funatic fractions. *Logo Exchange 5*(2), 6–8.

Describes Logo procedures to create a Fraction Maker for demonstrating fractional regions and addition with fractions.

———. 1986, November. Fraction line frolics. *Logo Exchange 5*(3), 4–8.

Describes Logo procedures for creating a number line and comparing fractional values. Addition and subtraction with fractions are included.

Usiskin, Zalman P. 1979, January. The future of fractions. *Arithmetic Teacher 27*(5), 18–20.

Usiskin refutes the argument that common fractions will become obsolete by exploring uses of fractions that will persist regardless of what calculating machines may do with them.

Usiskin, Zalman, and Max S. Bell. 1984, February. Ten often-ignored applications of rational numbers. *Arithmetic Teacher 31*(6), 48–50.

Facts about rational numbers help teachers and students understand and use them.

■ **NOTES**

1. National Council of Teachers of Mathematics. 1989. *Curriculum and Evaluation Standards for School Mathematics.* Reston, VA: National Council of Teachers of Mathematics, 57. Used by permission.
2. NCTM, 91. Used by permission.
3. NCTM, 94. Used by permission.
4. NCTM, 57. Used by permission.
5. MECC, 3490 Lexington Avenue North, St. Paul, MN 55126.
6. Society for Visual Education, Inc., Dept. VR, 1345 Diversey Parkway, Chicago, IL 60614-1299.
7. Davidson & Associates, Inc., 3135 Kashiwa St., Torrance, CA 90505.
8. Queue, Inc., 338 Commerce Drive, Fairfield, CT 06430.
9. DLM Teaching Resources, P.O. Box 4000, One DLM Park, Allen, TX 75002.
10. MECC, 3490 Lexington Avenue North, St. Paul, MN 55126.

CHAPTER 13

Fractional Numbers Expressed as Decimal Fractions and Percent

Knowledge of and skill in using decimal fractions and percent should become a prominent part of each person's mathematics repertoire. Children encounter decimals as they use calculators and digital time pieces, see them on odometers of cars and bicycles, and deal with the metric system of measure. They frequently encounter a sale situation in which prices are indicated in terms of percent off the original price. Articles in newspapers and magazines and news reports on television frequently include statistics and other forms of numerical data reported in decimal and percent form. Children should learn that decimals and percent are commonly used in many professions and occupations. Success in adult everyday-life activities, such as using credit cards and automated teller machines wisely, is dependent on a good understanding of decimals and percent. This chapter discusses materials and procedures for helping children learn about decimal fractions and percent and their applications in realistic situations.

In this chapter you will read about

1. the NCTM standards that apply to developing children's understanding and use of decimal fractions and percent;

2. materials and procedures for introducing decimal fractions to children;

3. materials and procedures for helping children learn how to round decimal fractions and relating these to common fractions;

4. how a calculator can help children understand decimal fractions;

5. materials and procedures for teaching children the four operations with decimal fractions;

6. using estimation for learning how to place decimal points in products and quotients involving decimal fractions;

7. examples of problem-solving activities involving decimals;

8. computer and calculator activities dealing with decimal fractions;

9. the meaning and uses of percent;

10. materials and procedures for introducing percent;

11. problem solving with percent.

NCTM STANDARDS THAT PERTAIN TO DECIMAL FRACTIONS AND PERCENT

Kindergarten Through Grade Four

Standard 12: Fractions and Decimals   In grades K–4, the mathematics curriculum should include fractions and decimals so that students can:

- develop concepts of . . . decimals;
- develop number sense for . . . decimals;
- use models to relate fractions to decimals . . . ;
- use models to explore operations with . . . decimals;
- apply . . . decimals to problem situations.[1]

Grades Five Through Eight

Standard 5: Number and Number Relationships
In grades 5–8, the mathematics curriculum should include the continual development of number and number relationships so that students can:

- understand, represent, and use numbers in a variety of equivalent forms (. . . , fraction, decimal, percent, . . .) in real-world and mathematical problem situations.
- develop number sense for . . . decimals, . . . ;

- understand and apply ratios, proportions, and percent in a wide variety of situations;
- investigate relationships among fractions, decimals, and percent.[2]

Standard 6: Number Systems and Number Theory In grades 5–8, the mathematics curriculum should include the study of number systems and number theory so that students can:

- understand and appreciate the need for numbers beyond the whole numbers;
- develop and use order relations for . . . decimals, . . . ;
- extend their understanding of whole number operations to . . . decimals. . . .[3]

Standard 7: Computation and Estimation In grades 5–8, the mathematics curriculum should develop the concepts underlying computation and estimation in various contexts so students can:

- compute with . . . decimals, . . . ;
- develop, analyze, and explain procedures for computation and techniques for estimation;
- select and use an appropriate method for computing from among mental arithmetic, paper-and-pencil, calculator, and computer methods;
- use estimation to check the reasonableness of results.[4]

THE NCTM STANDARDS

The NCTM standards indicate that initial instruction about decimal fractions should begin in the primary grades. The intent is not to make young children proficient in either their understanding of decimals or operations with them but rather to lay a firm foundation that will enable children in higher grades to avoid misconceptions and procedural difficulties. Because children's understanding of decimal fractions and the equivalence between them and common fractions develops slowly, it is important that teachers use physical materials, diagrams, and real-world situations over a period of years in order that children can relate their learning experiences to oral language and symbols.[5] Work with decimals continues, and percent is usually introduced in the upper grades of elementary school.

INTRODUCING DECIMAL FRACTIONS

Decimal fractions are one of three ways to represent fractional numbers. Activities with concrete materials will help children relate decimals to what they already know about common fractions and the Hindu-Arabic numeration system and emphasize the connection between decimals and common fractions as ways of representing fractional numbers. In the primary grades it is essential that children see models of decimal fractions, such as they do with common fractions. Once students have some concept of both common and decimal fractions they can learn about common and decimal fractions simultaneously, using the same models. This approach has several benefits. First, children learn that common fractions and decimal fractions represent the same kind of numbers rather than viewing them as being unrelated, as is often the case when the two fractions are studied separately. Second, it saves time, because many of the same concrete and pictorial materials can be used simultaneously to develop an understanding of both types of fractions. Third, as students model the two types of fractions with concrete, pictorial, and written representations, they have opportunities to discuss mathematical ideas and learn to appreciate the values of the two forms of notation.

Once it is clear that children are ready to learn about decimal fractions, familiar concrete aids should be used for developing their understanding. Cuisenaire rods or base-ten blocks are useful if they are available. Children who are accustomed to these materials will know that any particular piece can be named as a unit. Therefore they can use a tens flat from a Cuisenaire or base-ten set as a unit. Ten rods cover a flat piece, so each rod is a tenth of the flat, while 100 small unit cubes cover a square, and each one is a hundredth of a flat.

Paper marked with ½-inch squares can be cut to make an activities kit. Each child can make a kit, which consists of squares that are ten units along each side, at least ten strips that are ten units long, and 100 small unit squares. If squared paper is unavailable, a pattern on duplicating masters can be used to make copies for each child.

Tenths

When a group of students is ready to work with decimal fractions their first kit of materials should contain either commercial flats and rods or squares and strips cut from squared paper.

A lesson like Activity 13.1 can introduce the new fractions. The notations 0.1 and 1.0 are used in the activity. It is common practice to put a zero in front of the decimal point when a decimal fraction is written. The zero helps make it clear that the numeral indicates a decimal fraction. When no zero is written it is easy to overlook the decimal point and misread the numeral. A zero after the decimal point, as in 1.0, also has significance. It indicates that a unit has been separated into ten parts and that all ten parts are being considered; it should not be omitted.

Students should engage in additional activities with the rods or paper materials and alternative devices until they have a well-developed understanding of tenths and decimal notation for tenths. Lessons based on Activities 13.2 and 13.3 can be used. These activities are also suitable for review of decimals by students in higher grades.

ACTIVITY 13.1   Introducing Tenths

- Tell the children that for this lesson each flat from a Cuisenaire base-ten set or each square of paper represents one unit.

- Have children lay ten rods or strips of paper on top of a unit piece.

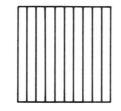

- Have the students verify that there are ten rods or strips on the unit piece. Ask a volunteer to give a number name for one rod or strip. If students lack the background to do this because they have not been introduced to common fractions, you will need to tell them that each piece is ⅒ of the unit piece.

- Ask volunteers to give names for two of the smaller pieces, then three pieces, four pieces, and so on until nine pieces have been named. You may need to tell the students that two pieces are ²⁄₁₀, three pieces are ³⁄₁₀, and so on to ⁹⁄₁₀ if they are unfamiliar with common fractions.

- Children who know about common fractions can write a numeral to name one of the small pieces on the chalkboard. Accept either ⅒ or 0.1 (.1). If ⅒ is written, ask if anyone can write the same number another way. Likewise, if 0.1 is written first, ask for the alternate notation. If neither name is given, you write them and point out that 0.1 and ⅒ are two names (numerals) for the same number.

- Do the same for the other fractional parts up to 0.9.

- Tell the students that 1.0 is the numeral to use when a unit has been cut into ten parts and all ten parts are being considered.

ACTIVITY 13.2   Fraction-Strip Tenths

- Give students duplicated copies of fraction strips marked in units and tenths.

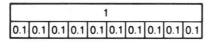

- Present instructions like these orally or in writing.

—Write both the common and the decimal fraction numerals for three tenths pieces.

—Show how many of the tenths pieces represent this decimal fraction—0.7.

—Write the decimal fraction that tells how many tenths you have if you start with three tenths and count five more tenths pieces.

Activity 13.3 has students count beyond 1.0. Once students have counted beyond 1.0 on a number line, they should also use Cuisenaire rods or base-ten materials or their paper kits to represent decimals greater than one. A number such as 1.3 is represented as a flat and three rods.

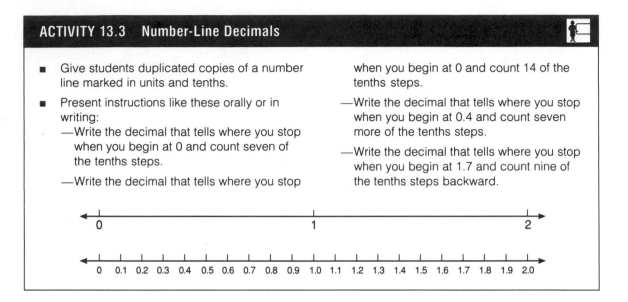

ACTIVITY 13.3   Number-Line Decimals

■ Give students duplicated copies of a number line marked in units and tenths.

■ Present instructions like these orally or in writing:

—Write the decimal that tells where you stop when you begin at 0 and count seven of the tenths steps.

—Write the decimal that tells where you stop when you begin at 0 and count 14 of the tenths steps.

—Write the decimal that tells where you stop when you begin at 0.4 and count seven more of the tenths steps.

—Write the decimal that tells where you stop when you begin at 1.7 and count nine of the tenths steps backward.

Hundredths

Children's understanding of the decimal fraction representation of hundredths is developed through extension of activities with tenths. The same materials are used except that pieces to represent hundredths are added to the kits. See Activity 13.4.

ACTIVITY 13.4   Introducing Hundredths

■ Display a unit region. Separate it into ten congruent parts; review the notation for decimal tenths.

■ Separate each tenth into ten congruent parts so that there are 100 parts.

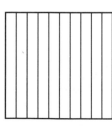

■ Discuss the fact that there are now 100 congruent parts. Introduce the notation for one hundredth: "0.01."

■ Have students count 24 of the parts and display this sequence of numerals as they count:

0.01, 0.02, 0.03, . . . , 0.24.

■ Name decimal fractions for students to represent with kit materials: 0.15, 0.36, 0.98, and so on.

■ Show representations of decimal fractions with models; have students name each fraction.

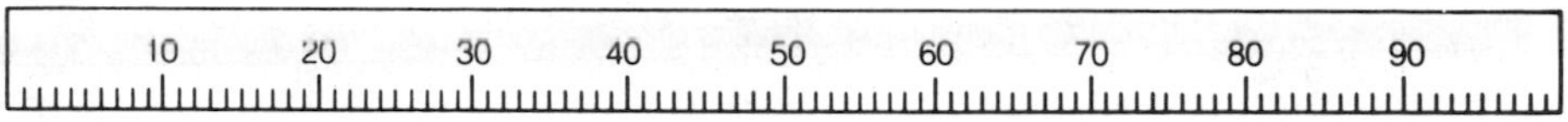

Figure 13-1
A meterstick shows tenths and hundredths of a meter.

A meterstick separated into decimeters and centimeters is useful for helping students understand tenths and hundredths (Figure 13.1). Students can examine the stick to note that there are ten decimeters and 100 centimeters. Have a student or the class in unison repeat the names "one-tenth, two-tenths, three-tenths, . . . , ten-tenths" as each student moves a finger along a stick. Help them note that there are ten hundredths (centimeters) in each decimeter.

Smaller Decimal Fractions

Concrete materials like those used for tenths and hundredths are impractical for representing fractional numbers smaller than hundredths. However, students can see a large unit region that has been marked to show 1,000 parts to extend their understanding of notation to include thousandths. From there it is not unreasonable for students to *imagine* that a unit has been cut into 1,000, or 10,000, or even 100,000 parts as they deal with the smaller decimals. In the same way that a number line can be used to help students realize that there is no smallest common fraction, one can be used to help them realize that theoretically a unit can be cut into smaller and smaller pieces to represent smaller and smaller decimal fractions and that there is no smallest decimal fraction.

■ ROUNDING DECIMAL FRACTIONS

Greater emphasis on estimation as a means of solving some problems and assessing the reasonableness of computation means that students need to know how to round decimal fractions to the nearest whole number or another decimal unit. For example, to determine the reasonableness of the product of 3.8 and 12.4, students can round 3.8 to 4 and 12.4 to 12 and estimate the product to be 48. The only reasonable answer for this multiplication is 47.12. The product 4.712 is too small, while the product 471.2 is too large. A number line is useful for helping students learn to round decimal fractions, as in Activity 13.5.

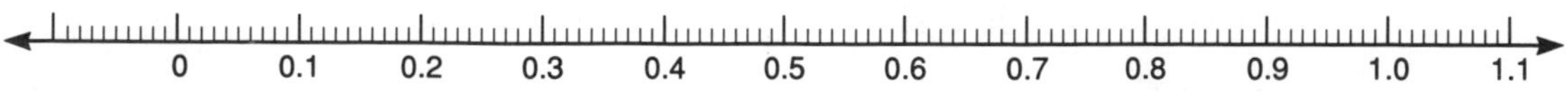

Figure 13-2
A number line can be used to show how to round decimal hundredths.

A number line that shows hundredths can be used in a similar way to show how to round hundredths to tenths (Figure 13.2). The same rules apply for these numbers as for tenths.

ACTIVITY 13.5   Rounding Decimals to Whole Numbers

- Display a number line that is marked in tenths.

- Write a decimal on the chalkboard: 2.3.

- Have a student point to the location of 2.3 on the number line.

- Ask, "Is 2.3 nearer to 2.0 or 3.0 on the number line?" Point out that since 2.3 is nearer 2.0, it is rounded to 2.0, or 2.

- Repeat with other mixed decimals until students can generalize that if the number in the tenths place is 4 or less, the decimal is rounded downward. If the number in the tenths place is 5 or more, it is rounded upward.

- Point out that a decimal less than 1 is rounded to 1 if the number in the tenths place is 5 or more. Decimals less than 0.5 are not rounded to whole numbers.

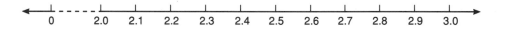

EXTENDING PLACE VALUE TO INCLUDE FRACTIONAL NUMBERS

Kits of structured or squared-paper materials and other learning aids provide a basis for developing the concept of decimal fractions as numerals for fractional numbers. By using these materials, children learn that 0.3, 0.13, and 1.3 are equivalent to the common fractions ³⁄₁₀, ¹³⁄₁₀₀, and 1³⁄₁₀, respectively, and that each pair of numerals names the same number. These same activities and the ones that follow should also be used to show that decimal fractions are a part of the Hindu-Arabic numeration system. These activities help students see that decimal fractions provide place-value positions to the right of the ones place to accommodate numbers smaller than one.

Using Place-Value Devices

Activity 13.6 uses a place-value pocket chart, a proportional aid, to help students realize that decimal fractions are an extension of whole numbers in the Hindu-Arabic numeration system. In Activity 13.7 a classroom version of an abacus, a nonproportional device, is used. This abacus can be made from pieces of coat-hanger wire stuck in a two-foot piece of 2-by-4 wood and wooden beads. When an abacus represents decimals, a rod other than the one on the right side indicates the ones place.

ACTIVITY 13.6   Place-Value Pocket Chart

- Display both a pocket chart and a set of kit materials. Show a set of kit materials with three unit and four tenth pieces. The pocket chart contains three bundles of tenths pieces and four single tenth pieces.

Ones	Tenths

- Point out that the three bundles of tenths pieces represent three units, while the single pieces represent four tenths. Write the numeral 3.4 on the chalkboard and have students discuss its meaning.

- Repeat with other decimal fractions, including some with no tenths and some with no units. In the first of these pocket charts, there are no units; the correct numeral for this is 0.5. In the second chart, there are no tenths; the numeral is 4.0.

Ones	Tenths

Ones	Tenths

- Dictate or give written numerals for numbers like 1.5, 4.7, 5.0, and 0.3 for children to represent with kit materials and the pocket chart.

ACTIVITY 13.7   Decimals on an Abacus

■ Display an abacus with the decimal point between the first and second rods on the right. Point out that the second rod represents the ones place.

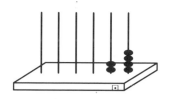

■ Have a student name the number represented by the beads. Have each student represent the same number with kit materials. Write the number on the chalkboard.

■ Display beads for similar numbers, such as 0.6, 4.2, and 5.7 and have each student represent them with kit materials. Write each number on the chalkboard.

■ Display an abacus with the decimal point between the second and third rods on the right. Point out the change and have the students name the places to the right of the decimal point as tenths and hundredths.

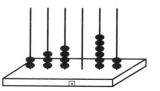

■ Have a student name the number represented by the beads. Have each student represent the number with kit materials. Write the number on the chalkboard.

■ Display similar numbers, such as 2.46, 8.09, and 23.96, have students represent each one with kit materials, and write each one on the chalkboard.

ACTIVITY 13.8   Decimals on a Calculator

■ Represent a whole number and decimal fraction with kit materials or on a place-value device. Have a student name the mixed number.

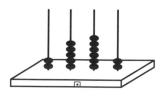

■ Demonstrate how the mixed number is entered into a calculator. For the number shown

on the abacus, enter [2], [5], [.], [6], and [2].

■ Have students read the mixed number displayed on their calculators—"two, five, point, six, two" and "twenty-five and sixty-two hundredths."

■ Represent other decimals and mixed numbers for students to enter into their calculators and read.

Using a Calculator

One of the first activities students do with a calculator is to learn to enter whole numbers. They learn that to enter a number like 243, the numbers 2, 4, and 3 are entered in that order. Activity 13.8 not only does that, but it also reinforces students' understanding of decimal numbers. Activity 13.8 deals with entering decimal numbers, and Activities 13.9 and 13.10 provide experiences with decimal fractions for pairs of students.

ACTIVITY 13.9   Counting with Decimals

- Each pair of students has a calculator.
- One student enters a decimal number—for example, 0.6. This student then tells the second student to count by tenths to a number such as 1.3. (This can be done by pressing $\boxed{+}$, entering 0.1, and pressing and counting $\boxed{=}$ until 1.3 is reached.)

- The second student tells how many times $\boxed{=}$ was pressed before getting to 1.3.
- The second student gives a number and similar set of directions for the first student to complete.
- Have students repeat with decimal hundredths.

ACTIVITY 13.10   Wipeout with Decimals

- Each pair of students has a calculator.
- The object is to "wipe out" a number in a particular place-value position in one move. For example, when shown the number 23.42, students are to wipe out the 4 in the tenths position in one subtraction. To do this, students must know that "4" represents 4 tenths and that it can be wiped out by subtracting 0.4 from 23.42. The 4 tenths are wiped out, leaving 23.02.

- Write numbers like these on the chalkboard or have them on cards for each pair of students.
- Variation: Have students use a 0–9 spinner to generate numbers to wipe out. Each player gets four spins to get as close to zero as possible in each place-value position.

WIPE OUT TENTHS	WIPE OUT HUNDREDTHS	WIPE OUT THOUSANDTHS
62.6	23.45	61.304
21.934	23.59	22.498
43.186	52.092	324.897

Connecting Whole Numbers and Decimals

Activities like the ones in Activities 13.11 and 13.12 help intermediate-grade students to complete the connection between place value for whole numbers and place value for decimals. As the first activity is done, emphasize that it is the ones place and not the decimal point that is the point of symmetry for place value in the Hindu-Arabic numeration system. Also, point out that each place-value position has a value that is ten times greater than the position to its immediate right and a value that is one tenth as much as that of the position to its immediate left, regardless of where it is in relation to the ones place.

By the end of grade six, some children will be ready to learn an even more mature way to represent decimal fractions. Those with a mature understanding of negative numbers can learn exponential notation, as in the final form that follows:

$$343.68 = (3 \times 10^2) + (4 \times 10) + 3 + (6 \times \tfrac{1}{10}) + (8 \times \tfrac{1}{10^2})$$
$$343.68 = (3 \times 10^2) + (4 \times 10^1) + (3 \times 10^0) + (6 \times 10^{-1}) + (8 \times 10^{-2})$$

EXERCISE The NCTM recommends that work with decimal fractions begin in the primary grades. Which of the decimal fraction concepts and activities for developing them discussed so far in this chapter do you believe are suitable for primary-grade children? Defend your selection.

ACTIVITY 13.11 Place-Value Chart

- Display the chart. Point out that the ones place is in the center of the chart.

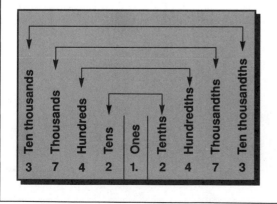

- Ask, "What is the value of the 2 at the left of the ones place?" (2 tens.) "What is the value of the 2 at the right of the ones place?" (2 tenths.)

- Repeat with the 4s in the hundreds and hundredths places and the 7s in the thousands and thousandths places.

- Discuss that the ones place is the point of symmetry, or balance, and that the tens place is to its immediate left and the tenths place is to its immediate right, the hundreds place is two places to the left and the hundredths place two places to the right, and so on.

ACTIVITY 13.12   Expanded Notation with Decimals

- Write these expanded forms on the chalkboard to review how to express a number
  such as 6,382 in expanded notation.

$$(6 \times 1,000) + (3 \times 100) + (8 \times 10) + 2$$
$$(6 \times 10 \times 10 \times 10) + (3 \times 10 \times 10) + (8 \times 10) + 2$$

- Put a display like this on the chalkboard.

  2.36 = _____ ones _____ tenths _____ hundredths

  0.46 = _____ ones _____ tenths _____ hundredths

  2.482 = _____ ones _____ tenths _____ hundredths _____ thousandths

- Have students fill in the blanks for each expanded number.
- Use examples like these to stress more abstract symbolism.

  4.68 = 4 + (_____ × 0.1) + (_____ × 0.01)

  2.43 = 2 + (4 × _____) + (3 × _____)

  2.006 = 2 + (_____ × 0.1) + (_____ × 0.01)
               + (_____ × 0.001)

■ COMPUTING WITH DECIMAL FRACTIONS

Students who have a good understanding of fractional numbers and their decimal fraction representations will experience little difficulty when they begin to compute with decimals. The computational process for each operation is identical to the one for whole numbers. Realistic situations along with concrete materials will make each operation meaningful to students. The realistic problems, whether real or hypothetical, help students recognize the types of situations that involve decimal fractions and grasp the importance of knowing how to do each operation.

Addition with Decimal Fractions

When addition with decimal fractions is introduced through realistic situations and familiar models, students quickly see that addition with decimals is like addition with whole numbers. Models help them see that addends are written in algorithms with numerals in each of the place-value positions aligned in a column and that addition is done one place-value position at a time, beginning with the position on the right. Activities 13.13 and 13.14 illustrate addition situations with tenths and hundredths. A number line is used to model the first situation, while base-ten blocks are used for the second one.

ACTIVITY 13.13   Adding with Decimal Tenths

"Jamelda earns pocket money by using her bicycle to do errands. She measures distances in kilometers with a metric odometer. For one errand she recorded the distances 0.7, 0.3, and 0.8 kilometers. How many kilometers did she ride for that errand?"

■ Have students write a mathematical sentence for the situation.

$$0.7 + 0.3 + 0.8 = \square$$

■ Display a number line marked with tenths and have a student show the three stages of Jamelda's errand. Have the student tell how far she rode.

■ Write an algorithm, as shown at right.

$$
\begin{array}{r}
0.7 \\
0.3 \\
+\ 0.8 \\
\end{array}
$$

■ Add the numbers in the algorithm.

$$
\begin{array}{r}
0.7 \\
0.3 \\
+\ 0.8 \\
\hline
1.8 \\
\end{array}
$$

■ Repeat with similar addition situations.

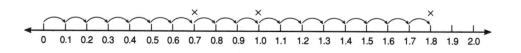

Subtraction with Decimal Fractions

A teacher should not let the fact that subtraction with decimals is done in the same way as subtraction with whole numbers lead to the belief that realistic situations and concrete models are unnecessary as the operation is introduced. Students need to see situations that lead to subtraction and to use models that make the regrouping process clear. Each of the following examples can be modeled with any of the concrete materials with which children are familiar. Paper-kit materials illustrate Activity 13.15, while base-ten materials are used in Activity 13.16.

ACTIVITY 13.14   Adding with Decimal Hundredths

"Juan bought two packages of ground beef. One package weighed 0.87 of a pound and the other weighed 0.95 of a pound. How much ground beef was in the two packages?"

■ Have students write a mathematical sentence for the situation.

$$0.87 + 0.95 = \square$$

■ Have students work in pairs and use base-ten blocks to model the situation.

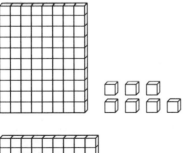

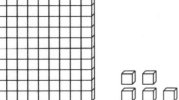

■ Have the students model each of the decimals; then have them combine the parts to show the total.

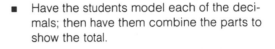

■ Write the algorithm on the chalkboard and add.

$$
\begin{array}{r}
0.87 \\
+\ 0.95 \\
\hline
1.82
\end{array}
$$

■ Repeat with similar examples.

"Jack's pumpkin weighed 4.6 kilograms. He cut a piece that weighed 1.9 kilograms from the pumpkin. What was the weight of the part of the pumpkin that remained?"

■ Have students write a number sentence for the situation:

$$4.6 - 1.9 = \square$$

■ Have students work in pairs to show 4.6 with kit materials.

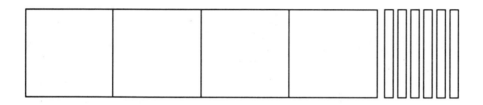

■ Point out that it is not possible to remove 1.9 from 4.6 without regrouping the 4.6.

■ Have students remove 1.9 of the pieces.

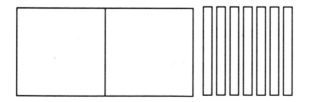

■ Write and complete the algorithm.

```
              3  1
   4.6       4̷. 6
 - 1.9      - 1. 9
            ───────
              2.7
```

■ Give additional examples for pairs of children to work on their own. Monitor their work.

"Chen had 42.36 grams of sulfur. He used 25.82 grams for a science experiment. How many grams of sulfur were left?"

■ Have a student write a number sentence for the situation.

$$42.36 - 25.82 = \square$$

■ Have students work in pairs with base-ten materials to show 42.36. (A large cube represents tens, a flat ones, a rod tenths, and a small cube hundredths.)

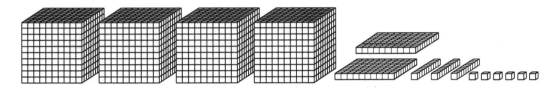

■ Discuss what must be done in order to show the subtraction with the materials. (The pieces in tens, ones, and tenths places must be regrouped.) Show the regrouping.

■ Have children remove pieces to show the subtraction of 25.82.

■ Write and complete the algorithm.

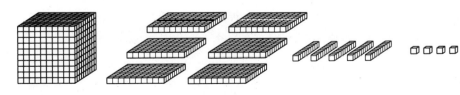

■ Give students other examples to complete on their own. Monitor their work.

Multiplying with Decimal Fractions

Because fractional numbers expressed as decimal fractions are multiplied using the same algorithm form as whole numbers, teachers must guard against having the process become mechanical for students. Introductory work with such multiplication should be presented within a familiar context relevant to some aspect of children's lives. Estimation is also an important aspect of making multiplication of decimals meaningful to students.

There are three possible situations when multiplication with decimal fractions is done: (1) a decimal is multiplied by a whole number, (2) a whole number is multiplied by a decimal, and (3) two decimals are multiplied. A meterstick is used to model the first type of situation in Activity 13.17, a strip of calculator tape is used for the second situation in Activity 13.18, and a set of overlays for an overhead projector models the third situation in Activity 13.19.

ACTIVITY 13.17   Multiplying a Decimal by a Whole Number

"Josie is repairing her railroad track layout. She needs six pieces of wire, each 0.6 of a meter long. How much wire does she need for her layout?"

- Draw lines that are each 0.6 of a meter end to end on the chalkboard with a meterstick to illustrate the situation.

- Point out that this is a repeated-addition situation. Six-tenths can be used as an ad-

dend six times. Write the multiplication sentence:

$$6 \times 0.6 = \square$$

- Discuss the meaning of the answer: 3.6 meters.

- Repeat with additional examples of wires of different lengths and quantities.

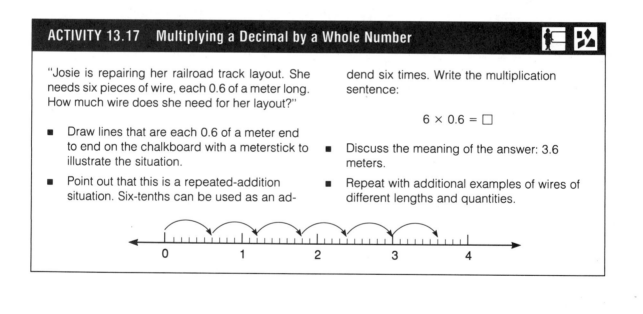

ACTIVITY 13.18   Multiplying a Whole Number by a Decimal

"A piece of ribbon that is 4 meters long is cut so that 0.2 of the ribbon is removed. How long is the piece of ribbon that is removed?"

- Illustrate with a 4-meter-long piece of calculator tape, marked to show the four meters.

Activity 13.18   *continued*

- Mark the piece of tape into ten congruent parts to show tenths of the entire piece. Shade two of the tenths to indicate the 0.2 that is cut off.

meter is removed when 0.2 of four meters is removed.

- Write and complete the multiplication sentence: 0.2 × 4 = 0.8

- Measure the shaded parts in relation to one meter. The model shows that 0.8 of one

- Present similar examples for children to complete and discuss.

ACTIVITY 13.19   Multiplying a Decimal by a Decimal

"Art foil comes in sheets that are 10 centimeters square. Sarah has 0.7 of a full sheet. If she uses 0.3 of this piece for an art project, how much of an original sheet will she use?"

- Project a square that is separated vertically into ten congruent parts. Shade 0.7 of the square.

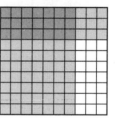

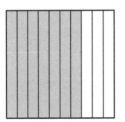

- Point out that the answer is represented by the 21 parts that are shaded twice. Each of the 21 parts represents one of the 100 parts into which the entire unit was separated, so the product is 0.21.

- Write and complete the multiplication sentence.

$$0.3 \times 0.7 = 0.21$$

- Lay a second square that has been separated horizontally into ten congruent parts on top of the first square. Shade 0.3 of this square.

- Present similar examples for students to complete and discuss.

After students use models to visualize the three types of multiplication situations, they will be ready to multiply by hundredths. They will now need to learn a meaningful way to determine where to place the decimal point in each product. Eventually they should be guided to generalize that the number of decimal places in a product equals the sum of the decimal places to the right of the ones place in each of the factors.

Before students use the generalization, they should use estimation to help them understand it. Exercises like those in Activity 13.20 will provide the guidance they need in understanding the generalization.

Exercises containing examples like these, where students underline the correct product for each combination, can be given to students who need practice in making decisions about where to place decimal points in products.

$2.4 \times 6.8 =$	16.32	1.632	163.2	1632
$10.6 \times 3.68 =$	3900.8	390.08	39.008	3.9008
$9 \times 2.98 =$	2682	268.2	2.682	26.82

Activities such as these should be followed by a discussion in which questions help students discover and formulate the generalization about determining the number of decimal places in a product.

■ "How many decimal places are there following the ones place in the first factor of this sentence?"

■ "How many are there in the second factor?"

■ "What is the sum of the number of decimal places in both of the factors?"

■ "How many decimal places are there to the right of the ones place in the product?"

■ "How does that number compare with the sum of the number of decimal places in the two factors?"

■ "Look at the next sentence. What do you notice about the number of decimal places to the right of the ones place in the two factors and in the product?"

ACTIVITY 13.20   Estimating Decimal Products

■ Write a multiplication sentence on the chalkboard.

$$0.9 \times 2.1 = \square$$

■ Ask, "What is 0.9 rounded to the nearest whole number?" (1.) "What is 2.1 rounded to the nearest whole number?" (2.) "What is the product of 1 times 2?" (2.)

■ Write the product of 0.9 and 2.1 without the decimal point: (189.) Ask, "Where should the decimal point be placed to indicate the correct answer?" (1.89.) Discuss why 1.89 is the answer. (0.189 is too small and 18.9 is too large.)

■ Have students estimate, then compute answers for examples like $5.7 \times 8.4 = \square$, $12.9 \times 10.4 = \square$, $25.23 \times 10.2 = \square$.

- "Now look at the remainder of the sentences. What do you notice about them?"

- "Someone tell me how to determine where to put the decimal point in a product when there are decimals in the factors."

Dividing with Decimal Fractions

Students' understanding of division with decimals is enhanced when the new division is related to division with whole numbers. As is the case with whole-number division, there are two situations involving division with decimals. Division with decimals determines either the size of each group when a set is divided into a given number of groups (partitive division), or the number of groups when a set is divided into groups of a given size (measurement division). The algorithm form used for division of whole numbers is also used for division with decimals. The new element for students is the need to place a decimal point in a quotient. As with other new topics, division with decimals should be introduced in relevant settings and with meaningful materials; Activities 13.21 and 13.22 provide some suggestions.

ACTIVITY 13.21   Partitive Division

"A rope is 16.4 meters long. If Juanita cuts it into four pieces that are the same length, how long will each piece be?"

- Display a piece of calculator tape that is 16.4 meters long. Ask, "What does the problem tell us Juanita did with her piece of rope?" (She cut it into four equal-sized pieces.) "How can we do that with this piece of calculator tape?" (Fold it in half, then fold it in half once more.) Fold the paper.

- Write the division sentence for this situation: $16.4 \div 4 = \square$.

- Write the algorithm:

$$4\overline{)16.4}$$

- Ask, "Will each piece of rope be at least one meter long?" (Yes.) "Two meters long?" (Yes.) "Three meters long?" (Yes.) "Four meters long?" (Yes.) "Five meters long?" (No.)

- Show division of 16 by 4 in the algorithm:

$$\begin{array}{r} 4 \\ 4\overline{)16.4} \\ \underline{16.0} \\ 4 \end{array}$$

- Ask, "After we divide sixteen by four, what is left to be divided?" (0.4.)

- Show this division in the algorithm:

$$\begin{array}{r} 4.1 \\ 4\overline{)16.4} \\ \underline{16.0} \\ 4 \\ \underline{4} \\ 0 \end{array}$$

- Measure the parts of the calculator tape to confirm that each one is 4.1 meters long.

- Discuss how this division is like finding ¼ of 16.4. (Each of the parts is ¼ of the original piece; they are identical situations.)

- Repeat with similar partitive situations.

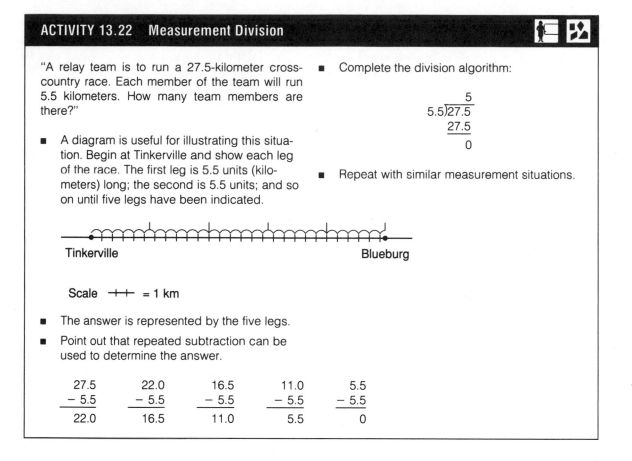

ACTIVITY 13.22 Measurement Division

"A relay team is to run a 27.5-kilometer cross-country race. Each member of the team will run 5.5 kilometers. How many team members are there?"

■ A diagram is useful for illustrating this situation. Begin at Tinkerville and show each leg of the race. The first leg is 5.5 units (kilometers) long; the second is 5.5 units; and so on until five legs have been indicated.

Tinkerville   Blueburg

Scale ++ = 1 km

■ The answer is represented by the five legs.
■ Point out that repeated subtraction can be used to determine the answer.

27.5	22.0	16.5	11.0	5.5
− 5.5	− 5.5	− 5.5	− 5.5	− 5.5
22.0	16.5	11.0	5.5	0

■ Complete the division algorithm:

$$\begin{array}{r} 5 \\ 5.5\overline{)27.5} \\ 27.5 \\ \hline 0 \end{array}$$

■ Repeat with similar measurement situations.

Students can use estimation as one way to determine where to place the decimal point in many quotients. Estimation is not helpful in all situations, however. It cannot be used for a sentence such as 0.045 ÷ 0.06 = □. The following ideas help students learn a general rule for placing decimal points in quotients.

■ To estimate the quotient for a pair of numbers, as in the sentence 29.52 ÷ 6 = □, students should think "29.52 is rounded to 30; 30 divided by 6 equals 5, so 29.52 divided by 6 will be about 5." When the quotient is determined, students should place the decimal point so that the answer is 4.52. Students can complete a written exercise with sentences like the following by using estimation and putting a decimal point in the correct place.

$$69.3 \div 3 = 231$$
$$811.8 \div 22 = 369$$
$$20.74 \div 3.4 = 61$$

- Students who know that common fractions can be used to express division can rewrite a decimal fraction division, such as $6.3 \div 0.3 = \square$, as a common fraction: $^{6.3}/_{0.3}$. When both numerator and denominator are multiplied by 10, the fraction becomes $^{63}/_{3}$. The fraction can be rewritten in algorithm form so the division can be completed. This process is the mathematical justification for the caret method of placing a decimal point in a quotient. When both divisor and dividend are multiplied by 10 or a power of 10 so that the divisor is changed to a whole number, the decimal point in the quotient can be placed immediately above the decimal point in the changed dividend. This is illustrated in the margin: a caret (ˆ) indicates the new position of the decimal point in the divisor and dividend. Students should use this procedure after its justification has been made clear to them.

$$
\begin{array}{r}
4.98 \\
6.3\overline{)31.3_\wedge 74} \\
252 \\
\hline
617 \\
567 \\
\hline
504 \\
504 \\
\hline
\end{array}
$$

Eventually students should be guided to make this generalization: The number of decimal places to the right of the ones place in a quotient is the difference between the number of places to the right of the ones place in the dividend and the number in the divisor. When students compare this generalization to the one about how to determine the number of decimal places in a product, they will see that the processes stated in the two generalizations are the inverse of each other. As with multiplication and division of whole numbers, time spent on calculation with multidigit decimals should be limited. Estimation and calculator skills are more useful and should be used in place of paper-and-pencil computation.

■ DECIMAL FRACTIONS: PRACTICE AND USE

Once students understand decimal fractions and operations with them, they need opportunities for periodic practice. Computer and calculator activities, as well as textbook exercises, can be used.

Computer Activities

Computer programs provide both practice and application formats. *Fractions, Decimals, and Percent*[6] is a program that includes computation with both common and decimal fractions, work with percent, and word-problem exercises involving the three forms of representing fractional numbers. Students act as FDP detectives to find and release a captured FDP agent by solving word problems using fractions, decimals, and percent. *Decimal Discovery*[7] deals with the meaning of and operations with decimals. When students select a correct answer, a spouting oil well lets them know. Students are motivated by arcade-like action to escape a dungeon in *Decimal Dungeon*.[8]

Calculator Activities

Activities 13.23 through 13.26 include a variety of calculator activities that provide practice with decimal fractions.

Textbooks for intermediate grades provide exercises for paper-and-pencil practice. These pages can be used when such practice is deemed necessary for particular students.

Students should see many practical applications of decimal fractions outside of mathematics lessons. As students learn about the metric system,

---

ACTIVITY 13.23   Reading Words for Decimal Fractions

- Write each of these decimal number words and the decimal numerals on the chalkboard or duplicate them to distribute to students:

  two and five tenths
  four and three tenths
  six and nine tenths
  five and seven tenths
  _____
  19.4

  sixty-one and forty hundredths
  seventy-five and sixty-seven hundredths
  four and twenty-one hundredths
  ninety-six and nine hundredths
  _____
  237.37

- Instruct each student to enter the decimal numbers for the words in the first list into a calculator, pushing the plus key after each entry. The numbers will have been read and entered correctly if the sum equals the decimal number at the bottom of the list. Have students do the same with the numbers named by the words in the second set of numbers.

ACTIVITY 13.24   Placing Decimal Points

- Write each of the multiplication and division examples on the chalkboard or duplicate them to distribute to students.

21.3	0.78	0.789	3.621
× 4.8	× 4.3	× 26.3	× 0.4
10224	3354	207507	14484

$$\frac{263}{3)7.89} \qquad \frac{654}{3.8)248.52} \qquad \frac{0051}{0.9)0.459} \qquad \frac{632}{2.7)170.64}$$

- Instruct students to use the processes of rounding off and estimation or counting decimal places to determine where to place the decimal point in each example. Have them check their estimates by computing the actual answers with calculators.

ACTIVITY 13.25   Checking Products

- Organize the class for a cooperative-learning activity.

- Duplicate these multiplication combinations and distribute them to students:

0.4 × 9	3.6 × 1
0.12 × 30	1.8 × 2
1.0 × 36	0.04 × 0.9
9 × 0.04	0.3 × 12
120 × 0.03	6 × 0.6
18 × 0.02	40 × 0.09

3 × 1.2	60 × 0.6
2 × 1.8	0.05 × 720
4 × 0.9	18 × 0.2
0.6 × 0.6	36 × 0.1
72 × 0.5	360 × 0.01

- Instruct students to put check marks next to combinations that they believe equal 3.6. Have them use calculators to check their work.

ACTIVITY 13.26   Batting Averages

- Organize the class for a cooperative-learning activity.

- Duplicate this table of baseball statistics to distribute to each group.

MAJOR LEAGUE BATTING

Player	Team	Times at Bat	Hits
Hatcher	Astros	564	167
Concepcion	Reds	279	89
Raines	Expos	530	175
Clark	Giants	529	163
Joyner	Angels	564	161
Mattingly	Yankees	569	186

- Have a student tell the class how a player's batting average is determined, or tell them that it is found by dividing the number of hits by the official number of times at bat.

- Have groups use calculators to determine the batting averages of the six players listed in the table.

- Extend the activity into a project by having each group adopt a major league baseball team. Have the groups locate information and determine the current batting average for each of their team's players. Have them maintain a chart on which they update each player's average once a week and show the weekly changes in their players' averages.

they will have opportunities to deal with decimal fractions. (Activities for learning about measurement are presented in Chapter 14.) Many science situations involve measurement, so it is natural to integrate them with activities designed to help students learn about the metric system. Students should be encouraged to find newspaper and magazine articles that show how decimal fractions are used in everyday situations. Bulletin board displays or notebooks can be prepared to organize their findings. Students can write entries in journals to describe their encounters with decimals during a week's time.

EXERCISE   Baseball batting averages are used in Activity 13.26 to illustrate an application of decimal fractions. Name other situations, sports oriented and otherwise, that can be used to demonstrate other uses of decimal fractions.

■ PERCENT

The pervasive nature of percent makes it important that students acquire a good understanding of its meaning and uses. In practice, percent is used in various ways, and its applications in business, government, science, and industry and in many aspects of daily life are numerous. In one day, these uses were encountered by one of the authors: A luncheon speaker reported that 13 to 14 percent of the forest fires in California in 1988 were started by arsonists. A *New York Times* article reported that prices in factory-outlet stores are 25 to 60 percent below regular department store prices. One California county reported that 10.4 percent of its population receives Aid-to-Families-with-Dependent-Children assistance. A discount store advertised triple reductions during a three-day sale: a 40 percent discount over regular department store prices, a red-tag discount of 25 percent off that price, and an additional 25 percent reduction off the red-tag price.

Meaning of Percent

Percent expresses a ratio between some number and 100. For example, when 15 is used as a percent, it is an expression of the ratio between the numbers 15 and 100; it is symbolized as 15%. The symbol % indicates a denominator of 100; the word **percent** names the symbol and means **per hundred,** or **out of 100.**

A state or local government often uses a sales tax as a means of raising revenue. A tax of 6 percent means that for every 100 cents (one dollar) of the purchase price of an article, a tax of six cents (0.06 of a dollar) will be collected by a merchant and turned over to the state. This setting provides a basis for discussing terms used in connection with percent. When a $10.00 item is sold, the cost is the *base* to which the tax is applied, 6 percent is the **rate** of tax, and 60 cents is the tax, or **percentage.**

Percent and *percentage* are often confused, and many children—and adults as well—are uncertain about the distinction between them. Because confusion is likely, a teacher must make it clear that percent indicates the *rate* (of sales tax, fires started by arsonists, or whatever), whereas percentage indicates the *amount,* or *quantity* (of tax, of fires started by arsonists, or whatever). Base and percentage always represent numbers that refer to the same units, such as interest or sales discount, and percent is the rate by which the percentage compares with the base.

A sales tax provides the basis for discussion of another potential point of confusion. A sales tax of 5 percent is common. If a 5 percent tax is raised to 6 percent, the increase is 20 percent. If, at a later time, the tax is reduced to 5 percent, is the *rate* (percent) of decrease the same as the *rate* of increase? In both cases, the *amount* was the same; the tax went up a penny, it came down a penny. The number lines in Figure 13.3 show that the rates in this increase-decrease situation are different. In (a) the first line represents the original sales tax, which was 5 cents for every dollar spent (5 percent). This line is a unit because 5 cents was the entire amount of tax for each dollar before the increase. The second line in (a) shows the sales tax after it was changed to 6 percent. The amount of the increase in the length of this line is the same as one of the five parts of the unit line. One of five is 20 percent of the whole, so the *rate of increase* was 20 percent.

In (b) the top line represents the new sales tax. It represents a unit, because the rate is now 6 cents for every dollar spent. The amount of decrease in the second line is the same as the length of one of the six parts in the unit line. One of six is 16⅔, so the *rate of decrease* was 16⅔ percent, not 20 percent.

Figure 13-3
Number lines showing: (a) When a sales tax is increased from 5 cents to 6 cents, the rate of increase is 20 percent. (b) When the tax is decreased from 6 cents to 5 cents, the rate of decrease is 16⅔ percent.

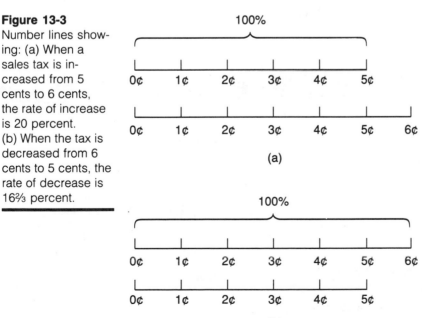

Introducing Percent

Before students begin work with percent, they must have a clear under-standing of fractional numbers and decimal fraction representations of them. Children can be introduced to percent through activities with already familiar learning aids, such as Cuisenaire or base-ten materials or squared-paper kits. The key point to make during early work is that percent means *per hundred,* or *out of 100,* so a Cuisenaire or base-ten flat or a square from a paper kit will serve as a unit, and small cubes and squares can serve as hundredths. Activity 13.27 uses Cuisenaire materials.

Poker chips with magnets affixed to them and a magnetic board are useful for showing percent examples. One hundred chips can be arranged in combinations of blue, red, and white on a board so students can name the percent of each color. The chips can be exchanged easily to show other combinations of 100 chips.

Once students have been introduced to percent, they should have op-portunities to practice renaming common and decimal fractions as percent and percent as common and decimal fractions. Computer programs provide opportunities for practice. *Percents/Decimals* [9] offers 16 different lessons, in-cluding two that deal with equivalent percents, decimals, and common frac-tions. *Conquering Percents* [10] has students work in a computer department store, where they learn ways to represent percent and equivalent decimals and common fractions. A series of programs called *Math Computational Series* [11] has activities dealing with percents that offer exercises in convert-ing fractions and decimals to percent. Check Appendix B for companies to call or write for catalogs of software.

Paper-and-pencil activities can be prepared for additional practice. An

---

ACTIVITY 13.27   What Does Percent Mean?

- Have students work in pairs with a flat and 100 small cubes from a Cuisenaire set.

- Tell them that the flat is a unit, or whole.

- Say, "Put fifty cubes side by side on top of the flat. What part of the flat is covered with cubes?" (½, or 0.50.)

- Write the common fraction and the decimal fraction on the chalkboard. Tell the students that another way to express the same amount is 50 percent. Write 50% next to the ½ and 0.50.

- Have students put these small cubes on the flat, one set at a time.

16 cubes   45 cubes   33 cubes
9 cubes   68 cubes

- After each set has been placed, have a stu-dent write its common and the decimal frac-tion representations on the chalkboard. You write the percent after each pair of numbers.

- Have students cover the flat with 100 cubes. Ask, "What percent should I write to show how much of the flat is covered?" Write 100% on the chalkboard.

activity sheet with examples like these can be duplicated for distribution to students who need the practice.

Name _____   Date _____

1. Rename each decimal fraction as a percent:
   a. 0.65 = _____   b. 0.21 = _____   c. 0.95 = _____
   d. 0.08 = _____   e. 0.86 = _____   f. 0.30 = _____

2. Rename each common fraction as a decimal:
   a. ¼ = _____   b. ½ = _____   c. ¾ = _____
   d. ²⁄₁₀ = _____   e. ⁶⁄₁₀ = _____   f. ¹⁄₁₀ = _____

3. Rename each common fraction as a percent:
   a. ¼ = _____   b. ½ = _____   c. ¾ = _____
   d. ²⁄₁₀ = _____   e. ⁶⁄₁₀ = _____   f. ¹⁄₁₀ = _____

4. Rename each percent as a decimal fraction:
   a. 13% = _____   b. 47% = _____   c. 99% = _____
   d. 5% = _____   e. 60% = _____   f. 21% = _____

5. Rename each percent as a common fraction:
   a. 20% = _____   b. 50% = _____   c. 19% = _____
   d. 75% = _____   e. 90% = _____   f. 5% = _____

Extending Understanding of Percent

Not all percents arise from situations in which 100 is conveniently present, as in the introductory activities given above. Therefore, once the basic concept is well established, students' work should focus on activities that deal with groups other than 100. In Activity 13.28, poker chips are used to develop understanding of such groups.

ACTIVITY 13.28   What Is the Percent?

■ Begin by showing ten magnetic chips, four blue and six white.

■ Ask, "What part of the set of chips are the blue chips?" (⁴⁄₁₀ or 0.4.) "Who can tell what percent of the chips is blue?" (40 percent.)

Ask the responding student to explain how the answer was determined. If no answer is given, ask, "What must you do to change ⁴⁄₁₀ to a fraction with a denominator of 100?" (Multiply both numerator and denominator by 10.) "When you do this, what fraction is equivalent to ⁴⁄₁₀?" (⁴⁰⁄₁₀₀.) "⁴⁰⁄₁₀₀ is what percent?" (40 percent.)

(continued)

Activity 13.28 *continued*

- Put a second set of 10 chips so there are 20 on the board.

⬤⬤⬤⬤⬤◯◯◯◯◯

⬤⬤⬤⬤◯◯◯◯◯◯

- Ask, "Are the blue chips in this set 40 percent of the set?" (Yes.) Discuss this situation to confirm that 40 percent is correct.

- Repeat with other sets that have the same ratio of blue chips to total chips.

- Complete a table to show the ratios of $4/10$, $8/20$, $12/30$, ... , $40/100$.

4	8	12	16	20	24	28	32	36	40
10	20	30	40	50	60	70	80	90	100

- Repeat with other combinations of chips. (Make the dividend of each ratio 10 or a factor of 100 to make conversion to 100 easy.)

Working Percent Problems

Students who successfully complete the activities already discussed are ready to learn how to solve percent problems. There are three ways to solve percent problems: the proportion method, the case method, and the unitary analysis method. The proportion method is the most meaningful and easiest one for elementary school children to learn and is the only one included in this book. It is based on the idea that a single expression can be used to solve a problem, regardless of whether it is the base, the rate, or the percentage that is the unknown.

$$\frac{\text{rate}}{100} = \frac{\text{percentage}}{\text{base}}$$

A situation involving a 200-acre farm, with corn planted on 50 acres, provides a setting within which to work to develop a meaning of the proportional method. A diagram of the farm will help clarify the situation for students (Figure 13.4).

"What percent of a 200-acre farm is planted in corn when there are 50 acres of corn?" When the number of acres planted in corn (percentage) and the total number of acres (base) are known, the percent (rate) must be determined. Set up an equivalent relation that includes the rate and 100 on one side.

$$\frac{\text{rate}}{100} = \frac{50}{200}$$

"Twenty-five percent of a 200-acre farm is planted in corn. How many acres of corn were there?" When the percent (rate) and total number of

Figure 13-4
A simple drawing can illustrate a percent situation.

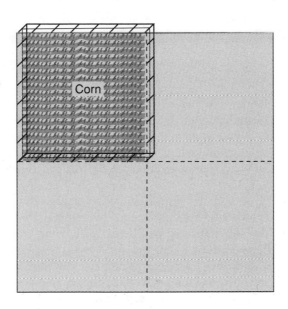

Corn

acres (base) are known, the number of acres planted in corn (percentage) must be determined.

$$\frac{25}{100} = \frac{\text{percentage}}{200}$$

"If 50 acres of corn is 25 percent of the entire farm, how many acres are there on the farm?" When the percent (rate) and number of acres planted in corn (percentage) are known, the total number of acres (base) must be determined.

$$\frac{25}{100} = \frac{50}{\text{base}}$$

In the example used here the solutions are not difficult. For the first situation—$^n\!/_{100} = ^{50}\!/_{200}$—students will see that 100 is one-half of 200, so the value of n will be one-half of 50, or 25. Point out on the diagram that the 50-acre corn field is ¼ of the total acreage and that ¼ is equivalent to 25 percent. For $^{25}\!/_{100} = ^n\!/_{200}$, they will know that 200 is twice as large as 100, so n is twice as large as 25, or 50. Students should see on the diagram that the acres planted in corn are ¼ of 200 acres, or 50. For $^{25}\!/_{100} = ^{50}\!/_n$, they will see that 50 is twice as large as 25, so n is twice as large as 100, or 200. The diagram shows that the 200 acres are four times as many as the acres planted in corn—50. The Math Explorer™ calculator makes the process of computing answers easy for children. To find the rate in this example, they multiply 50 by 100 and divide the product by 200. Pressing ⬛% converts the quotient to 0.25, or 25 percent. Similar operations are used to find the percentage or the base.

Figure 13-5
Number line for solving proportion problems

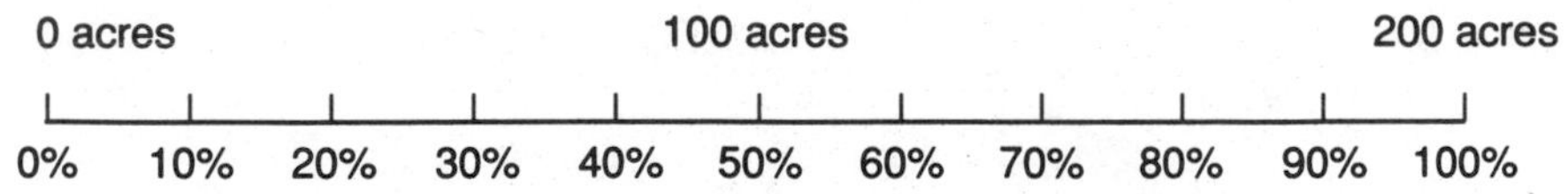

| 0 acres | | | | | 100 acres | | | | | 200 acres |

| 0% | 10% | 20% | 30% | 40% | 50% | 60% | 70% | 80% | 90% | 100% |

A number line is a way to solve the problems in this situation graphically. Draw a line with percent marks along the bottom. Put the number that represents the base above the 100. When 200 is above 100, 100 will be above 50, 50 will be above 25, and so on across the top. Students can use numbers above and below to determine missing terms in the proportion. (See Figure 13.5.)

Students need many opportunities to engage in problem-solving activities represented with real objects and diagrams to develop confidence in their ability to solve percent problems. The computer program *Conquering Percents* [12] offers students the opportunity to role play an employee's job in a computer store where they determine prices of merchandise, discount rates, and the amount of discounts. Newspapers contain many examples of uses of percent. Students can clip articles and advertisements from papers and prepare an interesting bulletin board. After a bulletin board has been assembled, discuss the many different situations in which percent is used.

EXERCISE   Briefly describe a situation other than the corn field that can be used to practice the proportion method of dealing with percent problems. How can the situation be illustrated by you or children?

■ SUMMARY

The fractional number system includes all of the positive and negative integers and numbers between integers that can be expressed in the form a/b, where a is any integer and b is any integer other than zero. Fractional numbers can be expressed with common fractions, decimal fractions, and percent. Fractional numbers greater than zero are included in the elementary school curriculum. Ways to introduce decimal and percent representations are presented in this chapter, along with ways of teaching operations with decimal fractions and problem solving with percent.

Work with decimal fractions and percent extends the understanding of fractional numbers and ways to express them. Decimals express numbers smaller than one that have denominators of ten or a power of ten. The denominator is not written but is indicated by the number of numerals there are to the right of the ones place in a decimal numeral. Structured materials, such as Cuisenaire and base-ten sets, unit-region kits cut from paper, and number lines are aids students can use to learn the meaning of decimal fractions. Once the meaning of decimals is understood and students can write decimal numerals accurately, they are ready to learn to round decimals to the nearest whole unit or to another decimal, and to add, subtract, multiply, and divide fractional numbers expressed as decimals. The algorithms for computing with decimals are like those for computing with whole numbers. Real-life situations and work with learning aids will help students extend their uses of the algorithms to include decimals. Carefully developed procedures to determine where to place decimal points in answers should be used rather than teacher-dictated rules. Computer programs provide both developmental and application activities. Calculators should be used for routine computation and practice. Textbooks can be used for practice activities. Applications of decimal fractions to science and measurement situations should be integrated to help students learn how they are used for practical reasons.

Percent is used to express a ratio between some number and 100. Carefully sequenced activities will help students understand the meaning of percent. Special attention needs to be given to the meanings of percent (rate), base, and percentage. The proportion method of solving percent problems is recommended in this book. Instruction about it can be related to earlier work with equivalent fractions and the use of proportions in problem solving.

■ STUDY QUESTIONS AND ACTIVITIES

1. The third standard for grades five to eight, "Mathematics as Reasoning," includes this statement: "[R]easoning shall permeate the mathematics curriculum so students can understand and apply reasoning processes, with special attention to . . . reasoning with proportions. . . ."[13] Write a paragraph in which you explain how you think work with percent can contribute to the development of this standard with fifth- and sixth-grade students.

2. Estimation is recommended as a way to help students learn how to place a decimal point in a product or quotient for computation with decimal fractions. Explain the thought process a child might use to estimate a product or quotient for each of these examples:

   a. $\begin{array}{r} 4.8 \\ \times\ 2.3 \\ \hline 1104 \end{array}$ b. $\begin{array}{r} 36.2 \\ \times\ 1.08 \\ \hline 39096 \end{array}$ c. $\begin{array}{r} 48.36 \\ \times\quad 51 \\ \hline 24799008 \end{array}$

   d. $3.2\overline{)21.8240}\ ^{682}$ e. $33\overline{)9.966}\ ^{302}$

   Explain why rounding off is not useful for making estimates in examples like these:

   f. $\begin{array}{r} 0.341 \\ \times\ 0.682 \\ \hline 232562 \end{array}$ g. $0.36\overline{)0.0072}\ ^{2}$

   Describe a process for placing the decimal point in each of the two preceding examples.

3. Jacqueline Dewar explains a model for solving percent problems (see the For Further Reading section). Demonstrate through drawings and written explanation how that model could be used to solve these problems:

   a. A mixture of coffee beans weighs 50 kilograms. If 48 percent of the beans are grown in Hawaii, how many kilograms of coffee are from Hawaii?

   b. A mixture of coffee beans contains 24 kilograms of coffee grown in Hawaii. If this is 48 percent of the entire mixture, what is the total weight of the mixture?

   c. A mixture of coffee that weighs 50 kilograms has 24 kilograms of coffee grown in Hawaii. What percent of the mixture is coffee from Hawaii?

4. Thomas Carpenter and his associates (see the For Further Reading section) evaluated students' work on the decimal fraction portion of the *National Assessment of Educational Progress* test and identified weaknesses. They indicated the implications of the test results for teachers. What do they say is needed to improve instruction about decimal fractions? Describe materials you believe should be available so students can overcome the weaknesses identified by these authors.

5. Look at advertisements in newspapers for examples of sale discounts expressed as percent. Make a chart which shows the original price, the amount of savings, and the final price for items costing $10, $25, $40, and $75. Also note the interest rates for savings and for loans. Create other charts to show savings on $1,000 and interest paid on a loan of $1,000.

■ FOR FURTHER READING

Carpenter, Thomas P., and others. 1981, April. Decimals: Results and implications from National Assessment. *Arithmetic Teacher 28*(8), 34–37.

The results of this NAEP test indicate that students lack a clear understanding of decimal fractions. This and other weaknesses are reported, along with implications of the test's results for classroom teachers.

Cole, Blaine L., and Henry S. Weissenfluh. 1974, March. An analysis of teaching percentage. *Arithmetic Teacher 21*(3), 226–228.

Describes the relationship between the ratio method and the case method of solving percent problems. Explains the ratio method and gives a brief outline of the background to understand it.

Dewar, Jacqueline M. 1984, March. Another look at teaching percent. *Arithmetic Teacher 31*(7), 48–49.

The author explains how a simple drawing can be used to illustrate the meaning of and operations dealing with percent. Examples of different types of problems are used to demonstrate how the drawing works.

Fisher, John W. 1975, February. Deci-deck. *Arithmetic Teacher* 22(2), 149.

The deci-deck card game provides practice in naming equivalent common fractions, decimal fractions, and percent. Several card games are possible with the deck.

Hiebert, James. 1987, March. Research report: Decimal fractions. *Arithmetic Teacher 34*(7), 22–23.

The author reviews recent research dealing with instruction about decimals. He concludes that most students do not develop a sufficient understanding of decimal fractions to understand rules and procedures for dealing with them. He stresses the importance of using concrete materials during introductory work and developing sufficient understanding of decimals so students can use estimation to determine the reasonableness of results when computing with decimal fractions.

Klein, Paul A. 1990, May. Remembering how to read decimals. *Arithmetic Teacher 37*(9).

A procedure for helping students to read decimal fractions after meaning is developed and presented.

Payne, Joseph N., and Ann E. Towsley. 1990, April. Implementing the *Standards:* Implications of NCTM's *Standards* for teaching fractions and decimals. *Arithmetic Teacher 37*(8), 23–26.

Model activities for meeting the standards for common and decimal fractions are presented.

Priester, Sharon. 1984, March. SUM 9.9: A game for decimals. *Arithmetic Teacher 31*(7), 46–47.

A card game—ONO 99—served as the inspiration for SUM 9.9, which is a game for practicing addition and subtraction with decimal fractions. The card deck and rules are explained.

■ NOTES

[1] National Council of Teachers of Mathematics. 1989. *Curriculum and Evaluation Standards in School Mathematics.* Reston, VA: National Council of Teachers of Mathematics, 57. Used by permission.

[2] NCTM, 87. Used by permission.

[3] NCTM, 91. Used by permission.

[4] NCTM, 94. Used by permission.

[5] NCTM, 57.

[6] Society for Visual Education (SVE), 1345 Diversey Parkway, Chicago, IL 60614-1299.

[7] Cambridge Development Laboratory, Inc., 214 Third Ave., Waltham, MA 02154.

[8] Cambridge Development Laboratory, Inc.

[9] Dorsett Educational Systems, Inc., P.O. Box 1226, Norman, OK 73070.

[10] MECC, 3490 Lexington Ave. North, St. Paul, MN 55126.

[11] IBM Educational Systems, 4111 Northside Parkway, Atlanta, GA 30327.

[12] MECC.

[13] National Council of Teachers of Mathematics. 1989. *Curriculum and Evaluation Standards for School Mathematics.* Reston, VA: National Council of Teachers of Mathematics, 81.

Measurement

The active involvement of children with measuring instruments in realistic situations is an essential ingredient in helping children understand measurement systems and tools for measuring. The National Council of Teachers of Mathematics expresses the need this way:

Measurement activities can and should require a dynamic interaction between students and their environment. Students encounter measurement ideas both in and out of school, in such areas as architecture, art, science, commercial design, sports, cooking, shopping, and map reading. The study of measurement shows the usefulness and practical applications of mathematics, and students' need to communicate about various measurements highlights the importance of standard units and common measurement systems.[1]

Measurement at all levels of the elementary school should involve students in activities where they investigate measurement concepts and develop skills in using instruments to measure many objects in their environment. Activities begin in the kindergarten and primary grades as children compare the length, capacity, and weight of familiar objects and containers. They are continued throughout the grades, with a variety of cooperative-group and teacher-led activities providing the means for students to extend and deepen their understanding of all areas of measurement. In addition to presenting examples of activities for children, this chapter includes a discussion of the meaning of measurement and characteristics of the metric and English systems of measure.

In this chapter you will read about

1. the meaning of measurement and two measuring processes;

2. the characteristics of the metric system and the English (customary) system, and the advantages of the metric system over the English system;

3. activities and procedures for building a foundation for measurement;

4. activities for developing the concept of linear measure with standard and nonstandard units;

5. commonly used weight (mass) measures and activities for developing the concept of weight;

6. area measure and activities for learning to measure the areas of plane figures;

7. volume measure and procedures to use in determining the volume of figures such as cubes and rectangular prisms;

8. the meaning of angular measure and activities for helping children learn to measure angles;

9. activities that promote children's understanding and use of estimation in measurement;

10. setting up a metric mini-Olympics;

11. activities dealing with temperature;

12. developmental activities for time and its measures;

13. activities for understanding and using money for exchange.

STANDARDS THAT PERTAIN TO MEASUREMENT

Kindergarten Through Grade Four

Standard 10: Measurement In grades K–4, the mathematics curriculum should include measurement so that students can:

- understand the attributes of length, capacity, weight, area, volume, time, temperature, and angle;
- develop the process of measuring and concepts related to units of measurement;
- make and use estimates of measurements;
- make and use measurements in problem and everyday situations.[2]

Grades Five Through Eight

Standard 13: Measurement In grades 5–8, the mathematics curriculum should include extensive concrete experiences using measurement so that students can:

- extend their understanding of the process of measurement;
- estimate, make, and use measurements to describe and compare phenomena;
- select appropriate units and tools to measure to the degree of accuracy required for a particular situation;
- understand the structure and use of systems of measurement;
- extend their understanding of the concepts of perimeter, area, volume, angle measure, capacity, and weight and mass;
- develop the concepts of rates and other derived and indirect measurements;
- develop formulas and procedures for determining measures to solve problems.[3]

 ## WHAT IS MEASUREMENT? _____

When students count discrete objects, such as marbles or apples, whole numbers are sufficient to determine a total. Continuous objects, which are measured, cannot always be measured by whole units. While a football field can be measured in yards, the yard measure would not be an appropriate unit to determine the wingspan of a hummingbird. Even inches are too large to measure the wingspan of the tiniest hummingbirds. Thus, fractional numbers, either as common fractions in the English system or decimal fractions in the metric system, are sometimes needed to measure continuous objects. Measurement is the process of attaching numbers to the physical qualities of length, capacity, volume, area, angles, weight (mass), and temperature. Time is also measured, but it lacks a physical quality. Each measuring unit must have the same attribute as the object being measured. A yardstick and a meterstick[4] both have the attribute of length and are used to measure length or distance. A square inch has the attribute of being two-dimensional and is used to measure area. Each object is measured by applying a unit of measure one or more times to the object. When a meter is used to measure the length of a playing field, the number of times the meter is applied along the length of the field determines the measure of the field. The unit need not be applied one unit at a time, as would be done if a meterstick was used, but can be laid out many units at a time, as would be done if a metric measuring tape is used.

Two Types of Measuring Processes

Two types of measuring processes exist: direct measurement and indirect measurement. The processes for determining many measures of length and capacity are direct, made by applying the appropriate unit directly to the object being measured. This direct process is referred to as **iteration.** Iteration is illustrated by the use of a measuring cup to determine the amount of cider squeezed from 20 apples. The quantity of cider is determined by pouring cider into and emptying the cup and counting the cupfuls until all of the cider has been poured. The amount of cider is expressed in cups.

Weight (mass), temperature, and time cannot be measured in the direct manner just described. Their characteristics, or properties, require an instrument that measures each one by translating the measureable property into numbers indirectly. Thus one type of weather thermometer has a number scale aligned with a tube that contains a liquid. The liquid expands (and rises) when it is warmed as the surrounding air becomes hotter; it contracts (and goes down) when it is cooled as the air becomes cooler. The temperature is determined indirectly by reading the numeral on the scale that indicates the height of the liquid at that time.

Measurement Is Approximate

Although the counting of discrete objects is exact, all measurement is approximate. The approximate nature of measurement stems from the fact that for every unit of measure there is, theoretically at least, a unit that is smaller. During their study of common fractions students use number lines to develop an intuitive understanding that there is no smallest fraction. During their study of measurement they can use this understanding to conclude that all measurement is approximate. Any unit of measure can be divided into one that is smaller and hence more precise. When a football field is marked off with yards as the unit of measure, it is 100 yards long. However, if a unit smaller than a yard, such as an inch, is used to measure the field, it might measure 3,598 inches, or slightly less than 100 yards.

▇ TWO MEASUREMENT SYSTEMS

The English, or customary, system of measurement has been used in the United States since early settlement of the continent and the foundation of the country. In more recent years efforts have been made to convert the country to the metric system, but none has been totally successful. Although President Gerald Ford signed the Metric Conversion Act of 1975, change-over was not mandated; it was to be voluntary. Changes occurred in some areas of manufacturing and commerce, but resistance prevented its spread to other areas. Even though use of the metric system will continue and may increase in some areas, the English system seems entrenched in everyday use. So children need to learn the basic units of measure for both systems.

The English System

The English system is a standardized system of measurement. The units of measure for length, weight (mass), and capacity remain constant within each type of measurement. However, no common relationship exists between the units for any type of measurement and between one type of measure and another, such as between length and capacity, as in the metric system. Tables for the various types of measurement reveal the lack of relationships within the system (see Tables 14.1, 14.2, and 14.3).

Table 14.1

LINEAR MEASURE		ENGLISH SYSTEM
12 inches (in)	=	1 foot (ft)
3 feet (ft)	=	1 yard (yd)
36 inches (in)	=	1 yard (yd)
5,280 feet (ft)	=	1 mile (mi)
1,760 yards (yd)	=	1 mile (mi)

Table 14.2

WEIGHT MEASURE		ENGLISH SYSTEM
16 ounces (oz)	=	1 pound (lb)
2,000 pounds (lb)	=	1 ton (T)

Table 14.3

CAPACITY MEASURE		ENGLISH SYSTEM
2 tablespoons (tbsp)	=	1 fluid ounce (fl. oz)
8 fluid ounces (fl. oz)	=	1 cup (c)
2 cups (c)	=	1 pint (pt)
2 pints (pt)	=	1 quart (qt)
2 quarts (qt)	=	1 half gallon (gal)
4 quarts (qt)	=	1 gallon (gal)

Metric System

In contrast to the English system, which developed over a long period of time and for which units were derived from such things as human body parts, grains of barley, and the distance a person could run before tiring, the metric system was created in a systematic way during a relatively short span of time in the late 1700s. In 1790 the National Assembly of France directed the French Academy of Sciences to devise a system having an invariable standard for all measures. The Academy derived its unit by measuring the distance from the equator to the North Pole and then used one ten-millionth of the distance as the length of a *meter*. A prototype, or standard, rod with a length of one meter was made from platinum. Other common units were derived from the meter. Tables 14.4, 14.5, and 14.6 show the uniform relationships between units within a type of measurement and between two different types of measurements.

Base units for capacity, weight, and area were established at the time the base unit for linear measure was established. A *liter*, the base unit for capacity, is the volume of a cube that is one decimeter on each side; this is a cubic decimeter (dm^3). A *kilogram* is the base unit of weight (mass) and was originally determined to be one cubic decimeter of water at 4 degrees Celsius, the temperature at which water is most dense. The standard for a *kilogram* is now a platinum-iridium solid kept in France. The base unit for land area is the *are* (a), which is 100 square meters (m^2). A *hectare* (ha) is 100 ares. Volume is measured in *cubic centimeters* (cm^3) and *cubic meters* (m^3).

A detail of interest coming from the 1960 Eleventh General Conference on Weights and Measures, at which time the International System of Units (SI) was established, was a redefinition of the meter. It is approximately the

Table 14.4

LENGTH MEASURE		METRIC SYSTEM
10 millimeters (mm)	=	1 centimeter (cm)
10 centimeters (cm)	=	1 decimeter (dm)
10 decimeters (dm)	=	1 meter (m)
1,000 meters (m)	=	1 kilometer (km)

Table 14.5

WEIGHT MEASURE		METRIC SYSTEM
1,000 milligrams (mg)	=	1 gram (g)
1,000 grams (g)	=	1 kilogram (kg)
1,000 kilograms (kg)	=	1 metric ton (t)

Table 14.6

CAPACITY MEASURE		METRIC SYSTEM
1,000 milliliter (mL)	=	1 liter (L)

same length as the original meter, but is now defined as 1 650 763.73 wave-lengths[5] in vacuum of the orange-red line of the spectrum of the krypton-86 atom. This standard was adopted because it is unvarying and indestructible and can be reproduced in any laboratory possessing the proper equipment.

Characteristics of the Metric System

One significant characteristic of the metric system has already been mentioned: the fact that measures of capacity, weight, and area are all based on the meter.

Another important feature is that the metric system is a decimal system. This means that for each type of measure there is an interrelationship of units based on multiplication or division by ten. This scheme is essentially the same as the Hindu-Arabic system, a fact that should be capitalized on to help children develop their understanding of the metric system. Table 14.4 shows this attribute through the equivalence of the various units. Two units of linear measure were omitted from this chart—dekameter and hectometer between meter and kilometer—because they are seldom used. Other units of capacity and weight such as dekaliter and hectogram are seldom used. The units of measure shown in the six tables for the two measurement systems show the units of measure commonly studied by elementary school students. Other units of measure studied in these grades are square meter and square centimeter; square inch, foot, and yard; cubic centimeter, meter, inch, foot, and yard; second, minute, hour, day, and year; and temperature with degrees Celsius and Fahrenheit.

Advantages of the Metric System

The metric system has several advantages over the English system.

- It is similar to the base-ten system of numeration.
- It is simple and is easy to use.
- There is a uniform set of prefixes that apply to units of measure in each area of measurement. Once learned and understood, they can be used with meaning regardless of the area of measurement being used.
- There are a relatively few units of measure that are frequently used—meter, gram, liter. They and their few subdivisions and multiples are all of the units most people need to know.
- The metric system is widely used. In fact, the United States is the only major nation not using the system.

■ EARLY MEASUREMENT ACTIVITIES

Work with measurement is spread over all of the years children are in school. The earliest work is largely informal and investigative in nature. Activities 14.1 through 14.4 suggest ways teachers can help children build a foundation for later work with both nonstandard and standard units of measure in capacity, weight, time, temperature. Each activity uses easily obtained materials.

ACTIVITY 14.1   Capacity

- Prepare clear plastic or glass containers by gluing rubber bands around them at different levels. Put two to six pounds of rice, a funnel, and a scoop in a plastic tub or large cardboard box.

- Children use the scoop and funnel to fill each container to the rubber-band level.

- This activity is not designed for children to count the number of scoops required to fill each container. However, some children may want to do this, so pencils and squares of paper should be provided for them to record their counts.[6]

ACTIVITY 14.2   Heavier and Lighter

- A commercial or homemade balance beam gives children opportunities to compare pairs of objects to determine which is heavier or lighter.

- Children's first work with the balance beam should be exploratory. They will learn to make it balance by putting an object in one pan and other objects in the second pan un-

til the crossbar is level. They also see the crossbar go down at one end when the object in one pan is heavier than the object in the other pan.

- Set up pairs of objects—toy car and wooden block, chalkboard eraser and small bag of rice, small rubber ball and box of pencils—so children can determine which is heavier and which is lighter. Prepare a mat on which children can place objects as they work.

Lighter	Heavier

ACTIVITY 14.3 Passage of Time

- Use four or five cans alike in both shape and size. Punch a hole in the bottom of each can: a small hole in one, a larger hole in another, and in-between sizes in the others. Paint each can a different color or glue colored construction paper to each one. Put water or clean, fine-grained sand in a plastic tub.

- Have a child select a can, fill it, and hold it so the water or sand drains through the hole. (If sand is used, the child will need to gently shake the can to drain all of the sand.)

- Ask questions as the children observe what happens:
  —"Does the red can drain quickly or slowly?"
  —"Which can drains more slowly, the red can or the blue can?"
  —"What is the color of the can that drains the fastest?"
  —"Can you put the cans in order from quickest to slowest?"
  —"What can you tell me about the size of a hole and the speed with which a can empties?"

ACTIVITY 14.4 Temperature

- Outdoors on a sunny day provides a setting for an investigation and discussion about temperature. Choose a location where there is a sidewalk, some grass, and a patch of dry ground, and select a time when one part of each is in sunlight and another part in shade.

- Have the children remove their shoes and socks and walk on the sunny sidewalk. Talk

about how it feels. Have them walk on the shady sidewalk and compare its feel with that of the sunny sidewalk.

- Have the children walk on the sunny and shady portions of the other surfaces. Discuss differences in temperature, if any, between each spot and the others. Can the children order the six locations from warmest to coolest?

INTRODUCING NONSTANDARD UNITS

Children's understanding of measure begins as they engage in activities such as those already described. Such activities should continue until children attain the state of maturity called conservation. Children who conserve quantity or length understand that the volume or length of an object does not change, even if the object's position is altered. Children are generally able to conserve at about eight or nine years of age. Once children are ready for measurement activities, their first work can be with nonstandard units.

Activities with nonstandard units bridge the gap between exploratory work and the introduction of standard units. Two goals for work with nonstandard units are to help children recognize the need for a uniform set of measures and to lay the groundwork for their understanding of the various types of measures. A variety of small linear objects can be used to lay the foundation for linear measures in either system of measurement. New pencils are used in Activity 14.5. When a single object, rather than many, is used to measure the length of something, the iteration process is used. (Iteration is explained earlier in this chapter.) A child's cutout foot provides a useful nonstandard unit of measure for introducing the process of iteration. The activity also lays a foundation on which to build children's understanding of the need for a uniform system of measurement. Walnuts, Unifix cubes, wooden blocks, or small bags of rice can be used as nonstandard units for experiences with weighing objects on a balance scale. Nonstandard units of capacity can be made by spray painting cans different colors. Children use them with rice in a plastic tub to gain experience in filling one container from another and counting containers. Squares cut from cardboard containers provide the means for investigations about area. Once each measurement concept is introduced and children understand a process, problem cards can be used for additional investigations. Children can be engaged in many different activities as they work in small groups with problem cards such as those used in Activities 14.5 through 14.9.

ACTIVITY 14.5   New-Pencil Measurements

- Have children work in pairs. Give each pair eight to ten new lead pencils.

- Select an object such as a desktop to measure. Demonstrate how to put pencils end to end to find the length and width of the desk in pencil units. Stress the importance of not leaving gaps between pencils or having pencils overlap.

- Have each pair lay out pencils to determine the length and width of a desk. Discuss the results and correct any misunderstandings.

- Use problem cards to direct children's measurement activities.

MEASURING WITH PENCILS

Use new pencils from the box to answer the questions.

1. How long is the reading table? How wide is the reading table?

2. How wide is the door to the hallway?

3. Can you figure out a way to find out how high my desk is? If you can, tell how high it is.

Use a sentence to answer each question.

ACTIVITY 14.6   Foot Units

- Have children work in pairs to draw and cut out outlines of each other's foot.

- Demonstrate how to use a "foot" unit to measure a table top or height of a desk using iteration.

- Have each pair of children measure a common object, such as a desktop.

- Once iteration is understood, give problem cards to direct children's activities.

- During a class discussion, talk about the students' measures for common objects. When the number of units for a given object—such as the length of the chalkboard tray—are not the same, introduce the fact that not every "foot" unit is as long as every other one. Some "foot" units are longer than others, so the length of an object varies, depending on the length of the "foot" used to measure it.

- Make a chart on which the children's "foot" units are ordered from shortest to longest.

MEASURING WITH "FOOT" UNITS

Use your "foot" units to answer these questions.

1. How high is the filing cabinet? How wide is the cabinet?

2. How long is the chalkboard tray?

3. How long is the classroom? How wide is the classroom?

Use a sentence to answer each of the questions.

ACTIVITY 14.7   Nonstandard Weights

- Set up a weight center with a balance scale and a box each of walnuts, wooden blocks, Unifix cubes, and small bags of rice for children to use as units of measure. Have a collection of objects to be weighed: book, softball, child's sneaker, bag of carrots.

- Demonstrate how units of each type are used to "weigh" one of the objects. Stress

the importance of having the two pans be as evenly balanced as possible. (With some objects it may not be possible to make the arm completely horizontal.)

- Provide problem cards to direct children's activities.

(continued)

Activity 14.7   *continued*

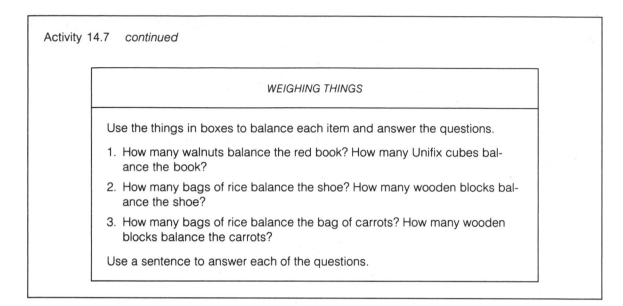

ACTIVITY 14.8   Colored Can Units

- Select cans so that one has four times the capacity of another, one has a capacity twice another, and so on until there are five or six cans. Paint all cans of the same capacity the same color; paint each size of can a different color than other-sized cans.

- Demonstrate how to fill one can with another by filling a larger can from a smaller one and emptying the contents of a larger can into smaller ones. Stress the importance of filling each can level to the top. Have children count as you fill and empty the cans.

- Provide problem cards to direct children's activities.

FILLING AND EMPTYING CANS

Use cans and rice to answer the questions.

1. How many blue cans does it take to fill one red can?
2. How many yellow cans can you fill from a green canful of rice?
3. Does it take more of the yellow cans or more of the green cans to fill a red can?
4. What is the order of the cans from largest to smallest?

Use a sentence to answer each question.

ACTIVITY 14.9   Covering with Squares

- Cut 6-inch by 6-inch squares from pieces of cardboard.

- Demonstrate how to cover the surface of a table or desk with squares. Stress the importance of not having squares overlap or leaving gaps. Have children count the squares. If there are pieces sticking over the edge of the surface, have them make two counts.

One count is of squares that are within the edges of the surface; the other count is of all of the squares. (Select surfaces for children to cover on which cards fit with no more than a little of the square sticking over the sides of the surfaces.)

- Use problem cards to guide additional activities.

MEASURING WITH SQUARES

Use the cardboard squares to answer each of the questions.

1. How many squares does it take to cover the tile surface at the entrance to our room?

2. How many squares cover the carpet in the listening center? Do the squares all stop at the edge of the carpet? How many squares are entirely on the carpet? How many squares are there altogether?

Use a sentence to answer each of the questions.

EXERCISE   Problem cards are used in Activities 14.5 through 14.9 to direct students' activities with nonstandard units. Select a type of measurement—linear, area, weight, or capacity—and a nonstandard unit for it; prepare a problem card to direct activities with your nonstandard unit.

■ STANDARD UNITS OF MEASURE

Children need to learn both the metric and the English system of measure. The premise of this book is that children learn about measurement best when they have frequent opportunities to measure objects. Rather than reading about a measuring process, such as linear measure, children should use an appropriate instrument to actually measure objects. As they work, they learn that 10 centimeters equal one decimeter and that 12 inches equal one foot. Once children are familiar with the units in one system, they can learn comparable units for the other system.

The time children need to learn both systems need not be extensive. Children who understand the basic concepts of measurement and can use the various instruments can apply their knowledge to situations, both actual and contrived, in which they make measurements. A teacher can create many situations in school that require children to measure in art, social science, science, and physical education.

In the past students spent much of the time devoted to measurement on rote exercises in which units from one system were converted to the other. The benefits of such exercises are few; students recognize this and consider the time spent on them to be worthless. There are a few relationships between units in one system and the other that children will learn as they use instruments of measure. For example, as they use yardsticks and metersticks they learn that a meter is slightly longer than a yard. As they weigh objects, they find that a kilogram is slightly more than two pounds. As they fill and empty containers they learn that a liter is a little more than a quart. This is useful information they acquire in meaningful ways rather than through rote exercises.

Measurement activities with standard units in this chapter use metric system units except with time and money. English units can be used for each activity, too, so teachers should prepare materials and set up learning centers for both systems.

The progression from working with nonstandard units to standard units goes smoothly for children experienced in working in cooperative-learning groups and learning centers or a laboratory setting. Instead of pencil or cutout-foot units for linear measure, now they use centimeter and meter rulers. Sets of kilogram weights replace walnuts and other nonstandard units, and liter containers replace cans.

Linear Measures

There are wooden and plastic rulers, including centimeter rulers and meter sticks. Some have only metric units, with whole centimeters along one edge and millimeter units along the other, while others have metric units along one edge and English units along the other. It is recommended that the first ruler used by children be one with no numerals and that contains only whole-centimeter units along one edge. The absence of numerals forces children to count units and not rely on numbers to determine the length of an object. These can be made by duplicating the ruler on tagboard and cutting them out (Figure 14.1). See Activity 14.10.

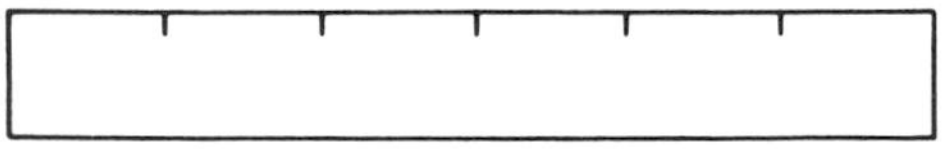

Figure 14-1
Ruler for use by children. Only unit segments are marked.

ACTIVITY 14.10 Using Whole Units

- Select objects with measures that are a whole number of centimeter units. Some ready-made articles to use are 35-mm film boxes, ballpoint pens, books. You can cut sticks, sharpen pencils, and trim paper edges so they have centimeter dimensions.

- Demonstrate how to use the centimeter ruler. Stress the importance of having the end of the ruler at one end of the object; also emphasize careful counting. To count, begin at the end and count points along the ruler until the opposite end of the object is reached.

- Use problem cards to direct children's activities.

USING CENTIMETERS

Use the tagboard ruler to measure the items and answer the questions.

1. How many centimeters long is the plastic pen?

2. How many centimeters long is the yellow spoon?

3. How many centimeters long is the film box? How wide is the film box? Is the end of the film box shaped like a square?

4. How many centimeters long is the strip of blue paper?

5. What are three things in the room that are less than 20 centimeters long?

Use a sentence to answer each of the questions. Compare your answers with those of another group of students. If there are any disagreements, measure the things that are involved to determine why there are differences.

Not all linear measurements will be a whole number of centimeters long. For example, the pencil in the upper part of Figure 14.2 is slightly longer than 4 centimeters, while the one in the lower part is slightly less than 4 centimeters. Measured to the nearest whole centimeter, each of the

Figure 14-2
Unit rulers are used to measure the length of two pencils. Each pencil has a measurement of 4 units.

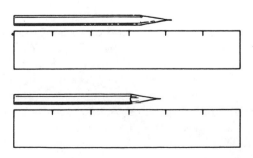

Figure 14-3
This pencil might be recorded as having a measurement of 5 units by some children and 6 units by others.

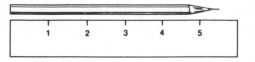

pencils is 4 centimeters long. When the endpoint of an object lies near the midpoint between two units, children must make a judgment about the length of the object. The pencil in Figure 14.3 might be reported as being 5 centimeters long by one child and as 6 centimeters long by another child. Each child can interpret the measure of the pencil differently and yet still give a correct measure for it. Numerals have been added to the ruler in Figure 14.3, so that children can now determine the measure of an object with numerals rather than by counting.

Work with meters follows that with centimeters. The first meter stick should be a stick that has no marking along the edge. Pieces of pine molding cut one meter long serve nicely. Problem cards similar to those illustrated earlier can direct students' work in cooperative-learning groups. The length and width of a classroom, the distance from classroom door to principal's office, and other places inside the school building can be determined by groups of children.

A trundle wheel is a special device for determining lengths or distances. It is a wooden or plastic wheel with a meter or yard circumference attached to a handle. The wheel is rolled across a surface, beginning with the starting arrow on the ground. At the conclusion of each rotation a "click" indicates one meter or yard. Children can work in groups with a trundle wheel to determine the measurements of such things as hallways, sidewalks, playgrounds, and distances in and around their school.

Eventually children should work with meter sticks subdivided into decimeters and centimeters, and with metric measuring tapes and millimeter rulers. Now children will measure all sorts of objects and use the devices to measure in science, art, physical education, and other curricular areas. Measurements will be recorded in different ways, depending on the children's maturity and understanding. For instance, a child's height might be recorded as 148 centimeters or 1.48 meters. Mixed units are not used to record measurements. The above measurement would not be recorded as 1 meter 48 centimeters, or 1 m 48 cm.

Most textbooks contain activities to help children learn how to convert a given metric measurement to another unit by multiplying or dividing. Through these activities children learn that to convert 148 centimeters to meters they divide 148 by 100. To convert 458 meters to kilometers, they divide 458 by 1,000. To convert 1.67 meters to centimeters, they multiply 1.67 by 100. When children are given such assignments, a calculator should be used to ease the task of dividing or multiplying and help students concentrate on processes rather than computations.

One of the NCTM standards for measurement indicates that students should learn how to estimate measurements so that they can make reasonable approximations of the meter, decimeter, centimeter, millimeter, and kilometer. A two-part activity, where children first record their estimates of the length of familiar objects and parts of their school and then measure each object or school part to determine the measurement, is good for developing skill in estimating linear measurements.

Another way to meet this standard is to help children establish standard reference measures based on familiar objects. A dime is approximately one millimeter thick. The width of the nail on a person's little finger is about one centimeter. The chalk rail in most classrooms is approximately one meter above the floor. Activities 14.11 and 14.12 help children establish personal reference measures for longer distance measures. In the first, each child determines the average number of steps she or he takes to walk ten meters. In the second they use knowledge of their steps to estimate a distance of 50 meters.

The best way for children to get a "feeling" for a kilometer is to walk the distance several times. Locate landmarks that are approximately one kilometer from school—a child's house, a store, a playground, a bridge. As the children walk the distance from school to one of the landmarks, help them note the time it takes. By doing this, the children can determine about how long it takes to walk a kilometer.

ACTIVITY 14.11   Your Step and Meters

- Measure a distance of ten meters in the classroom or a nearby hallway.

- Have each child walk from one end to the other, counting each step. The walking is done ten times.

- Have each child determine the average number of steps required to walk ten meters.

- Provide opportunities for students to use their paces to determine the approximate distance between places on the school grounds.

ACTIVITY 14.12   How Much Is 50 Meters?

- Take the children to a playground and align them along a line marked on the hardtop (or the edge of a sidewalk).

- Instruct the children to wait for your signal, then walk across the playground until each one thinks he or she has walked 50 meters, when each one is to stop.

- Have a pair of children use a metric trundle wheel or a metric measuring tape to measure 50 meters.

- Have each child note his or her location in relation to where the children who measured 50 meters are standing and evaluate his or her estimate.

- Have the children estimate other distances this way: 100 meters, 75 meters, and other reasonable distances. Have them evaluate each estimate.

Weight (Mass) Measures

Technically, weight and mass are not the same. Weight is the force exerted on an object because of gravity, whereas mass is the quantity of matter of which the object is composed. Thus a given object will weigh less on the moon, where the force of gravity is less, than it will on earth. It will have the same mass in either place, because the quantity of matter remains the same. However, even though a technical difference exists, it is common practice to consider weight and mass to be the same. Therefore the term that is commonly used—*weight*—will be used in the rest of this chapter.

The basic unit of weight is the kilogram. This basic unit has a prefix, unlike meter and liter. Table 14.5 shows the common units of weight in the metric system. By the time children complete elementary school they should be able to identify these units and name some common things that weigh about a gram or kilogram. They may encounter metric tons in social studies, where a country's production of copper and iron might be reported in that unit.

Two types of scales should be available, balance scales and spring scales. Commonly used versions of these scales are pictured in Chapter 3. In order to weigh objects on a balance scale, a set of weights is needed. A commercial set of brass weights might contain these units: one 500-gram, two 250-gram, two 100-gram, two 50-gram, four 10-gram, two 5-gram, and five 1-gram. A teacher can duplicate the large units by filling small bags with clean sand and the smaller units by using lead fish weights. Kitchen-type spring scales weighing up to 5 kilograms and a platform bathroom scale should be available. Two learning centers where groups of children practice weighing objects should be available, with one learning center containing a balance scale and such things as plastic fruit, pencils, red rubber erasers, and plastic animals, and the other containing a spring scale and bathroom scale and plastic bags of carrots and beans, boxes of paper, and other heavier objects. Problem cards can direct the children's activities (Figure 14.4).

Students who use scales to weigh objects will develop a sense that enables them to determine when something weighs about a kilogram. They will know that a gram of something is really a very tiny amount. They will be able to use that knowledge to judge the reasonableness of results when they weigh something and have a good sense for an amount when they read about the weight of things reported in metric units.

Capacity Measures

The liter is the basic unit of capacity in the metric system. It is a derived unit based on the decimeter, or tenth of a meter. A cube with inside dimensions of one decimeter has a volume of one cubic decimeter (dm^3), or 1,000 cubic centimeters (cm^3); this is one liter. Any container that has a capacity of one cubic decimeter has a capacity of one liter. Plastic containers of various sizes

Figure 14-4
Problem cards for
weight activities

WEIGHING WITH GRAMS

Use the balance scale and weights to answer the following questions.

1. What is the weight in grams of the plastic apple?
2. What is the weight in grams of the red eraser?
3. What is the weight in grams of the ballpoint pen?

Use a sentence to answer each of the questions.

WEIGHING WITH KILOGRAMS

Use the spring scale and the bathroom scale to answer each question.

1. How many kilograms does the bag of carrots weigh?
2. How many kilograms do ten mathematics books weigh?
3. How many kilograms does the bag of dried beans weigh?
4. How many kilograms does the box of paper weigh?

Use a sentence to answer each of the questions. Compare your answers with another group of students. If there are any disagreements, reweigh the objects that are involved to see if one group was wrong. Could a difference be the result of the way each group interpreted the measurements, rather than an error?

---

are inexpensive and can be purchased for classroom investigations (see the photographs in Chapter 3). The metric containers in which soft drinks, medicines, and other products are sold should not be overlooked. By choosing carefully, a teacher can accumulate a useful set of containers for children's activities. A learning center is used for activities with the problem card in Figure 14.5. It has a variety of common containers, some metric and some not. There should be at least one graduated liter container. Several smaller metric containers are desirable, but not necessary. The nonmetric containers can be vegetable and fruit cans; catsup, vinegar, and detergent bottles; pickle jars; and similar cans and bottles. There should be containers that hold both more and less than a liter without labels that indicate the amount of contents. Label each container with a letter A, B, C, and so on. A similar center can be set up so children can deal with milliliters. Specially prepared milliliter containers are available from school supply companies. Small plastic medicine containers cost little or nothing. Children can use these containers to determine the capacity of small bottles, such as those that hold liquid food coloring, spices, and perfume.

Figure 14-5
Problem card for
capacity activity

MEASURING CAPACITY

Use the containers to complete the activities.

1. List the letters of the containers you believe hold less than a liter. List the letters of the containers you believe hold more than a liter. Do you believe any of the containers hold just one liter? If so, list their letters.

2. List the letters of the containers in the order you believe is correct from smallest to largest.

3. Use the graduated liter container and other metric containers to determine the capacity of each container. Do not fill a container higher than the bottom part of the neck. Write the letter of each container and its capacity on your paper.

4. Check your estimates against the actual measurements. List the letters of containers for which your estimate was incorrect, if any.

5. Check your ordering of the containers. If you were mistaken about the placement of any of the containers, write the correct order now.

Area Measure

The units of measure for the area of an interior region bounded by a closed plane figure are derived from linear units. The metric units commonly studied in the elementary school are derived from the centimeter and meter. A square unit with one-centimeter sides is used to measure the area of small regions and a unit with one-meter sides is used to measure the area of larger regions. A square centimeter is designated by "cm²" and a square meter is designated as "m²." Goals of instruction are for students to be able to (1) name these two units and write their designations, (2) measure small regions directly by using square-centimeter grids and cardboard square-meter pieces and indirectly by measuring the sides of a region and using the formula $A = l \times w$ to determine the area, and (3) help children learn to determine areas by estimation.

Materials for a learning center consist of clear plastic pieces with a one-centimeter grid marked on each one, corrugated square-meter pieces, sheets of paper that can be measured with no parts of the centimeter grid overlapping and pieces where the grid overlaps (see Figure 14.6), and papers with irregular regions drawn on them (see Figure 14.7). Letter each piece of paper. Problem cards (above right) can be prepared to direct the students' activities.

AREA MEASUREMENT

Use the plastic grid to complete the activities.

1. Write the letter of each piece of paper that has a whole number of square centimeters. Write the area next to each letter.

2. Write the letter of each piece of paper that has parts left over when you measure its area. Write the approximate area of each piece next to its letter.

Compare your measures with those of another group of students. If there is any disagreement, remeasure the pieces that are involved to see if one group was wrong. Could a difference be the result of the way each group interpreted the measurements, rather than being an error?

MEASURING WITH SQUARE METERS

Use the square-meter pieces of cardboard to answer the questions.

1. What is the area of the carpet in the listening center?

2. What is the area of the four-square game area in the multipurpose room?

3. What is the area of half of the volleyball court in the multipurpose room?

Compare your answers with those of another group of students. If there are any disagreements, remeasure the surfaces that are involved to see if one group made an error. Could a difference be the result of the way each group interpreted the measurements, rather than being an error?

Figure 14-6
Plastic grid to determine areas. In (a) the grid fits a region with no overlap. In (b) the grid lines overlap the region.

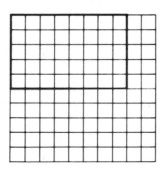

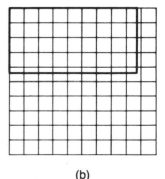

 (a)   (b)

Figure 14-7
Irregular plane region for a measurement activity

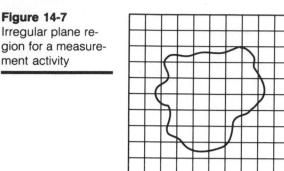

Children will find that not all regions can be measured in an exact number of square-centimeter or meter units. The problem cards give children opportunities to discuss situations where each of two groups may have a different measure in a particular situation because of the interpretation they made. Children need help in dealing with such situations. Teacher-led discussions about the area for the region in the second drawing in Figure 14.6 should present these steps:

- Count the units that are entirely within the region—there are 32.

- Count the units that are entirely or partially within the region—there are 45.

- Point out that the region's area will be at least 32 and not more than 45; a good estimate is 38 square units.

A similar process should be used to estimate the area of the irregular region in Figure 14.7.

Before they leave elementary school, children should learn a general formula for determining area. For regions such as squares and rectangles, the process is to multiply the measure of one edge by the measure of the other edge. By now students should know how to determine the product for an a-by-b array. That knowledge can be connected to the work with area so that children readily understand the formula $A = l \times w$.

Teacher-led activities such as Activities 14.13 and 14.14 will provide the instruction children need to learn and understand processes and formulas for determining areas of parallelograms and triangles.

Students need opportunities to estimate areas. As pointed out earlier, the width of a small fingernail is approximately one centimeter. Students can use "fingernail" centimeters to estimate the area of small regions. They can use their paces to estimate the area of larger surfaces.

ACTIVITY 14.13   Area of a Parallelogram

- Give each child a piece of paper cut in the shape of a parallelogram similar to the one shown in (a).
- Instruct the children to fold and cut off one end of the parallelogram as in (b).
- Show that when the cut end is put at the opposite end, the figure forms a rectangle as in (c).

- Review the formula for finding the area of a rectangle, and point out that it can be used to determine the area of a rectangle. (The formula for a parallelogram is sometimes stated as $b \times h = A$, where b represents the base, h the height, and A the area.)
- Give the children parallelograms cut from construction paper to measure and determine the area.

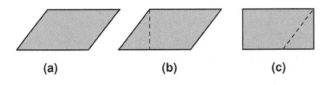

| (a) | (b) | (c) |

ACTIVITY 14.14   Area of a Triangle

- Give each child a pair of congruent triangles.

| (a) | (b) |

- Demonstrate how to join the two triangles to make a parallelogram.
- Review the formula for determining the area of a parallelogram.

- Point out that the area of the triangle will be ½ of the area of the parallelogram. The formula is:

$$A = \frac{b \times h}{2}$$

Give the children other triangles cut from construction paper to measure and determine the area.

Perimeter Measure

The perimeter of a plane figure is determined by finding the measure of each of the figure's segments and adding the numbers. Children frequently confuse perimeter with area and use the formula for determining area when working with perimeter and vice versa. One way to prevent this confusion is to relate the word *perimeter* with the word *periscope*. Nearly all fifth-

and sixth-grade children know that a submarine's periscope is used to look around the surface of a body of water. Point out that the prefix *peri-* means "around," so perimeter means "measuring around." Once the meaning is clear, children can use centimeter rulers to determine the perimeters of book covers, desktops, and other small regions. The perimeters of classrooms, playing areas marked on the playground, and larger regions can be determined by using meter tapes or a metric trundle wheel. It is then easy for students to determine that the perimeter of a square is represented by $4s = P$, of a rectangle by $2w \times 2l = P$, and of an equilateral triangle by $3s = P$.

Volume

Fifth- and sixth-grade children should learn about the volume measure of closed three-dimensional figures by making direct measurements of small containers with base-ten or Cuisenaire cubes. The small cubes in either set have edges one centimeter long and a volume of one cubic centimeter (cm^3). When a box that is seven centimeters long, three centimeters deep, and three centimeters wide is filled with cubes (Figure 14.8), students can determine the volume by counting the cubes. Direct-measurement activities help students understand that the formula $l \times w \times h = V$ is used to determine the volume of a regular solid figure. Once this formula is understood, students' understanding of area applied to triangles and other regular regions can be connected with finding volume for a figure such as a triangular prism (Figure 14.9). Once the area of the triangle has been determined, the height (h) can be multiplied by the base (B) to determine the volume. The

Figure 14-8
A rectangular solid (box) filled with cubes helps children learn the formula for finding the volume of the solid.

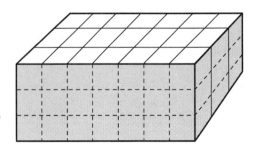

Figure 14-9
Children can find the volume of a simple geometric solid by using the formula $V = B \times h$.

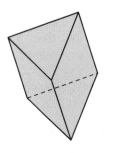

more general formula $B \times h = V$ can now be used for determining the volume of any regular solid.

A cubic meter made from square-meter pieces of corrugated paper taped to form a cube introduces students to the concept of a cubic meter. Once students visualize what a cubic meter is, they can measure their classroom to determine its approximate volume in cubic meters (m³). (They should estimate the height of the classroom for this activity.)

Measuring Angles

Another type of measure taught in elementary school is the measure of angles. First, the nature of this type of measurement must be explored so that students understand angles and degrees. The *degree* is a new type of measure that must be understood if its use in measuring angles is to be meaningful. One way to explain the meaning of a degree is shown in Activity 14.15.

After students understand the basis for measuring angles, the standard protractor can be introduced. A demonstration at the chalkboard with a large protractor or an overhead projector with a clear plastic protractor

---

ACTIVITY 14.15 What Is a Degree?

- Show the model of a rotating ray with an overhead projector.

- Tell the children to imagine a ray that is rotated around its endpoint so that it makes a complete rotation.

- Say, "As the ray moves around the circle, it makes 360 momentary stops, much like some second hands stop momentarily as they move around the face of a clock. What part of the entire circle is the distance between each pair of stops?" (⅟₃₆₀th.)

- Point to the ray and the dotted line representing a stop. Explain that the angle formed by the ray and the dotted line is one degree of measure.

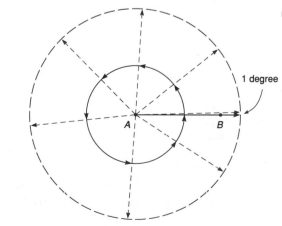

1 degree

A   B

Figure 14-10
The correct align-
ment of a protractor
to measure an angle

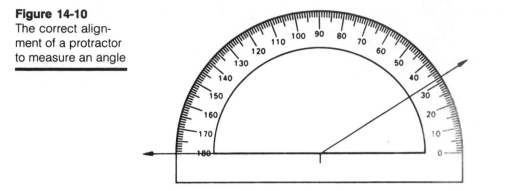

helps students see how to use the device. A demonstration protractor is pictured in Chapter 3. As students observe the demonstration, they should discuss the meaning of the marks and numerals on the protractor. After the
correct alignment for measuring is demonstrated with several angles (Figure 14.10), each student should receive a protractor and page with duplicated angles to measure. A teacher should walk among students as they use
the protractors to help those who have problems and praise those who are
working correctly.

EXERCISE   Activities with various types of standard units of measure illustrated in this
chapter use metric units. Would you begin activities with standard units
using the metric system or the English system? Defend your choice.

■ MINI-OLYMPICS

A class or intermediate-grade mini-Olympics is an entertaining way to provide opportunities for students to practice and apply measurement skills.
The event can be conducted either indoors in a multipurpose room or outdoors. Students can work in cooperative-learning groups to prepare soda-
straw bridges (Activity 14.22). Some class time is needed for them to get
their construction underway, then group members can work during free
time and before and after school to complete it.

Before the Olympics begins, students should select events; limit each
student to two or three, plus the soda-straw bridge event. Students who will
referee each event must be named. Supplies, including materials for each
event; forms for recording individual performances and a large chart for
results for each event; and prizes, if any, must be collected and prepared.

Activities 14.16 through 14.22 suggest events for a metric mini-
Olympics.

ACTIVITY 14.16   Cotton-Ball Put

- The object is to "put" a cotton ball the farthest.

- Each contestant has a cotton ball about the size of a tennis ball (a foam-rubber ball can be used). A contestant stands at a line and "puts"—that is, tosses the ball like a shot put tossed at a track meet. The distance for each put is measured to the nearest centimeter.

- The winner is the contestant to put the cotton ball the greatest distance.

ACTIVITY 14.17   Soda-Straw Javelin

- The object is to hurl a soda straw the farthest.

- Each contestant has a plastic soda straw. A contestant holds the straw between the thumb and middle finger of the throwing hand. The forefinger is at one end of the straw. The arm is extended and swung in an arc to hurl the straw. Measure from the starting line to the straw's nearest end with a centimeter tape.

- Winner is the contestant whose straw goes the greatest distance.

ACTIVITY 14.18   Paper-Plate Discus

- The object is to throw a paper plate the farthest.

- Each contestant has a paper plate. (Be certain just one type of plate is used.) A contestant stands at a line and throws the plate with a discus-throwing motion. (An alternate way of throwing is to use a frisbee-throwing motion.) Measure each throw with a meter tape to the nearest edge of the plate.

- The winner is the contestant whose plate goes the greatest distance.

ACTIVITY 14.19   Standing Broad Jump

- The object is to jump the farthest.

- Each contestant stands with feet together and toes on a line. A contestant moves to a crouching position with hands swung back parallel to the ground, then jumps. Measure the jump from the line to the contestant's nearer heel with a centimeter tape.

- The winner is the contestant with the longest jump.

ACTIVITY 14.20 Standing High Jump

- The object is to make the highest mark on a wall.

- Each contestant holds a piece of chalk in one hand and stands with that hand next to a wall. To jump, a contestant moves to a crouching position, then jumps as high as possible. The contestant makes a mark at the top of the jump. Use a centimeter tape to measure a jump.

- The winner is the contestant with the highest jump.

ACTIVITY 14.21 Build a Clay Bridge

- The object is to make the longest "bridge."

- Contestants compete in pairs. Each pair has a 100-gram piece of Plasticine clay; a judge verifies the weight.

- A bridge consists of a strand rolled from the clay. It is stretched between two chairs, with no more than 10 centimeters of the strand on each chair.

- The winner is the team that makes the longest bridge that remains in place for at least 10 seconds without breaking. Teams have three opportunities to roll out and erect a bridge. The longest strand is a team's official entry.

- Measure each bridge with a centimeter ruler.

ACTIVITY 14.22 Build a Soda-Straw Bridge

- The object is to build a bridge that will hold the greatest weight.

- Bridges are built in advance. These conditions apply:
  —A bridge may contain no more than 50 straws held together with glue.
  —Two or more straws may not be glued side by side to increase their strength; straws may be cut.
  —A bridge must be at least 75 centimeters long and 20 centimeters wide.
  —There must be a 10-centimeter-square piece of cardboard at the center.
  —There is no prescribed form for a bridge.

- On Olympic day, each bridge is placed to span the distance between two chairs. No more than 5 centimeters of an end may rest on a chair. Metric weights are stacked on the cardboard square at the center of each bridge.

- Winner is the team that constructed the bridge that supported the greatest weight before it collapsed.

■ MEASURING TEMPERATURE

Children in the second and third grade will learn to use the thermometer by reading thermometers and recording temperatures during daily activities connected with weather study. In the higher grades, there are opportunities for children to use thermometers as they engage in science studies. By the end of elementary school, children should read temperatures indicated on a Celsius thermometer, know that the freezing point of water is 0 degrees centigrade and that the boiling point of water is 100 degrees centigrade, and be aware of some temperatures closely associated with their lives—the normal body temperature is approximately 37 degrees centigrade, an outdoor temperature of 10 degrees centigrade is a cool day, while a temperature of 30 degrees centigrade indicates a hot day (Figure 14.11).

Primary-grade children should use large, easy-to-read alcohol thermometers. A teacher can make a demonstration thermometer by printing the scale on a large piece of stiff cardboard or Masonite painted a light color. The alcohol is represented by a piece of red cloth, made by sewing a strip of red cloth to a strip of white cloth, inserting the ends into slits cut at the top and bottom of the scale, and sewing the two ends together so the

Figure 14-11
Demonstration thermometers to help children learn how temperature is determined. The thermometer at left shows metric (Celsius) units, and the one at right shows standard (Fahrenheit) units.

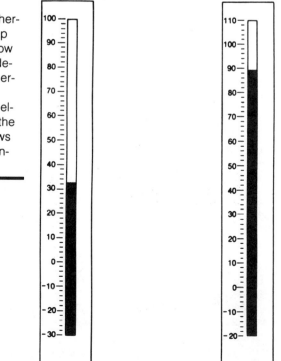

band is taut. After one child has read the temperature on a real thermometer, another one can set the temperature on the demonstration thermometer so the entire class can read it.

▉ LEARNING ABOUT TIME

Instruction about time deals with two aspects of the subject: the concept of time—which includes an understanding of duration of time and the sequence of events in a given period of time—and the mechanics of reading calendars and telling time on a time piece. Piaget's research indicates that some children are ready to develop a full understanding of time by the age of nine, while others are not ready until ten and eleven.[7] Before this time, children have a poor sense of duration of time and many misconceptions about the sequence of events. Activities with sand or water flowing through holes in cans, described earlier, are aids for developing a sense of duration. Sand-filled timers, such as for timing eggs, are another aid. An activity with shadows cast on a simple sundial aids in developing understanding of both duration and sequencing concepts; see Activity 14.23.

ACTIVITY 14.23   Sundial

■ Prepare a sundial by standing a pencil on a square piece of cardboard with Plasticine clay.

■ Note the event that occurs just before or after each observation: "school begins," "math class begins," "recess," "lunch time," and so on.

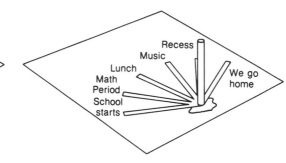

■ Set the sundial in a south-facing window (or outdoors) when a school day begins. Mark the position of the shadow. Periodically observe the sundial to note the position of the shadow. Have a child mark the shadow's position at each observation.

■ Repeat the activity for a week; be certain observations are made at the same time.

Activity 14.23   *continued*

- Repeat the activity for a second week, but make observations on the hour each day.

- Use the marks on the sundial to help the children understand the sequence of events in their school day.

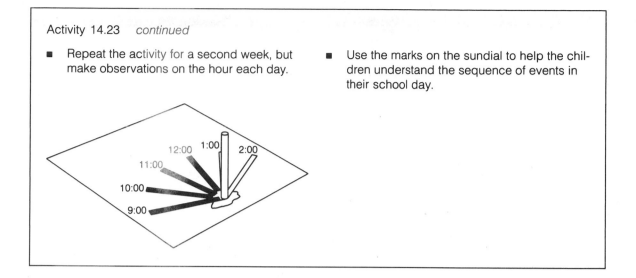

Follow the sundial activities with discussions that deal with the order of events, and later, the sequence of hours.

- "This morning we did some work with subtraction, and we made some paper-bag puppets. Which did we do first?"

- "We did three different things this morning. Who can tell me what we did first?" (Listened to a story.) "What did we do next?" (Played a math game.) "What was the last thing we did?" (Saw a film about animals.) "The game came after the story and the film came after the game. Did the film come before or after the story?" (This latter question helps children see that if event *B* follows event *A*, and *C* follows *B*, then *C* follows *A*. This deals with transitivity, a difficult concept for young children to understand.)

- "What is the first hour marked on our sundial?" "What is the last hour?" "What hours are in between?" "Let's name the hours in sequence." (9 o'clock, 10 o'clock, 11 o'clock, . . . , 2 o'clock.) "Let's look at the clock and see where those times are on it."[8]

Duration and sequence are also features of children's study of the calendar. They learn that calendars indicate days of the week, the number of each day, and the month of the year, as well as the year itself. Many teachers incorporate study of the calendar into seasonal events on a bulletin board. For the month of February, birthdays of famous Americans and Valentine's Day are featured. Calendars such as the one in Figure 14.12, which can be purchased or teacher-made, can be the basis for daily discussions. When a new date is posted, children can talk about such things as the year, month,

Figure 14-12
Classroom calendar
with removable tabs
for recording dates

March						
Sun.	Mon.	Tues.	Wed.	Thur.	Fri.	Sat.
	1	2	3	4	5	

and day of the week; the number of the day; the number of days that have already passed during the month, and events for the day.

Children's understanding of time can be enhanced by seeing an entire calendar as one continuous number line. Cut a large calendar and glue or staple the strip for each week to a long piece of calculator tape. Do not leave a gap between the last day of one month and the first day of the next. Center each month's name above its set of numerals. Affix the new calendar to the walls above chalkboards. Labels for each child's birthday and for significant school days and holidays provide a basis for discussion of past and upcoming events. Compare the number of days between Halloween and Thanksgiving to the number between Thanksgiving and Christmas and Christmas and New Year's Day; count the days until the next birthday; and so on.

Instruction about telling time should be built around activities with traditional clocks. Telling time with a digital clock should be learned but not at the expense of learning about regular clocks. A clock or watch does more than tell time; it helps us determine how much time has passed since, or is left before, a certain event. A person who says, "A half hour has passed since we began our walk at 3:00" has noted that the minute hand has moved halfway between 3:00 and 4:00. "It is 2:00; we have 45 minutes before the plane leaves at 2:45." A clock face makes it easy to see that 45 minutes remain before the plane leaves.

A recommended sequence of activities for learning to tell time is completed by end of the primary grades and has this order:

Figure 14-13
Clock without hands
for introducing
clocks to children

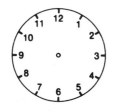

■ Begin with a large demonstration clock marked with black numeral hours. Talk about the sequence of numbers. Children should note that 12 is at the top and 6 is at the bottom. The numerals between 12 and 6 and between 6 and 12 should be noted. Prepare a worksheet with one large clock face but no numerals. Children write the numerals at each hour mark (Figure 14.13).

Figure 14-14
Clock face showing
hour hand only

- Add a black hour hand to the clock. Point it at the 12. Tell children that when the black hand points directly toward a number, it tells the hour. Point it at different numbers and have children tell the hour (Figure 14.14).

- Show a clock that has black hour numerals and a black hour hand, red minute marks, and a red minute hand. Have children point out differences between this and the first clock. Tell them that when the hour hand points to a numeral and the minute hand points to 12, the time is the hour shown by the hour hand. Set the clock at different times to indicate hours; have children name each hour. Show and discuss two ways of writing time to the hour: 9:00 and 9 o'clock.

- Use a clock with synchronized hands to show the direction the hands move. (Demonstration clocks are available from school supply businesses. Inexpensive mechanical alarm clocks can be used.) Start both hands at 12. Have children watch the hands as you turn them. Discuss the fact that while the minute hand makes one complete turn, the hour hand moves from 12 to 1. Repeat, beginning at other hours.

- Practice reading the time to the half hour. Emphasize the fact that the minute hand always points to 6 and the hour hand is halfway between two numerals. Set the hands at different half-hour positions for children to read. When the minute hand is at 6 and the hour hand is half way between 2 and 3, have them read the time as 2:30.

- Introduce reading time to five-minute intervals. Skip-counting by fives will help children see the sequence from 12:00 to 12:05, and on around to 12 again. Also point out that five minutes pass as the big hand moves from 12 to 1, 1 to 2, and so on. To help children realize this and to grasp the meaning of five minutes, have them watch the classroom clock. Remind them often to keep their eyes on the big hand as it moves from one numeral to the next as five minutes pass. Tell children how to read the clock when the big hand points to a numeral, and show them how to write the time, for example 6:20 and 8:45. Eliminate expressions such as "quarter past five," "half past nine," and "a quarter to ten"; express these times as "5:15," "9:30," and "10:45," and read them as "five-fifteen," "nine-thirty," and "ten-forty-five," respectively. These figures indicate time in airplane and train schedules, television guides, and other written materials and on digital timepieces.

- Introduce times to the minute, using procedures like the ones already mentioned.

Worksheets such as the one illustrated in Figure 14.15 can accompany lessons during which children learn to tell and write times.

Children in the middle grades should continue to practice until they can tell time accurately. Some will need demonstration-clock and worksheet

Figure 14-15
Worksheet for pri-
mary-grade children
learning to tell time
to the hour and half
hour

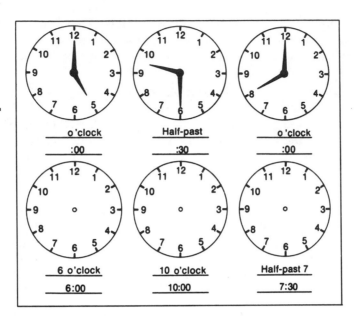

activities until they tell time accurately; others will need no special help. Class activities in the middle grades should also include topics such as the establishment of uniform time zones around the world, the history of telling time, and precision instruments—such as electronic timers—that record time. These topics can be included in social studies and science units taught in the middle grades.

EXERCISE   Classroom activities with time usually focus on learning to read time on clocks, with little or no attention to duration or passage of time. Why do you believe this is so?

■ LEARNING ABOUT MONEY

Children receive allowances and spend money at early ages. They need to know the value of each coin and bill in order to use their money properly. Instruction begins in grade one with activities designed to acquaint children with small coins. By the end of grade three, children have experiences with all coins and small bills. Textbooks for these grades often contain realistic pasteboard models of coins. Models of coins and bills are available from school supply businesses (see Chapter 3). Textbooks also contain pages of exercises for which children write the amounts of coins represented by pictured coins and indicate amounts of change for simulated purchases.

Even though children work with realistic models and workbook pages, they do not always grasp the relationships between pennies and nickels, nickels and dimes, and so on. These many-to-one and many-to-many matchings are confusing because there is no physical relationship between one coin and another to make their relationship clear. The set of proportional materials described here offers one way to show relationships between all coins and a dollar.

- Cut a square with 30-centimeter sides from tagboard. Mark a ten-by-ten grid on it.

- Cut these pieces: ten small squares, 3 centimeters by 3 centimeters; five rectangles, 3 centimeters by 15 centimeters; five rectangles, 6 centimeters by 15 centimeters; four squares, 15 centimeters by 15 centimeters; and two rectangles, 15 centimeters by 30 centimeters. Use cutout pictures of coins or rubber stamps with coin images to mark the small pieces. A penny goes on each small piece, a nickel on each 3-by-15 piece, a dime on each 6-by-15 piece, a quarter on each large square, and a half-dollar on each large rectangle. Glue a model of $1 on the large square.

Use these proportional materials for developing an understanding of each coin's value and of relationships among coins and for change-making activities. Have children work in pairs with a kit to complete teacher-led activities that include these types of experiences:

- Cover large pieces with smaller pieces. "How many pennies cover a nickel?" "How many nickels cover a dime?" "What different combinations cover a quarter?"

- Use the pieces to represent different amounts of money. "Show me seven cents." "Show me thirty-two cents." "What are the fewest coins you can use to make sixty-seven cents?"

- Introduce numerals for indicating the values of different coins: 1¢, 5¢, 10¢, 25¢, 50¢. (Do not introduce the decimal values 0.01, 0.05, 0.10, 0.25, and 0.50 until values greater than $1 are introduced.) Show an amount of money with numerals, say 53¢, and have children represent it with coins.

- Use the $1 mat and coin pieces for change-making activities. Display a picture of a small toy and a price. If the toy's price is 35 cents, the children put 35 cents worth of pieces in the upper left corner of the mat. The amount of change received from a dollar is the value of the uncovered part of the mat. If the purchase is made with 50 cents, the change is represented by the uncovered portion of the half of the mat on which the coin pieces are located.

- Gradually abandon the grid pieces in favor of real coins or models as children show they are ready for the change.

Children who are familiar with coins and small bills need to maintain and expand their understanding by regularly engaging in real or contrived activities that require the use of money. Children can work in cooperative-learning groups to complete the simulated activities. These are typical of the activities that are recommended for older children:

■ Give each child a real or simulated menu from a favorite fast-food restaurant and an activity sheet to guide the work:

—Choose your favorite lunch. List each item and its cost. What is the cost of your favorite lunch?

—If you pay for your favorite lunch with a five-dollar bill, how much change will you receive?

—What combinations of three items can you buy for less than $4?

■ Plan seven days of simple menus from foods listed in grocery advertisements. Students must decide on foods and estimate quantities, then use calculators to determine the sum for all of the costs. Use all of the totals to see what the average weekly cost of the menus is for the entire class.

■ Use a calculator and mail-order catalog or circular to create a shopping spree for students. An imaginary $100 is given each student or group; the student or group prepares a shopping list. Remind intermediate-grade students that the cost of a sales tax must be figured into the total. A local tax chart or the ⎍ % ⎍ key on the calculator can be used to figure the tax.

■ Older students can set up and operate a school supply business. Pencils, paper, notebooks, erasers, school T-shirts, and other related items can be stocked and sold.

■ One teacher helped students organize a "corporation" for which they sold stock to teachers, parents, and others to purchase hot-food dispensers for the school's adult lunchroom. The children learned about time purchases, accounting procedures, profits and losses, inventory control, stock dividends, and other aspects of running a business.

Programs for computers offer practice in making decisions about money. With *Parking Lot: Time and Money*[9] students play the role of a parking lot attendant. They receive and park cars, retrieve cars, and collect money. They must determine the length of stay and cost; accidents and delays in retrieving cars result in financial losses. *Money Squares*[10] provides practice in counting and using money in four different settings using a tic-tac-toe format. Scholastic[11] has produced a program in which students apply a variety of mathematics concepts, including money, as they shop in three different malls. *Math Shop Jr.*™ is for grades one to four and *Math Shop*™ is for grades four to eight. *Exploring Measurement, Time and Money—Level 1*[12] includes activities with the "Moneyboard and Sticky Store" to help students count money, read price tags, pay for items, and make change.

EXERCISE Do you believe the time and effort needed to develop and use proportional materials to help children learn the value of money is worthwhile? Defend your position.

■ SUMMARY

Two systems of measure are used in the United States. When the Metric Conversion Act was signed by President Ford in 1975 it was anticipated that a change to the metric system would occur. However, public resistance to the change was so strong that after changes in some areas, further changes did not occur. Today both the English and metric systems are used and should be learned by students. The English system has a long history. While it is a standard system, it lacks uniformity among and between units. The metric system was created in the late 1700s by the French Academy of Sciences. It is based on the meter, which is a one ten-millionth of the distance from the equator to the North Pole. Other units are derived from the meter. The metric system is based on powers and subdivisions of ten.

Children's first experiences should be exploratory; they should pour water, sand, and rice from one container to another, feel temperature differences, and order objects by length, height, capacity, and size in order to build background for understanding time, temperature, and linear, weight, area, and capacity concepts. Nonstandard units are used to introduce the meanings of different measures—linear, weight, capacity, area, and time. Later, various commonly used metric and customary units are introduced, and students learn the instruments and processes for using each one. Teacher-directed lessons and cooperative-learning groups working with problem cards in learning centers help students understand standard units. By the time children complete elementary school, they should be able to name commonly used metric and customary units, describe the structure of the metric system, and use measuring instruments accurately. Special units and activities are used to introduce and develop concepts related to time and reading clocks, and to understand and use money effectively.

■ STUDY QUESTIONS AND ACTIVITIES

1. In the NCTM standard for measurement at the beginning of this chapter there are four goals for grades K–4 and seven for grades 5–8. Write each goal on a piece of paper. Identify at least one activity from this chapter for each goal and describe briefly how the activity helps meet it.

2. Read the article by James Hiebert (see the For Further Reading section) about the difficulties children have with measurement. Write

down the major problems he lists. What kinds of experiences are needed to overcome these difficulties? Identify activities in this chapter that address each of the problems. List any other activities you are aware of that address these problems.

3. In an age of digital clocks, should children still learn to tell time with conventional clocks? Discuss this question with two or three acquaintances. What is the consensus, and what reasons are given? Many textbooks teach terms such as quarter past and quarter before the hour. How do you feel about teaching these terms? Do you believe children have trouble with this terminology? Is two-fifteen and two-forty-five better phrasing for children in a digital age?

4. John Bradford (see the For Further Reading section) describes a way to use Cuisenaire rods and plastic grids to help children learn the value of each U.S. coin. Read the article and compare his materials and procedures with the tagboard model described in this chapter. Which materials would you prefer to use with second-grade children? Why? Do you think that one set of materials would be better than the other for working with older children who have not learned the value of each coin and how to make change? If so, which set and why?

5. Read Marion Walter's article (see the For Further Reading section). Use her examples as a basis for designing problem cards dealing with perimeter and area that are suitable for mature fifth- or sixth-grade students.

■ TEACHER'S BOOKSHELF

Nelson, Doyal, and Robert E. Reys, eds. 1976 Yearbook. *Measurement in School Mathematics*. Reston, VA: National Council of Teachers of Mathematics, 244 pages.

■ FOR FURTHER READING

Bradford, John W. 1980, March. Making sense out of dollars and cents. *Arithmetic Teacher 28*(7), 44–46.

Cuisenaire rods and plastic hundred-grids serve as models for coins and dollar bills. Procedures for moving from concrete models to a written code for representing money are described.

Classon, Robert G. 1986, January. How our decimal money began. *Arithmetic Teacher 33*(5), 30–33.

Provides a historical perspective on our money system.

Daane, C. J. 1980, February. Primary coin activity cards. *Arithmetic Teacher 27*(6), 34–36.

Coin sheets and a coin trading board are the materials needed for six games, with emphasis on pennies, nickels, dimes, and quarters.

Fay, Nancy, and Catherine Tsairides. 1989, September. Metric mall. *Arithmetic Teacher 37*(1).

A set of learning activities based on a shopping mall theme provide a variety of measuring experiences.

Girard, Kimberley. 1989, April. Popcorn and mathematics. *Arithmetic Teacher 36*(8), 3–4.

Uses unpopped and popped corn for learning about volume and weight.

Hart, Kathleen. 1984, May. Which comes first—Length, area, or volume? *Arithmetic Teacher 31*(9), 16–18, 26.

Cognitive development provides clues for teaching about measurement concepts.

Hiebert, James. 1984, March. Why do some children have difficulty learning measurement concepts? *Arithmetic Teacher 31*(7), 19–24.

Children's misunderstandings about measurement provide information for teachers about the kinds of activities needed.

Hildreth, David J. 1983, January. The use of strategies in estimating measurements. *Arithmetic Teacher 30*(5), 50–54.

Systematic approach to estimation of measurements increases skills with processes of measurement.

Horak, Virginia M., and Willis J. Horak. 1983, January. Teaching time with slit clocks. *Arithmetic Teacher 30*(5), 8–12.

Suggests activities for time concepts and telling time with student-made slit clocks.

Lindquist, Mary Montgomery. 1989, October. Implementing the *Standards:* The measurement standards. *Arithmetic Teacher 37*(2), 22–26.

A variety of activities for various grade levels are suggested as ways to meet the NCTM measurement standards.

Nelson, Glenn. 1982, May. Teaching time-telling. *Arithmetic Teacher 29*(9), 31–34.

The author's approach to teaching time is one that simplifies the process by eliminating many of the confusing terms that inhibit learning. His simplified materials and terminology, along with a sequence for teaching time telling, are illustrated and discussed.

Riley, James E. 1980, October. It's about time. *Arithmetic Teacher 28*(2), 12–14.

Activities dealing with duration and sequence of time are described.

Steffe, Leslie P. 1971, May. Thinking about measurement. *Arithmetic Teacher 18*(5), 332–338.

Piaget's theories of cognitive development and some of their applications to learning the meaning of measurement are discussed in this thought-provoking article.

Walter, Marion. 1970, April. A common misconception about area. *Arithmetic Teacher 17*(4), 286–289.

The common misconception is that figures with common perimeters will have the same area regardless of the measures of their sides. The examples given here can serve as the basis for several problem-card activities to challenge mathematically mature fifth- and sixth-grade students.

■ NOTES

[1] National Council of Teachers of Mathematics. 1989. *Curriculum and Evaluation Standards for School Mathematics.* Reston, VA: National Council of Teachers of Mathematics, 112. Used by permission.

[2] NCTM, 51. Used by permission.

[3] NCTM, 116. Used by permission.

[4] *Meter* is the accepted spelling in the United States for the basic unit of length, and *liter* is the spelling for capacity. Children should also learn that alternate spellings, *metre* and *litre,* are used in many countries.

[5] The comma is omitted from numerals for large or small numbers in SI. Large numbers appear as indicated here, and small ones appear as 0.362 45. This practice is followed because the comma serves as a decimal point in some countries.

[6] Mary Baratta-Lorton. *Workjobs.* 1988. Menlo Park, CA: Addison-Wesley, 22–23.

[7] Richard W. Copeland. 1979. *How Children Learn Mathematics: Teaching Implications of Piaget's Research,* 3rd ed. New York: Macmillan, 209.

[8] This activity is adapted from Charles S. Thompson and John Van de Walle. 1981, April. A single-handed approach to telling time. *Arithmetic Teacher 28* (8), 4–9.

[9] Queue, Inc., 338 Commerce Dr., Fairfield, CT 06430.

[10] Cambridge Development Laboratories, Inc., 214 Third Ave., Waltham, MA 02154.

[11] Scholastic Inc., 2931 East McCarty St., P.O. Box 7502, Jefferson City, MO 65102.

[12] IBM Educational Systems, Department PC, 4111 Northside Parkway, Atlanta, GA 30327.

CHAPTER 15

Tables, Graphs, Statistics, and Probability: Tools for Data Handling

Every day newspapers and television news programs include headline stories which present numerical information. Information is presented with numbers and percentages, as descriptive statistics, or in tables or graphs. The information may describe current events or opinions, but often predicts or forecasts future events. Understanding how information is collected, recorded, reported, and analyzed is a skill that informed citizens must have in order to make decisions about homes, jobs, savings, purchases, and voting. In the last twenty years, the importance of tables, graphs, and statistics as tools for data collection and analysis have become apparent. The topic of probability is also necessary because many events are better interpreted when people understand whether they are expected or unexpected, usual or unusual happenings. The NCTM standards make it clear that these topics should be part of mathematics in elementary school.

In this chapter you will read about

1. the importance of understanding data in today's world;

2. how students learn to collect, organize, report, and analyze data based on their experiences;

3. activities to teach students how to make picture graphs, bar graphs, line graphs, and circle graphs;

4. how basic statistical concepts are part of the data handling activities;

5. experiments that provide students with ideas and vocabulary about probability;

6. how students can use the computer to assist in their organization and analyses of data.

NCTM STANDARDS THAT PERTAIN TO TOOLS FOR DATA HANDLING

Kindergarten Through Grade Four

Standard 11: Statistics and Probability   In grades K–4, the mathematics curriculum should include experiences with data analysis and probability so that students can:

- collect, organize, and describe data;
- construct, read, and interpret displays of data;
- formulate and solve problems that involve collecting and analyzing data;
- explore concepts of chance.[1]

Grades Five Through Eight

Standard 5: Number and Number Relationships
In grades 5–8, the mathematics curriculum should include the continual development of number and number relationships so that students can:

- represent numerical relationships in one- and two-dimensional graphs.[2]

Standard 8: Patterns and Functions   In grades 5–8, the mathematics curriculum should include explorations of patterns and functions so that students can:

- describe, extend, analyze, and create a wide variety of patterns;
- describe and represent relationships with tables, graphs, and rules;

- analyze functional relationships to explain how a change in one quantity results in a change in another;
- use patterns and functions to represent and solve problems.[3]

Standard 9: Algebra   In grades 5–8, the mathematics curriculum should include exploration of algebraic concepts and processes so that students can:

- represent situations and number patterns with tables, graphs, verbal rules, . . . and explore the interrelationships of these representations;
- analyze tables and graphs to identify properties and relationships.[4]

Standard 11: Probability   In grades 5–8, the mathematics curriculum should include explorations of probability in real-world situations so that students can:

- model situations by devising and carrying out experiments or simulations to determine probabilities;
- appreciate the power of using a probability model by comparing experimental results with mathematical expectations;
- make predictions that are based on experimental or theoretical probabilities;
- develop an appreciation for the pervasive use of probability in the real world.[5]

■ UNDERSTANDING DATA WITH TABLES AND GRAPHS

The *National Assessment of Educational Progress*[6] shows that many children do not use tables and graphs effectively in solving simple or moderately difficult problems. The importance of constructing tables and graphs as an important problem-solving skill is discussed in Chapter 5. Making a table or graph of observations allows patterns of information to become more apparent. Children need skills in making tables and graphs with data from their own experience so that they can read and interpret them when prepared by others. Work with tables, graphs, statistics, and probability begins with children's firsthand observations and data collection and should be exploratory in nature. The materials needed are readily available and inexpensive. Sheets of centimeter-square or inch-square paper, colored cubes, dice, spinners, picture stickers, pens and markers, compasses, and protractors are the materials needed for graphs that elementary school children make.

Sources of data are varied. In kindergarten and primary grades, children's birthdays, shoe sizes, means of getting to school, weight, height, hair and eye colors, favorite television shows, and favorite foods are meaningful topics. Some first- and second-grade teachers maintain a table of children's tooth loss and graph each month's total. Students can make up many questions from such a table and graph.

Intermediate-grade children are interested in many of the same topics as well as new ones: favorite recording and recording star, sports, and clothing, for instance. Children can also prepare graphs on science and social studies topics. During plant growth experiments, a daily or weekly record of growth can be made. In social studies, children can prepare graphs in several forms to compare farm products of different states or countries.

Data for tables and graphs should first be collected by children through surveys and later from research in reference books. Whenever possible, the data collection should relate to a topic being studied so that children can build data handling skills and use the information to answer questions. Information can be organized in many different forms including tables and charts. Object graphs, bar graphs, line graphs, and circle graphs have different purposes and different levels of difficulty.

Object and Picture Graphs

Kindergarten and primary-grade children's first graphs may arise from their classification activities. After sorting shoes into different categories, a natural extension is to make a graph. Activities 15.1 through 15.3 describe lessons growing out of classroom data collection. The same lessons can be repeated many times with different topics. Children begin with the experience of collecting data through classification of objects and organizing them into separate lines; then they use cubes or other objects and drawings or pictures to present the data.

ACTIVITY 15.1   Heads of Hair Graph

■ Ask three or four children with different hair colors to come to the front of the class to start the classification.

■ Ask a child to stand and have the rest decide whether he or she should stand with one of the existing groups or start a new group.

■ When all of the children are in groups, have each group line up facing out from a wall.

■ Ask which of the lines is longest, shortest, and so on.

■ Have the children return to their desks and give each one a square of construction paper about 2 × 2 inches or 5 × 5 centi-

meters. Ask them to draw their head and hair color on the paper.

■ Prepare a posterboard with the hair color categories on it. As the students finish coloring their square, tape the squares on the poster so that each one is in the correct line. When the poster is completed, ask the children for a title for the graph.

■ Have children make up questions that could be answered with the chart. Ask other teachers to construct a chart with children in their rooms and have students compare the charts and ask questions about comparisons.

Black hair					
Brown hair					
Blond hair					
Red hair					

ACTIVITY 15.2   The Shoes We Wore Graph

■ Have children look at their shoes. Let each one pick out a Unifix cube which most closely resembles the shoe color.

■ Put Unifix cubes in a box.

■ Ask the students to tell some questions they could ask about the color of the shoes. List several of their questions on the chalkboard or overhead projector.

Activity 15.2   continued

- Tell them they can answer the questions by organizing the Unifix cubes during center time. Ask them to record their answers to the questions on paper or in their mathematics journal. Suggest that they use squared paper to make a picture of the Unifix lines.

- After all the children have had a chance to complete their journals, organize the Unifix cubes into stacks on a table. Ask the children to compare their answers to the stacks of Unifix cubes. Use the questions which were posed and have children answer the questions from the data.

- Repeat the shoe color activity for several days or with types of shoes instead of color. The children will decide which colors of cubes stand for athletic shoes, dress shoes, sandals, boots, and so on.

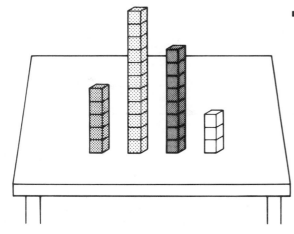

ACTIVITY 15.3   Our Favorite Pets Graph

- Have a collection of plastic animals, stickers, or pictures for cats, dogs, fish, birds, hamsters, turtles, horses, and so on.

- Let each child select the type of animal which they would like best as a pet.

- Use the plastic animals or pictures to make a graph.

Our Pets		
🐕	🐕 🐕	
🐈	🐈 🐈 🐈 🐈 🐈 🐈 🐈 🐈	
🐟	🐟 🐟 🐟	
🐕	🐕 🐕 🐕 🐕 🐕 🐕 🐕 🐕 🐕	
🐁	🐁 🐁	
🐹	🐹	
🐢	🐢	
🐦	X X X X	

(continued)

Activity 15.3   *continued*

- Use the graph for counting and comparing.
  —"How many children like cats? dogs? fish?
  —"Do more children like dogs than cats? dogs than horses?"
  —"How many fewer turtles are there than fish?"
- Have the children count the number of animals in each line. Record the results on a simple table with tally marks.

Our Pets	
Horse	| |
Cat	~~||||~~ | |
Fish	| | |
Dog	~~||||~~ | | | |
Mouse	| |
Guinea pig	|
Turtle	|
No pet	| | | |

In moving from an object graph to a picture graph the teacher must be careful to keep the pictures or symbols the same size. Precutting the squares is one way to establish an equivalent size for each item on the graph. Children also need help to start their picture graphs on a baseline at the bottom or at the left of the graph and to avoid overlaps or gaps as they place their stickers or pictures.

Intermediate-grade children should work with more complex picture graphs. In the pet picture graph, a picture for each pet is reasonable. In other situations, the information makes it difficult to represent them accurately with individual pictures. When many responses are gathered, the graph becomes too large with one picture for each response. For these graphs, one picture may represent two, five, or 100 responses. In Activity 15.4, children complete a large survey about favorite television shows.

ACTIVITY 15.4   Favorite Television Programs

- Develop with your children a survey of favorite television programs for the entire school or grade level. Arrange with the principal and other teachers for your students to collect information. This might be done with ballots, by sending students into the classes, or setting up polling booths in the cafeteria or front hall of the school.
  —Assist the children as they collect and tally the information.

Activity 15.4   *continued*

Sesame Street	⊞ ⊞ ⊞ ⊞ ⊞ ⊞
Family Ties	|||
Alf	⊞ ⊞
Cosby Show	⊞ ⊞ ⊞ |||

Murder, She Wrote	||

- Ask the children what would be a good symbol to represent television programs. They might suggest a picture of a television.

- Ask how many tally marks each television symbol might represent. They might suggest that one symbol represent 2, 5, or 10 responses. Have them discuss how many television symbols would be needed for set of tally marks using 2-to-1, 5-to-1, and 10-to-1 ratios.

- After they have determined a matching rule (2-1, 5-1, or 10-1), ask how to show the other numbers. If the rule is 10-1, they should suggest half of a television for 5 and a smaller part for 2.

- Have teams of three or four children make picture graphs using the rules which were decided.

Sesame Street	📺 📺 📺
Family Ties	[
Alf	📺
Cosby Show	📺 [

Murder, She Wrote	[

- Discuss the results of the poll. Let the children suggest questions which could be answered from the information collected.

- Post the graph in the cafeteria for all the students to see.

- Extension: Have the children note the networks for each of the programs. Using the top ten programs, compare the popularity of the networks in the school. Compare the results of the school poll to the national results of television ratings available each week in the newspaper *USA Today*.

Bar Graphs

Children who have made and interpreted object and picture graphs will find bar graphs easy to use and interpret. Information collected in Activities 15.1 through 15.4 with objects and pictures can also be expressed with bar graphs. Primary grade children can use paper squares to take information from picture graphs to bar graphs. Each item represents one square on the graph. Activity 15.5 uses hard candies to move directly from the object into a bar graph.

The shoe color graph can be extended into a long-term project. Children learn to make a bar graph using squares of colored paper that match the shoe's colors and placing them on a sheet of paper. Later squares of the same color are used so that children have to label each column of the graph

---

ACTIVITY 15.5   Colorful Bar Graph

- Give each student a package or assortment of colored candy pieces.

- Ask them to sort the candies by color.

- Give each a piece of squared paper and ask them to line up each group of candies into a column from the bottom edge leaving spaces between each column. Each candy piece should be in one square.

- Ask them to color the square under each candy piece. As they color each piece, they may put it back in the bag for snack time.

- Have pairs of children compare their graphs and write a statement that tells how the graphs are alike and different.

- Extension: Make a huge bar graph for the whole class. Have children color in the squares representing the number of each color they had.

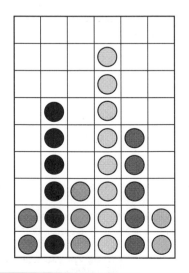 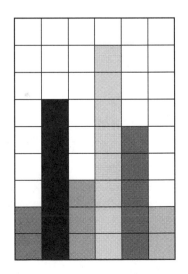

to indicate the colors. A table can be prepared to record data about the number of shoes over a period of several weeks as in Figure 15.1. Then the information can be placed in a computer spreadsheet program that has a graphing feature. Bar graphs are then generated by the program. These graphs can be compared to the bar graphs students make on a daily basis as shown in Figure 15.2.

Figure 15-1
Table with data concerning colors of children's shoes

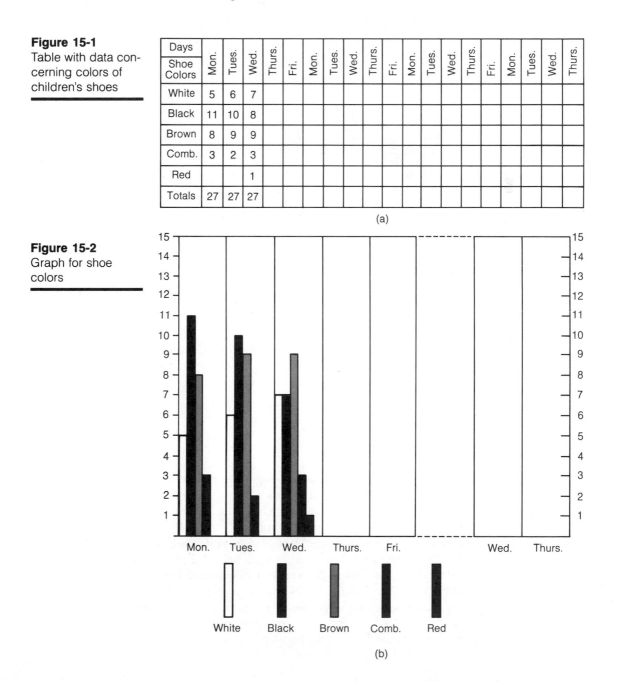

(a)

Figure 15-2
Graph for shoe colors

(b)

Figure 15-3

Line graph with data concerning color of children's shoes

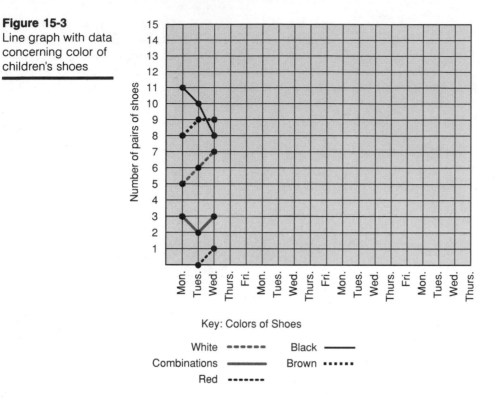

Key: Colors of Shoes

White ------- Black ———

Combinations ———— Brown ••••••

Red -------

Several graphing programs are now available. *Microsoft Works*[7] and *Appleworks* 3.0[8] have graphing built in. Older version of *Appleworks* can be used with add-on products such as *Time-Out Graphs*[9] or *Graphworks*.[10] *Easy Graph*[11] is a stand-alone program. Another way to extend the project is to have children compare color of shoes and the weather. If they keep track of each day's weather, students can see if there is a connection between shoes and the type of weather.

Line Graphs

Line graphs are useful for showing patterns and trends or changes in numerical information. Data comes from various sources. An almanac includes much information that can be used for line graphs, such as population for major cities at ten-year intervals since 1900. A plant growth experiment might give the height of plants over a three week period. A newspaper may give rainfall totals or new car sales for the last year. Students can do surveys of favorite foods several times during a year to see if the favorites change with the season. Problems involving relationships in which one value changes as another value changes (rate pairs) can be graphed, as in Activities 5.13, 12.24, and 15.6. In the elementary school most of these relationships result in linear graphs, although the one illustrated in Activity 6.7 contains a curved line.

Line graphs are usually introduced in the intermediate grades. A fourth-grade class that has been keeping track of shoe colors for several weeks can plot the information on a line graph. Each point of data is placed at the intersection of the day and the number of shoes of that color in Figure 15.3. Each color of shoes is shown with a different line and a key to the color is included. Activity 15.6 describes how students might create a line graph to show a rate-pair table.

One use of line graphs is to see if there is any relationship between two sets of data. In a study of population and area, the population of each state or province could be plotted with its area. Students look for any connections between the sets of information.

ACTIVITY 15.6   Making Ornaments

- Present the problem. "Our class is going to make holiday ornaments to sell. Each ornament will have seven gold stars. How many stars will be needed for the ornaments?"

- Let groups of children work on the solution for a few moments. Many will suggest multiplication as the operation to use. Some may place the multiples in a rate-pair table.

Number of ornaments	1	2	3	4	5	6	7	8	9
Number of stars	7	14	21	28					

- Show the children how to draw a horizontal and vertical axis on an overhead projection grid. Label the horizontal axis ornaments and the vertical axis stars and number them both. The vertical axis should be numbered in units of 10.

- Have the children place several ordered pairs from the rate-pair table or using multiplication: (1, 7), (2, 14), (3, 21), and so on.

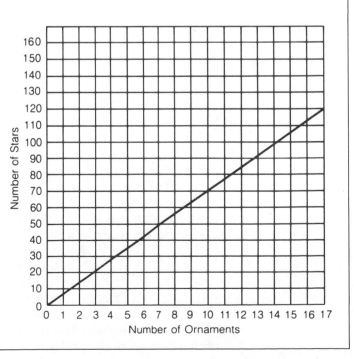

(continued)

Activity 15.6   *continued*

■ After several points have been plotted, ask the children if they see any pattern in the graph. When someone mentions that all the points are in a straight line, use a straight edge and lightly project the line. Have children read the graph, and check some of the points to see if the relationship is maintained.

■ Engage the children in discussion about which method is easiest to use: the rate-pair, the multiplication, or the line graph method.

■ Some children may be ready for the term **linear relationship,** meaning that the relationship fits on a line. Present several other tables of information and ask the groups to decide if the information is linear.

cost	16¢	32¢	48¢	64¢					
number	1	2	3	4					

kilometers	85	170	255	340					
hours	1	2	3	4					

EXERCISE   Collect examples of picture, bar, and line graphs from newspapers and magazines. Write five questions that could be answered for each example.

Circle Graphs

Circle graphs, often called pie charts, are used to portray information so that the relationship of each part to the whole is clearly shown. Each part of the circle, or portion of the pie, displays the part/whole relationship. These graphs can be introduced as early as third grade. The children might keep a record of about how an average day is spent: sleeping, eating, reading, playing outside, watching television, school, homework, and so on. Activity 15.7 describes how children make a pie chart of these daily activities.

Information related to science and social studies can be used to create circle graphs. Information from newspapers and almanacs about sales or profits from different stores; ethnic make-up of the cities, states, or provinces; and major categories of governmental spending and income are often shown in circle graphs. As children organize data for a circle graph, they must first establish what is the total or whole to be considered. For the circle graph about hours, 24 hours in the day was the total. In other instances the total comes from the data. When they gathered information about shoes, the total was the number of students in the class. When dealing with sales or populations, the whole is the total sales or the total population.

The next step is to determine the fractional parts of the whole that each part of the data represents. These can be expressed as either common or decimal fractions. The final step is to show each fraction as a part of the

ACTIVITY 15.7   Our Hours Circle Graph

- Create a 24-hour record sheet for children to keep. For each hour, they should write in the activity or activities which occupied the hour.

- Have each child summarize the daily record sheet in categories such as Hours Sleeping, Hours in School, Hours Playing Outside, Hours Watching Television, Hours Eating, and so on.

- Have the children check that they have a total of 24 hours.

- Give each one a circle which has been cut into 24 equal sections. Ask the children what each section represents. (One hour.)

- Have the students add a legend which shows what each color represents.

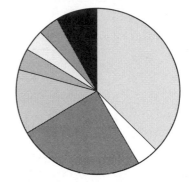

My Time

	Sleeping	37.5%
	Eating	4.2%
	Studying	25.0%
	Playing	12.5%
	Watching TV	4.2%
	Chores	4.2%
	Dress, bath	4.2%
	Other	8.3%

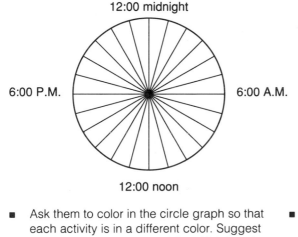

- Ask them to color in the circle graph so that each activity is in a different color. Suggest that they start with the activity which has the most hours.

- Display all the graphs and ask children to compare theirs to their friends'. Ask them to make up and answer five questions from the graphs.

circle. Fractions such as halves, thirds, fourths, eighths, and sixths should be very familiar to students. Figure 15.4 shows a chart on how a student's allowance is spent using familiar fractions.

At other times the data cannot be shown with these familiar fractions. When this is true or when greater precision is necessary, the number of degrees in a circle is used to figure the portion of a circle for each part of the data. To determine the number of degrees for each part of a circle graph, 360 is multiplied by the fraction for each part of the data. A protractor is then used to measure and mark the angles for the graph. Activity 15.8 shows how a table of information about shoes can be shown on a circle graph.

Figure 15-4
Circle graph for
allowances

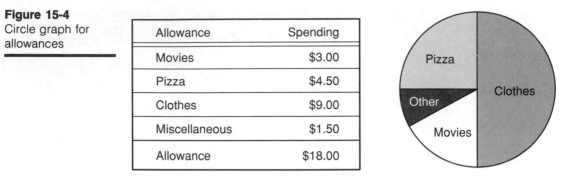

Allowance	Spending
Movies	$3.00
Pizza	$4.50
Clothes	$9.00
Miscellaneous	$1.50
Allowance	$18.00

(a)

(b)

ACTIVITY 15.8   Shoes in a Circle

- Display the table of shoes and have the students pick one day's data.

- Have them note the total number of students who were in the class that day. Tell them that the number of the children is the denominator for each fraction.

- Write fractions for the graph using the number of each type of shoe as the numerator.

- In the next column, have the students use calculators to determine the decimal equivalent for each fraction.

- In the final column, have the students calculate the number of degrees for each portion of the graph by multiplying 360 degrees by each decimal fraction.

- Have students use a protractor to measure the degrees for each portion on a duplicated circle.

- Have students color the graph and prepare a legend.

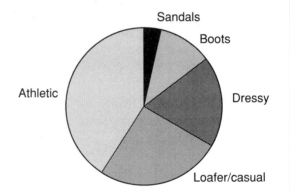

Types of shoes	Number	Fraction	Decimal			Degree
Atheletic	11	11/27	0.41	×	360	147
Loafer/casusal	7	7/27	0.26	×	360	93
Dressy	5	5/27	0.19	×	360	67
Boots	3	2/27	0.11	×	360	40
Sandals	1	1/27	0.04	×	360	13
Total students	27	27/27	1.00			360

Children should first construct graphs using both the fractional part and computed part procedures. Once they understand and can construct circle graphs, students should learn to use computer graphing tools to generate circle graphs. Most computer graphing programs can be used to create circle graphs, as well as line and bar graphs, from spreadsheet information. Computer programs are faster and they make graphs more accurately than humans can by hand. A program for using Logo to draw a circle graph is found in Appendix A.

EXERCISE   Make a time log of your day and sketch a 24-hour pie chart. Compare your graph with one made by a classmate.

▓ STATISTICS

Statistics are a way of describing, summarizing, and analyzing numerical information. Tables and graphs provide the basis for the simple statistics that elementary children learn. Even children in the primary grades can answer statistical questions during the construction and discussion of tables and graphs. In fifth and sixth grades, a formal study of statistics may be appropriate. The mode, the high and low terms in a set of data, the range, the median, and the mean can be incorporated easily into a study of tables and graphs.

When students collect information on surveys, they ask two kinds of questions: questions with word answers that fit the different categories of the survey and questions that are answered by numbers.

- Questions with word, or category, answers
    —What is your favorite kind of pizza? (pepperoni, mushroom, or cheese)
    —What pet would you like to have? (horse, cat, or fish)
    —What kind of shoes are you wearing? (dress, blue, or leather)
- Questions with number answers
    —How many brothers and sisters do you have? (0, 1, 2, or 10.)
    —What was your highest score on Yahtzee? (193, 250, or 394.)
    —How tall are you? (58 inches or 121 cm.)

A first lesson in statistics should help children recognize the difference between the two kinds of questions and answers. The way information is described is based on the kind of information that was collected: categorical or numerical.

The term *mode* can be used to describe both categorical and numerical information. The most frequent response in a set of data is called the **mode.**

The mode provides the answer to questions like these about categorical and numerical information:

■   Which type of shoes did most people wear? How many wore that type?

■   What was the favorite type of pizza? How many liked that type best?

■   Which pet would most people like to have? How many people would like to have that pet?

■   What number of brothers and sisters do most people have?

■   In Yahtzee, what is the most frequent high score?

■   How tall are most people in the class?

While mode applies to both categorical and numerical information, certain statistical terms apply only to numerical information. The concepts of high and low should be introduced. **High** refers to the largest number, the highest score, or the tallest child, whereas **low** refers to the smallest number reported, the lowest score, or the shortest child. Subtracting the low from the high gives the statistical measure called the **range.** Discussion of the highs and the lows and the range in data is natural in dealing with bar graphs.

■   What is the largest number of brothers and sisters that anyone in the class has? the smallest number?

■   What is the highest score on the game? the lowest score? What is the difference between the high and low score?

■   What is the largest population in a province? the smallest population? What is the difference between the largest and smallest?

■   What is the largest area of a state? the smallest area? What is the difference between the largest state and the smallest?

A classroom height chart provides a good source of statistical questions. As children line up by height, they also note the tallest and the shortest in the class. A chart of heights is a good way to graphically present the range of heights in the class. A height chart can also be used to introduce another statistical concept, the **median,** or middle number (Figure 15.5). If all the children's heights are marked on a chart, they can find the middle height by counting from the top and bottom until only one or two children's heights are left. When only one height is left, that height is the median height. If there are two heights left, the median is halfway between the two and no child has the exact median height.

The question "How tall are people in this class?" is hard to answer concisely. The median is one useful way of summarizing all the heights in the class. Some students are taller and some are shorter, but most people are in the middle. Therefore the middle height is a good way to tell someone

Figure 15-5
Chart of children's heights

Inches	Students
70	March 10
69	
68	
67	
66	L
65	J
64	
63	R, T, K
62	W
61	Y, K, S, M, B
60	C, V, W, L
59	J, A, P
58	E, D
57	
56	O
55	H
54	
53	Z
52	N
51	
49	
48	

about heights in the class. The **average,** or arithmetic **mean,** is another number that summarizes all of the heights. If children determine the sum of the heights and divide it by the number of students, they find the mean. Simple situations can be used to introduce the concept of average.

- What is the average number of brothers and sisters in the room?
- What is the average allowance of students in the fifth grade?
- What is the average score for the past ten spelling tests?
- What is the average area of states? of provinces?

A book students will enjoy reading is *On An Average Day,*[12] which lists the averages in over two hundred categories of events which take place each day of the week in the United States:

- Americans eat 24,657,534 hot dogs.
- Americans travel 1,144,720,833 miles by air and 5,205,479,452 miles by car.
- 596,164 hundred dollar bills are printed.

These statistics can develop into many interesting investigations, such as "What is the average number of hot dogs eaten in the school cafeteria each day?" and "What is the average number of miles driven each day by each student's family?" Magazines and newspapers also report statistics about sports, income, employment, housing prices, and want ads that can be used in classroom projects.

Statistical concepts can also be explored with computer spreadsheets. All spreadsheets have functions for sorting high to low, adding, subtracting, and determining averages. Fifth and sixth graders can enter areas and populations of cities on the spreadsheet. Then they can analyze the data and answer many questions with simple calculations. Activity 15.9 describes a spreadsheet for an interdisciplinary activity about rainfall.

ACTIVITY 15.9   The Rain Is Plain

- Have the children obtain data on rainfall for their community for the last ten years and put it in a table and enter it into a spreadsheet. A local weather station or newspaper will supply the data.

- After the children have collected the raw data, have them generate questions about it.
  —Which year had the most rain in the last ten years? Least rain?

  —Which month had the most rain in the last ten years? Least rain?

  —Which months have the highest average rainfall? Lowest average?

  —Which year had the most rain? The least?

- Make a copy of the spreadsheet on a new file so that students can experiment with the data without changing the original. Use the spreadsheet program to calculate monthly and yearly totals and averages. Use the sort or arrange function to compare the most and least rain for each month and year.

- Create graphs of the rainfall data with a graphic program. A bar graph is good to show the monthly average rainfall. A line graph is useful for showing the rain for any month of the last ten years. A circle graph can be used to compare rainfall by seasons.

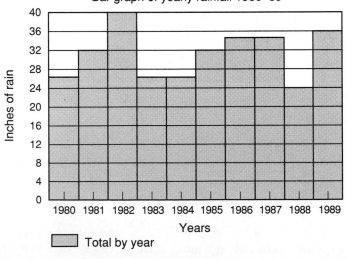

Bar graph of yearly rainfall 1980–89

(x-axis: Years 1980 1981 1982 1983 1984 1985 1986 1987 1988 1989; y-axis: Inches of rain, 0 to 40)

☐ Total by year

Activity 15.9 *continued*

MONTHLY RAINFALL (IN INCHES)

	1980	1981	1982	1983	1984	1985	1986	1987	1988	1989	MONTHLY TOTAL	MONTHLY AVERAGE
January	1.57	0.14	1.66	1.87	0.17	1.08	0.00	1.78	1.17	1.04	10.48	1.05
February	0.63	3.30	1.03	0.90	0.79	2.61	1.10	4.06	0.00	3.50	17.92	1.79
March	0.76	1.86	2.04	2.06	1.48	3.77	0.84	1.99	5.15	1.54	21.49	2.15
April	0.35	3.95	3.38	2.19	0.62	6.15	3.24	0.32	2.83	0.32	23.35	2.33
May	6.67	3.54	13.22	3.21	1.44	1.69	3.87	10.17	0.71	4.54	49.06	4.91
June	0.26	4.59	7.41	5.05	1.78	7.07	7.61	2.43	2.80	8.60	47.60	4.76
July	0.03	1.33	0.92	0.19	0.92	0.21	0.77	2.78	0.84	3.19	11.18	1.12
August	0.26	2.29	0.71	0.19	3.07	1.75	2.10	2.40	0.58	6.17	19.52	1.95
September	10.23	1.49	2.06	0.00	0.80	1.46	6.77	2.23	7.04	5.01	37.09	3.71
October	1.65	7.83	1.99	7.79	6.24	3.69	4.37	0.11	0.76	2.25	36.68	3.67
November	1.57	0.86	2.73	0.91	3.32	1.11	3.03	1.66	0.51	0.03	15.73	1.57
December	1.94	0.30	2.22	0.89	5.03	0.11	0.91	4.84	1.11	0.28	17.63	1.76
TOTAL BY YEAR	25.92	31.48	39.37	25.25	25.66	30.70	34.61	34.77	23.50	36.47	307.73	
AVG BY MONTH	2.16	2.62	3.28	2.10	2.14	2.56	2.88	2.90	1.96	3.04		30.773

Activity 15.9   *continued*

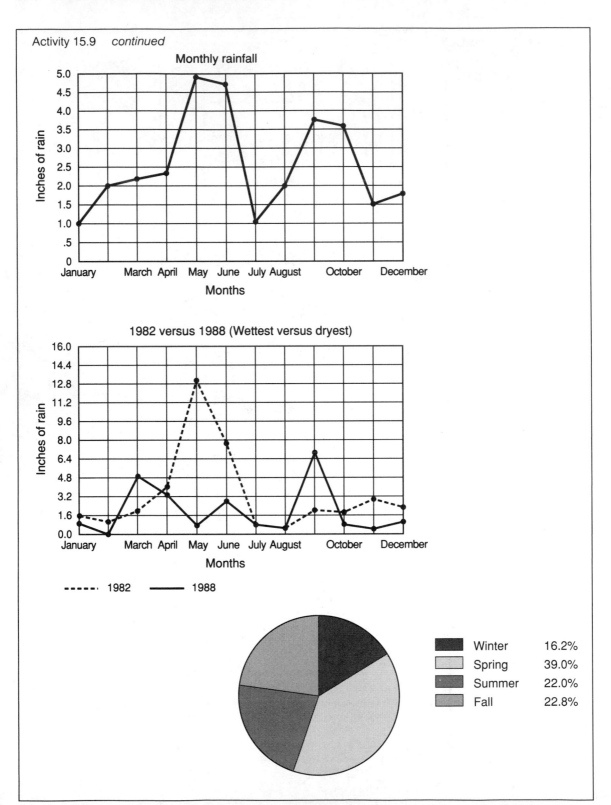

Monthly rainfall

1982 versus 1988 (Wettest versus dryest)

----- 1982   —— 1988

	Winter	16.2%
	Spring	39.0%
	Summer	22.0%
	Fall	22.8%

EXERCISE   Survey the heights of fifteen fourth grade students: 128 cm, 156 cm, 132 cm, 141 cm, 135 cm, 142 cm, 148 cm, 141 cm, 151 cm, 143 cm, 139 cm, 137 cm, 145 cm, 140 cm, 134. From the data set, determine the high, low, range, median, mean, and mode.

▪ PROBABILITY

Probability is the study of chance. Many decisions are influenced by **historical probability,** which is based on past events, or the **mathematics of chance,** which is based on the arithmetical probability of an event occurring. Probability activities enhance problem-solving and investigation skills. When children carry out probability experiments, they construct tables, search for patterns, perform computations, estimate, communicate the results, and draw conclusions. Finally, probability activities add fun, variety, and challenge to the elementary mathematics program.

Probability deals with the chances of an event occurring. If I plan a picnic in July, what are the chances that it will rain? If I roll one die, what is the chance that the top number will be 6? Information about the probability of rain in July or snow in February is based on statistical analysis of rainfall and snowfall. Data gathered over more than 100 years show that the chances of rain in the Central Valley of California and the high plains of Texas for July are nearly zero. A picnic in either of those places is unlikely to be rained out. However, rain in Hawaii or in North Carolina would be more likely based on historical information. Information about the probability of getting a 6 is based on the mathematics of chance. The die (singular form of dice) has six sides. Each of the sides is equally likely to be on top after a die is rolled. Therefore the chances of getting a 6 are 1 in 6, or $\frac{1}{6}$, or 16.6 percent.

Probability Investigations

Many of the probability experiments make predictions based on observations or compare theoretical results to observed results. Many informal experiments can be done in primary grades with pennies or dice. In the upper grades, children are ready for more advanced experiments and more formal explanations. Most activities can be simplified or made more complex to account for the interest and mathematical background of students.

A simple way to begin is with a penny. Children may not be able to flip a penny, but they can shake it up in a container and dump it onto a mat. On each penny flip or trial, the result is either heads or tails. The children can make a tally of the heads or tails for 40 trials as in Figure 15.6. After flipping the coin many times, children begin to have an intuition about the probabilities associated with it. On each flip, the chances of head or tail are equal. In the long run, the number of heads and tails will be the same.

Figure 15-6
Tally of coin flips

Heads   ︲︲︲ ︲︲︲ ︲︲︲ |||

Tails   ︲︲︲ ︲︲︲ ︲︲︲ ︲︲︲ ||

Flipping a thumb tack or tossing an old shoe in the air can be used to see what are the probabilities of getting a head or shank on the thumb tack or the sole up or down on the shoe. This leads to a discussion of "fair" chances. The chances of getting a head or a tail are fair, or the same, while those for the other devices are unfair because the chances of getting a head or shank and sole up and sole down are not equal.

Working with pairs of dice and spinners also helps develop understanding of probability. Two dice are used in Activity 15.10. An extension of this activity can be made by using three or four regular dice and tetrahedral or icosahedral dice. Children should record data in charts as they work. A Logo dice rolling experiment is in Appendix A. Probability spinners usually are divided into three, six, or eight equal spaces. Spinners with unequal areas can also be used to investigate the notion of fairness of events (Figure 15.7).[13]

Sampling is another probability technique that involves choosing a few items out of a larger number of items and drawing some conclusions based on the sample or samples. Children can use a collection of colored beads, or blocks, for a sampling experiment. Activity 15.11 describes a simple sampling procedure which can be used to estimate the color of the total group. Activity 15.12 extends this activity with a cumulative sampling strategy.

ACTIVITY 15.10   Rolling Dice

- Give each team of children a pair of dice and a chart. Have the children guess which of the numbers will be more frequent or less frequent when rolling two dice. (Students with experience rolling one die often guess that all the numbers will be the same.)

- The children roll the dice and determine the total. Each time the dice are rolled, the total is recorded in the proper column of the chart.

- Ask the children why some of the numbers came up more frequently than other numbers. If they are hesitant, you may ask how many ways the dice can make two and how many ways the dice can make seven.

- Extension: Have children predict what the results would be with three dice, then toss the dice to check their predictions.

Tally Sheet											
2	3	4	5	6	7	8	9	10	11	12
I	I	I	I	I	I	I	I	I	I	I
	I	I	I	I	I	I	I	I	I	
		I	I	I	I	I	I	I		
				I	I	I	I			
				I	I	I				
					I					

Figure 15-7
Probability spinners

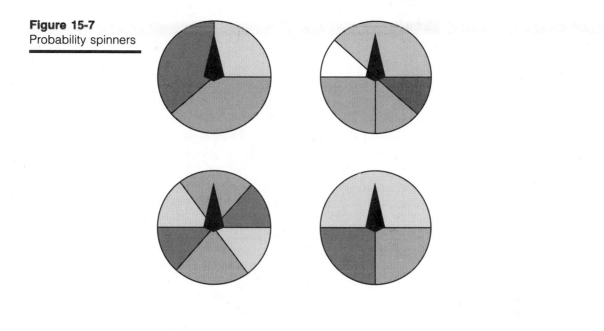

ACTIVITY 15.11   Marbleous

- Prepare a bag or box with 100 same-sized marbles of three or four different colors.

- Have a child draw one object from the bag and make a tally mark by its color on a piece of paper. Return the marble to the bag, shake, and repeat until 50 draws have been made.

- After 50 draws, have the students study the total for each color and guess how many of each color are in the bag.

- Use the totals to create percentages:
  —14 blue in 50 draws = $^{14}/_{50}$ = 28% or 28 blue marbles of 100

  —12 red in 50 draws = $^{12}/_{50}$ = 24% or 24 red marbles in 100

  —24 yellow in 50 draws = $^{24}/_{50}$ = 48% or 48 yellow marbles in 100

- Count the objects in the bag to find out how accurate the estimate was.

- Variation: Try the experiment again drawing only 30 marbles out. How accurate is the prediction? Then try 20 and 10 draws. Which is the most accurate? Which is the most work?

Tally Sheet		
Color of marbles	Count	Total
Red	~~HHt~~ ~~HHt~~ |||	14
Yellow	~~HHt~~ ~~HHt~~ ||	12
Blue	~~HHt~~ ~~HHt~~ ~~HHt~~ ~~HHt~~ ||||	24

ACTIVITY 15.12 Five at a Time

- Prepare a bag of objects (marbles, cubes, counter) with different proportions of colors.

- Instead of drawing out single objects, have the children draw out five at a time and tally them.

- After each draw, calculate a running total for each color and use it to estimate the fraction for each color.

- After four or five trials of five objects, estimate the percentages and number of objects in the bag. Draw four more times and estimate again. Count the actual objects to check the estimates.

	Red	Green	Black	Yellow
TRIAL 1	3	1	0	1
TRIAL 1 %	$3/5 = 60\%$	$1/5 = 20\%$	0%	$1/5 = 20\%$
TRIAL 2	2	2	1	0
CUMULATIVE %	$5/10 = 50\%$	$3/10 = 30\%$	$1/10 = 10\%$	$1/10 = 10\%$
TRIAL 3	3	0	1	1
CUMULATIVE %	$8/15 = 53\%$	$3/15 = 20\%$	$2/15 = 13\%$	$2/15 = 13\%$
TRIAL 4				

Probability experiments can be extended by using different objects and varying the number of trials. A coin tossing experiment is an extension that leads to an interesting pattern as the number of outcomes increases. When a single coin is tossed, only two possible outcomes happen: heads or tails. When two coins are tossed, the outcomes can be two heads, two tails, or one head and one tail. However there are two ways to get one head and one tail. Actually four possible outcomes are possible: T-T, H-H, H-T, or T-H. For three coins eight outcomes are possible (Figure 15.8). The combinations for 1, 2, and 3 coins are shown in triangular arrangement in Figure 15.9. After working out combinations for three, a teacher may ask students to look for a pattern. If they do not see it, try combinations for four coins and ask again. Soon the students will see that each line has sums from the previous row in it. Extend the pattern to 10 coins and see what happens to the number of possibilities.

Figure 15-8
Possible results of
flipping three coins

T-T-T

T-T-H

H-T-T

T-H-H

H-T-H

H-H-H

Figure 15-9
Pascal's triangle

			1			
1 coin		1		1		HT, TH
2 coins		1	2	1		HH, HT, TH, HH
3 coins	1	3	3	1		HHH, HHT, HTH. THH, HTT, THT, TTH, TTT
4 coins		————————				
5 coins		————————				

The arrangement of numbers is called Pascal's triangle after the seventeenth-century mathematician, Blaise Pascal, who studied and wrote about it. Problem cards can be made for students to investigate many interesting questions based on Pascal's triangle.

- What is the sum of each row of the triangle? Can you describe the sequence of numbers that includes each sum?

- When 6 coins are tossed, what is the probability of getting 3 heads and 3 tails? What percent of the possible outcomes is this?

- What is the probability of getting 4 heads and 4 tails when 8 coins are tossed? What percent of the possible outcomes is this?

- Will the percent of possible outcomes for 5 heads and 5 tails when 10 coins are tossed be greater or less than the percent for 4 heads and 4 tails when 8 coins are tossed? Why do you think this is so?

- When you toss 7 coins, what is the probability of getting 3 heads and 4 tails? What is the probability of getting 4 heads and 3 tails? Is each of these probabilities the same percent of the total outcomes? How do you explain this?

Another classroom project on probability could be an interdisciplinary unit on weather. Science, social studies, and language arts are combined in a unit described in Activity 15.13.

In Chapter 3, a mathematical investigation was suggested about the chances that two people in a group would have the same birthdate. With 366 possible dates, the probability that two birth dates of 30 people would fall on the same date seems unlikely. Students in the upper elementary

---

ACTIVITY 15.13   Whether Weather Interdisciplinary Unit

- Have children keep a record of the weather forecast for several weeks. Bring to their attention phrases such as 50 percent chance of precipitation, 10 percent chance for snow, partly cloudy, mostly cloudy, little chance of rain, and so on.

- Keep a chart of weather forecast and actual weather.

- Compare the forecast and actual weather to the forecast for their area from the *Farmer's Almanac*.

- Have students keep track of various factors which affect local weather: storms, winds, mountains and valley terrain, bodies of water.

- Invite a weather forecaster or someone with meteorology as a hobby to the class. Question them on how forecasts are developed.

- Make a classroom weather station with simple weather instruments such as thermometer, wind sock, and so on.

---

grades could do this project to see how often two people in a group might have the same birthday. An investigation will show that the probability of two people in groups of 30 or more having the same birthday is very high. A similar, but simpler, problem in Activity 15.12 models the birth date problem.

ACTIVITY 15.14   Two the Same

- Prepare ten bags or boxes, each with ten different items in it. Each of the ten boxes should contain the same items.

- Have a student pick an object from the first bag and note what it is.

- Pose the question, "How likely is it that an item picked out of the second bag would be different from the item taken from the first bag?" (The likelihood of it being different is 9 in 10 or $\frac{9}{10}$ and the likelihood it is the same is 1 in 10 or $\frac{1}{10}$.)

- Pose the question, "How likely is it that an item picked from the third bag would be different from either the first or second item?" (The third item would be different from the first item $\frac{9}{10}$ times and different from the second item $\frac{8}{10}$. The combined probability would be $.9 \times .8$ or $.72$.)

- Have the student act out the problem several times. Start with the first bag and choose, go to the second bag and choose, then the third, fourth, and so on. Stop when a match is made. Have them make a table of the results.

- Students will find that they usually have a match by the seventh item and occasionally as early as the third item.

- Create a chart to show the probabilities for the experiment. Ask the students if they see any patterns in the chart.

- Have students use calculators to finish the pattern established to calculate how likely it is that two of the items will match on the sixth, seventh, eighth, and ninth picks.

- Ask how the results of the probability table and the results of their data collection are similar. (They should see that the likelihood of getting two items the same from the fourth box is about 50 percent.)

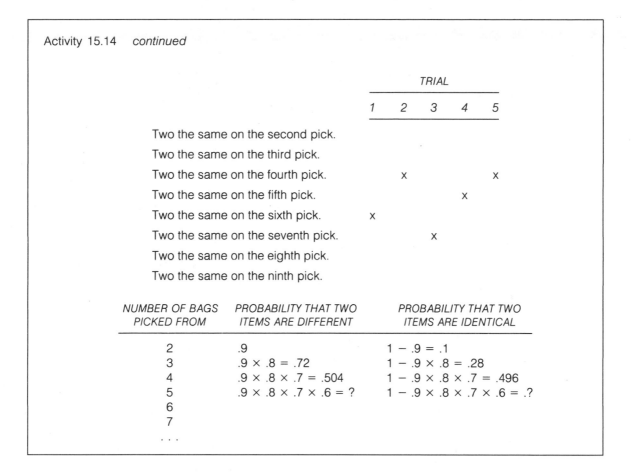

Activity 15.14   *continued*

	TRIAL				
	1	*2*	*3*	*4*	*5*
Two the same on the second pick.					
Two the same on the third pick.					
Two the same on the fourth pick.		x			x
Two the same on the fifth pick.				x	
Two the same on the sixth pick.	x				
Two the same on the seventh pick.			x		
Two the same on the eighth pick.					
Two the same on the ninth pick.					

NUMBER OF BAGS PICKED FROM	PROBABILITY THAT TWO ITEMS ARE DIFFERENT	PROBABILITY THAT TWO ITEMS ARE IDENTICAL
2	.9	1 − .9 = .1
3	.9 × .8 = .72	1 − .9 × .8 = .28
4	.9 × .8 × .7 = .504	1 − .9 × .8 × .7 = .496
5	.9 × .8 × .7 × .6 = ?	1 − .9 × .8 × .7 × .6 = .?
6		
7		
. . .		

The birth date problem is explained in exactly the same way, but the numbers are not nearly so congenial. The probability of two people having different birth dates is $^{364}/_{365}$ which is close to 1.0 or 100 percent. The probability of two people having the same birth dates is $1 - {}^{364}/_{365}$ or close to 0. When the pattern is extended, the results are as shown in Table 15.1.

Table 15.1
Likelihood of two people having the same birth date

NUMBER OF PEOPLE	PROBABILITY THAT TWO DATES ARE DIFFERENT	PROBABILITY THAT TWO DATES ARE IDENTICAL
2	100%	0%
10	88%	12%
15	75%	25%
20	59%	41%
30	29%	71%
40	11%	89%

Probability Terms

Children develop understandings of many concepts through probability experiments and investigations. Terms such as event or trial, likely event, impossible event, certain event, or equally likely event are ones that fifth and sixth grade students comprehend and use in their work. As children engage in the experiments, actions should be identified correctly. An **event** or a **trial** occurs each time a draw from a bag is made, die is rolled, or coin is tossed. When one coin is tossed, the outcome will be either heads or tails. The probability of heads or tails is equally likely, so there are two **equally likely events.**

If three beads are drawn from a bag containing three equal combinations of red, blue, and yellow, you are more likely to draw beads of different colors than you are to draw three beads of the same color. Drawing three red beads is an **unlikely event.** If 90 beads in the bag are red and only ten are yellow and ten are blue, however, it is more likely that three red beads than beads of three different colors will be drawn. Drawing three red beads is a **likely event.** If all the beads in the bag are red, drawing out a red bead is a **certain event.** However, in this case, the chance of drawing a yellow bead is zero; drawing a yellow bead is an **impossible event** when only red beads are in the bag.

Children's experiments also provide opportunities to develop the concept that each event can be assigned a number that indicates the event's probability of occurring. The likelihood of an event occurring is assigned a number on a scale from 0 to 1. The less likely an event is, the closer to 0 it is; while the more likely an event is, the closer its number is to 1. An **impossible event** has a probability of 0, and a **certain event** has a probability of 1. The probability of snow in the middle of summer in Arizona is close to zero; while the probability of an airplane from San Francisco to New York flying over the Mississippi River is close to 1. Flipping coins gives equal probability of heads and tails; the probability of heads is 1 in 2, or ½. Another way of stating the probability of getting heads is 50 percent. The probability of getting a 5 when rolling a six-sided die is 1 in 6, ⅙, or about 17 percent.

EXERCISE Activities 15.10 through 15.12 are investigations into probability concepts. Select one of the activities and design a problem card to direct students' work with that investigation.

■ SUMMARY

Much information is provided the public in tabular and graphic form. The ability to use tables and graphs effectively is a valuable problem-solving and reasoning skill. Children need to develop an understanding of tables and graphs and skill in using them. Children themselves provide the source of most of the information they need for collecting, organizing, and reporting in tables and graphs. Birth dates, heights, eye colors, and favorite pizzas, ice-cream and television shows are examples of information which children can collect. Primary children learn to construct and read object, picture, and bar graphs. Older children use picture, bar, line, and circle graphs. Picture graphs may also have scales so that one picture represents many responses.

Statistics in the elementary school can come from children's graphs. As children describe the information, they use statistical concepts such as the most frequent (mode), the range of responses from the lowest to the highest, the middle or median answer, and the average, or mean. Descriptive statistics help students summarize and communicate main points about the information they have collected.

Probability experiments also help develop important problem solving skills. Children perform experiments, record and organize data, examine data for patterns, establish numerical odds, and make predictions from their observations. Probabilities are derived from mathematical sources and from analysis of previous events. Mathematical probability deals with the mathematics of chance such as flipping coins. Statistical probability is based on accumulated data that pertain to particular events, such as rainfall or temperature. Children's work with probability should be largely exploratory; formal instruction should be limited to mature students in upper grades of the elementary school. A teacher should use correct terminology so children develop a vocabulary about probability.

■ STUDY QUESTIONS AND ACTIVITIES

1. Children should serve as the source of most of the data used in making tables and graphs. Think of ten topics in addition to the ones which are listed in this chapter about which children could collect information. These could involve other children in the classroom or school, teachers, the school building, the parking lot and street, while coming to school, or things and people at home.

2. Look at Activities 15.1, 15.2, and 15.3. Select another topic and write an activity plan for constructing a table and graph using that topic. Make a list of five to ten questions children could ask and answer based on the table and graph.

3. Collect data on number of pairs of shoes owned by students in your class. Have them list the shoes in categories: dress, casual, athletic, and so on. Work in groups to create a table and three graphs from the information.

4. Take a poll of heights of students in your class and describe the results using the mode, the range, high and low, the median, and the average.

5. Have a fellow student make a collection of 50–100 objects in a bag or box. Complete Activities 15.11 and 15.12 with your collection. Compare your predictions with the actual number of objects in the bag or box. Which method of sampling worked best for you?

6. Use Pascal's triangle to answer the questions on page 547.

■ TEACHER'S BOOKSHELF

Heymann, Tom. 1989. *On an Average Day*. New York: Fawcett Columbine.

Shulte, Albert P., and James R. Smart. 1981 Yearbook. *Teaching Statistics and Probability*. Reston, VA: National Council of Teachers of Mathematics.

National Council of Teachers of Mathematics. 1979. *Organizing Data: Dealing with Uncertainty*. Reston, VA: National Council of Teachers of Mathematics.

■ FOR FURTHER READING

Bestgen, Barbara J. 1980, December. Making and interpreting graphs and tables: Results and implications from national assessment. *Arithmetic Teacher 18*(4), 26–29.

The National Assessment of Educational Progress *test indicates that children can read tables and graphs for single bits of information but have difficulty interpreting graphs and solving problems with information from them. The author offers five suggestions for improving children's ability to interpret and use information from graphs.*

Burns, Marilyn. 1983, March. Put some probability in your classroom. *Arithmetic Teacher 30*(7), 21–22.

A teacher's curiosity about a statement in the Sunday paper provided the basis for a probability activity for her sixth graders. Her procedures and children's responses are described.

Dickinson, J. Craig. 1986, December. Gather, organize, display: Mathematics for the information society. *Arithmetic Teacher 30*(4), 12–15.

Four graphing activities are described. In the first, a teacher helps children select a topic and design a graph. The second uses Easy Graph, a simplified graphing program, whereas the third and fourth use BASIC or Logo languages to write simple programs for graphs.

Fennell, Francis (Skip). 1984, March. Ya gotta play to win: A probability and statistics unit for the middle grades. *Arithmetic Teacher 31*(7), 26–30.

A ten-day gaming unit designed to acquaint fifth- to eighth-grade children with games of chance is described. Children are introduced to many probability terms and concepts.

Horak, Virginia M., and Willis J. Horak. 1982, September. Collecting and displaying the data around us. *Arithmetic Teacher 30*(1), 16–20.

Activities based on personal, home, and school grounds data are used with a variety of graphs. Easily made graphs are pictured and described.

———. 1983, May. Take a chance. *Arithmetic Teacher 30*(9), 8–15.

> *This article deals with mathematics associated with probability. The simplest ones are suitable for primary-grade children, whereas the others are more appropriate for the intermediate grades.*

Johnson, Elizabeth M. 1981, December. Bar graphs for first graders. *Arithmetic Teacher 29*(4), 30–31.

> *A sequence of seven activities that ends with the construction of a bar graph is described. In addition to the graph itself, children deal with important concepts like "more than," "less than," "as many as," and so on.*

Nibbelink, William. 1982, November. Graphing for any grade. *Arithmetic Teacher 30*(3), 28–31.

> *Introducing and making coordinate graphs that are suitable for children in all elementary grades. Step-by-step directions using a variety of data indicate how to use the graphs in different grades.*

Shaw, Jean M. 1984, May. Dealing with data. *Arithmetic Teacher 31*(9), 9–15.

> *Children as young as six can learn about statistical concepts, such as measures of central tendency, measures of dispersion, and correlation, with the activities described in this article. Ways of displaying and interpreting data are discussed.*

———. 1984, January. Making graphs. *Arithmetic Teacher 31*(5), 7–11.

> *Graphing experiences based on children's lives are described, and ways to help children interpret and make predictions based on their data are suggested.*

Vissa, Jean. 1988, December. Probability and combinations for third graders. *Arithmetic Teacher 36*(4), 33–37.

> *Possible word combinations are the first step in an investigation of probability and combinations.*

Woodward, Ernest. 1983, March. A second-grade probability and graphing lesson. *Arithmetic Teacher 30*(7), 23–24.

> *Dice and paper grids provide the means for introducing second-grade children to the concept of probability through graphing the outcomes of multiple rolls of the dice.*

Zawojewski, Judith S. 1988, March. Research into practice: Teaching Statistics: Mean, median, and mode. *Arithmetic Teacher 35*(7), 25–26.

> *Tests and other research data indicate that 13-year-olds have a weak understanding of mean, median, and mode. The author identifies five things teachers can do to improve students' understanding of the concepts.*

 NOTES

[1] National Council of Teachers of Mathematics. 1989. *Curriculum and Evaluation Standards for School Mathematics*. Reston, VA: National Council of Teachers of Mathematics, 54. Used by permission.

[2] NCTM, 87. Used by permission.

[3] NCTM, 98. Used by permission.

[4] NCTM, 102. Used by permission.

[5]NCTM, 109. Used by permission.

[6]John Dossey, Ina Mullis, Mary Lindquist, and Donald L. Chambers. 1988. *The Mathematics Report Card: Are We Measuring Up?* Princeton, NJ: Educational Testing Service.

[7]Microsoft Corporation, 16011 NE 36th Way, Box 97017, Redmond, WA 98073-9717.

[8]Claris Corporation, 5201 Patrick Henry Dr., Santa Clara, CA 95052.

[9]Beagle Brothers, Inc., 6215 Ferris Sq., Suite 100, San Diego, CA 92121.

[10]PBI, 1155 B-H Chess Drive, Foster City, CA 94404.

[11]Grolier Electronic Publishing, Inc., 95 Madison Ave., New York, NY, 10016.

[12]Tom Heymann. 1989. *On an Average Day.* New York: Fawcett Columbine.

[13]George Bright, John G. Harvey, and Margariete Montague Wheeler. 1981. Fair games, unfair games, in 1981 Yearbook *Teaching Probability and Statistics.* Reston, VA: National Council of Teachers of Mathematics, 49–59.

■ INTRODUCTION TO LOGO

Logo was developed over a fifteen-year period (1965–1980) by a group of computer scientists, mathematicians, and educators in the Artificial Intelligence Laboratory at the Massachusetts Institute of Technology (MIT). Seymour Papert, a member of the design team who studied with Piaget, is a primary proponent of Logo and its uses in school. His book *Mindstorms: Children, Computers, and Powerful Ideas* outlines a vision of how computers should be used. He believes that computers should be used as "tools for thinking" and that children should be in control of the computing environment.[1]

Most uses of computers—tutorials, drill and practice, and even many games—put the computer in charge of children. Logo, on the other hand, allows the child to control the computer and direct the action of the computer with simple, English-like commands. Logo serves as a learning tool for exploring important concepts in arithmetic and geometry. With only a few commands, a child can draw shapes and pictures while learning about lines, points, angles, and equality. Simple numerical ideas using the four basic operations can be explored.

As the students grow in confidence with the basic commands, they begin to draw more complex designs and pictures. In planning and executing such designs, they employ important problem-solving skills such as looking for patterns, breaking a big task into simpler pieces, and working by guess and check. The structure of Logo allows them to program, save, and recall each part of the big task. The teacher's role is that of facilitator and collaborator. As children need commands and information, the teacher provides that information without interfering with the thinking and problem solving of the child. Students invent more projects in Logo as they become more proficient with the language.

The *turtle* is a symbol that many people associate with Logo. The turtle originally was a small hemispherically shaped floor robot that responded to commands such as FORWARD, BACK, RIGHT, and LEFT. The robot moved around the room and could draw a line on the floor to show its path. On the computer screen, the turtle is either a small turtle shape or a triangle that responds to the same commands and leaves a line on the screen to show where it has moved.

If a child types FORWARD 25, the turtle moves forward 25 spaces on the screen. If the child types RIGHT 75, the turtle pivots to the right 75 degrees. By continuing to move the turtle around the screen, the child explores the turtle world of angles, lines, and shapes. Primary children may continue this exploration for several months before moving on to more focused projects. Intermediate students who are being introduced to Logo may go through this phase in two or three days.

Drawing a square is one of the first Logo projects which children attempt. After several tries, they discover that four lines and four turns are needed, that all the turns must be 90 degrees, and that all the lines must be the same length. Younger children may accidentally create what they call a square corner or may try out many combinations before they find 90 as the correct number. Older students can use knowledge gained about the angles of squares to complete the figure. For both ages, the drawing of a square makes information about squares meaningful in a new way. They are using angles and sides to make something happen on the computer screen.

A square can be drawn with eight commands.

FORWARD 40 LEFT 90
FORWARD 40 LEFT 90
FORWARD 40 LEFT 90
FORWARD 40 LEFT 90

After a square is drawn, students notice that the commands are a pattern and ask for a shorter or easier way to draw the square. The teacher takes this as an opportunity to introduce the REPEAT command. REPEAT requires a number and a list of commands to be repeated in square brackets.

Figure 1
Turtle moves

HOME
FORWARD 25
RIGHT 75
FORWARD 10

Figure 2
Square

FORWARD 40 LEFT 90
FORWARD 40 LEFT 90
FORWARD 40 LEFT 90
FORWARD 40 LEFT 90

REPEAT 4 [FORWARD 40 LEFT 90]

Students then go through the same process to make other shapes. Task cards or pictures of shapes challenge students to draw regular polygons. First they work with individual commands to determine the correct angles and sizes; later they write the command with REPEAT. Logo Activity 1 is a sample task card for shapes.

LOGO ACTIVITY 1   Making Shapes

FORWARD   BACK   RIGHT   LEFT   HOME

Use turtle commands to draw a square, an equilateral triangle, rectangles, a pentagon, a hexagon, an octagon, and a circle. What other regular shapes can you draw?

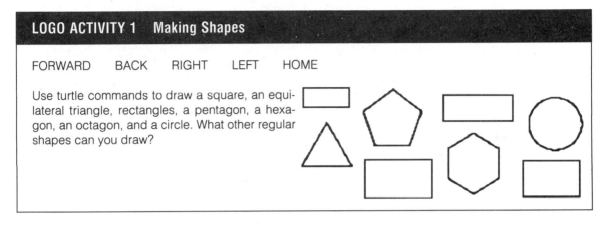

Drawing a square leads to triangles, circles, and hexagons. The length of sides and the size of angles must be figured out either through trial and error or through using generalized information such as the Rule of 360. The Rule of 360, also known as the Total Turtle Trip Theorem, holds that the sum of the angles which the turtle turns while traveling around a closed figure is 360 degrees. Some older students may see this relationship quickly, but many students need time and guidance to extract this generalization.

Another set of Logo commands are useful for controlling the turtle on the screen. Sometimes students want to move around the screen without drawing. The command for this is PENUP. When it is time to draw again, PENDOWN is used to lower the imaginary pen again. Logo also has pencolors which allow the turtle to draw in several colors. The commands for changing the pen color and erasing the graphics screen should be found in the user manual for your version of Logo.

Logo is not limited to the commands which were originally part of the language. Each student adds new commands which are developed as part of bigger projects. After drawing a square with the REPEAT command, the square can be made into a new command by defining a procedure. Defining a procedure means writing a small program by giving a name to a group of commands that complete a particular task. Rather than typing the commands for drawing a square each time, the program called SQUARE includes all the commands needed to draw the square.

```
TO SQUARE
REPEAT 4 [FORWARD 80 LEFT 90]
END
```

Logo Activity 2 describes how to create a pentagon procedure.

LOGO ACTIVITY 2   Shape Procedures

To create a procedure, you must name it with TO and a word which describes the procedure, write the commands to make the shape, and stop it with END. Here is an example for a PENTAGON.

After typing END, follow the directions in your user's manual for defining a procedure. After making several different shapes with REPEAT statements, make each of them into procedures.

```
TO PENTAGON                          Naming Step
REPEAT 5 [FORWARD 40 RIGHT 72]       Description
END                                  Completion
```

The new procedure draws a square when the command SQUARE is typed. The shape could have been named BOX or WINDOW depending on its use in the project. Children usually create and save procedures for all the basic shapes. With each new project, they encounter new problems that are solved by breaking down a complex idea into many smaller and easier ones. They may need special procedures for the drawing. Logo Activity 3 challenges students to find the shapes and put them together to make a picture. When students recognize that they can use the squares, triangles, and rectangles already created to draw a picture, they see the benefits of breaking down a big task into many smaller ones.

LOGO ACTIVITY 3   Many Shapes

What are all the shapes seen in this picture? Create procedures for each of these shapes. Use the pen commands and pen colors to draw a picture like this one. Make up your own picture with shapes.

Some teachers use activity sheets or problem cards with shapes and designs to suggest projects. Some textbook series now include Logo activities or offer supplemental Logo workbooks. Task cards may suggest investigations that might not be discovered independently. Such materials should be evaluated to make sure that they provide opportunities for children to extend procedures, create new projects, and explore concepts while they are working in Logo. Logo Activity 4 is a task card on perimeter. A teacher has created Logo procedures and saved them on a file disk to draw SHAPE1, SHAPE2, and SHAPE3 for this task card which the student can trace by moving the turtle around it.

LOGO ACTIVITY 4   Trace the Shape

SHAPE1, SHAPE2, and SHAPE3 have been saved on the File Disk. Trace each shape with the turtle and record the length of each side. Add up the total number of steps the turtle takes around the outside of the shape. Compare your total to that of three other students. How close were all of you?

   Add all the right turns to make a shape. Then add all the left turns. Find the difference. What did you discover?

◼ LOGO EXPLORATIONS

Explorations and investigations provide experiential background for mathematical ideas introduced formally later. Tracing the shapes in Logo Activity 4 allows children to explore perimeter in the first or second grade, although the term *perimeter* may not be used for two more years. Logo activities can be used to explore many concepts such as variables, fractions, graphing, statistics, probability, area and perimeter, divisibility rules, functions, and algebra. Several Logo procedures that can be used for mathematical explorations follow. Most of them can be modified easily and adapted to children's ideas.

Simple Drill

A simple drill program is written by randomly selecting two numbers from 0 to 9. This example is for addition, but it can easily be modified for multiplication with the terms product and the multiplication operator (*) substituted for the +. Working on subtraction drill will lead to work with negative integers.

```
TO DRILL
MAKE "FIRST RANDOM 10
MAKE "SECOND RANDOM 10
PRINT [WHAT IS THE SUM OF]
PRINT :FIRST
PRINT [AND]
PRINT :SECOND
WAIT 10
PRINT :FIRST + :SECOND
END
```

Mystery Rule

This Logo program is written by one student or the teacher for another student. It is a function machine that allows a person to type one number in with the procedure. The computer prints another number out on the screen. A student tries to figure out what operations cause the value to change.

```
TO MYSTERY.RULE :NUMBER
PRINT :NUMBER + 4
END
```

One student will type MYSTERY.RULE 7 and the computer will print 11. After several examples, the student should recognize that 4 is added each time. Many other rules can be developed which may be harder for students to figure out. Note that each time a variable name is used in the procedure to hold the place of a number or value, the variable is preceded by a semicolon (:NUMBER).

```
TO JOHN.RULE :NUMBER            TO ANITA.RULE :NUMBER
PRINT :NUMBER + :NUMBER −2      PRINT :NUMBER * :NUMBER
END                            END
```

Rods

Draw pictures of rods of different length by typing ROD with the number of the length in multiples of 10. Using the rod program, addition and subtraction can be drawn. Subtraction is a negative value.

```
TO ROD :LENGTH
REPEAT 2 [FORWARD 10 RIGHT 90 FORWARD :LENGTH RIGHT 90]
RIGHT 90 FORWARD :LENGTH LEFT 90
END
```

ROD 30
ROD 10

ROD 30
BK 10
ROD −20

Fraction Action

With this simple fraction maker, students can see how squares are cut into equal parts. Type FRACTIONSQUARE 5 to cut the square into 5 equal pieces. How could it be changed to make a rectangular fraction bar?

```
TO FRACTIONSQUARE :NUMBER
REPEAT 4 [FORWARD 50 RT 90]
REPEAT :NUMBER [RT 90 LT 90 FORWARD 50/:NUMBER
  BACK 50/:NUMBER]
END
```

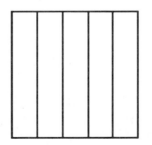

FRACTIONSQUARE 5

Pie Chart

A variation on the fraction maker is a pie chart that can be used to make a circle graph. If you wish to have 40 percent of the pie chart shaded in, you would type PIECHART 40 100. You can then change the pen color and finish the rest by typing PIECHART 60 100. If you wanted 4 parts of 11 total shaded, the chart would be drawn with PIECHART 4 11 and PIECHART 7 11.

```
TO PIECHART :PART :WHOLE
REPEAT 360 * :PART / :WHOLE [FORWARD 40 BACK 40]
END
```

PIECHART 40 100

Rolling Dice

Several simple procedures allow children to simulate rolling dice. DIE represents the number rolled by one die. ROLLDIE 20 would print 20 rolls of one die. ROLLDICE 20 prints 20 rolls of two dice.

```
TO DIE
OUTPUT 1 + RANDOM 6
END
```

```
TO ROLLDIE :NUMBER
REPEAT :NUMBER [PRINT
   DIE]
END
```

```
TO ROLLDICE :NUMBER
REPEAT :NUMBER [PRINT DIE + DIE]
END
```

■ DIFFERENT VERSIONS OF LOGO

Since Logo was introduced for microcomputers in 1981, many different versions of the language have been developed commercially. Two families of Logo have been most popular and widespread in schools: Versions of Logo have been developed by LCSI[2] and Terrapin[3] for a variety of computers and in Spanish. Improvements have been made regularly to take advantage of additional memory and improved computer hardware.

LCSI VERSIONS	TERRAPIN VERSIONS
Apple Logo	Terrapin Logo
Logo II for Apple	Commodore Logo
IBM Logo	PC Logo for IBM
LogoWriter	Logo PLUS

Most of the commands and much of the structure of the language are the same for all versions for different computers. All of the versions of Logo come with tutorial and reference materials that list the commands needed in each version of Logo. Both of the major Logo companies also publish a variety of teaching materials for Logo. In addition, resources are available from several other sources to stimulate project ideas for teachers and students.

■ LOGO BIBLIOGRAPHY

Bull, Glen, Steve Tipps, and Tim Riordan. 1985. *Nudges: Projects for IBM Logo.* New York: Holt, Rinehart, and Winston.

Bull, Glen, Steve Tipps, and Tim Riordan. 1986. *Nudges: Projects for Apple Logo.* New York: Holt, Rinehart, and Winston.

CLIME (Council for Logo in Mathematics Education). A special interest group of the National Council of Teachers of Mathematics. Quarterly newsletter from 10 Bogart Avenue, White Plains, NY 10606 (914-946-5143).

Harvey, Brian. 1987. *Computer Science: Logo Style.* Vols. 1, 2, and 3. Boston: MIT Press.

Logo Exchange. A monthly newsletter from International Society for Technology in Education. 1787 Agate Street, Eugene, OR 97405-9905 (503-686-4414).

Tipps, Steve, and Glen Bull. 1985. *Beginning with Logo.* Englewood Cliffs, NJ: Prentice-Hall.

Tobias, Joyce, Jerry Short, Sharon Burrowes, and Tom Lough. 1985. *Beyond Mindstorms: Teaching with IBM Logo.* New York: Holt, Rinehart, and Winston.

Watt, Daniel. 1983. *Learning with Logo.* New York: McGraw-Hill.

Watt, Molly, and Daniel Watt. 1986. *Teaching with Logo: Building Blocks for Learning.* Menlo Park, CA: Addison-Wesley.

■ NOTES

[1] Seymour Papert. 1980. *Mindstorms: Children, Computers, and Powerful Ideas.* New York: Basic Books.

[2] Logo Computer Systems Inc., PO Box 162, Highgate Springs, VT 95460 (800-321-5646)

[3] Terrapin, Inc., 376 Washington Street, Maiden, MA 02148 (617-322-4800)

SUPPLIERS OF MATHEMATICS SOFTWARE

BLS, Inc.
Woodmill Corporate Center
5153 West Woodmill Drive, Suite 18
Wilmington, DE 19808
1-800-545-7766

Cambridge Development Laboratory, Inc.
214 Third Avenue
Waltham, MA 02154
1-800-637-0047
1-617-890-4640 (MA)

Davidson & Associates, Inc.
3135 Kashiwa Street
Torrance, CA 90505
1-800-556-6141
1-213-534-2250 (CA)

D.C. Heath and Company
School Division
125 Spring Street
Lexington, MA 02173
1-800-334-3284

DLM
One DLM Park
P.O. Box 4000
Allen, TX 75002
1-800-527-4747
1-800-442-4711 (TX)

Dorsett Educational Systems, Inc.
P.O. Box 1226
Norman, OK 73070
1-800-654-3871
1-405-288-2301 (OK)

Educational Activities, Inc.
P.O. Box 392
Freeport, NY 11520
1-800-645-3739
1-516-223-4666 (NY)

Hartley Courseware, Inc.
Box 419
Dimondale, MI 48821
1-800-247-1380
1-517-646-6458 (MI)

Houghton Mifflin
One Beacon Street
Boston, MA 02108

IBM Educational Systems
Dept PC
4111 Northside Parkway
Atlanta, GA 30327

The Learning Company
6493 Kaiser Drive
Fremont, CA 94555
1-800-852-2255

Looking Glass Learning Products Inc.
276 Howard
Des Plaines, IL 60018-1906
1-800-545-5457

MECC
3490 Lexington Avenue North
St. Paul, MN 55126
1-800-228-3504, Ext. 527
1-800-782-0032, Ext. 527 (MN)

Micro-Learningware
Rt. 1, Box 162
Amboy, MN 56010-9762
1-800-222-5113
(on dial tone dial 53276)
1-800-247-0454 (MN)
(on dial tone dial 53276)

MicroMedia Publishing
6 Arrow Road
Ramsey, NJ 07446
1-800-922-0401
1-201-825-8888 (NJ)

Midwest Publications
P.O. Box 448
Pacific Grove, CA 93950
1-800-458-4849

Milliken Publishing Company
1100 Research Blvd.
P.O. Box 21579
St. Louis, MO 63132-0579
1-800-325-4136

Mindscape Inc.
3444 Dundee Road
Northbrook, IL 60062
1-800-221-9884

Optimum Resources, Inc.
10 Station Place
Norfolk, CT 06058
1-800-327-1473
1-203-542-5553 (CT)

Queue, Inc.
562 Boston Avenue
Bridgeport, CT 06610
1-800-232-2224
1-203-335-0908 (CT)

Random House Media
Dept. 517
400 Hahn Road
Westminster, MD 21157
1-800-638-6460
1-800-492-0782 (MD)

Scholastic Inc.
2931 East McCarty Street
P.O. Box 7502
Jefferson City, MO 65102
1-800-541-5513
1-800-392-2179 (MO)

Scott, Foresman and Company
1900 East Lake Avenue
Glenview, IL 60025
1-800-554-4411

Spinnaker Software Corp.
One Kendall Square
Cambridge, MA 02139
1-800-323-8088

Springboard Software
7808 Creekridge Circle
Minneapolis, MN 55435
1-800-445-4780, Ext. 2000

Sunburst Communications
39 Washington Ave.
Pleasantville, NY 10570-2898
1-800-431-1934
1-800-321-7511 (NY)

SVE (Society for Visual Education, Inc.)
Dept. VR
1345 Diversey Parkway
Chicago, IL 60614-1299
1-800-829-1900

Tandy Corporation
1700 One Tandy Center
Fort Worth, TX 76102

Square One TV: This is the television
program about mathematics produced
by the Children's Television Workshop
and broadcast on public television. Information can be obtained by writing:
    Children's Television Workshop
    1 Lincoln Plaza
    New York, NY 10023

■ SUPPLIERS OF MATHEMATICS
LEARNING AIDS

Creative Publications
5040 West 111th Street
Oak Lawn, IL 60453
1-800-624-0822

Cuisenaire Company of America, Inc.
12 Church Street. Box D
New Rochelle, NY 10802
1-800-237-3142
1-914-235-0900 (NY)

Dale Seymour Publications
P.O. Box 10888
Palo Alto, CA 94303
1-800-USA-1100
1-800-ABC-0766 (CA)

Delta Education, Inc.
P.O. Box 915
Hudson, NH 03051
1-800-258-1302

DIDAX Inc.
Educational Resources
Peabody, MA 01960
1-800-458-0024
1-508-532-9060 (MA)

Educational Insights
19560 S. Rancho Way
Dominguez Hills, CA 90220
1-800-367-5713
1-213-637-2131 (CA)

NASCO
1901 Janesville Ave.
Port Atkinson, WI 53538
1-414-563-2446

INDEX

Abacus. *See* Material, place value
Addition:
  activity
    common fraction, 420,
      421–422, 424
    decimal fraction, 458, 459
    whole number, 273, 274, 276,
      277, 278, 279, 280, 282–283,
      285, 286, 287, 288, 289, 291,
      296, 304–305
  calculator
    common fraction, 424
    decimal fraction, 467, 468
    whole number, 270, 284, 292,
      303–305
  common fraction, 418–425
  computer, 284, 303–304, 467,
    559, 561
  decimal fraction, 458
  meaning, 272
  property. *See* Property
  relationship to multiplication,
    270, 317, 318, 321–322, 334
  relationship to subtraction, 270,
    276, 278, 298
  terminology, 275
  whole number, 192, 265–268,
    272–297
  algorithm, 241, 270, 279
    with regrouping, 290–293
    without regrouping, 289–290
  basic fact, 108, 288
    defined, 281
    introduction, 273–274
    practice, 171, 283–286
  estimating sums, 247, 293–295
    compatible numbers, 295

    front-end addition, 294
    rounded numbers, 294
  mental arithmetic, 295–297,
    343
  readiness, 272–273
  reinforcing learning, 168–171,
    275–279, 281–283
  sentence, 274, 289, 290, 291
  sequence for teaching, 267–268
Addition Logician (software), 303
*Agenda for Action: Recommendations
  for School Mathematics in the 1980s,*
  123
Algebra, 179, 365
Algorithm, 231
  defined, 267
  reasons for teaching, 270–271
  See also Addition; Division; Multi-
    plication; Subtraction
Anxiety. *See* Mathematics anxiety
Appleworks 3.0 (software), 532
Arithmetic Teacher, 4, 56, 83
Ashlock, Robert, 105
Assessment, 97–113
  conference, parent / guardian, 97,
    105–106
  interview, 94, 95, 96, 97, 99–103,
    110
    Piaget-type, 96, 100–102
  listening to students, 94, 95
  National Council of Teachers of
    Mathematics statement, 97–98
  observation, 94, 95, 96, 97,
    98–99, 111–112
  parent / guardian conference, 97,
    105–106
  record keeping, 99, 111–113

  anecdotal, 111–112
  forms, 111, 112
  for grades, 112–113
  test, 106–111
    commercial, 106–107
    diagnostic, 107–111
      example, 109, 110
      intermediate grade, 109–111
      primary grade, 108–109
  work product, 97, 104–105
  written work, 94, 97, 100
Associative property. *See* Property
Attitude. *See* Mathematics attitude
Attribute blocks. *See* Material

Baratta-Lorton, Mary, 32, 192
Baratta-Lorton, Robert, 168
Base ten blocks. *See* Material, place
  value
Basic facts. *See* Addition; Division;
  Multiplication; Subtraction
Box™ Introduces Fractions (software),
  418
Box™ Introduces Numbers (software),
  241
Brownell, William, 25
Bruner, Jerome, 25, 27
Brush, Lorelei, 10
Building Thinking Skills, 51
Building Your Math Skills, 304
Bumble Games (software), 388
Bunny Hop (software), 241
Burns, Marilyn, 171

Calculator, 5, 77–81, 98–99, 144,
  145, 146, 239, 245, 270, 271,
  284–285, 292, 302, 303–305,